PROLOGUE

All teachers are inspired by the idea, _____ _____ ..opeiui, that we are getting something across that someday, someway, will benefit our students, make their life better, and give them the tools that they need to understand a very difficult world.

In psychology, students flock to our courses, eager to learn the lessons of life, how their mind works, and how to understand others. They want to understand what the world is really all about. Yet what they learn is often that they must memorize vast amounts of data and studies that make little sense in how to apply what they learn to the real world. They memorize what they need to know to pass a test, not what they need to know to understand life.

"You need at least a Masters Degree to get into the deep woods."

In a study by the prestigious PEW Research Center, America ranks 24th in the world in science. We are behind every civilized nation on earth. Why?

https://www.pewresearch.org/fact-tank/2017/02/15/u-s-students-internationally-math-science/

You can see the effects of this in our culture's response to global warming, in the rejection of immunization to Covid-19 and wearing masks, by as much as one-third of our country. The anti-science bias shows up in the response to our politics, our beliefs, and our personal opinions, on every topic.

A series of studies from MIT and Harvard suggest we are not doing well at what we hope to accomplish; we may not even get across the most important and most basic knowledge of any subject.

A brilliant series of studies called *"Minds of Our Own"*, produced by Harvard, MIT, the National Science Foundation, and the Smithsonian Center for Astrophysics, shows how dire the problem is. As the graduates of science and engineering at Harvard and MIT listen to the message of how they are the *"premier institution of science and engineering in the world"*, the graduates applaud themselves.

And it is true. Students come from throughout the world to study science and engineering at Harvard and MIT. Yet as the creme de la creme of American science come off the stage, after receiving their diplomas, they are met with a series of simple questions most cannot answer.

https://www.learner.org/series/minds-of-our-own/

"Can you take a flashlight battery, a flashlight bulb, and a wire and make the bulb light up?"

All of them predict they can. Yet when given a battery, bulb, and wire, most of them fail. Only a few seem to understand the principle of positive and negative ions meeting in the filament of the bulb to make it light. *"It speaks to a very basic understanding of electricity."*

https://www.learner.org/series/minds-of-our-own/1-can-we-believe-our-eyes/

When the graduates are given a piece of wood and asked what the wood is made up of, most say; *"water, minerals from the soil, and light for energy."*   But that is not the case. The wood comes from the air. When told that wood comes from the air, most act with disbelief. In fact, plants take in carbon dioxide (CO_2). In photosynthesis, they give off oxygen, and the carbon atoms, densely packed together, become the wood.

Photosynthesis is taught in every biology class in high school, but what do they really understand? In a study in a high school classroom, the biology teacher selects one of the brightest students in class. The experimenters ask him to describe what wood is made of. Like the college graduates, he says, "water, minerals from the soil, light". Then, the biology teacher spends a week talking about photosynthesis. Next, the experimenters asked the student again. He gives the same answer; 60% water and 40% minerals, or maybe 70% water. The actual source, carbon in the CO_2 in the air, is lost in translation.

https://www.learner.org/series/minds-of-our-own/2-lessons-from-thin-air/

The serious studies at Harvard and MIT should be seen by every teacher. They force us to re-evaluate how we teach and how we test.

Part of the problem is that people have *"a mind of their own"*. They come into class with preconceived ideas, and learning does not change their ideas. They may remember what they learn long enough to pass a test, and then it is gone. They revert to their previous ideas.

It seems that the belief that air has no weight, was a critical error that made it impossible for the students to understand that the carbon in CO_2 creates wood. Even more so in psychology; "common sense" and personal beliefs prevent learning even the most basic facts of psychology.

If you want to test yourself, I have a series of questions in Chapter 10 on *Cognition (p. 213)*, to see how you compare to the average college student. It deals with two of the most important psychological reasons why we fail to learn; the primacy effect of prior ideas, and how difficult it is to put together two simple ideas we have learned, if we have never seen that exact example before. It suggests we do not "think", we answer questions, just as the question about what wood is made of, from how the mind has learned to *perceive* the question. Just as we may perceive an illusion like the Necker cube, we *perceive* the question, based on our past experiences.

The professionals in the Harvard and MIT study describe the problem best:

> *"Why are students unable to learn?', is the critical question. Even the best and brightest often fail to grasp the most basic of ideas that we teach. "*

> *"By every indicator I see, we are not effective overall in the education of our youth, and we are paying a tremendous amount of money for it."* Science educator Earl Carlyon

> *"All young children know how to acquire meaning, that's the way they learn the language, without any special coding. But when they get in school they start learning to memorize, learning to pass tests rather than learning for understanding. Then the problem begins and it continues right through the university." Prof. Joseph Novak Cornell University.*

> *"I think we are teaching knowledge in bits, chunks, fragments. Meaningful understanding means not learning something in a shallow way, like a friend's telephone number that you keep in your mind long enough to dial it and then it's gone." Prof. Kathleen Fisher San Diego State Univ.*

"Just because you can explain something doesn't mean you understand the science. You have to be able to predict what will happen. That's the power of science." Prof. Philip Sadler, Harvard Univ.

"We try to teach maybe ten times more, than what kids can actually learn in our science classroom." *Prof. Philip Sadler, Harvard Univ.*

We have excellent textbooks in psychology, yet they are crammed full of far more than students could ever learn. Every revision proudly adds hundreds more studies. This creates more confusion, with more to memorize, and fewer examples that make for understanding. By forcing too much on them to memorize, we shortchange understanding. These texts would be most valuable as a fourth-year survey course.

"Every (scientist) gets a narrower and narrower field of knowledge in which he must be an expert in order to compete with other (scientists). The specialist knows more and more about less and less and finally knows everything about nothing." Nobel Laureate Ethologist Konrad Lorenz

We still teach by rote memory. The tests themselves are constructed to require students to memorize vast numbers of facts that will fit into a multiple-choice exam; and divide them into As, Bs, and Cs. But this does not test for understanding. Students are drowning in a tsunami of trivia.

Our schools have glorified sports, with weekly pep rallies for the football team, cheerleaders who cheer for the team, and the band that plays for the team. Majorettes that lead the parade for the team. Science has become just another pain the students must suffer through. The value of science is left out of our educational system, suffocating the spark of interest in students.

"Anti-science is now the leading killer of young and middle age adults in the United States." Dr. Peter Hotez, Baylor College of Medicine, on the refusal of nearly 1/3 of Americans to get vaccinated against Covid-19. CNN *01-11-2022*
https://www.healthsystemtracker.org/brief/covid-19-leading-cause-of-death-ranking/

The textbooks we use are bloated with studies, but low on examples. It should be the other way around.

"Examples are not another way to teach.
Examples are the only way to teach."
Albert Einstein

For a remarkable lecture on how learning occurs in students, see the following by Dr. Norman of UW School of Medicine and Public Health. Dr. Norman gives explicit examples of the essential need for multiple examples, in different circumstances, before a deep understanding can develop.

https://www.youtube.com/watch?v=cwaWHeyK_aM

Students and teachers can benefit from his lecture by thinking of multiple examples from life, the news, or personal experience, that illustrate the basic principles of psychology.

Few of my students are going to become PhDs in psychology. Most will become parents. Many will become teachers, or nurses, or car wash attendants. But all of them need to come away from a psychology course understanding what we know about how the mind works, and how it applies to the real world, not just memorizing terms in a textbook.

"I hope none of you are feeling stress about this test. It's only 50% of your grade, 60% of your future and 100% of your self esteem."

Yet, we teach our introductory psychology courses as if they were all going to become PhDs in psychology. We owe it to all of our students to give them information to understand life; the need for science, not just the bare bones of science, their need to understand interpersonal relations, how their own mind works, how others think, how our mind depends on our unique experiences. Instead, we ignore the misinformation, the politics, and the anti-science bias in our culture, as if psychology has nothing to say about the most serious issues of our time.

"The whole effect of our educational system is to dumb down and eviscerate any curiosity and interest. We serve, on a hardboard platter, the bland knowledge, void of understanding, censored to avoid offending, lame with interest..."

How To Escape Education's Death Valley | Sir Ken Robinson
https://www.youtube.com/watch?v=wX78iKhInsc

Out school system, with its enthusiastic pep rallies for "our" team, it's cheerleading for "our" team, and the band playing for "our" team, has made sports into the thing valued by most of our students. It has made science, and reality, into a boring, even painful, experience, that most must suffer through just to escape the prison that, by law, they must endure for twelve years. When they finally escape after twelve years, the only things they have learned to value as adults are sports and socializing with their friends.

From the mind of genius to the suicide bombers of today's news, from science to sex, understanding is essential to psychology. Memorizing facts is not what psychology is about. By reducing the number of studies, and emphasizing more stories and examples, this is an attempt to give students an edge on what they come to class for; an understanding of their minds and that of others. By knitting together the value of the studies we cover, with the examples, hopefully, they will come away with a better understanding of psychology.

We need to emphasize understanding and examples more than terms to memorize. There are still terms to memorize, such as the parts of the brain. But even here, the stories of **how** we know what the parts of the brain do, are as important as just learning *what* they do. Learning **how** we know is the essence of understanding science, and it makes it easier to remember than just memorizing words.

Years from now, students will probably have forgotten the studies about what the Frontal Lobes do, but all of us still remember the story of what happened to Phineas Gage when a steel rod was blown through the frontal lobes of his brain.

They will only dimly remember the Formal Scientific Techniques, but they will remember how the best doctors in America opened a vein to bleed George Washington of 40% of his blood (he died), and Sear's Electric Belts, and witch hunts, and demon possession, and what all that says about ***why*** we need the scientific methods.

They will learn nothing from teaching a dog to salivate to a bell, or memorizing CS, CR, UCS, and UCR; it will be lost to their mind as soon as they walk out the door. But they will remember how the Russians trained dogs to kill tanks in WWII and why this applies to the Kamikaze pilots, the suicide terrorists of 9/11, today's politics, and interactions with others. From those stories, we hope they will have formed an understanding of *how* we know what we know about the mind.

"Everything cool is to be found in the deep woods."

They may not remember the subtle force of words associated with emotion, but they will remember why a man who lived in a hole in the ground, eating rats for 30 years, received *"over 100 marriage proposals from awestruck women."* Yes, really. They will learn why one of Picasso's paintings recently sold at Sotheby's auction for 157 million dollars, while the same painting with your name on it would devalue the canvas it was painted on. And they will remember why Scarlett Johansson's "snot" sold for $5,300 on eBay. Yes, really.

They will remember how motion pictures control the emotions in your brain as adrenalin shoots into your blood, as you watch the Zombie apocalypse in a theater, and how that applies to politics, interpersonal relations, peer group pressure, anxiety, and the Salem witch hunt (see chapters 2 and 8).

Some in psychology have become successful by criticizing one point of view and showing their own to be superior (biological, behaviorism, developmental, cognitive, evolutionary, neuroscience, etc., etc...) No other science does this. We need to integrate all of the best of these approaches into a Unified Field in psychology. The "New" in this approach involves integrating perceptual psychology and culture as an essential basis of understanding how the mind works (Ch. 8 and 9).

I have tried to replace many of the less important studies with more examples of the most important principles and how they interact. But there is a great deal to learn in psychology. It turned out to be more difficult to reduce the information than I had imagined.

These are the bits and pieces that make up a deep understanding of how our mind works. I hope I have done them justice. Welcome to the deep woods...

1 THE ORIGIN OF SCIENCE

of ESP, Witchcraft, and Placebos

Extrasensory Perception • Hippocrates • Placebo Effects • Medicine's Era of Witchcraft • Psychology's Era of Word Magic •
Science • Rules of Evidence • Methods of Science

Before psychology could speak with the accent of science, before it could even pretend to produce results that bear the hallmark of knowledge as distinguished from opinion, it had to acquire new methods of collecting and elaborating its data. It had, in short, to learn the scientific method and in doing so to move from its armchair to the laboratory.

E. Heidbreder *Seven Psychologies*

In 447 BCE, the Greek historian Herodotus set down in writing an account of what must have been one of the first attempts by anyone to apply a scientific test to a problem of psychology. Herodotus is often called the "father" of modern history, because he was the first to write about his country, with all its problems and mistakes, without the glorification of their country and king that others had let pass for history. The problem he described involved extrasensory perception. Can some people know what is happening even though they are not present at the time? Can some predict the future?

Left: Herodotus the Greek Historian

The experimenter in Herodotus' account was Croesus, King of Lydia. Lydia was a highly cultured and powerful Greek city-state on the western edge of Turkey, between Persia and Greece. Historically, Lydians are famous as the first known civilization to use coins as money rather than simply to barter for goods—say, by trading wheat for pigs or chickens. Lydia lay at the doorstep of the mighty Persian empire, and Persia was gobbling up all the nearby states. Croesus likely knew they would get around to him.

Croesus wanted to know what would happen if he and his allies engaged in a pre-emptive attack on the Persian empire. Could he destroy them, before they got to him?

Croesus was not naïve. He knew the Persians were powerful. Before he would make any plans to attack them, he wanted to know the outcome of the war in advance. In our history, mystics, oracles, seers, and soothsayers, who claimed to predict the future, were abundant. To Croesus, the problem was, how do you tell a good mystic from all the people who only claim to have the power?

Croesus devised a test, a fairly ingenious test for his time. He assembled all of his scribes. Each was instructed to go to a specific oracle on a specific day at a specific time and ask the psychic what Croesus was doing at that moment. The scribes were instructed to record the answers and return them to Croesus. The logic was impeccable. Since only Croesus would know what he was doing, the psychics who answered correctly must have the power.

Above, is the temple of Apollo, where the Oracle of Delphi gave her predictions.

One scribe journeyed to the Oracle of Delphi, another to the Seeress at Ammon, throughout the known world, his test was spread; to Greece, Egypt, Jorden, and every other place where an oracle of reputation was known to live. On the appointed day, the scribes asked their question, recorded the answer, and on their return, they told Croesus of the answers they were given.

Of all the answers Croesus heard, only one rang true. The Oracle of Delphi, known as the Pythoness, answered that Croesus was making, in effect, a lamb stew. Croesus was impressed, for this was what he had been doing at that hour of the day. He had made it with his own hands, unknown to anyone.

Certain that the Oracle of Delphi was a true mystic, Croesus surrounded the oracle with much gold and sacrificed three thousand of every sacrificial beast to Apollo. Thus, ensuring her cooperation, he proceeded to ask the crucial question. What would happen, he asked, if he took his armies into battle against the Persian Empire?

The oracle replied that if Croesus attacked the Persians, he would destroy a mighty empire.

Armed with the knowledge that the greatest oracle in the world had given him knowledge of the outcome in advance, Croesus assembled his armies and led them against the Persians. The battle commenced. The fighting was hard. As the dust of battle cleared, from amidst the cries of the wounded and the stench of the dead, Croesus could see that the oracle had been right a second time. Croesus had destroyed a mighty empire—unfortunately for Croesus, it was his own.

The study of ESP by Croesus showed the beginnings of a spirit of scientific inquiry. Croesus was unwilling to accept other people's accounts about the abilities of the many oracles—he wanted to put their claims to a controlled test. He asked a question that none of the oracles could have known the answer to, only he knew the answer. And he sampled more than one oracle.

But two things prevented his study from being a good example of the scientific technique.

First, to be scientific, it must be **Reproducible**; Croesus did not try to reproduce the original successful prediction. Replication is essential in science. And, he asked only one question. The Oracle might have answered correctly by chance alone. If he had asked a dozen or more questions, he might have discovered that her answers were largely by chance.

Second, **Unclear Results.** Her answer could be interpreted in more than one way. She never specified what would actually happen, only that one empire would win. No matter who won, she would be right.

A single positive finding, even several positive findings, cannot be considered good evidence. It must be possible to repeat the same study time and time again with the assurance that the same or similar results will occur predictably, not accidentally. It would then be possible to compare the results of these studies with what might be expected by guessing—that is, by chance alone.

Her prediction could be interpreted in any way that one wished to interpret it. Immediately after his defeat on the battlefield, Croesus sent a messenger to the Pythoness at Delphi asking why he had lost the war. Her reply was (Herodotus, transl.):

It is not possible even for a god to escape the decree of destiny. Croesus has been punished for the sin of his fifth ancestor, who, when he was one of the bodyguards of the Heraclites, joined in a woman's fraud, and, slaying his master, wrongfully seized the throne.

Ambiguous statements that can be interpreted in more than one way are impressive cerebral magic perhaps, but they are of no value in adding to scientific knowledge. Predictions that would bring gasps of amazement from all when correct could easily be excused by the seeress when wrong.

Even the lamb stew the Oracle had predicted the first time could have been interpreted as a mess with his plans.

If the excuses could be tested and found to be true, they might then have scientific validity. We could then specify the conditions under which the predictions worked and did not work. But the conditions themselves can be couched in phrases that make them impossible to test and hence impossible to disprove.

Croesus was not alone. For tens of centuries, we have sought shortcuts to the future. We have stared in awe at mystics and magicians who seem to have supernatural power. Each year, we hear accounts of supernatural happenings and often we see at least one whose caption reads:

PSYCHIC POWERS OF_____MYSTIFY SCIENTISTS

Similar news headlines have appeared like clockwork since the beginning of the printed word.

PROPHACIES OF NOSTRADAMUS

One of the most recent revivals of prophecy were the predictions of Nostradamus. In 1555 A.D. he published some 942 quatrains that some believe have predicted events in the future. With that many quatrains, it is perhaps not surprising that *nine* of his quatrains seem to have come true.

One of the most celebrated is the report that he predicted the rise of Hitler and WWII. That prediction is based on the following quatrain:

> *Beasts ferocious with hunger will cross the rivers,*
> *The greater part of the battlefield will be against Hister.*
> *Into a cage of iron will the great one be drawn,*
> *When the child of Germany observes nothing.*

Some say this is predicting the invasion of Poland that began WWII when "Beasts ferocious" (tanks?) crossed into Poland. They say Hister was a reference to Hitler. But Hister is actually the Latin name for the Danube River. Nostradamus' critics note that his interpretations have been added later by his more enthusiastic followers. It is easier to predict the future, with the advantage of hindsight.

WHEN THE WORLD ENDED: *2012*

A similar example frightened much of America. Hollywood even made a movie about it called *2012*. The Maya calendar ended abruptly in December of 2012. Surely this must be a prediction of the end of the world. Could Hollywood and the *Dresden Codex* both be wrong?

Yet if you look at the Maya writings, the book, the Dresden Codex, sometimes called the Maya "Bible", the last day of the calendar ends abruptly on December 21, 2012. When the Maya described the last days on their calendar, it ended with a giant alligator (sky caiman) throwing up alligator vomit all over the world. For those who feared the world would end in massive alligator vomit, it must have been a dire prediction.

https://www.nbcnews.com/business/business-news/mayan-doomsday-marketers-see-opportunity-flna1c7608708

For NASA's comment on the end of the world, too often ignored in favor of the more sensational idea of the end of the world, see: https://www.nasa.gov/topics/earth/features/2012.html

But the Maya believed in cyclical rebirth, so it might never have been considered the end, only a new beginning.

Or, maybe, the Maya just got tired of making their calendar at that point and decided to go celebrate with a crock of Cepe'.

The image at the left, often used as an example of the Maya calendar, is actually a much later Aztec style calendar.

2012 has come and gone. Hollywood is still making movies. Ancient Aliens still walk among us, at least on the History Channel. Ghosts and Bigfoot have infiltrated Sci-Fi and the Travel Channel. Pass the Cepe'.

"What is your sign?" Aquarius? Scorpio? Taurus? Today, many people still believe that your "stars" determine your personality and perhaps your future. All science, from astronomers to psychologists, long ago abandoned any chance that either is true.

"The fault... is not in our stars, but in ourselves." Shakespeare

WHEN PROPHECY FAILS

In their book *When Prophecy Fails*, Psychologists Leon Festinger, Henry Rieken, and Stanley Schachter infiltrated a group of people whose leaders predicted the end of the world at a specific date. They wanted to know what would happen when that date came, and the world did not end (Chapter 20).

At first, the believers excused their failure by saying that they may be off on the date, but as more time passed, and it became increasingly clear the world was still spinning on, there was a marked change in their opinions.

Those whose belief was least, who had the least investment in the group, often quit the group. But those believers who were most convinced, some of whom had given away their possessions, continued to believe, sometimes even stronger. They excused the failure and went on looking for more "signs". They often became even more unwilling to change:

"A man with a conviction is a hard man to change. Tell him you disagree and he turns away. Show him facts or figures and he questions your sources. Appeal to logic and he fails to see your point."

This is not just a comment on one group and their inability to see any other facts. We see this again and again in our value judgments of others, our prejudices, our personal opinions, our politics, our religions, and every disagreement we have. What happens when people who refuse to consider any reality other than the ideas that others have imbedded in their mind become our politicians, our police, our bosses, our leaders?

The understanding of how easily people come to believe in the end of the world prophecy is critical to understanding how it is possible that 900 followers of the Reverend Jim Jones willingly committed suicide by drinking the poison they mixed into the Kool-aide in Jonestown. Hence, the term *"they drank the Kool-aide"* as a term for when people accept something without evidence. And it helps to understand how 36 followers of the Heavens Gate prophet in California, committed suicide, believing that they would be taken aboard a spaceship hidden in the wake of the Hale-Bopp comet, if they had enough faith. Understanding the power of words, associated with emotion, is basic to understanding the way the mind works. This important issue will be covered in Chapters 8 and 9 on the Mind Code and Perception.

The first ideas that others embed in our brain are the criteria by which we judge all things. We see this daily in our politics, where facts have no meaning unless the facts happen to support our bias. No amount of argument seems able to get past our personal beliefs.

"The aim of science is not to provide infinite wisdom, but to limit infinite error." Bertolt Brecht

He did not always fit in well
with the group think of the other scientists.

To foretell the future, the British read the tea leaves in the bottom of the pot. Before the battle of Masada, to know the outcome in advance, the Romans read the entrails of goats, spread out on the ground. The readings usually went well for the Romans. Primitive societies may "throw the bones". Today, some read the movements of the stars or the lines in your hand. How could events of pure chance come to control people's beliefs? See Chapters 2 and 8.

ESP AND SCIENCE: *Scientific Studies*

There are scientific studies that some believe provide evidence that ESP exists. This is the "scientific" evidence that is often written up in the popular media. However, the media rarely explains what the evidence is.

One example of this type of evidence is provided by an early study of ESP, sometimes called the *sheep versus the goats* study, conducted by Schmeidler and McConnell. The study tested the ability of two groups of subjects to predict the suits of cards. The two groups comprised those who believed in ESP (sheep) and those who did not (goats).

Twenty-five cards were in the deck. There were five different suits in this deck. The experimenter turned over each card, one at a time, and concentrated on the card that was exposed. The subject, who could not see the cards, tried to pick up mental clues about each card and then guessed its suit.

Over many trials, with twenty-five guesses for each run, the "Laws of Chance' would predict that the average person should score 5.00, guessing the suits of five cards correctly out of every twenty-five, purely by chance. What the researchers found was that subjects who did not believe in ESP, the goats, got 4.86 calls correct on the average, while those who believed in ESP, the sheep, got an average of 5.23 calls correct.

The differences between the two groups are statistically significant. Such results would not be expected to occur by chance over five times in one hundred (the .05 level).

The Schmeidler-McConnell study also raised its own questions. While differences between chance (5.00) and the result of 5.23 may suggest a small but significant degree of ESP, how do we account for the below-average performance of the nonbelievers? Is there such a thing as negative ESP? Or is there an unconscious bias in the way each group calls the cards that could account for the results of both groups?

It is difficult for many scientists to accept the idea that studies whose validity is based on violating the laws of chance can be accepted, especially when the results are so small.

"Even a blind chicken can find some corn"
Unknown Sage

Iverson et al. threw over twenty sets of dice from four different manufacturers over four million times. They measured the number of times the dice came up odd or even in each run of 20,000 throws, and compared the result to what would be expected by chance. They found a built-in bias in the roll of the dice, greater than would be expected by chance alone, and with no ESP at all.

SCIENCE AND PSYCHOLOGY
CAN PREDICT THE FUTURE. Yes, really.

Is it possible to predict the future? Yes, it is. And if you bear with me, I am about to show you how it is done using science. No, it is not a trick, it is a very real demonstration of how science and psychology can do things the supernatural cannot.

Let us try an experiment. Below are four numbers 1-2-3-4. See if your mind can *predict* what number most people would think of when they see this example. Circle which of the following numbers you think most people would circle.

1   2   3   4

After you circle one of the numbers, next circle which of the following numbers you like the most:

1   2   3   4   5   6   7   8   9   10

In the first example, if you were choosing by chance alone, each number would have an equal statistical chance of being picked. 25% would circle 1, 25% would circle 2, 25% would circle 3, and 25% would circle 4.

Most people would think of number 3. What number did you circle?

In fact, more students who are asked this question will circle number 3. Does that prove that you have ESP? That you can predict the future? Actually no, it proves the advantage of science. Simple systematic observation tells us that the majority of students, about 51%, will always pick number 3. Even if they are only asked to circle ANY one number. It has nothing to do with ESP, it has everything to do with science; having done this study repeatedly, that allows us to make a prediction, that violates the laws of chance, based on the scientific method of *systematic observation*.

The next most common number circled is number 2. Numbers 1 and 4 are rarely picked. In state lotteries, numbers 2 and 3 are the most commonly picked numbers. Yet in Japan, number 1, Ichiban, has a cultural bias. Ichiban means the first, the best.

Interestingly, if psychologists run this study again, on the same students, most of them will pick a different number. It is as if they are trying to prove they have free will, that they can make their own choice. That too, is predictable.

In picking a number from 1 to 10, again statistics clearly say that each number, if picked at random, would have a 10% chance of being circled. But we never choose at random. Any number has a chance. Yet number 7 is most commonly picked. Why? Perhaps because it is so commonly heard in our culture; "God rested on the 7th day", lucky 7 in dice, 7 days of the week, 7th son of a 7th son, Snow White and the 7 Dwarves...

Culture changes the value of what is embedded in our minds.

Even in an apparently free choice of numbers, we are influenced by our past experiences in our culture. All of this happens without our awareness. The role of culture is profound.

Numerology is the belief that numbers have magical significance in your life. There is no evidence for this, but people believe it because other people do.

In China, the number 8 has magical properties. It is their lucky number. In the year 2008, thousands of couples across China picked the number 8 and chose to get married on the 8th second of the 8th minute of the 8th hour, of the 8th day, of the 8th month of the year 2008, believing this would bless their marriage.

If you live in Haiti, Voodoo dolls may have magical significance. It is the location of pins in the Voodoo doll that brings bad luck to whoever is doing black magic to you. Did you know you can buy Voodoo dolls on Amazon.com? There are over 808 hits on Voodoo dolls or Voodoo doll pins.

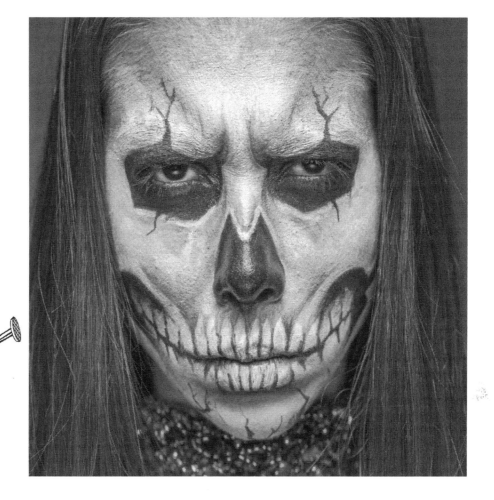

PSYCHOLOGY CONTROLS THE BIOLOGY OF YOUR BRAIN

Of course, Voodoo is not real. And yet, if you believe it is real, that has even more powerful control over your mind than the Hollywood versions of the Zombie Apocalypse that sends a chill up the spine of Americans watching Zombies in a movie theater. How this can happen is a critical issue in psychology (see chapter eight on *The Mind Code*).

At the witch trials of Salem, when the accused witch, almost all of them elderly women, was brought into the courtroom, the girls of Salem began to point at the accused and shriek "Witch! Witch!". At that moment adrenalin would have shot into the bloodstream of the spectators. Their heart would jump; just as today, we still respond in a movie theater to a Hollywood horror. The spectators were convinced by the reaction of their own bodies of the guilt of the accused. What else could possibly explain the feelings in their own body? Psychology (the emotion generated by the words of the girls), controlled the biology of their bodies. And that controlled their mind. See Chapters 2 on Learning and 8 on Perception for details.

Psychology controls the emotions in your brain. Simply understanding that may help give us greater control over our own brains. If you do not believe in Voodoo, it has little effect on you; although you may still feel a twinge of uncertainty. If you do not believe in witches, the idea has no power over you, and you are no longer a danger to your elderly neighbors.

In our seemingly free choice of numbers, culture is the culprit, not ESP. Science gives us an advantage in being able to predict something that is seemingly statistically impossible to predict, by observation and experimentation. Simply repeating this study again and again, gives us the power to predict. That is the value of science over ESP.

Could it be that similar studies with cards and ESP are measuring a similar bias and not ESP? The same problem exists in many scientific studies as well. Psychology has accepted that if a study is significant at the .05 level, meaning that, statistically, it may occur by chance only 5 times out of a hundred, that somehow that is good evidence. Not necessarily.

THE CIA and THE KGB:
THE *"MEN WHO STARE AT GOATS"*

The American Central Intelligence Agency learned from its sources in Russia that the Soviets were studying Psychokinesis, the ability to manipulate matter using the power of the mind. Our government was afraid we were losing the edge. Were the Russians again ahead of us just as they had beaten us into space with their Sputnik space program?

The U.S Army launched a top-secret, ten-year, ten-million-dollar program to try to catch up with the Russians. Would we be able to? Or were they too far ahead?

Hollywood has already made a movie about the study titled, *"Men Who Stare at Goats"*, starring George Clooney. The title was based on an actual study in the program that had psychics stare at a goat in the next room, from behind a one-way glass.

The psychic was asked to focus their psychic energy on the goat to destabilize the goat. Sometimes it took hours. Sometimes it took minutes. But eventually, the goat would begin to twitch, then jerk, then its movements became uncontrollable and it fell to the ground jerking and twitching. After some minutes, the goat would recover and stumble around, as if in a drunken stupor, until it returned to normal.

I have seen some of the films of the Russian psychic that convinced the Russians that Psychokinesis, the ability to control matter with the mind, actually works. A lady psychic was brought into the laboratory. She was made to disrobe and put on a laboratory smock, to ensure that she had nothing concealed that might influence the outcome. Then she was led downstairs into a bare room with a concrete floor and concrete block walls. In the middle of the room were nothing but a folding table and a hardback wooden chair.

After she was seated at the table they brought in a Russian navy compass, sealed in a wooden box, with a glass top. The psychic would focus her energy on the needle of the compass. She moved her hand about six inches above the glass of the compass. At first, nothing. But then the needle of the sealed compass would twitch and jerk and twitch. There is a lot of twitching and jerking in psychokinesis. As she moved her hand in a circle, the needle of the compass would start to turn with her hand. As she moved her hand faster and faster above the compass, the needle would spin faster and faster. As she slowed, the needle would slow. When she stopped, the needle would stop.

What else could it be but the power of mind over matter?

At the same time, in America, our psychics were showing even more remarkable powers. Uri Geller had demonstrated, before the physicists at Lawrence Livermore Laboratories, America's nuclear laboratory, that he could bend spoons and keys with this mind. The scientists were convinced he could not have tricked them. Yet it was beyond anything known to physics.

Uri Geller made a fortune showing his ability before groups of awe-struck celebrities in Hollywood. At one gathering, he would ask everyone present to get out their keys. Then he would go through several keyrings staring at the keys. Finally, he would remove one key, ask the owner to place his finger on the end of the key, put the key down on the table, and he would rub the long end of the key, barely touching it with his fingers, while focusing his mind on the key, all the while the camera was on the key.

After several moments, he might ask if the key was getting hot. Soon he would pull his fingers back from the key and the audience would gasp at seeing a very sharp bend in the key. He could then flick the long end of the key with his finger and make it bounce up and down on the table.

Did Geller have psychokinetic power? Was he proof of what the Army was looking for? It was all very impressive to the Army. Or was there another explanation?

James Randi is a world-famous magician who has made a living exposing psychic tricks. He made an offer of $100,000 of his own money to anyone who could show psychic power under strictly controlled conditions. Today, that offer stands at $1,000,000 of his own money. *"No one has ever been able to collect even one cent of that money"*, Randi says. Could Geller?   Geller did not take Randi up on his offer.

Randi demonstrated that he could do the same thing by taking a key off of Dick Patton's keyring and, on camera, easily bent the key, barely touching it with his fingers as he rubbed the end of the key.

How did Randi do it? He claims no psychic powers. He says it was just a trick. But he stood by the magician's oath to tell no secrets.

I have no magician's oath, so I have no problem telling you how it can be done. I have done it in class, the same way. Ask first for students to get out their keyrings. Find one you like and remove the key. Have them put their finger on the head of the key and you stroke the long end of the key. As you slowly move your fingers back from the key, it seems to continue to bend in front of your eyes.

How is he/she going to get into their house tonight?

But the secret is not in what the audience thinks they are seeing. The secret is in what happened the night before. You see, there are only three basic types of house keys; the Kwikset, the Schlage, and a mortice style. So, you rummage through your old keys, find a Schlage and a Kwikset, ones you don't remember what they were for, place each one at an angle at the L of the base of a concrete step, and whack it with a hammer until you have a nice parabolic bend.

Then you simply palm the already bent key in class, and ask students to get out their keyrings. Kwikset is one you can always find, and the easiest to bend. Make a show of taking one off of someone's keyring, and slide it into the palm of your hand.

Then push just the head of the already bent key out. Ask the person to put their finger on the head (this helps, because it keeps the already bent key from flopping around) and stroke the long part of the key gently with your fingers. Keep the already bent end of the key covered with your fingers, and gradually move your fingers back. The nice parabolic bend makes it look as if it is bending in real-time as you gradually slide your fingers back.

But the real reaction comes when I tell the audience how the trick is done.

"Aaaaw! It's Just a Trick!!!"

"Aaaaw, it's just a trick." Students often react with disappointment. People want magic and mystery. They demand entertainment. But the purpose of science is not to awe people, the purpose of science is to find out how reality works.

We are fed a constant diet of X-Men and Supermen and Harry Potter and John Wicks and superheroes and sports heroes and special effects. The mantra of Hollywood and most of television seems to be; "Millions for special effects, not one cent for reality."

We live in a fairy tale of our own creation.

Reality cannot compete with the sensationalism that tickles our emotions.

> We often demand magic and superheroes... reality seems boring by comparison.

The prestigious PEW research institute found that America ranks 24th in the world in science; the worst of any civilized nation on earth. The failure of our educational system to get across to our species the *value* of science has created an illusion we cannot escape.

https://www.pewresearch.org/fact-tank/2017/02/15/u-s-students-internationally-math-science/ft_17-02-14_stem_table/

"Rather than 'Great Books', could you show me the 'Mediocre But Fun to Read Books'?"

America is behind Estonia, Slovenia, Poland, Czechoslovakia, and 20 other countries in science. Singapore, Japan, and Estonia are the top three in science. China is rising fast.

We are overwhelmed by magic and mystery. We expect it. We demand it. We are disappointed by reality. We have been fed a diet of sensationalism for so long, that reality is boring. Yet the sensational world of superheroes and fairy tales has done nothing to help our species.

We have made more progress in the last 100 years than in tens of thousands of previous years combined. Only the methods of science have provided the development of agriculture, medicine, and research that has improved the human condition.

Immunization and antibiotics and medical technology have dramatically reduced the death of millions from the plagues that took the lives of so many of our youth. Science and technology applied to agriculture have brought about a great abatement from the famine that took the lives of millions.

Yet we still cannot escape the emotions, the Limbic System tickling, that controls what people seek.

In every area of science, from agriculture to the invention of antibiotics and immunization, figuring out how things work has made our species a success. Science keeps our children from dying of starvation and disease. Amazing people does not help. Yet in the "real world" entertainment rules. Hollywood and sports and politics have proven that sensationalism is where the money lies. Tickle, tickle.

So, What About The Russian Psychics and the Goats?

It is important to understand **why** we need the Scientific Methods, before we even get to *what* the Methods are.

The woman who so easily moved the needle of a compass with the power of her mind amazed many. How could anyone fake this? Yet this is not a new trick. Even though they made her disrobe and put on a laboratory smock, they forgot about the shoes. She was wearing the old heavy shoes that Russian women were once famous for. All that would be needed is to take off and cut out part of that big heel, hollow out part of the rubber, insert a powerful magnet in the heal and seal it back up.

When she sat down at the card table, she only had to cross her legs under the table, one foot in her lap, putting the magnet close to the underside of the table. Then, as she moved her hand, faster and faster over the compass, the movement of her hand and body masked the movement of her foot under the table.

The KGB did not tell us what happened to the psychic after they found out.

And the goats? How could anyone possibly fake that? This was left out of the film, but the Army discovered that the farmer who sold them the goats had sold them his defective goats. These goats had a rare psychomotor seizure disorder that was genetic. Several times a day, unpredictably, they would jerk and twitch, fall to the ground, and minutes later, gradually recover. Psychic power had nothing to do with it.

The Hollywood sequel? *Goats who Stare at Men*?

After ten years and ten million dollars, the U.S. Government concluded that there was no useful value to ESP.

But there is a useful value to science and psychology.

Psychologists, as scientists, have developed a callous skepticism from decades of exposure to those less honest than James Randi. Too often, persons claiming to have the power of mind over matter—and having satisfied many an audience as to the truth of their claims—are found to be merely masters at deception. Such deception is usually quickly eliminated in a psychology laboratory, but it sometimes creeps through the most carefully constructed safeguards.

An interesting aside from this, some years ago a woman called the psychology department at the university. She said she was certain that her grandson had ESP and wanted to find a psychologist to test him. The secretary ran up and down the halls of the department trying to find someone to talk to her, or test the grandson. Nobody even wanted to talk to her. Finally, the secretary found a graduate student who was willing to try. We never heard the outcome.

Learning itself creates bias. The only question is whether that way of looking at reality is *accurate* and if the information it is based on is *adequate*. That is why we need the scientific methods.

"We must always have an open mind,
but not so open that our brains fall out."
Bertrand Russel's Nobel Prize Acceptance Speech

If you want to know why ESP is unlikely, read Chapter 6 on the Prime Mover, the neurons that power the brain, and Chapter 4 on how we know what the brain does, from studies of brain injury.

Perhaps even better, examine your own mind as it struggles to remember what you thought you learned on the next exam. Neurons have difficulty communicating, even *within* our own brain.

Even when findings can be shown to be statistically unlikely, occurring by chance perhaps only once in 300,000 times, that cannot be considered proof of what is being investigated. The odds of winning the lottery and getting the extra number right are truly astronomical, yet someone eventually always does.

Scientists have been studying ESP for over a century. To date, the scientific evidence of ESP indicates that its effect is so slight that, even if it exists, its importance to human behavior cannot begin to compare to the importance of other *known* influences on our behavior.

When studying for an exam, do not try to read the teacher's mind. Instead, do it the old-fashioned way; *study*.

There is one way that sometimes will allow you to read the teacher's mind about what is most likely to be on the exam; many of the best teachers often spend the most time in class going over what they consider the most important material. If you focus your mental energy on the areas they cover, that might turn out to be what is on the exam. No guarantees. Every teacher is different. Many teachers hope you will read the textbook for the important details. Hope springs eternal. So, they use the questions made up for them by the textbook publisher.

We can be sure of one thing. We will continue to be deluged with reports of those claiming to have supernatural power. At present, despite media reports to the contrary, no psychic has done anything that cannot easily be duplicated by a good magician. Houdini himself did some of the same things as psychics being touted today, but Houdini did not claim to have special powers.

Houdini spent much of his life debunking claims of psychics that they could get in touch with your dead relatives, for a fee. He was so successful at exposing these fake mediums, that mediums almost disappeared from the media until they reappeared in the late 1990s on the Sci-fi channel.

The doubt that scientists express about the validity of ESP is not mere prejudice, it results from seeing so many frauds in the media, and also what we know about the human brain. Indeed, skepticism reflects a sharp awareness of our recent past when our readiness to believe in supernatural forces ruled our thoughts. This was an era so difficult to overcome that, having escaped its emotions, none want to go back.

FOR THOUSANDS OF YEARS, MENTAL ILLNESS WAS BELIEVED TO BE CAUSED BY DEMON POSSESSION

Emotional disturbance was widely considered to be "caused" by possession by demons. Demoniacal possession was, in turn, believed to be the work of Satan. The following is an account written by a medical doctor in 1836 (Oesterreich). Note the similarities between this and the Hollywood movie, *The Exorcist*:

The voice coming from her professed to be that of an unhappy dead man, her individuality vanished, to give place to another. So long as this lasted, she knew nothing of her individuality, which only reappeared (in all its integrity and reason) when she had retired to rest.
This demon shouted, swore, and raged in the most terrible fashion. He broke out especially into curses against God and everything sacred.

Bodily measures and medicines did not produce the slightest change in her state, nor did a pregnancy and the suckling which followed it. Only continual prayer (to which moreover she was obliged to apply herself with the greatest perseverance, for the demon could not endure it) often frustrated the demon for a time.

During the five months all the resources of medicine were tried in vain. On the contrary, two demons now spoke in her; who often, as it were, played the raging multitude within her, barked like dogs, mewed like cats, etc. Did she begin to pray, the demons at once flung her into the air, swore, and made a horrible din through her mouth.

Prayer was also particularly disagreeable to this one. If the woman wished to kneel down to pray, the demon strove to prevent her with all his might, and if she persisted, he forced her jaws apart and obliged her to utter a diabolic laugh or whistle....

She was able to eat nothing but a soup of black bread and water. As soon as she took anything better, the demon rose up in her and cried: "Carrion should eat nothing good!" and took away her plate. She often fasted for two or three complete days without taking a crumb of food and without drinking a drop. On those days the demon kept quiet. Through distress, suffering and fasting, she had grown thin and was little more than a skeleton. Her pains were often so great, by night as well as day, as to beggar description, and we like herself were in despair over them.

Notice that the doctor is describing the events *as if* he actually *saw* the "demon" doing these things. All he saw was the individual doing this. He assumed demons were the cause, therefore he wrote his assumptions about what he believed he was seeing. Observations are not valuable unless they are precise.

Following the movie, *The Exorcist*, psychologists saw an increase across America in the number of people who believed they were possessed by demons. Many *imitated* the symptoms they saw in *The Exorcist*.

Following the movie *Jaws*, about people being eaten by a great white shark, beaches across America reported a decrease in attendance.

"That werewolf film had a profound effect on you."

> Albert Bandura, in a classic study of learning, showed that children exposed to violence, tend to *imitate* that violence.

For centuries, we have credited supernatural forces with our own emotions, loves, hates, and desires. Such powers were believed to be the causes not only of disease and emotional disturbance but of all-natural phenomena. Famine, storms, drought, wind, and other happenings were attributed to supernatural forces. The Greeks attributed thunder and lightning in storms to the power of Zeus. Even today, in the twenty-first century, such beliefs linger in our legal contracts. Insurance contracts still refer to floods, hurricanes, tornadoes, and hailstorms as "acts of God."

"Everywhere man blames nature and fate, yet his fate is mostly but the echo of his character and passion, his mistakes and his weaknesses."

Democritus (2,440 years ago)

Fearsome-looking Gargoyles surrounded the churches in the Middle Ages. Above, and below, Gargoyles, several of many around the Cathedral of Notre Dame in Paris. People believed it would scare off demons. It must have worked; all the demons have disappeared.

Throughout history, eyewitness accounts of dragons abound. The Nights of the Round Table in England were portrayed as fighting off dragons to save the princess. Countless tales abound of people seeing dragons flying against the sky. Eyewitness accounts of demons, succubus', sea monsters, and monsters of all types were the reading fare of an educated public.

Today, all of this has been replaced by Zombies, Bigfoot, UFOs, ESP, Ancient Aliens, Ghosts, and countless other supernatural ideas. The mind is a fertile place for fiction. Hollywood has combined with "reality TV" to give us nothing but emotions that grab our attention.

Dragons took on an international flavor, showing up not only in England, but in Slovakia, China, and even in America, in the form of Quetzalcoatl, the feathered serpent of the Aztecs. Anthropologists note that this myth may have come from the separate discoveries of fossils of dinosaurs found in the rocks. The Smithsonian describes how a Chinese historian, Chang Qu, in the 4th century had mistakenly labeled a Stegosaurus fossil as a dragon (Stromberg). These fossils had been dead for over 60 million years. Human nature, and our fertile imagination, were all that may have been needed to make people see dragons everywhere.

For centuries, the development of science as we know it was paralyzed by superstition, fear, beliefs, and emotions that blinded us to what was there. We wove elaborate stories around these myths, just as if the myths were true. What are the forces that shape such superstitions? How much of what we believe is determined by unlikely coincidences or by our own expectations?

"Our system went down because someone stepped on a crack in the sidewalk."

Psychologists, even more than doctors, must worry about how such effects may influence human perception. Much of the magic and ritual of primitive societies has its origin in such effects. Science itself emerged from the ashes of myths and magic. Before we can understand psychology—before we can approach it as a science—we must explore the operation of these influences on our perception, beliefs, and behavior.

Despite the lack of scientific evidence for ESP, many people believe in it because of a personal experience with something that seems to be ESP. Most of us have had the experience of having a "feeling" that something will happen only to find that it does happen. We may be thinking of a friend when suddenly the phone rings and we discover the friend has called. Can such "feelings" be mere coincidence?

A college professor who commuted thirty miles a day to and from college notes that sometimes he got a feeling that he might have an accident and should stay home that day. The feeling was especially strong on days when the weather was rainy. In three years of commuting, he never had an accident. What would have happened if he had? He says he probably would have become a strong believer in "feelings."

Most of us make predictions of various kinds every day, but we are most likely to remember the rare predictions that turn out right and ignore the hundreds that are wrong. We may be thinking of someone, and suddenly the phone rings. Just who we were thinking of. This may only have happened once, but we tend to remember this and forget the many times we were thinking of someone and nothing happened.

This tendency is responsible for the fame of a great many mystics. The psychic Jeanne Dixon, for example, has made dozens of predictions since she reportedly predicted the assassination of President John Kennedy. Most of her predictions have been either grossly inaccurate or obvious to anyone who has studied the circumstances surrounding the predicted event.

In 1960 Dixon predicted that Fidel Castro would be deposed within ten years. Almost all of us believed he could not last. Castro outlived her prediction by over forty years.

She predicted that America would land on the moon within ten years. We did, but President Kennedy had made the same prediction before Dixon.

Her followers, however, notice only the successes, while the many failures are quickly forgotten. This is the same human characteristic that gives the Las Vegas slot machines such powerful control over behavior. Even though the machines only pay back three out of every four dollars put in them, on average, we tend to notice the wins and ignore the losses. Thus, by ignoring the losses, most players come away feeling like winners.

ORIGIN OF THE EXPERIMENTAL METHOD

Medicine and its Era of Blind Beliefs

When George Washington came down with an upper respiratory infection, they called in three of the best doctors in America. They opened a vein and bled him. Even after he asked them to stop, they continued to bleed him because they thought it was working.

By the third bleeding, they had removed 80 ounces or 2.36 liters. That was 40% of his blood.

He died.

https://www.pbs.org/newshour/health/dec-14-1799-excruciating-final-hours-president-george-washington

For thousands of years, doctors would open a vein and bleed a patient to make them well. How is it possible that we never realized we were making people worse?

This is a story of the two oldest and most long-lasting theories of disease in the world, ones you probably will not learn in medical school.

1.   THE POISON THEORY

2.   THE THEORY OF HUMORS

The oldest theory of disease, still found in America today, is the Poison Theory. For thousands of years, our ancestors have observed that if you eat tainted meat, you get sick, you throw up, you may live or you may die. If you eat certain berries or fruit, you get sick, you throw up, you may live, you may die. If you eat certain mushrooms, you get sick, you throw up, you may live, you may die.

The corollary to the poison theory is that, if you believe poisons in the body cause disease, then the way to cure disease is to purge the body of those poisons.

Out of these simple observations our ancestors long ago came to believe that *all* illness is caused by poisons in the environment. Among the Zoe Indians in South America, they regularly drink Cepe', a fermented drink that makes them throw up, "to cleanse themselves" of the poisons in the body.

https://www.youtube.com/watch?v=XMLbCYCMp2w

If you look at the video above, about 1/3 the way through, you see the Zoe dancing around naked while singing chants. Some of the people in the picture are drinking Cepe', an alcoholic drink that makes them throw up. It is a lot of naked people dancing and throwing up. Just like Spring Break in College.

Even today, if you go to any pharmacy in America, you will find, "Colon Cleansing Kits" to rid you of whatever toxins might be in your body. A recent example on the internet is a man trying to sell you such methods by telling you that everyone has between five and twenty pounds of "toxic poop" in their system. In California, there are "Hi-Colonic Centers" you can go to if you want to flush the poisons out.

Yet most doctors long ago abandoned the poison theory of disease after the "germ" theory was proven by Pasteur, Koch, and Jenner. Most will tell you the body can eliminate normal "toxins", unless you actually drank poison, then you had better get to a hospital.

This idea persists only as a failure of our educational system at every level. We fail to teach **why** we need science. One more reason why America ranks 24rd in the world in science.

The second longest-lasting theory of disease is Hippocrates' Theory of Humors. In a desire to find out what powers the human body, Hippocrates did autopsies on the deceased. With no microscope, all he found were what he called "Humors" flowing in tubes. Blood in the veins and arteries. Black Bile in the liver, Yellow Bile in excrement. And Phlegm in the gastric juices and what we cough up. He speculated that an imbalance of these four humors would cause disease.

The corollary of that is that if you believe an imbalance of bodily humors is causing the disease, then the way to cure disease is the restore the balance of bodily humors. This gave a justification to the already common practice of bloodletting.

"...let him have also all sorts of plasters, potions, and purging medicines, so contrived that they may keep some considerable time, and likewise such as may be had and used whilst they are fresh."

Hippocrates

Even the best and brightest minds are not always correct.

If you had examined the little black bag physicians carried around with them through the 1880s, you would have found they used both techniques, purging the poisons, and restoring the balance of humors, to "cure" whatever ails:

- A razor for bleeding. A jar of leeches, for more precision bleeding, was kept in their office.

- Enemas and laxatives, to flush out the poisons or restore the balance of humors.

- Emetics, to make you throw up the poisons, or restore the balance of humors.

- Poultices, like a mustard plaster, to draw out the poisons, especially for colds and the flu.

    After four days, they would take the mustard plaster off of your chest and the yellow mustard would now have turned a grody greenish-black. People would say, "See, it has drawn out the poison!" "Now you are getting better, aren't you?" Today, we have ads on TV saying wearing white cotton "foot pads" inside of your shoes will draw the toxins out of your body, "See, the pads have turned black."

- Laudanum, was the miracle drug that worked for every ailment. Laudanum was a mixture of opium, often dissolved in alcohol. It made people feel better.

https://www.sciencedirect.com/topics/neuroscience/laudanum

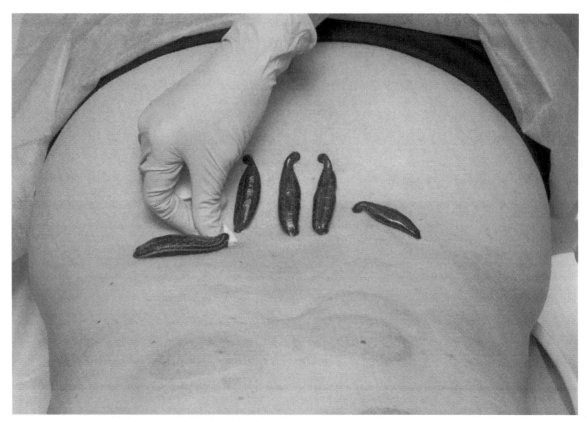

In some countries, leeches are still used for bloodletting. Note the hot cup marks to supposedly draw out the toxins.

Why was bleeding so popular? Why did both patients and doctors swear by it? Red blood cells carry oxygen to the brain. If the brain is starved of oxygen, its first reaction is to go into la-la land. It is similar to what happens in deep-sea diving; if you go up too fast, without stopping to decompress along the way, nitrogen builds up in the blood and displaces the oxygen. You end up with what is called "Nitrogen narcosis" or "rapture of the deep" and may swim off and drown.

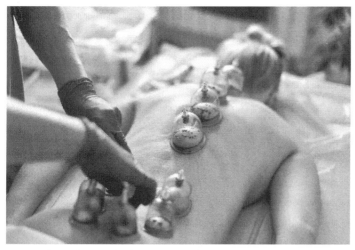

Bloodletting is like a cheap drunk. Patients swore by it. Doctors were impressed that their patients seemed to feel better. Of course, it did not make the patients better, it actually made them worse.

Many died, but the dead never sue. Doctors were convinced it was working for almost any disease. There were no complaints from the dead.

Left: In parts of the world, punctures are made in the skin and hot cups are put over them to create a vacuum to suck out blood.

The same problem came up repeatedly in medicine. Until the beginning of the 20th-century doctor's miracle drug was Laudanum. Laudanum was widely prescribed for everything from a toothache to menstrual cramps to gunshot wounds. People swore by it. What is Laudanum? It is a tincture of Opium, with both morphine and codeine alkaloids. You could find cocaine, marijuana, opium, and more at any pharmacy. Until early in the Twenty Century, when the Harrison Act was passed by Congress in 1914.

Most claimed it had healing powers that were beyond anything anyone else could claim. In fact, they cured nothing, but they made people feel better. If a pill made people feel better, they would want to take more of it. If they want to take more of it, by definition, that is addiction. Today, we have made addiction a crime.

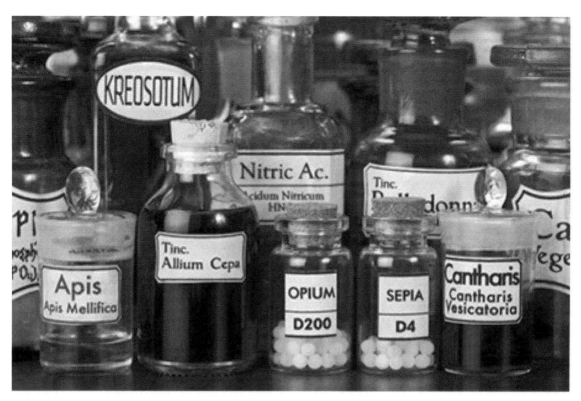

That created Medicine's first Croesus style confrontation with reality. How do you tell if a medicine is actually working? Or does it only make you feel better?

SNAKE OIL AND ELECTRIC BELTS
A CURE FOR CANCER?

Countless thousands of products, from Snake Oil to Electric Belts, have claimed to cure everything from impotence to cancer. How do they prove their claims? They avoid giving any evidence, except to use "testimonials" from "satisfied users."

In the 1903 edition of the famed Sears-Roebuck & Co. catalog, it was claimed that "... *The Heidelberg Belt seeks the weak, diseased part at once. It produces an invigorating current of magnetic and galvanic current...*" Further, the ads claimed the belt was effective for "...*seminal and vital weakness, nervous debility or impotence, stops almost immediately the unnatural waste or loss of vitality.*" A special loop to cover the sexual parts hinted at the belt's value as a sexual energizer, and Sears promised to mail the belt in a plain brown wrapper to avoid embarrassment to the user. It was the Viagra of the day, except it did nothing, much like ground Rhino horn and tiny feet in China, the effect was all in the mind of the user.

More than this, the Electric Belt claimed to cure almost anything, including cancer: *"The stomach attachment for indigestion, constipation and general debility of the stomach is invaluable. Promotes the digestive organs, tones up the liver and strengthens the assimilative power. Even that terrible disease, cancer of the stomach, has been known to be arrested, to yield to and be cured by the wearing of a genuine Heidelberg Electric Belt."*

The following is from the 1903 Sears Roebuck catalog advertisement for the Heidelberg Electric Belt. Note the very first paragraph begins with *"testimonials from the cured."* And the very last paragraph promises "numberless *letters from people who have used the Heidelberg Electric Belt and realized wonderful benefit from its use."*

rent is desired for such troubles in an aggravated form, we urge by all means our Giant Power 80-gauge Belt at $18.00.

OUR $4.00 HEIDELBERG ELECTRIC BELT comes complete with stomach attachment and spiral suspensory. The stomach attachment for indigestion, constipation and general debility of the stomach is invaluable. Promotes the digestive organs, tones up the liver and strengthens the assimilative power. Even that terrible disease, cancer of the stomach, has been known to be arrested, to yield to and be cured by the wearing of a genuine Heidelberg Electric Belt.

ent and spiral suspensory. Our price..$4.00
ent and spiral suspensory. Our price....................................... 6.00
ent and spiral suspensory. Our price....................................... 8.00

Although Electric Belts were abandoned long ago, there are repeated episodes of fake products making similar claims all the way to the present. One enterprising individual was fined a million dollars for running TV ads claiming that Coral Calcium can cure cancer. But much more slip through the fingers of a badly staffed and poorly funded Food and Drug Administration (FDA). It is simply exhausting to sort through all the bogus claims in ads. Those who claim such cures say they are only exercising their rights, partly protected by the First Amendment, the right to freedom of speech.

Most Americans believe that the FDA would not allow a product to be advertised if it has no value. Yet the FDA is not allowed to test or approve products for market if they are natural cures (like Electric Belts?) or Vitamins or Minerals or Homeopathic treatments. Congress took away that ability from the FDA, in a return to what we were like 100 years ago. Sometimes the government can take action after a product has been found to be dangerous or deceitful, but that may take years before the product can be removed from the public.

A few years ago, absurd claims were being made for "ionized bracelets" backed only by "satisfied users". Hack claims from Palm readers to Tarot card readers to the infamous "Smiling Bob" commercials, hinted at amazing ability to help you. Help you do what? Often, they did not even say what they could do, they just hinted and spoke of "satisfied users".

A lawyer's disclaimer in the fine print at the bottom of the screen stated that "this product is not intended to diagnosis, treat, cure, or prevent any disease." Some of these commercials, such as the "Smiling Bob" commercials, are studied today in the Marketing departments of Universities. Perhaps as an example of how gullible we all are when we have no real evidence to go on.

The fact that such claims are continuing to occur today, is a testament to the failure of our educational system to educate our children to understand the reality around us. From the public school system to our universities, little is taught about our history of fiction invented by our own minds.

Placebo Effects: Never underestimate the emotion of feeling someone knows how to make you better. This feeling, is *known* in medicine as the *placebo effect.* *Placebo* means "I shall please" in Latin.

> *"The patient, though conscious that his condition is perilous, may recover his health simply through contentment with the goodness of the physician."*

Hippocrates

Henry Beecher is credited with being one of the first to use the placebo effect as a medic in World War II. After running out of pain-killing morphine, he replaced it with a simple saline solution but continued telling the wounded soldiers it was morphine to calm them. It reportedly helped calm them. That is a purely psychological effect.

We know that big placebo pills work better than small placebo pills. Red placebo pills work better than white placebo pills. All of that is psychological.

Yet there is more to the placebo effect than just psychology. We all know from experience that we may come down with a cold or flu. For several days we get worse, then we start to get better. After a week or so, we are well.

Our body can often heal us even if we take no medicine at all. If we happened to take a placebo in the middle of the disease, we might start to get better, yet mistakenly believe it was the placebo that made us better.

It was once considered possible that placebos helped make us better. But extensive studies have failed to find any beneficial medical effect. Except, maybe, in psychology. The normal placebo effect works on about 20% to 30% of patients. In psychological depression, it seems to work 50% of the time. What does that say about psychological depression having psychological causes?

To find out if a medicine helped, or if we just imagine it is what made us better, we must have a method to find out if it worked. How can we do this?

"The patient in 9C wants you to confirm my optimism."

Pharmaceutical companies must take the placebo effect into account every time they review the effectiveness of a drug. Usually, the drug companies themselves are tasked with the job of doing scientific studies, not the FDA.

Yet for every scientist who can testify that a drug lacks the advertised curative power, the manufacturer can often put many people forward who will honestly swear that the product indeed works for them. In study after study, companies have compared the reactions of subjects who used a product under investigation with those of people who took nothing. Each time, the patients who took their product reported feeling much better than those who took nothing.

When the product users were compared to a placebo group, however, the truth emerged. In such a study, two groups of patients were given capsules, but they were not told what the capsules contained— only that they were testing a product for its usefulness in treating their condition. One *experimental* group of patients was given capsules containing the drug company's product. A second *control* group was given only placebos, so-called sugar pills. A third *control* group of patients received nothing. After some time, the groups were compared.

The group that received nothing had improved slightly: One does sometimes get better without help. Both the product group and the placebo group reported *significantly greater improvement* than the group that received nothing. Thus, the placebo or sugar pill group may have felt as much improvement as the group that used the product "specially formulated" to cure whatever ailed them.

If there is no difference between the Placebo group and the Experimental Group that received the actual medication, then the effect of the medicine is likely just a placebo effect itself. Despite the placebo studies, it has proven difficult to get such useless claims removed from the market. After all, they do something, even if it is psychological.

"Some patients respond to the magic wand."

In 1994 congress passed a bill removing all control the FDA had over "natural" cures, "homeopathic" cures, and vitamins and minerals. This created a rush of bogus claims for such products that overwhelms reality to this day. https://sgp.fas.org/crs/misc/R43062.pdf

Some Congressmen claim they did so to "get government off the backs of the people" by removing government control. Yet it only benefited those selling the products and left all of us without protection from bogus products.

Companies still sell millions of dollars' worth of such products to "satisfied" users each year. Congress reversed decades of protection from bogus products with the stroke of a pen.

Today, companies sell vast numbers of vitamins, minerals, wrinkle reducers, even testosterone "boosters" that have no real scientific evidence to support their claims. They are not reviewed by the FDA, yet they sell billions of dollars of products to unsuspecting customers.

Any day now Electric Belts could make a comeback. Oops, they already have; an hour-long ad for "ionized" bracelets implied that they have the power to "restore the ionic balance" and reduce the body's pain. Hour-long shows of "satisfied" users spoke of the miracle cure for their aches and pains. They claimed that "when you have pain in any part of your body it is because of an imbalance of ions". Many people believe that if you see something on TV it must be true. Really?

https://www.youtube.com/watch?v=eOVuyMVyT5I

WORD MAGIC: The "Nominal Fallacy"
The Belief that, by Having Named Something,
We Have Somehow Explained it.

In a study of how children view the world, Jean Piaget found that two to three-year-old children believe that *the name of an object is inherent in* the *object itself.* Indeed, in the history of many philosophies, one of the early debated topics dealt with whether or not the name of the object is derived from the essence of the object itself ("A rose, is a rose, is a rose... ").

The importance of words went far beyond the object. Words became the answer. And the first "answer" we concocted made a god of our own words. Psychologist Frank Beach called this the "*nominal fallacy*" —the fact that by merely naming something, we somehow feel that we have explained it.

We see this in adults as well as children. If we see a disturbing mass shooting on television news where many people are killed, we often hear people say, "Why did he do that?" and the answer we may hear is, "He was crazy."

"Oh! He was crazy. That explains it." No, crazy is just a word. It explains nothing.

When we get a bit more sophisticated, people may say, "He was schizophrenic."

"Oh! He was schizophrenic. That explains it." No, schizophrenic is just a word. It explains nothing.

Psychology has been studying schizophrenia for over one hundred years. To this day, we have only a vague understanding of it. We know there is a genetic link. Psychiatrist E. Fuller Torrey and others have found that if one identical twin has schizophrenia, the other identical twin has a 50 to 60% chance of having schizophrenia. But what about the other 40 to 50% who have identical genes, but do not have schizophrenia?

More important still, FBI statistics have noted that of the mass shootings in the United States, only 17% have a diagnosis of "mental illness", another term that is poorly defined. Yet our culture has a bias against the idea of "mental illness" and is too ready to jump to the conclusion that this explains the mass shootings.

"Just because your doctor has a name for your problem, doesn't mean he understands it."

Franz Kafka

At the turn of the century, the word *instinct* was believed to explain many things. Why do people engage in sexual activity? Because they have a sex instinct. Why are people aggressive? Because they have an instinct for aggression. Why are some people good at music? Because they were born with a music instinct. How do people know good from evil? They know it instinctively (or a little voice tells them). How do you know what is truth? You just know it instinctively or through "common sense".

Word magic is not the only obstacle to the development of science. Another superstitious belief is *animism: the* belief in an indwelling force or spirit that exists in living or nonliving matter.

Jean Piaget found young children believe inanimate objects have the same feelings and emotions as they have. If a child attributes feelings to a doll made of a piece of wood, for example, he or she may cry if Dad steps on the wood. If a little girl drops her doll, she may show the same emotion as if she herself had fallen, including consoling the doll.

William James cites the case of a deaf person who believed, as a child, that the sun and moon were the gods he was taught about in religion. Because the gods appeared wherever he went in the neighborhood, he believed they followed him around personally all the time. Interestingly, the sun and moon were revered by most of our ancestors.

Historians and anthropologists have found identical beliefs in our own history back to the Greeks and in virtually every primitive society studied. The Greeks attributed human features to the gods (the causes?) of thunder and lightning. The sun, moon, and many other inanimate objects were once believed to be gods. They endowed gods with human emotions and desires, including jealousy and duplicity, and they fought furiously when the divinity of their gods was questioned; as in the execution of Socrates for questioning their beliefs. Socrates was convicted of corrupting the minds of his followers by a vote of 501 of his fellow citizens in the democracy of Athens. A second vote was taken, and the sentence of death was pronounced.

Science has grown at the expense of our belief in the supernatural. We no longer believe that supernatural forces control our lives. Witches and demons have no value either as explanations or causes. Yet this separation of science from the supernatural has come slowly, and elements of demonology have been present in all aspects of human history at one time.

Astrology once ruled astronomy. As knowledgeable an astronomer as Kepler had to bend a knee to astrology by feeding information on the movements of the stars to the court astrologers, to satisfy his employers and his stomach. In Kepler's era, people saw little value in astronomy unless it could predict the future, and the thoroughly disproven notion that the movement of the stars influences the life of the individual is not uncommon even today. Yet astronomy has progressed only by disassociating its methods from the supernatural.

Biologists once believed that living matter was distinct from non-living matter because living matter possessed an innate force, which they called "elan vital" or "vital spirits." Those were just words. The discovery of the cell, the basic component of all living tissue, threw that concept into question. Living matter seemed to be composed of other living matter. Recently, the discovery of the inorganic origins of organic matter has shed more light on the problem. Our search for "vital spirits" has proven fruitless; they have been relegated to the status of "demons."

Science has followed a zigzag evolutionary course—not a smooth or easy one. Only by separating itself from superstition has science been able to make progress.

Our ancient beliefs in demons, witchcraft, astrology, dragons, and voodoo are void of evidence to support them. Old beliefs have been replaced by beliefs in Bigfoot, Ancient Aliens, ESP, UFOs, ghosts, Zombies, fake news, and more. No sooner is one claim refuted than it is replaced by more. It never seems to end.

"There is nothing so absurd that it cannot be believed as truth if repeated often enough."

William James, often called the "Father of American Psychology"

In America, the Zombie Apocalypse is more popular than science. One more reason we rank 24th in the world in science.

Our educational system has failed, at every level, to get across the **value** of science. Only the boring, pedantic, methods are allowed to be taught in our public schools. Yet, we have made more observable progress in just the last 100 years than in tens of thousands of years before. Why?

What is it that makes the scientific methods more successful than any other methods?

- Pictures and cartoons are presented as illustrations and do not necessarily represent actual studies.

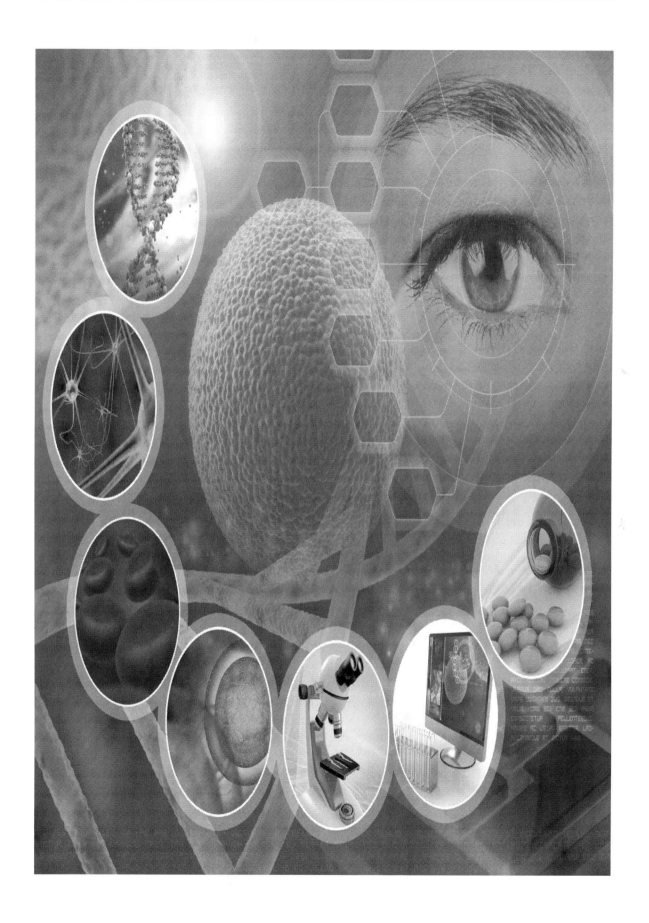

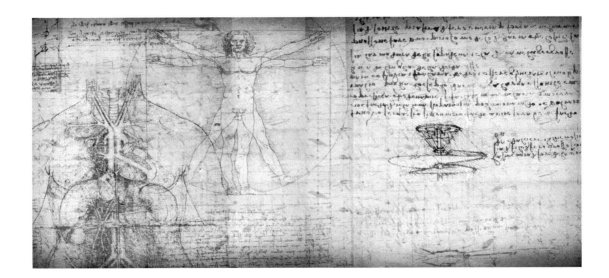

2 RULES OF EVIDENCE

Experiment is the interpreter of nature. Experiments never deceive. It is our judgment which sometimes deceives itself because it expects results which experiment refuses. We must consult experiment, varying the circumstances, until we have deduced general rules, for experiment alone can furnish reliable rules.

Leonardo da Vinci

WITCHCRAFT, DEMONS, AND RULES OF EVIDENCE

For all but a small period of our history, supernatural powers have been seen as the cause of all unexplainable happenings. If an apparently healthy man or woman were suddenly to die, they did not think *"it must be a heart attack"* or *"it must be a stroke"*. They believed that witchcraft and black magic were proven by such a death.

The idea that natural causes such as heart attacks or stroke could be responsible is only a recent historical development.

The witch trials of our early history abound with testimonials that declared that an accused "witch" had passed by a home in which a mysterious death occurred only hours later.

In one case at Salem, court testimony by her neighbor, revealed that the accused "witch" had been seen touching the white picket fence outside the house of a man's farm. The next day, his best milk cow died. Such testimony was considered to be convincing evidence of the guilt of the accused, and many an innocent person met death after being caught in a web of such circumstantial evidence:

The mere coincidence of events was accepted as meaning that one had caused the other. These were not witches. They were our grandmothers. They were not even what we have today, people claiming to be "witches" because they think it gives them some sort of supernatural power. The vast majority of those put to death were elderly women whose appearance and behavior made them seem frightening to others. Most had outlived their relatives. Their only crime was to be old. Some of the accused were suffering from mental or physical traits that made them a source of fear or hatred in the community. Some were simply different, and were suspected for their nonconformity.

The hold that witchcraft once had over our minds is difficult to conceive today. Yet the most widely distributed book of past eras was the *Malleus Maleficarium* (Hammer of Witches), which instructed the reader on how to ferret out witches. It was widely taught that you could always tell a witch by her peculiar mannerisms, so one should always watch for people with peculiar mannerisms. And we did. We found them everywhere.

The impact of witchcraft on the western mind is the subject of a carefully documented survey of the phenomenon by the Nobel Prize-winning historians Will and Ariel Durant (p 577-8):

> *An epidemic of witchcraft fears swept southeast France in 1609. Hundreds of persons believed themselves possessed by devils; some thought themselves changed into dogs, and barked. A commission of the Bordeaux Parliament was appointed to try suspects. A method was devised to discover the spots at which devils had entered the body of the accused: he was blindfolded, needles were stuck into his flesh, and any place where he failed to feel the injected point was judged to be the port of entry. Hoping to be pardoned, suspects accused one another. Eight were convicted, five escaped, three were burned; and spectators swore later that they had seen devils, in the form of toads, issuing from the heads of the victims. In Lorraine 800 were burned for witchcraft in sixteen years; in Strasbourg 134 in four days (October 1582). In Catholic Lucerne, 62 were put to death between 1562 and 1572; in Protestant Bern, 300 in the last decade of the sixteenth century, 240 in the first decade of the seventeenth.*

> *In Germany Catholics and Protestants competed in sending witches to the stake. It is incredibly and yet reliably reported that the Archbishop of Trier had 120 persons burned at Pfalz in 1596 on the charge that they had made the cold weather last devilishly long. A cattle plague in the Schongau district (1598) was ascribed to witches; the Bavarian Privy Council at Munich urged inquisitors to "show more earnestness and severity in your proceedings"; in consequence 63 witches were burned, and the relatives of the victims were required to pay the cost of the trials. At Hainburg, in Austria, 80 were executed for sorcery in the two years 1617-18. In 1627-29 the Bishop of Wourzburg is said to have put 900 witches to death. In 1582 Protestant editors reissued, with their approval, the Malleus Maleficarum (Hammer of Witches) which the Dominican Inquisitor Jakob Sprenger had published in 1487 to guide in the detection and prosecution of witches. Elector Augustus of Saxony decreed (1572) that witches were to be burned to death even if they had injured no one. In Ellingen 1,500 witches were burned in 1590, in Ellwangen 167 in 1612, in Westerstetten 300 in two years; there were similar ecstasies in Osnabruck in 1588, in Nordlingen in 1590, in Wurttemberg in 1616; these latter statistics, however, are derived from contemporary newssheets notorious for inaccuracy. German scholars estimate a total of 100,000 executions for witchcraft in Germany in the seventeenth century.*

In the previous picture you see what people saw as demons in the smoke, leaving the bodies of the burning "witches". You or I may look at clouds and see a dog or a horse or a UFO. These people were not looking for dogs or horses or UFOs, they were looking for signs of witchcraft, witches' "familiars"; toads, demons, black cats. Spectators swore they saw the "evidence" everywhere they looked. Above, you see a woodcut presumably showing the "demons" rising from the smoke from the burning of our grandmothers.

After enduring the agony of a trial, the accused were often convinced of their own guilt. They wept. They confessed their sins. They begged forgiveness. They prayed to God. Those who sat in judgment deliberated their fate. The "witches" were sentenced to die. The last American "witch" died in Salem in 1693 (Hansen).

The terror of witchcraft stormed through our minds even into the age of Galileo and Kepler. It continued over one hundred years after Columbus, well into what historians have called the "Age of Reason." However, the scholars we credit with beginning the Age of Reason were unique, and represented the best, most educated minds of their era. They were not "average" nor could they be considered representative of their age.

Even the best-educated scientists often believed in the supernatural. The chemist Robert Boyle (1627-91), who developed Boyle's Law on the behavior of gases, recommended that coal miners be interviewed about the demons they met while working underground.

The few people and clergymen who expressed doubts about the treatment of witches often found themselves accused of heresy and reminded of the Biblical admonition that "*Thou shall not suffer a witch to live*" (Exodus 22:18 KJV). No one dared to try to stop the hysteria, for fear of being accused of being, "One of them!"

WITCHCRAFT AT SALEM VILLAGE.

In America, the fear of witches culminated in the famous witch trials of Salem. Three hysterical young women testified before the Salem juries about the horrors the witches had forced them to endure. The witches, most of them elderly women, themselves hysterical with fear, were brought into the courtroom to face their accusers.

As soon as the accused witches were brought into court, the young women cried, some fainted, as in the drawing above, and others pointed at the accused and shrieked, "*Witch! Witch!*"

For the spectators who were watching, the shriek of "Witch! Witch!" was convincing. Adrenaline and cortisol shot into their bloodstream. A chill went up their spine. Their heart jumped. Today, the same thing happens in America among theater goers in a movie from Hollywood about witches, zombies, demons and more. We know this is just Hollywood making a buck off of our fears, but up until recently, everybody believed the stories were true.

People were convinced that these women were guilty by the reaction of their own bodies. The emotions that surged through the mind of the spectators condemned the accused. See Chapter 8 on The Mind Code for how this can happen.

PSYCHOLOGY CAN CONTROL THE BIOLOGY OF OUR BODY

There is no more important lesson than to understand how that happens. *Understanding* gives us some protection from the emotional manipulation of Voodoo, Witch hunts, Politics, Hollywood, and the emotional put-downs of others that lead to depression and anxiety.

Today we know that same feeling just from sitting in a movie theater as Hollywood uses drama on the screen to control the emotions in our bodies. But we know that is only Hollywood trying to make a dollar off of our fears or anger. Back then, they believed it was real. They were convinced by the feelings in their own brain, their emotions, of the guilt of the innocent. *That* is why it is important to understand psychology.

Today, we see the same emotions in our politics, convincing people their fears are real. In one study fully 23% of political supporters said they believed that Congress and the media are controlled by "*a Satan worshiping cabal of pedophiles*". Yes, really.

https://www.businessinsider.com/23-of-republicans-believe-satan-worshiping-pedophiles-control-us-government-2021-5

They accused Anderson Cooper of CNN of drinking the blood of children. Cooper confronted one former believer, finding it incredible that anyone could have believed that. They do.

In 2021 Forbes noted that 15% of all Americans believe the debunked QANON conspiracy theories.

https://www.forbes.com/sites/tommybeer/2021/05/27/nearly-30-of-republicans-believe-american-patriots-may-have-to-resort-to-violence-to-save-us-study-finds/?sh=d97e31af91f6

Members of Congress who failed to go along with their beliefs were often booed, vilified, or even received death threats from their own constituents. Congressmen often cowered in their offices, afraid to speak out against what was happening.

What does that tell us about how easily the human mind can be convinced with nothing but words? See The Mind Code in Chapter 8 for what psychology knows.

The great enemy of the truth is very often not the lie — deliberate, contrived and dishonest — but the myth — persistent, persuasive, and unrealistic. Too often we hold fast to the cliches of our forebears. We subject all facts to a prefabricated set of interpretations. We enjoy the comfort of opinion without the discomfort of thought.

President John F. Kennedy

RULES OF EVIDENCE

"Science is a way of thinking much more than it is a body of knowledge."

Carl Sagan *COSMOS*

Out of centuries of witch hunts and court trials that convicted people based on the slimmest of circumstantial evidence, came Rules of Evidence that determine what can and cannot be admitted in court as evidence against you. Science also had to develop Rules of Evidence that determine what can be useful evidence.

In court, eyewitness testimony is still admitted as evidence and is often considered the most convincing evidence. He/she was there, he/she *saw* it happen. Even today, studies have shown that the most common reason for innocent people being convicted of crimes they did not commit is eyewitness testimony.

In medical science, eyewitness testimony was thrown out as a scientific method after the realization that Placebo Effects, such as testimonials from "*satisfied users*" that they were saved by bleeding or electric belts, or Magic Elixirs, cannot be scientific evidence. The Rules of Evidence in science are far more strict than the Rules of Evidence in a court of law.

Of 375 people in prison who were found innocent by DNA evidence, 69% were due to eyewitness testimony.

https://innocenceproject.org/eyewitness-identification-reform/

What are the Rules of Evidence in science? Beliefs, no matter how convincing they seem, are not enough. The beliefs that determined the behavior of the witch hunters, doctors of humors, and kamikaze pilots were never subjected to the test of science. In science, we must have *rules of evidence,* better than those in a modern court of law, that aid us in separating facts from coincidence, hard evidence from hearsay testimony, bias, and belief. What are the *Rules of Evidence* that make science different from any other approach?

Science is *a method of testing reality through our senses.* It differs from magic and the supernatural because it deals with data that conform to what may be called the *rule of able,* which is that all scientific data must be (1) Observable, (2) Recordable or Measurable (3) Reproducible, and ideally, (4) Predictable.

1. OBSERVABLE

We must be able to *Observe* something before we can study it. We cannot observe ghosts or demons or witchcraft. Yet there are many things that we cannot observe that we have discovered ways to make observable.

In 440 BCE the Greek Ionian philosopher Democritus proposed that all matter is composed of minute invisible particles he called *atoms.* He had no understanding of what an atom was by today's standard, but physics honored his memory by using his own term, *the atom,* to refer to one of the smallest particles of matter. Democritus had no way of proving his theory of the atom. He could not prove that the air was composed of atoms. In fact, he had a problem proving that air existed at all.

> *"Nothing exists except atoms and the void, everything else is opinion."* Democritus

Ionian philosophers believed that there are four basic elements: air, fire, earth, and water. What is air? You cannot see it. You cannot touch it. You cannot smell, taste, or hear it. In the era of Democritus, not everyone believed that air existed. Oh, certainly if the wind blew the leaves in the trees, there was something there *then.* Spirits moving through the void. Zeus sneezing. But when the wind does not blow, what is there? If people cannot even agree on the operational definition of the subject, then how can it be studied? Could you demonstrate the existence of air with only the crude equipment available to the Ionian philosophers? How?

The Ionian philosopher Empedocles sought to reduce the question of its existence to something *point-at-able,* which could be seen by all. This would have achieved the first essential task in removing that question from the realm of the philosophical and placing it squarely in the field of science.

Empedocles could take a wineskin, then squeeze on the sides of a wineskin. Wine would have come out. Everyone believed in the existence of wine. Why? Simply because anyone could see, touch, smell, or taste it. In short, it was *point-at-able,* observable by our senses.

But suppose that Empedocles, having emptied the wineskin, then plumped up the bag. What is inside it now? "Nothing," most would say. "We saw all the wine come out". No," Empedocles could respond. "It is full of air."

If he then took a hollow reed, inserted one end in the opening of the wineskin, stuck the other end of the reed into a bowl of water, and squeezed on the sides of the bag, what would come out? Bubbles, of course, can be seen and even touched by any observer. In short, air could be reduced to something point-at-able, which everyone could see—and agree—was there. He did demonstrate that air is a substance, but in a somewhat more difficult manner, this example is simpler.

His observations would have satisfied the second major "able." That is, they would have been easily *reproducible* by anyone using the same equipment under the same conditions. One would not have to wait for spirits to move the leaves of trees before air could be studied. It was reproducible on demand.

From this point, Empedocles could proceed to another major "able" in science: Anything that is point-at-able, may be *measurable.* His measure might be as crude as counting the air bubbles and comparing the count from this bag with that from bags of varying sizes. From this, he might have formed a law regarding the volume of air as related to the size of the bag, or he might even have discovered Boyle's law on the behavior of gases.

LEARNING: WHAT WE CANNOT SEE

Psychology is about learning. What is learning? We cannot see learning as it happens. We are not aware of learning the language we speak. It is not something we have to be taught in a classroom. Yet, it is clearly learned. It is as impossible to observe learning as it is to observe air. Yet Pavlov was one of the very first to show we can study learning scientifically, as effectively as physics can study air.

Pavlov paired a bell (actually a metronome at first) with meat. Bell-Meat, Bell-Meat, Bell-Meat. After just six pairings, the dogs responded to the Bell by itself, with the maximum amount of saliva; an Autonomic Nervous System response from the Parasympathetic branch of the brain. The brain of the dogs responded to the Bell as if it were Meat, in *anticipation* of meat.

Using bells and saliva, he took learning, which no one could see happening, and made it into something observable that could be studied scientifically. It was an object lesson on how to make something we cannot see into something observable that we can study. It was a beginning.

MONUMENT TO PAVLOV AND PAVLOV'S DOG.
Simple association makes learning possible. Pavlov made the connection between biology and psychology.
Thorndike, Skinner, Piaget, Bandura, Bruner, and many more, went on to continue the success in making learning observable.

Microscopes and telescopes have made it possible for scientists to observe the germs that cause disease and the formation of stars in space. Technology has moved forward with science, and science has benefited from technology.

2. RECORDABLE *OR MEASURABLE*

At its simplest, a measurement may involve only keeping a record, in writing or in pictures, of the behavior you are observing. This record will allow for future *comparisons* to the observations of other scientists.

Someone once noted that if something exists, it exists in some degree. And if it exists in some degree, it can be measured. To aid science in formulating reproducible laws of nature, from which we can predict, it is useful to measure what we are talking about. But sometimes we take the idea that it must be measured too far.

Measurement itself is only a method that allows for more precise *comparison*. It is not an essential need for science, but it has proven invaluable in medicine and physics.

"Not everything that counts can be counted, and not everything that can be counted counts." –
Unknown source, often attributed to Albert Einstein

**"What if we don't change anything at all ...
and something magical just happens."**

Even in business, measuring your success is essential. Magic does not just happen. Knowing what works and what does not work is basic.

3. REPRODUCIBLE
THE AXE SCIENCE WIELDS
THAT SETS IT ABOVE OTHER METHODS

It is not enough to accept another person's word that something is true. Unless it is something that anyone else, using the same methods, can reproduce and get the same or similar results, it is not science.

In 2003, a team of biologists from Korea announced that they had produced human stem cells from a clone of a human blastocyst. This was an enormous accomplishment. Human stem cells can regrow human tissue. Biologists from all over the world eagerly sought to expand on the research.

But no one could reproduce the results. After years of trying, the original work was declared a fraud.

Since then, other scientists have been able to make stem cells out of other cells. It is a huge accomplishment, but it relies for its validity, on the fact that the study can be reproduced.

Scientists make mistakes. Mistakes are basic to all human learning. But no result is accepted because someone important says so. There are always other scientists who will attempt to reproduce the results. If it cannot be reproduced, it is not science. Every scientist knows others are waiting to critique their study.

You rarely see such fraud in science because scientists know that, eventually, it can be discovered.

4. PREDICTABLE

CAN WE PREDICT A FUTURE WE HAVE NEVER SEEN?

Finally, what is observable, recordable, and reproducible may ideally be *predictable*. One may predict what will happen from our data even in situations never experienced. NASA took the laws and mathematics developed by Sir Isaac Newton, and safely put men on the moon even though we had never done this before.

Centuries after the age of Democritus, Leonardo da Vinci (1452-1519) predicted that a sunken ship could be raised from the canals of Venice by pumping air from the surface into airtight bladders inserted into the water-filled compartments of the ship. As the balloons were inflated, they would have displaced the water and eventually rise to the surface, bringing the ship along with them. But in his day, they could not make balloons big enough or air-tight enough. Today, the U. S. Navy uses this same technique as the most effective means of raising a sunken ship.

Da Vinci took the Air, that Empedocles studied (pure science), turned the bag upside down, and made it into a useful idea (applied science), even though it took centuries for technology to improve enough to make it useful. Pure science is "knowledge for the sake of knowledge". You never know when it will prove valuable.

Physics began with simple techniques that permitted the formulation of far-reaching laws, although it was not until the era of Galileo that scientific methods became systematic. Aristotle had once proposed that heavy objects fall to the ground more quickly than lighter objects. That was considered "common sense". Galileo sought to test this commonsense proposition. In a famous experiment, unfortunately apocryphal, but a great example, one light, and one heavy object were dropped from the tower of Pisa (he actually used an incline board). Anyone who wanted could observe the outcome: Both objects hit the ground at exactly the same time. Galileo helped advance physics by designing other simple, yet scientific experiments *that everyone could see, point at, and agree on.*

A second great advance in physics was made by Newton, who formulated laws of motion and gravity by which we can predict and thus understand these physical phenomena. Extrapolation (predictions) from Newton's laws allowed NASA to land men safely on the moon, even though we had never had this type of experience.

Much the same is true in biology. The invention of the microscope made it possible to see microorganisms. But a problem then arose. Where did the microorganisms come from? Did they generate spontaneously? That is, did they spring forth from nonliving matter? Or were they produced only by the reproductive systems of other living microorganisms?

How could we reduce these complex questions to things that were Observable Louis Pasteur (1822-95) was faced with the same type of problem as Democritus. The existence of the microorganisms had been demonstrated, but no one could agree on their origin. Pasteur knew that if a nutritive solution were boiled long enough, the microorganisms would die. The nutritive solution would be sterilized, and life would no longer be present. If, however, the solution was exposed to the air for several days, it would soon be teeming with microorganisms.

Again, Empedocles's discovery of air has proved useful.

Did they appear spontaneously from the nonliving solution? Many influential scientists believed so. Pasteur, however, believed that they floated through the air and landed on the nutritive solution, where they began to grow and reproduce. The problem was how to demonstrate this, one way or the other, to everyone's satisfaction.

Pasteur hit on the idea of boiling two flasks of a nutritive solution, leaving one of the sterile flasks exposed to the air but covering the second one to keep out the microorganisms he believed to be present in the air. Days passed. Microorganisms began to grow in the exposed solution, but none grew in the covered solution.

Pasteur was convinced that the microorganisms came from the air. When he demonstrated this to his fellow scientists, however, they were not impressed, quickly pointing out that no life grows in an air-tight environment. Any microorganisms that generated spontaneously in the sealed flask could not be expected to grow. Pasteur's experiment had failed to control this factor. He had not provided the two flasks with equal treatment.

Pasteur tried again. How could he allow air into both flasks and still keep out microorganisms from the air? A hint from a colleague provided the answer. Pasteur used a flask with a long, curved beak that would admit air but trap microorganisms in the curve of the beak. The beak on a second flask contained no such germ-trapping curve. Now air could easily go into either flask. Microorganisms grew only in the straight-necked flask, while none grew in the curved-beak flask. Pasteur had succeeded this time. His results were difficult to dispute.

The problems of psychology are similar. We may ask, "What is more important to human knowledge—what we are born with, or what we learn from experience?" Once we have a question, we must reduce it to something we can see, something we can agree on. In devising their studies, psychologists try to reduce a complex question to simple point-at-able elements. As we shall see in later chapters, studies by Pavlov, Watson, Harlow, Piaget, Bruner, (See Chapter 8-10 on learning and cognition) as well as studies by biologists, neuroscientists, and zoologists such as Lorenz and Tinbergen (See DNA in Chapter 11) and others are attempts to take questions about learning, that— like the "air" of the Ionian philosophers— no one could see or agree on, and make them into something that everyone can see.

Is Science Built into the Brain of a Child?

Piaget provides one of the best examples of what science is all about. He describes the behavior of a two-year-old child named Laurent. Laurent is sitting on the floor. Laurent picks up a ball. He drops the ball. He watches it bounce. He picks it up again. He drops the ball. He watches it bounce. Over and over, he does the same thing.

Piaget is doing an observational study. Simply observing and describing what Laurent does.

Laurent, this two-year-old child, is doing an experiment.

He picks up the ball. He *Observes* what happens when he drops a ball. He *Repeats* the experiment over and over. He *Records*, or remembers, what he observes. Out of this series of *Observations*, *Repetitions*, and *Recording* his observations, his brain can *Predict* something about the behavior of a ball in a gravitational field. He doesn't think in those terms, he just gets pleasure from curiosity by observing reality. But he is behaving like a little scientist.

It is as if the methods of science are built into the biology of the brain. *Curiosity, exploration, memory, and the ability to predict from past experiences*, come easily to a two-year-old.

Even Pavlov's dog could easily predict the future by learning that food always followed Pavlov's ringing a bell. The biology of his brain triggered saliva, in anticipation of food.

As a child gets older, words replace simple observation as the main source of knowledge. Words, emotions, and perceptions, combined with our fertile imagination, take on a force of their own. We saw this in our history of electric belts, dragons, witches, demons, and more. Words can make learning easier, yet words often mask the reality of what is happening. Words take on a force of their own. They mask the value of science, by inflating the value of sensationalism.

Hollywood, politics, and the media now provide the ideas implanted in the minds of our culture. Our educational system has failed to teach the lessons of history we need to protect ourselves from the mind's overwhelming addition to fiction and sensationalism. Trivia rules. From *Ghost Hunters* to Vin Diesel's *The Last Witch Hunters,* to vampire movies and Alien invasions, there is little to be found about science that you cannot count on the fingers of one hand. The *value* of science is missing from our culture and our education at every level. Our schools make science boring.

In our schools, science is its own worst enemy; constantly making itself more difficult, more boring, and more a captive of jargon. Nowhere has this been more true than in psychology and its effort to look more and more "scientific", to the exclusion of any association with the reality all around us.

"Every kid starts out as a natural-born scientist, then we beat it out of them."

Carl Sagan

Even a child can do science as well as Empedocles.

She does something. She **observes** the effect. She does it *again and again* **(reproducible).** She *remembers* **(records)** the outcome. That allows her to **predict** what will happen the next time.

"Look, look. Come see what I have found." All scientists are eager to show others their discoveries. Nobel Laurate, physicist Richard Feynman, spoke of the *"tremendous excitement of knowing, even for a brief while, something about how nature works that no one else knows."* Emotions drive the effort. Knowledge is its own reward.

"We are in the position of a little child entering a huge library filled with books in many different languages. The child knows someone must have written those books. It does not know how. It does not understand the languages in which they are written. The child dimly suspects a mysterious order in the arrangement of the books but doesn't know what it is..."

Albert Einstein

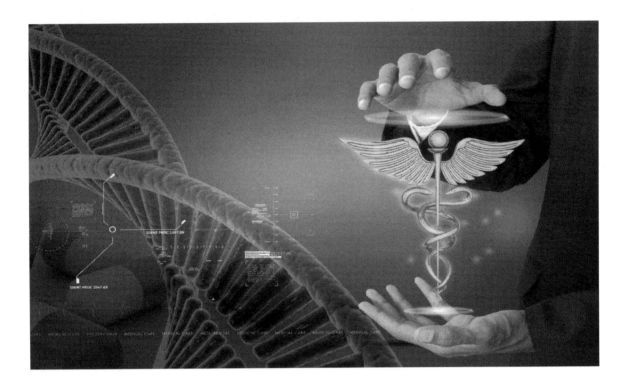

3 THE METHODS OF SCIENCE

Observation, Experimentation, Correlation...

We live in a society exquisitely dependent on science and technology, in which hardly anyone knows anything about science and technology.

Carl Sagan (COSMOS)

I. SYSTEMATIC OBSERVATION

Perhaps the oldest, and one of the most successful, methods of science is that of simple *systematic observation* of what we want to study. This is the method used by Copernicus, Galileo, Darwin, Alexander Fleming, Margaret Mead, Jane Goodall and so many more.

Our ancestors at Stonehenge, the Maya at Chechen Itza, and many more, systematically observed the movements of the sun and may have used these observations to learn the best times to plant their crops on which their civilization had come to depend. Measurement helped. Wooden markers of the sun's position, were eventually replaced by the stone markers at Stonehenge. If crops were planted too soon, or too late, they could fail. Those simple observations may have saved the lives of many from starvation. Blood sacrifice to their gods did not help.

Leonardo da Vinci made exquisite drawings of his ideas and the corpses he dissected, trying to understand what life was all about. These drawings and his notes became a record that inspired others who followed to make their own observations and compare their observations to those of da Vinci. This is the basis of the scientific method.

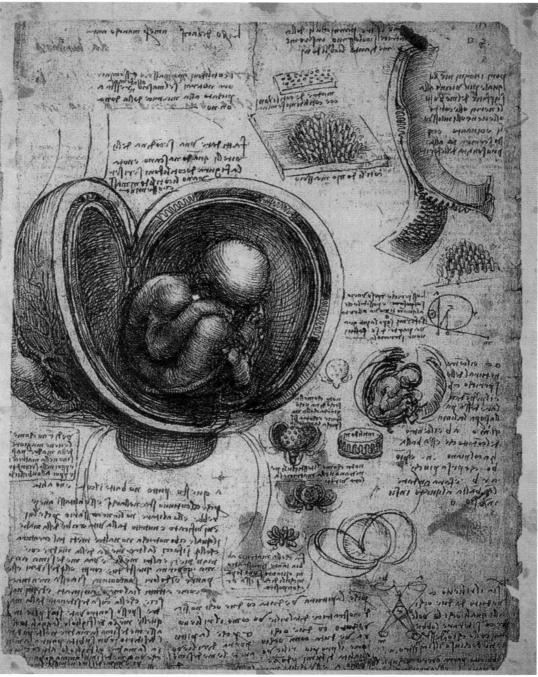

Goodall and the Chimps of Gombe

Jane Goodall wanted to know how Chimpanzees behave in the wild. We know how they behave in captivity; they fight, they mate, they make faces; they throw feces at the visitors, and they get excited when they see the visitors jump and squawk. That is the reason zoos have clear plexiglass between the Chimpanzee cages and the visitors.

Goodall wanted to know how they behave in their native world. So, she took herself to Gombe Stream Reserve in Africa, sat down under a tree, and, after the Chimps had gotten over the excitement of the novelty of her presence, she began to take notes on what she observed.

The importance of the *notes* must not be ignored. The notes are a record that could be read by other scientists and used to contrast and compare to their own observations. Without such a record, the observations might be useless to science. Later, Hugo van Lawick came along with a video camera and made movies the two could show to millions of people on National Geographic. A video record is even more valuable for contrast and comparison than notes. And science could be shared with the world.

The media made Jane Goodall famous for her discovery that chimpanzees could make and use tools. She describes her own excitement over observing a chimp use a long grass straw, poke it down a hole in a termite mound, and wait patiently while the termites crawled onto the straw. Then they would lick the termites off of the straw, not unlike a child licking malted milk off of a straw in a milkshake.

Goodall had confirmed the striking work of psychologist Wolfgang Kohler who, forty years earlier, discovered that Chimpanzees in his research station on Tenerife (see chapter 10 on Cognition) could learn to put two lengths of bamboo fishing poles together to lengthen a short single pole, and be able to use the longer length to rake in a banana.

The chimp, Sultan, found that he could use his teeth to sharpen the end of a pole to make it fit into another pole. On their own, the Chimps found they could use the pole to poke at the chickens in cages across from their cages. The chickens would jump and squawk. The Chimpanzees seemed to think that this was all kinds of keen.

Although it was not noted by Kohler, the behavior of the chimps seemed to be remarkably similar to the behavior seen in eight-year-old children who bully other children and use name-calling to get a rise out of others. Are they doing it for their own entertainment, like the chimpanzees? Or is their behavior reinforced by the laughter of others around them when they put other kids down (like politicians using words to trash their opponents as their supporters laugh)?

Kohler's observation that chimps could bite the end off of a stick, to make it into a weapon or a tool, was recently demonstrated by Jill Pruetz and Paco Bertoleni who found that Savanna chimps in Senegal, would bite the end off of a stick to sharpen it, and use it to hunt Bush Babies (another primate the size of a squirrel) for food. One source of this is in this view of *evolutionary psychology*:

https://www.youtube.com/watch?v=T-pUwQ4mfiY&t=485s by professor Bill von Hippel.

Yet two of the most important discoveries of Jane Goodall were largely ignored by the media, censored to this day, perhaps because it tells us something we do not want to hear. In one of her discoveries, what was truly revolutionary is that the chimps form into hunting bands, track down and isolate a Colobus monkey of a different species, and kill the smaller Colobus monkey. As soon as they killed the monkey, the hunting party would break out into shrieks of joy, jumping up and down in something close to exaltation. Then they ate the helpless monkey. It reminds one of nothing so much as a football player spiking the ball in the end zone and doing a little dance. The NFL had to outlaw such behavior when it was used to make fun of their opponents. Today it still happens, but it is often fined.

There is no evidence that any NFL player was ever killed and eaten by his opponents, although Soccer fans in Argentina stormed onto the field after their team lost, and stabbed to death one of the opposing team's players. A half dozen spectators were killed in a stampede following a soccer match between Germany and England, which led to the Dutch banning both teams from playing there. Even from high school, I can remember a couple of fistfights and one stabbing, not among the players on the field, but among the fans, under the stands, after the game. Emotion rules.

It is not uncommon to see militia groups such as the Taliban in Afghanistan or ISIS in Syria celebrating their own atrocities against those they see as infidels. It is not unlike the feeling of the heroism of our ancestors over destroying the "witches", and celebrating what they have done as heroic. They saw themselves as heroes, as did their society. In chapter 20 on *The Social Order,* psychologists will attempt to clarify how much of this is built into our DNA and how much is learned.

Our politics are not much different. Remember the attempted coup of January 6, 2021? And the joy the participants expressed after the takeover of the capital, parading around with a Confederate flag and threatening to "hang Mike Pence"? Some 140 police officers were injured in the attack. One had a heart attack, and four committed suicide in the weeks that followed. The difference is only one of degree. And even the anger and separation of those who got the Covid-19 vaccine, vs. those who refused to do so or even to wear a mask, is a telling story of how our mind works.

Science provides the information it takes to think. By far the most important work of Jane Goodall and others is still censored by the media. See Chapter 20 on The Social Order for more of her important work that was left out of her important discoveries. Few wanted to believe it. Now we know she was not exaggerating. We will cover this topic on *The Gombe Chimpanzee Wars* in the chapter on Social Psychology, in our study of prejudice and war.

2. EXPERIMENTATION

The Dirt Simple Secret of Modern Medicine

So, how do we know if bleeding people works? How do we know if Sears' Electric Belts work? And what about Laudanum? And Dr. John's Snake Oil, the Magic Elixir? Just asking people how they feel does not work.

If you have a medicine that, say, claims to improve your memory or cure the common cold, and you have hundreds of satisfied users who believe that it does, what do you see on television? The company only puts on television those true believers who are the most enthusiastic.

What was missing from medicine for tens of thousands of years was a simple method, that no one ever thought to use. For centuries we believed it was enough to have satisfied users. Yet we all get better from the common cold after a few days. And we all have better memories if we just took a memory improvement drug because we now focus our mind more intently on what we want to remember.

What was missing from medicine was a way to account for the fact that we all get better *even* if the medicine does not do anything. The way to find out if it works is to have something to *compare* it to. In medicine that becomes the Placebo Control Group. That means no one in either group knows who gets the sugar pill and who gets the real medicine until the experiment is over. In psychology, it is just the Control Group or Comparison Group. Consider this example:

Experimental Group: Gets the actual medication or treatment.   RESULT 64% improve.

Control Group: Gets the Placebo pill or baseline treatment: RESULT 25% improve.

If the RESULTS (the *Dependent Variable* --whatever you are measuring) come out something like the above example, then the difference between the group that got the actual medication or treatment and the group that only got the placebo is, roughly, the actual effect of the medicine.

But if there is little or no difference between the two groups, that suggests the medicine does not work.

Just use a comparison group. *That is dirt simple.* Dirt Simple. Yet it took us tens of thousands of years to figure that out. How could we have been so stupid for so long? That says something profound about the way the human mind works.

Of course, there are other considerations when comparing an Experimental Group to a Control Group. They must both be similar and, as much as possible, free of bias.

- *Random Groups*: assign members at random to each group to avoid bias.

- *Matched Groups*: ensure the groups are matched for age, sex, problems, or other variables.

- *Double-Blind Studies*: A Placebo Control is a single-blind study. Ideally, you should have a second blind, on those who run the study. Even the doctors doing the study, should not know if the people are getting a Placebo or the real medicine or treatment. That is to prevent bias. Not uncommonly, a doctor who knows which patients got the actual medication and which got the placebo, may react differently to each. The reaction of the doctor, having enthusiasm for the one he knows got the real meds or being deadpan to the patient he knows got the placebo, can bias the results.

HOW DO YOU TELL WHEN AN AD IS BOGUS?

1. If the ad only presents enthusiastic people who claim it works, it is unlikely they have any factual evidence that it does work. Companies only show the ones who are the most enthusiastic about the result. The majority who got no benefit may be ignored.

2. If the ad claims to have scientific evidence for its value, but does not tell you what the scientific evidence is (how the control group compared to the experimental group, and the statistics), then the value of the product is probably not very impressive.

3. *"Figures don't lie, but liars' figure"* Mark Twain. To sell a product, many exaggerate the claim, by focusing only on the most enthusiastic users and the most impressive statistics.

4. *The most common bogus ads today often involve ads for vitamins, minerals, wrinkle reducers, testosterone boosters. Rarely do you see any evidence other than simple association presented as evidence. Coincidence is not evidence.*

WHY IT IS SO HARD TO TELL
IF WHAT WE SEE ON TELEVISION IS HONEST?

Until the early 1970s, the number one artificial sweetener in America was Saccharine. It was found in diet soft drinks, cookies, candy, ice cream, and more.

Then, a study came out in the press that said scientists had found a 50% increase in urinary tract tumors associated with saccharine. Immediately, there was a national panic. Diet drinks and foods with saccharine were being dumped at closeout prices. Quickly, Nutri-sweet or aspartame replaced Saccharine as the main sweetener.

But it was years before the full story of that study came out. It turns out that two groups of 100 rats each were used in the study. The experimental group of 100 rats was fed the equivalent of 800 times the amount of saccharine an average adult would consume in a lifetime of drinking diet soft drinks. That is not an unusual procedure, Q & D or Quick and Dirty, studies are often done first to see if something might cause a problem.

The Placebo Control group of 100 rats was fed an equal amount of a placebo, usually corn starch.

They found the group fed saccharine had 6 urinary tumors. The group given the placebo had 4 urinary tumors. That is a 50% increase in the number of urinary tumors associated with saccharine. That was statistically significant.

Was that actually significant? Or did Stephen Hawking get it right in his quip?

"It was recently discovered that research causes cancer in rats."

Stephen Hawking

To understand any study, we need to know, not just the percent of the difference, but all of the statistics in the study. It took over a quarter of a century before the FDA could give saccharine a clean bill of health. Now you can find it on your grocery store shelf. But it no longer has the value it once had. It was replaced by Nutri-sweet (aspartame).

A 50% increase in tumors sounds dramatic. But if the public is not educated to understand the value of the statistics, they cannot know what questions to ask or what the statistics mean.

If they are not told what the statistics are, even scientists cannot understand what the evidence means.

Yet the statistics in this study were dirt simple, even obvious, when we were told the facts.

"OCCAM'S RAZOR:" The Law of Parsimony

William of Occam was one of the first to note that we should strive for the simplest explanation, that explains the most information, with the fewest unnecessary assumptions.

"Any intelligent fool can make can make things bigger and more complex... it takes a touch of genius—and a lot of courage, to move in the opposite direction."

E. F. Schumacher

"Truth is ever to be found in the simplicity, and not the multiplicity and confusion of things."
Isaac Newton

"If you can't explain something to a six-year-old, that means you don't really understand it."
Attributed to Richard Feynman by his students.

A theory should be simple enough to explain the evidence, but no simpler.
Albert Einstein

Yet in our schools, we have continued to make science more and more difficult to understand. Teaching students about methods and math have discouraged far too many, and left most without the real-world examples they need to understand the simple reality of science.

THE FORMAL SCIENTIFIC METHOD

"Research is what I am doing when I don't know what I am doing."

Werner von Braun

In our textbooks, and in the American Psychological Association (APA), the formal methods of science are emphasized:

1. RESEARCH:
First, do your research. You want to know everything that has already been learned about the subject you want to study. *"Do not keep re-inventing the wheel"*. Out of what you learn from the studies that have already been done, new ideas and questions will emerge.

Previous Research must be briefly, but clearly, presented in the proposal.

2. HYPOTHESIS:
Formulate your hypothesis.

A Hypothesis is commonly presented in an If–Then statement. "IF I do this... THEN, based on my research, I expect this will follow..."

Nobel Prize Physicist Richard Feynman, in a film describing to his students the methods of science, said;

Feynman: *"...first you guess..."*

Students: (laugh)

Feynman: *"Don't laugh. That is what we do..."*

Then he describes how the guess must be tested and, if the guess does not fit the data, *"It must be thrown out..."*

A Hypotheses is a guess, but it is an educated guess, if you have done your research.

3. DESIGN YOUR STUDY:

Design a study tight enough to evaluate whether your hypothesis is valid or not. It may be just as useful to find an idea does not work as it is to find an idea that does. In real life, the trial and error of problem-solving have far more errors than successes. Yet we can learn from our mistakes.

"At least we know that idea didn't work."

4. RUN YOUR EXPERIMENT:

Everything you do must be described in detailed terms, detailed enough that anyone reading your work could, using the same techniques and measures and samples, reproduce your work and get the same or similar results.

5. ANALYZE YOUR RESULTS:

How do you interpret your results? Are there other possible interpretations?

The whole purpose of statistical analysis is not so much to prove something, but instead *to use precise data to illustrate your findings.* Remember the story of the rats with urinary tumors? Without knowing all of the statistics of the study, even a scientist cannot understand anything from just knowing the results.

Too often students come away feeling like a failure if their research does not work out as predicted. Figure out where you went wrong. Point it out to others.

Thomas Edison reportedly experimented with over 100 elements, from silk thread to tungsten, before he found one that worked best in an electric light. All of us experiment constantly with life, and interpersonal relations, to find out what works best for us. Failure is more common than success. Trial and Error is universal.

The above is just the FORMAL scientific method. In real life scientists rarely write any of this down, they just guess, do their study, and look at the results. The FORMAL method is what you have to do if you want to get grant money to do research. If you want to publish your results, you must write up your results in the formal way, or no APA publication will publish your results.

There is probably a good reason for requiring that studies be written up in a formal manner. In some studies, you cannot even tell what it is that the psychologist is trying to do. Writing down a clearly stated Hypothesis, and explaining the Research it is based on, makes the study far easier to understand, and maybe forces the experimenter to think about what they are doing.

Kudos for being precise.

Experiments allow for control of all the extraneous variables that might otherwise interfere with our observations. By controlling all the variables, it makes it easier to see "cause and effect".

But experiments are not always the best way to do psychology. Simple Observation of human behavior can be more accurate and more relevant than trying to bring this into a laboratory. If we can combine both, we would be a better science.

The formal scientific method used by psychology has its critics:

> *"A biologist, if he wishes to know how many toes a cat has, does not 'frame the <u>hypothesis</u> that the number of feline digital extremities is 4, or 5, or 6,' he simply looks at a cat and counts. A social scientist prefers the more long-winded expression every time, because it gives an entirely spurious impression of scientificness to what he is doing.*

Chemist Anthony Standen

3. CORRELATION

Every textbook on statistics says the same thing, *"Correlation is NOT Causation"*. The fact that two things occur together does not mean that one thing causes the other: This association is basic to human superstition.

WHY COINCIDENCE IS CONVINCING

A remarkable example of the fallacy of our belief that coincidence can prove anything is provided by George Metcalf in his analysis of *"The Dangers of Bread"*.

http://www.geoffmetcalf.com/bread.html

In a humorous analysis of a Cincinnati Enquirer headline, *"Smell of Baked Bread may be Health Hazard"* he describes the following facts, and yes, they are all generally facts:

1. *More than 98 percent of convicted felons were bread eaters.*

2. *Fully half of all children who grow up in bread-eating households score below average on standardized tests* (if the 50th percentile is average).

3. *More than 90 percent of violent crimes occur within 24 hours of eating bread.*

4. *Bread has been proven to be addictive. Subjects deprived of bread and allowed only water actually begged for bread after only two days.*

George Metcalf was being humorous with his analysis of the dangers of bread, yet what is striking is that every example he gave is basically true.

The point is not that bread is dangerous, we all eat bread, not just the 98% of convicted felons. We all know from experience that bread is not dangerous, it does not make us commit a violent crime…

The point for us is that ***if we did not know what bread is,*** that kind of evidence would be terribly convincing. If we simply substituted another word for bread, like an illegal drug, or a politician; vast numbers of people would eagerly believe it. It is much like the *Malleus Maleficarum*, the book that described in detail how to detect a witch, yet it is quite useless.

"Figures don't lie, but liars' figure." Mark Twain

Yet the same kind of "guilt by association" has been used by everyone from witch-hunters to politicians today to convince people that the most absurd ideas are correct. From QANON conspiracy theories, to associating political opponents with emotionally charged words, to TV shows hawking aliens, ghosts, and supernatural forces, we are all too easily convinced by nothing but words associated with emotions. Reality is boring by comparison. Our schools have failed to provide us with the very knowledge we need to understand this world. Perhaps it is no wonder that we are 24th in the world in science.

Ignorance combines with arrogance to produce a certainty that is hard to argue with.

We often hear students and even police officers say "I don't believe in coincidence." Yet, from the witch hunts to the centuries of bogus "cures' to the overwhelming superstitions of our species, coincidence detracts us from reality.

WHAT CORRELATIONS ARE GOOD FOR:

Correlations may *suggest* a possible relationship. They can also be useful to show associations with known variables.

Every test devised by psychologists is based on correlation. A test gives you a score. What does that score mean? How do we know? Academic achievement tests such as the SAT scores are correlated with grades (success in school). I.Q. tests are correlated with ability. Personality tests are correlated with observations of friends, relatives, or psychologists. Most of these correlations are only at the .24 to .42 level. Correlation is not a great measure of any of these, but it is the measure we have.

It is not enough to tell someone what their score is. We also need an honest appreciation of what that score does *not* tell us.

4. CASE STUDIES

Case studies have been especially useful in our studies of how the brain operates. In the next chapter, you will see how Hippocrates studied soldiers who have received head wounds in battle. Such simple studies tell a remarkable tale about what the brain does, and even what our conscious mind is, and is not.

The story of Phineas Gage, who survived a steel rod being blown through his frontal lobes (in chapter 4) found no change in his apparent intelligence, consciousness unimpaired, yet a strange change occurred in his personality.

Psychology has a long history of studying psychological problems in individuals with psychological problems or even just our ability to work problems. Yet psychology's problems with such studies are closer to the problems medicine had with separating placebo effects, or other extraneous variables, from what we are observing.

5. EXTRANEOUS VARIABLES

Other methods have the flavor of science if not always the accuracy. Public opinion polls are notorious for the fact that people often change their minds, and other events change the outcome. In the election of 2016, the best of our opinion polls predicted, just before the day of the election, that Hillary Clinton would defeat Donald Trump by 3%. In fact, she did defeat Donald Trump by nearly three million votes. Who became President? Why?

Still, the reliability of any opinion poll depends on having an accurate sample of the actual voters or a random sample of the opinion of the overall population. It is only scientific, based on the value of the sampling procedure. It is not a major scientific method, but still very useful.

Occasionally, the artificial environment of an experiment, may interfere with the responses of the subject. This is why natural or systematic observation is also essential for an understanding of what is actually happening.

"Relax and react spontaneously to the flier."

6. THEORY: Not What You Think...

"I Have a Theory..."

People seem to think that having a theory is nothing more than having an opinion. In science, a theory must be based on hard evidence, a reason to think something may be true, and that it can explain other information. It is not just an idea that comes out of our mind, or is based on something we heard on television.

Today, the ruthless use of simple associations to "prove" something is seen in shows that claim aliens were responsible for building the remarkable stone monuments of past civilizations. How did the aliens get here? In stone space ships? And in shows hawking ghosts and spirits as the cause of happenings. "WOW! Did you hear that?" What else could that noise be except a ghost?" Noises in the woods at night? "What could it be? It must be Bigfoot". Those are opinions, without evidence to base it on. Without evidence for the basic assumption, they are not theories.

Yet such shows get tens of millions of dollars more in advertising revenue and viewers than any science show. Except for the occasional shock and awe of a color picture of stars or a colorful nebula, reality is too rare in the media we live in.

First comes the evidence. Then, Theory allows us to extrapolate beyond our data, to project an idea onto other examples. But it must be based on hard evidence, not just an opinion.

A theory may allow us to see farther than we otherwise could, and build on our knowledge. But it is only as good as the evidence on which it is based.

Theory allows us to infer relationships, sometimes from the simplest evidence.

"I think we're on different career paths."

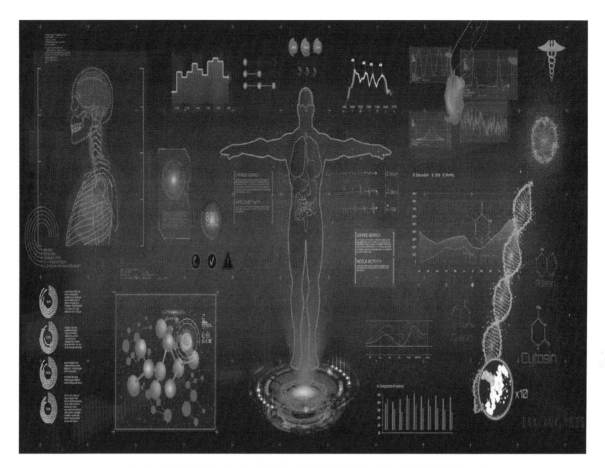

THE FRAMINGHAM STUDY

One of the most successful examples of the use of the scientific methods came from the medical research done at Framingham. Researchers enlisted almost the entire town of Framingham, Massachusetts in a multi-generation extensive study of medical tests. They took every known measure of health; temperature, blood tests, blood pressure, urine samples, weight, etc. in an attempt to determine what would predict heart health.

5,000 subjects were followed for decades. The studies began in 1948 and continue to this day. The study is still going on with the children of the original participants, with new data on genetic effects.

From these dirt simple studies of blood pressure and blood samples, what they found was transformative. Using only the most basic measures of health, they determined that (1) cigarette smoking causes cancer and heart disease, (2) high blood pressure causes heart disease, and (3) high cholesterol levels are related to heart disease. Since heart disease and cancer are the two major killers in medicine, the discoveries were profound.

All of this, blood pressure, weight, smoking, and more, are dirt simple discoveries. Yet they are more important than anything we lauded in bleeding people, electric belts, or Dr. John's Magic Elixir. The dangers of cigarettes were argued for decades before it was accepted throughout the country. For decades, every time the press mentioned the harmful effects of cigarettes, they would put on an opposite view, to be "fair and balanced". The first discussions of global warming suffered the same fate. But that was neither fair nor balanced.

Later studies found that reducing smoking and taking medication to control high blood pressure and cholesterol, could help prevent the major causes of death. Yet it took decades for the results of the study to become known to the general public. At first, no one even wanted to criticize the cigarette industry or the fast-food industry. But today, the success of this dirt simple study is a legend.

SCIENCE AS A MIXTURE OF MANY DISCIPLINES

Perhaps the wisest of all analogies to explain the interdependence of all disciplines comes from an old story from India of blind men trying to describe an elephant. One blind man grabs hold of the tail and describes the elephant as thin and long, like a snake. A second grabs hold of a leg, and describes the elephant as round and stout and firm, like the trunk of a tree. A third blind man grabs the trunk and describes the elephant as like a squirming fire hose. A fourth grabs hold of the stomach and describes the elephant as huge, round, and floating in the air.

Each of the men in this example has acquired a fraction of reality. None has the whole picture. That is why it is critical for scientists to know our History, Biology, Brain, Psychology, Sociology, and Culture. Knowledge must be a synthesis of all bits and pieces of information that describe the human mind. Together we must examine all of the evidence we have, and search for more.

That is why we need a *unified field* of biology, brain, learning, behavior, cognition, perception, sociology, cultural anthropology, and history, to interpret what our mind is all about.

Although not as concentrated as the Framingham study, psychologists are involved in studying the brain, behavior, perception, learning, and social interaction in an attempt to discover the basic underlying causes of behavior and human problems. Even human *history* is a critical piece of evidence that is often ignored. Many of the areas of psychology studies may seem dirt simple, but that is often where the most important information is found.

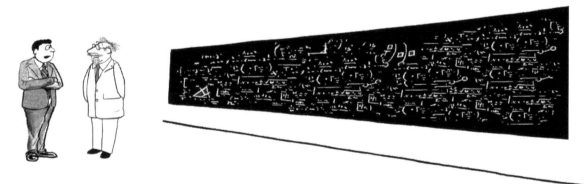

**"For my profile I'll be talking about the science you ...
but what about the fun you?"**

"Science knows no country, because knowledge belongs to humanity, and is the torch which illuminates the world. Science is the highest personification of the nation because that nation will remain the first which carries the furthest the works of thought and intelligence."

Louis Pasteur

Progress in science has not come easily. Our first tentative steps to figure out how the brain works tells a story of the difficult task of understanding life. Yet an understanding of the brain and behavior is to our success as a species.

But something happens when speech comes into play. The same ability to use words that have given us such an advantage over other species in communicating ideas and education, has also created the greatest superstitions and fears. Words have led to bloodletting and witch hunts and wars.

We seem to lose the ability to do science when the emotional effect of *words* takes over. Unable to escape the words others have embedded in our minds, we ignore reality, fear it, and evade it as much as possible. We must pay as much attention to the ignorance and arrogance produced by words, as to their success.

"Everybody's a mad scientist, and life is their lab. We're all trying to experiment to find a way to live, to solve problems, to fend off madness and chaos."

David Cronenberg

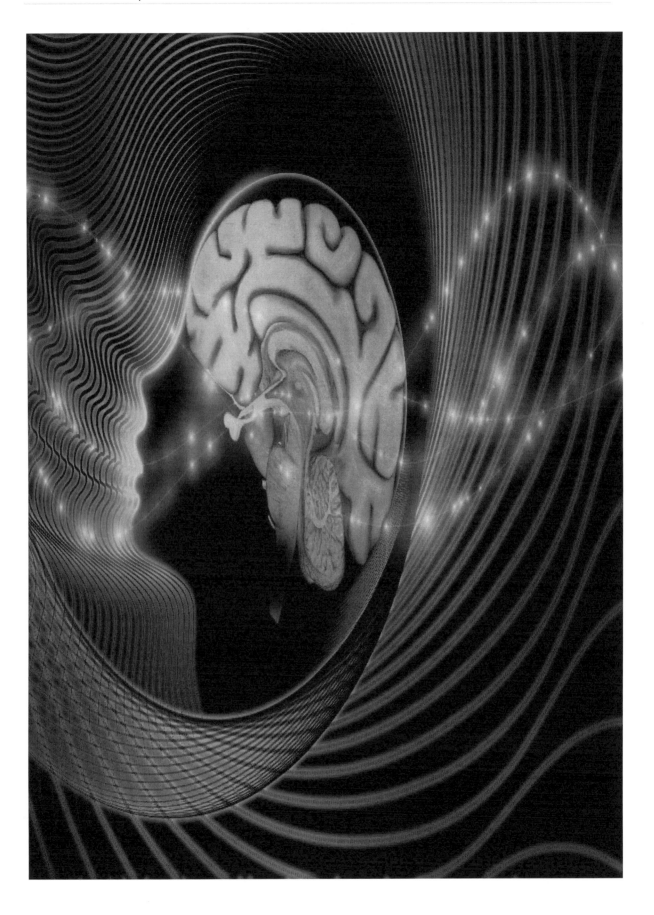

THE BIOLOGICAL FOUNDATION OF THE MIND

The brain is the seat of our stored knowledge and our behavior. The brain coordinates the interaction between our body and our environment. In discussing the biological aspects of behavior, textbooks often begin with the neurons and sensors before going into the studies of the brain. However, scientists first learned about the functioning of the brain by studying patients who had suffered head wounds, epilepsy, and brain tumors. Only much later did the importance of the neuron and the functioning of the sensors become apparent. By taking the reader through the early probing of the brain first, we leave open much of the mystery of the brain as it appeared to early researchers. The questions they raised were often about the source of power for the brain, the neurons.

The chapters in this part have been organized around the major questions that have troubled brain researchers. How can we study the brain itself? How does the brain provide us with "consciousness"? Does our "mind" exist independently of our body?

Our knowledge of how electronic computers operate is providing us with a new model of how the brain functions. Yet many of the mysteries that excited the imagination of the ancient Greeks are still unexplained.

In all the knowledge of the universe that is being revealed to us by our probes into space, there is nothing that can surpass the importance of the knowledge we are gaining from our probing of the inner space of the human brain. It is here that we are finding clues to the mind that can be found in no other way—clues that will influence our concept of human nature for centuries to come.

An understanding of the biology of the mind is basic to our understanding of human psychology.

Chapter 4 • The Human Brain: Probing the Surface of the Brain

Chapter 5 • The Prime Mover: The Neuron and the Computer

Chapter 6 • The Sensors: Sensation and Perception

Chapter 7 • The Conscious Mind: The Ghost in the Machine?

4 THE HUMAN BRAIN

PROBING THE SURFACE OF THE BRAIN

HIPPOCRATES • FRITCH AND HITZIG • BROCA * WERNICKE * PENFIELD •

PHINEAS GAGE • MALMO • LURIA

The Location of the Mind • Mapping the Cerebral Cortex: Sensory Cortex, Motor Cortex • Probing the Brains of Conscious Patients • The Silent Mass: The Frontal Lobes

> *"Some people say that the heart is the organ with which we think and that it feels pain and anxiety. But it is not so, men ought to know that from the brain and the brain alone, arise our pleasures, joys, laughter and jests, as well as our sorrows, pains, griefs and tears. Through it, in particular, we think, see, hear, and distinguish the ugly from the beautiful, the bad from the good, the pleasant from the unpleasant, the brain is the interpreter of consciousness. "*

Hippocrates circa 2,450 years ago *The Sacred Disease*

It is as important to understand ***how*** we know what we know about the brain as it is to understand *what* the brain does. *How* is the very essence of science, the understanding that leads to knowledge.

How could Hippocrates possibly have understood the role of the brain in pleasure, joys, laughter and pain, grief and tears, over 2,000 years before we began to catch up to him in our culture? Hippocrates said that *"the proper school of a surgeon is war"*. By observing soldiers who received head wounds in battle, he dramatically learned how important the brain was in controlling everything there is to know about us.

Even today, with Positron Emission Tomography (PET scans), radioactive dyes and functional Magnetic Resonance Imaging (fMRI) that allow us to see deep inside the brain without the need for surgery, we still go back to the methods of old to tell us the purpose of the structures of the brain. Brain damage from strokes and head injury are still the basis of such knowledge. PET scans and fMRIs make it easier to locate the problems inside the brain.

Hippocrates' declaration of the importance of the brain was ignored in the centuries that followed. Indeed, the heart replaced the brain as the central organ of thought and feeling. Aristotle declared that the heart is the seat of the mind, or soul, as it was called by the Greeks. After all, the heart is palpable. It works unceasingly. In agitation it speeds up; in relaxation, it slows. The brain makes no response when poked or probed, no life-giving fluid gushes forth when penetrated. It does not move, flinch, or secrete bile. To all appearances, the brain is silent, devoid of action.

Aristotle saw the massive blood vessels servicing the brain and concluded that the brain is just a radiator, not unlike the radiator in your car, that functioned to cool the blood. The heart, he said, is the seat of intelligence. Man needed a bigger brain to cool our hot blood. The knowledge that Hippocrates had based on observation was lost.

"There are in fact two things, science, and opinion; the former begets knowledge, the latter ignorance." Hippocrates

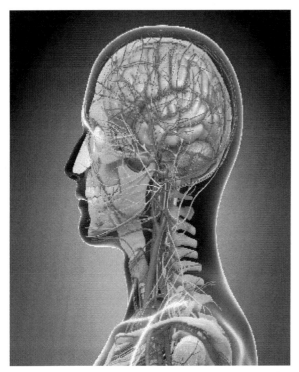

For most of the last 2000 years, the heart was considered to be the seat of the psyche, a popular concept that was essentially unchallenged until the 18th century. The impact of this belief is still felt today in our valentine vocabulary of emotion, which speaks of heartache, heartbreak, affairs of the heart, and *"in your heart you know he's right"* (from the 1964 presidential campaign).

By 1749, William Harvey's classic studies of the blood's circulatory system had taken much of the awe and mystery away from the function of the heart. The world slowly came to accept the heart as little more than a sophisticated pump that lub-dubs the nourishing blood to the tissues of the body. Our culture has only recently begun to catch up with our science.

Old myths, now written into law, arose to plague us. In 1973 a heart transplant surgeon and medical team were indirectly accused of murder in a court trial because they removed the beating heart of a man, whose brain had been destroyed by a gunshot, for a transplant. By law in many states, death is still ruled to occur when the heart stops beating. Yet modern techniques make it possible to keep the heart alive indefinitely, long after the brain has ceased its function. No heart transplant team was ever indicted on such a charge, but it is a telling comment on what we have believed in the past.

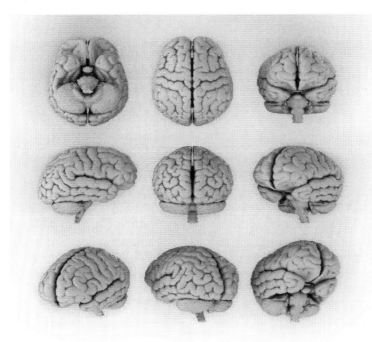

The human brain consists of about three pounds of nerve tissue; nothing but cells, neurons and glial cells. Under the skull, the brain's surface is normally covered with a thick membrane, the dura matter, and under that is a network of veins and arteries that supply it with essential oxygen and nutrients. The brain cells can live only a matter of minutes without oxygen. The blood supply itself contains enough oxygen to keep the cells alive for several more minutes without a new supply of oxygen. If the blood vessels are damaged in an accident or blocked by an internal stroke, then the cells fed by the blood supply will die.

If the blood vessels and membrane are removed from the surface of the brain, a complex series of hills and valleys, called convolutions, will be seen. It has sometimes been said that the more intelligent the animal, the more complex the convolutions. Less intelligent animals do have smoother brain surfaces. However, the depth and complexity of the convolutions are related to brain size, more than intelligence.

The dolphin has a brain as large as that of a human, and every bit as complex in its convolutions. The brain of an elephant is four times the size of our own; that of the blue whale is five times as large.

Larger brains appear to be more convoluted to allow greater surface area for the cortex, that is the conscious mind, and to allow the blood vessels, lying deep within the convolutions, to supply the essential oxygen to the cells lying within its mass. By folding in upon itself, the cortex provides inlets for the major blood vessels as well as greater surface area.

"Primum non nocerum." (First, do no harm)" Hippocrates

These are the first eight great discoveries about the human brain that lifted the veil of ignorance that has kept us in the dark for so long. Generally, in order of their discovery:

1. THE SACRED DISEASE -- HIPPOCRATES

"People think that epilepsy is divine simply because they don't have any idea what causes epilepsy. But I believe that someday we will understand what causes epilepsy, and at that moment, we will cease to believe that it's divine. And so it is with everything in the universe"
Hippocrates

The Greeks believed that epilepsy (a seizure disorder) was a sacred disease. The Oracles of Delphi were selected from people who had a seizure disorder. When under the trans-like state of a seizure, they believed that the Oracle could communicate with the gods. For over a thousand years the Oracles of Delphi at the Temple of Apollo, were believed to be capable of speaking to Apollo and could answer questions about the future. Their behavior had to be interpreted by a cadre of priests, who often couched the answer in riddles that you had to interpret.

Compared to our own history, the Greek's view of epilepsy was relatively quaint. For over a thousand years in our history, we believed people with a seizure disorder were possessed by demons and treated them accordingly.

Surgeons who trained in Hippocrates' *"school of war"* would have observed that soldiers who had never before had a seizure would, if they received a head wound in battle, often start having seizures. The seizures were related to scar tissue in the brain. Later surgeons discovered that if you surgically removed the scar tissue, the seizures would abate, at least until new scar tissue grew.

Seizures can originate at any point in the brain, most commonly in the cortex, the surface of the brain, and usually always on just one side. If the seizure is close enough to the motor cortex, it may disrupt the ability to control our muscle functions (a psychomotor seizure).

Seizures are sometimes preceded by a feeling, and generally dissipate after a few minutes. If the seizure is in an area away from the motor function, it might disrupt some of our sensory input, such as vision or hearing or touch.

Today, most seizures are effectively controlled by medication; Dilantin, Tegretol, Phenobarbital, Neurontin, and even deep cranial stimulation and vagal nerve stimulation. None of these were available in the time of Hippocrates or when we were treating seizure disorders with exorcism because we believed they were caused by demon possession.

Epilepsy

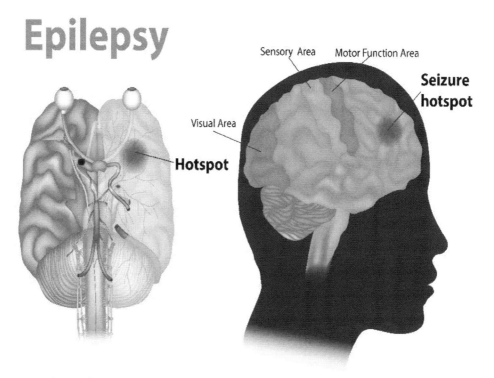

Hippocrates understood that disease was not caused by the anger of Zeus, but had natural causes that we would one day discover. Now we know they can be caused by brain injury, high body temperature, or more rarely, they can be genetic. More than any other fact, it was his rejection of supernatural causes of disease that earned him the title of "father" of modern medicine.

Understanding how we know, gives us an insight into how science works.

2. THE LEFT SIDE OF THE BRAIN CONTROLS THE RIGHT SIDE OF THE BODY

"And if incision of the temple is made on the left, spasm seizes the parts on the right, while if the incision is on the right, spasm seizes the parts on the left..."

Hippocrates *On Wounds in the Head*, trans. E. T. Withington, Vol. 3, 33.

How do we know this: How could Hippocrates possibly have known this over 2, 400 years ago, before we had any way of seeing inside the brain? Hippocrates gained his insight into the importance of the brain from his study of soldiers who had received head wounds in battle. He found that in some cases an injury on one side of the brain would produce paralysis of the opposite side of the body. An injury on the left side of the head might produce paralysis of the right arm or leg, or even of the entire right side of the body. This curious observation was repeatedly made by physicians in the centuries that followed, but the very absurdity of such a fact seems to have left us more baffled than enlightened.

"War is the school of the surgeon" Hippocrates

The value of this knowledge continues to this day. It is common to see doctors in a hospital or nursing home extend both their hands to a patient and say, "Squeeze my hands". This is a "quick and dirty" way of testing for a stroke. We know strokes, a blockage of blood vessels in the brain, are usually always localized on only one side of the brain. If one of the patient's hand's squeeze is more limp than the other, it suggests a stroke on the opposite side of the brain. It is not a complete test as it only works if the motor area of the brain is affected by the stroke, but it is still useful information.

In 1870, at the University of Berlin, one of the first major experimental studies on the brain was performed. Two Prussian physiologists, Fritsch and Hitzig, began to probe the surface of the brain with an electrical stimulus. In a series of studies, they put dogs under an anesthetic, cut away portions of the bony skull covering the brain, and applied an electric probe to the brain's surface, the cortex, along the motor areas of the brain.

As they probed along a diagonal line near the center of the left and right sides of the brain, they found that gross motor movements occurred on the opposite side of the body. Probing the left side of the brain moved the right foreleg, paw, or hind leg. Probing at different points along the line produced movements of the jaw, twitches of an eye, and movements to the right or left.

As surgeons in the Prussian Army, Fritsch and Hitzig stimulated the same areas of the brains of unconscious soldiers, whose brains had been exposed by their wounds. The soldiers' bodies responded in the same way as those of the dogs in the laboratory. Further studies demonstrated beyond any doubt that the same order of control in the cortex of a dog is also present in cats, sheep, monkeys, and humans.

Clearly, the brain controlled the body. Furthermore, the left side of the brain controlled the right side of the body, and the right side of the brain controlled the left side of the body.

The remarkable similarity of the brains of animals and humans has been highly beneficial to all experimenters working in brain research, and improved techniques of electrical stimulation have allowed the mapping of motor areas in the brains of animals and people. The mapping is so accurate that stimulation of specific areas of the brain can produce independent movement in separate fingers of the human hand.

The work of Fritsch and Hitzig raised many questions. They extensively probed the brain, and yet they found no point other than this motor area that produced any responses. The rest of the brain, almost 90 percent of it, was mysteriously silent. This finding may have led some to the mistaken conclusion that we only use 10 percent of our mental powers and the rest remains deeply hidden.

3. BROCA'S AREA
THE CENTER OF MOTOR SPEECH:

In the 1860s, the French surgeon Paul Broca encountered a unique patient named Leborgne. As a young man in his thirties, Leborgne had lost his ability to speak. No physician of the day could understand why this should be. Over the

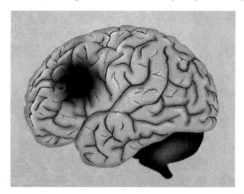

years, the man suffered from increasingly severe seizures, and eventually, his right arm and leg became paralyzed. Now in his fifties, Leborgne came down with a serious illness, unrelated to his physical and verbal problems, and had been sent to Broca for help. Broca was unable to help and the patient died. Broca performed an autopsy and discovered that a large area of the brain had been destroyed in the left cerebral hemisphere.

A second and very similar case later came to Broca's attention. By comparing the area of overlap of the injury of one patient to that of the second, Broca successfully outlined the area of motor speech that now is known as Broca's area. The area where the overlap of injury was greatest was a walnut-sized section of the frontal lobe just in front of the motor area that controls the movement of the lips, tongue, and jaws.

The damaged area in the above outline approximates the damage Broca found in his patients. It is directly in front of the part of the Motor Cortex that controls the movement of the lips, tongue, and vocal areas. It is found only on the left side of the brain.

In the years that followed, Broca's findings were repeatedly confirmed by other surgeons. But out of the many findings, a remarkable pattern began to emerge. All the patients who were unable to speak had suffered damage to the left side of the brain.

Damage to the same area on the right side alone had no such effect. We have since learned that human language ability is generally located in the left side of the cerebral cortex-even in left-handed people. We have also learned that people with damage limited to Broca's area can still understand speech and can write.

Broca's Area was important because it showed us that there are very specific areas of the brain devoted to very specific abilities. Broca's area makes speech possible. Yet we are not unique. Mynah birds and parrots can speak. African parrots are especially talkative. They can imitate any language. But their verbal ability is limited, they cannot understand words. They are not using words as symbols for other ideas.

4. WERNICKE'S AREA: THE CENTER OF UNDERSTANDING SPEECH

Speech is exceptionally important to understand because it is the ability of humans to communicate that gives us an ability that other animals do not have. We can use words to communicate with others. Words from Broca's Area can trigger a host of meanings in the Wernicke's Area of another person.

Like Broca, the German physician Wernicke also had two patients with problems. Unlike Broca's patients, these patients could speak. They could pronounce words clearly and distinctly. Unlike Broca's patients, they could not understand a word they said or a word you said to them.

Both of Wernicke's patients would, on autopsy, be found to have damage to an area only inches behind Broca's area, just above the sensory area for hearing on the temporal lobe.

Approximate area of the brain damaged in Wernicke's patients. Today, this may be referred to as Receptive Aphasia.

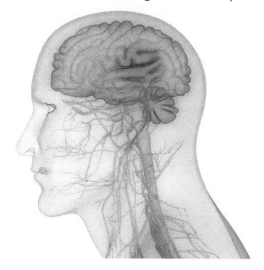

One of the first clients I ever worked with was a young man with no apparent problems at all. He was physically normal, able to work with tools or anything you could show him to do that he could imitate. If you spoke a sentence to him, he could repeat the sentence in perfect English and perfect diction. People often thought him to be completely normal.

But even though he could speak perfectly, he could not understand a word you said to him, or a word he said to you. It was difficult to believe that he could be so limited only in one area. I gave him a WAIS IQ test to find out. His lack of understanding of verbal ideas meant he could score no higher than an IQ in the 50s. Even on the Performance section of the WAIS, often thought to be nonverbal, he was limited. Damage to Wernicke's Area is profound. Yet his ability to imitate what you showed him, or the words you spoke, was still remarkable.

Today, psychologists use such information to make a diagnosis of Aphasia. Broca's Aphasia is also called Expressive Aphasia. Wernicke's Aphasia is also called Receptive Aphasia.

Of the two, Expressive Aphasia is often the most difficult because of our culture's dependence on language. I have often thought this young man might have done well as a hunter, say 100,000 years ago, before humans developed speech. It may suggest too, that just because our ancestors used tools, does not mean they could speak.

It might also suggest that at least two mutations had to take place (for Broca's Area and Wernicke's Area) before we developed the communication ability we have today. Separate mutations in the right side of the brain, for visual-spatial ability, might have occurred first, to facilitate tool making. This would be an interesting case study for an anthropologist.

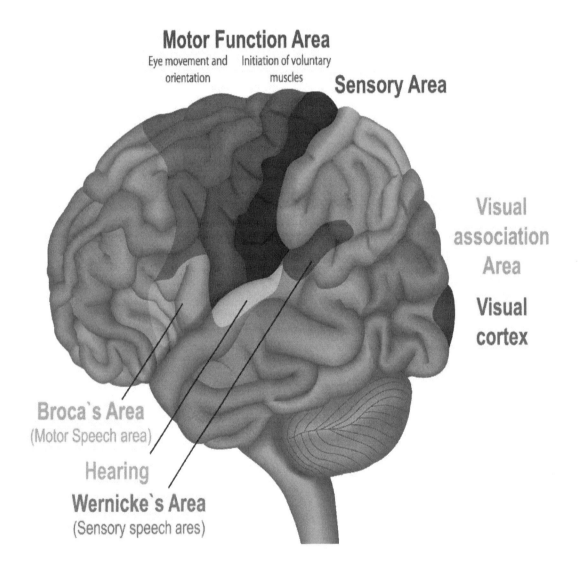

The most recent discoveries of a new generation of cognitive neuroscientists, using fMRIs and methods of seeing the activity of neurons in the brain, have found that there is a tract of nerve cells joining Broca's area and Wernicke's area that is activated when we speak. Other areas of the brain also make simultaneous connections with the visual and auditory cortex as well as other areas. These areas do not act in isolation but as a coordinated unit.

5. SENSORY CENTERS IN THE BRAIN

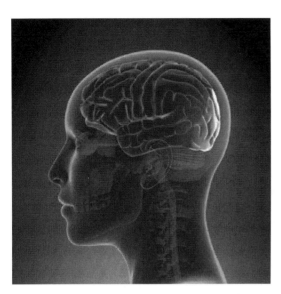

In a short few years after the experiments of Fritsch and Hitzig, the mysterious 90 percent began to give way. In 1873, D. Ferrier (1886) found that vision resides in the back of the brain, in the occipital lobe, which makes up about 20 percent of the rear of the cortex. When the eyes were intact but the occipital lobe was damaged, they now had great difficulty in learning tasks requiring sight. Destruction or damage to other areas of the brain showed no such visual impairment.

Left is the visual cortex of the brain, the occipital lobe, at the back of the brain, where Ferrier located the center of vision in the brain. The optic nerve runs from the back of the eyes, through the optic chiasm to the rear of the brain. This area of the cortex is where we become conscious of what the eyes see.

6. THE PHANTOM LIMB PHENOMENON

Back to the mysteries of observing soldiers who received wounds in battle; one of the most remarkable is the discovery that individuals who have had a leg or arm amputated, still report feeling as if the limb is still there. They have marked pain in the neuroma that forms at the point of the amputation, as nerve axons attempt to regrow, but regrow only in a mass. They report feeling touch on the missing foot or calf even though it no longer exists. Why?

What we know is that the feelings that come from our limbs are felt in the sensory cortex of the brain. The brain itself is the source of the feeling, not the limb. That is hard for us to imagine as the brain so clearly reacts as if the pain we feel in our foot, is actually in our foot. But that is an illusion.

Sensations in the Mind: By the turn of the century, great progress in local anesthesia made possible a breakthrough in brain exploration. Local painkillers, roughly similar to the Novocain used by dentists to deaden an area around a tooth, now made it possible to deaden only one area of a patient's skull. Because the brain tissue itself has no receptors that produce the sensation of pain, the surgeons could electrically probe the brain while the patient was still conscious. That means the patient could tell you what he or she experienced. This allowed the surgeon to know which areas needed to be removed. It also allowed the gradual mapping of much of the cortex by electrically stimulating the brains of conscious patients.

THE MISSING 90%
STARTS TO GIVE WAY

Fritsch and Hitzig could not find any reaction in many of the brain areas they had probed. However, their subjects had been unconscious and unable to describe what they experienced. In 1909, Harvey Cushing (1936), an American surgeon, applied electrical stimulation to an area of a human brain just behind, and parallel to, the motor area stimulated by Fritsch and Hitzig. The conscious patient reported feeling sensations of touch and tingling on the opposite side of his body. The sensations felt as if the body were being physically stimulated on that side, even though nothing was touching him. Cushing had discovered the sensory cortex. Although his instruments were crude and his research was limited by the technology of the era.

Cushing's findings posed a question that begged for an answer: Could we accurately map the functions of the entire brain with this technique?

Patients suffering from intractable seizures, sometimes as many as 300 a day, often could not be helped by the medications typically used for seizures. To stop the seizures, required the removal of areas of the brain where the seizures originated. To do so required that the surgeon know which areas were good and which areas needed to be removed. How could he know this?

In the late 1940s, the Canadian neurosurgeon Wilder Penfield and the Swiss neurologist Walter Hess, working independently, began to systematically map the sensory cortex discovered by Cushing. They began their work on patients that were suffering from brain tumors or epilepsy, which required correction by brain surgery. The electrical probe was to become a valuable tool that would enable surgeons to discover which parts of the brain tissue could safely be removed with the least damage to the good brain tissue.

While the surgery was in progress, the patients could tell the surgeon what they were experiencing. After comparing the results of a great number of cases, Penfield traced out a remarkably specific road map of cortical functions. When he probed the uncovered brain at a point on the temporal lobe just above the front of the left ear, the patients reported feeling sensations on the right side of the chest. Continuing upward on a diagonal line toward the top rear of the head with the electrode, Penfield elicited sensations on the opposite side of the body in the mouth, the tongue, teeth, gums, and jaw.

7. MAPPING THE SENSORY CORTEX

Sensations in the lower lip, both lips, upper lip, face, nose, eyes, thumb, index finger, middle finger, ring finger, and little finger, were reported along a line between one-third and two-thirds of the way up. As Penfield probed toward the top along the same line, sensations were reported in the hand, wrist, forearm, elbow, arm, shoulder, neck, trunk, hip, and at the very top, the leg. On the same line, but now continuing down into the cleft between the left and right cerebral hemispheres, sensations in the foot and toes and genitals were reported.

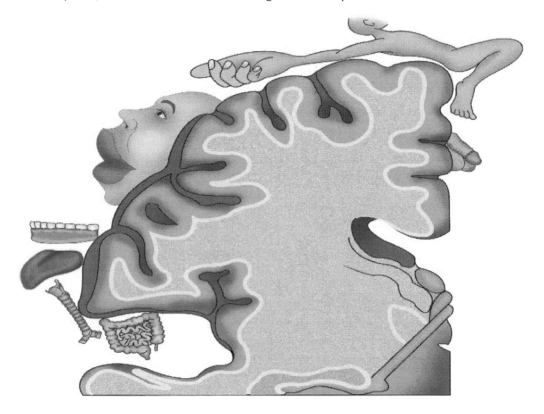

The Sensory or Somatosensory Cortex above as mapped by Penfield. Note that the size of the area on the brain corresponded to the sensitivity of the skin. The most sensitive areas are the lips, tongue, fingers, and deep down the cleft, the genitals. Larger areas like the trunk and legs, even though they are massive, have fewer sensory receptors.

These sensations occur in the same order for all humans. The order reflects a reversed image of the body. The feet and legs, which are the farthest from the brain, are represented at the farthest possible point from their origin, the top of the brain. Conversely, areas of the body that are closest to the brain-the mouth, tongue, and lips-are connected to the area of the brain nearest to them.

In addition, the area of the brain where stimulation produces sensation in the lips is over four times as large as the areas that produce a sensation in the legs and trunk, even though the latter is much larger physically. Similarly, the areas of the brain devoted to a single finger are as large as that devoted to the leg. This should not be too surprising. The sensory end organs responsible for touch are very heavily concentrated in our fingers and lips but are quite sparse elsewhere. We use our fingers to discriminate among textures, for example, but cannot make such fine distinctions with our thighs.

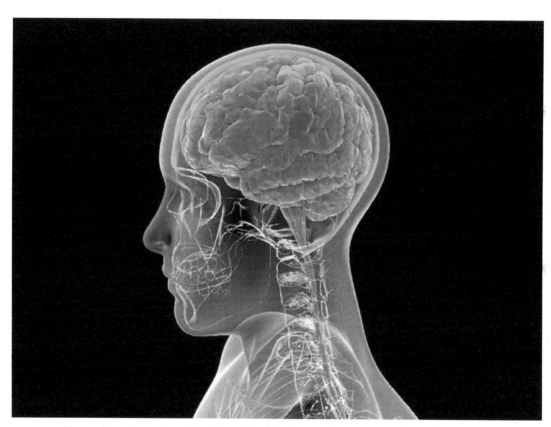

Above, the motor cortex, (Front, in red) and the Sensory Cortex mapped by Penfield and Hess

(Rear, in blue, if you have color).

8. MAPPING THE MOTOR CORTEX

Directly in front of the sensory line is the motor cortex stimulated by Fritsch and Hitzig. Penfield's delicate probing of the motor cortex produced equally specific responses. Beginning in front of the ear and continuing on a diagonal line exactly parallel to the sensory line, stimulation would produce movement in the throat, tongue, jaw, larynx, lips, face, eyelid and eyeball, brow, neck, thumb, the separate fingers, hand, wrist, elbow, shoulder, trunk, hip, knee, ankle, and toes.

The motor areas were similar but not identical to those of touch. Areas of the motor cortex that control frequently used body parts such as the jaw and ankle are larger than on the sensory cortex. Again, their relative locations on the motor cortex appear to be the same for all humans, and similar for dogs, cats, horses, chimpanzees, and the laboratory rat.

In probing the motor area of the cortex, Wilder Penfield was surprised to hear a clear, sustained vowel cry from the patient. Similar vowel sounds, sometimes with a consonant, have been elicited by stimulation of the motor areas. No intelligible word has been produced by stimulation of the brain. However, electrical stimulation of certain motor areas will produce interference with the speech of a conscious patient. In many cases, the stimulation will cause patients to repeat a word they have just spoken. At other times, patients showed confusion while counting. In one case, a patient jumped from six to twenty during stimulation but resumed correct counting with the number seven when the electrical current was turned off.

In still another case, electrical stimulation of one area seemed to produce a temporary aphasia known as the tip-of-the-tongue phenomenon. Shown a picture and asked to identify it the patient began to say,

"That is a . . . I know. That is a. . . . ".

The patient could demonstrate what the picture was by making gestures but was unable to come up with the correct name. When the current was turned off, the patient could immediately identify the pictures.

INSIDE THE BRAIN

1. MEMORIES

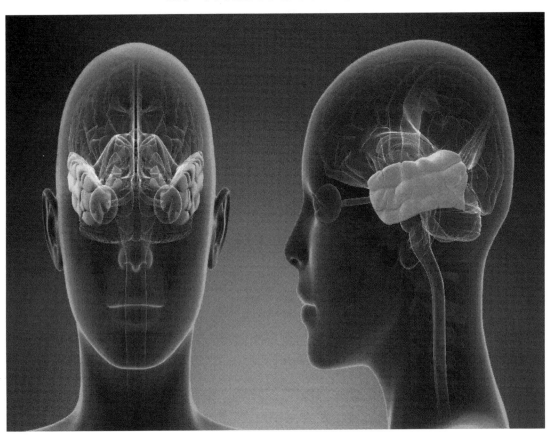

The most striking finding in Penfield's study of the cortex was the discovery that memories, much like a video replay, could be triggered by electrical stimulation of the temporal cortex on either side of the brain.

On stimulation of the surface of the right temporal lobe, above the right ear, one woman exclaimed that she saw a familiar memory from an office. She could see the desks, herself, and a man leaning on a desk with a pencil in his hand was calling to her. She recalled all the details she had noted at the time of the actual event. However, she and other patients were unable to recall any information that was not specifically noticed at the time. Apparently, such information goes unrecorded.

After surgical removal of much of the area of the same patient's right temporal lobe, electrical stimulation was applied to the underlying area, the hippocampus, which is known to be associated with consolidating memory into long-term memory.

Stimulation produced a memory of the place where she was accustomed to hanging her coat where she goes to work. Another patient reported listening to an orchestra. For as long as the electrical impulses continued, the patient heard music and reported feeling as though she were in the theater where she had heard it. Yet another patient reported a beautiful church scene where she had been on Christmas Eve some years earlier.

THE THREAD OF TIME

Once the memories begin, the patient has no control over them. They progress inexorably like a videotape replay within one's own mind. They cannot be started or stopped voluntarily. The experience always goes in forward chronological sequence, unfolding progressively, moment by moment-always forward and never backward-for as long as the stimulation continues.

As soon as the electrical current is turned off, the images stop, as if a television had been unplugged. Sometimes, re-stimulation at the same spot will cause a replay of the same memory, beginning at the same point in the memory on each successive stimulation. Penfield and Roberts (1959, 54-55) provide a poetic analogy of their findings:

> The thread of time remains within us in the form of a succession of "abiding" facilitations. This thread travels through ganglion cells and synaptic junctions, it runs through the waking hours of each man, from childhood to the grave. On the thread of time are strung, like pearls in unending succession, the "meaningful" patterns that can still recall the vanished content of a former awareness.
>
> No man can voluntarily reactivate the record. Perhaps if he could, he might become hopelessly confused. Man's voluntary recollection must be achieved through other mechanisms. And yet the recorded patterns are useful to him, even after the passage of many years. They can still be appropriately selected by some scanning process and activated with amazing promptness for the purposes of comparative interpretation. It is, it seems to me, in this mechanism of recall and comparison and interpretation that the interpretative cortex of the temporal lobes plays its specialized role.

Milner and Penfield suggest that stimulation of the cortex triggers electrical activity in numerous other underlying structures, including the hippocampus. It would be a mistake to conclude that the memory traces are localized in the temporal cortex of the brain. Memories seem to be scattered throughout the brain rather than localized. But research has found that one area of the brain is crucial for memory; the hippocampus.

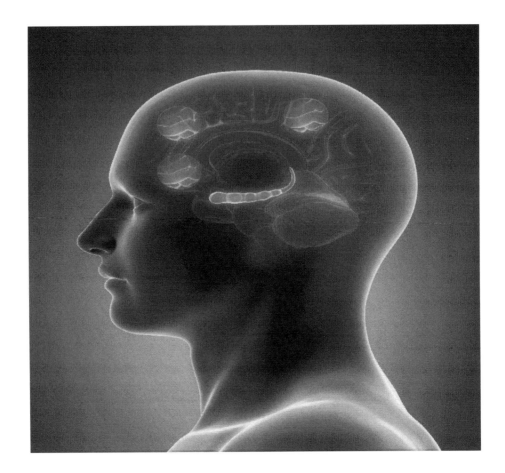

Above: at bottom, the multi-segmented hippocampus, at the top, encoded memory is within all areas of the brain—vision, hearing, touch, all provide the information we find in memories.

"People like us, who believe in physics, know that the distinction between past, present, and future is only a stubbornly persistent illusion."

Albert Einstein

Einstein knew that the past and future do not exist independently of our brain; contrary to what many have suggested in Science Fiction movies. Einstein's prediction that time would pass more slowly at high speeds, such as the speed of light, has often been misinterpreted as suggesting time travel. That is not what Einstein meant.

We have machinery in the brain that allows us to remember the past, in bits and pieces. But the past does not exist, except as a memory.

The future does not exist, except to the extent that our past experiences allow us to predict the future. When the Bell rings, we might anticipate, based on our experience, that food will follow. Yet, only the present exists, past and future are *"only a stubbornly persistent illusion."*

Old memories are scattered throughout the brain. But deep within the brain, is a segmented, worm-like structure, the Hippocampus. When damage occurs, what we observe is difficulty in consolidating working memory or short-term memory into long-term memory. This is not uncommon in dementia such as Alzheimer's disease. That means the individual may not remember what you or they just said only minutes earlier, although they may remember earlier experiences in their life in detail.

2. THE HIPPOCAMPUS: "50 FIRST DATES"

The Hollywood movie, *50 First Dates,* was loosely based on an actual case. This was a girl who developed a brain infection at the age of eight. Somehow her brain recovered except for the hippocampus, the area of the brain that consolidates short-term memory into long-term memory. Now, she could remember almost nothing for more than a few minutes. She says the other children at school made fun of her. Each day she would forget what happened and it would happen again.

At one point she tells how later in life she was out on a date, excused herself to go to the restroom, and when she came out, she could no longer remember who she was with. She was so ashamed that she had to sneak out of the restaurant.

To all appearances, she was an attractive, bright girl with no problem. Other people could not understand her behavior and she had to try to explain part of her memory was gone. She learned to substitute a journal for her memory loss. Each moment she would have to write down everything that happened to her and everything she had to do the next day, or she would forget. That notebook became her memory. Then, she had to remember to read it throughout the day to remind her.

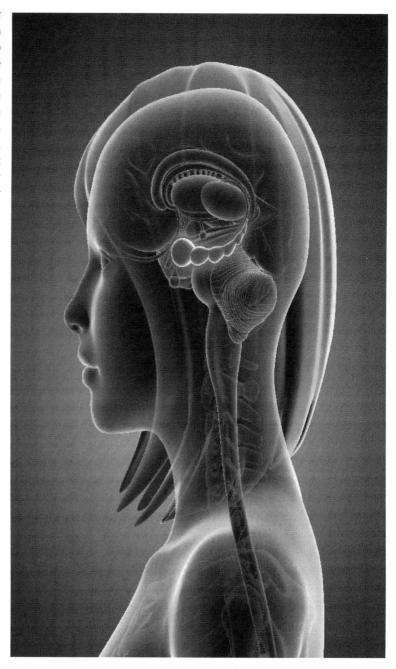

Yet this young woman managed to finish college using her notes as her memory. If she can do it, college students have no excuse.

The hippocampal areas of the brain are difficult to visualize. Imagine that the left side of the brain is represented by a side view of the right-hand glove of a boxer. The overly large area of the glove that protects the right thumb is roughly similar in outline to the left temporal lobe of the brain. If the hand in the glove were resting in a normal position the hippocampus would lie along the thumbprint inside of the glove. The hippocampus creates a bulge on the inner side of the temporal lobe that is about the size and length of your little finger. There is a hippocampus in both the left and right lobes of the brain.

Over two hundred patients have had to undergo surgery in which one of their two hippocampal regions has been removed. In none of these cases was there any apparent problem created by the loss of one hippocampus itself, although there were often other problems related to the removal of surrounding areas.

By 1960, a series of reports by Wilder Penfield and Brenda Milner began to indicate that some very unexpected side effects can be attributed to this area. These problems were found in only three very special cases. In these cases, unknown to the surgeon who removed one of their hippocampal areas, the one remaining hippocampal area had suffered a severe injury that left it almost useless. These patients now had no hippocampal area in the brain at all.

The patients were a 28-year-old laborer, a 41-year-old civil engineer, and a 47-year-old physician. After the patients had fully recovered from the effects of surgery, they were given I.Q. tests. No loss of intellectual ability was apparent, but the examiners found that now the patients could remember almost nothing that happened to them more than five minutes earlier. When the physician was shown drawings he had prepared only a half hour earlier, he did not remember having drawn them.

Other memory disturbances also occurred. One patient could recall nothing that had happened to him for four months before the operation. A second patient lost all recall of the previous eighteen months. Yet, for the most part, their memory of their past seemed as intact as it had ever been and they could recall instances in their life as clearly as before the operation. The single most impressive result was their inability to remember anything that happened to them after the operation.

Short-term memory or working memory was not affected by the removal of the hippocampal areas. Only the ability to store that short-term memory for recall later was missing.

You are using short-term memory, or possibly sensory memory, when, having looked up a phone number in the phone book, you remember the number only long enough to dial it. If it turned out that you dialed the wrong number you might have to go back to the phone book again. When this short-term memory goes into permanent storage, it becomes long-term memory-as you might use when asked to recall the street address where you lived ten years ago.

The evidence suggests that the hippocampus is the area that allows short-term memory to be consolidated into long-term, permanent storage.

Behind the forehead lies the massive area (25 percent) of the cerebral cortex known as the frontal lobes. To Penfield and Roberts, the frontal area appeared strangely silent. Electrical probing of this area produced no sensations, no feelings.

Electrical probing of the brain has provided insight into the functions of many parts of the cortex. If the occipital (visual) lobe at the rear of the brain is stimulated, sensations of light are reported. When the top edge of the temporal (auditory) lobe is stimulated, sounds are reported; while stimulation of the front edge of the parietal (tactile) lobe produces sensations of touch. It seemed as if electrical stimulation studies might be able to unravel the mysteries of the brain. However, electrical stimulation studies began to turn up new mysteries.

Stimulating huge areas of the frontal lobe of the cortex resulted in no observable behavior and no reports from their patients. Furthermore, a large area, known as the parietal association area, roughly in a triangle between the tactile, auditory, and visual areas of the cortex, gave little or no evidence of their function when stimulated electrically. The question of the function of these areas remained unsolved.

3. THE FRONTAL LOBES:
THE GREAT SILENT MASS

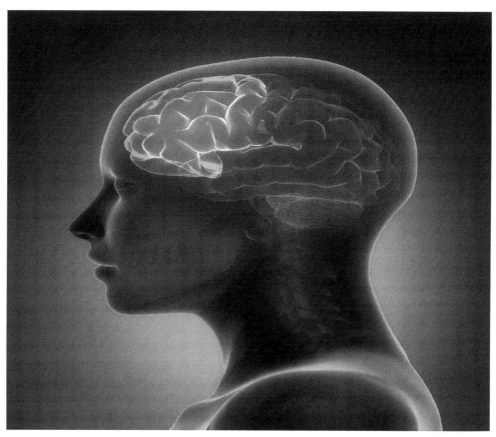

Of all the areas of the brain that differentiates humans from other animals, none is more striking than the frontal lobes. The great mass of brain tissue above our eyes makes a strikingly different profile for modem humans compared to the low forehead appearance of the apes and early Neanderthal and Homo Erectus species. In the animal kingdom, there is a general rule that the more intelligent the animal, the more likely it is to have a larger frontal "granular" area. Humans have the largest such area in proportion to the rest of the brain. We are followed by apes, monkeys, dogs, cats, rats, and so on down the line in decreasing order of the percentage of their cortex devoted to the frontal area.

The correlation between intelligence and the physical differences in the brains of humans and other animals gave rise to the often-heard cliche that people with higher foreheads are more intelligent. Evidence from studies of humans does not support this notion. Increases in the size of the frontal lobe may indicate, not intelligence, but the tendency of some animals to form social groups. Humans, monkeys, and dogs, for example, have proportionately larger frontal lobes than animals that do not form social groups. Or possibly both. The need to function in a group, and even to recognize other members of that group, may require an increase in some form of brain function.

In humans, and probably other primates, there is an area at the base of the temporal lobe that is specialized in facial recognition, essential to a social group. Damage to this area results in the loss of ability to recognize even people we have known for life.

But probing the frontal lobe produces no feeling, no movement, how can we investigate the function of these silent areas? Occasional unfortunate accidents do provide us with insight into what the function of the frontal lobes are in humans.

4. FRONTAL LOBE FUNCTION:
THE PHINEAS GAGE SYNDROME

The first case in medical history involving damage to the frontal lobes has become famous as the "American crowbar case." In 1868, a 25-year-old foreman named Phineas Gage was employed as a foreman of an excavating crew. As Gage was tamping down a dynamite charge with a steel bar, the charge went off prematurely. The steel bar, some three and a half feet long and over an inch in diameter, was blown out of the hole, passed under Gage's left cheekbone and out the top of his head at a point between his eyes and several inches up from the bridge of his nose. Gage was temporarily knocked unconscious, but Gage was up and speaking in a few minutes.

His men carried him to the road, helped him into an oxcart, and supported him in a sitting posture while he rode three-quarters of a mile back to his hotel. He was able to get out of the cart by himself, and the doctor who examined him reported that he seemed quite alert. Indeed, the doctor remarked with astonishment that the only problem he seemed to be having was exhaustion due to the hemorrhage from his bleeding. Otherwise, he seemed "perfectly conscious."

In a follow-up study, Doctor J. Harlow (1868) reported that Gage seemed to have recovered his physical health. Gage had no pain in his head but described a "queer feeling," which seemed difficult to pinpoint.

Before his injury, Gage was reportedly in very good health, well-liked by his men, and a very shrewd businessman, who was energetic and persistent in executing his plans. His employers regarded him as their most capable foreman. After his accident, however, marked changes in his personality began to occur. Dr. Harlow (1868, 339-40) now described him as:

> *"Fitful, irreverent, indulging at times in the grossest profanity (which was not previously his custom), manifesting but little deference for his fellows, impatient of restraint or advice when it conflicts with his desires, at times pertinaciously obstinate, yet capricious and vacillating, devising many plans for future operations, which are no sooner arranged than they are abandoned in turn for others appearing more feasible"*

The destruction of the frontal lobes seemed to leave Gage unable to control or inhibit his behavior. He became profane and reckless and seemed to disregard the social consequences of his behavior. He could make plans, but he

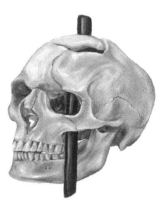

could not carry them out effectively. Could it be that the frontal lobes are involved in the conditioned control over behavior? Could this be the center of the social control for the excitation and inhibition of behavior? Or could it somehow, too, be connected with the "will" or volition that allows us to carry out the plans we make?

Left: a drawing showing the path of the crowbar that passed completely through his head. He lived for many years.

The answers to such questions do not come easily. In Gage's case, other areas of the brain related to emotion may also have been damaged. It is difficult to know precisely what produced Gage's difficulty in behavior. Scientists who study such cases of brain ablation are put into a situation a little like the scientist in the now proverbial story of a scientist who was attempting to investigate the function of a grasshopper's legs.

As the story goes, he took his tweezers, pulled off the grasshopper's two front legs, put him down on the table, and yelled "Jump." The grasshopper jumped, and the scientist dutifully recorded his observation in his notebook. He then pulled off the grasshopper's second two legs and yelled, "Jump." The grasshopper again jumped, and the scientist recorded his observation of the grasshopper's behavior. He then pulled off the last of the grasshopper's legs, placed the grasshopper on the table, and again yelled "Jump." The grasshopper did not jump. The scientist recorded in his notebook: "When all the legs of the grasshopper have been removed, the grasshopper becomes deaf."

When dealing with studies of brain damage, or neuropsychology, this is not as farfetched as it seems.

Two clients I worked with showed very similar behavior to that described by Harlow. Both showed great difficulty in controlling their temper and often got into trouble for such behavior. Both showed little regard for other people's feelings, would at times hit a weaker person and claim they deserved it, or even that the person they hit had provoked it, although that was not what others reported. They could say "I'm sorry" when they thought they were going to get into trouble, but moments later repeat the same actions. Both had records of EEGs showing abnormal electrical activity in the frontal lobes.

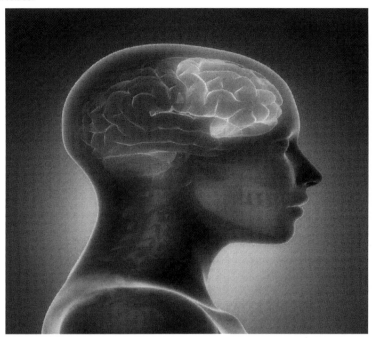

The Gage case is of interest more for what did not happen after his injury than for the changes in his personality. There was no apparent loss of consciousness. His memory remained intact. He seemed to be capable of thinking and carrying on a conversation. At the time, there were no apparent changes in his intellectual ability, or at least they were not obvious in the crude observations of his era. So, we seem almost back where we started, with the mystery of a great silent mass.

Since Phineas Gage had his unfortunate accident, hundreds of studies of damage to the prefrontal and frontal lobes have been made. With the publication of *The Frontal Lobes* in 1948, the results of a symposium of all the big guns in the field of neurosurgery, a first step was made in a scientific analysis of the functions of the frontal lobes.

Reports of striking personality changes were common, for a prefrontal lobotomy (surgical separation of the frontal lobe from the rest of the brain), and many were quite different from those described for Gage, or patients whose frontal lobes were intact even though damaged. Patients who were once active and reliable became passive, compliant, and seemingly frivolous in their behavior.

5. PRE-FRONTAL LOBOTOMY

Yet studies others have done of patients who have had surgery to separate the frontal lobes from the rest of the brain, a pre-frontal lobotomy, showed quite different results; these patients became passive. These studies were done seventy years ago when pre-frontal lobotomies were done to reduce the patient's schizophrenia or aggressive behavior. Today, they would be considered barbaric and unnecessary as Major Tranquilizers, now known as Antipsychotic medication, is as effective, less permanent, and less barbaric.

We know so little about the functioning of the brain that we cannot be sure that in interfering with one area that we have not interfered with an important secondary area. For example, if an accident to the jaw were to destroy the nerve cells leading to the vocal cords, the victim could not speak and might appear unintelligent. Could we then conclude that the vocal cords are the center of intelligence? Probably not. We have similar problems in interpreting the effect of damage to areas of the brain. Damage to one area of the brain might only show that someone has cut the telephone cable leading into one particular city and not that damage in this area would control the entire communication network.

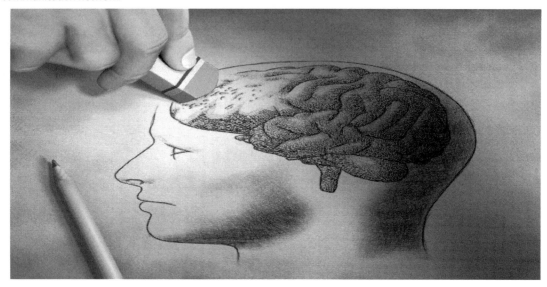

Robert Malmo describes one patient's plight in detail. After surgical removal of her frontal lobes, her former astute budget management deteriorated. When she attempted to buy groceries at the supermarket, she often ended up buying only meat and forgetting to buy anything else. On taking her groceries home, she often left them out of the refrigerator so that they spoiled.

When her husband returned from military service overseas, he was staggered by the change in her personality. Formerly, she had taken complete responsibility for the home, the children, and the housework. Now she avoided responsibility, and her husband had to do most of the work. Formerly she had argued with him about various marital problems, but now she agreed with anything and everything he said. Malmo quotes him as saying, *"I have what most men want, a wife who agrees with me about everything, but I don't like it!"*

It is still difficult to understand how frontal lobe brain damage can lead to aggression and uncontrolled behavior in some, such as Phineas Gage, yet in a specific operation, a pre-frontal lobotomy that separates 20% of the frontal lobe from the rest of the brain, it leads to passivity and lack of concentration.

Continuity, Planning, and Follow-Through

For Malmo's patient, what seemed to lack was more "will" or motivation than ability. Emergencies that came up seemed to jolt the patient into her formerly responsible self. At one time, when it was necessary to move across the country, she was able, on her own, to sell all of her furniture, do her own packing without help, buy a railway ticket, and successfully make the move. Malmo notes that the patient seemed to have believed that unless she acted firmly and quickly, she would be kept on at the hospital for observation and perhaps cannot go to her new home with her family. However, once she became established in the new home, she again became quite passive.

This lack of motivation seems to be common in such cases. In a second case, a very capable waitress was soon fired from her job following the removal of her frontal lobes. In her description of what happened, she said that she just did not have the drive or push she once had to wait on several tables at the same time.

Employers of such patients have similar reactions. They frequently describe their employees as "stupid" and unable to follow simple instructions. Yet when intelligence tests are given before and after the removal of the frontal lobes, often very little difference in the I.Q. scores is apparent. Their memory is intact, their ability to do mathematics is unimpaired, and their reasoning powers are adequate.

One change that shows up following a lobotomy is a tendency to give increasingly concrete responses when defining words on vocabulary tests. For example, Malmo reports that one patient defined the word stanza before the operation as "poems, verse." After the operation, it was described as "a heading of something or a beginning of a sentence." The word plural, originally defined as "more than one," now was described as something with "s" on it. Even this intellectual difference is comparatively slight, however. It is certainly not what one would expect with patients who have had only 20 percent of their cerebral cortex disconnected.

So, what is the function of the frontal lobe? Is it the seat of human "will"? Is it what allows us to intentionally carry out a plan of action? Some simple, yet effective, tests by Malmo provide a clue. Malmo asked a female patient to count up to sixteen and then stop at that number. He then asked the patient to do the same to twenty-two and finally sixty-one. The patient had no difficulty in carrying out these tasks. It was a different matter, however, when a test was interrupted at any point. Malmo told the patient:

> I want you to count up to six. While you are counting, I shall ask you to stop and do something else for me. After I have done this, I shall ask you to continue counting up to six.

> Examiner: "Now count up to six."

> Patient: "One-two-three-four."

> Examiner: "Stop. What letter comes after B?"

> Patient: "C."

> Examiner: "All right. Now finish counting."

> Patient: "What am I supposed to do? D-E-F-G."

> Examiner: "That's enough now."

Malmo considered it remarkable that the patient's most conspicuous failure occurred on what appeared to be the easiest of all the tests given her. He concluded that the patient was easily distracted and showed an inability to maintain a set toward the goal in the face of distraction.

In short, it seemed as if the patient could not ignore irrelevant stimuli and concentrate on relevant stimuli. This distractibility may have been the major factor in the inability of such patients to carry out their plans or intentions. They were often fired for seeming to be unable to carry out simple instructions. But was their problem a lack of motivation, or lack of "will"? Or was it more likely that it was their ease of distractibility, or their inability to maintain a set toward a goal?

Other problems also arise. The surgical removal of the frontal lobes may have interfered with areas related to the limbic system, which underlies the frontal lobe. This system is related to emotional behavior and might well influence the motivation and the emotionality that made up the apparent personality changes.

Furthermore, the frontal lobes might serve as an association area between the motor cortex and underlying areas of the brain, such as the hippocampus, which is involved in memory. In the present state of our knowledge, we can only speculate about how much of the changes in behavior and cognition result from the function of the frontal lobe per se and how much of the changes result from damage to the underlying structure.

New speculation was added by the world-famous Soviet neurologist Alexander Luria, at the Burdenko Institute in Moscow. Luria had patients with frontal lobe damage place their heads in position in a device that would allow an accurate recording of their eye movements. They were then allowed to look at a picture of several people inside a house. Cameras automatically recorded the eye movements of the subjects, how long they spent looking at any given point of the picture, and exactly at what part of the picture they were looking.

Luria found marked differences between normal individuals and those who suffered damaged frontal lobes. Normal individuals spent most of the time looking at the faces of the people in the picture. Patients with damaged frontal lobes moved their eyes aimlessly across the figures.

When asked how old the people in the picture were, the normal subjects looked first at the faces of the people and then at their clothing. The patients, on the other hand, moved their eyes rapidly back and forth across the picture in a sort of scanning motion, but with no concentration on faces or clothes. When asked to memorize the clothing the people in the picture were wearing, normal subjects showed a very definite eye movement up and down the figures in the picture, while the patients again moved their eyes aimlessly back and forth across the screen. When asked to judge the wealth and status of the people in the picture, a normal person would look at the condition of the house and its furnishings. Again, the patients displayed aimless, undirected visual activity.

Luria speculates that the frontal lobes are related to a sort of feedback mechanism by which the brain continually alters motor behavior, in this case, the scanning motion of the eyes, in response to stimuli-the pictures shown to the subjects. Without such feedback, the brain is incapable of directing "voluntary" behavior.

At present, the function of the frontal lobes is still at least partly a mystery. We know more about what this area does not do than about what it does. The frontal lobes appear to be only indirectly related to emotion and intelligence. There is some evidence to show that they may be involved in "willful" motor behavior, concentrated attention, and perhaps in the feedback between motor and sensory areas.

There is still another possibility, however. Humans, of all the animals, have the largest frontal areas in the brain. One of the marked differences between humans and other animals is our ability to plan for the future and carry out those plans. Individuals with damaged frontal lobes may be capable of planning for the future, but they seem to lack the ability to carry through on those plans. Like many of the lower animals, they live in the present, in the here and now, without the ability to carry through on behavior that requires sustained, concentrated attention. Although this characteristic may be a simple result of damage to a feedback mechanism, the possibility remains that it is related to one or more functions of the frontal lobes.

Certain other mental abilities are essential for our uniquely human behavior. For example, try multiplying two 2-digit numbers in your head, without pencil and paper. For example, multiply 12 X 18 in your head---Notice what you have to do to come up with a solution.

Did you find it necessary to stop and mentally picture the two numbers in your mind? Did you then find it necessary to mentally reproduce the problem in your mind, almost like chalking it on a blackboard? Can you imagine how difficult it would be to solve problems if we were unable to hold such images in our minds while working out possible solutions to them?

6. ASSOCIATION AREAS OF THE BRAIN

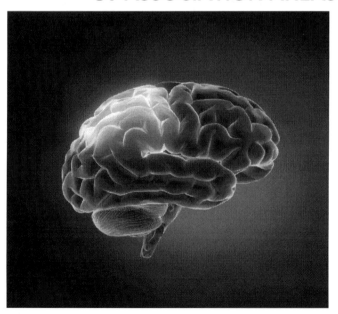

Although once thought of as a "silent" area of the brain, we know these areas are critical areas that allow for associations being made between vision, hearing, and touch. The greater the number of associations, the better the learning. Our schools reflect this in teaching the alphabet, A is for Apple (*hear* the word Apple, *see* the Apple, even *touch* the Apple and the letter A as well. These associations make learning easier for children. But it is also true of adults. Perhaps too often we make the mistake of thinking that adults learn differently from children.

There are similar association areas in the temporal and frontal lobes

7. THE CEREBELLUM: The Little Brain

The Cerebellum, or little brain, lies at and just below the back of the brain. This area is even more heavily convoluted than the rest of the brain. It is critical for fine motor movements of the type found in riding a bicycle or picking up a pencil off of the desk. Athletes and babies rely on this area of the brain because the repeated practice of basic motor movements are recorded in this area.

Damage to this area of the brain can produce symptoms of cerebral palsy, involving shaking or muscle tremors, when attempting to engage in motor activities such as speech, writing, playing a guitar, or motor activities. Movements may be jerky instead of smooth.

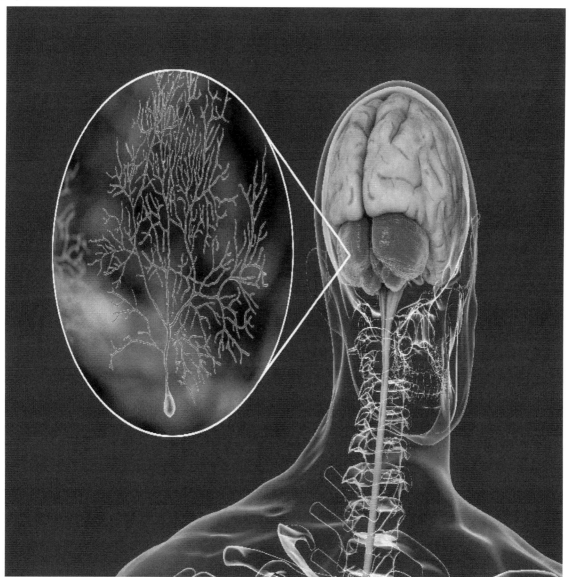

Above the unique Purkinje neurons that control our learned automatic motor movements in walking, writing, or athletics. Also found in heart tissue.

The kind of question you might get on an exam over such parts of the brain might be; *"Ron was involved in a motorcycle accident that damaged his brain. Today he can no longer play his guitar or ride a bike. What area of the brain is more likely to be damaged?"*

A. Broca's area, B. Thalamus, C. Cerebellum, or D. Sensory Cortex?

8. INSIDE THE BRAIN:
FROM THE SPINAL CORD UP

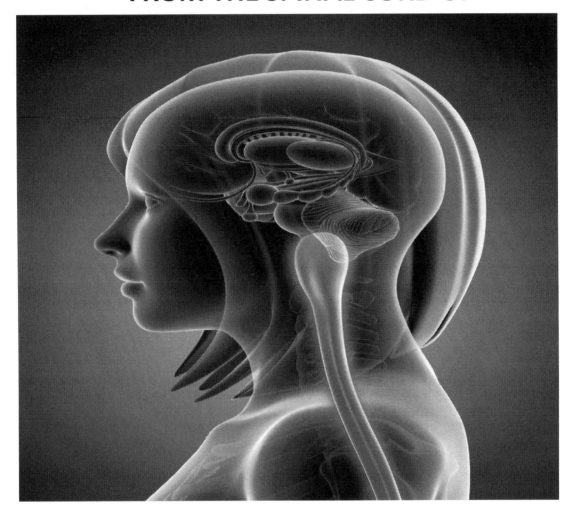

The spinal cord carries all the messages from our proprioceptive feedback, sensors in the muscles, and our senses of touch, up to the sensory centers in the cortex. It also carries all of our intentional motor movement down from the motor cortex on the surface of the brain, through the thalamus and cerebellum, to all the muscle groups of the body.

If the cord is cut, we lose the ability to feel or move, although we may be quite conscious.

The Medulla is the next part of the brain at the top of the spinal cord. This is an automatic center for control of the heart, breathing, and essential life functions. As long as this area is intact, the body may still function. Breathing and heart rate can continue, even if the rest of the brain is dead.

The incoming sensory nerves and the outgoing motor nerves enter the Thalamus, a major central relay station for all the nerve impulses going to and from the cortex. It probably had far more important functions than we realize, but because so much traffic goes through it, it is difficult to determine if it does neural processing as well.

THE PONS of the Medulla is a bulbous mass consisting of the cell bodies of neurons that send and receive electrical impulses from throughout the body, via the thin axons coming out of the cell bodies.

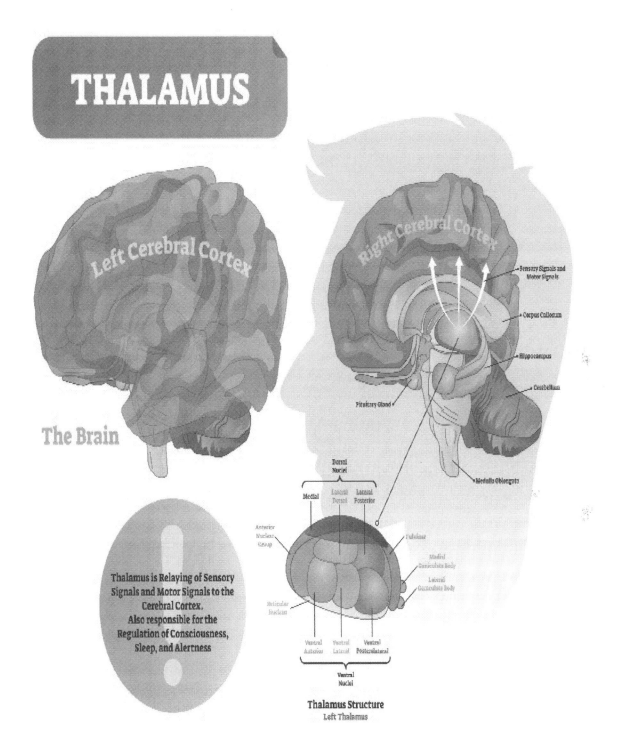

THALAMUS

Thalamus is Relaying of Sensory Signals and Motor Signals to the Cerebral Cortex.
Also responsible for the Regulation of Consciousness, Sleep, and Alertness

Thalamus Structure
Left Thalamus

9. THALAMUS

The Thalamus consists of two egg-shaped bodies, one each on the left and right sides of the brain. Inside, are Thalamic nuclei that have separate functions, but their exact functions are not always clear.

10.   HYPOTHALAMUS AND HOMEOSTASIS

Coming out of the Thalamus is it's smaller brother, the *Hypothalamus*, a major center of control for many bodily functions; Temperature regulation, blood pressure control, hunger, and sugar intake, thirst, pleasure, and sex, and it regulates the Pituitary gland's release of hormones related to reproduction, ovulation, the menstrual cycle and more. It does this massive job by sensing hormones, temperature, pressure, and chemicals in the blood. This forms a feedback loop that tells the Pituitary gland to release hormones as needed or to damp down functions as needed.

The hypothalamus contains multiple nuclei, clusters of cell bodies, that perform much of its complicated functions. One major question that arises from all these studies is, how does the brain "know" when to make changes in eating or drinking, blood pressure or body temperature, or any of the many automatic functions that must be carried out many times each day?

Mechanisms that control hunger seem to operate as a homeostatic control over behavior. *Homeostasis* refers to a balance, the body's ability to maintain an equilibrium between two extremes. A familiar example of this mechanism is the thermostat, which controls room temperatures, maintaining a balance between heat and cold. The first thermostats consisted of a coil of metal with one loose end projecting between two contact points. As the room heats, the metal expands. When it expands enough, it contacts the point above the metal end and activates the air conditioning. As the room cools, the metal contracts, breaks contact with the air conditioning unit, and eventually contracts enough to make contact with the point that turns on the heating unit.

By oscillating between the two extremes, the thermostat keeps the room at a balanced temperature. The mechanism is a purely automatic consequence of the physical properties of metal. Neither the supernatural nor intelligence is involved.   In the brain, that type of homeostatic mechanism is controlled electronically.

Two forms of homeostatic mechanisms seem to operate in the brain. First, we have seen how electrical stimulation of on/off centers in the *hypothalamus* activates body mechanisms for heating and cooling to maintain a constant body temperature, for hunger and satiation to regulate appetite, and other body mechanisms as well. Operation of hypothalamic centers involves electrical firings of both *on* and *off* controls.

Second, glands such as the *pituitary gland,* which also has electrical on/off controls over its activity, secrete chemical substances that travel through the bloodstream, causing other glands in the body to release hormones. The hormones return through the bloodstream to the pituitary, causing it to inhibit or increase hormone production as needed.

As body hormone levels rise and fall, the pituitary gland increases or decreases its level of stimulation, and consequently maintains a homeostatic balance among the secretions of the other glands of the body.

The hypothalamus appears to contain remarkably sensitive on/off control centers for regulating body temperature. If a small amount of liquid that is warmer than body temperature is injected into the blood supply leading to the hypothalamus, all the effects of the body's cooling mechanisms will appear automatically. The individual will sweat, or pant; there will be an increased blood flow to the skin to diffuse the excess heat.

HYPOTHALAMUS

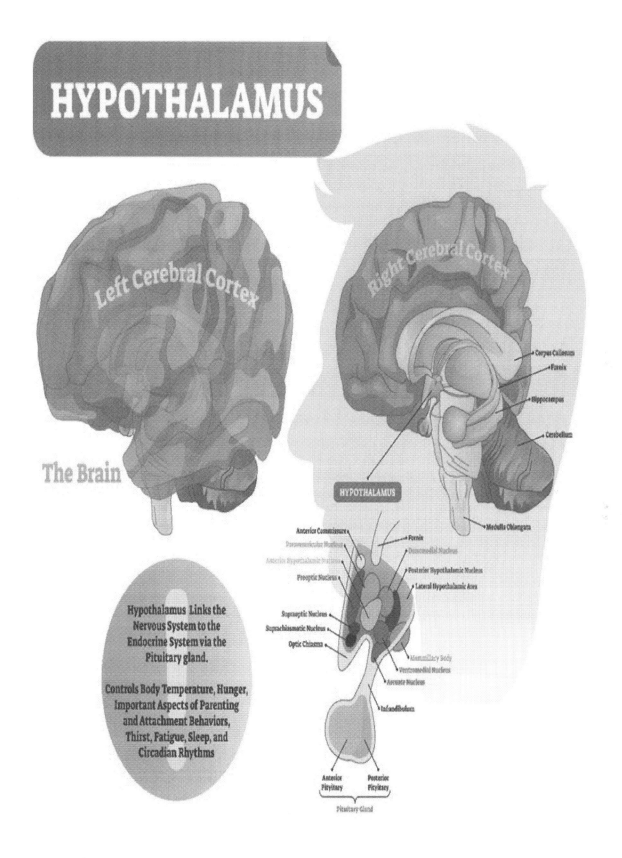

The Brain

Left Cerebral Cortex

Right Cerebral Cortex

HYPOTHALAMUS

Corpus Callosum
Fornix
Hippocampus
Cerebellum
Medulla Oblongata

Hypothalamus Links the Nervous System to the Endocrine System via the Pituitary gland.

Controls Body Temperature, Hunger, Important Aspects of Parenting and Attachment Behaviors, Thirst, Fatigue, Sleep, and Circadian Rhythms

Anterior Commissure
Paraventricular Nucleus
Anterior Hypothalamic Nucleus
Preoptic Nucleus
Supraoptic Nucleus
Suprachiasmatic Nucleus
Optic Chiasma

Fornix
Dorsomedial Nucleus
Posterior Hypothalamic Nucleus
Lateral Hypothalamic Area
Mammillary Body
Ventromedial Nucleus
Arcuate Nucleus
Infundibulum

Anterior Pituitary
Posterior Pituitary

Pituitary Gland

11. THE PITUITARY GLAND

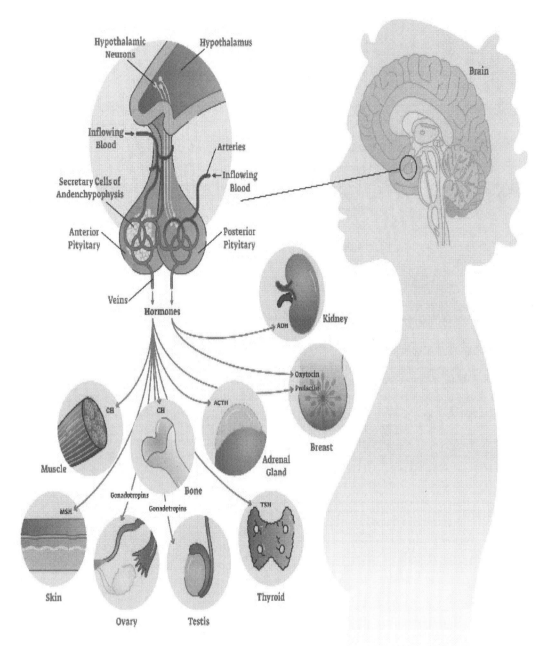

HORMONAL CONTROLS

The Pituitary Gland sits on a stalk that comes directly out of its control center, the Hypothalamus. Sensors in the Hypothalamus tell the Pituitary to start or stop releasing a variety of hormones into the bloodstream.

One of the interesting facts about the Pituitary gland is that this same configuration, the Pituitary gland sitting at the end of a stalk, leading from the Hypothalamus to the bulbous mass, the Pituitary itself, is identical in most animals, even birds, in its shape. This shows the close association of all animal species. An apparatus that formed perhaps a billion years ago, is still essential today.

12.   THE AMYGDALA:

The Fight or Flight Response

The Amygdala is an almond-shaped structure sitting next to the end of the Hippocampus, one of each on each side of the brain. It is a major center of emotion along with the Limbic System. The fact that it is next to the part of the brain that consolidates short-term memory into long-term memory may be significant.

Fear or anger releases cortisol into the blood and makes for a stronger memory. This is a problem in cases of Post Traumatic Stress Disorder, and Child and Spousal abuse, as this can create a memory that can interfere with the individual's ability to function. Frontal view below.

THE FIGHT OR FLIGHT RESPONSE: In one series of studies, there is a video of how an electrical impulse can change curiosity into fear in a cat. The cat has an electrode implanted in the fear center of the Amygdala. When a mouse is put into the cage with the cat, the cat immediately starts toward the mouse. When the experimenter stimulates the fear center with a mild electric current, the cat suddenly jumps back. The mouse panics and starts running around the cage.

The cat starts running away from the mouse, trying to avoid it at all costs.

https://www.youtube.com/watch?v=FoJGYegL9rc

https://www.youtube.com/watch?v=IyLGLxfPRCs

In a separate series of studies, an electrode is inserted into the anger or rage center of the Amygdala in a lower-ranking monkey in a monkey cage. When the rage center is triggered, the lower-ranking monkey attacked the Alpha monkey, driving him off of his perch and chasing him around the cage. When the electrical current is turned off, both monkeys are left looking around, as if unsure of what happened.

When the "rage" center of the Amygdala is triggered through an electrode in a cat, the cat will display all the features associated with a major struggle for life; the Fight or Flight syndrome. It will hiss, arch its back, put out its claws, and, like the spectators at Salem, its hair will stand on end, making it appear larger to its adversary. The latter has no advantage in humans however, as we have little hair, we just experience it as a chill going up our back.

In Chapter 8 on The Mind Code, we will see how psychology has found ways to trigger the same kinds of responses (fear or aggression or pleasure) by simple Stimulus-Stimulus associations without the need for wires, electrodes, or surgery. Watson demonstrated, in a famous study with little Albert, how simply pairing a loud noise, that trigger a fear reaction, with a furry animal, resulted in little Albert having a fear reaction to any furry animal, even a ball of cotton.

The Amygdala does not act alone. It is mediated by the Hypothalamus. The Frontal Lobes, as in Phineas Gage's syndrome, provide learned social controls over aggression and fear. See Chapter 8 and 9 for details of learned controls over our emotions. Much like the story of the grasshopper, it is more complex than we may think.

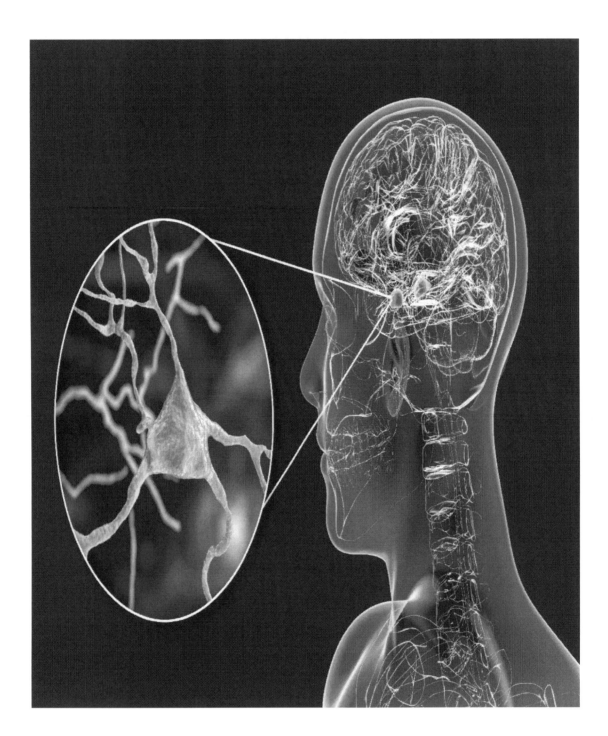

Above, the amygdala, one on each side of the brain, is an area specifically associated with the emotions of fear and aggression; the very basis of the *Fight or Flight* mechanism of the brain. It is next to the Hippocampus, the area of the brain that consolidates short-term memory into long-term memory. The more emotionally charged an experience is, the more likely it is to be embedded in our long-term memory. This can benefit us by ensuring that learning takes place, but it can also be a significant problem as in Anxiety Disorders or Post-Traumatic Stress Disorder (PTSD).

While electrical stimulation of the amygdala is impressive, psychologists have discovered how to elicit the same emotions without wires, without electrodes, just by emotional conditioning. So have politicians. More in Chapter 8 on learning and chapter 20 on war and Social Psychology.

13. THE VENTRICLES:
The Empty Spaces in your Brain

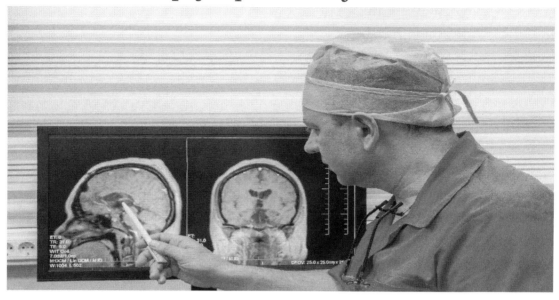

The surgeon points to the center of the brain. In the picture to the right and below you can see a black butterfly-shaped area in the direct center of the picture. This is not a structure; these are empty spaces known as the ventricles.

The ventricles, the black butterfly-shaped area in the center, are filled with cerebrospinal fluid.

Their function is to provide cerebral-spinal fluid to bathe the brain and spinal cord and possibly act as a shock absorber.

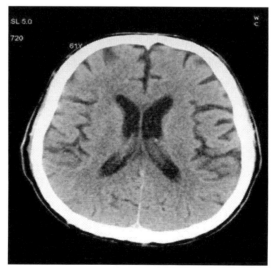

One of the unique features of the ventricles is that they tend to enlarge when damage inside the brain occurs. Next, you can see the "normal" butterfly-shaped ventricles on the left and that of Huntington's Chorea on the right.

This enlargement of the ventricles takes place when cells in the brain die and the fluid inside the ventricles expand to fill in the empty space. We see this in medical disorders such as Huntington's disease and sometimes schizophrenia.

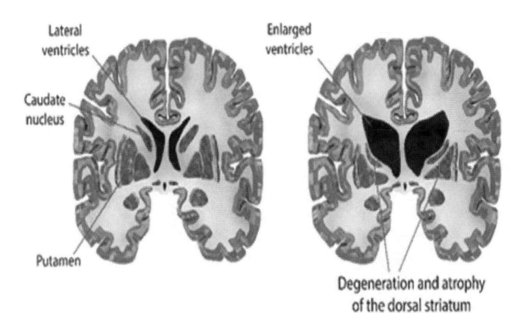

Healthy brain

Lateral ventricles

Caudate nucleus

Putamen

Huntington's disease

Enlarged ventricles

Degeneration and atrophy of the dorsal striatum

Psychiatrist E. Fuller Torrey found the same thing in patients suffering from schizophrenia. In his studies of identical twins, where one had Schizophrenia and their identical twin did not, he found these enlarged ventricles tended to be present in the twin with Schizophrenia.

However, this is not of diagnostic value. Normal people differ in their ventricle size. The difference is most clear in comparing identical twins. As we get older, our brain shrinks, and our ventricles enlarge, yet we are not more likely to become schizophrenic with age.

The significance of these findings is that it shows that schizophrenia is an actual brain disease. Even this is not always certain, as there is still disagreement whether all the problems we label "Schizophrenia" are different disorders that should not be characterized under the same category as schizophrenia.

The most common symptoms of schizophrenia are hallucinations or delusions, or disorganized thinking, or all of the above.

In addition, there is Paranoid Personality Disorder, which has some of the same symptoms as Paranoid Schizophrenia, but it is not Schizophrenia. We also have Schizoaffective Disorder, which is a mood disorder but has some of the same symptoms as schizophrenia. And more, there is Schizophreniform Disorder which is the short-duration version of Schizophrenia, that only gets diagnosed if you get over your diagnosis of Schizophrenia within one to six months. And chronic Undifferentiated Schizophrenia which sort of seems like long term Schizophrenia, but we cannot get a good symptom pattern. Are these all the same?

Torrey found that if one identical twin has schizophrenia, their genetically identical twin has a 50 to 60 percent chance of also having schizophrenia. If it were totally genetic, we might expect a 100% chance. We still do not know what differs the ventricles in one from the other 40 to 50 percent.

If one child in a family has schizophrenia, there is a 10 to 12 percent chance that one of the other children in the family will have schizophrenia. That means, on the average, about one of every 10 children such couples have could have schizophrenia. Genetic transmission is far less than the general public believes.

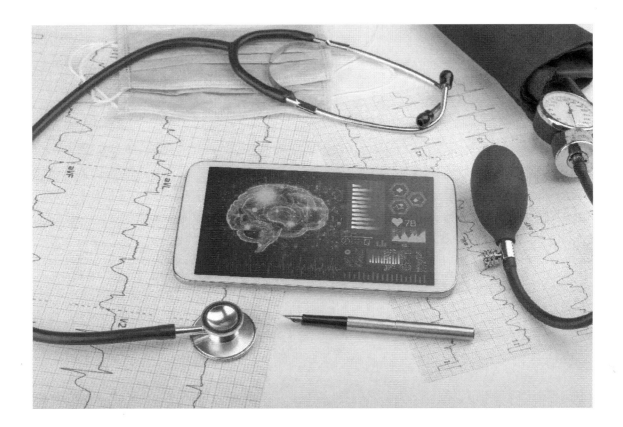

14. DIAGNOSES?

Even in medicine, diagnoses are not as easy as the public may suppose. We have great diagnostic tests for something such as Diabetes. Yet other disorders are almost impossible to diagnose. When the dreaded Ebola virus hit America for the first time, the first case showed up at a hospital in Dallas, Texas. He was diagnosed as having a bad case of the flu and sent home. Two days later, he died of Ebola. Doctors were not even thinking about Ebola as a possibility. The same thing happened in Florida with the first cases of Anthrax spores that were sent through the mail. It was immediately diagnosed as the flu. He died days later of Anthrax.

The first cases of Covid-19 were dismissed as just a case of the flu. The Delta mutation of Covid-19 mimics the common cold early in the symptom pattern. Upper respiratory diseases have a similar pattern in their early stages. Colds or 100 different varieties of the cold virus, the Flu, and dozens of varieties of the flu, Hantavirus, Anthrax, multiple varieties of pneumonia, and even allergies and asthma have all had similar symptom patterns, especially in the early stages.

Psychiatrist Daniel Amen speaks of his brain scans of 83,000 patients, including 500 criminals, 90 of whom were murders. He says that undiagnosed brain damage is a major player in anger problems. This may be seen in the lack of control over anger in Phineas Gage with Frontal lobe brain damage.

Amen also shows images of two depressed patients. One has extensive activity throughout the brain. But the second showed only normal activity in the brain. Both have similar symptoms of depression. We still have no ability to use brain scans to diagnose depression. Other problems may present similar symptoms, but there is an interesting suggestion from depressed patients that there may be more than one form of depression, even when the symptoms are identical.

We were fortunate to have found tests that can detect the coronavirus Covid 19, yet to this day we do not have a single reliable diagnostic test that can test for any psychiatric disorder; not Schizophrenia, Depression, or Anxiety disorder; nothing. Psychological diagnoses all rely on a symptom pattern to get a label. Not exactly an ideal technique, but something we need to be honest about. We must not get enthralled by our own word magic.

15. COGNITIVE NEUROSCIENCE OR NEUROPSYCHOLOGY

The relatively new area of neuropsychology has provided us with the shock and awe of beautiful multicolored pictures (artificially colored) to show the inner firing of groups of nerve cells. Using fMRI and PET scans provides a dramatic view of the interaction of parts of the brain we could never otherwise have known.

• It is now being used to map the human brain.

• These studies have shown, for one example, that there are nerve tracts going from the temporal cortex and Wernicke's area to the Motor cortex and Broca's area. These areas "light up" (the neurons absorb more oxygen or use more energy) when we engage in verbal processing.

• Professor Nancy Kanwisher of MIT has a remarkable series of lectures describing how this has been used to tease out how we know there are many specialized areas of the brain. These are a series well worth watching if you are fascinated with the function of the brain itself. Not since the initial discoveries of Broca and Wernicke and Penfield's mapping, have we had such a complete view of how the brain works. Professor Kanwisher has used her own brain to show how the brain functions.

She has found that the brain seems to have many highly specialized areas that involve facial recognition, music, thought, and more.

https://www.youtube.com/watch?v=5Yj3nGv0kn8

https://www.youtube.com/watch?v=ZueXhzQS1k4

•   One perhaps surprising discovery at MIT involves the relationship between language and thought. Different parts of the brain "light up" when we are *thinking,* then when we are *speaking*.

•   It would be very interesting to see if the same or different parts of the brain light up when we are *thinking* compared to when we are **perceiving.** See Chapter 9 on Perception.

•   Her associate, Rebecca Saxe, found that there are specific parts of the brain that "light up" when we *think about what other people are thinking about us*. Wow!

https://www.youtube.com/watch?v=IAiB6kmnxeM

16. WHAT NEUROPSYCHOLOGY CANNOT TELL US

No matter how complete our map of the human brain becomes, it will never tell us about the origin of our knowledge, beliefs, or the emotions associated with words. It cannot explain the behavior of a Kamikaze pilot or a suicide bomber, it cannot tell us why we speak English or Swahili, or where our prejudices or interests come from.

Even if we know everything about Broca's area and Wernicke's are, and what genes control their function, that still tells us nothing about the languages we speak or how words can lead to love or war. The emotions associated with words come from our experiences in our environment.

•   Cognitive neuropsychology has taken over what is researched in the major institutions of this country. If you look at the areas of psychology of professors at MIT and Stanford, there is virtually no psychologist who has any interest other than cognitive neuropsychology. This narrow focus could set psychology back a quarter of a century.

•   Learning the entire genetic code of humans, as important as that is, tells us nothing about what genes do without going to low tech, looking at different genetic traits in different individuals and corelating those observations with the individual genes. The same is true of neuroscience, knowing everything about the brain, still tells us nothing without knowing the experiences of individuals.

•   Neuropsychology, by itself, gives us no insight into personality differences, what makes for genius, why we love or hate or feel the emotions of shame or guilt.

•   Only the low-tech methods of basic *psychology, sociology, and cultural anthropology* can provide us with an understanding of the emotions and beliefs that control our mind.

•   In every final analysis, we have to go on to the simple, *learned*, associations and perceptions that are encoded in our minds. See Chapters 8 and 9 about learning and perception for the powerful effects of experience on our mind.

Brain Anatomy
Worksheet

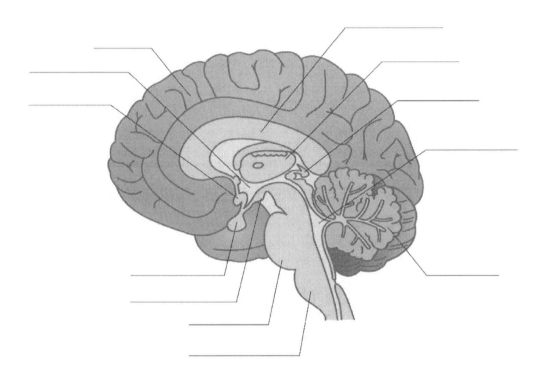

Can you describe the function of six of the areas above?

STUDY FOR AN EXAM: In the above diagram you might be expected to know the (1) names of the brain parts, (2) the function of the brain parts, and (3) *how* we know what the function is.

Spinal Cord	Thalamus	Corpus Callosum
Cerebellum	Hypothalamus	Pituitary Gland
Medulla	Ventricles	Hippocampus

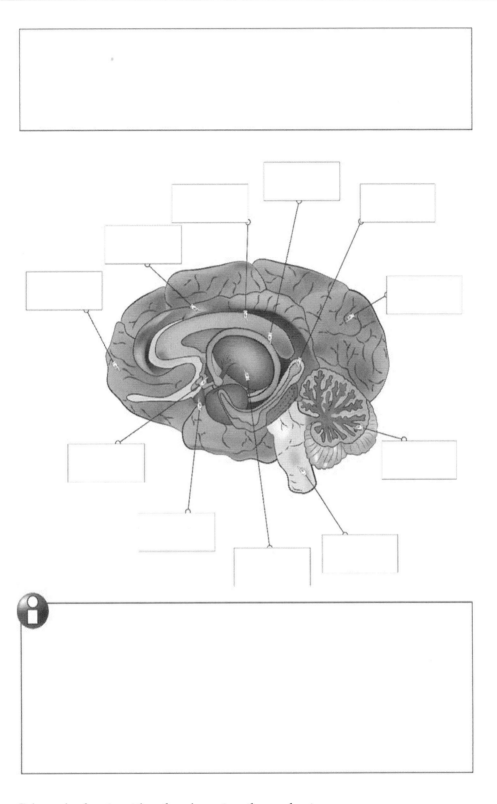

Science is about putting the pieces together as best we can.

But what is it that powers the brain? The critical issue next.

5. THE PRIME MOVER

The Neuron and The Computer

DA VINCI • DESCARTES • GALVANI • VOLTA • GOLGI • WEINER

What Is the Source of Power? • The Nerve Cells • The Wires, The Synapse: The Go/No-Go Relay. • Neural Interaction

Specialized Cells • Cybernetics: Brain and Computer

...when I feel pain in the foot, the science of physics teaches me that this sensation is experienced by means of the nerves dispersed over the foot, which, extending like cords from it to the brain, when they are contracted in the foot, contract at the same time the inmost parts of the brain in which they have their origin, and excite a certain motion appointed by nature to cause in the mind a sensation of pain, as if existing in the foot hence the mind will feel pain in the foot, just as if it (the mind) had been hurt.

Rene Descartes, 1641 *Meditations on the First Philosophy*

SEARCH FOR WHAT POWERS THE MIND

Hippocrates and Leonardo da Vinci were both consumed with trying to find the mystery of what powered the human body. They knew about "nerves" but they had no idea what a nerve was or how it could power the body and mind. What they called nerves were massive cables carrying thousands of nerve fibers to every part of the body.

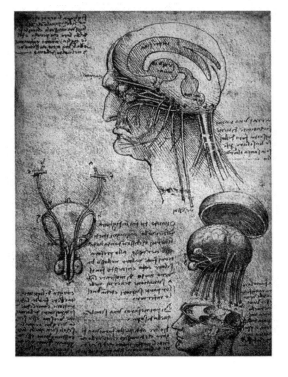

Rene Descartes knew there were nerves in the body connected to the foot in 1641, yet no one knew how nerves worked. Extensive dissections of corpses found little that would provide the answer. Hippocrates found only what he called *Humors*, flowing in tubes (Blood, Black Bile, Yellow Bile, and Phlegm) which only led to misinformation.

Da Vinci wrote carefully detailed notes and drawings of birth, death, and the brain. Yet he found nothing in the brain that would explain the difference between the great mystery of life and death. A man could be alive one minute, animated, talking, full of humor and pathos, and dead the next. What was the difference?

Da Vinci's quest to uncover the secrets of life led him to extensive drawings of dissections to illustrate his findings. Yet both Hippocrates and da Vinci failed to find the secrets to life they sought.

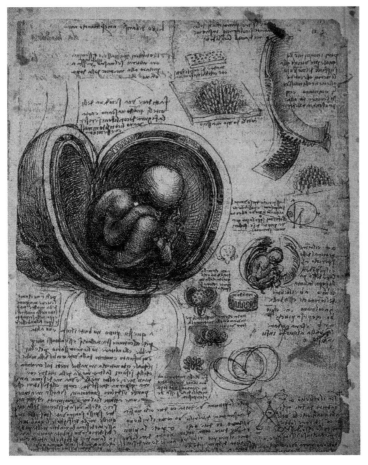

Extensive studies of the brain itself found nothing. It was a great silent blob, little more than a mass of semi-hardened jelly. When Anthony van Leeuwenhoek invented the microscope, scientists again turned their attention to the brain.

When the early explorers of inner space turned their microscopes on the human brain, they found nothing. The brain tissue apparently contained nothing as fascinating as a drop of rain. Not until the late 1800s did the brain begin to give up its secrets under the prodding of an Italian physician, Camillo Golgi.

Golgi found that treating brain tissue with silver salts would permanently stain the individual cells, thus making them visible under the microscope. The sights that Golgi saw proved as remarkable as any wonders of the heavens.

Golgi saw cells within the human brain. Some had cell bodies shaped like plump pyramids with threadlike tentacles branching off from each corner of the pyramid. Some of the cells were associated in groups for obviously specialized purposes.

At about the same time, the Spanish physiologist Santiago Ramon y Cajal drew remarkable, detailed illustrations showing that the threadlike projections of the cells made contact, by the hundreds, with other cells within the brain. For decades, a controversy raged as to whether the nerve cell's connections formed one continuous network, like a fishnet, or whether they were connected in on/off relays like a telephone switchboard circuit.

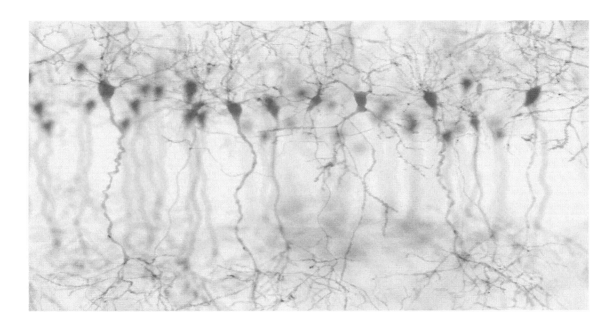

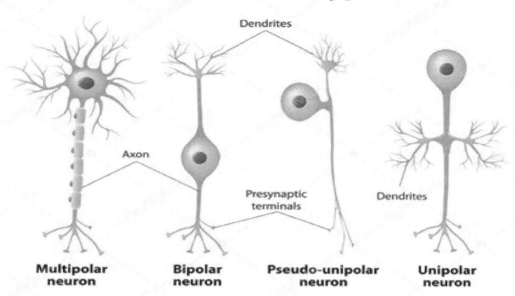

Basic Neuron Types

Dendrites

Axon

Presynaptic terminals

Dendrites

Multipolar neuron   **Bipolar neuron**   **Pseudo-unipolar neuron**   **Unipolar neuron**

1. ELECTRICITY POWERS THE BODY
Galvani's Frog

Newton's reference to "standing on the shoulders of giants" is a profound metaphor for the importance of how previous discoveries are essential in leading to new discoveries.

The discovery of what powers the body began with a seemingly irrelevant finding that biology teachers across our high schools often show in the lab, yet students may not grasp the importance of that simplistic discovery to everything we now know about how the brain works.

While doing an experiment on static electricity in the 1700s, Luigi Galvani was astonished that a nearby leg that had been cut from a dead frog suddenly jumped when touched with a steel scalpel.   How could the leg of a dead frog come suddenly to life?

Taking an invention much like Benjamin Franklin's lightning rod, he attached one end of the sciatic nerve coming out of the leg of a dead frog to a metal pole and the other end of the leg to an iron hook.   In the middle of the lightning storm, the leg jumped.   This became the idea that "*animal electricity*" controls the movement of the body via the nerves.   The sciatic nerve is a cable that contains the axons from many hundreds of nerves from the brain and spinal cord, throughout the body.

Mary Shelley began her enduring novel, Frankenstein, based on the lightning rod of Benjamin Franklin and the idea that electricity could bring a dead frog back to life.   In the story, the monster's brain was hooked up to a lightning rod on the roof, and the jolt of electricity brought the dead back to life.   It does not work, of course.   Yet Galvani's experiment led to countless products promising to, like the Heidelberg Electric Belt from Sears, restore virility, cure cancer, and revitalize almost any part of your body.   The seemingly miraculous power of electricity became one more tool of the grifters.

Today Galvani's name is associated with important scientific concepts that bear his mark. *Galvanic current,* and the instrument used to measure this current, the *galvanometer;* have been named in his honor. Galvani's contribution to our story was in revealing that the forces that power the body could be removed from the realm of speculation and placed in the realm of experimentation.

The most sensitive instrument in a "lie detector" is the GSR or Galvanic Skin Response.   The GSR measures any changes in the electrical activity across the surface of the skin.   It does not detect lies, it detects fear and the activation of the Fight or Flight response of the Autonomic Nervous System.   Of course, anyone accused of a crime could easily respond with fear, whether they are guilty or innocent.   That is why it is not allowed as evidence in a court of law; either for you or against you.

So, if it is not allowed to be presented as evidence in a court of law, then why do so many police agencies use it?   In hope of scaring a subject into confessing.   It is even legal for the police to lie to a subject to try to get him to confess; such as telling him he failed the lie detector or that his friend has already confessed and implicated him as the mastermind.   Yes, really.   It has already been vetted before the Supreme Court and judged legal.   But if you lie to a police officer, that is a crime.

2. THE MYSTERY OF HOW ELECTRIC POWER IS GENERATED

Shortly after Galvani made his discoveries, Alessandro Volta (1745-1827), an Italian physicist, demonstrated that electric current can be reliably produced by sandwiching sheets of copper and zinc between sheets of wet cardboard soaked in brine (salt water).   Volta created the prototype of today's automobile battery.   If you examine an automobile battery, the sandwiching of different types of metals in a "wet cell" battery will look remarkably similar to the technique used by Volta.   The implication of Volta's discovery for biology quickly became clear.   Electricity was not a magical or supernatural phenomenon.   It could be produced reliably and consistently with natural materials.   Could it be that the natural chemicals and materials of the body also produce an electrical current that moves the body as Galvani's electrical stimulus moved the leg of the frog?

The discoveries of Galvani and Volta had begun a new movement that, although they were not aware of it, would eventually remove the aura of the supernatural surrounding the power source of the body.

With the invention of the microscope in the early 1600s, scientists turned their attention to the wonders of an infinitely small universe that promised as great a store of excitement as that witnessed by Galileo when his telescopes opened up the heavens.   The extent of the microscopic universe was proving to be fantastic.   A single drop of pond water contained hundreds, even thousands, of living organisms-from the famous single-celled amoebas to an infinite number of grotesquely beautiful creatures that we could never have imagined in our wildest fantasies.

When the microscope was turned from pond water to living tissue, an equally great surprise was in store.   All living tissue, bone, muscle, heart, lungs, and skin were composed of millions of tiny units, which we now call *cells*.   Specialized cells secrete protein that make up our hair and fingernails.   Bone marrow cells produce bone out of calcium.   The Isles of Langerhans are special cells that secrete insulin.   Muscles are composed of cells that move on stimulation.   Each cell was remarkably similar in construction to the single-celled organisms such as the amoeba.

The radical implications of this discovery quickly became apparent.   Each cell within any tissue of a living organism was alive and functioning in its own specialized role, not unlike the unicellular organisms observed in the pond water. The difference was that the cells of the body functioned as a cohesive unit, and each depended for its existence on the adequate functioning of the whole.

3. THE POWER of the MIND:
The Neuron

The human brain consists of one thing, and one thing only -cells.   The active cells in the brain are the *neurons,* highly specialized cells of many types, which generate and conduct their own electrical impulses.   There are between 86 and 100 billion nerve cells in the brain.   Neurons vary in shape and size, and they may range from a tiny body one-thousandth of an inch in diameter to as large as one-hundredth of an inch (or roughly 10 to 100 microns).   The neurons are much like wires that generate and transmit an electrical impulse, a series of dots, to and from the brain and throughout the entire body.

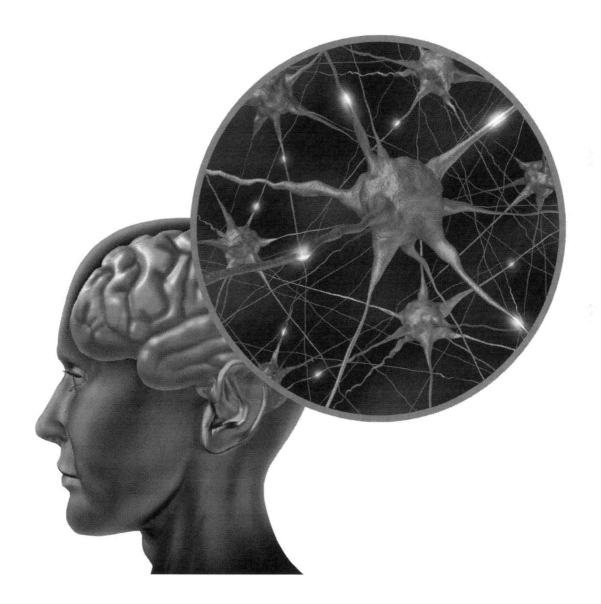

Besides about 85 billion Neurons, there are approximately twice as many Glial cells that provide physical support for the Neurons and also provide immune function, repair damage, maintain the blood-brain barrier, and more.

Most of the actual power of the brain, however, comes from the unique properties of the Neurons, that allow them to generate and conduct electrical impulses in the brain and throughout the body.

NEURON

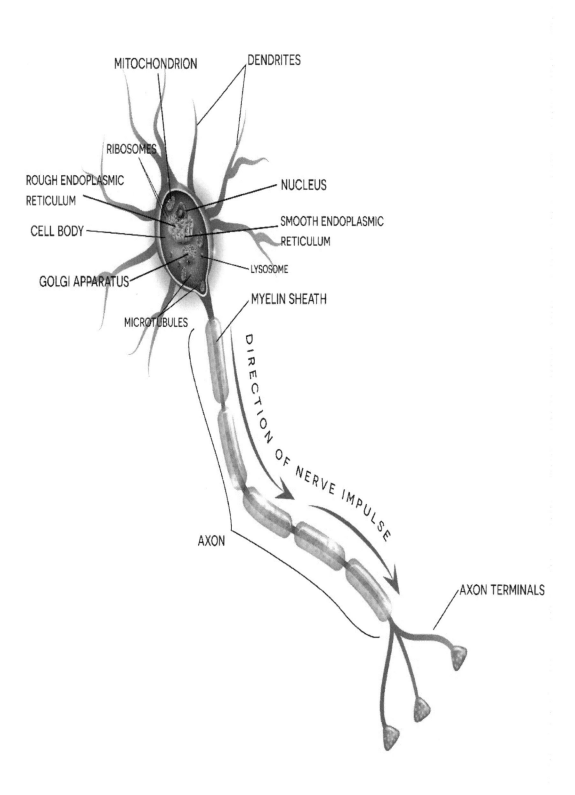

THE AXON: So long as the positive ions are kept on the outside of the· cell membrane, the axon, the "wire" of the membrane, is said to be *polarized.*

A stimulus, such as an electrical probe of the cell wall or the pinching of a nerve's axon, allows a rush of the positive ions into the membrane, and the axon depolarizes (fires) in sequence, along its entire length.

The positive ions form an electrical impulse and sweep like an ocean wave down the length of the axon. Immediately after the crest of the wave passes any point of the axon, an internal mechanism of the neuron throws out the positive ions, restoring its polarity and allowing another impulse to follow almost immediately behind the first wave.

The effect is much like that of lighting a fuse. The flame of the fuse travels along its entire length. And the point where the sodium enters the membrane is, roughly speaking, the point of the flame on the fuse. But unlike the fuse, the axon immediately regenerates itself.

Since the electrical charge of the axon is conducted by positive and negative ions, no destruction takes place as it does in the burning of a fuse. The axon's ability to immediately repolarize itself, by pushing the positive ions that entered, back outside the axon. This allows the transmission of as many as two hundred impulses per second on a single axon, although an axon rarely operates at this high a frequency. The speed of the electrical impulse itself can be measured by placing electrodes at points along a major nerve, such as the nerve in the leg.

The nerve impulse will be carried along the axon at a speed of up to two hundred miles per hour. The speed is incredibly slow when compared to the speed of electricity carried on a wire or in a computer, but it should be noted that the axon is not a wire, and that the axon spends much of its time generating the electric current by the exchange of positive and negative ions. Yet two hundred miles per hour is relatively fast when you consider that the nerve impulse rarely has to travel more than six feet in the average human.

Each axon fires according to the all-or-none law. Each electrical impulse is of approximately equal strength regardless of the strength of the stimulus that fired the neuron. Different axons may vary in the strength of their impulse, the larger the diameter of the axon, the greater the intensity of impulse it can carry. But each axon generates only one impulse strength. In effect, the nerve cell speaks to the brain only in a series of dots of electrical pulses of equal intensity. By analogy, each bullet you shoot from the barrel of a gun is identical in velocity and strength to the others, regardless of how hard you squeeze the trigger of the gun. Only by varying the number of bullets fired, does one achieve a difference in effect.

More than this, hundreds of axons from other neurons may converge on a single cell. One neuron may be connected to 1,000 other neurons in a network. Whether that cell may fire or not, its graded potential depends on how many other cells are firing excitatory or inhibitory chemicals at the same time. The input coming into a single cell creates a far more complex reaction than what a computer is capable of, yet the computer is far faster, and math is its main strength.

Spontaneous firing of nerve cells also occurs. Individual axons depolarize regularly, sometimes several times per minute. This phenomenon is observable even in axons that have been completely removed from the organism and kept alive in a solution of nutritive fluid. The effect of this spontaneous firing may be much like that of the idling of a car motor. So long as only single neurons are firing at random, their spontaneous discharge has no noticeable effect. When thousands of them operate simultaneously, however, an effect on behavior is observed. As in the car with an idling engine, where motion must await an engagement of the gears, engagement of other neural systems must occur before neural discharges will cause any overt action.

At a distance from the cell body, the axon eventually divides into many branch-like tentacles. In the motor nerve cells leading from the spinal cord to the muscles, these axon terminals connect with the fibers of the muscle tissue itself. Electrical impulses traveling along the *neuro-muscular* axon cause fibers in the muscle tissue to contract, resulting in movement.

Multipolar neuron

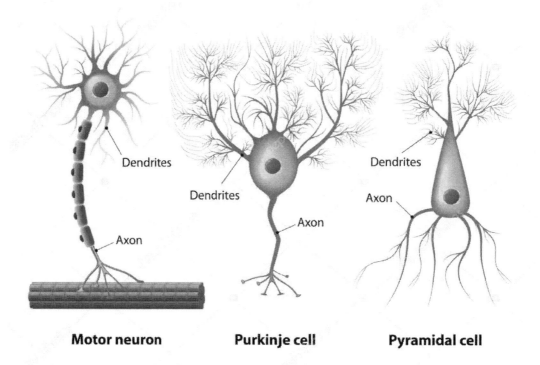

Motor neuron   **Purkinje cell**   **Pyramidal cell**

Myelinated or insulated neurons innervate the muscles. Purkinje cells are highly complex cells found in the cerebellum or little brain. This is the area of the brain responsible for skilled muscle movements as in sports, riding a bicycle, or typing. Pyramidal cells are in the cortex, the 1/2 inch or so of the gray matter surrounding the surface of the brain.

All cells maintain an electrical potential difference between the inside and outside of the cell membrane. The neuron is different from other cells only in its highly specialized means of transmitting an electrical impulse from one point to another. The axons and dendrites of the neuron are electrical wires of a sort that generate an electrical impulse and carry it along the entire length of the fiber.

If we examine an axon or dendrite fiber in cross-section, we find a thin hollow tube with an outer membrane approximately one molecule thick. If we insert a tiny microelectrode into the giant axon of the sea squid and place a second electrode against the surface of the axon, we would find an electrical difference of about minus 70 millivolts. Every cell in the body has the same electrical potential difference between the inside and outside. The neuron is a specialized cell that can act as a wire to carry an electrical charge to other neurons.

The key to the power of the neuron lies not with the axon or dendrite alone. Rather, it consists of the electrical potential difference between the inside and outside of the cell membrane. -70 millivolts is the *potential* electrical impulse. All cells have a potential difference between the inside and outside of -70 millivolts. But the neuron is a specialized cell that transmits an electrical impulse to other areas.

Careful measurements show the outside of the neuron has relatively more positive than negative ions, whereas the inside of the neuron has relatively more negative than positive ions. The resulting situation is much like that of a dry cell flashlight battery with an interior core of carbon (positive) surrounded by chemicals (negative). In effect, connecting the positive and negative poles of a flashlight battery, as when you turn on the flashlight, will cause an electric current to flow. Neurons only send a series of blips (on/off), not a continuous flow of electricity.

The hotdog-shaped insulation is the myelin sheath, composed of fatty tissue, to prevent one electrical impulse from jumping to an adjacent nerve. The nodes in between the myelin sheath allow the electrical impulse to jump from one node to the next and speed transmission.

Myelinated axons are the White Matter of the brain. The Grey Matter is composed of short, non-myelinated axons and are found in the half-inch or so of the surface of the cerebral cortex. That is what we think with. That is where we consciously perceive reality. Yet, there are also myelinated neurons in the main sensory areas of the cortex.

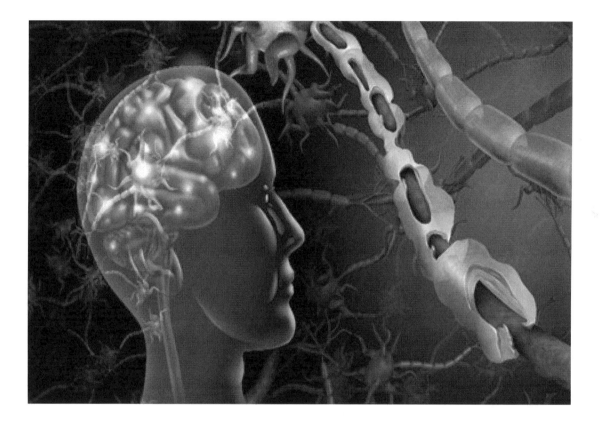

Above, the "hot dog string" of the myelin sheath is typically white, and is often called the "white matter" of the brain, as opposed to the "grey matter" or non-myelinated neurons in the cortex; the surface of the brain. The myelin sheath is composed of fatty tissue for insulation. In patients with Multiple Sclerosis, the myelin sheath surrounding the motor axons deteriorates.

If this insulation is damaged (above, left axon), the electrical impulse may not reach the muscles it is attached to. It may even short out or trigger an adjacent neuron. This slow deterioration may occur over decades, only gradually becoming worse.

4. HOW POWER IS GENERATED BY CHEMICALS

A flashlight battery has a central core of carbon, positively charged, leading to the nipple at the top of the battery. Surrounding the carbon core is a chemical matter that is negatively charged. A wire runs from the spring base of the batteries (negative) to a switch. A second wire runs from the switch to the metal around the base of the bulb. The top of the nipple,

positively charged, contacts the bottom of the bulb.   When the switch is
turned on, negative ions meet positive ions in the filament of the bulb,
and the bulb lights up.   This is the simple task that Harvard and MIT
graduates did not understand.

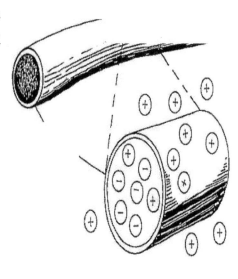

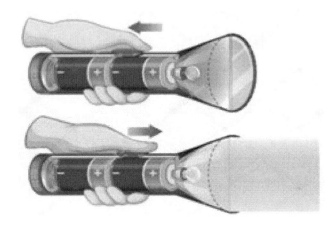

Neurons in the brain do not light up, but they do send an electrical impulse down the axon. Positive and negative ions are the key to the similarity. A Non-Myelinated Axon is above on the right. Positive ions predominate on the outside of the axon. Negative ions are on the inside. When the positive ions enter the membrane and contact the negative ions, an electrical charge is generated and carried down the axon like an electrical impulse on a wire.

The amount of electrical discharge by any single neuron is small, only a fraction of a volt (70 mv).   However, when the specialized cells fire simultaneously, the resulting electrical discharge can be tremendous.   With the famous electric eel, a mass of such specialized cells runs along most of its entire length from the head, positively charged, to the tail, negatively charged.   This is capable of a collective jolt of as much as 400 volts, more than sufficient to stun a horse.   In most animals, however, the amount of electric current given off outside of the body is not perceptible.

This current can be recorded by specialized machines such as the electroencephalograph (EEG), which can measure waves of minute electrical discharges of masses of neurons within the brain, and record them from outside the body.   It cannot, however, read your mind, it only measures gross general electrical activity. The importance of this in understanding the conscious mind is seen in Chapter 7.

THE SYNAPSE: A COMPLEX SWITCHING NETWORK

At the point where the branches of an axon contact another neuron or muscle tissue, the axon branches end in an end bulb and a *synapse*. Between the end bulb of the axon and the cell body or dendrite of the next neuron is a chasm known as the *synaptic gap*. This gap is so tiny that it can only be meaningfully measured by the use of an electron microscope.

In the 1940s, a great controversy arose whether the electrical impulse continued at this point to stimulate the next neuron, or whether the electrical impulse stopped at this point and caused the release of certain chemicals, which crossed the gap to stimulate the point on the other side. Studies demonstrated that the chemical *acetylcholine,* when administered at a neural-muscular junction, would cause a discharge of the motor nerve cells and a contraction of the muscle, just as Galvani had observed in the leg of a frog.

Extensive experimental studies later showed that neuromuscular synaptic bulbs themselves release acetylcholine, which causes a contraction of the muscle tissue. At neuromuscular synapses, receptor sites directly across from the synaptic end bulb pick up the acetylcholine and aid the depolarization of nerve and muscle tissue. Also present is an enzyme called *acetylcholinesterase,* which acts to neutralize the acetylcholine almost immediately after it has fired the muscle fiber.

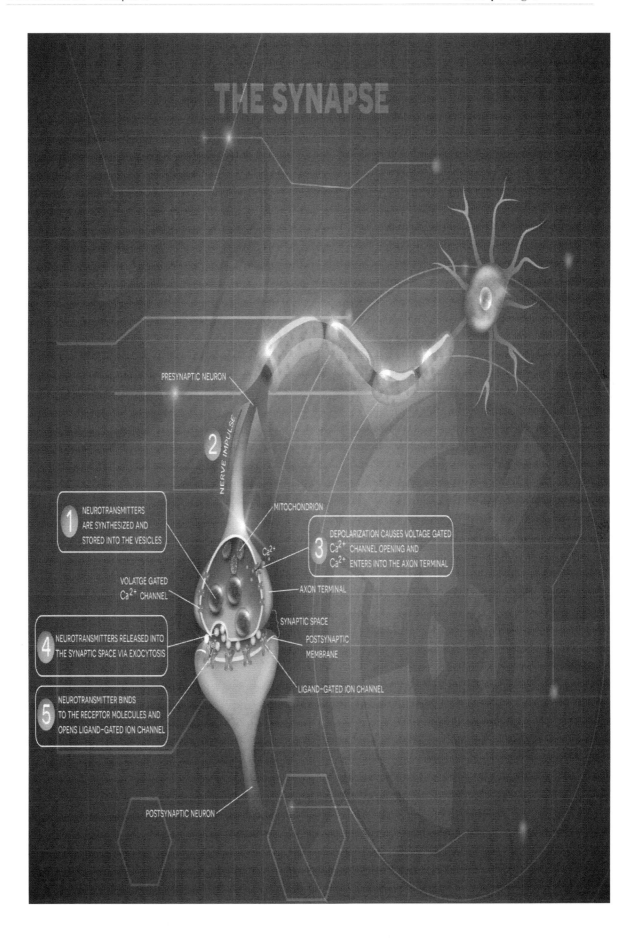

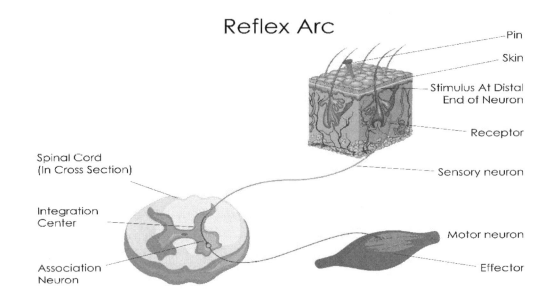

Reflex Arc

5. NEUROTRANSMITTERS

ACETYLCHOLINE The first clearly identified chemical that jumps the gap at the synapse is predominately involved in muscle movement, but also in some forms of memory. If we were to flood a muscle with acetylcholine, the muscle would contract. The electrical impulse would release acetylcholine across the synaptic gap, and if enough were released, the muscle fibers it innervates would contract, again, like Galvani's frog.

As soon as the acetylcholine is released, a second chemical, acetylcholinesterase, neutralizes the neurotransmitter. Without acetylcholinesterase, the neurons would fire continuously.

In South America, natives boil down the extract from plants to make a black tar-like substance called curare. They put the tar on the darts they use in their blowgun. When an animal is struck with a dart, it begins to lose control of its muscles. After only minutes it will fall to the ground, often alive and conscious, but unable to move its muscles.

The same type of enzyme is used by zoo keepers to render animals, even lions, and elephants, motionless so they can be helped with medical procedures. If too much were given, it could cause the animal to lose the ability to breathe, so the amount will vary based on experience or body weight.

GAMMA AMINOBYUTERIC ACID GABA is perhaps the most common neurotransmitter. This amino acid is secreted at the synapse and functions to *inhibit* the nerve from firing. Whether the nerve cell fires depends upon how much excitatory chemicals it receives and how much inhibitory chemicals it receives.

In combination with the excitatory transmitters, GABA allows a diverse range of responses that are potentially more elaborate than the simple ones and zeros of a computer. Instead of just an all-or-none, on or off, the firing of a cell, the control of the cell becomes more adaptable.

DOPAMINE is a wide-ranging neurotransmitter that is found in areas of the brain associated with everything from pleasure and reward to the ability to control fine motor movements. When this transmitter is depleted or the receptors that respond to dopamine are reduced, this may cause a disorder known as *Parkinson's Disease*.

Parkinson's Disease is something we are more aware of today because celebrities such as Mohamed Ali the boxer, Michael J. Fox, and even a former Pope have had the disorder. Mohamed Ali was formerly known for his "rope-a-dope" style, and he would stand still and allow his opponent to hit him in the face, to tire out the opponent, or to show he could take it. We now know that Parkinson's disease is not uncommon in boxers and others who have endured head trauma, although it has other causes as well.   In boxing, it has been known as "punch drunk" and rarely shows up until later in life.

If you watched Mohamed Ali long after his original diagnosis, you would have seen him standing, waiting, slightly bent over, with his hands circling uncontrollably in what psychiatrists call a "pill-rolling" tremor.   If someone with advanced Parkinson's disease were to walk, you might see them stumbling forward, leaning into their walk, or even running a bit to keep ahead of falling.

Parkinson's disease

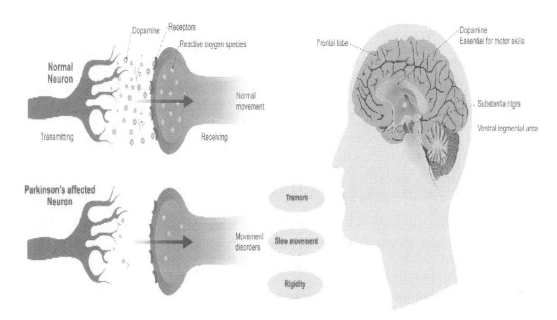

L-dopa is a medicine that crosses the blood-brain barrier and supplies the much-needed dopamine to the brain.   It works almost miraculously in the early stages of the disease, but over the years it gradually loses its effectiveness.

But since Dopamine can be important as a neurotransmitter for anything from pleasure to memory to fine motor movement, we know nothing about why Dopamine is so widely used by the brain. Is it really what creates "pleasure" as some experimenters claim? Or is it just another neurotransmitter that serves to fire specific neural circuits?

ENDORPHINS AND ENCEPHLINS Are the body's opium, morphine, and heroin equivalents. These drugs fit into the same receptor sites for pleasure and relief of pain as these neurotransmitters. They kick in normally, only under extreme stress or pain. Athletes sometimes call this the "second wind". Just when they feel they cannot go another step, their body may release these transmitters to give them a dramatic boost.

A colleague of mine who is a runner, tells me they kick in after she has run about two miles. I don't think I have run two miles total in my life, but I will take her word for it.

SEROTONIN is widely associated with mood, although the evidence is not clear. For fifty years pharmaceutical companies have touted medications such as Prozac, Paxil, Wellbutrin, and now many more as a treatment for depression because they make more Serotonin available at the synapse.   These drugs are called SSRIs or Selective Serotonin Reuptake Inhibitors because once Serotonin is released into the synapse, the drugs prevent it from being reabsorbed (reuptake inhibition) into the end bulb. Thus, they make more Serotonin available in the synapse for the next impulse... which makes it more likely that the next impulse will fire the cell.

SSRIs are often prescribed for depression but, contrary to the general impression, these drugs do not make you happy. If a drug made you happy, it would be illegal. Because you would want to take more of it. That is the very definition of addiction. What SSRIs do is to make

more Serotonin available at the synapse, by preventing it from being reabsorbed. One of the side effects of this is sleeplessness, at least until the body adapts.

The most recent studies on the effect of SSRIs on depression by Seymore Kirsh and others suggest that these drugs do not work any better than a placebo, except on the most severely depressed individuals. Other evidence suggests there may be more than one type of depression.

There are at least 40 other neurotransmitters, but our knowledge of even the few we are aware of is limited.

6. DIAGNOSIS IS NOT EASY

Pseudo-Parkinson's Disease: Has the same symptoms as Parkinson's Disease, and is caused by the same underlying problem that affects Dopamine in the brain. However, it is not Parkinson's Disease and is curable. All nurses and even just relatives should be aware of this problem because it can be caused by too much psychoactive medication or seizure medication.

I worked with a client who was suddenly hospitalized for an unrelated problem. After she came out of the hospital a variety of bizarre symptoms were reported. She was cursing at staff, refusing to take her medication, refusing to bathe or take care of herself, refusing to get out of bed or come out of her room, slurring her words, shuffling her feet, crying, unsteady on her feet, and "lying on staff".

The reported symptoms could have been anything. Cursing staff and lying about staff is sometimes a result of arguments with staff.

Refusing to take her medication, refusing to bathe or care for herself, and even lying about staff may occur in Schizophrenia. Was she delusional? Or was it paranoia? Was it disorganized thinking?

Refusing to bathe or take care of herself, crying, and refusing to get out of bed, could all be Major Depression.

Slurring her words, unsteady on her feet, could have been alcohol or drugs.

Or was it dementia?

Or was it that she was not getting enough of her medication, Depakote, a seizure medication, often used for Bi-Polar.

Any of these were possible. I was no Sherlock Holmes. We called a staff meeting. Everyone was there. She was there, staff were there, the nurse was there, the family were there, the social worker was there, and I was there.

As I sat and watched her throughout the meeting, I had no clue about all of the problems I was hearing. Then, suddenly, when she excused herself and got up to go to the restroom, the symptoms stood out. She was shuffling her feet, leaning into her walk, her hands were doing a "pill-rolling" tremor... all the symptoms of Parkinson's disease. Even the "mask-like" appearance of her face when she tried to laugh now made sense.

I asked the doctor to reduce her Depakote levels. He looked at the charts, and found that her previous Valproic Acid levels, a measure of the effectiveness of Depakote, had always been way too low, not too high. It made no sense that medication levels that low could cause this. He doubted that had anything to do with it, but he went ahead and dropped the level.

Within days her behavior problems stopped. He had to reduce it again to return her to normal.

What happened? It made no sense. The Valproic Acid levels in her blood should have told the story.

What happened was incredibly simple, yet impossible to catch. No one knew that she had rarely been taking her Depakote. Every time the doctor saw her, he ran a Valproic Acid test to determine if her levels were in the therapeutic range. Every time the levels came back low. So, he gradually kept raising her medication, and she continued *not* to take it.

Then she was hospitalized; if you know anything about hospitals, you know they make sure the patient is taking all of the medication their doctor prescribed. When she came out of the hospital, she was on record high levels of the medication she had not been taking.

This is an important caveat for anyone in the medical profession or psychology or even just for relatives. If someone has been doing well, and all of a sudden there is a dramatic change, the first thing you should consider is their medication. Were they forgetting they took the medication and then taking a second dose? If it were a child, were their parents doing the same? Did they just believe that if a little medication was good for them a whole lot more would be even better? That is an all-too-common mistake. Is there a new medication that interferes with or adds to the effect of the old?

In one case a teen began hitting his grandmother and himself. He had never had such a problem before. It turned out that his grandmother had forgotten she had already given him his medication and gave him additional doses. Sometimes, if a client has problems, their parents think that they should give them more medication to "help" them. Not a good idea.

There are so many extraneous variables in the professions that it helps to be aware of as much as possible. Psychiatrists routinely check for medication side effects every time their patients return for a refill. The test may be as simple as having them extend their hands to check for tremors. Or observing for tardive dyskinesia by watching for repetitive motor movements, jerking or twitching, in their face or lips.

Yet there are still things that are missed. One of the things you often hear about is the so-called "psychotic break", where a patient who is doing well suddenly goes "off the deep end." Often this results in more medication being prescribed. Yet the psychiatrist rarely hears about the causes, but there usually is one.

One day I got a panicked call from our staff. A client had "gone off" in a facility, trashed a thousand-dollar computer and copy machine, threw a computer monitor through the wall, and generally terrified everyone. I got there at the same time the police did. The one fortunate thing about both our jobs is that the drama is usually over by the time we get there.

I talked to him to be sure he was calm and walked him to the police car. I got a call later saying they were not going to hold him. The next morning, we had a nice talk, he was now in good spirits, and I took him to see the psychiatrist.

The psychiatrist asked him, "How are you doing?"

He replied, smiling, "I'm fine doc. How are you?"

Psychiatrist: "Are you having any problems?"

He replied, still smiling, "No. I'm fine."

Not exactly the most complete information. As it turned out he was angry and upset at his job supervisor who, others told me, had been angry and stubborn and acting like a jerk. This is one of the most common causes of people exploding in school or on the job when they are treated unfairly or bullied by other students or supervisors and no one will listen to their side of the story.

Yet we always blame the kid who was bullied or the employee who was belittled and not the environment. Without any doubt some people are unreasonable and difficult to get along with in the best of times, but it is not always their fault, look to the environment first. Be suspicious of the term "psychotic break" as it is often used to cover our own lack of awareness of the actual causes.

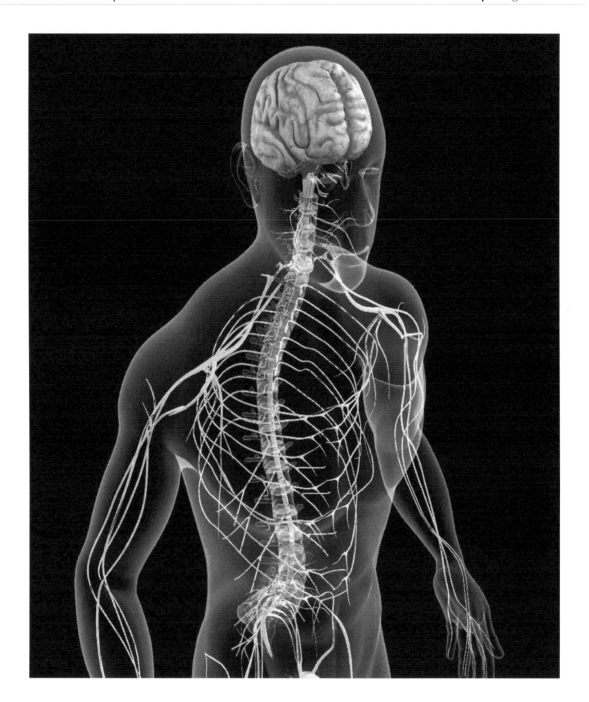

7. THE BRAIN CODE

Some may think it unlikely that simple neural switches could account for the great range of human behavior. Yet every ability the computer has is based on only two digits, ones and zeros (I and 0). If you have a CD with music on it, there is no music on that CD, only an infinite number of ones and zeros. If you have a DVD with motion pictures on it, there is nothing on that DVD but an infinite number of ones and zeros. The CPU reads the ones and zeros and translates that into controlling every pixel on the screen, every tone and voice, and everything you see and hear.

The earliest form of code is morse code, which consists of only dots and dashes. Every letter of the alphabet is assigned a different series of dots and dashes, just as every letter a computer reads is assigned a different series of ones and zeros. Yet a telegrapher can, using only dots and dashes, send an entire book across wires to another telegrapher who can decipher the code into a complete book.

The DNA code that writes the entire of the human genome into a living person, consists of only four base pairs; Adenine-Cytosine or Cytosine-Adenine, Thiamine-Guanine or Guanine-Thiamine. Yet with only four letters in the DNA code (A, C, T, G) it can reproduce an entire human being.

In the brain, the "code" consists of nerve cells firing or inhibited from firing (on or off) and graded potentials, determined by how many excitatory or inhibitory cells fire or how frequently they fire. The human brain is far more variable than a computer, but also far more fallible in its infinite superstitions. See Chapter 8 for details.

THE CYBORG ANALOGY

The end of World War II brought vast new developments in computers, internal guidance systems, and servomechanisms. It did not take long before someone recognized the striking resemblance between these automatic mechanisms and the functioning of the brain.

In 1948, Norbert Weiner's *Cybernetics,* published at the Massachusetts Institute of Technology, proposed a compelling and far-reaching parallel between the computer and the human brain. Weiner's comparisons, although tentative, were exciting and opened the door to a new area of speculation and study-*cybernetics*-which may be described as the comparative study of natural and man-made automatic control systems. The basic elements of Weiner's analogies are summarized below. Today, it is one basis for a new view of Cognitive Psychology.

The Digital Computer There is a marked similarity between the electronic switches of a digital computer and the neurons of the human brain. Computers originally used thousands of electric switches that either allow an electric current to flow (open) or prevent it from flowing (closed), *although today's computers use ones and zeros for the same effect*. Each switch transmits its current or it does not, in an all-or-none fashion. As we have seen, neurons too may either allow current to flow (fire excitatory impulses) or prevent it from flowing (fire inhibitory impulses). Furthermore, a neuron may itself either fire (open?) or not fire (closed?) in an all-or-none fashion, depending on the amount of stimulation it receives.

Today, computers use ones and zeros to compute information. When you press the "W" key on the computer keyboard it does not send a "W" to the screen. It sends a series of eight binary digits; such as 01101011 from the central processor, which instructs the video processor to recreate a "W" on the screen. The keyboard, a form of sensory input, instructs the computer. Or we must feed programs that others have already created for us, into the computer.

Without a program being fed into the computer, like a word processor or a spreadsheet, the computer has been described as nothing but a very expensive doorstop. Today, we have forgotten that the first computers from Apple and IBM had no programming at all. They were a tabula rasa, a blank slate, with potential. Even the disk drive that was used to load programs into the computer had to have DOS the Disk Operating System, installed first, before the computer could have programs loaded into it.

The electronic switches in a digital computer are arranged in banks, and setting off one switch can trigger an entire series of switches in sequence. When neurons fire, they too may trigger sequences of other neurons to which they are attached, These, in turn, may fire still more neurons. The effect may be much like that of the retrieval process in the memory banks of a computer, or even the calling up of stored subroutines of computer programs. Thus, a single switch, or a single stimulus that fires a neuron, may call on thousands of switches, or neurons, triggering additional sequences in turn.

Feedback:

Feedback distinguishes a computer from a simple reflex. Similar to the homeostatic mechanism that controls body temperature, feedback is an electronic version of Purposeful Behavior. Feedback is the *DO LOOP* in a computer program. Feedback directs the brain.

When we move our bodies, we get feedback from sensors in the muscles. We also *get* visual feedback because we see any change in the scene that resulted from our movements. A blind person walking alone through a maze of traffic has no visual feedback--he can walk, but he has no visual information that would tell him how he is doing. He must rely on feedback from other senses; such as touch, with a cane, or hearing from echoes in the environment. Only when it is possible to see or feel the effect of our movements is it possible to direct our motor behavior purposefully.

A form of electronic homeostasis is provided by the gain control of a car radio. Once the volume is set, it will automatically remain the same whether you drive near the radio station or many miles away. The volume is maintained because there is a feedback loop between the radio output and input. As the volume (output) gets higher, it is damped down to a preset level.

WILL CYBORGS EVER REPLACE US?

Some have said that when computers become so advanced that they can cross the singularity and become self-aware, they may reason that humans are the greatest threat to the planet and decide, on their own, to exterminate the threat. Movies such as *Terminator* with Arnold Schwarzenegger, have suggested that super-intelligent robots could replace us, after exterminating the threat to the planet.

Yet it is unlikely that this could ever happen, unless... of course, we forget to put a couple of OFF switches in their programming. Could our species possibly be that stupid? Actually, humans have no hardwired OFF switches in our programming that would prevent us from exterminating ourselves. Some say we have an ON switch. See Ch. 20.

8. ENRICHED OR IMPOVERISHED ENVIRONMENTS CHANGE THE BRAIN

Other theories of how memory traces are made in the brain are that there is a change at the synapse that makes it more or less likely to fire the attached nerves. We also know that experience creates more synapses in the brain. Studies by Rosenzweig and others have found that rats raised in an "enriched" environment have heavier and denser brains than those rats raised in an "impoverished" environment.

The "impoverished" environment rats were raised in a standard wire cage with no social or environmental additions. The "enriched" environment allowed the rats freedom to play with other rats, platforms to jump on, and objects to play with. These rats not only had heavier and denser brains (presumably with more neural connections) but the areas of the brain that were most affected turned out to be the areas involved in *vision and motor movements*; just the areas you might expect from the larger, more social environment they were raised in.

9.

COMPUTER SCIENCE AND ITS CONTRIBUTION

Although the brain is not like a hardwired computer, it shares remarkable similarities to a computer.

- **SWITCHING**: The Neurons that power the brain work in a simple ON or OFF function, much like a computer, with the addition of graded potentials.

- **DECISION MAKING:** Perhaps the most dramatic semi-similarity is how both computers and the brain make decisions. Computers use an IF-THEN decision diamond or DO LOOP to make a decision. In a flow chart, in the Decision Diamond, the computer compares two numbers or patterns, (IF X = Y, THEN go on to the next step. IF X does not equal Y, THEN go back to a previous step in the program.)

- **CONTRAST and COMPARISON**: Similarly, the human mind compares and contrasts two variables. This allows the brain to make a "choice" as to whether the two variables (or stimulus patterns) are similar or not. This is most evident in Approach-Avoidance conflict, where a decision is often made on the relative positive or negative emotions, or in switching perspectives as in the Necker cube (see ch9).

- **PRE-PROGRAMMED PROCESSING**: Like a computer, the brain is biologically structured to process information. As in Broca's area and Wernicke's area, etc.

- **LEARNED PROGRAMS**: Just as a computer must have DOS or a Disk Operating System loaded into itself before new programs or information can be fed into it, so does the human mind. Learning programs the brain; and creates new learning sets or concepts. New concepts make new learning possible without the need for new biological programs in the brain.

DESPITE THE SIMILAR FUNCTIONS OF THE COMPUTER AND THE BRAIN, THERE ARE ALSO DRAMATIC DIFFERENCES.

- **EMOTION**: This is a primary force that controls human motivation. There is no comparable method in the computer. Curiosity, Pleasure, Fear, Anger, and all of the various combinations of these that produce excitement, shame, guilt, etc. are unique products of the brain and experience. Although it is possible to simulate emotion in a computer, this tells us absolutely nothing about the programs and emotions that life and society feed into the human mind.

• Only the low-tech methods of learning in *psychology, sociology, and cultural anthropology* can tell us how the brain uses emotion and comparison to make the brain into a useful, programmed mind.

• **LINEAR VS MULTIPHASIC** Computers are linear, one step after another. They compute far faster than the brain. The brain is linear and non-linear, with every neural connection having many connections, which seems to make for greater flexibility and allows the processing of patterns.

• **PSYCHOLOGY** (Learning) picks up, where biology leaves off. Sociology and cultural anthropology come in to provide the next level of information about how the brain is shaped by experience.

• **LEARNED PROGRAMS** The mind itself is structured by its experiences in a way that is unlike a computer. The new experiences structure the brain itself (as in our unique perceptions), and determine what the brain is capable of "seeing" or experiencing, as in language or cultural illusions (Ch. 9 & 11).

Next, is how information is programmed into the brain by our environment; **The Sensors**.

6 THE SENSORS

HOW WE KNOW THE OUTSIDE WORLD

We have not yet begun to understand how my brain gives me consciousness... In fact, all I know is what my mind gives me in perception and memory and imagination. By seeing, hearing, and touching I come to know the world of nature and as a scientist I try to understand that world, including even my own brain. The really interesting features associated with that world like color, sound, smell, form, pain, are not in the world at all but come to my mind as interpretations of signals to my brain in a manner that is completely beyond any scientific comprehension.

Sir John Eccles, Neurophysiologist The *Mind of Man*

"If a tree falls in the forest, and there is no one around to hear it, does it make a noise?" This seemingly philosophical question strikes at a powerful understanding of the human brain that few today grasp. Yet it is an important two-part question that hits at the comment of biologist Sir John Eccles. To understand the brain, you must understand this question.

YOUR HOMEWORK ASSIGNMENT: *Tonight, just before you go to bed, stare at the light in the ceiling for about 10 seconds. Then turn out the light. In total darkness what do you see? An afterimage of light. It moves as you move your eyes. How can you see light in total darkness? This can only happen because the machinery of the brain itself is producing what we call light.*

One can imagine Democritus and his fellow Ionian philosophers/scientists, sitting around a campfire late at night, drinking wine *"only in moderation"*, watching the flames flicker in the fire. Then, when they look off into the dark, they still see the flames flickering in the dark of night, even when they do not exist. The light exists only in the brain itself. What we call "light" is created by the brain itself.

In 430 BCE, the Greek philosopher Democritus posed a riddle: He stated that *"By convention sweet and by convention bitter, by convention hot, by convention cold, by convention color: in reality, all that exist are atoms and the void"*; To Democritus, the atoms that touch our senses are not the same as the *sensations* of sweet, bitter, hot, cold, and color that we experience. His insight is echoed in the comment by Sir John Eccles above.

Democritus believed that our perception of reality is based on sensations that result from atoms thrown off from the objects in our environment. He believed that these particles pass through the pores of the body to the mind. He thought all senses are forms of touch and that what we know results from the changes produced in our mind by the forces that act on it.

Although we have a different view of this today, the question is not as arcane as it seems. Indeed, it has come back to haunt us with a vengeance. Sir John Eccles, awarded the Nobel Prize in physiology, pays homage to this same question when he notes that *"the really interesting features associated with that world like color, sound, smell, form, pain, are not in the world at all but come to my mind as interpretations of signals to my brain."* For all its simplicity, no science fiction writer could have posed a question more astounding in its implications than that.

It is that same fascination that, to this day, inspires physicists and biologists to try to understand the great mystery of nature. How is it possible the brain can produce what we see? How is it possible that the brain itself produces what we call light and sound and color and pain and pleasure from nothing more than the sensations that the brain experiences?

Before we finish this chapter, you should be able to partly answer that question about the tree falling in a forest, as a two-part answer. By the end of the chapter, you should see at least a partial answer to what gives us consciousness. Although, to this day, we have no idea how the machinery of the brain creates light, color, sound, pain, hot, cold, or emotions.

We must remember that we do not observe nature as it actually exists, but nature exposed to our methods of perception... theories determine what we can or cannot observe... Reality is an illusion, albeit a persistent one.

Albert Einstein

1. THE SENSE OF TOUCH

Democritus believed that touch is the most basic sensation. And understanding touch is basic to being able to understand the other senses, although not all are the same as touch.

Embedded just under the surface of the skin are specialized nerve endings that respond to (1) pressure, (2) pain, (3) warmth, and (4) cold.

TRY THIS EXPERIMENT: Lightly touch the hairs on your arm with your fingers. Do not touch the skin. The hairs themselves have no sensation of touch at all. You can cut them with a razor and they do not respond. But what do you feel when you brush those hairs?

Nerve endings that are sensitive to pressure or stretch, wrap themselves around the base of each hair follicle in the skin. The hair follicles themselves are totally insensitive to pain or pressure. However, if you lightly brush the tips of the hairs without touching the surface of the skin, you can feel the repeated firing of the stretch receptors attached to the base of each follicle. There is perhaps no better example of the localized sense of touch than these specialized sensors.

If someone pokes at the surface of your skin with a very fine hair, you find that different areas of the skin vary widely in sensitivity. In some areas, such as the small of the back, you might feel no sensation at all. You might be totally unaware that the hair was pressing against your skin. In other areas, such as the lips, genitals, and fingertips, a rich supply of sensory nerve endings provides an immediate awareness of even the lightest touch.

Cross section of human skin, showing a sensory nerve ending wrapped around the base of a hair follicle. The Root Hair Plexus moves when the hair is touched. This causes the attached nerve to fire, sending an impulse to the sensory cortex of the brain. We experience this as touch.

This is basic to understanding, because a mechanical touch is all it takes to send positive ions into the nerve cell, which depolarizes along its length, until the electrical impulse ends up on the sensory cortex mapped by Penfield.

Other highly specialized nerve endings are triggered by different stimuli:

Pacinian Corpuscles are fired by pressure, as are sensors in the urinary bladder as well as proprioceptive sensors in the muscles.

Organs of Ruffini are fired by warmth.

Krause's End Bulbs are fired by cold.

Free nerve endings produce the sensation of pain.

SENSORY RECEPTORS IN SKIN

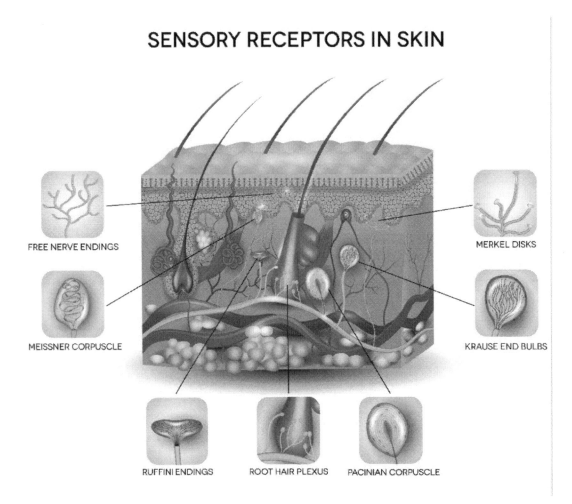

FREE NERVE ENDINGS

MERKEL DISKS

MEISSNER CORPUSCLE

KRAUSE END BULBS

RUFFINI ENDINGS   ROOT HAIR PLEXUS   PACINIAN CORPUSCLE

There is a smooth muscle attached to the base of each of the hairs. When the Fight or Flight portion of the Amygdala is triggered, as it may be in a horror movie in the movie theater, the little hairs on the back of your neck may stand on end. This is of little value in humans, but you see this in cats and other species as a defense mechanism; when all the hairs are standing upright, it makes the animal look bigger and more menacing to its opponent. This may make the opponent think twice before attacking. For humans, it is just a quaint reminder of what our ancestors at Salem felt when the girls started to shriek, "Witch, witch!"

Our skin sensors are pretty good at helping us navigate the real world, but they are only a pale imitation of physics. The sensation of hot or cold depends on the surface temperature of the skin and the temperature of what we touch. If the surface temperature of the skin is 98 degrees, and we jump into a bath that is 100 degrees, we may feel that the intensity of the heat in the tub is tremendous. Yet after a few minutes, our skin adjusts, and the temperature of the water no longer seems nearly as high as when we first touched it.

Similarly, if the outside temperature is 100 degrees and we enter an air-conditioned building where the temperature is 70 degrees, the building will feel cool; if the outside temperature is 30 degrees, however, the 70-degree inside temperature will seem pleasantly warm. Thus, the same stimulus, a temperature of 70 degrees, feels quite different depending on our earlier experience.

The skin does not appear to contain any sensory receptors that respond specifically to the sensation of "hot." It has been shown that the sensation of "hot" is a combination of stimulation of receptors that respond to warmth, cold, and pain. There is a remarkable illustration of this possibility. If two copper tubes or micropipettes are twisted around each other for their entire length, with warm water running through one tube and cold water through the other, the tube with warm water will feel warm and that with cold water will feel cold. If you touch both of them together, with the warm and cold water running through, however, the sensation will be one of "hot."

Internal Body Sensors

The senses of touch provide one of the best examples of the earlier contention of Democritus and Sir John Eccles that the interpretation of sensations lies, not in reality, but in our mind. If you place a chili pepper on your tongue, what sensation do you feel? The sensation is one of heat, often one of very intense heat. If you apply the chili pepper to a scrape on the back of your arm, you again will feel a sensation of heat where the skin is raw. But what would happen if you took a thermometer and stuck it into the chili pepper? Would the mercury in the thermometer rise? Would you get any kind of heat at all? No, there is no heat in a chili pepper. The heat is in your mind.

Where there is no caloric energy, no radiation, by all laws of physics there is no heat. Yet identical reactions can be obtained by touching dry ice, which is certainly not hot, or by rubbing the so-called" deep heating rubs," which are used by athletes as muscle relaxants, into the surface of the skin. The deep heating rubs actually do not penetrate beyond the surface of the skin, but they give the sensation of heat and perhaps a placebo effect that allows muscular relaxation. Yet again, neither case involves anything that could be considered heat by any law of physics.

Proprioceptive Feedback:

Even with your eyes closed, you can reach out with your hand and trace circles or squares in the air. With reasonable accuracy, you can even touch your nose with your forefinger. This ability comes from *proprioceptors,* sensory receptors embedded in the muscles and tendons of your limbs. We often are not conscious of the stimuli to which these deep receptors respond, nor of the responses themselves, yet they are crucial to our behavior. The movement of your muscles guides the cerebellum in the coordination of the endless number of fine motor movements needed to type on a keyboard or execute the most intricate of athletic skills.

As increasingly heavy amounts of pressure are applied, the sensation of pressure gives way to one of pain. Pain is the body's way of signaling the mind that tissue destruction is taking place. The sensation of pain sometimes occurs before actual tissue destruction, which gives the brain a chance to remove the body from the painful stimulus. The surface of the human skin is heavily saturated by free nerve endings that respond to pain, yet they are remarkably absent in such areas as the brain. The probing of most areas of the brain of a conscious patient produces no sensation of pain or pressure.

In the British Navy, several hundred years ago, after a man was flogged with a cat-a-nine-tails, the follow-up procedure was to throw a bucket of salt water over the wounds on his back. What did the victim feel? Intense pain. Yet there had been no additional tissue destruction. How does salt produce this reaction?

Salt consists of sodium chloride. When it is placed on a moist area of the wound, the salt breaks down into sodium and chloride, and sodium overpowers all neurons that are exposed. The neurons will continue firing until the salt is washed away or the body naturally dissolves the salt and carries it off. The sensation this produces is one of extreme pain. An electric shock to the surface of the skin, such as that delivered by a cattle prod, will similarly fire pain neurons. Yet the shock itself produces no tissue damage whatsoever.

It is well known that a scrape or burn over a square inch of skin can be far more painful than an inch-deep cut. The intensity of the pain depends on the number of neurons involved, rather than on the extent of tissue damage alone. In the case of a scrape, a large number of neurons are involved-and firing-whereas a more severe and more dangerous cut may involve comparatively few neurons. This is one reason that major surgery can sometimes be done with no anesthetic other than the questionable one of acupuncture.

Hypnosis, Selective Attention, and Pain

The sensation of pain also depends on psychological factors. We may become so intensely involved in a task such as repairing an automobile or working with machinery that a cut or scrape may go unnoticed until the job is finished. Minutes or even an hour may pass before we notice a sudden throbbing where the skin has been injured. The cut may have been there all along and yet, while we were preoccupied with one particular activity, the mind somehow prevented the pain. It seems as if the intensity of the concentrated attention is enough to inhibit the sensation of pain.

This same phenomenon may be observed in several other areas of perception. The student who is engrossed in reading a particularly interesting book may be able to fully concentrate despite the noise of a radio in the background, whereas a student with less interest would simply not be able to "tune out" the irrelevant incoming stimuli. This type of selective attention may be the major factor in the reduction of pain that is associated with hypnosis or acupuncture. The patient who is concentrating on the voice of the hypnotist or the pain of the acupuncture needle may simply psychologically "turn off" pain from other areas. It is not magic; it seems to be only our brain's ability to focus so selectively that other incoming stimuli are ignored by the brain.

2. THE SENSE OF HEARING:
Written on the Wind
The Auditory Signal

What is sound? We know what we subjectively experience as noise, but what is it that produces this noise?

Sound consists of waves. What are waves? Waves are the vibration of air. What is air? Air consists of molecules; oxygen, nitrogen, etc. Airwaves are created by the vibration of air molecules.

If you hit the tip of a tuning fork, its metal tines will begin to vibrate, producing a noise. The vibration of the metal tines sets up waves of air molecules, which radiate out from the tuning fork in much the same way as the ripples that form in a pond when you drop a stone in the center. Ripples of pressure radiate out from the point where the stone cut through the still surface of the pond, each ripple displacing the water in front of it and thus causing more ripples.

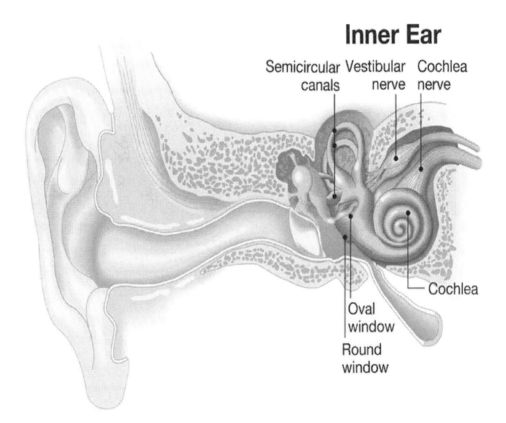

The amount of mechanical pressure exerted by the sound, or by the stone that causes the ripples in a pond, is referred to as the amplitude of the sound. No matter how great the pressure, the air molecules that begin the vibration do not travel far beyond their source. Instead, they move as a wave, with each point triggering a vibration in the next series of air molecules.

The reason that sound can be heard at great distances is that the vibration of one set of air molecules sets up a vibration in the set nearest it, which, in turn, vibrates the set nearest it, and so on. But each group of air molecules that are vibrating tends to do so around their resting state. They do not move far. If they did travel longer distances, each speech would be like a gust of wind. Instead, the airwaves travel in a way similar to the waves in water if you drop a pebble into the water.

THE DOPPLER EFFECT: Seeing Into the Universe

An important property of sound is the Doppler effect. Take a train whistle as an example. Every time the train whistle is sounded it has the same tone to those who are aboard the train no matter what the speed of the train, for sound waves are traveling at the same relative speed as the train itself. However, if you are standing near the track listening to the whistle of an approaching train, the sound waves will be greatly compressed as the train speeds toward you.

The speed of the train is added to the speed of the sound waves, and the whistle sounds very shrill and high-pitched. Immediately as the train passes, however, the sound waves are spread out farther because the source of the sound is moving away at a fast rate. The previously shrill sound is now quite low and deep. Yet to the engineer who is operating the whistle, no change in sound has occurred.

It is all relative.

Astronomer Edwin Hubble used the same Doppler Effect with light to determine that the Galaxies outside of our own Milky Way Galaxy are all moving away from us at varying speeds. The "Red Shift" of the color of these Galaxies shows that they are not stable, but in motion, and moving away from us. This is seen as hard evidence of the "Big Bang" that sent all matter throughout the universe. If you imagine a balloon with spots on it, as the balloon inflates, each of the spots moves away from us at a greater distance. The more the balloon expands, the greater the distance.

Causes of a lack of Hearing

The Human Receiver When the vibration of the air molecules hits the membrane inside the ear this sets up a vibration in the fluid in the cochlea of the inner ear. The pressure waves trigger tiny hair cells in the cochlea, which fire in much the same manner as the pressure cells at the base of hair follicles when you run your fingers across the tips of the hairs on your arm.

Different hair cells in the inner eat fire to different frequencies of sound, but they all fire in the same mechanical fashion. What is remarkable is that on reaching the brain, impulses from the hair cells in the cochlea are translated into what we call sound, whereas impulses from the nerve endings at the base of the hair follicles in the arm are translated into what we call touch.

Deafness can result from one of two causes. If there is damage to the sensory receptor in the ear, the auditory neurons will be unable to pick up the vibrations of air molecules and translate them into electrical impulses. The potential for sound exists in the form of sound waves, but it is simply not picked up by the receiving apparatus.

Second, deafness can be produced by damage to the neurons that lead from the cochlea to the auditory cortex of the brain or by damage to the auditory cortex itself. The sound waves are picked up by the receptor cells and may be translated into electrical impulses, but the impulses either do not reach the brain or the brain itself is unable to receive them,

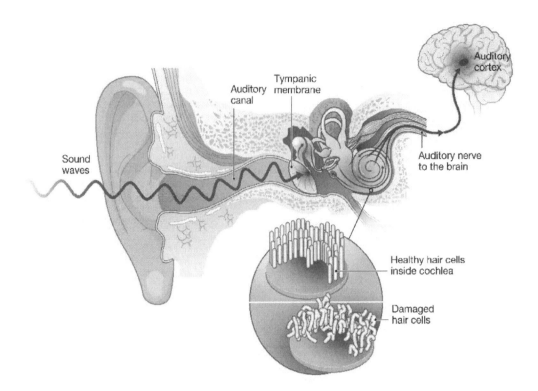

Although sound waves are present, the perception of sound is not possible without the sensory receptors to pick up the sound waves, the auditory neurons to convert them into electrical impulses, and the auditory cortex, which receives and processes those impulses.

More remarkable still is the fact that when the auditory neurons leading from the cochlea are electrically stimulated, a conscious patient will report hearing sound. We thus can bypass both the sensory receptors and the auditory neurons, and go directly to stimulate the brain, yet the sound is reported by the patient.

Why? There is certainly no vibration of air molecules. There is nothing that by any law of physics we can call noise. Yet the patient perceives noise. Can you explain this phenomenon based on what you have already learned?

3. TRANSDUCTION:
CHANGING ONE FORM OF ENERGY INTO A DIFFERENT FORM

Radar represents a rough analogy of how human vision operates. The radar machine emits a specific band of high-frequency electromagnetic radiation, which is beamed out into space where it bounces off clouds or metal objects such as planes. The radiation that bounces off an object is reflected back to a receiving device, which picks up the specific wavelength of the object and automatically transduces it into a blip of light on the radar screen. The blip of light does not exist in nature. Machinery picks up the radar waves and from them reproduces a model, or representation, of what is out in space. The model is the blip on the screen.

The human eye functions something like the receiver part of a radar unit. Electromagnetic radiation, produced by the sun or electric light bulbs, is reflected or bounced off the objects in the environment. The photons that hit the surface of the retina then fire, which in turn translate this form of energy into the electrochemical impulses that are received by the brain and translated into what we subjectively call light.

We cannot see Radar waves. This is a frequency of Electromagnetic Radiation that cannot be seen by our visual sensors. However, scientists have developed a way of *transducing* (changing) one form of energy (Radar frequency) into another form of energy (visual frequency). The light energy shows up as a blip on a radar screen. That blip represents a plane in the sky, even though the blip is neither a plane nor a radar wave. The light is what the radar machinery has changed into a visible light we can see.

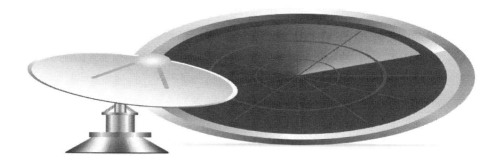

The brain itself routinely changes the same form of energy, light waves, or sound waves, or touch, or taste (an electrical impulse) from the sensors, into a completely different form of energy (an electrical impulse) that travels to the brain.

The brain itself receives only electrical impulses. The visual imagery stops at the retina. The auditory information stops at the Cochlea. The information from the senses of touch stop at the surface of the skin. Only electrical impulses ever reach the brain.

How the brain transforms this electrical energy into what we call light, color, sound, and touch, is a mystery beyond anything we can explain.

RECEPTORS

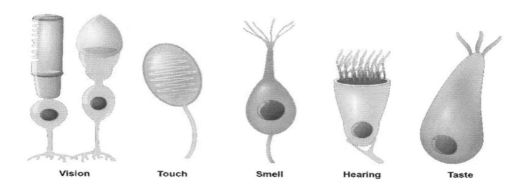

| Vision | Touch | Smell | Hearing | Taste |

These human sensors *transduce* one form of energy (touch, sound, smell, light) into a different form of energy, an electrical impulse that travels down an axon to reach the sensory centers in the brain.

In the world of electronics, we repeatedly see the use of one form of energy as a transmitter, which can then be transduced by specialized receivers into a second form of energy that the human organism, via its receptors, can receive and respond to. Radio waves of the type used by AM, television, and FM stations are forms of directed electromagnetic radiation.

The radio waves themselves do not contain any form of sound. They are electromagnetic radiation, not mechanical vibrations of air molecules. The radio or television receiver contains transducers that convert this form of energy into electrical currents, which carry impulses to the speaker where they are converted into the mechanical vibrations of air that we know as sound.

Highly specialized radio receivers pick up one frequency of one radio station while ignoring others close to it on the frequency scale. In the human eye, there appear to be receivers known as *cones* which similarly respond to highly specific wavelengths of light but respond considerably less to other wavelengths.

4. THE VISUAL SENSORS

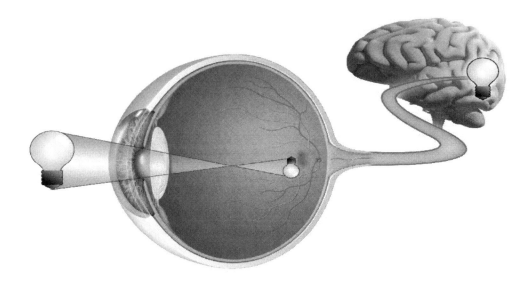

Between the ultraviolet and infrared ranges of the electromagnetic spectrum, there is a very narrow band of radiation to which the human eye is sensitive. Called the *visible spectrum,* this band ranges between roughly 400 and 700 millimicrons in length. Electromagnetic waves outside these lengths are not perceived by the human eye. The waves are there, but they are not in the visible spectrum; like the nearby frequency that is "ignored" by a radio receiver, they are not picked up by the human eye.

Nothing in nature sends out directed electromagnetic radiation in the same manner that a radio station does. What happens is that particular frequencies of electromagnetic radiation are reflected (and sometimes absorbed) by objects in the environment. The receptors in the human eye pick up only specific reflected wavelengths but do not fire when exposed to other wavelengths.

Light and Color Sir Isaac Newton (1642-1727) was among the first to study the nature of light. In a darkened room, he punched a small hole in a curtain through which a beam of light could pass. He placed a small prism, a triangular-shaped piece of glass, in the path of the light, which passed through the prism and onto a white sheet. As the light passed through the prism, it broke up into shades of violet, green, yellow, and red, which were apparent on the white sheet. These are the basic spectral colors, and they are the same colors you see when light passes through the beads of rain in a distant thunderstorm or the fine spray mist of a garden hose.

Newton also was impressed by the changes in the shape and size of the ray of light reflected on the sheet. No longer was it a round single point: It had spread out into a band far wider than the original source of light that struck the prism. Newton realized that the white light that we see is not white at all but consists of all colors of the spectrum.

5. THE COLOR SENSORS

In a series of studies, Newton demonstrated that when the rays of color were sent back through a second prism, they emerged on the far side as a pure white light. With today's projectors, we can project pure light sources-colors of blue, green, and red-onto the same spot on a screen. Where the three colors overlap, we see a very definite gray-white color. This phenomenon can only be seen by using pure light sources. A mixture of tempera paints would have quite a different effect, since tempera paint would be dealing with reflected light and not projected light.

Newton realized the important implications of his discoveries: Color was not a property of the objects in the environment; color was a property of the light that struck these objects. In a darkened room, he let the spectrum from the prism fall on a green leaf. The leaf appeared green only when it was held in the green portion of the spectrum; otherwise, it was colorless.

The leaf absorbed all other colors and reflected only green. Newton's demonstration that color is a property not of objects but of light itself, presaged a revolution in our thinking about the nature of sensation and perception.

Early in the 1800s, a Bavarian physicist and optician named Joseph von Fraunhofer developed a double-prism spectroscope, a breakthrough in physics. The spectroscope was a sort of microscope that enabled him to carefully examine the colors in the visible spectrum that Newton had only seen with the unaided eye. To his amazement what he saw were a great number of fine black lines, differing in degrees of thickness. These spectrum lines are known as *Fraunhofer lines.*

Fraunhofer later developed a method of measuring the incredibly tiny distances between the lines, with the help of a physicist, Augustin Fresnel. Fraunhofer realized that the distance between the lines represented the wavelengths of the light rays. He was able to accurately measure the wavelength of a band of red light at 637 millionths of a millimeter.

This and similar measurements later led to the realization that all forms of electromagnetic energy are but different frequencies, or different wavelengths, of the same basic energy form.

When light reflected by images in the environment passes through the lens of the eye, it is focused on the retina of the eye. The retina has millions of specialized sensory nerve endings, transducers that change electromagnetic radiation into the electrical energy that can be received and processed by the brain.

These transducers are more commonly known as *rods* and *cones* In animals having color vision, such as birds, primates, and humans, cones tend to predominate at the sharpest point of visual focus in the retina--the *fovea centralis.* Color vision was an advantage to animals that fly through trees or swing through trees. In the human eye, there are over six million cones for color vision and a hundred million rods for black-and-white vision.

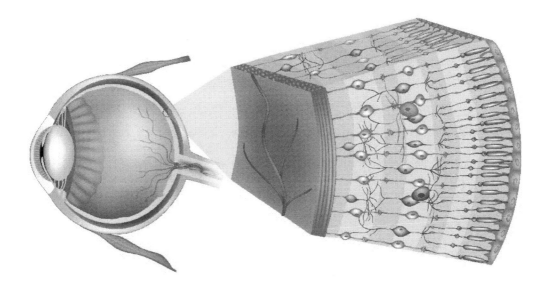

The rods tend to be sensitive to dim light, whereas the cones are most useful in well-lit areas. Cones also tend to respond to specific frequencies of bright light. The relative sensitivities of rods and cones can be demonstrated in a simple experiment. If you look directly at a distant star, the dim light will fall directly on the fovea, which consists of cones, and the star will be difficult to see. If, however, you look slightly to one side of the star, the light will fall on either side of the fovea where there are more rods, which respond to the dim light. Thus, it is easier to see a distant star by looking slightly to one side of it than by looking at it directly.

Physiologist George Wald discovered that the rods absorb *photons,* which are increments (quanta) of electromagnetic radiation. The photons cause a chemical change in the composition of each rod, (rhodopsin) and its sensory neuron depolarizes, firing an electrical impulse to the back of the brain. The electromagnetic radiation stops at the retina of the eye, however. Again, what the brain receives is not light, but the electrical impulses transmitted by the neurons.

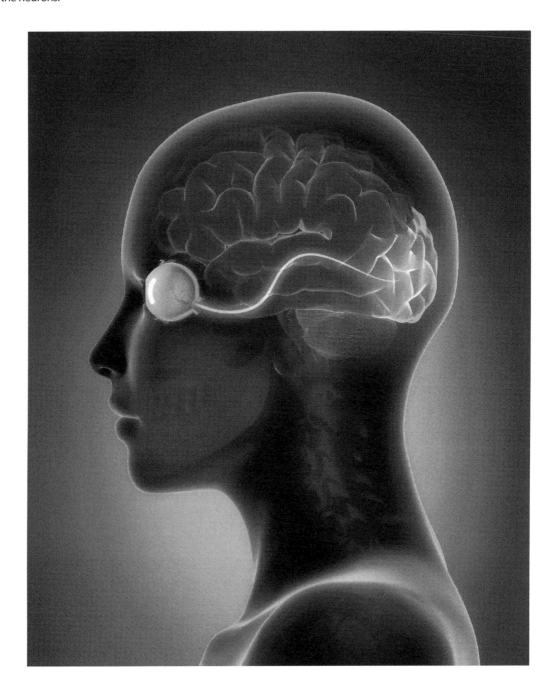

6. THE ELECTROMAGNETIC SPECTRUM

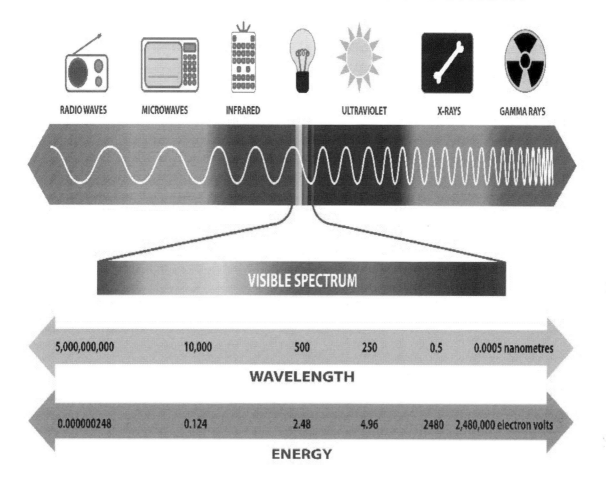

The entire electromagnetic spectrum indicates the remarkable relationship between the various forms of electromagnetic energy. Gamma-ray radiation is among the most penetrating of all wavelengths. Such radiation can strike and alter the structure of genes, causing genetic defects ranging from the absence of limbs, mental retardation, and blindness to less noticeable genetic disorders from hemophilia to birthmarks. Seriously detrimental genetic mutations occur in over 3 percent of all human births. The radiation that produces genetic defects affects everyone equally whether you are an American, an Armenian, a Russian, or a Chinese. Even if you are a Cocker Spaniel, all species are subjected to the same risk of radiation-induced genetic damage.

There are over 6,000 known, cataloged, genetic disorders in humans. The majority of genetic disorders, however, are quite minor and normally go unnoticed. In rare cases, such mutations may even be beneficial to the organism. These are the mutations that lead to the individual differences on which Darwin's principles operate.

One of the most familiar forms of radiation is the wavelengths known as x-rays, which we have turned into a valuable tool in medical diagnosis. Unlike visible light, which is reflected by objects in the environment, x-ray radiation is capable of passing through many objects. Emitted in a highly concentrated beam, x-rays can penetrate muscle tissue and are recorded on a film plate on the other side of the object being x-rayed. Very heavy tissue, such as a bone or teeth, absorbs more radiation than does muscle tissue, skin, or the hollow portion of a bone or tooth.

The x-ray picture through which the electrons have passed easily, in contrast to the darker or intermediate gray areas, the bones, where more electrons have been absorbed. The study of x-rays is an excellent example of how it is possible to investigate a form of electromagnetic radiation that is not normally visible to the human eye.

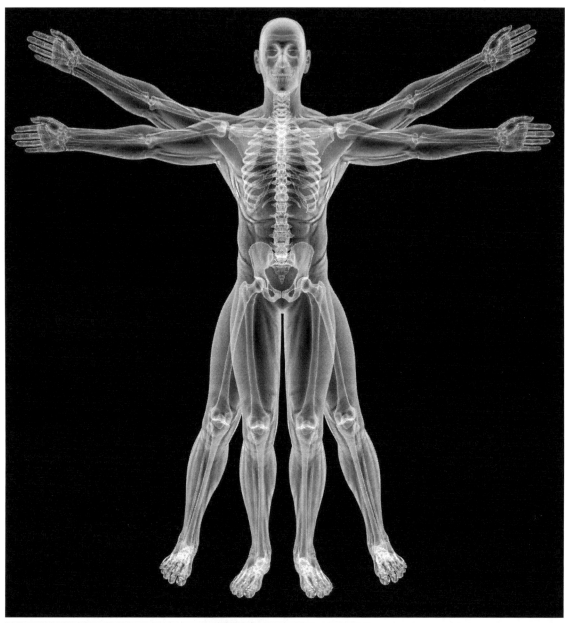

Ultraviolet radiation, as with most forms of radiation given off by the sun, is largely absorbed in the upper atmosphere before it reaches the surface of the earth. Yet a sufficiently large amount of it does get through. Ultraviolet radiation is what stimulates the human skin to "tan," thus producing a barrier against the burning of the skin by further exposure to the sun. Over a long period of time, ultraviolet radiation may produce skin cancer. Dark skin, associated with individuals from tropical areas, reduces the risk of skin cancer. White skin, associated with individuals from northern areas, increases the ability of the skin to produce vitamin D, which helps prevent rickets but makes them more susceptible to skin cancer.

In sex cells or a fetus, if gamma rays strike the DNA, it may eliminate one of the base pairs. The DNA may attempt to repair itself. If it repairs itself with the same base pair, nothing will change. If it repairs itself with a new base pair, a mutation may result. If it is unable to repair itself, a spontaneous abortion may occur. About 10 to 20% of babies are spontaneously aborted, even if the mother does everything right. This is known as a miscarriage. Yet this is so little known that many women from actress Brooke Shield to princess Megan Markle, have reported serious feelings of depression following a miscarriage, as if it were their fault. This happens regardless of what we do or fail to do, it is nature's failure. But society has failed to educated people to understand this.

https://www.mayoclinic.org/diseases-conditions/pregnancy-loss-miscarriage/symptoms-causes/syc-20354298

As with x-rays, ultraviolet radiation becomes visible only when special sensing devices are used. Photographers can encounter ultraviolet rays when attempting to take pictures at high altitudes in the mountains. The radiation shows up on color film as a distinct haze, and the photographer is often surprised to find that what appeared to be a sparkling landscape through the viewfinder now seems nothing more than a misty fog in the distance. Special UV lens filters are available which help to eliminate this ultraviolet haze.

Beyond the ultraviolet rays are infrared rays, which can also be picked up on special photographic film. Our skin picks this radiation up as "heat". Every object in the environment that gives off heat-from the human body to the metal in an idling automobile engine gives off infrared rays. Although these rays are less intense than the heat given off by the sun, they are of much the same order.

This phenomenon is the basis for various heat-sensing devices developed to track missiles, locate and destroy enemy aircraft, and detect ground troop movements from the air. Films specially sensitized for this type of radiation make it possible to photograph the heat given off by a running engine in total darkness. Even after the vehicle has been moved; it is possible to photograph the engine heat that had been absorbed by the sidewalk and surrounding air.

Again, all this may occur in what is total darkness to our eyes. The fact that the human body gives off heat in varying amounts has been exploited in photography techniques that allegedly capture the aura or halo around the human body. Such photography shows nothing supernatural, and results from such techniques can be duplicated simply by dilating or constricting the peripheral blood vessels at the surface of the skin.

In World War II special machines were devised to bounce infrared rays off objects in the environment. When equipped with a special sensing device to transduce the infrared radiation into light visible to the human eye, these "sniper scopes" could be used in the dead of the night to locate objects that otherwise would not be visible.

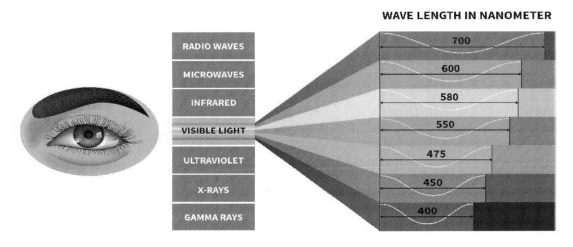

WAVE LENGTH IN NANOMETER

7. COLOR VISION:

The Frequency Receptors

The rods and cones of the retina

In a world where the vast majority of animals see reality in shades of gray, with occasional shades of yellow-green, humans share with other primates and the birds the ability to perceive the world in color. Color vision is especially useful to animals who have to navigate through the trees, as birds and early primates have. Color vision is believed to result from the highly specialized responses of the cones to different frequencies of electromagnetic radiation. The exact process by which this occurs is still unknown, but we know the cones absorb photons of light, causing chemical changes, and firing the nerve cell in much the same way as described for the rods.

TRICHROMATIC THEORY:

Three Types of Cones, different frequencies

There are two basic theories of how the incoming light is translated into color vision: (1) the *trichromatic,* or three-color theory; and (2) the *opponent-process* theory.

It is possible to reproduce virtually every color gradation by combining pure light sources of the three primary colors, blue, green, and red. The trichromatic theory assumes that there are three types of primary color receptors (cones), each sensitive to wavelengths in one of the three parts of the spectrum. The measurement of electrical impulses from the retina itself suggests that this assumption may be correct. The cones fire in numbers and combinations that depend on the wave-length of the light reaching the retina. When pure light sources of the three primary colors overlap, all cones fire and the result is "white" light.

The trichromatic theory has difficulty accounting for color blindness, which is found in about 7 percent of all males and 1 percent of all females. The most common color blindness is the inability to discriminate between reds and greens. Presumably what has happened is that the red and green color receptors respond equally to the same stimuli.

According to the trichromatic theory, however, we see yellow when the cones fire that are sensitive to wavelengths of red and green. How then, can someone who is blind to red and green nevertheless discriminate the color yellow?

OPPONENT-PROCESS THEORY

In the 1870s, Ewald Herring formulated a new theory to explain the facts of color blindness, as well as the mystery of color afterimages. Herring proposed that instead of three separate color receptors, there are four-red, green, yellow, and blue.

Further, the color receptors that are sensitive to red and green function together in pairs, as do the receptors sensitive to yellow and blue.

The advantage of Herring's theory is not readily apparent until one examines the phenomenon of color afterimages. The color receptors sensitive to a particular wavelength can tire in much the same way as lifting a heavy weight will fatigue the arm. If you stare at the color red for about thirty seconds, and then focus your eyes on a white piece of paper, you will see a very clear afterimage that is not red but green. Similarly, if you stare at something green, thus fatiguing the green sensitive receptors, the afterimage you see on a white sheet will be red. Identical results are obtained for the other paired colors-blue and yellow. To try this experiment, turn to the inside of the back cover and stare at the United States flag printed there in black, yellow, and green. Then look at a sheet of white paper. What do you see?

In normal vision, stimulation of one member of a pair, say red, inhibits the other member of the pair, the green. But after color adaptation takes place, then looking at a field of white reflected light will cause the remaining color process to overcompensate, resulting in the experience of the complementary color to which it has been paired.

After years of research, the phenomenon of color vision has still not been fully explained. At present, it looks as though both the trichromatic and the opponent-process theories are correct. The best information is that the trichromatic theory operates in the retina itself, while the opponent-process theory operates behind the retina, in a complex interconnection of neurons.

8. "IF A TREE FALLS IN THE FOREST..."

Now we are ready to take on the questions of "If a Tree Falls in the Forest..." and Sir John Eccles-and a host of new ones as well. What happens when a tree falls in the forest? To answer the question, it is necessary first to distinguish between the physical definition of sound and our perception of it.

In physics, sound is defined as the vibration of the molecules of the air. The fall of the tree will certainly set up vast waves of vibrations of air molecules. As we have seen, however, what we call *sound* can be produced in the human mind without these vibrations. When a tree falls or a whistle blows, the resulting vibrations stop at the cochlea, where they are transformed into electrical impulses. The electrical impulses, not the mechanical vibrations, are what reach the brain. Sound is a product of the machinery of the brain.

A similar problem exists when we try to define what we call light. As with sound, electromagnetic radiation never reaches the brain. The photons stop at the retina of the eye, where they are *transduced* into electrochemical impulses of the same type as those generated by the auditory neurons. Much like a computer, touch, hearing, and vision all rely on exactly the same type of electrical impulses going to different areas of the brain. Furthermore, we do not even need electromagnetic radiation to produce what we subjectively call light.

A familiar example is provided by the detective struck from behind by the butt of a gun as he enters a darkened room. The result? He "sees stars." A blow to the back of the head is sufficient to fire the neurons that cause the sensations of light. Identical reactions can be produced in a somewhat less distressing manner, one can see light in a totally darkened room by simply pressing hard on the eyeballs until the pressure begins to fire the neurons that are normally fired only by photons striking the retina. When an electrical probe is inserted into the visual neurons, an electrical stimulus can produce light.

The fact that cones respond only to specific wave lengths suggests that these brain cells are highly specialized in their response.

If other cells that receive sensory impulses are equally specialized in their functions, the area of the brain where the neurons terminate would be of extreme importance to allowing vision or hearing. The visual system is so complex, however, that it is impossible to say with certainty that how much of such specialized neural responses are a product of the visual cortex alone or of the visual system as a whole.

9. WHAT THE BRAIN RECEIVES:

SENSE	CELLS	STIMULUS	WHAT THE BRAIN RECIEVES
TOUCH	NERVE CELL	PRESSURE	ELECTRICAL IMPULSE
HEARING	CILIA CELLS	PRESSURE	ELECTRICAL IMPULSE
VISION	RODS/CONES	CHEMICAL CHANGE	ELECTRICAL IMPULSE

We are still left with one of the mysteries of brain research. Why do identical electrical impulses produce marked differences in the quality of sensation that we perceive? We know that different senses are received in different ways; hearing is sequential, vision is both sequential and a pattern.

Left: The sense of smell comes from chemicals floating through the air. Democritus guessed at atoms going through the air. Since the chemicals are made up of atoms, he was largely correct. Scents go almost directly to the brain itself.

Thus, anything you inhale is rapidly reacted to by the brain. Some drugs can directly damage the brain cells. We saw this again with Covid-19, an inhaled virus that led to a loss of the sense of smell as one of the first symptoms.

Scent is basic to the sexual behavior of most mammals, including our dogs, cats, and deer. The scent emitted during the "mating season" triggers sexual behavior in the estrus cycle. In humans, there is much less likelihood of scent being related to sex, even though French perfumes were often made from the sex glands of animals, which led to the near extinction of the Tibetan Musk deer, prized for its musky scent.

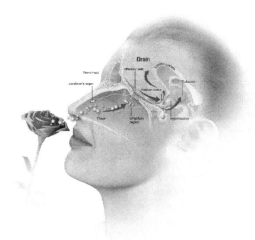

The physiologists and their microscopes have reduced the human mind to the complex interaction of nerve cells. Yet science does not detract from the great importance of the human being by attempting to show how the mind works through the interaction of the brain cells. The working of the human brain is a tremendous thing--tiny cells, neural networks, everything working together to produce human behavior. Although we have partly answered the question posed by Democritus, each answer and each discovery have raised a host of new questions that are as fascinating today as the nature of sensation in the Golden Age of Greece.

10. THE SIGNAL AND THE EXPERIENCE

The Brain Receives Only Electrical Impulses From all the Senses

The brain only receives the electrochemical impulses transmitted by the nerve cells. Not until these impulses reach the brain are they translated into what we perceive as touch or light or sound or smell. How can sensors that rely on such similar means of electrical communication possibly convey such widely different sensory experiences?

Several factors seem to be involved:

(1) the nature of the sense organs that receive the external stimuli,

(2) the frequency of firing of different neural connections,

(3) the patterns in which the neural connections fire, and

(4) the different locations in the brain where the neural connections are processed.

The eye and ear, for example, respond to entirely different types of stimuli. The ear responds only to mechanical vibrations- not to electromagnetic radiation. The receptors of the eye will fire to electromagnetic radiation, but they will not usually fire to a noticeable degree purely because of mechanical vibrations. Neurons of the eye and ear also differ in their pattern and frequency of firing and the different processing centers in the brain.

TOUCH: Is a simple stimulus that varies in frequency, or how often the nerve(s) fires.

SOUND: A variety of different frequencies that occur in sequence.

VISION: Light varies in frequency, sequence, and especially in producing a pattern.

Must we explain these differences based on what we now know about the interaction of cells? Or are there some factors, as yet undiscovered, that will eventually provide a revolution in our understanding of how the mind perceives the myriad variations of our environment. There is no hint of what new revelations may be forthcoming, and thus we must make the best of the information we do have.

To this day, we cannot explain how these complex nerve impulses produce what we subjectively call touch, sound, light, and color. Perhaps someday one of those reading this text will be awarded the Nobel Prize for figuring it out.

The reflected light from objects in the environment passes through the lens of the eye and is focused on the retina in definite shapes, patterns, and sizes, which vary in shading from black to gray to white. The neurons that are exposed to the lighter shades fire almost continually.

In contrast, neural firings in the ear, occur not in projected images, but in a sequence. One frequency follows another frequency as sound waves strike the cochlea, just as words in a sentence follow each other. We interpret visual stimuli from changes in the patterns and sequences of neural firing. Auditory stimuli, however, are more likely interpreted as a combination of sequence and frequency rather than pattern.

The senses of taste and smell also respond to very specific stimuli in the form of chemicals, which are quite different from the stimuli associated with hearing and sight. Furthermore, the chemicals that trigger the sense of taste may be quite different from those that trigger the sense of smell.

There is another possible explanation for the differences between the sensations. It may be that the auditory cortex of the brain to which the auditory neurons send their impulses is quite different than the area of the brain where the visual processing ends up, in the visual cortex. In other words, the cells of the visual cortex may respond to the electrical impulses that they receive in a manner quite different from that in which the nerve cells in the auditory cortex respond to the electrical impulses from the auditory system.

In an extreme example, this theory would suggest that if you hooked up the auditory neurons to the visual cortex, you would "see" noise as light; by hooking up the optic nerve to the auditory cortex, you could "hear" light as noise.

In contrast, the theory that the major differences are due to the nature of the receptor and the pattern and frequencies of nerve firings would predict that in such an arrangement, we would merely see in our auditory cortex where the optic nerve was now positioned and hear in the formal visual cortex where now the auditory nerve would be. There seems to be some truth in both theories, but no one is yet prepared to say exactly what is happening.

The discovery by Hubel and Weisel that some nerve cells in the visual cortex respond to horizontal lines, others to vertical lines, and still others to lines of specific lengths suggests that these brain cells are highly specific in their response.

If other cells that receive sensory impulses are equally specialized in their functions, the area of the brain where the neurons terminate would be of importance to allowing vision or hearing. The visual system is so complex, however, that it is impossible to say with certainty. It seems likely that there is much processing of the sensory input before it ever reaches the cortex.

We are still left with one of the mysteries of brain research. Why do seemingly identical electrical impulses produce marked differences in the quality of sensation that we perceive? Must we explain these differences based on what we now know about the interaction of cells? Or is there some factor, as yet undiscovered, that will eventually provide a revolution in our understanding of how the mind perceives the myriad variations of our environment? There is no clear hint as to what new revelations may be forthcoming, and thus we must make the best of the information we do have.

The physiologists and their microscopes have reduced the human mind to the complex interaction of nerve cells. Yet science does not detract from the great importance of the human being by attempting to show how the mind works through the interaction of the brain cells. The working of the human brain is a tremendous thing-tiny cells, neural networks, and everything working together to produce human behavior.

Although we have partly answered the question posed by Hippocrates and Sir John Eccles, each answer and each discovery has raised a host of new questions that are as fascinating today as the nature of sensation in the Golden Age of Greece.

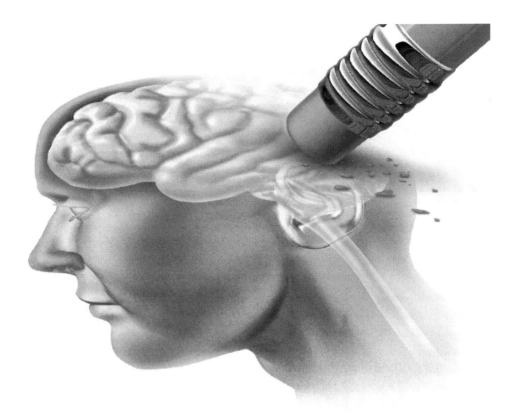

7 THE CONSCIOUS MIND

"THE GHOST IN THE MACHINE"

"... I was faced with a great puzzle. I was studying some of those patients with large chunks of their brain removed and could find nothing wrong with intelligence, consciousness unimpaired, which was indeed, a very great puzzle. In the years that followed, I developed what might be called, I think fairly, a crackpot theory; that thinking consisted of the interaction between brain cells, nothing more, that consciousness and intelligence is a function of the interaction of brain cells... it implied that man is a complex organism, complex beyond my imagining, complex beyond, beyond any of the words of the mind and all this with no evidence of the supernatural at all."

Donald O. Hebb, Psychologist, Chancellor, McGill University

The Mind of Man

One great lingering mystery of the human brain is: What causes consciousness? Textbooks have often noted that we have no clear ability to study consciousness so, instead, we study altered states of consciousness; sleep, drugs, and hypnosis.

Yet there seems to be at least a partial answer to the question of consciousness, although not every psychologist will agree. The electroencephalograph (EEG) gives us only a gross measure of brain wave activity in the brain. It cannot tell us anything about specific thoughts or why we behave as we do. But it does give us an informative picture of what is related to varied states of consciousness.

1. BRAIN WAVES AND CONSCIOUSNESS

In normal wakefulness, the alpha waves dominate with a frequency of 9 to 13Hz. But Beta waves are fast frequency waves that occur only when we are awake and *focusing* our attention on a problem, cycling at 15 to 30 times per second.

One Hz is equal to one cycle per second. If you are paying attention, your brain is now cycling 15 to 30 times each second as you read this.

When we are asleep, we see slow waves of around 2 cycles per second sweeping across the brain. In dreaming, spindle bursts of up to 12 Hz may occur.

Gamma waves are the most extreme form of excitation, at 30 to 80 Hz. They occur when we are intensely interested in what we are focused on, to the exclusion of other input. This is often accompanied by an emotion; from love, which may make us silly, to the Fight or Flight response, involving anxiety or anger, even to a breakdown of our ability.. This may make us on edge, ready to make an instant move, or to focus on a problem of importance to us.

The speed of the waves that scan across the brain is dramatically correlated with the state of consciousness.

HUMAN BRAIN
WAVES

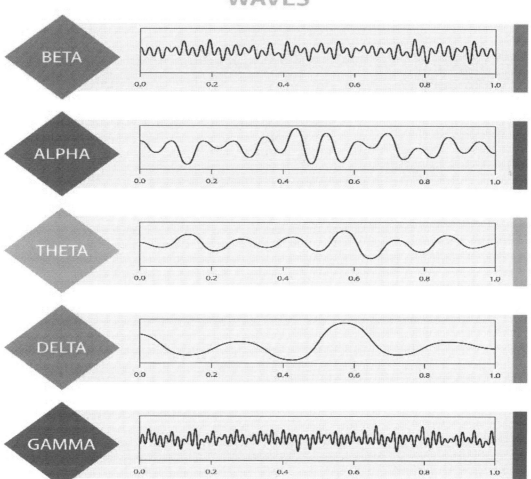

This has led to the theory that the brain waves function as, or indicate, a "Google Scan", coursing through the cortex at high speed when we are focused, slowing somewhat for a restful state of being awake. And finally dropping down dramatically for sleep and a loss of conscious focus.

Alphabet, the parent company of Google, is working on creating an Artificial Intelligence, a computer that can mimic the thinking of the human mind. Of course, a computer does not perceive reality in the same way, with the same mechanism.

There is one remarkable similarity between a computer and the brain, that is, the use of contrast and comparison, such as what a computer does at a "decision diamond" in a flowchart, or a choice point (it compares two variables, or patterns, to determine whether to go on to the next step, or to return to a previous step.

As in an internet search engine, the waves may course through our brain, picking up bits and pieces of information, generalizing it into a thought or idea, and pushing this to the forefront of our awareness. As the brain waves drift slower, we gradually lose our train of thought and lose our consciousness.

By this analogy, our memory system is like the internet, a depository of vast quantities of information, often generalized into concepts or ideas, awaiting only a scan for a word, action, or concept. The brain waves are a scanning device that flutters through the cortex, picking up those bits and pieces of information and presenting them as a completed action or thought.

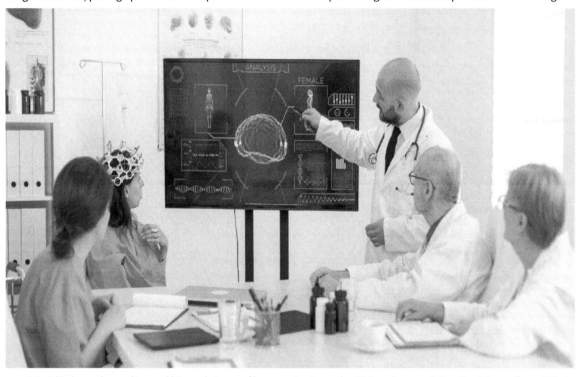

Most likely, we have glimpsed bits and pieces of how our brain works. Yet we have only touched the surface. What about how we perceive reality itself? See Chapter 9,

This has led to the theory that the brain waves function as, or indicate, a "Google Scan", coursing through the cortex at high speed when we are focused, slowing somewhat for a restful state of being awake. And finally dropping down dramatically for sleep and a loss of conscious focus.

Denis Gabor developed the holograph based on interference patterns instead of a picture. This led to the possibility of memory being analogous to a hologram, spread throughout the brain. Karl Pribram, in his book *Languages of the Brain*, developed this idea as organized waves from the cortex to the basal ganglia.

Alphabet, the parent company of Google, is working on creating an Artificial Intelligence, a computer that can mimic the thinking of the human mind.

Similar to an internet search engine, the waves may course through our brain, picking up bits and pieces of information, generalizing it into a thought or idea, and pushing this to the forefront of our awareness. As the brain waves drift slower, we gradually lose our train of thought and lose our consciousness.

By this analogy, our memory system is like the internet, a depository of vast quantities of information, often generalized into concepts or ideas, awaiting only a scan for a general word, action, or concept. The brain waves are a scanning device that flutters through the cortex, picking up those bits and pieces of information and presenting them as a completed action or thought.

All of this relates to the comment by Donald Hebb that began this chapter. If consciousness is a result of the rapid scanning of the cortex, a scan that allows us to make our way through the world, then it makes sense that there is no one area of the brain where consciousness is found. Instead, consciousness is spread throughout the brain, read by the scan of associations in all areas of the brain.

To see another modern interpretation of consciousness, check out the following:

Your brain hallucinates your conscious reality | Anil Seth
https://www.youtube.com/watch?v=lyu7v7nWzfo
And also check out *The Neuroscience of Consciousness*
https://www.youtube.com/watch?v=xRel1JKOEbI
Or go to youtube.com and search for Special Parts of the Human Brain.

2. SELECTIVE ATTENTION AND CONCENTRATION

In a brilliant study by Donald Broadbent, he arranged headsets that would play different stories in each ear. Students were told to only listen to the story in the left ear, others were told to only listen to the story in the right ear. Then he would have them answer questions about both stories.

Those who were told to only listen to the story in the left year, could mostly only answer questions about that story, not the other story, and vice versa.

Selective Attention to only one thing, seems to shut out incoming input from our other senses. It may work the same way with pain, as long as we are focused intently on, say, the voice of the hypnotist, or the work we are doing.

4. TWO BRAINS AND THE CORPUS CALLOSUM

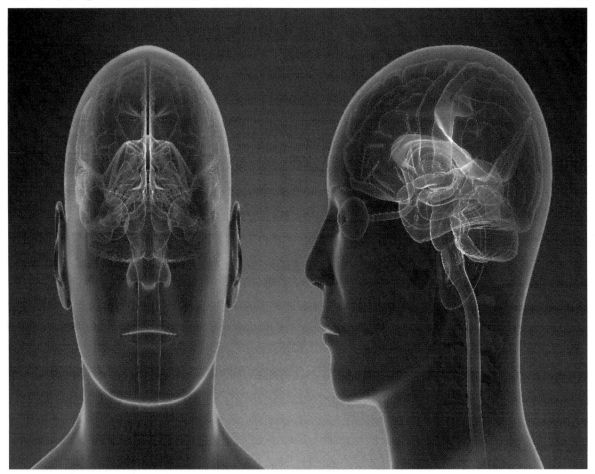

The brain of man, like that of all animals is double, being parted down its centre by a thin membrane. For this reason pain is not always felt in the same part of the head, but sometimes on one side, sometimes on the other, and occasionally all over.

Hippocrates in *The Sacred Disease*, trans. W. H. S. Jones

We have two arms, two legs, two eyes, two ears, and two nostrils. It should come as no great surprise that we also have two brains. Hippocrates noted this from his dissections of animals and humans. Yet it took 2,400 years to realize just how remarkable this is. We theoretically have the capability of having two conscious minds within the same body.

In the normal course of life, this is of no concern, as the left and right brains are exposed to the same experiences throughout life. The information received from one brain instantly crosses over to the other brain via the corpus callosum.

Seizures involve the firing of massive numbers of nerves. They typically begin on one side of the brain, cross over the corpus callosum to the other side of the brain, and debilitate the other side as well. Intractable seizures can happen over a hundred times a day.

Where it is not possible to control such seizures with medication, one useful technique is to sever the connection between the two brains. This does not stop the seizures, but it limits the seizures to only one side of the brain, where the problem lies. The other side is still conscious, and able to maintain some control during the seizures.

Before doctors ever used the split-brain method on humans, studies were done on cats. They trained a cat with both the corpus callosum and the optical chiasm separated, to ensure that the visual information only went to one or the other side of the brain. Then they trained a cat on a visual task with each eye. When a patch was placed over the left eye of the cat, it learned to always find food-for example, behind a certain object-by using its right eye. If the patch was then taken from the left eye and placed on the right eye, the animal was unable to perform the same task that it had performed easily before.

The visual information received by the right eye went to the right side of the brain, and that received by the left eye went only to the left side of the brain. Because there was no means within the brain of exchanging information, the left eye and the left brain did not know what was seen by the right eye and the right brain. It was as if they were operating within two separate animals.

The implications of this finding for psychology is interesting. It should now be quite easy to do a classic hypothetical study in psychology. Beginning with a young animal with a severed corpus callosum, would it not be possible to train one side of the brain to react fearfully to certain stimuli and the other side of the brain to react positively to the same stimuli? In effect, you would have two animals within one body exhibiting markedly different reactions to the same stimuli. The centuries-old question of the difference between one's biological individuality and one's learning experiences could then be studied.

In the adult human patient, however, both sides of the brain have grown up with the same experiences. Both sides have experienced the same reality. Both sides have had the same experiences and the same memory. Stimuli are tagged with the same emotion, and words have the same meaning. The two sides cooperate, and instead of responding differently to the same stimuli, they respond with a relatively good degree of coordination. Thus, the differences are far more subtle in an adult with the two sides separated, and can be revealed only through careful testing.

Roger Sperry and Michael Gazzaniga have conducted extensive tests of more than half a dozen patients who have undergone the operation to sever the nerves of the corpus callosum. Their experiments indicated the existence of a dual consciousness. For almost all people, the left side of the brain is the verbal side of the brain. The right side of the brain has only limited ability to control speech. The left side of the brain normally dominates our speech and directs our behavior.

The functions of the two sides of the brain and the role of the corpus callosum can be studied by observing the patient's responses to tactile, visual, and auditory stimuli presented to one side of the brain or the other. If we place a plastic number in the left hand of a patient whose corpus callosum has been severed, the patient can feel it but cannot verbally indicate what the number is. This is true because sensation from the left side of the body goes to the right (nonverbal) side of the brain. The patient can, however, signal the number by holding up the same number of fingers on his or her left hand. Patients do this with unfailing accuracy, yet they are unable to say verbally the number the left hand has felt.

The verbal left side of the brain has received no sensory feedback from the left hand; it knows only what the *right*-hand feels. It has not seen or touched the number held in the left hand. It cannot tell what the number was, and it cannot guess with accuracy any better than chance

If visual stimuli are presented to the left side of the brain, then the patients can say what it is that they see. If they see something only with the right side, they cannot tell you what they see, they cannot even guess at it. Yet, they may be able to indicate with their left hand, perhaps by writing, what it was that they saw.

In one case, Sperry and Gazzaniga used a special stimulus-presenting device that presented slide pictures to just the right side of the brain. One picture happened to be that of a naked lady. This picture was shown to a female patient, who immediately reacted by giggling and blushing. Yet the verbal side of her brain did not know what was going on. She responded by saying, in effect, *"I don't know what happened. I know something happened, but I don't know what it was."*

Observations of patients with split brains give some indications of a dual consciousness even under more ordinary conditions. In one case, a patient was working on a task with his right hand, a task involving drawing or spatial relations, which were better handled by his left hand. He was surprised to find that his left-hand kept interfering with the task his right hand was trying to do. As he tried to do the problem with his right hand under the direction of his verbal brain, the left-hand kept butting in to try to correct mistakes the right hand was making.

All this poses a problem for psychologists who advocate that we find our "real self." If there can be two of us within the same body, then what does this mean to our individuality? Of course, normally we do not have to worry about this. So long as both sides function simultaneously- that is, so long as they are connected, they cannot function independently as separate selves. But the demonstration that dual consciousness is possible is a shocking discovery for most of us.

For a more extensive review of the important information about the brain go to this hard science example of both the discoveries and the problem of being too close to the forest to see the trees by a pioneer in brain research, Michael Gazzaniga:

https://www.youtube.com/watch?v=tz-L2Ll85rM

ART AND THE RIGHT BRAIN

The right side of the brain also has some unique functions. Normally, right-handed individuals can write or draw better with their right hand than with their left. When the corpus callosum has been severed, however, the situation is reversed. Now they can draw as well with their left hand as they ever could (that is, not well, but as well as ever), but their ability to draw with their right hand may be impaired. They may even be unable to draw pictures of circles or squares or boxes, though they can do so, as poorly as ever, with their left hand.

This finding suggests that the right side of the brain normally controls spatial relations and communicates its knowledge to the left side of the brain across the corpus callosum. When the callosum is severed, the left side of the brain is on its own and its ability to draw seems quite limited according to Gazzaniga.

Musical ability also seems to be associated with the right cerebral hemisphere. The Russian composer, Vissarion Shebalin suffered two strokes that damaged the left side of his brain and rendered him unable to speak. Yet he was able to compose music and play music with one hand. Over the next few years, he completed his fifth symphony, which colleagues hailed as a masterpiece.

One of the first clients I ever worked with was Leon Blox, a man whose art was once displayed in the Capitol rotunda in Austin. Yet he was unable to make change for a dollar and his tested I.Q. was in the 50s. I retested him again as I thought it must be a mistake. But no, he scored in the 50s again. I.Q. tests favor verbal ability, this area was compromised in his brain. Yet his artistic ability was still intact.

Studies such as cases like Shebalin and Blox, has led investigators to note that the left side of the brain is most closely associated with symbolic abilities such as verbal concepts and math, whereas the right side is more closely associated with imagination, patterns, and spatial perceptions, as in art and music.

This would have required mutations that allowed the right side of the brain to recognize **patterns**; Patterns of visual stimuli (art) and patterns of auditory stimuli (music).

Damage to one side of the brain may leave the other intact, and still able to function.

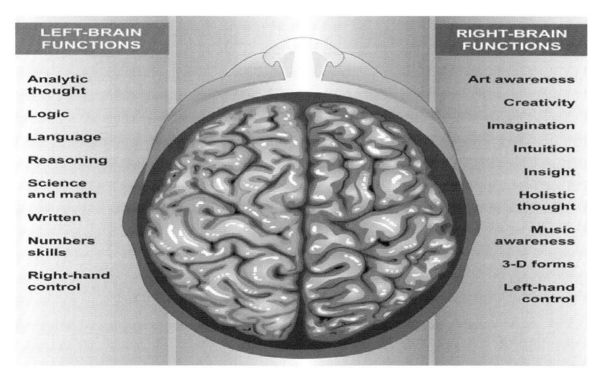

There is still some uncertainty about whether creativity, intuition, and insight are localized in the right side of the brain, but the two sides have different processing abilities. As a general rule, the left side of the cortex is associated with *language and math*, both essential to your score on an I.Q. test, while the right side is associated with *pattern recognition* such as visual-spatial relations, as in art and music. Pattern recognition involves sequences of tones, as in music, and both *sequence and pattern recognition* in art (or tool making).

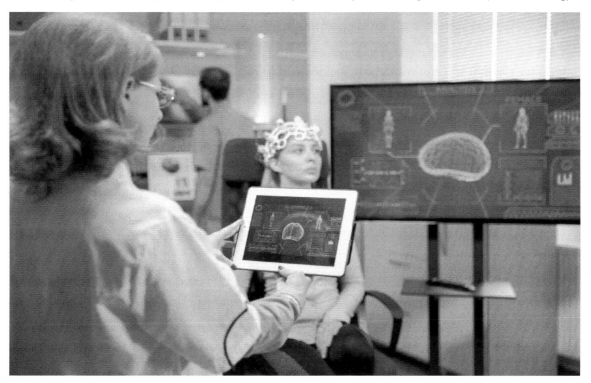

5. THE DILEMMA OF ANTHROPOLOGY
HUMAN EVOLUTION, MUTATIONS, AND THE BRAIN
Processing *Patterns* Of Vision And Hearing

The stories of Shebalin and Blox suggest that before we became "fully" human, it would not only have required new mutations to our DNA to produce Broca's Area and Wernicke's Area in the left side of the brain, but also mutations that gave the right hemisphere of the brain the unique abilities that allow for spatial perception and musical coding or pattern recognition. The right brain mutations would have also been related to our ability to produce tools (arrowheads, axes, sewing needles, better shelters, etc.).

This suggests that at least three major mutations, or even multiple mutations, would be required to give us the unique abilities of the human brain. First, for Broca's area, to give us the ability to mimic words and sounds. Second, for Wernicke's area to give us the ability to process sounds (by associating sounds with the real world). And third, at least one "*pattern*" mutation that would have given the right side of the brain the ability to process visual stimuli into *patterns* (art) and auditory stimuli into *patterns* (music).

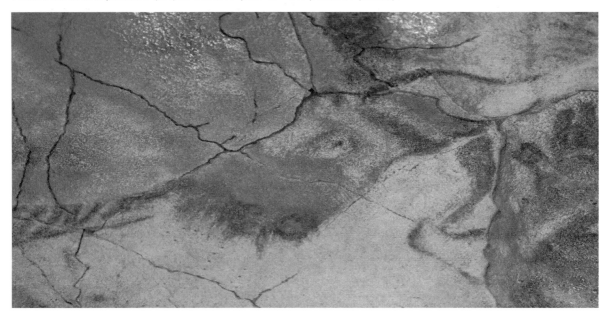

Cave drawing of a primitive bull (Auroch) from Altamira Spain, approximately 30,000 years ago.

It may not be necessary to have unique mutations for other abilities, simply associating them with the three types of major mutations may have been enough to dramatically increase the brain's ability to process information. The greatest difference in size between chimpanzees and humans is in the association areas of the frontal lobe, temporal lobe, and parietal/occipital lobes.

We can no longer assume that walking upright or having a larger brain can indicate when we developed our current ability. Neanderthals had a brain size of 1650 ccs compared to modern man's 1350ccs. it is not the size of the brain, but the mutations that gave us unique biological programs for processing information. This presents a difficulty for anthropologists who hope to identify which of the human ancestors became "fully" human. The remarkable human ability to process flint into arrowheads (over 100,000 years ago), or produce the extraordinarily beautiful cave paintings dating from 35,000 to 40,000 years ago indicates that this ability might have come before speech. The ability to "flint knap" or knock off pieces of flint to make an arrowhead, would have required the spatial and pattern recognition of the right side of the brain. This may have further evolved into the ability to represent symbolic images in art. Yet this seems to have been separate from the verbal ability of the left side of the brain. There is no clear fossil record of the origin of these separate abilities.

6. HYPNOSIS

Hypnosis has a shadowed history. Accounts of hypnotic regression to an earlier age, or even to a previous life, have little evidence to support their claims. Using hypnosis to dig up earlier "repressed" memories has sometimes led to grossly misleading information.

https://www.scientificamerican.com/article/hypnosis-experts-cast-doubt-on-famous-psychological-experiments/

However, there are some things we know that seem important. First, not everyone can be hypnotized, only about 20% of subjects can go into a trance-like state which resembles a stage of "hypnogogic" sleep where we are partly asleep and partly awake, as if we are aware of relatives talking elsewhere in the house, but still are in a state of semi-sleep. It may be that most of us do not want to give up our self-control and resist going into a deeper state.

But one thing that has been confirmed about hypnosis is that those who are hypnotizable can endure the pain that the rest of us would not. How can this be? Pain is pain?

Think about this, has there ever been a time when you were working in the garden or working on your car and you cut yourself but did not notice it at the time? Later, when you relax, you suddenly notice the pain? The brain can focus so intently on what we are doing that we do not notice other stimuli, even pain.

Students may experience this when they are studying (or more likely, playing games on the computer) and the other relatives are talking, yelling, or playing the TV loudly, yet we hardly notice because of our intense focus on what we are doing.

All of this is related to the studies of Donald Broadbent that first showed that if students were told to concentrate on the story being played through headphones, but to ignore the story being played in the other ear, they could selectively attend to such a degree, that they could only answer only the questions about the story they were paying attention to.

7. MURDER, FEAR, EVIL SPIRITS AND THE ELEMENTS OF PSYCHOLOGY

In a study of how fear spreads, a television series, *Unexplained History*, hired a hypnotist, John Pullum to work with seven people who volunteered for a night at a "haunted" house. They prepared the subjects by saying that someone was killed here and found buried in the walls of the house. The subjects were told they were to test the hypnotist who was claiming to be a psychic, to see if he had psychic powers; although that was not the real test.

https://www.youtube.com/watch?v=aEeJKWgA7yQ

The people were then allowed to overhear the hypnotist/psychic loudly talking to the producer saying, *"Don't B--- S--- me, I know someone was killed in this house",* to give the subjects the impression that the hypnotist was psychic (the "power" of suggestion).

After a few tests, the volunteers were told that something happened at a place outside the house, and they were given a pendant to hold to see if it moved, presumably indicating a spirit presence. One at a time the students went out to sit alone in the dark, holding the pendant.

Of the seven students, only three found the pendant moved. Two said they heard voices, like the voices of children off to the left. One said she heard running water, off to the left. All told their stories, all three felt a spirit presence, yet four had no psychic experiences.

At the end of the experiment, *all* seven people came to believe that there was a spirit presence even though four said they felt nothing. Why were all of them convinced even though only three said they had the experience? Because all heard the spooky account given by the three, and that was enough to convince all of the people.

Just *words* convinced them.

Finally, the hypnotist confessed he was not a psychic and that no one had been murdered in the house, the house was a movie prop, it was all a plant in an attempt to set them up for a Salem-style witch hunt, where all came to believe in witches from the testimony of a few. It worked out even better than they had expected.

We see this same use of associations with stories, with emotions, that are used on television to convince millions of viewers of ghosts, Ancient Aliens, UFOs, Big Foot, and even demons are real. Words are all it takes, especially when combined with emotional stories told by "eyewitnesses".

Politicians use the same techniques, associating words with emotions. One can imagine our primitive ancestors, sitting around a campfire, listening in awe to the shaman and storytellers of their tribe, entertaining them with stories of the supernatural. Today, the Shaman have been replaced by Hollywood, Politics, and the Media, peddling fiction to eager minds. It is a failure of our educational system at every level.

This illustrates many important ideas in psychology.

1. **Selective Attention**; focus everyone's attention on one idea. The effect of Selective Attention was demonstrated by Donald Broadbent's study of different stories told in each ear, yet they only remembered the story they were asked to pay attention to. Also seen in the above account, setting them up to think about someone being killed in the house, and in today's politics, where one idea is trumpeted even as more serious ideas are ignored.

2. **Power of Suggestion or simple association**: Using nothing but words, the idea of supernatural presence was communicated to all individuals that someone had been killed. Again, as in the example above. All it takes are words. How this can happen is the subject of Chapter 8 on the *Quest for the Mind Code*.

3. **Social Contagion**: Because three people *said* they experienced something spooky, *all* of them came to believe in their experience. All it took were *words*. The four who had no spooky experience, came to believe, because the other three people said they had a spooky experience.

   Yet we see all of these factors come into play in today's culture, without hypnosis, just with the three factors noted above. In politics, despite not having a shred of evidence, people came to believe because others believed. It was a recreation of the thousands of years of witch hunts, in real-time, something we could all see happening, even without a scientific experiment.

   We have seen this repeatedly in recent years when 900 people, in the reverend Jim Jones religious cult, committed suicide by drinking the poisoned Kool-Aid, hence the expression "they drank the Kool-Aid" when people believe something just because others do.

   We see it again in the Heaven's Gate cult where 36 convinced believers drank poison so they could be transported to a new plane of reality by going to the spaceship they were told was awaiting them behind the Hale-Bopp comet in the night sky.

   We see it in the election of 2020 so many came to believe that the election was stolen, just because others believed, and that Anderson Cooper, A CNN newscaster, was drinking the blood of children, and that the government was controlled by a "cabal of Satan worshiping pedophiles", and that the Pandemic of Covid 19 was just "Fake News".

   We see it today in how many Americans came to believe in ideas without evidence. Nothing is more important to get across to people than to understand how these things occur, to prevent our youth from believing, just because others do.

   Hypnosis is not some magical process beyond our understanding. It can be reduced to known processes of the human brain; selective attention, social contagion, and the power of words (suggestion or simple association) to focus our thoughts. All of these variables operate in our most basic perceptions of interpersonal interaction, learning, politics, and more.

8. SLEEP AND DREAMING

Throughout the night, people's eyes will rapidly move back and forth under their eyelids. If someone is awakened during REM sleep, they usually report they were dreaming. Researchers have studied sleep in the laboratory, keeping track of brain waves, sleep cycles, and REM sleep. REM stands for Rapid Eye Movement.

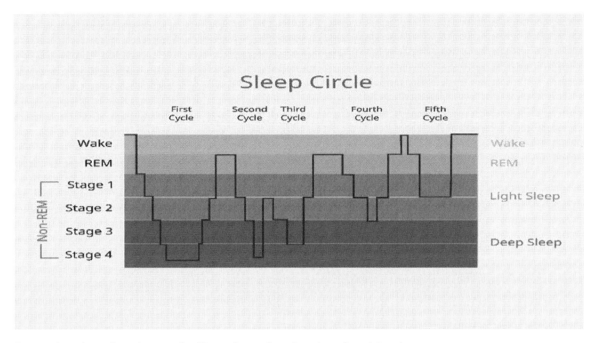

Researchers have found some significant facts after decades of studying dreams:

•   Dreams reflect our past experiences. Primitive societies do not dream about color television sets, they dream about fishing or planting, or whatever is common to their culture. I remember one of the few times I dreamed in color when I was about 12 years old. I dreamed we just got a new color television for Christmas. Yes, in the Dark Ages, TVs were once only black and white. When I got up in the morning, the dream was so vivid I ran into the living room to see the color television. But it was only a dream. Natives from the outback are unlikely to dream about television.

•   Dreams do not predict the future. As with being awake, we make predictions throughout the day about what may happen, but we mostly only remember the few when it happens to come true, not the times we do not get the color TV.

•   Dreams occur periodically throughout the night, as often as three to five times a night. We rarely remember any of them.

•   Even people who say they do not dream, report dreaming when awoken in a REM stage.

•   When asleep, the brain shuts down our motor movements to prevent us from acting out our dreams. In people who sleepwalk, this mechanism may not be working as well.

•   The feeling of falling, common in dreams, seems to result when one is in a state of half asleep, half awake, perhaps related to coming out of the damping down of our motor movements.

•   Dreams seem to function in a similar way to daydreams. If we are bored, the mind seems to wander to Cancun, etc., self-stimulating as a general way to avoid boredom. Babies REM far more than adults. It seems unlikely that they are dreaming in the same way as adults. Self-stimulation of the brain seems to be necessary for normal brain function. Dreams may be only a byproduct of that necessary stimulation.

•   Sleep seems to function as a time to recover from work as well as a means of consolidating memory in the brain.

We rarely remember our dreams for long. Sigmund Freud, who considered dreams as a window into our unconscious mind, found that he had to keep a paper and pencil next to his bed, so that he could immediately write down what he was dreaming about before it disappeared. If we do not rehearse the dream when we wake up, it will rarely go onto long-term memory. Much like studying for an exam.

Going to sleep in a sleep lab, where you know other people are watching you, is not easy. It may take several nights before someone becomes accustomed enough to relax.

"I read a story. Dr. Ehrlich is making rain sounds. Now why don't you just shut up and go to sleep?!"

"I think he's fake sleeping"

Children often have nightmares or even night terrors. It is important to reassure children that dreams are not real, they are fiction, just like the cartoons they see on TV.

Anxiety triggers nightmares, especially when they have heard stories of boogiemen, demons, zombies, and more from other children or on television. Reassuring them that dreams are not real, may help prevent the problem.

9. THE RETICULAR FORMATION: ESSENTIAL TO CONSCIOUNESS.

Coming out of the spinal cord is a mass of neurons that extends throughout the brain to the cortex. The Reticular Formation is essential to being awake. If this formation is severed as it comes out of the spinal cord, the animal will go into a coma. If an electrode is implanted into the Reticular Formation, and stimulated, the stimulation will wake up the animal.

This area of the brain appears to be intimately associated with what produces the conscious mind. Without stimulation, and the following arousal, consciousness could not exist.

Many neuropsychologists consider this to be a seat of the conscious mind, or at least an essential brain process that allows the conscious mind to function. This area is likely to be a major area of study in the effort to understand the conscious mind.

Yet what we mean by the conscious mind is more than simply being awake. It implies an awareness of what is going on around us, an ability to seamlessly make our way throughout the world on our own. This same Reticular Formation seems basic to controlling another brain function, the brain waves that determine the level of consciousness. This we can measure with an Electroencephalograph (EEG). The EEG allows us to monitor the stages of consciousness.

10. THE CONSCIOUS MIND

Psychologists and neurologists do not all agree as to what consciousness is. But this is the closest approximation of what the evidence suggests. Consciousness appears to be a combination of:

- **SCANNING**: The scanning mechanism of the brain allows us to immediately find a generalization of past stored information, (as in the scanning speed in an EEG) much like a google scan, that sets our ability to focus on specific information or a general image. The Reticular Formation, that keeps us awake and responds to novel changes in stimuli, may mediate the process.

- **ANTICIPATION**: The ability of the biology of the brain to anticipate what is going to happen next, based on our past experience (as in Pavlov's dog salivating to the bell in anticipation of food).

- **FOCUS**: The ability of the brain to focus our attention on whatever stimuli are most important or novel at the moment (as shown by Broadbent's study of students with headphones with different stories told in each ear, focusing only on one story) and also the P300 brain wave that reacts to novel stimuli. It grabs our attention.

- **SPEED:** The relatively high speed of neural connections that mask what is happening. This gives us an apparently *seamless continuity with the reality* around us.

Many psychologists believe that consciousness is the most important mystery in the human brain. Yet, the evidence suggests that almost all animals that have a cortex, and consciousness, a product of the brain itself, combined with our anticipatory experiences. That does not mean the same thing as self-awareness. We could make a good case that even humans are only vaguely self-aware. Perhaps the single most important human ability is not consciousness but our unique ability to use symbols (words, thoughts, sign language, codes) to communicate with others. See chapter 12 on *The Symbol* to attempt to analyze our verbal ability.

Even more basic, is to understand how the brain is programmed by our experiences in our environment in a way that makes it possible to anticipate what comes next. See *The Mind Code, Perception, and Culture* (Ch 8 and 9).

More basic still, is the fact that the environment changes the biology of the brain itself so completely, that we see different realities, based on our experiences. See the most recent evidence in Chapter 9 on *Perception,* dealing with cataracts in babies and how illusions became the potshards of our past experiences.

Perhaps the most viable explanation for the conscious mind is that it is based on a form of Google scan, related to the scanning waves of the brain. Stimuli we encounter can be scanned rapidly, allowing the brain to anticipate what to do next. Even Pavlov's dog could anticipate what would follow the stimulus of the bell.

"I'm trying to organize a stampede, but everybody's got her own agenda."

The relatively high speed of the neurons allows a largely seamless ability to make our way throughout the environment. It allows us to anticipate what will happen next, even without the need for conscious awareness.

As the speed of the scanning waves goes up, we have focused attention. As the speed of the scanning waves goes down, we lose our selective attention, and go toward an unconscious level of sleep. Yet, there is no general agreement as to what is happening in consciousness. Getting neuroscientists or psychologists to agree on consciousness, is a lot like "herding cats". Only much harder.

11. WHY DO PSYCHOLOGISTS SPEND SO MUCH TIME STUDYING THE BRAIN?

We study the brain because it tells us something profound about what the brain can do, and about what the brain cannot do. It is just as important to know the limits of the brain's ability as it is to know its strength.

What psychologists would want to know is not just about the chemicals in the brain, but about the wiring of the brain itself and our learned programs. With more than 85 billion neurons and trillions of connections, it is most unlikely that we will ever be able to trace a single thought in the brain. Yet knowing about these connections would tell us more than just knowing about what is at the synapse. Why do we study the brain instead of the programs in the brain?

Much of the reason is that recent studies suggest that memory may be encoded at the synapse, or by the growth of new synapses. Yet this may tell us little about what is important to psychology; which is the nature of the programs and memories in the brain.

It is a little bit like the Abraham Kaplan story of the drunk and the streetlight. A man comes along late at night and sees a drunk crawling around on his hands and knees under a streetlight.

He asks the drunk, "What are you doing?"

The drunk says, "I've lost my key, can you help me find it?"

So, the man gets down on his knees and crawls around with the drunk looking for the lost key. After a while, the man is ready to give up and he asks the drunk, "Where were you exactly when you lost the key?"

The drunk replies, "I was over there, in the alley."

Exasperated, the man replies, "If you were over there in the alley, why are you looking over here under the lamp post?"

The drunk replies, "Cause the light is better over here."

Why do we study the brain and neurotransmitters instead of brain programs?   Cause the light is better. And neural connections are too complex to track. Of course, we have learned a great amount about how complex the brain is with different chemicals for different purposes. The more we know the better off we are.

However, no studies of fMRIs or PET scans can tell us anything about the learned programs of behavior that are in the brain.

Yet, psychology has found ways of inferring what the connections are, without even looking inside the skull; by studying the relationship between stimuli and responses and intervening variables in the real world. Psychology, Sociology, and Cultural Anthropology all give us a window into how we have been programmed by the environment. Understanding that, is much of what the study of psychology is about.

Everything we can learn about the biology of the human brain is very important. Everything we learn about the influence or our biochemistry contributes to our understanding. Yet biology is not what the human mind is about. It is about the programs subtly embedded in the mind by the forces of society and experience. Only by understanding these forces can we understand the ideas, the emotions, the beliefs that shape our lives and determine our reality.

"All our knowledge has its origins in our perceptions." Leonardo da Vinci

Yet, our understanding of reality comes from our perceptions. How? Next, see Chapters 8 and 9 on how the mind is formed.

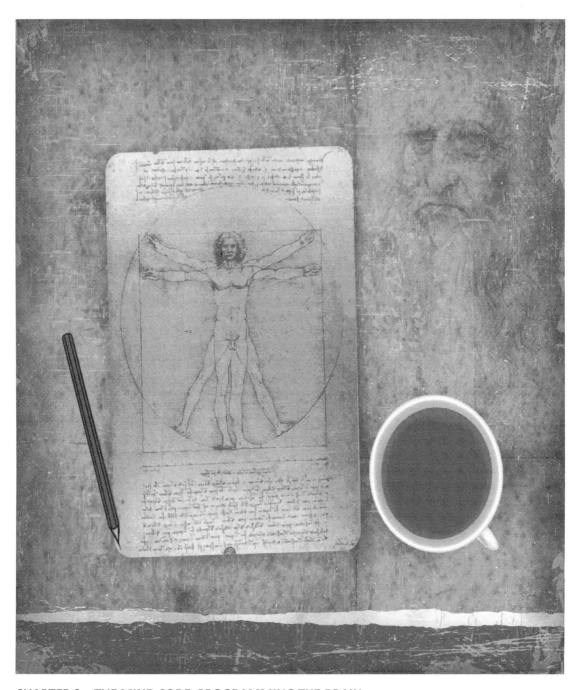

8 THE MIND CODE

HOW LEARNING PROGRAMS THE MIND

Russian Tank-Killing Dogs • Evolution of Behavior • Law of Effect • S-R Conditioning • Conditioned Emotional Responses • Video Replays • Subtlety of Conditioning • Reductionism in Science • Observational and Imitation

During a long period (of time) *groups of fishes will have been compared to each other in respect to their multiplicity, and groups of days to each other. But the first man who noticed the analogy between a group of seven fishes and a group of seven days made a notable advance in the history of thought.*

Nobel Laureate Alfred North Whitehead
Science and the Modern World

The realization of the analogy between the number of fishes and a similar number of days, and more, was the beginning of the science of mathematics. The realization that mathematics could apply to an almost infinite number of situations was a marked advance in science.

Spring 1941.   Poised in the forests of Central Poland, the Panzer divisions of Hitler's Panzer army awaited the orders that would send them into battle against the largest and best-equipped army they had yet faced.   Fresh from the rapid, almost bloodless fall of France, the Panzer groups were quickly shifted by Hitler to the Russian Front.   The speed and daring of the German plan took Stalin completely by surprise and led the German army to the brink of victory.

In America, a handful of scientists had already split the atom.   Spurred by the ever-present fear that the secret weapon threatened by Germany would turn out to be the atomic bomb, physicists worked feverishly to convert their knowledge of the atom into a weapon.   The significance of the atomic structure had been recognized by only a few of the world's scientists.   Their success is well known.

1. THE "ATOM" OF THE MIND?

Much less well known were the attempts of Ivan Pavlov, to split the "atom" of the mind-a phenomenon noted by the American learning theorist Edward Thorndike.   Just as the chemist has broken all matter into various combinations of molecules, and molecules into atoms, Pavlov and Thorndike were attempting to break behavior into its simpler, more basic components.   They were attempting to find principles that, like the principles of mathematics (seven fishes = seven days) or the atomic charts of the chemist, apply to an infinite variety of conditions. Pavlov and Thorndike had discovered what they believed to be the most elemental building blocks of which all behavior is composed, from which all is built.   As with atomic research, their discoveries, too, were turned to the needs of war.   For any discovery is only what humanity makes of it.   This "atom" would never be as spectacular as an atomic explosion, and even to this day, few have recognized its importance for our understanding of our own nature.

Ivan Pavlov

"Do not become archivists of facts.   Always search for the underlying cause of behavior." Ivan Pavlov

The first known intentional use of this knowledge as a weapon of war is recorded in the war diaries of the First, Third, and Seventh Panzer Divisions of the German Army, a story that is forcefully told by Paul Carell in his book *Hitler Moves East 1941-1943*.   The original product was crude and it never turned the tide of battle, but it illustrated well the basic components from which all behavior, including war, is built.

THE RUSSIAN TANK-KILLING DOGS

Field Marshal von Bock's Panzer Division moved rapidly across Russia.   The *blitzkrieg,* which was made possible by the mobility and speed of mechanized equipment, had already revolutionized warfare.   Like the French a year earlier, the Russians were psychologically unprepared to cope with the new German techniques.   The Russians were only prepared for a repeat of the static lines of war from WWI.   The Germans, under tank commander Heinz Guderian, used tanks in masses to cut through the thin lines of the Russians, then turn and come in behind them.   The shock of being attacked from the rear was too great and the Russian army fell apart.

The Russian T-34 tank, a well-kept secret, caught the Germans by surprise.   The T-34 was heavier and possessed more firepower than the German tanks, but its effectiveness was limited because the Russians' only used tanks to support the infantry, they ever saw it as a force on its own.   Weeks after the invasion began, the German tanks again moved east, where they would encounter yet another surprise.

The Panzer group captain from the German Third Panzer Division sat in the turret of his Mark III tank, which was flanked on either side by more of the fast moving iron machines.   Before them, the Russians were putting up stiff resistance under Stalin's "stand and die" order, but the German tanks were having an easy go of it.

As the tank commander cast a glance over the countryside, he suddenly saw two dogs hit the ground running. Watching the dogs as they ran from the bushes, he noticed satchels attached to their backs.   Messenger dogs, he probably guessed, perhaps carrying ammunition or medical supplies to partisans fighting behind the lines. He knew that French and British forces used pigeons for messenger service, and the Germans themselves had used dogs for guard duty and hunting prisoners.   But now there was something unusual, very out of the ordinary.

Dogs are invariably frightened by loud, threatening noises.   The loud diesel engines, the clank and clatter of steel against steel, must have been powerfully frightening to an animal that can barely stand to hear a police siren in the city.   But these dogs were not heading around the German lines: They were coming directly at the tanks.   Stunned for a moment, before he could warn the other tanks, he watched with amazement as the first dog picked out the nearest German tank and ran toward it.   Diving below the view of the tank crew, the dog ran behind and directly between the treads of the tank.

Within a split second, the captain saw a flash of light as a tremendous explosion ripped the tank, sending showers of dirt and steel into the air.

What would make a dog charge blindly into a stimulus as frightening as a tank?   What had the Russians done?   Had they discovered a "tank-killing" instinct?   Had they bred dogs for generation after generation to come up with an animal that would attack metal monsters on sight? Was it in the dog's genes, written into their DNA?

Had the Russians appealed to the territorial instincts of the dogs by planting fire hydrants around the German tanks, thus sending the dogs into a rage at the sight of their territory being invaded? Or, were the dogs so brainwashed by the appeals of Marxist-Leninist dialectical materialism that they were willing to die for Mother Russia?

COGNITIVE PSYCHOLOGY: STIMULUS GENERALIZATION IN ACTION

And what of the psychological effect of the incident on the tank crews? Imagine yourself as Lt. Heinrich Mueller, sitting in the turret of your tank at dusk.   The darkness obscures your vision as you try to stay alert; you strain your eyes and ears for any sight or sound.   Suddenly, a rustle in the bushes, a pat-pat of softly padded feet, and from out of the dark you hear the sounds of a dog, an "arf-arf".   A chill might go up their spine, like the chill that went up the spine of the people at Salem when the girls shrieked "Witch, Witch!"

After the word spread through the German troops, it would not be necessary to put charges on the dogs: Just release a few hundred mongrels into the German ranks late one night, and the imagination of the tank crews would do the rest.   Stimulus generalization in action.

Humans, being "smarter" than dogs, did not require any trials to reach their maximum level of fear.   It only required words.   Words *associated* with a terrifying event.

The fact that such remarkable behavior could be produced in a dog is of interest.   How did the Russians do it?   The answer lies in the principles underlying the basic learning process, but their usefulness in understanding behavior goes far beyond the simple training of animals.

HOW DID THE RUSSIANS CONVINCE DOGS TO ATTACK TANKS?

Every psychologist knows the story of how Pavlov conditioned a dog to salivate to the sound of a Bell. He used a metronome first, but Bell is so much easier to write. By sounding a Bell and following it with Meat, the dog would associate the Bell with the Meat. Normally, the dog would only salivate to meat placed on his tongue. But after 3 pairings of Bell-Meat, Bell-Meat, Bell-Meat an average of six drops of saliva appeared in his cheek tube. After six pairings they reached the maximum level of 12 drops of saliva.

But few psychologists know the rest of the story. Pavlov tried many stimuli, from a metronome and a music box, to a touch on the dog's flank, a word, and yes, eventually a bell. Any stimulus could come to elicit saliva Pavlov found that other stimuli could be used in place of the bell: Any auditory stimulus-a tone, the click of a metronome, even a spoken word. Any visual stimulus-a light, a pattern of stimuli. Any tactile stimulus-the touch of a brush to the dog's skin. Any stimulus could come to produce the same effect. Perhaps we could form a general law, in effect, that *"any stimulus that can be experienced by the animal can be conditioned to elicit saliva."*

Any stimulus? How about pain? That is a stimulus all organisms can experience.

Pavlov wanted to find out.   He rigged a device to elicit an electric shock, much like the shock you might get in winter if you walked across a rug and touched metal.   Shock-Meat, Shock-Meat-Shock-Meat and, after more trials, the shock by itself.   The dogs salivated to the shock alone.

By gradually increasing the level of shock (*gradual desensitization*) he reached a point where the dogs would salivate to fairly intense pain.   Instead of reacting with fear, as in the essential biological survival mechanism, the *Fight or Flight* response, they became excited and responded eagerly to the session.   Fifty shades of the Marquis de Sade, he had developed experimental induced machoism.

> *"Within a few weeks the dog would actually wag its tail excitedly, salivate, and turn toward the food dish in response to the electricity."*

Pavlov had discovered it was possible to reprogram the wiring of the brain. Even the most important biological survival mechanism known, the Fight or Flight response, could be controlled by a simple learning procedure.

It was not that the dogs enjoyed the pain, as some think of machoism, but that they enjoyed what had been associated with the pain.   And the positive emotion of food countered the negative emotion of pain.   Today, when others speak of retraining the brain, or of neuroplasticity, they often do not give credit to the origin of the idea, perhaps because this has been ignored by our textbooks.

Do you remember the Russian tank killers? Are you beginning to get some hint of how they were conditioned to perform in the presence of the German tanks? The behavior of the dogs seems, on the surface, to be very complex.   The conditioning technique used by the Russians may seem disappointingly simple when it is described.   But behavior, no matter how complex it seems on the surface, may be composed of many conditioned responses that are of no greater complexity than those observed in Pavlov's dogs.

2. CHAINING IT ALL TOGETHER

So, what did the Russians see in Pavlov's work? They took puppies from an early age and fed them near a running tractor. Gradually they moved the food dish closer and closer to the tractor.   This is Stimulus Desensitization.   Just as Pavlov had gradually increased the level of shock, the fear of the noise of the tractor being the same as the fear of shock.

The Russians started with young dogs-Dobermans, sheepdogs, and mongrels -which were fed only under certain stimulus conditions, specifically, in the presence of a tractor with the motor running.   At first, the dogs were fed some distance from the tractor.   Gradually, with each successive feeding, the food was moved closer and closer to the noisy tractor.   This is the same technique Pavlov used to gradually condition dogs to salivate to the painful stimulus of a strong shock.   After a number of such pairings of food and the noise stimulus, the dogs were eating under the body of the running tractor.

Eventually, the trainer hooked the food dish to a bar underneath the tractor, and the dogs were conditioned to eat as they ran along beneath the moving vehicle.   Russian prisoners interrogated by the Germans said that the dogs had been trained on tractors.   It is somewhat difficult to believe, however, that they had not received at least some training under tanks as well, since the stimuli presented by the two vehicles are quite different.

The rest was easy.   Saddlebags loaded with high explosives were strapped on their backs.   A magnetic detonator would trigger the explosives when the dogs came close to the tanks.   The dogs were pointed in the general direction of the German lines and actively sought out and, purely inadvertently, destroyed the tanks.

The meat had not been planted under the German *tanks; it had been planted in the "mind" of the dogs.*

There is a Russian film showing a German Shepherd dog eagerly lunging toward the tanks as the trainer had to restrain him until the tanks had passed.

The Russians claim the dogs killed some 200 German tanks.   They do not say how many Russian tanks the dogs killed by mistake.

3. CULTURE AND PSYCHOLOGY

Emotions are controlled by the same methods that control our saliva and our pupillary response; to far greater effect.

Could this only happen with a dog? Are humans too smart? Will free will save us.? In the battle of Okinawa in

WWII, some 2,800 Japanese Kamikaze pilots dove their Zeros into American battleships, damaging 368 of them, and dying in doing so.   An estimated 8,000 Japanese soldiers died in hopeless Banzai attacks against American tanks and machine guns.   Some 3,000 civilians on Okinawa committed suicide rather than surrender to American forces.

https://www.pbs.org/wgbh/americanexperience/features/pacific-john-chapman/

https://en.wikipedia.org/wiki/Kamikaze#cite_note-45

Why? Because they wanted to? That is not an answer that would satisfy any psychologist today.   Instead, we need to know about the cultural history of these willing suicide bombers; The Samori tradition, the Bushido code; death before the dishonor or surrender.   They were taught that dying for the emperor, for their country, was a great honor.

They were told that *"duty is hard, death is as light as a cherry blossom falling from a tree."* They had been programmed by their culture. Their country honored those who died for their country. Every culture glorifies their dead as having died for their country.   The dead are not there to question the idea.

The idea is implanted in the "mind" of the individual.   Their behavior reflects the power of that emotional conditioning.

We all have a tendency to think that the world must conform to our prejudices.   The opposite view involves some effort of thought, and most people would die, sooner than think.   In fact, they do so.

Nobel Laureate Bertrand Russell

Every culture seeks to indoctrinate its own children with the ideas most emotionally held in its culture.   Thus, ensuring that, as adults, they will never be able to think in any other way.

Death before Surrender

TOKYO (AP) Dec. 3, 1972-World War II ended 27 years ago, but it's still real for some Japanese soldiers holed up in former battlefield areas.

Officials estimate there may be between 300 and 3,500 former soldiers hiding in the jungles of Southeast Asia and one Pacific Island, either from ignorance of the war's end or blind loyalty to a military code which taught them death was preferable to surrender.

The tenacity of these stragglers to avoid capture or surrender has evoked sympathy and pain in this country.   For years, the Japanese have tried to live down memories of their country's war atrocities and charges that the Japanese character, feverishly nationalistic, is again leading the nation toward militarism.

The latest incident involving former Japanese soldiers occurred on Lubang Island in the Philippines last month.   Two stragglers, foraging for food, exchanged fire with a police patrol.   One of them, Pfc. Kinshichi Kozuka, a member of an intelligence-gathering unit, was killed; the other, believed to be his superior, Lt. Hiroo Onoda, was wounded, and escaped back into the jungle.

The incident numbed the Japanese who barely 10 months earlier listened in disbelief as Shoichi Yokel, an army sergeant captured near his subterranean hideout on Guam, related how he subsisted on a diet of bark, rats and fruits for more than a quarter of a century even though he knew of Japan's surrender.   He said he was ashamed to return home alive.   Commented the Mainichi Shimbun, a major daily: "We cannot really talk about peace or prosperity until we rescue all those who were alienated from their motherland by their tragic fate at the end of World War II."

Spurred by public demands for action, the government says it will try to trace missing soldiers and lure them home.   But officials say it may be a near-impossible task.   A similar rescue effort in the 1950s ended in failure.

Some stragglers are believed to have married local women.   Officials say it could be difficult for them to come home and admit openly what they consider the disgrace of having survived the war.

Others are believed to be aware of the war's end.   But, like Yokel, they may have become victims of their military discipline and they may now prefer to live out their lives in isolation.

"Then there are those who may genuinely believe the war is still going on," says an official.   "And they may consider all these attempts to lure them out as enemy traps to capture them."

Since his return to Japan, Yokoi has slowly recovered from the psychological shock of a changed Japan. He complained on his return that the Japanese had lost their reverence for their emperor, who until the end of the war was regarded as a God.   It was this respect for his emperor which helped sustain him in his jungle hideout, Yokoi explained.

WHY WOMEN LOVE A MAN WHO LIVES IN A HOLE IN THE GROUND AND EATS RATS

After thirty years in the jungle of the Philippines, Hiroo Onada was finally convinced to come out from his hiding. He received a hero's welcome on his return to Japan. The media reported that *"...he received over 100 marriage proposals from awestruck women."* For the members of his generation, refusing to surrender was viewed with respect and admiration. For the people of the Philippines, he was considered a war criminal for continuing to kill their people after the war was over. Any Stimulus—Any Emotion, in this case, it depended on how your culture led you to perceive that stimulus.

4. HOLLYWOOD AND POLITICIANS USE CONDITIONED EMOTIONS TO CONTROL YOUR MIND

In Steven Spielberg's masterpiece *JAWS* what happens just seconds before someone gets eaten by a shark? At first, there is no music at all. Then the music starts at a low tempo. The music picks up in tempo until... the moment someone is sucked under by a shark. Then, the music stops abruptly.

The next time the audience hears the music, the little hairs on the back of their neck may stand on end, adrenalin may start to enter their bloodstream, and some are on the edge of their seat. The music is the CS, like the bell, that controls the biology of their body.

Of course, Stephen Spielberg had no ulterior motive other than to provide an entertaining movie and maybe be remembered as the greatest director of all time. Yet, after the movie aired, attendance at beaches across the country went down.

At the Salem witch-trials, when the accused was brought into the room, the girls began to point at the accused and to shriek, *"WITCH, WITCH"*. The biology of the body of the onlookers then shot adrenalin into their bloodstream, their heart jumped. Hollywood does the same thing in their horror films, controlling the biochemistry in your blood.

Politicians have used the same method, attacking their opponents with words that have been associated with emotion. Accusing their opponents of *"stealing the election"*, despite not a shred of evidence to support that.

In fact, sixty lawsuits were brought and thrown out of court by judges because no evidence was presented. Yet people continued to believe this even years with no evidence to support it. Emotions tend to rule over reason.

Pavlov's work was the very basis of the understanding of the relationship between our biology and our psychology.

Yet if textbooks only teach about how he made a dog salivate to a bell, the entire importance of his discovery is lost.

5. ANY STIMULUS—ANY RESPONSE- (Almost)

(Already wired into the autonomic nervous system)

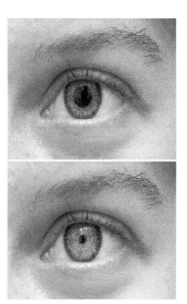

Learning controls the biology of the brain. Not just with the ability to control the Fight or Flight response, but basic responses that are rarely thought of as learned.

Look in the mirror at the pupil of your eye. Think; constrict-expand, constrict-expand. What will your pupil go? It will stare right back at you like you are stupid. But if you sit in a dark room, your pupil will expand automatically, to let in more light. If you have an experimenter sitting behind you with a bell, and a light switch, at random, have him sound the Bell, then turn the light on in your eyes. Your pupil will constrict to shut out the light. Turn off the light and your pupil will expand. Again and again, Bell-Light, Bell-Light, Bell-light.

After a while, he can sound the bell, without turning on the light, and your pupil will constrict: not to the light, but to the bell. Pavlov's Neuroplasticity in action.

New mothers often report that, after a while, when they hear the baby's hunger cry, they will automatically begin to lactate. The discovery that learning could control the biology of our autonomic nervous system was only the beginning. What came next was even more critical to understanding how the brain is programmed.

The spectators at the Salem witch trials felt the power of psychological control over their own bodies when the girls of Salem began to shriek, "Witch, witch". Yet they understood nothing about why a chill went up their spine and their heart jumped.

In the chapter on the Amygdala and the Fight or Flight Mechanism in the brain, we mentioned that you do not need to electrically stimulate the Amygdala with an outside electrode to elicit a fear or anger response. Psychology can do that without wires, without electrodes, just by classical conditioning.

6. THE GENESIS OF MOTIVATION

#classical conditioning #Kerplunk experiment #Little Albert #Stimulus-Response #behaviour #behaviorism #comparative psychology

Pavlov himself blew off emotions as just *"generalized excitement"*, it remained for an American, John B. Watson, to discover that the same techniques used by Pavlov generated an even more powerful control over emotions. Watson is famous, or infamous, for his experiment with "Little Albert". He first showed that Albert, this 1 ½ year-old child, was not afraid of anything. He would try to pet a rabbit or a mask, he had no fear. Watson began his experiment. While Albert was playing with his toys, they brought in a tame white rat. When Albert looked up at the rat, Watson would bang two pieces of metal behind him. The loud bang would startle Albert and he began to cry.

After repeating this several more times, Albert would begin to cry as soon as he saw the white rabbit, and attempt to get away. Not only this, but the fear *generalized*. Now, he would begin to cry if he saw a white Santa Clause beard, he would whimper at the sight of white cotton.

Of course, this is an unethical thing to do to a child, and no one

in psychology today would be allowed to do this. But it must be noted that back then, in the era of *"spare the rod and spoil the child"* no one thought anything of it because they were doing far worse to their own children. Many parents still do. In his autobiography, Winston Churchill noted that when he was a child in the school system, he was constantly being called up in front of the class for talking in class, bent over the desk, and beaten with a rod. He said, *"It did no good."*

Not only that, but in our own schools, to this day, coaches routinely use slogans to motivate their charges to endure pain, *"No Pain—No Gain"* and they may shame their players with, *"Don't be a wus!"* *"Hit 'em harder!"* Coaches in the big leagues think nothing of the harm that might be done.

In 2014 some 5,000 former NFL football players sued the NFL for long-lasting brain damage and more. The NFL settled out of court for 765 million dollars. In 2021 a high school coach was arrested and charged with manslaughter for the death of a student from heat exhaustion during his training.

The average NFL player only lasts 3 ½ years before they are injured or replaced with a

younger and hungrier buck. The joke among the NFL players is that NFL stands for Not For Long.

They are motivated to seek the cheers of the Sunday crowd. They are motivated to avoid the boos of the Sunday crowd. On top of that, they fear the disapproval of the coach and seek the "atta boy" of the coach as well as that of the other players.

With over 700 named phobias, there is simply no limit to the number of potential fears, even a fear of things that do not even exist, like ghosts and demons. Politicians have long made use of this fact by associating words that imply a negative emotion, with their opponents, even without a shred of evidence.

The methods the Russians used to motivate dogs to attack tanks are the same methods coaches use on our own children. Gradual desensitization to the ideas of pain ("No Pain—No Gain"). The emotional approval of the coach, the "way to go!" of one's fellow players, the roar of the Sunday crowd, all provide the primary motivation, the emotion, that controls our behavior.

Our entire society is a proving ground for Pavlov's classical conditioning and Watson's conditioned emotions. We are all at the mercy of society's emotions, they are embedded in our brains from an early age, when our brains cannot resist the effect. Can we be free to choose when we have no understanding of this?

The Positive Emotion: When Pavlov rang his bell, he observed only the motor or salivary responses of the dogs. He ignored what may turn out to be the more significant response that he was conditioning: the *positive emotional response.* The dogs not only salivated at the stimulus of the bell, they displayed marked signs of enjoyment.

If you hold a piece of meat up for your dog when it begs at the dinner table, it not only salivates and smacks its lips, but its entire body wriggles in anticipation; it whines, it shifts its stare nervously between you and the meat, uncertain whether the meat will end up in its mouth or yours. Its tail may wag with such abandon that its hindquarters may appear to "wag" as well.

You often get the same emotional reaction by rattling the chain collar or picking up the leash used to take the dog for a walk. The positive emotional response associated with going on a walk is fantastic. The new sights to see (at least newer than the backyard), the pleasure of nosing it with the cocker spaniel down the block, the joy of urinating on a communal fireplug, the thrill of embarrassing its owner by going to the potty on the neighbor's lawn-ah, paradise!

If you open the hall closet and inadvertently jingle the dog's chain collar, your dog may instantly appear from any room in the house and spring to the front door. Even while waiting at the door, the dog may leap about so vigorously that it is a struggle to get the collar on over its head. It is not just a response of saliva that Pavlov conditioned, but a profoundly powerful emotion as well.

Pavlov chose to attribute such behavior to generalized excitement. It has become increasingly clear, however, that a positive emotional response has also been conditioned-in this case, a response that can only be described as intense. Is the response being conditioned a reflexive one? Or is it an emotional response? At this point, the available evidence indicates that both reflexive and emotional responses can be conditioned, either separately or at the same time.

7. ANY STIMULUS-ANY EMOTION

The cow of all animals is most sacred.   Every part of its body is inhabited by some deity or other.   Every hair on its body is inviolable.   All its excreta are hallowed.   Not a particle ought to be thrown away as impure.   On the contrary, the water it ejects ought to be preserved as the best of all holy waters – a sin destroying liquid which sanctifies everything it touches, while nothing purifies like cow-dung.   Any spot which a cow has condescended to honor with the sacred deposit of her excrement is forever afterwards consecrated ground, and the filthiest place plastered with is at once cleansed and freed from pollution, while the ashes produced by burning this hallowed substance are of such a holy nature, that they not only make clean all material things, however previously unclean, but have only to be sprinkled over a sinner to convert him to a saint."

Sir Monier-Williams
Bramnism and Hinduism

In India, cows are sacred.   In America, we mulch them into burgers and eat them.   We wear their skins on our feet.   When McDonald's moved to India, they were greeted with wild protests, "Cow killers!", even though they were already serving vege-burgers.

It made front-page headlines in India; it was ignored in America.   It is all *relative* to what stimuli have been associated with which emotions.   Then, that emotion *generalizes* to other associated stimuli, as above.

Mahatma Gandhi offered a more modern version; cows are venerated, he noted, because they are *associated* with life-giving.   All life is sacred.   But it is a matter of association. Words that have been *associated* with positive emotions are then *associated* with any other stimuli.

In our culture, we may revere the bones of saints or a sliver of wood that we were told was from the "original" cross. We may even attribute miraculous healing powers to such relics.

In America, politicians do the same thing, associating themselves with all things positive and their opponents with all things negative.   And many believe their excreta are hallowed, even when the hard evidence shows their words to be puerile.

The fact that we can "feel" those emotions, that it tickles our limbic system, has created the illusion that those emotions reflect reality.

Words, associated with emotion, control the mind. It applies to our thoughts, our value judgments, our politics, our religion, our choice of a marriage partner, and our individuality. Few ever ask, "What is the hard evidence?" Even the press largely asks, "What is your opinion?" Unless we understand that evidence is vastly more important than personal opinion, we cannot control our own minds, we cannot do science.

"The obscure we see eventually, the completely obvious, it seems, takes longer."

Edward R. Murrow

Chains of learned responses described by Pavlov control the practice of athletes. Constant repetition trains the cortex of the cerebellum to learn these chains to perfection. You see this in learning to type, riding a bicycle, or playing sports. We also see it in driving a car; at first, we have to think about each move, every change of lane, and every glance in a mirror, but after a few years, we get in the car in the morning and daydream all the way to work. When we finally get there, we may be amazed and not even remember all the turns, because our automatic mind would move, turn, and brake automatically, all the while we are daydreaming.

Yet most of human motivation is directed by emotion, not by chains of conditioned responses. We seek what is associated with positive emotions and avoid what is associated with negative emotions. An unknown poet put it well, an echo of Thorndike's Law of Effect; I wish I could give credit:

"No matter how high or lowly the beast,
we all do what pleasures most or pains least."
Unknown Sage

The importance of psychology is in knowing that "what pleasures most or pains least" is not determined by reality, it is largely determined by the emotions *associated* with the words and ideas of others. Those words then determine our thoughts, our beliefs, and our very perception of reality.

Yet no one notices the evidence that we are saddled by the emotions others embed in our minds, via simple association. The emotions seem so obviously correct. We "feel" those emotions in the depth of our brain.

What Pavlov did not realize at the time was that a stimulus associated with an emotion creates a General Theory of Relativity (Any Stimulus-Any Emotion) that does not require the learning of specific reflexes or chains of learned responses to explain behavior. Most of what we have talked about, from the Kamikaze pilot to the responses of high school football players, is based on emotions that set a goal, that does not require a learned chain of responses.

Yet there is a third variable, not so apparent: The biological effect of novel stimuli on our brain. From Donald Hebb to Harry Harlow the effect of novel stimuli has been shown to create a variable degree of emotion. A moderate degree of novel stimuli triggers a "curiosity" response. We seek to approach. A strong degree of novel stimuli can create a dramatic Fight or Flight response. Children show a marked degree of fear when lost in a supermarket. Intense and directed fear can create anger and attack directed against whatever perceived danger we encounter.

Curiosity is often more powerful than conditioning. We can see this in spades when we try to teach a dog or a child. Any change in the environment grabs its attention, and spurs it to seek something besides what we are trying to teach. Some have confused this with invalidating the basis of learning. No, it is just one more extraneous variable we must consider. Cognitive psychologists have a term that describes this; children have, "A mind of their own."

Every emotion we feel comes out of our experience of stimuli associated with fear, anger, and pleasure in the biology of our brain. Such a simple fact, yet no one notices. The fact that Any Stimulus can trigger almost Any Response, even an emotion, is a notable advance in human psychology.

After a while there *is no need to experience an actual emotion*, the brain computes the emotions, associated with words, in a way that determines what we like or dislike or what makes us angry, just based on our past associations.

8. THOUGHTS CAN CONTROL THE BIOLOGY OF YOUR BRAIN

One of the most important studies ever done, both for understanding the mind and for understanding psychological problems of anxiety and depression, is a study that demonstrated how thoughts can control the biology of your brain.

Neal Miller, who developed the concept of bio-feedback, has demonstrated that even the very thoughts in our brain can be controlled by emotional conditioning. Miller wired volunteers to a machine that would deliver a mild electric shock. Then, he used a tachistoscope to present a simple symbol, a "T" or a "4" to the subject.

Every time the "T" was presented, a mild shock would follow. If a "4" was presented, they received no shock.

After the fear was established, they never gave another shock. Then, he presented a series of dots "." they were told to "think" T for the first dot, then "think" 4 for the next dot, over and over. No shocks were given. The fear response was recorded by the GSR emotional response".

Miller measured the fear reaction, to the thought, by using a GSR machine, part of what is used in a "lie detector". "Lie detectors" do not detect lies, they detect activation of the fear or anxiety response.

The subjects showed a fear response, just to the "thought" of "T", that continued for 25 trials, *with no shock being given. "Once bitten—25 times shy"?*

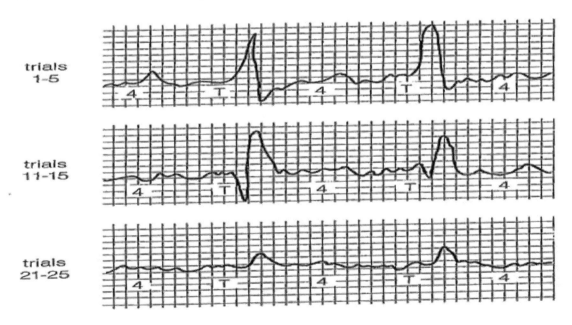

This study should have been a bridge between behavioral psychology and cognitive psychology, although it was largely overlooked by cognitive psychologists.

More still, this is a demonstration of the environment controlling the brain in a way that applies to the origin of anxiety disorders and depression. We know that those who have problems such as PTSD or those who commit suicide have had as much as four times more negative experiences as those who do not.

Note also, that this fear response can go into extinction. Behavioral and Cognitive behavioral psychology both use procedures designed to reduce or eliminate fears; such as gradual desensitization.

9. THE MIND CODE: THE POWER OF ASSOCIATION STIMULUS + STIMULUS = PERCEPTION

Learning at its most basic may be by a simple *association* between two stimuli. Some years ago, a vacuum cleaner company brought a new, space-age vacuum. Using sound-deadening materials along with baffles; they took their basic model and made it very quiet. They test marketed it alongside its standard noisy model, to prove it works just as well but was very quiet. Women would not buy it. Why?

Think about this, every time you rev the engine on your car, the more power it puts out, the more noise it puts out. The more noise it puts out, the more power it puts out. Every time you press 10 on your blender, the more power it puts out, the more noise it puts out. When you turn the electric fan on high, the more power it puts out, the more noise it puts out.

Power and noise are intimately associated. This is a Stimulus-Stimulus association that imprints on the mind so firmly that noise (S) = power (S), creates a new perception in the brain. Not just a thought, but an actual perception. Never in the entire of human history have we ever had motors until about a hundred years ago. Only within this short period has everyone born since 1900 had this learned perception imprinted on their brain. A vacuum that was not noisy simply was not *perceived* as powerful.

In my day when a teenager got his first car, he wanted to put a glass-packed muffler on it, because it gave it that deep-throated varoom, Varooom, VAROOOOOMMM, Babala, babala, babala... Aaaah, that was so cool. It was the very definition of cool to a teenage male. The sound made it seem like it was putting out more power. But noise did not make the car more powerful, it only made it noisier.

Yet we were motivated to seek noise just because of our perception that noise = power. Stimulus (noise) + Stimulus (power) = Perception. Even before we got a car, we would take a clothespin, put it on the strut of our bicycle wheel, and attach playing cards to the strut, so that when the spokes went around, they would make a brrrrrrrr, sound. Noise is *perceived* as power by the human mind.

10. THOUGHT OR PERCEPTION?

We do not "think" that *noise is power*, we actually experience (**perceive**) noise as power. Stimulus + Stimulus + Stimulus Generalization = Perception. One step beyond Pavlov's learned responses or even emotional conditioning is the idea that simple associations of stimuli can produce a *perception*, not just a response; more on that in the next chapter.

PABLO PICASSO AS A NAME (S)
ASSOCIATED WITH MONEY (S) AND FAME (S)

In January 2010, at Sotheby's auction in London, a painting by Pablo Picasso sold for 54 million dollars. One year later, another of Picasso's paintings sold at auction for over 110 million dollars. In 2015, one of his paintings sold for 179 million dollars. Why? What makes a painting with Picasso's name on it worth more than a painting with your name on it?

"I never heard of this Picasso fella. Give me five bucks and it's yours."

Decades ago, Pablo Picasso was interviewed with *Life* magazine and said something so profound that I tore out the page and memorized it. I still have it. What he said was this:

> "...I have not the courage to think of myself as an artist, in the great and ancient sense of the term. Giotto, Titian, Rembrandt were great painters. I am only a public entertainer who has understood his times and exploited as best he could, the imbecility, the vanity, the cupidity of his contemporaries. Mine is a bitter confession, more so than it may appear, but it has the merit of being sincere."

Pablo Ruiz Picasso, Life magazine

Picasso was being too hard on himself.   But he was also being painfully honest.   He took a CBS film crew on a tour of his studio in Spain.   He showed them how every morning, his associates would set up a row of easels and canvas on one side of a grand hall.   Picasso would start with the first canvas, go all around the room, and at the end of the day, he would sign each one.   His signature on a painting made it worth a small fortune.   My signature on the same painting would devalue the canvas it was painted on.   They couldn't even give it away.   Or, they would have to sell it at the flea market like damaged goods.

Picasso was honest enough that he told people, in no uncertain terms, in effect, "I mass produce this crap."   And it still sells.

Early in his career, Picasso painted perfectly normal pictures, such as his classic "The Patient" but it did not sell. The more bizarre he made it, the more famous it became.   People started paying attention.   Its value increased. Fame has a value all its own.

FAME HAS AN EMOTIONAL VALUE ALL ITS OWN: Jorden's shoes and Johansson's "Snot".

In 2021 a pair of old tennis shoes, worn by Michael Jorden in his rookie year sold for one and a half million dollars at auction at Sotheby's auction in London.

When Jay Leno had actress Scarlett Johansson on his late-night show, she came in with a cold.   Leno asked her to sneeze into a handkerchief and they would put it up for sale on eBay.   It sold for $5,300 dollars on eBay. Simple association between fame and Scarlett's "snot" gave it a value that your "snot" could never sell for. Fame, as with Picasso, makes something worth more, in people's minds.   Now if she could just make it art...

Fame has a value all its own.   Fame (S) attached to an individual (S) or even a part of them, makes us feel that that is somehow special.   Remember how a sacred cow, or a politician's excreta have been made holy (p. 163).

11. EVOLUTION OF BEHAVIOR

How Simple Random Behavior Evolves into Complex, Purposeful Behavior.

If an organism is not born with knowledge of its environment, how are the complex patterns of behavior developed that allow it to adapt to widely differing situations? Does knowledge suddenly appear full-blown after an animal thinks over past experiences? Or does the learning process require no more understanding than the simple instinctual response of a fighting rooster (see Chapter 11 on DNA and the preprogrammed response)? Just how *does* purposeful behavior occur?

Just before the tum of the century, a student at Harvard University began collecting cats; stray cats, alley cats, even his neighbor's cats.   The student was E. L. Thorndike, and the cats were the star performers in Thorndike's treatise on *Animal Intelligence* (1911).   His findings quickly became classics in the literature of psychology, for Thorndike it was uncovering a "law of nature," which he named the *law of effect*.   Thorndike intended his law of effect to become to psychology what Darwin's law of natural selection is to biology: *how simple, random, behavior "evolves" into complex, purposeful behavior.*

TRIAL AND ERROR LEARNING

The popular literature of the early 1900s abounded with miraculous tales of the intelligence of animals: Dogs lost hundreds of miles from home who unerringly found their way back home, and animals who went out of their way to warn their masters of fire or other disasters and saved the lives of their family. Tales of their insight, comprehension, and understanding frequently took on an aspect of super-animal, if not superhuman, intelligence. Such was our knowledge of the behavior of animals when Thorndike entered the field. But how much in these anecdotal tales is truth, and how much is the artificial creation of our human propensity for self-delusion?

Thorndike's subjects were stray cats, dogs, and chickens. He needed a problem to test their intelligence. The most famous of his problems was the "puzzle box," an orange crate with wooden slats as bars and, near the door, a looped string or foot pedal that, when moved, would spring the door open, releasing the animal. Outside the cage, the animal would find food and freedom as rewards for its success.

Into the puzzle box went the cats, one at a time, and Thorndike intently watched their progress. Each cat began by sniffing at the cage, sniffing at the corners, sniffing in the direction of the food outside the cage door. It clawed at the bars, paced the floor, purred, scratched itself, meowed, scratched, stretched, and scratched again. Eventually, in the process of nosing around the cage, it played with the string and pulled the loop of the string. The door flew open, and the cat got the reinforcement (Food and freedom).

When placed back into the puzzle box, the animal again repeated much of the irrelevant behavior. As trial followed trial, however, the random, purposeless behavior dropped out, and the pattern of responses associated with getting out; staying near the string, playing with the string, pulling the string, remained.

As Thorndike watched cat after cat, day after day, in similar puzzles, he soon found that the animals had no cognitive solution to the problem in mind at the beginning of the struggle. An inspection of the mechanisms that held the door shut did not enable the animals to "reason" out their escape. Instead, they exhibited random, purposeless behavior, hitting on the solution mostly by chance. Once they had tripped the release and escaped, "learning" occurred. The next time in the cage, they tended to repeat the same behavior patterns that had led to their release.

"To the intelligent man with an interest in human nature, it must often appear strange that so much of the energy of the scientific world has been spent on the study of the body and so little on the study of the mind; 'The greatest thing in man is mind,' he might say, 'yet the least studied.' Especially remarkable seems the rarity of efforts to trace the evolution of the human intellect from that of the lower animals. Since Darwin's discovery; the beasts of the field; the fowl of the air and the fish of the sea have been examined. The infinite pains by hundreds of workers in the effort to trace our physical genealogy, and with consummate success; yet few and far between have been the efforts to find the origins of intellect and trace its progress up to human faculty. And none of them has achieved any secure success.

It may be premature to try again, but a somewhat extended series of studies of the intelligent behavior of fishes, reptiles, birds and mammals, including the monkeys, has brought results which seem to throw light on the problem and to suggest its solution.

The process involved in the learning was evidently a process of selection; The animal is confronted by a state of affairs or, as we may call it, a "situation." He reacts in the way that · he is moved by his innate nature or previous training to do, by a number of acts.   These acts include the particular act that is appropriate and he succeeds, in late trials the impulse to this one act is more and more stamped in, this one act is more and more associated with that situation, is selected from amongst the others by reason of the pleasure it brings the animal, The profitless acts are stamped out; the impulses io perform them in that situation are weakened by reason of the positive discomfort or the absence of pleasure resulting from them. So, the animal finally performs in that situation, only the fitting act: ·

Here we have the simplest and at the same time the most widespread sort of intellect or, learning in the world.   There is no reasoning, no process of inference or comparison; there is no thinking about things, no putting two and two together; there are no ideas-the animal does not think of the box or of the food or of the act he is to perform.   He Simply comes after the learning to feel like doing a certain thing under certain circumstances Which before the learning he did not feel like doing.   Human beings are accustomed to think of intellect as the power of having and controlling ideas and of ability to learn as synonymous with ability to have ideas.   But learning by having ideas is really one of the rare and isolated events in nature.   There may be a few scattered ideas possessed by the higher animals.   but the common form of intelligence with them, their habitual method of learning, is not by the acquisition of ideas, but by the selection of impulses."

Edward. L. Thorndike *Popular· Science Monthly;* 1901

It seemed to Thorndike that a 'bond" had been formed by the association between pulling the string and what happened immediately afterward-the reward of food.   From one trial to the next, this 'bond" seemed to be "stamped in", eventually becoming a complete, integrated response.   There are exceptions to this generalization.   Some species-specific behavior is possible with some animals but not others.   For example, a raccoon learns more readily to wash its food before eating than a dog would because raccoons are biologically capable of such activities and engage in them normally.

Similarly, a cat would find it easier to learn to pull the looped string in Thorndike's puzzle than would a dog because cats are biologically structured in such a way that playing with a string comes naturally.

12. TRIAL AND ERROR IN COGNITIVE TASKS

Many tend to think of Trial-and-Error learning as something primitive, limited to animals trying to find food. But we see trial and error as basic, even to the most advanced cognitive behavior. Consider the behavior of dramatically different tasks by Thomas Edison and Albert Einstein.

Edison experimented with over 100 different filaments from cotton to silk before he found one, tungsten, that worked best. That is Trial and Error at its most basic.

Albert Einstein had to go back to the drawing board, experimenting with multiple mathematical formulas before he found one that worked with his General Theory of Relativity.

Every computer programmer knows that he or she must try different lines of code, run the code, to see if the final result is what he wants that program to do. Then, change the line of code, run it again and see if it works. That is Trial and Error at its most basic.

Above: Frustration or Success at Trial and Error. Emotion drives the effort. Trial and Error is basic to the most advanced thinking we all do; from Copernicus comparing models of the known universe, to Edison experimenting with over 100 different filaments for a light bulb, to Einstein trying different mathematical models until he found one that fit; to trying different commands in computer programming; trial and error is basic. The emotions of Frustration or the thrill of Success can also be seen in this understanding of the "Law of Effect".

13. THE "LAW OF EFFECT "

From his observations, Thorndike began to formulate the law of effect, which can be summarized as follows: *Behavior, followed by reinforcement (food or freedom, etc.), will tend to be strengthened; any behavior not followed by reinforcement will tend to drop out (become extinct, a* term Thorndike borrowed from Darwin's concept of evolution).   Not a very impressive statement for a "law of nature"? Freshmen psychology students are rarely impressed.   Come to think of it, seniors and graduate students rarely stand up and cheer either. Neither do learned professors.   One somehow expects something more grandiose, but the significance of this law is greater than is immediately apparent.

The significance of Thorndike's discovery is more apparent in a study by Guthrie and Horton. Although Guthrie and Horton did not believe that reinforcement is necessary for learning to occur (it is not), their study demonstrates the power of the association between a response, *any* response, and the result that follows it.   In this study, Thorndike's puzzle box was modified slightly by the use of a pole in the *center* of the cage, away from the door, that could be accidentally triggered by the animal backing into it, clawing it, chewing on it, or by any number of purposeless activities.   The release could be purposefully triggered as well.

The stage was set. A cat was dropped in. The cat scratched at the bars, purred, meowed, paced the floor, and sniffed at the walls.   Eventually, it grew tired of trying to find a way out.   It lay down, rolled on its back, and stretched.   Rolling on its back, it accidentally tripped the release.   The cage door flew open.   Escape followed.

"Any behavior followed by reinforcement will tend to be strengthened." What does the cat do the second time it is placed in the cage? Exactly. For trial after trial, photos taken at the moment of release showed the cats repeating whatever movements had led to release.   Not all rolled on their backs.   Some were clawing the pole when the release was triggered; they continued to claw the pole in trial after trial.   Some had accidentally backed into the pole tail first; they continued to back into the pole trial after trial.

Each animal had "discovered" its own method of escape, and each continued to use the method that had been followed by escape. No cognitive understanding of pushing the pole as the cause of their release was necessary: The cats had learned a response.

The Guthrie and Horton study is somewhat artificial.   The simplicity of the release mechanism seems to have minimized the natural evolution of the conditioned 'bonds" into purposeful behavior.   There was no room for error to drop out, because errors too were followed by escape.   In this apparent shortcoming however, lies the true significance of these studies; the reduction of learning to its most basic *beginning-the association between a stimulus and a response or between two stimuli.*

No organism begins with knowledge or understanding: At the most basic level, purposeful behavior evolves from random, irrelevant, trial-and-error behavior.   Identical behavior is found in human children and adults when exposed to completely new problems.   Thus, we have part of the technique with which the tank-killing dogs were trained: any behavior, with a few exceptions, can be learned.   The behavior does not have to be rational.   But that is only part of the picture.   How is it possible for a fear-producing stimulus, such as the noise of tanks, to produce a positive emotional response?

The cat first escaped when it rolled on its back and accidentally hit the pole that opened the door.   In trial after trial, the cats in the Guthrie and Horton study repeated whatever superstitious behavior had led to their escape.

This is not just for simple behavior.   Any computer programmer knows that Trial and Error is basic to their art.   You write a line of code, and run the code to see the effect.   You go back and change the line of code, and run it again to see if the outcome is more like the change you want.   Again and again, the programmer repeats the same process until the outcome is what they want.   Even artists learn their art by the same Trial and Error method, along with contrast and comparison to the outcome they want.

Isaac Newton, sitting under the now-proverbial apple tree, observed the proverbial fall of an apple.   A simple observation, one not likely to be impressive to the average person, yet Newton's systematic investigations of such simple phenomena led to a revolution in the science of physics.   Ask scholars to list a handful of the greatest people in the history of science, Newton is at the top of the list.   Many think that Einstein replaced Newton, no, he solved problems Newton had not, but Newton's ideas and calculations helped NASA send astronauts into space.

Perhaps the best examples of the value of the work of Pavlov and Thorndike come from the previous mention by Nobel Laureate Alfred North Whitehead, when he spoke of whoever first noted the similarity between a group of *seven* fishes and a group of *seven* days.   That was the beginning of math, something that can apply to a vast number of situations.   For Pavlov and Thorndike, their ideas could also apply to a vast number of situations.

14. THORNDIKE'S EVOLUTION OF BEHAVIOR BY THE "LAW OF EFFECT"

"In a very short time we have come a long way, from the simple learning of the minnow or chick to the science and logic of man. The general frame of mind which one acquires from the study of animal behavior and of the mental development of young children makes our hypothesis seem vital and probable.   If the facts did eventually corroborate it, we should have an eminently simple genesis of human faculty, for we could put together the gist of our· contention in a few words.   We should say: -

The function of intellect is to provide a means of modifying our reactions to the circumstances of life, so that we may secure pleasure, the symptom of welfare.   Its general law is that when in a certain situation an animal acts so that pleasure results, that act is selected from all those performed and associated with that situation, so that, when the situation recurs, the act will be more likely to follow than it was before;

that on the contrary the acts which, when performed in a certain situation, have brought discomfort, tend to be dissociated from that situation.   The intellectual evolution of the race consists in an increase in the number, delicacy, complexity, permanence and speed of formation of such associations.   In man this increase reaches such a point that an apparently new type of mind results, which conceals the real continuity of the process.   This mental evolution parallels the evolution of the cell structures of the brain from few and simple and gross to many and complex and delicate.

Nowhere more truly than in his mental capacities is man a part of nature.   His instincts, that is, his inborn tendencies to feel and act in certain ways, show throughout marks of kinship with the lower animals, especially with our nearest relatives physically, the monkeys.   His sense powers show no new creation.   His intellect we have seen to be a simple though extended variation from the general animal sort.   This again is presaged by the similar variation in the case of monkeys.   Amongst the minds of animals that of man leads, not as a demigod from another planet, but as a king from the same race."

Edward L.   Thorndike *Popular Science Monthly,* 1901

The discovery that the brain could be programmed by simple stimulus association, to an almost infinite number of responses, from saliva to pleasure to purposeful behavior, is a major advance in our understanding of the brain.

But Trial and Error learning is not just something that occurs in lower animals or a more primitive form of learning. Even computer programmers routinely use this in crafting a computer program.

Learning Computer Language is like learning Chinese to most students.   But even the most experienced programmer must do Trial and Error to get each line of code to do what they want.

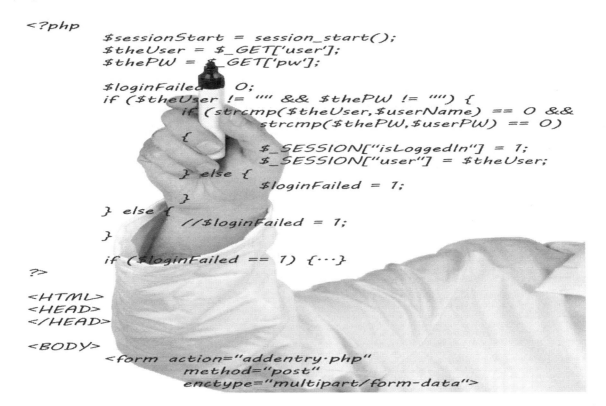

Yet the enthusiasm that comes from getting a computer to do what you want it to is what motivates much of such behavior. The end result—success—is an experience that brings a positive emotion.

15. THE BASIC STIMULUS-RESPONSE CONCEPT

Many prior discoveries had already been made, in psychophysics for example, of Broca's Area and Wernicke's area, but the significance of the work done by Pavlov for the science of psychology is perhaps most directly comparable to that of Newton for the science of physics. Mention any famous name in history, and Newton's name will almost certainly be included. What did he do that was so important? Newton demonstrated that the "laws" that govern the workings of nature were not the province of the gods, but could be known by humans. What is more, he demonstrated that these laws could be reduced to mathematical predictability. Never before in history had this been made so clear.

A revolution in psychology, as a science of behavior, began with an equally obscure observation. The apple was saliva, the observer was Pavlov. Ivan Pavlov, so the story goes, walked into his laboratory one day, and a dog being used as an experimental animal slobbered at the sight of him. To most people, this would not seem worth noting, but to Pavlov, it posed a question: Why had the dog salivated at the sight of him? Salivating at the taste of food, even at the sight of food, that makes sense. Salivating at the sight of an old physiologist? Hmmm.

A few years earlier, unknown to Pavlov, an American psychologist had observed a similar phenomenon while doing graduate work at the University of Pennsylvania. E. B. Twitmyer (1905) had been investigating the patellar tendon reflex, the knee jerk. In his experiment, Twitmyer would ring a bell and then release a small mallet that would strike the pressure receptors in the subject's tendon, triggering a knee jerk. While working with a subject, he accidentally hit the bell without releasing the mallet. Immediately, the knee jerked-without having been hit! Why?

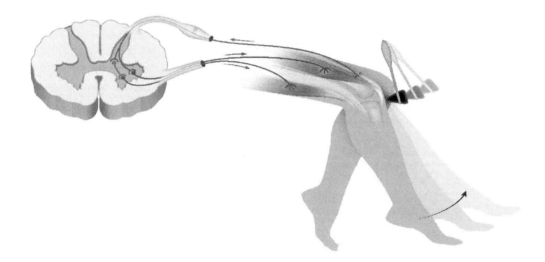

Did you jerk your knee?" He had not voluntarily jerked his knee; the reflex seemed to have operated on its own.

Have you guessed what Twitmyer was observing? This was a learned, or conditioned, reflex. Quickly realizing that he had made a significant discovery, Twitmyer dropped his original investigation and set out to study the phenomenon. He made note of his findings in his doctoral dissertation. No one noticed. In 1904, he reported his findings to the American Psychological Association; they listened, applauded politely, and left. Knee jerks? Simply not relevant, not meaningful. Discouraged, Twitmyer abandoned his research.

A few decades later, American psychologists would hastily revise their opinion of Twitmyer's discovery, but meanwhile the field had been left open to the again incidental observation of the Russian physiologist Pavlov. And when Pavlov caught the ball, he ran with it.

If the dogs salivated to a visual stimulus (Pavlov) that previously had been paired with feeding, would they salivate to other stimuli, say a noise? Pavlov rigged a restraining belt for the dog and a means of delivering meat powder directly onto the tongue of the dog. Another special device measured the drops of saliva as they came from the salivary gland. He sounded a bell. Nothing happened. The dog looked up inquisitively, but did not salivate. He sounded the bell again, immediately followed it with meat powder, and the dog salivated. Twice more he presented the stimuli: bell-meat, bell-meat. After the third pairing, he presented the bell alone. Seven drops of saliva appeared in the tube-saliva secreted to the stimulus of the bell alone!

Again, he paired the stimuli; bell-meat, bell-meat-and after six pairings, he again sounded the bell alone. Twelve drops of saliva appeared in the tube.   Further trials did not increase the strength of the response.   The dogs reached the maximum response of which they were capable after an average of only six pairings.

16. EXTRANEOUS VARIABLES

As always, many intervening variables interfere with learning.   Just as it is very hard to teach a dog anything if he is distracted by any novel stimuli or to get a child to do what you want him to do. It is difficult to get across an idea to a student who is daydreaming of being in Cancun or talking to the girl next to him.   That does not disprove the idea that learning is possible, only that it is more difficult than we hoped.

Parents often note the difficulty of using behavior modification on their own children.   That is very real.   But it is not proof of the failure of the principles, only of the power of other stimuli to distract our attention from the learning at hand.   Children have *"minds of their own"* and they are only interested in the sights and sounds that excite their own minds, not so much in the ideas we are trying to teach.

Galileo said that all objects fall at the same speed.   Others pointed out that if you drop a piece of paper and a book, which will hit the ground first? Does that disprove Galileo? No. It is the extraneous variable, *Air*, that keeps a piece of paper from following the discovery of Galileo. When astronauts landed on the moon, one of the experiments they demonstrated before the camera was to drop a feather and a rock in the airless world of the moon. Both hit the ground at the same time.

17. THE EARLY FAILURE OF S-R PSYCHOLOGY TO EXPLAIN BEHAVIOR.

It has to be noted that any attempt to teach a dog or a child is severely limited by any other stimuli. Curiosity overwhelms their selective attention.   Their attention is often grabbed by anything or everything. Developmental psychologists would say the child has "A Mind of Their Own." Yet the permutations of curiosity or the effect of previous experience do not invalidate the basic discovery.

Galileo said that all objects fall at the same rate, no matter how heavy or light they are. Critics quickly pointed out that a feather or a piece of paper do not fall at the same rate. But that is because other extraneous variables (the air) buoy up the paper or feather. Galileo's experiment showed that using light and heavy balls, they both hit the ground at the same time.   The air was simply one of many extraneous variables that gave a wrong impression.

Early in the history of behavioral psychology, the first behaviorists were excited by the prospect that it could be possible to make psychology so precise, so predictable, that we could predict every movement, every element of behavior.   In other words, we could mathematically predict behavior as effectively as the science of physics can predict the movements of atoms in space.   We fairly salivated at the thought of becoming a "real" science, like physics.

But even the best psychologists failed to find a mathematical formula that could predict behavior with mathematical precision. Many thought this was a failure of psychology to become a "real" science. Psychology attempted to be like physics, to reduce every element of behavior to mathematical equations. It was a dismal failure. We could not even predict the precise behavior of a rat in a maze. Random behavior is a variable in psychology.

Then, it turned out that physics was not so precise either. Heisenberg's *Principle of Uncertainty,* and *Chaos Theory*, and the *"Law of Chance"* and the variability of the Normal or Abnormal *Distribution Curves,* and Schrodinger's cat all pointed out the need for physics to rely on general principles, they could not predict the behavior of a single photon in a slot maze. Random chance was built into reality.

It made little practical difference. In the real world, the general principles work quite well.

Then, in an amazing argument between the upstart mathematician Kurt Godel and the world-famous mathematician David Hubel, it turned out that even mathematics was not perfect. They could not find a perfect resolution to every problem. Again, it made little difference to the real world of mathematics we live in. It was mostly a curiosity among the mathematicians.

But at least psychology was not alone. Nature is random. The Normal Distribution Curve provided us with a way to plot the variability. If we could hold curiosity and prior experience constant, if we could control the variables, then we could plot the outcome.

18. WHAT LEARNING THEORY CAN NOT EXPLAIN

Critics of the S-R, or S-S approach have pointed out problems that cannot be explained by this simple approach.

- Consider a "flashbulb" memory. Almost everyone can remember where they were the first time they heard of the Kennedy assassination or the attack on the Twin Towers on September 11. I can not only remember the event; I vividly remember the road I was on when I first heard of these events on my car radio and exactly where I was when I saw it on television later. It is not just a stimulus-response memory it is like a general impression of everything going on at the time. An image is implanted in my brain. It is like Darwin saying, *"…I remember the very spot in the road whilst traveling in my carriage…"* when he had his great insight. What kind of memory is a flashbulb memory? Is Sensory Impression the most basic form of learning?

- Studies show that we do better on exams if we take the exam in the *same* room we study in instead of a different room. Why?

- Edward Tolman noted we learn by what he called "Cognitive Maps" and "Latent" learning. How?

- We can condition an adult to fear a word in a laboratory, by giving a mild electric shock associated with that word, yet he will not fear that word outside of the laboratory. Why?

- You cannot teach an adult to fear a furry animal as easily as you can a child. Why?

- If you try to multiply two numbers in your head, say 12 X 13, you may find that you have to imagine the two numbers in your mind, even chalk it up like on a chalk board in your mind, to do this.

19. ESTES STIMULUS SAMPLING HYPOTHESIS:
How Nothing Becomes Something

Robert Estes did not start out to solve the problem of the century in psychology. He wanted to explain something more simple. Why did it take Pavlov's dogs six pairings of Bell-Meat, Bell-Meat, before they reached the maximum level of saliva? Why did the dogs not learn this simple response in one trial?

The question of one-trial learning was once a significant issue in psychology. Estes provided a remarkably simple answer to this profound question that also applies to the issue of "which came first, the Stimulus Impression or S-R learning". Imagine a dog in Pavlov's laboratory. The Bell sounds. He perks up his ears, a curiosity response. But it is not associated with anything yet.

What Estes realized is that the bell (S) is not the only stimulus going off just before the food is presented. Other dogs may be barking (S). Pavlov's assistant may be sneezing (S), the door may be creaking (S), the wind is blowing outside (S), people may be talking nearby (S), or anything that catches his attention (S, S, S).

As trial follows trial, most of these stimuli gradually drop out. The Bell will still sound, dogs may still be barking, the wind may still be blowing… but no sneezing, no squeaking door.

As trials continue, the one constant stimulus is the Bell associated with the Meat.

Many studies in psychology that never made sense now suddenly make sense; For example, we know that if you study for a test in the same room in which you take that test, you will remember much better than if you take the test in an unfamiliar room. We do not just learn the material; we learn the material as part of a complete Sensory Impression of everything that is going on. Many other stimuli present at the same time are learned, along with the initial impression.

I remember my grandmother going into the other room to get something, and then forgetting what she went in for. Then she had to come back into the room she came from, with all the stimuli present at the time she started out, to be able to remember what it was she forgot. I find myself doing the same thing. Somehow, just being in the same room you started from, with all the original stimuli, makes it much easier to remember.

When we have a flashbulb memory, it is a Sensory Impression on the brain. We are not learning just one S-S connection, but every impression that is going on at the time, even brief bits of a recording of everything going on at the time. Vision, sound, touch, and sometimes even taste and smell, all stimuli may all be recorded at the same time.

What this also would illustrate is that Sensory Impressions, as in Bumps and Dents, is the most basic form of learning. Then, only after the initial impressions, do Stimulus-Stimulus associations (light and shadow) develop.

Finally, Perception may develop out of the associations. So, the confusing part; stimulus-stimulus associations may become a perception, but out of many perceptions, perception may then become a concept or even a stimulus by itself. Something in-between "which came first, the chicken or the egg?" and Schrodinger's cat. Out of many perceptions, those perceptions may develop into concepts, ideas, schema, learning sets; whatever you want to call it.

20. THE SEQUENCE OF CONDITIONING

In psychology today, textbooks divide conditioning into two parts, Classical Conditioning by Pavlov and Operant Conditioning by Thorndike and Skinner. Yet a survey of psychologists across the nation showed that a clear majority of psychologists say they are not two separate forms of learning, but only different aspects of the same basic learning. If we look at a temporal, time-based, outline of the two procedures, we can see just how similar the two are.

Their similarities become evident if we outline them in terms of the sequential order of stimuli and responses as shown, not unlike the order in our memory discovered by Penfield and Roberts, or the order on a Video Replay of events.

Classical Conditioning (Pavlov, Watson)

TRIAL	STIMULUS		RESPONSE
1.	BELL --- ---	MEAT	SALIVA
2	BELL saliva	MEAT	SALIVA
3	BELL - Saliva	MEAT	SALIVA
4	BELL - Saliva	MEAT	SALIVA
5	BELL -SALIVA		

Operant Conditioning (Thorndike, Skinner)

TRIAL	STIMULUS	RESPONSE	REINFORCEMENT (Positive Stimulus)
1.	STRING (SEES)	PULLS STRING	Freedom/Food (Reduced Hunger, Etc.)
2.	STRING -	PULLS STRING	REINFORCEMENT, PLEASURE
3	STRING	PULLS STRING	REINFORCEMENT, PLEASURE
4,	STRING	(POSITIVE BY ASSOCIATION)	

In conditioning, the First Stimulus, becomes the cue that the Second Stimulus (or response) will follow. That enables the mind to react in anticipation of what to expect.

Psychologists would qualify this statement by noting that the animal must pay attention to the stimulus before conditioning occurs. If Pavlov's bell had sounded while the dog was busy looking over a strange new dog, conditioning might not have occurred. There are many such permutation effects that interfere with learning.

HOW DO CLASSICAL AND OPERANT CONDITIONING DIFFER?

In Classical or Pavlovian Conditioning, the environment is acting upon the individual—as in Steven Spielberg pairing music with someone being eaten by a shark. The music now elicits a response in your own body, even controlling the release of adrenalin, etc.

In Operant or Thorndike's Conditioning, the individual is *operating* on their environment. The rat presses a bar (an operation) and food results. We say "good morning" to someone, they smile and greet us. If they did not say "hello" to us when we said this to them, then our response of saying "good morning" to them, would quickly go into extinction. Just as if pressing a bar no longer gave the rat food, the rat would stop pressing the bar.

Yet, both forms are in a similar temporal sequence. When a questionnaire was sent out to chairs of psychology departments asking them if Classical and Operant Conditioning were two different forms of learning, or just part of the same learning process, the great majority of chairs responded they were both part of the same learning process, not separate forms. Yet it is still universally taught as if they were two different forms. What they both have in common is the simple *association between a stimulus and a response*.

Any stimulus? Any stimulus that trips the organism's neural sensors could be conditioned to produce salivation: *visual stimuli* such as color, patterns, and sequential presentations of patterns; *auditory stimuli* such as noise, loud or soft tones, words, sequential patterns of words, and even fluctuations in the tone of voice; and *tactile stimuli* such as heat, cold, pressure, pain, and even feedback from internal proprioceptive pressure sensors embedded in the muscles that cannot even be consciously experienced.

Very subtle changes in tone, pressure, light intensity, and color can be conditioned to become discrete, specific stimuli eliciting a specific response; as in discrimination training. Pavlov found a dog could be trained to salivate not only at a low amplitude tone but also when the tone changed only slightly in frequency.

Most learning does not occur in a laboratory with ringing bells, ticking metronomes, and meat powder. Pavlov was not developing a new technique. He was simply making clear, for the first time, exactly how conditioning (learning) normally occurs. In real life, conditioning is typically so subtle, so masked by the infinite variety of stimuli that can occur simultaneously, and by the infinite number of previous experiences that have formed, that it is difficult to even observe learning happening outside of a laboratory.

Any Response (R) If Pavlov could do nothing more than to make a dog salivate when he rang a bell or flashed a light, the conditioning phenomenon would be of little value. However, conditioning could be affected not only by any stimulus but by many different responses already wired into the nervous system; from knee jerks to pupillary response, to, as Watson demonstrated, our most basic *fight or flight* emotions.

21. OBSERVATIONAL LEARNING:

The Power Of Imitation (Modeling)

Albert Bandura demonstrated imitation, or modeling, a uniquely primate form of learning.

Albert Bandura is most famous for his Bobo doll experiment, where he found that children, exposed to a model of an adult hitting a Bobo doll, would quickly imitate the behavior they saw. Bandura himself came to regret that that was all he was remembered for. His most important work is often left out of the textbooks.

In a remarkable study by Albert Bandura, he found he could counter condition or desensitize the fear of dogs in children, a common childhood phobia, by showing them four, four-minute videos of a boy playing with a cocker spaniel. This important study is an exceptional method of applying a cognitive technique to accomplish the behavioral methods of Mary Cover Jones, who counter-conditioned and desensitized little Peter from his fear of dogs. Simply by showing videos, we could use this technique to counter fear in 40 or more individuals at once (Shepard). This bridges the gap between Behavioral therapy and Cognitive psychology, although it was often ignored by psychology.

Imitation gives us an ability rarely found in animals lower on the phylogenetic scale. Primates can learn by imitation, but it seems to reach its maximum in humans. For a real-life example of just how powerful it can be, check out this two-year-old baby trying to imitate Beyonce while watching her on television.

https://www.youtube.com/watch?v=c5BXdDdsPL4

Here is a baby, barely old enough to stand, trying his heart out to imitate Beyonce dancing in a television video. There are biological programs in the brain that allow us to imitate the behavior we observe in others. This is a step up from simple stimulus-response learning and the law of effect.

Scientists at the University of Parma, in Italy, have discovered "mirror" neurons in the brain that "act out" a scene we have just witnessed, by stimulating 20% of the same neurons in the person *watching* the video. The same areas of the brain that were active in the person in the video, would be seen in the brain of the person only watching the video. When one experimenter was licking an ice cream cone, the same areas of the brain of a monkey that was watching, began "lighting up" under the fMRI. These studies hold promise for Cognitive Psychology to give us a possible understanding of the unique properties of the brain.

Albert Bandura's studies on children acting out aggression that they had just observed, seem to have a neurological basis. Bandura's work began an interest in exploring what we imitate. We imitate parents, peers, Hollywood heroes, and political and religious ideas. The stories embedded in our brains by others have a profound effect on our behavior, and on what we believe. That influence applied to sex (see Bandura and Walters p370 in Ch. 19) and peer group pressure or social conformity, and in one of the most important studies ever, in psychotherapy (see Bandura's use of videos to counter 44 children's fear of dogs Ch. 22) and more.

BANDURA'S EXTENSIVE CONTRIBUTION TO PSYCHOLOGY

Although Bandura is most remembered for his experiments on imitation or modeling such as the Bobo doll imitation of aggression, this was only one of his studies in a long history of remarkable work. Much of his best work has been missed by textbooks. Perhaps his greatest work was his study that found he could counter the fear of dogs in 44 children by simply showing them a few minutes of film of a boy playing with a cocker spaniel over four days. Then, the boys could pet a dog which they never could before.

Thus, he was able to counter the fear with an observational study using only films, even on many children at once. This demonstrated that the behavioral work of Mary Cover Jones, in countering little Albert's fear of dogs, could be done simply and easily with only examples. This has broad implications for therapy, including in teens and adults. See Chapter 22 on Therapy or Shepard's *Forces of Mind*, for more extensive examples.

Bandura's work with observational learning bridged the gap between Behavioral psychology and Cognitive psychology in a way that is too little appreciated.

A stimulus is any sensation experienced by the organism: anything that triggers our sense of, sight or hearing or touch· or taste or smell. Equally important; internal thoughts *or* sensations of hunger or movement of our arms and legs ·will produce *proprioceptive* stimuli that the brain can experience. The common characteristic of these stimuli is that they all involve the discharge of electrical impulses by nerve cells within the brain.

A stimulus could be all of the stimuli that occur at the same time, not just a single stimulus. Even a whole mental image, such as the observational studies of Bandura, might be a stimulus.

We have briefly discussed the second and third classes of responses: emotional responses and video replays, or memory traces. The feedback from a response may itself become a stimulus for another response, leading to a chaining of responses.

A mother and son in the zoo have learned a new way to get food. She is begging for peanuts that visitors to the zoo toss to them. Her son has learned the same behavior, perhaps by imitation. None of this is in their genes, yet the remarkable ability of learning, and learning by imitation, make both able to secure food in a most unnatural environment.

22. MEMORY: THE VIDEO REPLAY

Reflexive and emotional responses are not the only responses possible. A stimulus may elicit a "memory trace" or perhaps a chain of "memory traces." The physiological basis of memory was first demonstrated in a series of remarkable studies by the Canadian neurosurgeon Wilder Penfield and his associates. Penfield and Roberts applied electrical stimulation to portions of the brains of human patients who had to undergo open brain surgery. As the brain has no pain or touch sensors, it is possible to operate under a local anesthetic that allows the patients to remain conscious and describe what they experience.

The surgeons touched an electrical probe to the surface of the brain, releasing an electrical current that discharged or fired nerve cells in that portion of the brain. When the electrical stimulus was touched to the side of the exposed brain, the patients reported vivid memories from the past: "Flashbacks" from former experiences, familiar scenes, faces, and events were often described in detail. But these experiences were described as more vivid than a dream, more true to life than a memory. It was as if the patients were describing a video replay of a past experience-complete with sensations of sight, sound, touch, and emotion.

There are no uncertainties about what the patients report. The replay they describe persists for as long as the electricity is flowing to the probe and stops the instant it is withdrawn. Sometimes the tape can be repeated after withdrawing the electrode by restimulating the same point. Each time the replay begins at the beginning, and it *always* unfolds in a forward sequence that is strikingly similar to the forward temporal sequence in conditioning studies.

Ordinarily, a memory trace might be elicited by a visual, auditory, or tactile stimulus from the environment, and not by direct electrical stimulation of the brain. This stimulus might be a word, a face, a pattern of stimuli, or even a thought. The fact that an ordinary memory is not as vivid as the one recalled under electrical stimulation is probably not surprising. Penfield and Roberts suggest that if all memory traces were as vivid as their patient's report, it might be impossible to think in the resulting confusion of overwhelming stimuli.

One problem with considering such memory traces as stimuli-produced responses is the difficulty of measuring or even observing such responses. However, even though this concept is not a part of traditional learning theory, mental images are of such importance that any theory failing to take account of them cannot hope to explain human behavior.

23. LIKE RAIN ON THE OCEAN:
The Subtlety of Learning

At about the same time as Pavlov and Thorndike were beginning to uncover the basic principles, an interesting example of the subtlety of the phenomenon was taking place in Berlin. A German named Von Osten proudly disclosed to the scientific world that he had a horse with an I.Q. at the genius level, at least for horses. Clever Hans, as the horse came to be known, showed remarkable powers of reasoning. He could add and subtract and even solve complex mathematical problems. He tapped the answers quickly, and usually correctly, with his hoof. Single taps with his right foot indicated single units, and single taps with his left indicated units of ten. The horse also could read and write. The alphabet was printed on a large chart (in German, of course, since Hans was a German horse) with the number of taps, in code, that would be equivalent to each letter. Questions were written on a blackboard, and using this code, Hans tapped out the answers, spelling words and even sentences.

Hans could even do square roots. Now, if a horse can do square roots, students have no excuse.

Scientists from across Europe marveled at Hans' remarkable behavior. Skeptics, however, watched Clever Hans, and they watched Clever von Osten.   Surely some signal-some means of cueing the horse was responsible for this unique behavior.

They knew that of all the domestic animals, cats, dogs, white rats, the horse was not the smartest of all creatures. Horses could not even make their way out of a barn on fire. Could it be that Hans was an exception? No, surely something was wrong.

One observer noted something of interest.   Clever Hans could do mathematical problems only if van Osten knew how to do them. He could spell only words von Osten could spell. The limit of von Osten's I.Q.   seemed to be the limit of the horse's I.Q.   Psychologist Karl Stumph finally proposed an experiment.   Von Osten was asked to step out of view while he asked Hans a question.   Clever Hans was instantly reduced to ordinary Hans.   Questions that had been simple for Hans were now only occasionally answered correctly (8% or at random).

Von Osten himself seemed surprised at Hans's difficulty.   Why was the horse's efficiency reduced? Were the psychic vibrations of his interrogators incompatible with Hans's cerebral wavelengths? Further observation revealed that von Osten tensed up when Hans started counting and relaxed when he reached the correct number.   As it turned out, the owner had been giving Hans very subtle cues as to when to stop responding. Immediately after Osten relaxed, Hans was rewarded for his success with a lump of sugar.   Hans slobbered copiously.

More than saliva had been paired with a stimulus.   Hans had been reinforced after the visual stimulus of van Osten's relaxation, and thus he was conditioned to tap until van Osten relaxed.   Other subtle cues, such as van Osten leaning slightly to one side or the other, would show Hans whether tapping with the left foot or the right foot would be followed by reinforcement.

Hans's entire repertoire of behavior can be reduced piece by piece to a conditioning phenomenon-a series of conditioning steps similar to that outlined earlier.   Von Osten never charged money for Hans's performances and, in fact, seemed genuinely surprised by Hans's difficulty in performing with other people.

It is generally believed that van Osten himself was unaware of the cues that Hans relied on and had not consciously trained him to perform.   In other words, he genuinely believed that Hans could read and write. Even granting that considerable coaching may have been given, the performance of the horse in response to such subtle cues is still quite remarkable.

THE S-R BOND:

The "Atom" of Psychology?

The S-R concept is a model of the association between a stimulus and a response, or a stimulus-stimulus association, in time and space, a model into which the temporal relationship between the environment and the organism can be fitted.

An awareness of the relationships between stimuli and responses makes it easier for us to see the controls over our behavior.   At present, we have only a vague understanding of the neural nature of the S-R bond.   We do not fully understand the physical nature of the memory trace.

The S-R and S-S concept of the association between stimuli has value as an ordering principle: It orders the complex relationship between the environment and behavior, just as mathematics is designed to order the complex physical world, and it clarifies the effect of experiences that otherwise would be lost in the disorder of complex behavior.

24. SCIENCE AS REDUCTIONISM

All of science is based on reductionism. In physics, the subject is *matter*. Matter is reducible to molecules. Molecules are reducible to the elements in the periodic table. These are reducible to the structure of atoms. Atoms are reducible to electrons, protons, and neutrinos, etc... These subatomic particles are reducible to quarks and maybe strings...

In biology, the subject matter is *living matter*. Living matter is reducible to organs; heart, lungs, liver, and brain. The organs are composed of organized groups of cells. All of the organs are composed of cells. Every part of the human body is composed of cells; Neurons in the brain, the Isles of Langerhans in the pancreas, bone marrow cells, cells that secrete protein to make fingernails, hair, bone. Cells are reducible to mitochondria, RNA, DNA, and the four base pairs of chemicals in the DNA code...

In psychology, there has been no easy agreement, yet we see similar reductionism. The subject of psychology is the Mind. The Mind is reducible to Concepts (Ideas or thoughts, schema, learning sets, cognitive maps, imitation, etc.) which are reducible to perceptions, which are reducible to associations (S-S, S-R). Or, is it possible that images in the brain are more basic than S-R associations? See the next chapter on perception.

SUBJECT	Reduces to:	Reduces further to:
Physics (Matter)	Elements------------Atoms--------------	Subatomic Particles
Biology (Living Matter)	Organs--------------Cells----------------	DNA, RNA, etc.
Psychology (Mind)	Concepts-----------Perceptions---------	Associations (S-S, S-R) MORE

Although psychologists may not all agree, it seems inevitable that reductionism will have to apply to psychology as it has to other areas of science. It seems likely that concepts, perceptions and associations can produce every aspect of learning we know, in a way that is roughly analogous to how changing the frequency of electromagnetic radiation can produce widely varying forms of radiation (X-Rays, Gamma Rays, Radio waves, light, etc.), including varied forms of color and frequencies for radio stations, etc. Nature tends to prefer the simplest mechanisms that produce the greatest variety.

The **MORE** would have to include Stimulus Generalization, Approach-Avoidance conflict, the Prime Experience, Selective Attention, Imitation, generalization, discrimination, learning concepts or sets, the relative speed of the neural action, and still MORE. All of which influence our perception of reality, out of which our conscious mind develops. All of these areas are subjects of study by psychologists.

The "WOW" factor, whatever the peer group, society, the news media, or Hollywood gets excited over, becomes embedded in the mind of the child. From sports to sex, it all happens with the same subtle method with which we learn the language we speak; Simple Association and Psychology's General Theory of Relativity (Any Stimulus-Any Response). It colors and controls our response to everything from sex to politics to religion. It winds its way through our everyday responses from interpersonal relations to our superstitions.

Any Stimulus—Any Emotion.

It is all relative.

Yet there is evidence that S-S or S-R associations may *not* be the most basic form of learning. See the next chapter on perception for details.

PRINCIPLES OF CONDITIONING

If you hear the term "Conditioned" think of "learned".

If you hear the term "Unconditioned" think of "unlearned" or natural.

An unlearned stimulus is one that elicits a natural response (saliva, fear, fight, etc.).

Unconditioned stimulus *(UCS):* The unconditioned (or unlearned) stimulus elicits an automatic, unconditioned response (UCR) from an animal.   All of us are pre-wired by our genes, in such a way that we give automatic responses to unconditioned stimuli such as food, water, pain, discomfort, sexual stimulation, novel stimuli, and a great many more. If paired with another UCS, many of these stimuli can also become conditioned stimuli.

Even memory could be considered as an unconditioned response to-novelty. That is, that novel stimuli or novel combinations of stimuli are automatically recorded (UCR) by the brain.

Conditioned stimulus (CS:) A stimulus (ex. Bell) that is paired with an unconditioned stimulus (ex. Meat) can become a conditioned Stimulus.   That CS that will elicit a conditioned response (CR) similar to the response previously elicited only by the food (UCS).

Conditioned response (CR).   if any Stimulus (CS) is paired with an unconditioned stimulus (UCS) then that stimulus will become a CS that will elicit a response (CR) similar to that previously elicited by the unconditioned stimulus (UCS); The CR is learned response, It is now similar to the unlearned response.

Stimulus Generalization: Once conditioned to respond, like little Albert learning to fear a tame white rat, this would generalize to similar stimuli (any furry animal even a ball of cotton).

Extinction: If the CS (like the bell) is presented repeatedly without being followed by the UCS (meat), the organism will gradually stop responding, and the response is said to have "gone into *extinction*." If the, CS of Pavlov's bell were to be presented repeatedly to a trained dog...   without following the CS with the UCS (meat), the dog would gradually stop salivating.

Extinction is not the same as forgetting: -The dog does not forget to respond; it learns that the meat no longer follows the bell; In effect, it *learns* not *to* respond.

Spontaneous recovery: Suppose that a response has gone into extinction.   Sounding the bell, no longer brings a response. Yet days later, if you now sound the bell again, the old response may return.

Chaining of Responses   Complex behavior, such as sports, can be composed of chains of stimuli.

Successive Approximations of the final behavior may be learned. Even in our schools, we teach math by first learning the 1, 2, 3s, then addition and subtraction, followed by multiplication and division, until algebra, etc...

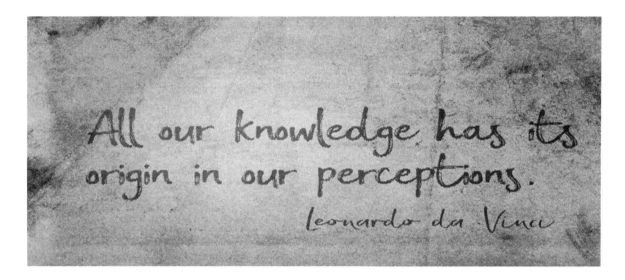

9 ORIGIN OF KNOWLEDGE
AND PERCEPTION
Innate Or Learned?

What Is the Source of "Knowledge"? The new Cataract Studies • The Brain Cannot See without Experience • Experiments in Perception • Learning Determines Perception

"We must remember that we do not observe nature as it actually exists, but nature exposed to our methods of perception. The theories determine what we can or cannot observe... Reality is an illusion, albeit a persistent one".

Albert Einstein

1. THE ORIGIN OF PERCEPTION

Psychologists Combs and Syneg tell of two graduate students who were coming home late at night, speeding down the highway, when suddenly the headlights fell on an object, about three feet around, on the road.

The passenger, seeing that the driver was going to hit the object, suddenly grabbed the wheel of the car and attempted to steer the car around the object. The driver fought just as hard to keep the car going straight toward the object. Why? Both saw the same object. Both had exactly the same sensation on the retina of their eyes.

The passenger was from the Rocky Mountain states and the object he saw on the highway was a boulder. If you are from Colorado, you know that boulders on the road are not uncommon. The driver was from the Plains states, and the object he saw on the road was a tumbleweed.

The moment of truth comes, of course, when you hit the object.

I have been driving on the road in New Mexico at night when a tumbleweed appeared on the road ahead. You cannot tell if it is solid, until you hit it.

This frames the difference between *sensation*, what the eye sees, and *perception*, what we have *learned* from our unique experiences.

To see a discussion of perception and an example of how our experiences read reality into our perception, see the World Science Festival: *The Reality of Reality: A Tale of Five Senses*:

https://www.youtube.com/watch?v=S1jn86eUX0E

2. WHEN THE BRAIN IS NOT PROGRAMMED, THE MIND CAN NOT SEE

Only very recently has a dramatic new wave of understanding of the age-old question of nature (biology) vs nurture (experience) been answered. Previously, psychologists and biologists have always assumed that the brain developed separately from experience; that the brain unfolded from the DNA without experience. New studies have found that the brain itself is dramatically dependent upon experience.

Not even psychologists suspected that the brain itself, needed experience from the environment before even the most basic perception of reality could emerge.

There are a series of studies of a rare condition where babies are born with a cataract in only one eye. Although rare, there have been some 200 cases of babies born with a clouded lens in only one eye, that completely obscured vision in that eye. We have learned that without experience from a very early age, the clouded eye will fail to develop the visual areas of the brain, even though the eye and brain are still quite normal.

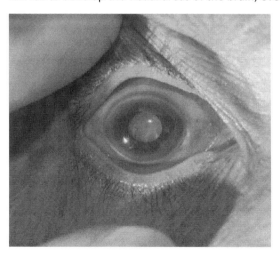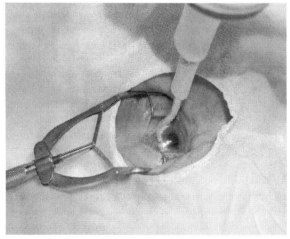

Further, the cataract must be removed within the first months after birth to prevent the permanent loss of vision in that eye. Not only does the cataract have to be removed, but a contact lens, and much later a new plastic lens, have to be inserted to replace the clouded lens.

Just as important, the normal eye must now be patched, sometimes for years, to prevent it from seeing, to force the brain to develop the neural connections it takes to allow the eye that had the cataract to see.

VISION CAN NOT DEVELOP WITHOUT EXPERIENCE

If the normal eye is not patched, the brain will ignore the new input from the eye that had the cataract, and focus all of its selective *attention* on the first good eye.   That would mean that the surgery to remove the cataract would not benefit the baby unless the eye that formerly had a cataract was now forced to develop.

This is similar to a condition found in older individuals called amblyopia, or "lazy eye".   If one is fitted with glasses or contacts, where one eye sees more clearly than the other, the brain will ignore the poorly fitted eye and focus all of its attention on the correctly fitted eye.

In an older child or adult this can be corrected with refitting and simple eye exercises.   But in a baby, this is so critical that the brain itself will fail to develop the neural processes needed for vision with that eye, and the eye may become useless.

For a visual example of what happens in the brain of a baby born with a cataract in only one eye see the PBS series on *The Secret Life of the Brain: The Baby's Brain* (about ¾ the way through.)

https://www.youtube.com/watch?v=U0L0mYi_ftc&t=87s

What is the source of knowledge? Note that Locke and Molyneux were talking about *knowledge*, which implies understanding.   They were not talking about the "instinctual" or reflexive processes that are already present in animals that control our search for food or sex.   The failure to distinguish between knowledge and instinct, has made it an unnecessarily difficult question for psychologists to argue over.   See the next chapter on instinct.

Learning does not just give the brain information to process, as in a computer, it changes the brain itself so completely that it creates a new reality in the brain. From the bits and pieces of our perception, the brain creates a reality; the mind "sees" what the brain has been shaped to see.

By this analysis, the brain is not the linear computer imagined by Turing, although the function is similar. Instead, it is closer to being a "holographic" computer, ruled by emotion, steeped in the prime experiences that are now "hardwired" into the brain by experience. **It is not just "programmed", the biology of the brain is actually sculpted. A child has more neural connections than an adult. As the brain grows through experience, some neuronal synapses are strengthened, while others wither and disappear; "Use it or Lose it". The result is a brain that has been sculpted by experience. This sculpting is known as "pruning".**

From birth to the age of three the number of synapses increases from an estimated 2,500 to 15,000 synapses on each neuron. https://www.ncbi.nlm.nih.gov/pmc/articles/PMC3222570/

https://learnbehavioral.com/blog/brain-plasticity-2

Yet no analogy is entirely adequate to describe what the brain does. Just as the chapter on the senses noted that we still cannot explain how the brain gives us color, sound, taste, smell, out of simple neural responses, we are not at a point where any analogy is complete. Perhaps a future neuropsychologist will enlighten us.

Even before the new studies on babies with a cataract in only one eye, there were strong hints from studies that showed how our very perception of reality is a product of learning, not our DNA.

3. LEARNED REALITY

HOW CAN YOU SEE 3-D IN ONLY 2 DIMENSIONS?

Above you see a steel plate with indentations. Are these markings dents, or are they bumps? Are the rivets dents or bumps? Look at the picture, especially the impressions on the right, and decide what the indentations appear to be. What do you see? They are dents from cannonball hits. Then, turn the picture upside down and look at it again.

Your impression may change from one form to the other, even while you look at it the same way. Upside down, the dents become bumps.

Why do you perceive it differently? In fact, it is a two-dimensional picture, not three-dimensional at all. Perceiving the photo as three-dimensional is itself a product of our past experience. We perceive bumps or dents (both three-dimensional perceptions) because of our prior experiences, not because of what our senses "see" in the picture.

No conscious thought is required. No conscious thought can prevent it. Your automatic brain presents this to your conscious mind.

Yet your conscious mind can sit back and observe how your brain works, quite independent of your conscious awareness. Our past experience creates our reality.

DO WE THINK OR DO WE PERCEIVE?

We do not just "think" these are bumps or dents; we actively *perceive* them as bumps and dents. We only "think" about it after the brain shows us what to perceive.

Whether you see bumps or dents does not depend on reality. You are seeing neither bumps nor dents. What you are seeing is a flat, two-dimensional picture. It has no depth. Yet, even though there is no depth in the picture, the brain actually "sees" (perceives) this as three-dimensional because of our past experience with light and shadow, in much the same way as people saw a tumbleweed or a boulder. How is this possible?

Past experience influences our perception of "reality," even though we have no conscious awareness of its influence. From years of prior experience with our environment, we are conditioned to perceive light as coming from above. If light comes from above, shadows are cast downward, not upward. Bumps cast shadows below them; a dent would be illuminated at the bottom and the shadow would be near the top on the inside.

What is significant about this illustration is that the effect, seeing dents one way or bumps the other, works even though the viewers are unable to explain why they interpret it this way. *It is not necessary to even think about the shadows for the effect to appear.*

Ekhard Hess devised an ingenious way to test the origin of this perception. He raised two groups of chicks, one on a plexiglass floor with light coming from above. The other is on clear plexiglass with the light coming from below. When grain was fed to the normally reared group, the top of the grain would be lit, and the bottom would be in shadow. When grain was fed to the second group, with the light below, the shadow would be on top and the bottom of the grain would be lit.

Then he tested each group with photographs. The normally reared chicks spent most all of their time pecking at the photo of grain with the light on top, not the photo with light coming from the bottom. The group reared with light coming from below, spent most of their time pecking at the photo of grain with the light coming from below. Each responded to the perception they grew up with.

About two in ten students can explain why they see dents one way or bumps another. If they are given longer to look at the picture and think about it, more students might catch on, but what is important is that our past experience can not only determine our perception of "reality" but it can do so without our conscious awareness of its influence.

Furthermore, even when we become aware of the past experience that has influenced our perceptions, the effect still works. We cannot change our perception just by knowing why it happens.

As we shall see later, our past experience has an even greater effect on our subjective impressions of good and bad, and on our thoughts and behavior. Again, this influence operates whether or not we are aware of it.

4. NEUROPLASTICITY
FLIP THE WORLD UPSIDE DOWN.
CAN THE BRAIN RECOVER?

In a series of studies by psychologists Ivo Kohler, P. K. Pronko, and others, they asked student volunteers to wear a pair of goggles for a week that would flip the world upside down. We know that the lens of the eye projects an upside-down picture to the visual cortex, but the brain interprets that as right-side up. If we went one step further, and flipped the vision upside down, would they be able to make it in this new world?

At first, the world appeared distorted. When asked to pour water into a cup from a pitcher, they faced the fact that not only did the table and pitcher appear upside down, but their arm and cup appeared upside down. When they moved their right hand into position, the hand and arm came in from on top. They spilled water all over the table.

Even walking proved difficult. They had to have another student follow them around campus to ensure their safety. Yet by the end of a week, some could ride a bicycle around campus.

Their brains had adjusted remarkably well to learning the new reality. But it took days of experience, much like a baby's first learning to make sense of its world. William James once described how the world would look to a newborn baby as *"a blooming, buzzing confusion."* He was criticized by many who still believe in inborn ability, but James's comment has proven closer to correct than his critics.

The remarkable ability of the brain to adapt to a wide variety of circumstances involved learning visual-motor coordination. But it is a critically important step to understanding what the brain is all about. Not just the language we speak and understand is determined by experience, but our very perception of reality is determined by our interaction with our environment.

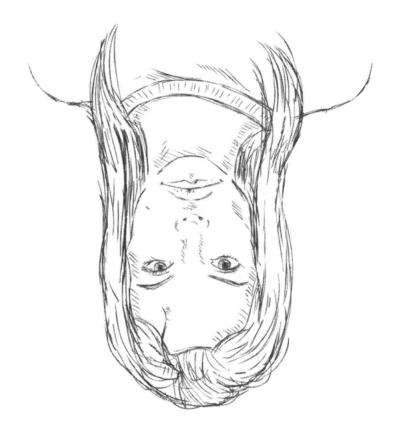

Focus on the above picture until you think you know what you are seeing. Does your conscious mind see anything unique about this picture? Turn the picture upside down to see what your conscious mind cannot see.

> First demonstrated by Peter Thompson of York University with a picture of Margaret Thatcher. This effect is common, even if done with an actual picture.

Why? Why is your conscious mind unable to see reality? Our conscious mind relies on the images and ideas that experience has embedded into our brain. We have few imprints in our brains for what people look like upside down. All we know is what she should look like right side up. So, when we see the above image, her mouth is actually right-side up. When we turn it upside down, then we see what our conscious mind cannot see.

The first ideas or images embedded in our minds become the template by which we judge all reality. Without the comparison with many upside-down faces, we would have nothing to compare and contrast it with. The brain's ability to generalize from our past experiences allows it to compare them to reality.

Our ability to perceive reality, like our ability to answer a question like, "Take two apples from three apples, what do you have?", depends entirely on our previous experience.

NOTE: It is not necessary to even think about the image for the effect to appear.

In Japan and China, the round "moon" face is considered the most attractive. The western ideal of beauty is quite different, the long slender face is considered most attractive. See the following for a dramatic example, not unlike the Necker cube. It is well worth seeing:

https://www.youtube.com/watch?v=pzpKG8NfSto

Perhaps more than any other example in psychology this illustrates just how tightly our conscious mind is controlled by our past experiences, and how our mind is determined by our learned perceptions.

To see an even more dramatic demonstration of just how dependent we are on the images embedded in our brain, see the end of this chapter on beauty.

https://www.youtube.com/watch?v=b7vOSoZSmOk

5. THE BRAINS OF COLLEGE STUDENTS NO LONGER SEE REALITY AS IT IS

One of the first insights into the question of the origin of human knowledge was provided by one of the all-time greats in psychology, Gordon Allport, author of two of the most readable and valuable books ever penned by a psychologist; *The Psychology of Rumor* and *The Nature of Prejudice*.

Gordon Allport and Thomas Pettigrew showed a simple geometric design to a group of college students. The design was that of a trapezoid, the Ames window illusion. That is an object that is like a rectangle but is dramatically shorter at one end than at the other. A wire through the center of the object was connected to a motor that would slowly turn the object around in a circle, always in the same direction. Go to youtube.com and search for the "Ames Window" or the "Ames room", another trapezoidal illusion.

Now, this was a simple, straightforward observation. Yet when college students in America are asked to draw the object they are looking at, they do not draw it as a trapezoid, which it is, but as a perfect *rectangle*. When they are asked to describe what the object is doing, they will tell you, every one of them, that the object is *flapping back and forth*, not going around in a circle.

Thousands of miles away in the heart of Africa are the citizens of the proud Zulu nation. These stoic warriors were once prized for their ability to run at a steady pace day and night and still be ready to fight, twenty miles away, on the next day. Only the Enfield rifle brought about their defeat at the hands of the British during the period of colonial expansion.

When the descendants of those Zulu warriors are today asked to look at the same geometric figure the college students saw, they draw it as a trapezoid, which is exactly what the figure is. When they are asked to describe what the figure is doing, they do not say that it is flapping back and forth. They see it as it is, as going around in a circle.

How could there be such an incredible difference between how American college students see a simple figure and how it is seen by African natives?

Do the natives have superior genes? Is it the result of centuries of biological selection that has honed their senses to the peak of perfection? Are they just genetically more advanced?

What about our college students? Why are they incapable of seeing reality? Are their senses so jaded by years of smoking weed that they can no longer see what is in front of their eyes? Is this your brain on weed? Have their brains turned to mush from the millions of cell phones attached to their ears? Are they the result of a decadent evolutionary backlash in which their senses are no longer capable of perceiving reality as it is?

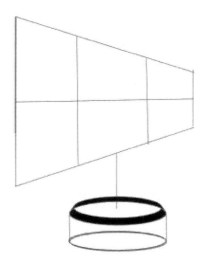

Why the difference in perception? Allport and Pettigrew found that if these same images were shown to the Zulus living in the city, with the identical genetic background to those living in the wild, that these Zulus who grew up in the city saw the same distortion of reality as the citified American college students. They drew it as a rectangle. They saw it slowly flapping back and forth.

Genetics was not the answer. The reason lay in the environment. Zulus in the wild grew up all of their lives without seeing squares or rectangles or signs or windows or even lines. They lived in round beehive huts with rounded roofs and doors. They tilled their soil in contoured furrows that clung to the rolling hillside of their fields.

But when Zulus were raised in the city, surrounded by rectangular windows and signs and doors in a world of western architecture, their brains began to see reality in the terms of their new sensations. Their exposure to rectangular signs and windows so biased their perception in favor of seeing rectangles that it was impossible to see it as it really was. Instead, they saw it the same way American college students saw it.

The windows and frames above are trapezoids in the picture, yet in our culture, our brain has learned to *perceive* them as rectangles.   Note the similarity between the black lines on the ceiling and the far wall of the room. This is similar to the Necker cube we will see next.

This trapezoid effect is no small illusion.   I have shown the actual illusion in front of classes of students and I have always been amazed at how complete the effect is, not just on students, but also on myself.   When I showed it to students, I was sitting where the students were in a fully lit classroom.

The effect was total.   It looked to me as if the object were flapping slowly back and forth instead of moving in a circle.   Even though I knew well in advance what to expect and why, even though I knew the motor that powered the machine could not possibly do anything but take the figure in a circle, I found it impossible to see the effect as it was.   If you see it in three dimensions, it is even more striking than the bumps and dents effect.

Again, no conscious awareness is necessary at all for the effect to work, and no conscious awareness seems to prevent it from working.   Even consciously trying to see the trapezoid as going in a circle did not seem to help, it still looked as though it were flapping back and forth.

To see an exceptional example of the trapezoid illusion in 3-D, even though the film is only 2-D see this recreated example by Veritasium:

https://www.youtube.com/watch?v=dBap_Lp-Ooc

Nor was this the only case where our college students were incapable of perceiving reality.   Many more have since been found.   Unfortunately, the trapezoid effect does not work in two dimensions on the printed page.   You would have to see it in real life or in the above example, to experience the effect.   But one that does work is famous as the Muller-Lyre illusion. If you look at the figure of lines,

you find that the center line on the right appears to be longer than the center line on the left.   The one in the middle looks halfway between.

But if you measure all three lines, you find that all are exactly the same length.   If you take the same illusion and show it to the Zulus, they will not be fooled by it.   Most will see the lines as the same length.   This effect is not as pronounced as that of the trapezoid but it is easier to show on the printed page.   The fact that most of our perceptions are accurate means nothing.   The accurate perceptions are formed in the same way as the "illusions" we have seen.   Yet seeing these illusions tells us volumes about how we learn to perceive reality.

Note the similarity of the lines at the top and bottom angles, to the angles of the top and bottom of the wall in the first picture. Richard Gregory noted that our experiences with the edges at the ceiling or floor creates the illusion of which is closer or farther away. Our past experiences with rooms and angles creates the illusion that the line is closer or farther away.

6. MAKING THE CODE VISIBLE:

What the Conscious Mind Cannot See

What kind of environment could lead to such widely different effects as the Muller-Lyre effect and the trapezoid effect? What elements of the environment lie encoded in our brain?

The key to decoding the Muller-Lyre effect was suggested by the Dean of perceptual psychology, Richard L. Gregory, professor of Neuropsychology at the University of Bristol. The angles provide the clue (and the *cue*). In the Muller-Lyre illusion, you will see the same angles present on the corner of a room or ceiling or buildings or in the inside of a book when the binding is facing toward you or facing away from you.

The Muller-Lyre illusion is based on a very similar distortion of angles, as you see in the trapezoid. The mind "reads" the angles at the end of the line as though they were the corners on the inside of a building or the edges of a box. This is what Zulus raised in the city saw that Zulus raised in the country did not see. Both lines in the center of the figure above are equal in length. Note the similarity to the trapezoidal windows.

In art, this would be called "perspective". Leonardo da Vinci used this masterfully to create the feeling of depth in his two-dimensional paintings. That was the real da Vinci code.

These effects have one thing in common. Whether the angles of the Muller-Lyre illusion, or the angles of the trapezoid, all involve experiences that we have with boxes, buildings, signs, and angles that are remarkably unique to our modern civilized environment, and often completely missing from the environment of our more primitive ancestors. Yet, within the space of a few years, a child's brain will adapt so totally to this new environment that their perception of the very stuff of reality is changed forever.

It is happening again. The dramatic changes brought about by computers, television and smartphones have created a generation that learns in a way that is quite different from previous generations. Learning by studying words in a book is going out the window. Students today expect to be entertained. They need immediate feedback. They need fast-moving information. Any educational system that fails to change to meet the novel way the human mind works is going to fail. We cannot compete with the glamor and flash of television and youtube.com unless we change how we present education to students.

Recently a student came by looking for a colleague whose office was next to mine. The colleague was not in. The student whipped out her cell phone and took a picture of the closed office door. For a moment, I was astonished; it made no sense to me. She told me she was actually taking a picture of my colleague's Office Hours that were posted on the door because that was easier than remembering them. Coming from a different reality, I had no clue.

7. ONLY WITHIN THE PAST 12,000 YEARS COULD WE SEE THESE IMAGES.   WHY?

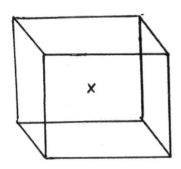

In our search for the origin of the mind, these images are much like the track of an electron or neutrino on a photographic plate or a subatomic particle in the Hadron supercollider to a physicist.   They are the track of a vanished reality, the imprint of experience that has touched our minds and forever altered how we experience reality.   Consider the two-dimensional Necker cube.

Is the X in the picture on the cube on the inside of the box or the outside of the box?   Move your eyes around the cube for about fifteen seconds or so, and you can make the cube go from inside out to outside in and back before going on.

You will find that the brain seems to automatically switch back and forth from one "insight" to the next without the slightest conscious effort.

As with bumps and dents, it is as if *you can step back and observe your brain functioning quite independently of any conscious effort on your part*.   No "thought" is required.

Again, we are seeing in three dimensions even when there is no third dimension.

It is unlikely that Zulus living in the outback could see this effect.   Only those who have lived in an environment full of boxes, angles, signs, and children's building blocks could see this effect.   However, once you have learned it, it becomes almost impossible to see it as *just* the two-dimensional collection of lines that it is.   Like the bumps and dents effect, it seems to be "three-dimensional", like a hologram imprint in the brain, read by our mind.

All the books on perception describe the Necker cube as an "ambiguous" figure.   Richard Gregory suggests that the brain makes two "hypotheses" about what the cube is and switches back and forth between the two.   But I do not think the hypothesizing theory is necessary.   This is not the ambiguous figure it has long been considered.   The brain cues on very specific stimuli, just as the bumps and dents effect is triggered by whether the shadow is at the top or the bottom.   Can you guess what it is in the Necker cube that cues the mind?

From your experience in reading this book, you may have guessed that it is the angles that cue the mind.   But

that is only part of the picture.   The brain takes its cue from the sides.   Try this experiment; First look at the *top* "side" and switch to the *bottom* "side".   Now go back and forth between those two.   You find that merely by looking from top to bottom, you can change how your brain sees the figure just as turning the bumps and dents picture up or down changed whether you saw bumps or dents.

Ah, but why should this be?   What does the brain see in one view that differs from the next?   The brain sees the side you are looking at as being the side *closest* to you.   *This is exactly the way the brain would see the side of a "real" box in "real life".*

The brain has made a generalized model of an actual box, vaguely analogous to a hologram, and uses that model for contrast and comparison to allow it to interpret any new experiences.

Once again: It is not necessary to even "think" about the box for the effect to appear.

8. CREATING SOMETHING OUT OF NOTHING?

Can the brain really make the jump from a vague outline to construct an image that is not there? Consider the following image.

Do you see two "invisible" squares in the next picture? Would the Zulu in the outback be able to see this?

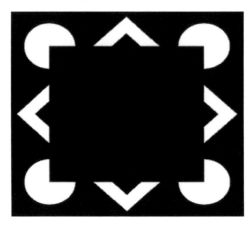

9. EDGE DETECTORS, OR LINE AND MOTION DETECTORS IN THE BRAIN

Hubel and Weisel won the Nobel Prize for their discovery of edge detectors, or line and motion detectors in the visual cortex of a cat.   The discovery that the visual cortex of the brain has neurons that respond only to a line moving one way, but not to a line moving another, is a major advance in our understanding of the brain. If you move your eyes around the next figure, you can see these line and motion detectors firing in your own brain without the messy need for brain surgery.   The fluttering of the lines is similar to the line and motion detectors found by Hubbell and Weisel.

David Hubel and Torsten Wiesel, at Harvard Medical School, found evidence of neural specialization that goes far beyond what anyone had previously expected. In their Nobel Prize study, they touched electrodes to the visual cortex of an anesthetized cat. While the cat was looking straight ahead, they moved lines on a screen in front of it. The lines registered on the retina of the cat's eye, and the electrodes were clicking repeated as the line crossed the retina. This enabled the experimenters to record the brain cells that were firing in response to the changes in visual stimuli.

Hubel and Wiesel found that some cells are so specialized that they fire only when a line moves in one direction, but not when it moves in the opposite direction. Furthermore, some cells respond to a line moving horizontally but not to one that is moving vertically (and vice versa). Still, other cells fire when a short line moves across the visual field, but they will stop firing-that is, they will be inhibited from firing-if the line is lengthened.

The brain contains a remarkable number of specialized cells that enable us to discriminate objects in the environment. Every object we see involves the firing of slightly different patterns of neurons. The differences among the shifting patterns provide the basis for the mind's ability to discriminate between different visual patterns. At the biological level, then, the brain is by no means a blank slate-a *tabula rasa*. However, the method by which the mind encodes these shifting patterns and makes them available for recall is still beyond our present knowledge of biology.

If you move your eyes around the next image, you can experience the firing of edge detectors, or line and motion detectors, discovered by Hubel and Weisel, by the fluttering of the image, in the visual area of the cerebral cortex of your brain, without the messy need for brain surgery.

The above image seems to combine the line and motion detectors firing, along with the brain trying to focus on an unfamiliar image.

10. DOES THE BRAIN REQUIRE EXPERIENCE BEFORE WE CAN SEE LINES AND ANGLES?

But another, far less noticed, discovery by Blakemore and Cooper found that even the edge detectors discovered by Hubel and Wiesel may not develop without experience. They raised kittens in a box that had only *vertical* stripes. When they attempted to test how they responded to similar lines in Hubel and Wiesel's study, they found these kittens seemed to have no horizontal line detectors, only vertical line detectors. When they held a pencil horizontally and moved it toward their eyes, the kittens ignored the pencil. When they moved the pencil vertically toward their eyes, the kittens immediately blinked and reacted to its movement.

The second group of kittens was raised in a box that had only horizontal lines. Their cortex seemed to have developed only *horizontal* line detectors, not vertical ones. They flinched only when a horizontal pencil was moved toward their eyes. They did not react to a pencil moving vertically toward their eyes. They seemed to have no vertical line detectors. They found only horizontal line detectors in the cortex of cats reared with only horizontal lines, and only vertical line detectors in those reared with vertical lines.

The implication is astonishing. It means that the line and edge detectors discovered by Hubel and Wiesel do not exist in the biology of the brain; they only develop out of the experience of the brain with lines and edges! Just as the Necker cube and the trapezoidal illusion could not be seen by the brains of Zulu raised in the outback, we can only see certain elements that our brain has already been programmed to see; programmed by experience.

We do not learn just an association between stimuli, or a Stimulus-Response association. We learn an entire perception of reality, imposed on our brain. Each of us has a slightly different perception of reality. Yet each of us shares some perceptions in common.

When you put this together with the discovery that the brain itself cannot see without previous experience, as in the babies with cataracts, it suggests that the human brain is far more like the Tabula Rasa (Blank Slate) than anyone ever suspected. Our very perception of reality is determined by the impressions experience leaves in our brain.

John Locke's idea of a "blank slate" referred only to knowledge, no one ever denied the biological processes, such as Broca's area and Wernicke's area, or other brain mechanisms. Knowledge implies understanding.

Left: From the bare angles of the origami, we see this as a person, leaning backward against a table.

Stimulus Generalization in your brain: From the vague outlines of the next origami the human mind can "see" or interpret the image to be a baby on the back of its mother. We cannot guess the species, bear or chimpanzee, but the brain takes the vague outline from our past experiences and we "see" an actual image instead of seeing only paper. This may be the *generalization* of many past experiences. Possibly a generalization picked up by a very fast Google scan of the memories in our brain.

Again: It is not necessary to even think about the images for the effect to appear.

We may dislike the idea that our reality is not as "real" as we perceive it to be.   But Einstein was at least considerably closer to the truth when he said, *"...reality is an illusion, albeit a very persistent one."* That is what makes it all the more important to try to see beyond the superficial, to understand what reality is, as best we can.

Our very perception of reality is determined by the images embedded in our brain by the culture and unique experiences we grow up with.   This suggests that Stimulus Generalization is a product of the machinery of the brain itself.   But the end product is a result of a composite of the images we see in our daily life.   Stimulus Generalization in action? This suggests the biology of the brain can extract data into an average, a generalized perception.   The average of our experiences becomes our reality.

Could this be the same principle that Behaviorists call "Stimulus Generalization", that Piaget called "assimilation", that Harlow called "learning sets"? If so, we would have a general principle that is found throughout the major learning theories.

What is it we have learned about how the mind is programmed into the brain by the environment? How much is learned? How much of learning is perception?

THE GREAT NATURE-NURTURE CONTROVERSY

"Let us then suppose the mind to be, as we say, white paper, void of all characters, without any ideas; how comes it to be furnished? Whence comes it by that vast store which the busy and boundless fancy of man has painted on it, with an almost endless variety? Whence has it all the materials of reason and knowledge? To this I answer in one word, from experience; in that all our knowledge is founded, and from that it ultimately derives itself.   Our observation about external sensible objects, or about the internal operations of our minds, perceived and reflected on by ourselves, is that which supplies our understandings with all the materials of thinking.   These two are the fountains of knowledge, from whence all the ideas we have, or can naturally have, do spring."

John Locke *Essay Concerning Human Understanding*

Suppose that a man, blind since birth, was suddenly given his sight.   Deprived of visual experience throughout his life, yet having experienced the world through all his other senses, what would he see on coming out of this cave for the first time? Could he tell the difference between a circle and a square? Would he recognize his sweetheart from a lamppost?

The basic ideas in these questions were posed to the scientific world in 1690 in a letter from William Molyneux to his colleague, philosopher John Locke.   Locke's ideas on human nature had already helped lay the foundation for the radical new view of the political nature of humanity that Thomas Jefferson later would use in the American Declaration of Independence.

In his *Essay Concerning Human Understanding,* Locke presented the groundwork for the great nature-nurture controversy.   Is our knowledge innate? Are we able to recognize shapes and forms naturally? Is it "natural" for a man to be sexually stimulated by the sight of a naked woman? Or do these stimuli acquire "meaning" only through nurture, and experience? Would they have no meaning without prior learning?

Locke and Molyneux believed that at birth, the mind was a *tabula rasa,* a blank slate, without content, knowledge, or understanding, and that only through experience could the environment acquire meaning.   Other equally influential people of their time believed that much the opposite was true, however: that we already possess knowledge of our environment at birth, knowledge of good and evil, form and motion, and how to react instinctively to a variety of situations.   In other words, nature had provided us with knowledge that did not require experience.

The questions raised by Molyneux could not be answered by science until relatively recently.   The answers, within this chapter, were to prove as revolutionary to our concept of human nature as Locke's political philosophy had been for the American Revolution.

Often, we think we are thinking, when we are only perceiving. We have become so conditioned to use the word "think", that we use it to describe anything that pops into our mind. Perception is more basic, and more powerful than we "think".

11. PERCEPTION AND BEAUTY

Among the Zoe tribe of South America, they consider the umbepo to be the essential mark of beauty among men and women. The umbepo is a one-inch thick by six inches long piece of wood that is inserted in a hole punctured in the bottom lip. It begins at the age of 5 and is constantly enlarged until it reaches the adult stage.

https://www.youtube.com/watch?v=aR_bUx3aCAo

BEAUTY IS DETERMINED BY THE SIZE OF YOUR FEET

For over one thousand years the Chinese standard of beauty was based on the size of a woman's feet. Four-inch "Golden Lotus" feet were considered the ideal of feminine beauty and sexuality. Mothers would bind their daughter's feet, often intentionally breaking the instep, to get their daughter's feet to fit into the standard of beauty. The practice was outlawed in the 1920s yet some continued to bind their own feet secretly, because they still consider it a mark of beauty. One woman said that she believed this is what gave her a good marriage. Beauty, like Any Stimulus-Any Response, or the 7,000 known languages, is *relative* to the culture we grow up in.

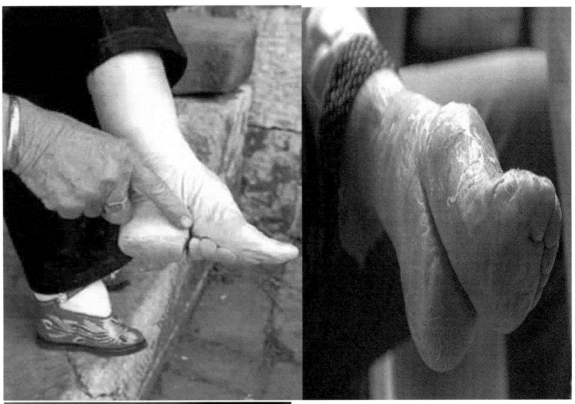

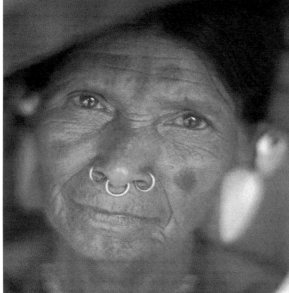

BEAUTY IS DETERMINED BY THE SHAPE OF YOUR FACE:

In Japan and China, the round "moon" face is considered the most attractive. The western ideal of beauty is quite different, the long slender face is considered most attractive. See the following for a dramatic example, not unlike the Necker cube, well worth watching:

https://www.youtube.com/watch?v=pzpKG8NfSto

Left: Among primitive groups, nose rings are very popular. Now, nose rings are making a fashion statement among American women.

BEAUTY IS DETERMINED BY THE SIZE OF YOUR LIP:

Beauty among our species varies more dramatically than anyone may imagine. Consider the ideal of feminine beauty among the Mursi: https://www.youtube.com/watch?v=Ulq9NrH6aFw

https://www.youtube.com/watch?v=2Mz1vaTeUSY

Among the Mursi tribe a woman who did not have a large lip plate would be considered unattractive.

As one young Surma male from another tribe said in a National Geographic special, *"I'd marry a woman with a big lip plate. We don't like women without lip plates."* The following YouTube video from the BBC shows the Suri tribe of the Omo valley, with young girls practicing glamor with sticks in their mouths, prepping for the lip plate that is deemed beautiful by their society. https://www.youtube.com/watch?v=2Mz1vaTeUSY&t=1s

Among the Highland hill tribes of Thailand, women wear rings around their necks as a mark of beauty. They start their daughters at about the age of five and add rings until their head is as much as a foot above their shoulders. The Pandung women of the Philippines and among tribes as far away as Africa, also consider the neck rings to be beautiful. BEAUTY IS DETERMINED BY... ANY STIMULUS-ANY PERCEPTION

Below, from the Venus of Willendorf 28,000 years ago (left) to the Venus of Vestonick (next), to the Czech Venus (right). Over 144 of these 4 ½ to 11 ½ inch figures have been found that represent the oldest and only form of the human figure ever found from this period. They have been found from Germany and Czechoslovakia almost

29,000 years ago, to Catal Huyuk, in Turkey, just 8,500 years ago. Fertility symbols?

The 19th century African explorer Sir Richard Burton tells of a tribe where the future brides of the chief were being kept in cages and force-fed fruit to make them big, to please the chief.

BEAUTY IS DETERMINED BY PERCEPTION

PERCEPTION IS DETERMINED BY CULTURE

CULTURE IS DETERMINED BY EXPERIENCE, and BLIND CHANCE.

THE STIMULUS GENERALIZATION THEORY OF BEAUTY

If you are beautiful, you are average. Out of a series of faces, the one judged most attractive was a computer-generated average of all the faces. Halberstadt, et. al.

https://journals.sagepub.com/doi/full/10.1177/0956797613491969

"It happens with no conscious awareness, and we have no ability to change our brain's perception. The experiences we have, seem to *generalize* from our experience to produce a *generalized image* in our mind, that we perceive as most attractive (or most accurate, as in our personal opinion on politics, religion, life...) All of this happens with no conscious awareness and we have no ability to change our perception. It is all relative, 'hardwired' by experience." Shepard, *MIND: The Untold Story...*

The "WOW!" EMOTION CAN COUNTER THE PAIN OF PIERCING OR TATTOOS.   - Cultural evidence of Any Stimulus—Any Response, described by Pavlov, Watson, and Perceptual Psychology. Like each of the 7,000 known human languages, it is all relative to the learning embedded in our brain by experience in our culture or peer group.

THE PERCEIVER

Do we actually think? Or does the brain shift words, which are associated with perceptions, in and out of consciousness, like looking at the top or bottom of a Necker cube? Does the relative speed of associations, mask what the brain itself is doing? See Ch. 10 on **Cognition** for the hard evidence.

12. GENERAL PRINCIPLES OF PERCEPTION AND LEARNING

1. **We are Each at the Center of Our Own Perception of Reality:** Each of us grows up as the center of our own background of experiences. No two are exactly alike, yet we have similar patterns of behavior. From our language to our politics, to our religion, to our concept of beauty, our perception of reality and our emotions are all relative to our past experiences.

2. **When it comes to knowledge and perception, the human brain is far more like a Tabula Rasa than we ever knew**. The studies of cataracts in babies, and the studies by Blakemore and Cooper of cats unable to see horizontal or vertical lines if they had not had experience with these lines, are profound demonstrations of the essential need for experience to form the brain itself.

3. **Learning does not just give the brain information to use in processing as a computer; it changes the brain itself so completely, that it creates a new reality in the brain. From this reality, our conscious mind "sees" what the brain has been modified to see. As in the cataract in one eye in babies and the study of kittens raised with only vertical stripes or other kittens raised with only horizontal stripes as well as cultural illusions.**

4. That is not to deny the importance of inborn programs in our brain that determine many things such as language (**Broca's area and Wernicke's area, etc. etc.)** but, John Locke's statement that the brain contains no knowledge or Einstein's statement that "All knowledge if from experience," are both closer to the nearly infinite malleability of the brain itself.

5. **Our visual and verbal illusions** (trapezoidal illusion and "take two apples from three apples, what do you have") illustrate our profound dependence on our previous experiences. The conscious mind sees the brain's generalized associations from prior experiences.

6. **Any Perception—Any Emotion?** Even our perceptions can elicit an emotion, as well as a response. We see this in what we like or dislike, and even our prejudice or attraction to others.   A perception under one circumstance, can also be a stimulus.

7. **Perceptions** result from our basic *generalized* stimulus patterns being associated with experience.

8. **Our thoughts,** can be a perception, flitting in and out of our conscious mind. The relatively high speed of the neurons, masks the underlying associations that create our thoughts.

9. The **"WOW"** factor, whatever the peer group, society, or Hollywood gets excited over, becomes embedded in the mind of the child or adult. From sports to sex, it all happens with the same subtle method with which we learn the language we speak; Simple Association and Psychology's General Theory of Relativity. It colors and controls our response to everything from sex to politics to religion. It winds its way through our everyday responses from interpersonal relations to our superstitions. Any Stimulus Pattern—Any Perception. It is all relative. The failure to understand that simple fact creates much human misunderstanding.

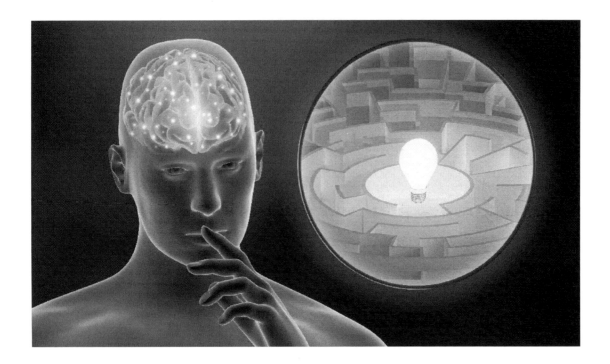

10 COGNITION

The Organization Of Knowledge

NASA • KOHLER • HARLOW • PIAGET • KENDLER AND KENDLER • PRIBRAM

• Insight: Sultan and Kohler's apes • Insight without Experience?
• Learning Sets: How Insight Develops • The Evolution of Knowledge
• Stages of Cognitive Development • Information Processing

"Knowledge is power." It is nothing of the sort! Knowledge is only potential power. It becomes power only when and if it is organized into definite plans and directed to a definite end.
Napoleon Hill

By 480 BCE, the armies of the Persian Empire were at the gates of Greece. At this turning point in civilization was born the Greek historian Herodotus, whose unbiased accounts of the wars have brought him the wide acclaim of many of today's scholars as the "father" of history. From the quill of Herodotus came a fascinating story, perhaps apocryphal, of a moment of human insight.

Early in the war between the West and the East, Croesus, King of Lydia, in Western Turkey, had joined forces with his neighbors in a preemptive strike against the growing menace of the Persian Empire.

The attack was well fought but poorly advised. Out of the deserts of Persia came the armies of Cyrus, mounted on camels. When the horses of the Lydian cavalry caught the scent of the camels they panicked. Unable to control their horses, the Lydians were forced to dismount and fight a delaying action while Croesus retreated to his palace at Sardis.

Sardis was besieged and fell before the angered and vengeful armies of Cyrus.

The soldiers of Cyrus quickly entered the town, looting its stores, and burning its buildings, taking whatever they wished.

Secure in his victory, Cyrus ordered that Croesus and his lieutenants be put to the torch. Bound and helpless, the once-mighty Croesus was tied to a stake in front of the palace where his word had once been law and lesser kings had once brought gold in tribute.

Before the fires were ignited, Croesus raised his head to the skies and repeatedly cried out, *"Solon, Solon!"* On hearing the cries of his enemy, Cyrus became curious and sent an aide to ask Croesus the meaning of his lament. But Croesus, who was about to be burned, had no interest in satisfying the curiosity of his tormentor. Croesus did not answer.

Croesus' silence must have intensified the curiosity of the Persians. For a long while, Croesus kept his silence. Finally, he spoke of Solon, an Athenian, who had once come to Sardis where he was shown the wealth and power of Croesus. Instead of being impressed, Solon had made light of Croesus' wealth, telling him, in effect, "all things must pass." On his funeral pyre, Croesus now thought of how true Solon's predictions had been. Further, he thought of how well they applied, not just to him but to every monarch.

When Cyrus heard this from the translators, he was profoundly moved. Only days before, Croesus had been a man, not unlike himself, who commanded thousands and who sat at the seat of wealth and power. Yet now Croesus was at the depths of poverty and the door of death. Cyrus may have thought, in effect, "There, but for the grace of the gods (or the camels), go I." The security of his victory may have seemed less certain. Perhaps seeing himself mirrored in the eyes of Croesus, Cyrus ordered that Croesus be released.

Now the drama was coming to a head. Croesus had saved his own life, but all around him the city of Sardis was being looted and burned. The Persian rage at the unprovoked attack by Croesus was being vented on his city. Croesus tried a ploy. The paraphrased interpretation went something like this:

Croesus (to Cyrus) "May I speak?"

Cyrus (by now very impressed with his captive's stories) "By all means, say what you have on your mind,"

Croesus "May I ask what it is that your soldiers are doing?" He points to the city in the background where smoke is rising from the buildings as the Persian soldiers put the torch to them and strip them of their wealth.

Cyrus (perhaps incredulously) "Why, they are looting your city!"

Croesus "Oh, no, my lord. They are not looting my city. It is no longer my city. It is your city. They are looting *your* city."

Cyrus was staggered by this insight. He now saw the situation from a completely new perspective. He ordered his soldiers to put an end to the pillaging of the city.

 Did Cyrus change his behavior toward the city as an act of conscious thought (cognition)? Or was his behavior skillfully controlled by Croesus?

This change of behavior could have been reversed, given a different stimulus. What if, for example, a general in Cyrus' army had told the Persian leader that stopping the looting now would surely lead to great resentment and disobedience on the part of his avenging troops that might cost Cyrus his command?

When the stimulus is outside the mind, we tend to say that it controls the organism. If the stimulus comes from within the mind, had Cyrus thought of either or both stimuli "by himself", we tend to think of it as "free will." We would say that Cyrus had thought over the options and came to a personal decision, that his behavior was not controlled by another.   For all practical purposes, there is no difference. The moment of insight may be provided by an outside stimulus or by the stimulus of one's own thought.

Just as important, the moment of "insight" in the brain occurs instantly, just like looking at the top and then the bottom of a Necker cube can change your perception of reality.

1. NASA AND THE MILLION-DOLLAR INSIGHT

Early in the space race between the U.S. and Russia, NASA was faced with a significant problem. We sent astronauts into space with paper and a ballpoint pen to record their observations. Back then, tape recorders were too big and bulky to send into space; now they fit in a chest pocket.

The astronauts quickly found that the ballpoint pen would not work in space. With no gravity and no air pressure, the ink would not flow. In the cold of space, the ink would freeze. What to do?

NASA spent one million dollars to develop a SPACE PEN. They spent months perfecting a new ballpoint pen. It was designed to be pressurized to counter the lack of air pressure; a special thixotropic ink was used to prevent freezing. In stainless steel, with a tungsten carbide ball, it was the ultimate in high-tech writing instruments. The Space Pen would write in zero gravity, upside down, in the coldest environment, even when the temperature outside their space suits was far below zero.

The Russians used a pencil.

This simple example tells us something about how the mind works. Americans were used to thinking in terms of hi-tech. We tended to go for the method that improved technology, of the ballpoint pen, to the degree that it would overcome all obstacles.

The Russians had always used a pencil. Pencils were cheap. From their schools to the space program, this solution came naturally.

Our past experiences determine the "insight" we would use when faced with a problem. The difference between the American and the Russian "insight" into problem-solving shows how dramatically our past experiences influence our cognition.

2. HOW EXPERIENCE CHANGES THE VERY NATURE OF LEARNING, THOUGHT, AND INSIGHT

In a review of how we think by Shepard (MIND: The Untold Story...), students were asked to write down their answers to the following questions. See how you compare to other college students.

1. *Take two apples from three apples. What do you have?*

    92% of my college students say "one" apple. They know they are right. They are absolutely certain. Is that correct? Read the question again.

    Even on the third reading of the question, few change their minds. It must be "one" apple. But the correct answer is "two" apples. Can you explain why that is the correct answer? Read it again.

    I use this question to illustrate a profound principle of how the mind works, the Primacy Effect. What does the mind do to answer that question? We go back to what most of us learned in first grade: "If you have three apples and you take away two apples, how many do you have left?"

    But the question does not say "take away" it says "take" and it does not ask how many do you have "left" it asks how many do you "have". If you take two, you have two.

    Many think this is a "trick" question. But no, it is a very straightforward question and an important rule of psychology. If you never went to first grade, you could easily answer that question.

    *What we have learned **first** takes precedence over any other possible answer to the question. We see this again and again in our reaction to the ideas of genius, politics, religion, sports, and personal arguments. In the entire of human experience, the primacy effect rules.*

    Over the years, as word has gotten out about this question, students are less likely to answer "one" and have learned from other students about the question. But, like Copernicus' insight, if you don't learn it, you don't know it.

2. *"What Four Words Appear Most Prominently on Every American Coin?"*

    You are an eyewitness to thousands of American coins. Answer one simple question: What four words appear most prominently on every American coin? Do not cheat by looking.

    Nearly 100% of college students know the correct answer. The four words are, "In God We Trust". So do all the professors who have been asked. They are certain of their answer. They have no doubt. Could everyone possibly be wrong? They are wrong. Try again.

    How is it possible that after tens of thousands of experiences with American coins, almost no one can answer this simple question? Because no one pays attention. The four words are, "United States of America".

    Both statements are on the coins, but that one is several times larger than the first; "most prominently". Yet we all remember, "In God We Trust" because it has been a headline in the news, we have heard it mentioned, it was controversial, it is emotional, therefore, it is seared into our minds, we remember it because of what we have heard, not because of what we have seen. This illustrates a second major principle of psychology; Selective Attention.

    The forces of selective attention and the primacy effect bias every judgment we have in interpersonal relations, politics, religion, and personal choice.

If you still think these are "trick" questions, let's try one that is absolutely straightforward. Here is a question that might determine if you are ready for College.

3. *Divide 30 by one-half. Then add 20. What is the answer?*

    More than 94% of my college students know the correct answer is 35. They are "pretty sure" of their answer. Is that what you got? Wrong. Try again.

    Even after trying again only a few students in most college classes will say that the correct answer is 80. Usually, those are math or science majors. Why is the correct answer 80? Can you figure this out? Read it again.

    Almost everyone's brain interprets this question as saying "Take half of 30" but it does not say that at all, it clearly says "Divide 30 by one half". If you divide 30 by one half (.5) you get 60. Add 20 and you get 80. But if you don't learn it, you don't know it. Once you learn it, you get pretty good at it. But having to figure it out on our own is very hard because our minds have never been taught that exact kind of question.

    Yet this is a profound question because of what it says about the human mind. All of us learned division in school. All of us learned fractions in school. But when it comes to putting two and two together to come up with an idea we have never learned, that is not easy. That is why the seemingly simple ideas of Copernicus, Darwin, and Einstein were so difficult for others to see.

    We cannot easily answer this question because most of us have never had a question just like this one. In every case of "genius" from Copernicus to Darwin to Einstein, they could put ideas together that no one had ever taught them. That is very difficult to do, unless they have taught you to do so, then it seems easy.

    Now let's go back to simpler questions. Here is a question that might determine whether or not you can get into medical school. And no, it is not a trick question.

4. *A doctor gives you three pills. He tells you to take one pill every half hour. How long before the pills are all gone?*

    Almost every college student knows the correct answer is one and a half hours. Is that what you got? Wrong. Read the question again.

    On the second try, some guess wildly at ½ hour, some guess two hours. No. The answer is one hour. How could the answer be one hour?

    Did you figure this out? Take one pill at 7:00 p.m. Take the second at 7:30 p.m. Take the third at 8:00 p.m. In one hour, they are all gone. We all learned math in school. Why is it so difficult to apply it to the real world?

    It seems likely that we are only really good at answering questions when we have learned exactly the same question before. It is very difficult to apply ideas in new situations.

5. *A rancher had 19 cows. The cows were struck by lightning. All but one of the cows died. How many were left?*

    92% of college students say "one". Even on re-reading the question, almost everyone says "one". After telling them that is wrong, students still say "one". Some wildly guess 18 or even 20. Wrong again. Read it again.

    Can you figure it out? The correct answer is 19. Why is 19 the correct answer? Can you explain this?

    This is like the first question about "take two apples". The mind automatically assumes that the question asks something it does not ask. We perceive the question based on past experiences. The question we hear is "how many were left alive" but that is not what the question asks, it asks "how many were left". There were 19 left; 18 dead ones and 1 live one.   But we have difficulty in trying to think in any way except what the mind believes (perceives) the question to be.   Einstein saw a whole new way of looking at the question of gravity.

College professors are not much better at answering such questions than anyone else.   All our responses depend on what we have learned, or what we failed to learn.   Unless we have learned the answers elsewhere, we are not very good at thinking outside the box into which our culture fits our mind.

3. COGITO, ERGO, COGITO COGITO:
I THINK, THEREFORE, I THINK I THINK.
The fact that we can think has created the illusion that we do think.

Experience changes the very nature of learning in the brain. What we have learned first, may increase learning ability, or interfere with learning.   It may prevent understanding new information, or facilitate understanding. We see this daily in our interpersonal interactions, our politics, our religions...

Words change the very nature of learning. Words and emotions can take precedence over reality.

"And you thought I was dumb?"

DO WE THINK, OR DO WE PERCEIVE REALITY?

Even words can elicit a perception in the brain. What we consider *thought* might only be the relatively high speed of our perception. Just as the Necker cube can switch back and forth from one perception to another, by looking at the top or bottom of the cube, our brain can manipulate our perception so rapidly as to create the illusion of "thinking".

The question of thought or perception makes a great deal of difference when you consider whether our perceptions, or our words, reflect reality at all.   Even if this makes little practical difference, it is a serious question when it comes to a deeper understanding of how our mind works.

4. THE ORIGIN OF COGNITION

But what is the creative process? And what about our ability to think and reason and change our mind? The question now becomes: What is the origin of thought? What happens at the moment of a sudden change in perspective? Is it different from the learning process observed by Pavlov and Thorndike? What about insight? What about creative thinking? Are there forms of learning that are more important than trial-and-error and conditioning?

Are we something more than the product of our experiences? Are we the person presented by Pavlov, Thorndike, and Skinner? Many psychologists think that our behavior cannot all be explained as the total of all our past stimulus-response experiences. What about our ability to change our mind? What about our thought processes? What about our creative ability? We can do more than respond reflexively to our environment. We can imagine things that never were. We can produce new and revolutionary creations.

That we are more than the sum of our separate past experiences has often been expressed in a Gestalt proverb that *"The whole is greater than the sum of its parts."* If you spread out all the separate components of a computer, this array of parts would not be the computer. The computer is the sum of its parts *plus* the organization of those parts.

When assembled and fed programs into its memory, the computer can do a great deal; without this organization, it is nothing. Inadequately wired, it is still nothing. By analogy, we too are more than the separate, discrete bits of data that are fed into us. We are that, plus the organization of these data.

If we wanted to learn about the functioning of a computer, we would have to study more than its parts. We would have to study the computer as it was being programmed and subsequently functioning as a whole. Similarly, if we wish to learn about human behavior, we must also study ourselves as we are "programmed" - to acquire knowledge-and we must study behavior as a product of the organized whole.

Human behavior is more than a simple stimulus-response reaction to the environment. Cognition, awareness, and thought all describe the process that allows us to "work" problems in our mind without having physically to go through the fumble and find of trial-and-error learning.

What is "thought"? Why do we "change our mind" rather than doggedly persist in reflexive behavior? What is this flexibility of behavior that allows us to solve problems "in our mind" without having to physically experience them? Do we have some innate power of reasoning that exists independent of experience?

5. BEYOND CONDITIONING
The Whole Is Greater Than the Sum of Its Parts

Off the coast of North Africa is a chain of underwater mountains, only their tips projecting above the ocean's swell. During the rainy season, every afternoon before dusk, the isles are cooled by moisture from the fast-rising clouds of summer rain squalls. When darkness comes, the jungle is pierced by night calls from amidst the trees. At dawn, the midsummer sun begins steam drying the liquid from the soul of the leaves. When evening returns, the cycle repeats itself.

Every mother's son or daughter dreams of spending a few years of his or her life on such an island with all the time in the world to do whatever he wants. For most of us, time and "maturity" rupture that fantasy. But German psychologist Wolfgang Kohler found himself in just such a place.

In the Spanish-owned Canary Islands, where Columbus stopped for provisions before his epic voyage to the new world, is an undistinguished island known as Tenerife. At the outbreak of World War I, Kohler was in the process of studying the behavior of chimpanzees at the Berlin Anthropoid Station on this equatorial island.   Kohler probably did not intend to stay in Tenerife for long, but war has a way of influencing the best-laid plans. Kohler stayed there for seven years.

What did Kohler do during those seven years in paradise? Kohler wrote of the personalities, foibles, and idiosyncrasies of our first cousins.   Before the end of the war, Kohler had published a massive collection of his observations on the learning process of apes.   And when Kohler wrote, he wrote well-or at least he had a good translator.   Kohler's *The Mentality of Apes* was one of the first works by a major psychologist that is readable from cover to cover.   It was almost ten years after the initial publication of his work, however, before it was translated into English.

It seemed to many of his readers that if Kohler's observations were accurate, Thorndike's meticulous studies of intelligence would have little application. Kohler believed that learning proceeded by sudden jumps or "insight" rather than fumble and find.   His studies indicated that the process of learning by trial and error was mechanistic, superficial, and irrelevant to most learning situations.

Was Kohler correct? Or, as other psychologists were to argue, had he missed something? The issue was joined. Was learning by trial and error or by insight? Was one more important than the other? Not since the nature-nurture controversy began had psychology seen a debate of quite this importance and magnitude.   And not until very recently have we come close to resolving the question.

6. INSIGHT:
The "Aha" Phenomenon

Is trial and error necessary for problem-solving? Kohler arranged a problem that would allow him to observe how the chimps solved a "new" problem. A young chimpanzee named Sultan was led down a corridor from the courtyard into a room.   While the chimp watched, Kohler opened a window onto the courtyard and dropped a banana outside the window onto the ground and out of sight of Sultan.

The chimp was familiar with both the room and the courtyard from prior experience. Would he know to retrace his steps back into the yard to get the banana, or would he stand at the window staring at the spot he last saw it? The problem had never been presented to Sultan before, but by the time Kohler had closed the window, Sultan was racing out of the door, and down the corridor to the playground. When Kohler got back to the window to observe his progress, Sultan was already enjoying the banana.

The observation was repeated using a dog with meat as a reward. The dog jumped on the window once and then raced out the door after the meat. Both the chimp and the dog had had previous experience inside and outside of the building, and although they had never performed this task, it was clear that no trial and error was necessary, but such a simple test was only the beginning of Kohler's studies. Kohler went on to more complex tasks involving the use of tools to solve problems.

The problem was how to get a piece of food placed outside the animal's cage and just out of its reach. Attached to the food was a rope which the chimp could pull with his hands or the dog could pull with his teeth. The task proved easy for the chimps. They quickly pulled the food into reach with the rope. But for the dog, this seemingly easy task proved to be impossibly difficult. Although showing the greatest interest in the meat, the animal would have starved to death before hitting on a solution.

Now Kohler's problems were becoming increasingly difficult. They were reaching a point at which even the chimpanzees could not immediately solve the problem. But this is exactly the point where Kohler began to observe the remarkable problem-solving moment-the point at which a seemingly insoluble problem gave way to the animal's "power of reasoning."

Kohler suspended a banana high off of the ceiling of the testing room. In a corner of the room were some packing cases. Then he introduced a hungry chimp. The chimp immediately spied the fruit, jumped at it repeatedly, threw sticks at it, and finally beat his hands angrily against the wall. Eventually he sat down and gazed blankly about the room. After a while he noticed the boxes. He began moving the boxes. Then in an

instant he pushed one of the boxes under the bananas, still not high enough, he sat down on the box. After a while he ran to get a second box, placed it next to the first, finally stacked it on top of the first box. This was still not tall enough. Then he ran get the third box, stacked it hurriedly, climbed up onto the shaky structure, and retrieved his prize.

The sequence of discovery was similar for most chimps: first, a period of single-minded and futile attempts to jump high enough to get the banana; then a period of rest or exploration; and lastly, a glance at the banana, the boxes, or both, and the rush to the prize. Still, great variation was noted in their behavior. One required five minutes.to recognize that the boxes could be used as a ladder, another took fifteen minutes, a third took an hour, and a fourth took over a week's worth of trials before solving the problem.

To Kohler, what was significant was the behavior of the animals at the moment before the problem was solved. The chimps did not pull the box under the fruit by accident, climb up on it by accident, and obtain the reward by accident. No trial and error seeméd to be involved. A chimp is playing nonchalantly with the boxes one moment, and the next moment he suddenly rushes to a successful completion of the task. The solution was (1) without trial and error, and (2) frequently quite sudden. The moment of solution was much like our human reaction on reading an idea in a book and hours or days later suddenly finding oneself thinking "Aha, so that's what it meant." Kohler called this "aha" phenomenon *insight*.

In a later version of the same experiment, Kohler was trying to get the chimpanzee Sultan to use a ladder to reach the fruit. Sultan had already mastered the fine art of stacking boxes, but this time no boxes were available. Try as he would, Sultan was simply not able to grasp the idea of how to use a ladder. Discouraged, Sultan shot a disdainful glance at the banana and gave up. Kohler may have lost his patience too, for he records that he walked into the testing room, and went over and pointed at the banana as if to say, "Come on, now. Don't you know what ladders are for?"

Suddenly, Sultan grabbed Kohler's assistant by the arm and pulled, tugged, and jerked him into position underneath the banana. Using the assistant's belt, shoulder, and head as handholds, Sultan scampered up this substitute for a stack of boxes, squatted briefly on his head, triumphantly snatched the banana, vaulted to the floor, and consumed his reward with gulps and lip smacking.

Once Sultan had perfected this easy technique, he was reluctant to give it up merely to further Kohler's scientific curiosity. When Kohler and his assistant refused to be led under the fruit, Sultan would throw a tantrum.

Later, when he was together with a group of chimps working on another suspended banana problem, Sultan attempted to try the same technique using another chimp in place of a human. But the other chimps were not aware of Sultan's insight, and were even less impressed by his technique. Unable to explain his purpose, Sultan tried to force the other chimps into position. But when Sultan tried to stand on their heads, they were not having any of this. Some of them panicked at this peculiar behavior. Others, too terrified to run, crouched flat on the ground while Sultan vainly tried to reach the fruit by leaping up and down on their shoulders.

By the second day, Sultan's idea had caught on with the group, and the other chimps began to *imitate* him. Kohler records with amused desperation how each chimp struggled to grip another, lifting their feet to climb, all wanting the reward but all refusing adamantly to sit still long enough to be a footstool while the other fellow got the goodies. Preoccupied with this method, they totally ignored new implements in the room that might have been used successfully.

Are humans likely to be more adaptable than Kohler's chimps in similar tasks?

The psychologist N. R. F. Maier provided an interesting comment on this question. Using adult humans as problem solvers, Maier suspended two strings from the ceiling of a room. The task for Homo sapiens ("wise men") was simple. All they had to do to earn the distinction of being "smarter than a monkey" was to tie the loose ends of the string together. But there was a catch. The strings were too far apart for a man to hold onto one string while grabbing the other at the same time.

What solutions did the humans come up with? Some reasoned that one string had to be made longer, so they could reach the second string. Others reasoned that if they could stand on boxes, they would be taller and the first string would pull farther. Nothing wrong with this logic at all, except for one minor detail:

There was nothing in the room that could be used to lengthen the string and nothing in the room they could stand on! The only object in the room was a pair of pliers, but the pliers were not long enough to help in lengthening the string.

The solution seemed clear. Lengthen the string or stand on boxes. But the obvious solutions did not work. The only possible solution was an ingenious one that is, if you happen *to* be the experimenter rather than the subject. If you tie the pliers to the end of one of the strings, and start the pliers swinging back and forth like the pendulum on an old clock, then while holding on to the other string it was possible to catch the one with the pliers.

Simple? Perhaps. But only a few of the sapiens were able to solve it. Most spent their time attempting the "obvious" solutions. Creativity was stifled. Most of those who caught on did so only after the string was set in motion by brushing against it. In part, the problem was difficult because it was novel: We are not used to the Maier string problem

In part the problem is a lack of experience with this type of problem. In part too, it was difficult because we already have a fixed idea of how pliers may be used (functional fixedness). This stereotype of the use of pliers may be so strong that we are unable to see other uses for them.   If we replace the pliers with a pendulum bob, the problem becomes easier to solve.

7. IMITATION, EMPATHY, AND MIND SET
Closure: Spatial and Temporal Proximity

Kohler found many similarities in the behavior of humans and apes.   Two examples are of importance here. First, Kohler noted that animals learn not just by doing or through trial and error, but by imitating the behavior of others.   Many instances of such imitation were observed.   Chimps learned to climb poles, vault poles, knock fruit down, and do other tasks more rapidly if they had observed another chimp doing the same thing.

Not only did chimps imitate other chimps; they empathized with each other's efforts to get the fruit offered as bait.   Kohler describes how one chimp in a cage watched another trying to lift fruit off a hook with a pole.   The caged animal went through all the motions with its hands while intently watching the progress of the worker. Similar behavior may be observed in people watching that all-important football game on television and physically empathizing with the quarterback as he is hit on the two-yard line vainly struggling for the goal.

Second, Kohler noted that once the animals had learned one way to solve the problem, they had great difficulty putting that learned idea aside and adopting a new, easier method of problem-solving.   Even when the old method no longer worked, as in the chimp's attempts to use each other as ladders, they continued to ignore sticks, ladders, and other implements that might have been used until they had thoroughly exhausted their preoccupation with the old method.   In short, they displayed stereotyped behavior, not unlike that of Guthrie's cats (Chap. 8) or Maier's people.

Kohler noted that problem-solving is at its best when both the problem and the solution are in view at the same time; in Kohler's terms, "closure" (putting the ideas together) was more likely.   Kohler found the chimps were much less successful at solving the box-stacking problem if the boxes were left outside the room.

In one such test, animals that had formerly been successful at box stacking were led past the boxes in the hall and into the testing room.   Would they "remember" the boxes in the hall while trying to reach the suspended fruit inside the room?   Even the resident genius, Sultan, had difficulty in such a test, and only after repeated tries to get the fruit in other ways did he "remember" the boxes in the hall and race out to get them.

Anthropologist Jane Goodall surprised some of her colleagues with the important discovery that chimpanzees in the wild not only use tools but "manufacture" them as well.   Goodall observed and recorded on film that chimpanzees will break off twigs from bushes, strip them of their foliage, and use them to draw termites out of the holes in the termite nests.   They place the stick in the hole, wait until it is covered with termites, and then withdrew the stick.   Like a child licking the milkshake off a straw, they run the stick through their lips, licking off the delicious termites.

Other anthropologists have noted that baboons will use rocks to kill scorpions. For food? How many more brain cells or mutations in their wiring diagrams would be necessary before they began making arrowheads or war clubs? Chimpanzees can make and use implements in the wild.

But psychologists are not so interested in that fact as they are in the *process* by which learning to use tools develops. And no one, not even the recent intrepid anthropologists, has been a more careful observer of this process than Wolfgang Kohler.

Kohler's apes had already mastered the art of using a pole to rake in a banana from beyond their reach outside their cage. This time, Kohler placed the reward farther than one pole's length beyond the cage. Two hollow bamboo poles of equal length were given to the ape. The poles fitted together, much like a short version of a cane fishing pole. Only by fitting them together could the chimp get the reward.

Sultan began the task. Straining through the bars, he groped with a single stick in the direction of the banana. When one stick did not work, he tried the other. Neither worked! Frustrated, Sultan made a futile gesture at adaptation. In a clear retreat to a once successful concept or learning set, he pulled a box toward the bars as if the box could somehow be useful for this problem. Quickly recognizing its uselessness, he pushed it to one

side. Next, in a close try, he took one stick and pushed it out as close to the fruit as he could. With the second stick, he pushed on the end of the first until he actually moved the fruit. Kohler notes some evident satisfaction in Sultan's behavior after just being able to move the objective even though he could not get it.

Jane Goodall found that chimpanzees in the wild will make a tool out of a stick to extract termites from a mound.

After some fumble-and-find attempts, a chimp will often suddenly discover how to fit two poles together to make a tool.

The first stick was returned to Sultan and a little coaxing was given. As the animal watched, the observer put one finger into the opening of the stick. But Sultan was not ready for imitation. He quickly tried the previous method of pushing one stick out with the other to touch the fruit.

An hour passed.   Kohler began to despair, remarking that it seemed hopeless.

Sultan was left with the sticks and the keeper was left to watch him.   Within five minutes after Kohler's remark, things began to happen.   First, Sultan connected the sticks while playing with them, without any apparent consideration of their value in getting the bananas.   Shortly thereafter, the keeper reports the moment of triumph:

> Sultan first of all squats indifferently on the box, which has been left standing a little back from the railings; then he gets up, picks up the two sticks, sits down again on the box and plays carelessly with them.   While doing this, it happens that he finds himself holding one rod in either hand in such a way that they lay in a straight line; he pushes the thinner one a little way into the opening of the thicker, jumps up and is already on the run towards the railings to which he has, up to now, half turned his back, and begins to draw a banana toward him with the double stick.

Kohler found that chimpanzees are not just users of tools, they are also makers of tools.   He describes vividly the inventive process in Sultan (p.   151):

> In Another experiment, further manufacture of implements is demanded of Sultan.   Besides a tube with a large opening, he has at his disposal a narrow wooden board, just too broad to fit into the opening.   Sultan takes the board and tries to fit it into the tube.   This is not a mistake; the different shapes of the board and the tube would tempt even a human being to try it, because the difference in thickness of both these objects is not obvious at first sight.   When he is not successful, he bites the end of the tube and breaks off a long splinter from its side, obviously because the side of the tube was in the way of the wood (" good error").   But as soon as he has his splinter, he tries to introduce it into the still intact end of the tube, a surprising turn, which should lead to the solution, were not the splinter a little too big.   Sultan seizes the board once more, but now works at it with his teeth, and correctly too, from both edges at one end toward the middle, so that the board becomes narrower.   When he has chewed off some of the (very hard) wood, he tests whether the board now fits into the round opening of the tube, and continues working thus (here one must speak of real "work") until the wood goes about two centimeters deep into the tube.   Now he wishes to fetch the objective with his implement, but two centimeters is not deep enough and the tube falls off the top of the wood over and over again.
>
> By this time Sultan is plainly tired of biting at the wood; he prefers to sharpen the wooden splinter at one end and actually succeeds so far as to get it to stick firmly in the sound end of the tube, thus making the double stick ready for use.   In connection with this treatment of the wood it must be remarked that contrary to my expectation, Sultan bit away wood almost exclusively from one end of the board, and, even if he took the other end between his teeth for a moment, he never gnawed blindly first at one, and then at the other. His way of dealing with the tube was also satisfactory.   The one opening of the tube that had been spoiled by breaking its side is thereafter left unheeded.   I had some anxiety for the other opening during the further experiment, but although Sultan, when the wood and splinter did not fit in, put his teeth into it several times, he never really bit into the side of the tube so that the opening could still be used.   I could not guarantee that each repetition of the experiment would turn out so well.   Sultan evidently had an especially bright day.

Kohler went on to note that the sharpening of sticks with the teeth as Sultan had done seemed to be well within the capabilities of chimps-even when not necessary to solve a problem.   One chimp named Grande was fond of sharpening sticks in such a manner and using them to poke at anyone who passed by her cage.   It required only one extra step (insight?) to make this practice useful, but what about this "extra step"? What is the origin of such thinking?

The sudden, insightful, problem-solving of Kohler's chimps seemed markedly different from the fumble-and-find behavior of Thorndike's cats.   Why? Do chimps learn through insight rather than trial and error?   Had Thorndike's puzzle box been too mechanical, too unnatural for insight to operate?   Or did Kohler's chimps have some advantage from past experience that Thorndike's cats did not?

Although Kohler's chimps did not seem to engage in trial-and-error behavior, their problem-solving behavior was often erratic, fumbling, and inept.   Kohler accurately recorded their inconsistencies, which would take on meaning many years later when Herbert Birch, of the Yerkes Primate Laboratory, tried to repeat Kohler's studies using chimpanzees that had spent most of their life in a cage rather than in the jungle.

When given the same problems as Kohler's chimps, the cage-teared animals had greater difficulty performing. Over a period of trials, they began to solve the problems.   There was little evidence of initial insight: Only after some experiences were the chimps able to demonstrate "insight" in using the sticks and boxes as tools.

Does thinking arise spontaneously from within the mind? Does it already exist, awaiting only the raw materials? Or does thinking require experience? We know that sudden, "insightful" learning does occur.   We know that some experience seems necessary before sudden, insightful learning takes place.   But how does thinking develop? To determine the role of experience in the development of higher mental processes, it is necessary to control the entire learning history of the animal.

8. THE EVOLUTION OF THOUGHT
The Learning Set

Perhaps one of the most significant findings in learning theory, and one of the least known, came from *The Learning Set* studies designed by psychologist Harry Harlow at the University of Wisconsin.   Harlow discovered what he considered one of the most basic concepts in the thought process: *the learning set*.

Harlow first had to control the learning history of his subjects.   If the pre-capture experiences of Kohler's chimps had aided their insight, there would be no way of knowing which experiences had been important.   Such control could only be possible by using rhesus monkeys reared in captivity, in a situation in which their entire learning history could be known.

Second, Harlow had to have problems for the monkeys to learn to solve.   He devised problems basic to learning itself; problems involving discrimination, transfer of training, and operant conditioning.   He began with a discrimination test.

Below: Harlow's problem tray with two stimuli, a square and a circle. A monkey was presented with a tray on which two objects had been placed.

The objects were different in shape, size, and color.   One of the objects always had a peanut or raisin as a reward under it.   If the monkey picked up the correct object, it got the reward.   The wrong object had no reward, and if the monkey picked it, the tray was withdrawn and the objects were presented again on a second trial.

The objects were switched from left to right, from trial to trial, to be certain that the animal was learning the object rather than the position.

The initial learning began with a slow fumble-and-find process.   The monkey's behavior was closer to that of Thorndike's cats than Kohler's chimps.   Over a series of trials with the same object, they learned that the reward was always under the square object and not under the round object.   They learned this well enough that they eventually chose the correct object on every trial.   It took them 30 trials to reach this level with the first two stimuli.

Harlow used not just two pairs of objects but many dozens of different pairs of objects-not just squares and circles but crosses and triangles, or X shaped and + shaped objects.   As soon as the monkeys had mastered one problem to perfection, they were presented with a new one.

 Harlow's problem tray with cross and triangle.

Now the question is posed. Having learned to work the first discrimination problem perfectly every time, would the monkeys be able to transfer the knowledge they acquired from the first task to the second task? Would they learn the second task more easily than the first? In other words, had "insight" developed? Or would it require as many trials to learn the new stimuli as it took to learn the first stimuli?

Two new stimuli were presented-objects the monkeys had never before seen. The second task began. Trial followed trial; success, failure, success, failure... On the second problem, almost as many trial-and-error failures were made as on the first, about 30 trials. Out of two possible choices, the monkeys started out making as many wrong responses as correct ones. Again, they finally mastered the problem to the extent that they were correct on every trial. Then they were presented with a third problem, a fourth, and a fifth.

Problem followed problem and as each one was mastered the succeeding problems were solved somewhat more easily. After fifty such problems, and many trials on each problem, the monkeys were able to pick the correct solution to completely new stimuli, after the first trial, 90 percent of the time.

After 300 trials, the monkeys could be presented with two new stimuli, never seen before, and learn which one was correct after only one trial. If they picked the correct stimulus the first time, they continued to do so; if they picked the wrong stimulus the first time, they picked the correct one on the second and continued to do so (insight?). Harlow called this phenomenon a *learning set*.

The results of Harlow's study are quite striking, and they suggest to Harlow that trial-and-error learning and insight are but two aspects of the same learning process. The study suggests that insight does not exist independent of prior experience. On the contrary, only through experience does insight develop.

In a variation on the basic discrimination problem, Harlow devised an oddity problem in which three objects-two of them identical-were presented at the same time. The test was to learn to always choose the unique object. This time, both monkeys and nursery school children were tested on a series of problems. Harlow allowed twenty-four trials on each task and then presented a new set of objects.

Again, the process of *fumble and find* predominated-not just for the monkeys but for the children as well. Gradually, their performance improved as they mastered problem after problem. Finally, they could learn in one trial. Remarkably, Harlow notes the monkeys did better than most of the children! Perhaps, however, the difference in relative achievement was because of a difference in the motive value of the reward.

Harlow's "learning set" concept is an organizing principle that explains much of learning and thinking: From repeated trial-and-error experience, an organized response set evolves. This learning set can apply to stimuli never experienced by the animal. The animal can now solve problems similar to those it has solved in the past without going through the laborious fumble-and-find process. Simple concepts or learning sets may now be combined into more complex ones, which may then apply to more complex problems.

This step-by-step process can be observed in the chimps studied by Kohler.

In learning to use the sticks to reach bananas outside of their cage, they relied on countless experiences of reaching for distant objects with their arms. Usually, they were successful. Thus a "reaching" learning set, if you will, Piaget would call it a schema, already existed. Second, Kohler noted they had often used sticks in play to touch distant objects and occasionally to poke at the observers as they passed. Combining these and probably other such elements of past experience led to the use of sticks to reach the banana.

Later, on more complex tasks, Sultan joined two sticks together in play, apparently by trial and error. He did not immediately use the joined sticks to reach the food, but it was only shortly thereafter before he "joined" the concept or learning sets together to solve the problem.

What about people? We have seen that nursery and preschool children go through a trial-and-error process in learning, although they may learn faster than Kohler's chimps.

Do human children display more "insight" than the chimps? Do they show evidence of a different, distinctly human type of learning? Of course, language gives humans a substantial advantage over the ape, but for now, let us stick to the type of problem-solving that both apes and humans can do before examining our unfair advantage.

9. HUMAN PROBLEM SOLVING
Children's problem box

Child psychologists Kendler and Kendler devised a simple but unique test of a child's ability to combine two ideas (concept or learning sets?) An apparatus was built and training began.

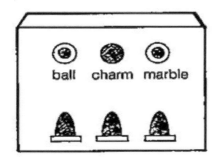

First, the child was shown that pressing the button on the left would deliver a steel ball into the cup.   Second, the child was shown that pressing the button on the right would deliver a marble.

The experimenter then closed off both side sections and opened the center section. The child was now shown that if a steel ball were put into the hole in the center section, a charm would be delivered into the cup.

Finally, all sections are uncovered, and the child is asked to get the machine to deliver a charm.   Will the child be able to combine the first and third concept or learning sets? Will the child push the button on the left, obtain a steel ball, and put the ball into the hole to get the charm?

Remarkably, preschool children have great difficulty in solving this problem.   Only 6% of the five-year-olds could solve this problem.   Not until they were nine years old could 50% of them solve the problem.

They do not seem to associate the steel ball they get by pressing the button with the steel ball that will get them the charm! The second concept or learning set with the marble may serve to interfere with the connection, but regardless, little insight is shown by preschool children.

If allowed to play around (trial and error), would they eventually catch on? Probably.   But only 6 percent of the kindergarten children and 50 percent of the third-grade children solved this problem on the first trial.

This is not to say that preschool children do not show "insightful" learning. They do. But given a problem never before experienced by them they resort to fumble and find, trial and error, just like adults.

Nursery school children and monkeys may learn by fumble and find and pyramiding concept or learning sets, but what about adults? Surely adults have reached an intuitive stage where reason takes over and such steps are no longer necessary.   Perhaps, but have we? Let us try a problem very similar to the one Harlow's monkeys had to master by fumble and find.   We have made it slightly more complex, since humans have had somewhat more experience than Harlow's monkeys.   But it is sufficiently unfamiliar that it will offer somewhat the same challenge to our thought processes without having to be tricky in any way.

Harlow used two stimulus objects with his monkeys, your problem has eight.

Harlow had a peanut under one of the objects as a reward. Your only reward will be the challenge of doing better than a monkey if you succeed. The peanut-cross problem is stated verbally so you can rely on past experience. Can you solve it with insight or intuition?

By the time you continue reading here, you will have already been through three notes and should be moderately exasperated. Why is the problem so difficult? Do you think it was that much harder for a human than Harlow's problem was for a naive monkey? What happened to all those years of public education, not to mention any innate insight we credit ourselves with having?

There seem to be two reasons the problem is difficult for the average student.

First, as in the case of Harlow's monkeys on their first trial, it is a new problem to us. Most of us have had no prior experience with this type of problem. So, we fumble as badly as Harlow's monkeys. After practice, of course, we could learn to work this type of problem with any stimuli.

But more than this, we are usually so certain that our first answer is correct.

Why? The answer seems to be that we have already formed a certain way of dealing with problems, a concept or learning set. When we try to apply our "logic" (the concept or learning set) to this problem, however, we fail because the problem cannot be worked by our standard concept or learning set. Nonetheless, as with many such problems encountered

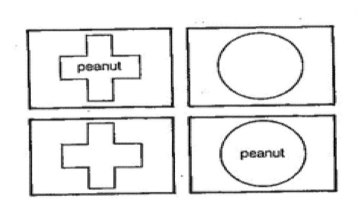

THE PEANUT-CROSS PROBLEM*

*Based on similar problems by P. C. Wason.

Here are four cards. Each card has a cross, with or without the word *peanut,* on one side and a circle, with or without the word *peanut,* on the other side. Which cards are the *only* cards will you have *to* turn over to determine if it is always true that:

Every card that has a "peanut" cross on one side has a circle without "peanut" on the other side.

Read the instructions carefully. When you are certain of your answer, but only when you are certain, check note 1 below. Pay attention to this problem because it Illustrates · two crucial points of learning.

NOTE 1: Did you figure that the cards that must be turned *over are* the "peanut" cross and the circle without "peanut"? Almost 100 percent of the people pick these two cards.

If you did, however, then you, like almost everyone, are still incorrect. Go back and reread the statement carefully, try again, then read note 2.

NOTE 2: Do you now think the answer should be both of the crosses? Or should it be both of the circles? Either answer is incorrect, if you are following the standard course of logic, you now think that the answer is all four cards. Right? But you are still incorrect.   You have just about run out of possibilities (fumble and find?), but go back and try again.   There is no trick to the logic of the problem, so do not blame it on that.   Then see note 3.

NOTE 3: Usually, by the third try, two or three students out of a class of thirty begin to understand the problem well enough to explain it.   Do you? The answer is that the "peanut" cross and the "peanut" circle must both be turned over.   Can you explain why?

Or did you get it right, as most of us do, by trial and error (mostly error)?

Our initial false conclusions might be explained as follows.   First, we start with a concept or learning set that makes certain assumptions.   That is, we assume that by turning over the "peanut" cross we can prove the statement that all "peanut" crosses have a no "peanut" circle on the other side.   And it either is correct or it is incorrect.   That conclusion is correct.

Unfortunately, we go on to the erroneous assumption that if the circle without a peanut has a "peanut" cross on the other side then we have proven the statement.   This is patently false.   It makes no difference what is on the other side.   If it is a "peanut" cross fine.   If not, who cares, since we have made no predictions about what is on the other side of circles without peanuts.

It is crucial that the circle with a "peanut" be turned over because if it turns out that it has a cross with a "peanut," the statement is flatly wrong! Remarkably, once we start out with the first learning set then, like Kohler's apes trying to use each other as a ladder, we ignore other ways of looking at the problem.

10. MENTAL TRIAL AND ERROR: "THOUGHT"

What did you do when you tried to solve the problem? A monkey might have physically turned the cards over. Humans do not have to.   We can turn the cards over in our mind.   We can imagine what could be on the other side without looking.   By turning the cards over in our mind by imagining all possibilities-we are free to work problems, by trial and error, in our mind.

"Thought" is no more free from error than physical trial and error.   Psychologists could make an excellent case that this form of logic is far more prone to error.   But if thought is based on enough physical experiences, as were the learning sets developed by Harlow's monkeys, then the thought process gives us a tremendous tool-- a shortcut for working on new problems.

In our daily life, we are continually turning over cards to anticipate the effect.

In social interaction, we may think about how another would react if we said one thing or did something else. We learn from experience to anticipate their reactions.   Often, we are wrong.   But by thinking out all possible reactions in advance, it increases the odds that we may be right.

ANALYSIS OF THE PEANUT-CROSS PROBLEM

Almost everyone notes at first that the "peanut" cross must be turned over, because if it has a circle without a peanut the statement is correct, and If it has a circle With a "peanut" the statement is false.   Therefore, to find out if the statements are true this card must be turned over.   So, most people are half right.   But then so was Harlow's monkey.

What people fail to note is that the "peanut" circle is every bit as crucial to our "proof" as the first card.   If the "peanut" circle has a cross without a peanut, then it matters little.   We have made no predictions about either card in the statement.

But if the "peanut" circle has a "peanut" cross on the other side then our statement is flatly false! After this has been pointed out almost everyone sees the logic in this.   The card must be turned *over.*   Why is it so difficult to see this before it was pointed out?

Students invariably want an explanation of why the other two cards do not have to be turned over, so bear with me.   First, the circle without "peanut"; could ·have either a cross with "peanut" or a cross without "peanut" on the other side.   These are the only two possibilities.   If it has a cross with "peanut", then fine, the problem statement is correct, but not proven.

Again, if it has a cross Without "peanut," who cares? *We* have not predicted crosses without "peanut." In other words, it does not matter which is on the other side of the circle without "peanut" because it cannot *disprove your* statement.

Interestingly, most of us have difficulty grasping the fact that finding a "peanut" cross on the other side is of no importance-it merely supports the statement.   What is important in this problem is which cards can *disprove* the statement (another learning set?).

For the same reason, the cross without "peanut" is of no importance.   We *have* simply made no predictions about crosses without peanuts.   Even if it has a circle with "peanut" on the other side; it in no way affects the prediction

11.   THE NECKER CUBE ILLUSION: "HOLOGRAPHIC" IMAGES IMPRINTED IN THE BRAIN

In Kendler's study, children had to (1) push a button to get a steel ball, and then (2) put the steel ball in a hole to get the charm.   The two were separated by an irrelevant task, having to press a button to get a marble.   This seems to have interfered with their learning to put the steel ball in the hole to get the charm.

After learning these two separate acts, the younger child could still not put the two together to get a charm.   It could be that the moment of insight was possible only when the two ideas occurred simultaneously, or in sequence, so that the mind, in effect, combined the two ideas.

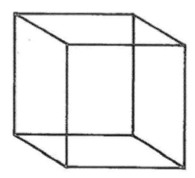

Consider an analogy of how this sudden change of perspective may operate. Above is a Necker cube. Look at the top first, then look at the bottom, until you see it flick back and forth from one side to another, and ask yourself which side represents the front of the box or the back of the box. Then, look at the left side and next at the right side.

If you look at the top of the box you will see it one way.

If you then look at the bottom of the box you will see it change, suddenly and dramatically. The front will become the back or the back will become the front.

Next, look at the left "side" of the box. Then look at the right "side" of the box. You will see it change dramatically.

No thought is necessary. No thought will prevent you from seeing this.

In fact, what we see by looking at the top and then at the bottom, this is exactly the way a "real" box would look in "real" life.

It is as if the brain has formed an almost 'holographic' image of a box, a generalized image from past experiences. What we are seeing is not a stimulus, but a complete image of the box, formed by the brain, from past experiences.

The automatic brain can instantly change its perception and deliver to the conscious mind a new perception. Note that your conscious mind is quite unnecessary for the effect to occur. Thought has nothing to do with perception.

12. INSIGHT VERSUS TRIAL AND ERROR

Our concept of how we solve problems has progressed somewhat as follows:

1. *Insight*: Kohler's studies indicated that learning can occur quite suddenly without any need for trial-and-error learning. This presented a problem for the stimulus-response theorists.

2. *Experience*: Birch demonstrated that the insight Kohler observed in his studies cannot occur without a considerable amount of trial-and-error experience. Animals raised in a Spartan Zoo, without experience with trees and sticks and vines, cannot easily perform.

3. *Learning sets*: Harlow systematically studied the experience that is needed before insight can occur. He concluded that experience with several similar problems allows the development of a "learning set" for dealing with one type of problem. This knowledge is then generalized to new but similar problems. In effect, the animal "learns to learn." The development of concepts or learning sets now allows the animal to solve problems suddenly, with "insight."

4. ***Cognition (vicarious trial and error):*** Humans can solve problems by turning ideas over within their minds (using symbols, words, etc.), without having to physically manipulate the environment as Harlow's monkeys did by turning over the cross or circle. Sometimes called *vicarious trial and error,* this cognitive ability to experiment with ideas in the mind is part of the thought process. We can construct mental models and test out their possibilities in our minds.

5. ***Creativity:*** Certainly, the mind can piece together ideas or dream up concoctions that have never before been experienced. The mind is at least as creative at imagining new ideas (most often incorrect, but occasionally brilliant ideas) as nature has been at genetically imagining new species of animals. The process of creativity is not a mystical one.

Two factors may prove basic to the creative process. First, is the trial-and-error process, and second, is the sudden coming together of two ideas or learning sets that had never before been considered in sequence in the mind. The latter could occur through vicarious trial and error or by an accidental thought, perhaps even by the capricious firing of nerve cells. we may avoid many mistakes and perhaps learn to produce the reaction we hope for.

A similar form of thinking may involve the use of visual models within the mind. If we can visualize a problem by using our past experience, the problem becomes easier to work. For example, what is the total number of doors, including closet doors, that you have in your house? Try to answer this question before reading further.

How did you solve this problem? Usually, we have to picture in our mind each room in our house and count each door. We reconstruct a visual model of our home in our mind.

Isaac Newton once said that he was unable to imagine anything of which he could not make a model. Newton was speaking of models made on paper as well as in the mind. Copernicus constructed a physical model of the solar system and compared it with the existing model.

Psychological theories are often models of behavior, based on past experience, that we construct to anticipate someone's behavior under certain stimulus conditions. In many such models, we are doing more than counting our doors. We generalize beyond our past experiences. We must guess at or imagine (through anticipation or generalization) things we have not experienced directly.

Most thinking seems to occur through thoughts involving words or concepts rather than through visual models. Such thinking may involve mathematics. For example, think of a six-digit number and try to multiply it by any two-digit number.

What do you have to do? Do you have to "write" it or visualize it in your mind before you can do the problem? Most of us do, although a few people have learned the mathematical concepts so well that the solution becomes reflexive or almost automatic.

Thought with words may follow similar steps. We first need to visualize a new idea or problem in concrete terms. Then, after an experience with this or similar ideas, the thought, if it is more familiar to us than mathematical symbols, may become as reflexive or automatic as that of a mathematics wizard.

13. THE CREATIVE MIND
LEARNING SETS and the PROCESS of Insight

Prior learning is essential before "insight" can occur.   The development of learning seems to be the basis of what is called "insight." But one question remains unanswered. In Kohler's chimps, as in people, the "moment of insight" is often sudden and unexpected. It does not develop gradually. At one moment, Sultan was standing inattentively beside his tools gazing at the goal.   The next moment he raced toward the tools and then to the goal.

Harlow's study demonstrated the role of prior experience, but it left unanswered the question of why this sudden change in perspective-a change that most certainly is crucial to the thought process itself.

One possibility may be suggested.   That is, insight is the sudden adding together of two concepts or learning sets or ideas that the mind had not previously considered in sequence.   Thus, insight may be a sudden switch to a new view of the same problem, as when Sultan put the two bamboo poles together in a straight line and suddenly saw them as a new tool.   A similar combination of two learning sets may occur to allow children to solve the Kendlers' problem-of the "insight" of putting the steel ball in the hole.

In the case of the rapid change in perspective with the Necker cube, how does this rapid change work? Why does it work at all? Why does the mind perceive the shaded area as obviously the *front* one moment, and obviously the *back* the next moment? It is almost as if one were listening to two arguments about a controversial subject and being convinced first by one, then by the other.   It seems as if the mind were automatically trying out all possible perceptual fits on this simple figure, as if trying to find the "correct" interpretation.

Note that no "conscious" activity is necessary at all.   The figure may move from one interpretation to the next without effort on our part.   Could it be that the moment of insight requires no more conscious effort than this? If we conceive of the mind as composed of video-taped memory traces, stimulus-response (S-R) bonds, or learning sets, is it difficult to imagine how these may trip in and out of sequence in much the same way as the Necker cube? Indeed, perhaps this is basic to the creative process in apes and people.

At present, psychologists are not in any general agreement on how creativity occurs.   Some psychologists have suggested that dreams are an example of the creative process at work.   The bizarre tree association of thoughts that occurs during dreaming may be an undirected form of the mirid's creative ability.   Certainly, we know that in dreams we can imagine things that we have never before experienced in quite the same way as they occur in the dreams. Is this imaginative process in dreaming a result of the spontaneous firing of nerve cells in the brain? Is it like our changing perception of the Necker cube?

Can creativity be explained by appealing to the ideas of learning sets? Or is creativity a more basic biological process of the brain? At present, there is no general agreement among psychologists. It seems likely, however, that in the final analysis, both learning processes and biological processes must be considered.

Comparatively little is known about the physiological aspect of creativity or of dreaming.   But what about the creativity of the people who have made major contributions to science?

14. CREATIVITY:

A study of the creative process in science may shed some light on creativity itself. Some of the most remarkable

discoveries seem to have resulted from a simple analogy that allows the scientist to suddenly view a problem in a completely different perspective. An example is the discovery of the helical structure of the DNA molecule. James D. Watson, who shared with F. H. C. Crick and M. H.F. Wilkins the Nobel Prize for the discovery of the structure of the molecule, described his insight as having involved first a stage of intensive study of everything available about his interest, followed by a period of almost complete abandonment of study during which he "goofed-off" to a considerable degree.

The first stage might be considered the acquisition of knowledge. The second stage is sometimes called the "incubation" period, during which ideas supposedly are generated unconsciously or at least some mental process occurs. There is little evidence that anything actually occurs during the "incubation" period, but the period is remarkably similar to that frequently described by Kohler in which a chimp, after repeated failures to work a problem, ignores the problem for a while and then suddenly sees the answer. Watson says seeing a spiral staircase on an old movie called *"The Spiral Staircase"* suddenly created a moment of insight about the shape of the DNA molecule.

Following the "incubation" period, the "aha" phenomenon seems to come on suddenly, although it probably is produced by some stimulus or thought. In Watson's case, the stimulus that triggered the insight reportedly was a movie he had seen with a spiral staircase in it. As with Sultan, the light bulb suddenly appeared above Watson's head, metaphorically speaking, and he rushed to the solution of the problem: Aha! Perhaps the structure of the DNA molecule is a double helix, rather than any of the conventional shapes we have tried to fit it to. With the base pairs like rungs on a ladder, each rung they found could only fit one set of base pairs.

Then the hard work began, to fit the known bases into base pairs that explained how a cell can divide itself accurately. Finally, the discovery must be tested. Will it work? Does it fit the existing data? Will experimental evidence confirm it? Will it bring in the banana?

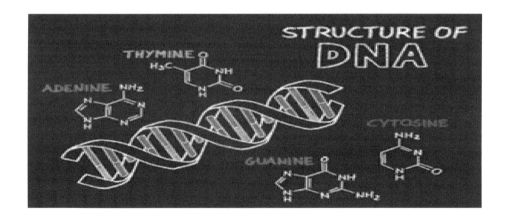

Thomas Edison once defined his genius as *"I percent inspiration and 99 percent perspiration"*. Undoubtedly, much effort must go into finding the "correct fit" once the idea develops. Edison already knew that a fiber would light, he was just looking for a material that would make it useful. He says he experimented with over 100 fibers before he found the most effective one.

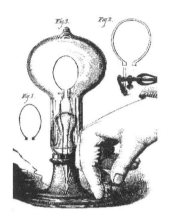

Further, not all discoveries fit into the sudden, insightful model of Watson. Nevertheless, the sequence of events; study, formulation of the problem, incubation, and insight, are repeated with remarkable frequency in the autobiographical accounts of great discoveries.

Copernicus did not record his moment of insight, but anyone who lays the Copernican model of the solar system alongside the Ptolemaic model can quickly guess at the shift in perspective that was involved. The shift is much more complicated than that of the Necker cube, but the analogy may well be correct. Copernicus took a step back from his Earth and viewed the system in its entirety. He was not limited by the existing concepts or learning sets that came from being earthbound.

Once Copernicus gained the insight that the Earth can be viewed as a planet, the behavior of other objects in space fell into place. From that point on, he began to see how astronomical data would fit into his theory. Remarkably, it did. Even Copernicus, you may remember, was bound by an existing concept or learning set-the belief that the orbits of planets in God's universe would have to be perfect. It remained for later astronomers to break with that idea and exchange it for a new one.

And what about Darwin? The two basic concepts in Darwin's theory are *natural selection* and *individual variation.* Neither idea was new. The facts of death were known to others of his day, Malthus for one. Reading Malthus' essay on population suddenly showed Darwin a dramatic new view of just how fragile life is. Anything that made it more likely that an organism would survive to reproduce its own kind, meant that the reproducers would inherit the earth. This became *Natural Selection.* The existence of *individual variations* was certainly recognized by Linnaeus and others of equal ability. But Darwin put these two concepts or learning sets together to get the charm. He achieved the sudden shift in perspective necessary to recognize the relationship between the two concepts.

After the insight of Darwin, it became relatively simple for others to comprehend what previously had not been apparent. Biologist Thomas Huxley verbally kicked himself for having so often seen the obvious but still missed the conclusion. Perhaps Huxley's reaction was not unlike that of most of us to the answer to the cross and circle problem.

When psychology's historian E. G. Boring was asked to pick the greatest psychologists of all time, he picked Charles Darwin as number one. Darwin demonstrated beyond any doubt, that humans are subject to the same laws of nature as all other animals. So is our psychology.

Often, however, persons living in the time of a great discovery-such as the contemporaries of Copernicus and Darwin, have difficulty changing their perspective. Existing concepts or learning sets can make the "obvious" too obviously correct, and emotional conditioning can prevent the thought necessary to grasp the new insight.

Thus, while learning sets are a crucial mental tool for the development of new knowledge, they may also prevent us from seeing new relationships. Similarly, emotions add spice to life, but they too may well cripple our ability to think. Can we perhaps understand our resistance to Plato, Copernicus, and Darwin, -perhaps even to comprehension of our own nature, -as being a result of the emotional conditioning of our culture and the learning sets we have already formed?

The first ideas society or parents or peers embed in the mind of a child sets the course of their very perception of reality, often for life, rendering them incapable of seeing any other point of view.

Can thought be reduced to a simple process of phasing learning sets in and out like changing perceptions of the Necker cube? Is the incubation period nothing more than a rest period during which we relax our emotions and learning sets to such an extent that, when we return to the problem, a shift of concept or learning sets is possible? Some of the evidence just reviewed suggests that these may be basic elements of creativity, yet much more may be involved.

Certainly, we hope to explain eventually the creative process as something other than a mystical phenomenon. As we have seen, however, much of the functioning of the brain is not fully understood, and no subject has been more difficult to grasp than that we so blithely have labeled *intelligence.* We not only have to consider the question of experience but also that of physiological development. Does experience constitute the only difference between a three-year-old, a seven-year-old, and an adult? What about physiological maturity?

DEVELOPMENTAL, INFORMATION PROCESSING, AND MEMORY

15. THE DEVELOPMENTAL PSYCHOLOGY OF PIAGET

Infants cannot be successfully toilet trained until they have physically matured enough to control the appropriate muscles for holding it all in. If they cannot control themselves physically, no amount of reward, punishment, or reason will be of any use. Also, children cannot learn to speak until they pass a certain stage of physical development. Thus, there are certain biological limits to learning. But what about cognition? Are there also stages that must be passed in physical development before learning can progress? Are these stages based on biology as Piaget believed? Or do they come from Learned experiences?

For more than fifty years, the French child psychologist Jean Piaget has studied cognitive development in children. Piaget's studies rival those of Kohler in the brilliance of his straightforward observations. From his research, Piaget has proposed four general stages of cognitive development in the child. The age at which each child goes through these stages may vary, but Piaget believes that the order is the same for all children. Each stage may be illustrated by the type of task a child can or cannot do.

STAGES IN COGNITIVE DEVELOPMENT

3 MONTH   6 MONTH   7 MONTH   9 MONTH   12 MONTH

1. Sensory-Motor Stage

From birth to two years of age, the infant begins forming the sensory impressions on which later intellectual development will depend. Piaget emphasizes that infants are not simply passive recipients of stimuli from outside-not just a blank slate. They are, in fact, active seekers of sensory stimulation. By moving about in their environment, they create their own stimulation (feedback).

B. F. Skinner describes an experiment that illustrates Piaget's point, although Skinner might cringe to see it interpreted this way. Skinner suggests that we observe an infant lying in his crib and wait for the child to make some natural motion, for example, raise his left arm. After the arm is raised, we turn on a flashing, attention-getting light as a reinforcement. We tum the light off when the arm is lowered, and on again when it is eventually raised. Before long, the infant-still lying in the crib-will be raising and lowering his arm as fast as Mom or Dad can tum on and off the light.

Skinner would say that the reinforcing stimulus (the light) is controlling the baby's behavior. Piaget, in contrast, would say that the baby is learning to control the stimulus. When the arm is raised, a light flashes, and the infant thoroughly enjoys his new-found ability to change the environment. So, the infant learns to control the light through his own behavior.

The difference in Skinner's and Piaget's interpretations of the same facts, as in the earlier story of Cyrus and Croesus, is the basis for a major controversy between *S-R* learning theorists and developmental psychologists, such as Piaget.

In seeking stimulation, a child of less than one year of age will follow moving objects with his eyes and by moving his head. If Mom holds a red ball with one hand and moves it across the infant's field of vision, the infant will follow it, but if Mom holds a piece of plain cardboard in the other hand and moves the ball behind the cardboard, the infant will stop tracking the ball the moment it disappears! The baby will begin to look elsewhere for other stimuli. It is as if the object, being out of sight, has ceased to exist. This behavior is in marked contrast to that of the infant of one year or older. By one year of age, the infant has learned the concept (learning set?) of *object permanence-that* is, that objects may still exist even though he can no longer see them.   The average one-year-old will even try to go behind the cardboard to find the ball.

OUT OF SIGHT, OUT OF MIND

If a baby under 9 months of age drops his rattle and it falls out of sight, the baby will not look for the rattle.   It does not seem to know that an object still exists if it cannot see the object.   If mother moves the rattle in front of the baby, the baby will follow the rattle with its eyes.   But if the mother moves the rattle behind a piece of paper, where the baby cannot see it, the baby will look away, as if the rattle no longer exists.

Between the ages of one and two, the concept of object permanence is only partial.   If the parent takes a rattle that the baby wants and places it in a cigar box, the infant has learned that the rattle continues to exist even though he cannot see it.   The baby will actively seek to get the rattle.

But what if the cigar box were placed behind a cardboard screen, and then the rattle removed and left behind the screen, would the baby know the rattle must be somewhere?

Would the baby look behind the screen where the rattle had been?   When the cigar box is presented to the infant, he will look inside, faithfully expecting the rattle.   Will he look behind the cardboard where the box has just been? Generally, not.   It does not occur to the infant that something could happen that he does not know about.

Harlow might say that the child has no learning set that would allow such an interpretation.   But by the age of two, the infant will look first in the cigar box, and if the rattle is not there, he will begin looking elsewhere for it. It could be that the preoperational child has learned a new learning set, a new concept.

The concept of Object Permanence does not appear automatically by age two.   It evolves gradually over many months.   This is a fact demonstrated by Piaget's own research.   Actually, we learn visual-motor coordination throughout our live, it is basic to athletics and even driving a car.

2. *Pre-Operational Stage*

Preoperational Stage Beginning at about the age of two, when the child first begins to talk.   Psychologists W. N. and L.A. Kellogg, who reared a chimpanzee in their own home alongside their own son, note that up to age two, the problem-solving and learning abilities of the chimp were somewhat ahead of those of their human

child--probably because of the chimp's faster rate of physical maturation.   By the age of two, however, the human child begins to leave his cousin behind in learning ability.

The major factor seems to be the development of the human child's ability to symbolize, to use words (or symbols, as in Braille, or sign language, or Morse code) to represent ideas and objects, and to use physical objects to represent other objects or ideas.   For example, the child learns to speak of (or indicate) "the ball," "the car," and "Mommy," even when the objects he is referring to are not present.

Similarly, a stick may become a model airplane or a car, a leaf may represent a boat, a doll may be treated as Mommy treats the baby, and so on.

The ape, in marked contrast, is usually limited to the present.   Chimpanzees and other mammals can operate only on stimuli that are physically "real."   Animals will usually not treat a doll or model as if it were real.   Except for the apes closest to humans, such as the chimpanzee and gorilla, animals do not seem to have a means of thinking about something that is not present for more than a few minutes.   They cannot use words to think about a car or doll that is not present.   They are limited by their spatial and temporal world.

EGOCENTRISM

From two to six years of age, children are markedly *egocentric* in their view of reality.   Egocentric does not mean selfish.   It is Piaget's term because the child perceives all reality through his own eyes, not through the eyes of others.   This applies not only to feelings and beliefs, but to a concrete perception of reality as well.

In one study by Inhelder and Piaget, some children were shown a scale model of three distinctly different mountain peaks arranged in a triangle pattern.   Each child could walk around the model to get a good look at all sides.   Then the child was seated facing one of the mountain peaks at a point of the triangle; the observer sat opposite the child.

The child was then shown several pictures of different views of the model and asked to pick the picture showing the *observer's* view of the model.   Almost invariably, the children chose the picture of what they saw from their chair, not the observer saw.   Time after time, this happened.   Why?   Apparently, children have formed no concept (or schema or learning set?) that would allow them to realize that the observer sees a different view of reality than they do.

Adults, of course, can work this concrete problem easily, but we often have the same difficulty as the child for understanding different beliefs, values, or ideas conceived in the minds of others.

CONSERVATION OF MATTER Age 2 to 6

A second major concept that has not yet formed in the child under seven years is that of *conservation*.   The classic example of this can be shown with a five-year-old child, two short fat glasses filled with water, and one empty tall skinny glass.

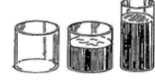

First, the child is shown two short glasses with the same amount of water in each.   He is then coaxed into saying that both contain the same amount of water, a fairly obvious fact at this age.   Then, before the child's very eyes, the water from one of the short glasses is poured into the tall skinny glass.

 Now, is there any difference in the amount of water in the short and tall glasses? Most children of this age will say, often spontaneously, that the tall glass has more water in it.   Interestingly, when the same type of study is done with children who are asked to count fifteen marbles into each glass, the five-year-old will still say that the taller glass contains more marbles than the shorter glass.

Clearly, a child's concept of shape and volume differs from that of an adult.   It all hangs on the word "MORE".   If mom asks a five-year-old if he/she wants "more" milk, then when she pours "more" milk into the glass, the level of the milk rises.   It seems to be more of a difference in learning, than a difference in development.   But as soon as the child goes to first grade, he/she learns a quite different association of the word "more".   In fact, our schools now teach the concepts of "more" than, "over" "under" "around" and "through".   The same concepts Piaget used to test five-year-old's, are now taught routinely in first grade, and even in kindergarten, largely because of Piaget's work.   Now they are learning a new idea, to replace the old idea.   That would be learning rather than development.

3   Concrete-Operational Stage   Ages 7-11

Not until around the age of around seven do children begin to recognize that "more" and "amount" are two different concepts.   They also learn an important *new* concept: that the shape of a container cannot in any way affect the amount of liquid it holds.   It may be incorrect to assume that five-year-old children are responding to a concept of *quantity* when they are asked which glass contains "more" liquid.

In fact, children could be responding to a simple S-R relationship.   When a child asks for more milk, more coke, or more juice, the usual result is that the level in his glass is raised.   Thus, "more" comes to be associated with the higher level of liquid in the glass.   Only much later, after numerous learning experiences in many different situations, does the concept of "more" take on the meaning of quantity.

Why?   What happens at the age of six that changes the mind of the child?   Is it age?   Likely more importantly, this is the age they start school.   And what do teachers teach in school?   They teach concepts of "more than", "less than", "around", "through", "over", "under".   The concepts tested by Piaget, are now taught in school.

An important point is illustrated by this study.   Children may be able to verbally express a concept; they may be able to say which glass has "more" water in it.   They may even be able to use a word correctly in many cases. Often, however, a child may parrot the verbal ideas of his elders without fully understanding the test of a child's ability to visualize a problem.

Parents and psychologists and teachers, in turn, may fail to recognize that the child's grasp of reality is limited by his experience.   Parents may fail to understand how their child could express an understanding of a concept so beautifully in one situation and fail so badly in another.   The child may simply have a different concept; a concept shaped and limited by his own experience.

By the age of seven, the child has mastered the set of conservation of quantity with liquid and with numbers. But does the child have difficulty with abstract ideas relating to space?   Inhelder and Piaget arranged a task in which glasses of colored water are presented to seven-year-olds.   The child is asked to predict what the surface of the water will do if the glass is tilted to the left.   Look at two glasses, one with the water surface drawn in. What would the surface of the water look like in the second glass if it were tilted to the left? (Try this one yourself.   You will be able to work it, but see if you do not experience at least a temporary intellectual pause before the moment of insight.)

 Can you work this problem?   What do you have to do to succeed?

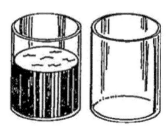

In Piaget and Inhelder's study you could not work the problem without stopping to construct a mental image, a visual image in your mind, of what the glass would look like if tilted to the left. It seems to be far more difficult for us to draw a hypothetical water surface level in a tilted glass when the glass we are looking at is still vertical.   Children are ordinarily not capable of doing this until they reach the age of nine.

4 Formal-Operational Period Ages 12 up

By the time children are twelve, they are capable of dealing with a great many hypothetical situations other than the semi-concrete problems discussed above. They are now capable of dealing with hypothetical "what if" types of problems they have never before experienced. This ability does not appear suddenly at any one stage, and we are still uncertain as to relative importance of biological growth and experience in its development.

How important is a child's physical age in determining whether or not the child can solve a problem? From what you know now, do you think that if five-year-old children were given enough demonstrations of the conservation of liquid, enough learning sets, they would be able to solve similar problems while they are still five? And if the five-year-olds were given enough experience in viewing the scale model of mountains from all sides, could they eventually pick the correct picture from the observer's viewpoint? At this point, you may be thinking of some experiments you would like to see done.

We know that young children have greater difficulty mastering abstract concepts, such as that of conservation, than do older children. For the moment, there still seems to be some uncertainty as to how much of this difficulty is due to physical immaturity and how much is due to the simple lack of experience.

But by the time a child has reached the formal-operations stage, is there any type of problem that an adult can work that a twelve-year-old cannot? Given the same knowledge or experience, that is. Can an adult without background in nuclear physics, mathematics, or psychological principles master the knowledge any more readily than a preadolescent child? The best guess, based on existing evidence, seems to be no. We have no evidence that the adult has any innate intellectual advantage in reasoning over the child who has at least reached puberty.

And we have much evidence that adults make precisely the same type of mistakes in reasoning as children do. If you were sharp in relating the material we have already been over, from Kohler to Piaget, to your own behavior you may well have recognized some similar examples in your own learning of new tasks.

The change in perspective that the five-year-old must learn in order to see the mountain peaks from the viewpoint of the observer is very much like the change in perspective that Copernicus had to make to see the solar system in a different perspective. Even today the average adult would have great difficulty demonstrating how Copernicus came by his ideas about the solar system, much less applying them by observation of the heavens. We believe that his ideas are correct because we have been told they are correct. But do we really understand them? Can we explain them any better than a five-year-old can explain conservation?

Knowledge does not spring forth automatically at a given age. It evolves with new experiences and new insights. We are continually adding to our understanding throughout our lives.

16. THE CONTRIBUTION
OF DEVELOPMENTAL PSYCHOLOGY

The biological development of the brain is clearly a factor in understanding human behavior. When we reach puberty, so much changes besides just our physical development. We become more independence seeking. We question the ideas of the adults. The allegiance of children changes from the parents to the peer group.   It is essential to understand all of this.   Some of this is clearly due to changes in the biology of the brain at puberty.   Yet much of this is also due to what we have learned outside of the home and the intense feeling of a need to fit in with the peer group.   Much of this is biological development, yet much of this is also learned, unintentionally, in our schools.

Developmental Psychology has given us a vast wealth of experimental studies that demonstrate what children know and what they do not understand.   One of the greatest contributions may be that they simply educated us to understand that the understanding of a child and the understanding of an adult are quite different.   It is important to know that what we think a child understands may only reflect our own perception of reality, not theirs.   It is important not to mistake our own mistakes in understanding for theirs.   And vice versa.

> *"When I was seventeen, I thought my old man was the stupidest person on earth.   When I got to be twenty-seven, I was amazed at how much the old man had learned in the last ten years."*

> Mark Twain

17. BEYOND DEVELOPMENTAL STAGES

No amount of neural data processing by the brain can be useful without prior experience as a base.   Stone and Church provided a simple demonstration of this fact in a study in which adults were asked to draw a picture of an island, not just the part of the island that is above water, but the part of the island that is below the water as well.   A majority of the adults, most of them from Hawaii, came up with something like the drawing below. What is wrong with the picture?   Do you think your opinion is due to previous learning about islands and underwater mountains in school or on television?

What does the part of an island under the water look like?   Natives living on islands all of their lives did not know.   They knew the land dropped off suddenly, but most assumed that it would be round like the boats in the harbor.   It was a good assumption (intuition?), like stimulus generalization, but it is wrong.

Even adults, like Piaget's children, cannot do problems they have not experienced.

18. WHAT ROLE DOES LEARNING PLAY?

Harvard psychologist Jerome Bruner has been a firm supporter of Piaget's studies, but he disagrees markedly with Piaget about the need for biological maturity. Is it necessary that children be over twelve years old before they are taught algebra? Is it necessary for children to be seven before they can grasp the concept of conservation of matter?

Do children have to be one-year old before they can form the concept of object permanence? Bruner thinks not. Because these concepts seem to depend on prior learning experiences, according to Bruner, a child given step-by-step concrete experiences with a variety of such tasks should be able to master them, much as Harlow's monkeys mastered the discrimination learning sets.

Bruner and Kenney have devised a step-by-step method of teaching quadratic equations to ten-year-olds. The method uses concrete materials, such as building blocks, to allow children to see the mathematical relationships visually, rather than have to imagine them in their minds.

Then, as with Harlow's monkeys, problem after problem is presented until the concept is formed. A child then can work an infinite number of quadratic equations that have solutions based on the newly formed concept.

Through similar techniques, the concept of object permanence has been taught months earlier than it is usually learned and the concept of conservation of matter years before it appeared in Piaget's subjects. It is possible that soon, psychologists will develop marketable games for parents to play with preschoolers that will speed up their ability to solve problems. Today's students learn as much about mathematics and history by the eighth grade as their grandparents had learned after graduation from high school.

If a child reaches maximum physical and intellectual development by or before puberty, some interesting possibilities arise. By the use of Harlow's learning sets, carefully metered out in Skinner's teaching machines, could we not teach a child of twelve or under the same amount that is learned in high school?

Principles of logic, higher mathematics, and other advanced concepts could be introduced at twelve, and children would complete today's college requirements by the time they are fifteen. Such advanced curricula and methods may be too much for today's educational systems to accomplish, but the idea is not farfetched. Before the year 2050 A.D., it may become a reality.

19. COGNITIVE PSYCHOLOGY

Cognitive Psychologists often see themselves as having replaced Behavioral Psychology, yet it is more accurate to say that they added an important new dimension to psychology. Cognitive psychology could never explain what Behavioral Psychology could explain, and Behavioral Psychology could not explain much of what Cognitive Psychology showed.

By selecting a few studies that only cognitive psychology could explain, it gave a mistaken impression that the advantage always went to their position. Perhaps more likely, both saw a portion of how the mind works, but not the whole picture.

• Wolfgang Kohler's extensive study of "insight" in chimpanzees was a major step toward recognizing that something was going on at a higher level inside the brain, although trial and error learning was clearly a part of the puzzle.

• Selective Attention, demonstrated by Donald Broadbent by having students wear headphones, playing different stories into each ear, were told to pay attention to only one story. When asked questions about what was happening in both ears, they were able to effectively answer those questions that were about the story only happening in the ear they were attending to.

• Tolman's studies of latent learning and "cognitive maps" strongly suggested that we learn far more than just a simple stimulus-response association. This presaged the realization that we may learn all sensory input, not just an S-R relationship.

• Piaget's experiments with human children provided a rich source of understanding of how children understand reality differently than adults; from their own experiences, and how this understanding changes throughout life.

• Studies of memory and the fallibility of memory by Elizabeth Loftus and others have found our memory is vague and easily re-written. Eyewitness testimony, often considered the best evidence, is a serious problem that has led to the jailing of innocent people. The number one cause of innocent people being convicted of crimes they did not commit, is eyewitness testimony.

https://www.oxfordbibliographies.com/view/document/obo-9780199828340/obo-9780199828340-0026.xml

The major contributions of cognitive psychology are important, but not paradigm-changing. They add to the paradigm.

21. WHAT COGNITIVE PSYCHOLOGY CANNOT DO

The failure of cognitive psychology to provide a bridge between basic learning (such as trial and error, and learned emotions) and cognitive processes, left their theories without hard evidence of how it fits into psychology.

• Piaget's concepts of Schema, Accommodation, and Assimilation are subject to the problem of the Nominal Fallacy: the belief that, by having named something, we have somehow explained it. Without a basis in hard evidence, these words have no meaning. Simply describing a term, does not explain it.

• Harlow's study of "learning sets" provided a hard evidence ground for going from simple association to cognitive psychology, but has been largely ignored by cognitive psychologists.

• More importantly, they ignore the most recent discoveries of cataract studies in babies that show the brain itself is profoundly molded by experience. **Without visual experience, the brain itself will never develop the ability to see. Experience itself changes the biology of the brain and our perceptions.**

• At its simplest, a "theory of mind" may only refer to a child understanding that another child may think differently than their own, which is the beginning of a critical understanding of people. Undoubtedly this happens early, but it is severely limited in its application. Understanding why others think differently is a lifelong process. Even adults fail to understand how or why others think differently.

• Studies that rely solely on how long an infant spends looking at one picture, rather than another, are not well grounded. Guessing what the infant is "thinking" is not scientific.

• Basic Trial and Error learning studied by Thorndike applies to every form of cognitive thinking, from computer programmers to Copernicus, Einstein, and others who used trial and error to find out what nature is doing. Edison himself experimented with some 100 different filaments before finding one that worked.

21.COMBINING BEHAVIORAL AND COGNITIVE PSYCHOLOGY

- Harlow's study of "learning sets" provided a hard evidence basis for going from simple association to cognitive psychology.

- Miller's demonstration that a conditioned fear reaction also applies to our thoughts. He found that just *thinking* about a symbol that had been associated with shock could carry a measurable GSR fear response for 25 trials.

That does not mean that an actual biological fear response is needed. The brain itself is quite capable of computing what we should fear without actually experiencing the fear.

- Martin Braine's work on Pivot and Open words showed how easily a child could create new sentences, never heard before, without the need for a new theory of creativity.

- The study by Shepard suggests that we usually respond with whatever ideas were the first ideas in our brain, the prime experience, and how we *perceive* a question, not with thought. Thought may only be perceptions that our ability to focus our attention makes easier to observe and manipulate.

- In a remarkable study by Albert Bandura, he found he could counter condition or desensitize the fear of dogs in children by showing them four-minute "Modeling" videos of a boy playing with a dog. This important study is a new method of applying a cognitive method to accomplish the behavioral methods of Mary Cover Jones, who counter-conditioned and desensitized little Peter from his fear of dogs. This bridges the gap between Behavioral therapy and Cognitive psychology.

Unfortunately, many have believed that one must accept one theory completely and reject the other. That has not been a success in psychology or in politics. Science has been so successful because it is based on the evidence, not the opinions.

22. INFORMATION PROCESSING THEORY:
The Brain and the Computer

One of the newest ideas in cognitive psychology comes from the study of computer data processing. The idea of the mind as an information-processing machine is set forth by Karl Pribram in *Languages of the Brain* and by George Miller, Eugene Galanter, and Karl Pribram in *Plans and Structure of Behavior*. The theory is based on the belief that the brain is biologically structured to process information in much the same way as a computer is structured to process information.

A computer is capable of making only one independent decision: It can proceed to the next operation or go to a different stage in the program. The computer's "decision" is based on a simple process of comparing two numbers or patterns of bits to see whether they are the same or different.

This step in a computer flowchart is known as an IF-THEN statement or a DO LOOP. Complex computer operations would be impossible without the computer's ability to make this simple go/no-go decision. All other computer abilities are mechanical mathematical functions provided by the programmer.

The human mind may make similar "decisions" by *comparing* one bit of information, or a pattern of information, to another.

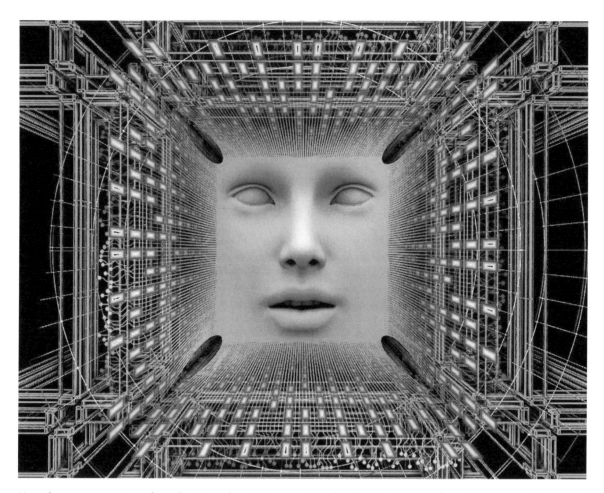

How does a computer make a decision when it is processing data? In its simplest form, in the following example, the process is: As the computer (1) reads data into the machine, it goes on to the next steps (2, 3, 4) and processes the data, followed by· the seemingly unimportant (5) adding of X = X + 1 in which whatever number X is at that point is increased by 1.

 The next step (6) sends the computer into the decision diamond where the number that X now equals is compared to a preset number-for example, the number in memory cell J. If X equals I, the computer "decides" to continue to the next step. If X is less than I, *then* the computer "decides" to go back and run through the data again, adding another X + 1 until X equals I. Then it will continue on with the next stage of the program.

Contrast and comparison are basic to our ability to think. The computer uses basic comparison to compare two variables (X and I). When the two are equal, the computer goes on to the next step. That is the only thinking a computer can do. It may be the only thinking we are capable of as well.

On a more complex level, information-processing theory suggests that the mind makes decisions in a similar way. That is, the mind decides on a solution to a problem by comparing a solution (means) with the problem (end). The means-end analysis proceeds somewhat like the numbers in a decision diamond. In a computer, the numbers are compared until they are equal; then the computer goes on to the next step. Similarly, the brain may compare images of the problem to images of the possible solutions to see if any match.

In the brain, the process involves (1) testing for a difference between the possible solution, and the problem, (2) operations to decrease the perceived difference (thinking?), (3) retesting for a difference, until (4) the problem is solved, and the brain goes on to something else. Miller, Galanter, and Pribram refer to this as a TOTE process: Test, Operate, Test, Exit.

On a simple level, this may be what was happening when Kohler's chimp Sultan tried to bite wood off one end of a stick to get it to fit into the opening in a second stick. Sultan bit, and tested by trying to fit them together; Test, Operate, Test Exit.   They did not yet fit, so he bit and tested, bit and tested until a final fit occurred and, EXIT.

On a more complex level, we may generate ideas or hypotheses about how to solve a problem.   Thinking out a problem (by imagining possible solutions) may require us to test and operate, test and operate, on a number of possible alternatives until the final fit occurs, the difference between means and end is zero, and the problem is solved.

INFORMATION PROCESSING THEORY

Problem Solving Sequence in a Computer Flowchart

Human Data Processing Sequence?

1. Acquisition of Knowledge
   Data A,B,C,D is read into the computer's memory cells.

2. Learning Sets are Formed (These may be viewed as problem solving strategies)

3. Learning Sets are Formed

4. Learning Sets are Combined
   Idea (I) Forms

5. X is the problem that is to be compared with the idea (I).

6. TOTE type mechanism for testing Idea (means) against the Problem (end).
   (Vicarious Trial and Error?)

7. Insightful Problem Solving
   (New Learning Set Formed?)

8. Behavior

Computer Sequence

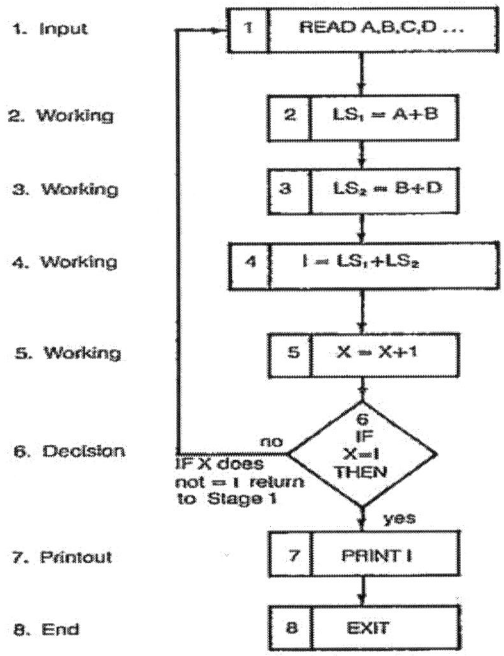

Stage	Box	Operation
1. Input	1	READ A,B,C,D ...
2. Working	2	$LS_1 = A+B$
3. Working	3	$LS_2 = B+D$
4. Working	4	$I = LS_1 + LS_2$
5. Working	5	$X = X+1$
6. Decision	6	IF $X = I$ THEN — no: IF X does not $= I$ return to Stage 1 — yes
7. Printout	7	PRINT I
8. End	8	EXIT

When computer programmers are developing a new program, they have to try one line of code (OPERATE), run the program (TEST), to see if it works, change a line of code (OPERATE), try another, run the program (TEST), over and over again before they solve a simple series of programming steps.   Trial and Error becomes the 99% Edison spoke of.

23. INFORMATION PROCESSING
IN THE BRAIN

One of the important points made by the information-processing theorists is that the brain is biologically built to perform information processing, as a computer is built to perform mathematical comparisons (the DO LOOP or a comparison of two variables).   The assumption is that the brain automatically performs information processing as a computer automatically performs its data processing.

But it is likely that the two do not operate the same way.   The brain seems to use contrast and comparison, basic to science, as a way of making it through the world. The computer works only with math, patterns, and wiring for comparison. The two are not the same, although it is a close analogy.

The brain is programmed by our DNA to allow us to *anticipate* what will happen next, just as Pavlov's dog salivated in *anticipation* of meat following the bell.   Yet without learning, the brain is nothing but three pounds of semi-hard jelly.

In "real" life, we are all doing much the same to make it in this world.   We are trying to figure out what works, what path to choose, what is really important, what we need to know and what is trivia.   We learn about life by Trial and Error, with a special emphasis on Error.   We get little help from our schools on the problems of life, we are left at the mercy of whatever ideas others give us; our parents, the press, our peers, Hollywood, and pretty much all of the random experiences we have in life.   These experiences make up the Rubik's cube of life.

24. SUDDEN
INSIGHT?

How does sudden insight occur? Perhaps it is as simple as the change in perspective we have when we view the top of the Necker cube and change to looking at the bottom.   It changes our perception instantly, with no thought required, something like seeing the box flip one way and then another.   Similarly, when two ideas suddenly fit, when x=y, then the mind sees a new possibility.   Yet the moment of insight can occur automatically, it may not require thought.

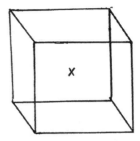

25. A SYNTHESIS OF CONFLICTING THEORIES?

Any attempt to satisfy all points of view runs the danger of satisfying none. But some synthesis of the ideas of Kohler, Harlow, Piaget, and others is essential if the problems of cognition and creativity are to be resolved. It seems likely that all these theories have grasped a part of the truth, not unlike the six blind men trying to describe an elephant just from touch. The following points may be suggested:

(1) Experience undoubtedly requires associations; a computer is of no value without data. *"All knowledge is from experience."* Einstein

(2) Experience changes the very nature of learning in the brain. What we have learned early on, as in *"take two apples from three apples"*, interferes with learning or even understanding new information. Or it may facilitate learning.   We see this daily in our interpersonal interactions, our politics, and our religions.

(3) Cognition may automatically be programmed from concepts or learning sets that allow knowledge to be generalized to new stimuli.

(4) Learning Sets or learned programs in the brain.   It may be that these concepts or learning sets have a biological basis not unlike that of the TOTE mechanism suggested by Miller et al.-that is, the learning sets are an automatic result of an innate data processing device. Or, they may be a result of the brain's ability to anticipate what comes next (Bell-Meat).

(5) Development of the Brain. Piaget's concepts may represent the development of learning as the brain matures physically and the data-processing machinery becomes plugged into a variety of learned programs for data processing.

(6) Creativity may involve a combination of the capricious firing of brain cells (dreams or imagination?), the fitting together of ideas or learning sets in sequence, mental trial and error, Necker cube sudden changes, and TOTE testing.

(7) And the brain's sudden change in perspective, as in the Necker cube, when the pieces fit (and Sultan gets the banana).   Each of the theories discussed seems to describe a part of the overall process.

This interpretation is presented as one possible interpretation of the research data. Many psychologists may not accept the idea that Harlow's learning sets are the same as the cognitive concepts of Piaget and Bruner and the heuristic methods that Newell and Simon discuss in *Human Problem Solving.*   Further, there is no general agreement that the mind functions in quite the same way as a computer flowchart.

Theories must be tested. Mystical explanations of our genius may be awe-inspiring, but few scientists doubt that the end result of the study of the human condition will be an explanation by simple, natural processes.

26. MEMORY

BLACK BART: Elements of Memory

In the early 1880s a highwayman, nicknamed Black Bart by the newspapers, was famous for robbing stagecoaches. He would often fell a tree on the road, and, when the stage rounded a corner and had to stop for the tree, he would leap out of the bushes with two guns and yell, in effect, "Your money or your life." In the bushes were gun barrels of his "gang" poking out of the shrubbery. The coach quickly gave up and only later learned the gun barrels were only black sticks to fool them into thinking they were surrounded.

There were many highwaymen back then, but Black Bart blew all of them off the front page of the press. Not that he was much different from the others, but, like the most famous boxer Muhammed Ali before every fight, he left a poem behind at the scene of every robbery. The newspapers hung on every word. This is one of the poems he left behind:

"I've labored long and hard for bread,
For honor and for riches.
But on my corns, I've stood too long,
You fine-haired sons-a-bitches.

Black Bart never killed anyone, unlike some of the more famous highwaymen. Yet he remained in the news long after they caught him. Why? It turned out that Bart had never before been a robber. He had come from back east, from New York. When the second Gold Rush started in California, he left his job and traveled West to the gold fields; like thousands of other Americans. There, he lost everything; Like thousands of other Americans. He turned to robbery, perhaps angry over being misled into thinking he too could make it rich. Many others could identify with that.

Black Bart's Poem illustrates some basic principles of memory.

1. **Emotion:** If you were asked on a test, to remember one of the lines of Black Bart's poem, which line are you more likely to remember? Most likely the last line. Why? It triggers an emotional reaction in your brain. From learning, to refusing to learn things that contradict the emotional ideas embedded in our brains, emotion is a profound determinate of what we will remember, or what the brain will refuse to learn. The source of emotion, the Amygdala, is just adjacent to the Hippocampus, the part of the brain that consolidates short-term memory into long-term memory.

2. **Novelty:** It is also an unexpected or novel stimulus, so it triggers a p300 wave in your brain. In an EEG, that P300 wave responds to any novel stimuli. If students are asked to read aloud a list of male names, while connected to an EEG, and suddenly came to a female name in the list (or vice versa), it would produce a spike in the P300 wave of the EEG, the brain's clear reaction to novelty.

3. **Pattern recognition:** Generally, a product of the right side of the brain, it responds to visual patterns or auditory patterns (sights or music), this seems to result in the *rhyme* of the poem grabbing our attention and making it easier to remember.

4. **Familiarity:** If we learn something about the background of Black Bart, such as his giving up his job for the gold fields, something hundreds of thousands of others had done, that makes it easier to identify (by association) with his problems.

5. **Similarity:** If we took a biology course in high school, learning the terms makes it easier to learn new, but similar, material in college.

THE SERIAL POSITION EFFECT

Hermann Ebbinghaus found that the first words we learn, in a list of words, are more likely to be remembered than the middle or last words. If you are given a list of, say, 30 nonsense syllables, and asked to memorize them. When tested on their memory we are most likely to remember the first words, and, secondly, the last words in the list. The words in the middle are most likely to be forgotten.

This example, often called the Primacy Effect has some similarity to the Prime Experience (also called the Primacy Effect) discussed earlier, however, this Primacy Effect deals with consolidating short-term memory into long-term memory, and the Prime Experience has to do with how the brain actually perceives reality (the first ideas in the brain become the criteria by which we judge all things).

THE FALLIBILITY OF MEMORY

Studies of memory and the fallibility of memory by Elizabeth Loftus and others have found our memory is vague and easily re-written. Eyewitness testimony, often considered the best evidence, is a serious problem that has led to the jailing of innocent people. The number one cause of innocent people being convicted of crimes they did not commit, is eyewitness testimony.

THE ZEIGARNIC EFFECT

A comparison of the *Zeigarnic effect* and the results of a study by Rosenzweig provides a classic scientific study of memory. In her original study, Zeigarnic arranged a variety of tasks, such as jigsaw puzzles, and gave these to children to solve.

She allowed each child to successfully complete one-half of the puzzles at random. On the other half of the puzzles, the children were interrupted before they could complete the task.

Zeigarnic later asked the children to recall the content of the tasks. She found that of 138 children:

> 11O of them recalled more interrupted tasks than completed tasks, *
>
> 17 recalled more completed tasks than interrupted tasks, and
>
> 11 recalled the same number of each.

Her findings, which have been replicated by many other experimenters, have been termed the *Zeigarnic effect:* that is, we remember the tasks we have not completed, while forgetting, those we have finished.

Then came Rosenzweig. Using the same basic technique as Zeigamic, Rosenzweig introduced a new element. He told college students that the puzzles were considered to be true measures of the students' I.Q. and ability, and that any puzzle not completed in the allotted time would be removed. Then he encouraged them to do their best and sat back to observe their behavior.

As in Zeigarnic's study, the students were interrupted, totally at random, on half the tasks without regard for the time or their progress. On the remaining tasks, the students were allowed to complete the work regardless of how long it took.

A control group of students received exactly the same treatment but without the ego involvement, that is, they were not told that their performance was an indication of their I.Q. and ability.

 When subjects from the two groups were asked to recall the tasks, a marked contrast emerged: The "ego-involved" students recalled more of the tasks they had successfully completed and fewer of the tasks they had failed to complete, while the control group exhibited the Zeigarnic effect, recalling more of the unfinished tasks.

The key is *ego-involvement:* When the students believed that completed tasks represented success and uncompleted tasks represented failure, this belief became a part of their social yardstick. The completed puzzles (positively reinforcing) were remembered, while the uncompleted puzzles (failure, negatively reinforcing) were repressed. We tend to ignore facts we believe are damning to our individual status, our ego, our feelings of personal adequacy.

We see this in our interpersonal relations, our politics, our religions, our everyday lives. What we can remember depends on many things, including our ego involvement as well as our biology.

27. NATURE OR NURTURE OR INTERACTION?

Until about 1920, it was widely believed that all behavior was the result of inborn instincts.   People spoke of "born" geniuses or "born" lovers or "born" bad to the bone.   Behavior was explained in terms of instincts: sex instincts, courting instincts, marriage instincts, moral instincts, and the like.   Learning was considered relatively unimportant.   Today, we have reverted to that simplistic use of Word Magic by those who say, "It is all in your DNA."

In the early 1900s, psychologists began to realize that instincts alone could not explain much of human behavior. A sort of revolution (sometimes identified as *behaviorism)* followed this realization, and everything--culture, manners, morals, even speech, and thinking--came to be interpreted as learned (nurture) rather than innate (nature).   Innate tendencies now were considered relatively unimportant,

In the 1960s, it became fashionable to speak of human behavior not as a product of nature or nurture, but as an interaction between the organism's biology (nature) and its environment (nurture).   Much growth and development are just such an interaction.   For example, your height depends on the inherited genetic code (nature) that sets a maximum limit on the length of your bones.

How tall you are also depends on your environment, however: If you live in an environment where protein is scarce, you may not grow as tall as if you had grown up in an environment where a high-protein diet (nurture) was common.   Today's male adult averages 5 feet 10 inches tall.   The skeletons (or suits of armor) of our European ancestors of only a few centuries ago, however, average about 5 feet.   Similarly, the Japanese diet improved after World War II, and the height of children raised in Japan since then is markedly greater.   In effect, then; height is not simply biologically set: It is determined by both nature and nurture.

Today, there is a tendency for psychologists to consider themselves "interactionists" or eclectic (parts of everything) psychologists rather than nativists or environmentalists.   An eclectic psychologist would be quick to point out that three-dimensional vision requires both the native equipment (the biological programs or structure of the brain and eyes) but also experience in the environment (feedback from moving and seeing, etc.).

It is certainly true that humans could not speak without the unique biological structure and programs in the brain that allow speech.   Yet our *language and the meaning and emotions attached to words,* is totally determined by the culture in which we grow up, -it is not biologically determined.

Our opinions, attitudes, religions, and other beliefs are also strictly products of our environment.   If one is comparing a chimpanzee's ability to speak with a human's speech, then the difference is overwhelmingly biological.   But if one is comparing one culture's language or beliefs with that of another culture, the difference is overwhelmingly learned. In either ease, calling it an interaction may distort what is happening. We must know how much is learned and how much is biological.

There are, then, at least three categories or conditions of human behavior: (1) *biological,* as in the structure of the brain or speech mechanisms; (2) *learned,* as in the specific language, behavior, or beliefs of a culture; and (3) an *interaction,* In varying degrees, of the two.   The problem may be to define our terms and determine which is important under which circumstances.

Does the environment acquire meaning only through experience? Even granting the considerable evidence that stimuli acquire meaning in higher animals only through experience, there still seem to be obvious contradictions to this idea.   How do young male birds "know" to stake out a territory during the mating season and defend that territory from other males? Why do they exhibit this behavior even when they have never had experience with fighting or mating or much of anything? Why do stags only beginning to bear antlers rush madly into battle in the rutting season? How do animals "know" how to care for their young? In short, what about our "instincts"?

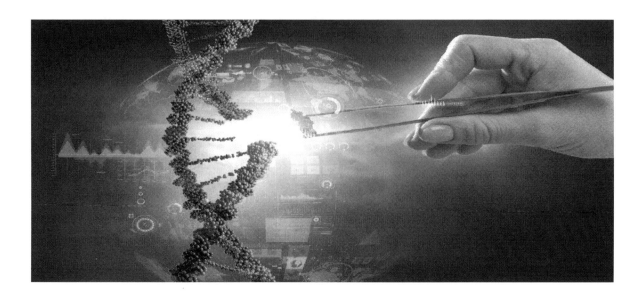

11 DNA

THE PRE-PROGRAMMED MIND

The DNA And Innate Patterns Of Behavior

TINBERGEN • LACK • LORENZ • BEACH • WATSON • HESS

"The Neuro-physiological organization we call instinct functions in a blindly mechanical way, especially apparent when its function goes wrong.
Nobel Laureate Konrad Lorenz

One of the continuing debates in psychology is over how much behavior is learned and how much is innate. Much of animal behavior is dictated by forces embedded in our DNA. Can we discover how much of this is learned, and how much is in our genes? And how much is an interaction?

1. WATSON'S MYSTERY AT BIRD KEY

Most psychologists would be shocked to find that John B. Watson's name was among the great naturalists of all time. His best work is left out of our textbooks. But his work in studying instincts marks him as one of the most thoughtful of all psychologists. Watson's work on Bird Key was recreated by the **BBC** in their series *The Great Naturalists*. It has recently been confirmed in similar species by the award-winning series on nature by Sir David Attenborough in his most recent work, *Seven Worlds*.

Bird Key is a small island off the East coast of America. Today, it is populated by many resort homes, but in Watson's time, it had nothing on it except terns, a species of bird. People could walk among the terns without panicking. There were no natural predators on the island and they built their nests in plain sight, in just a scrape in the sand on the beach.

Watson noticed that the turns would return to their own nest after flying out for food. How did they know where to return to? How did they know their own eggs from that of other terns?

Watson tried an experiment to find out. Taking a page from earlier work by Tinbergen and Fabre, once a tern was gone from its nest, Watson moved the tern's eggs four inches away from the nest. When the tern returned to its nest, would it sit on the nest or on its eggs?

The tern returned. She looked at the eggs. She looked at the nest. Then, she settled down on the nest, ignoring the eggs next to it. For a while, she even went through the motions of tucking the eggs in under her, although there were no eggs to tuck in.

Eventually, the tern would retrieve the eggs, but her attachment to her unique scrape in the ground was significant. Later, *Scientific American* would publish an article describing the egg retrieving "instinct". They found that the terns would retrieve an egg, by using its beak to scrape it in. They also found that if they placed golf balls around the nest, the tern would also retrieve the golf balls and sit on them until...

Watson thought the terns were making something like a photographic map of the scenery around the area to be able to return to exactly the same spot. To experiment with this idea, he waited until the tern had left the nest, and then patiently rearranged the scenery around the tern's nest. Rearranging the scenery confused the tern and required some while to adjust.

To Watson, it meant that the terns displayed no "knowledge" of what they were doing at all. It looked like a series of inborn responses that the birds carried out much like a series of reflexive responses. Today, we might call this a biological program in its brain. This realization led Watson, the pioneer of Behaviorism, along with much of American psychology, to reject the idea that animals were born with an understanding of what they were doing.

Recently, Sir David Attenborough showed an identical example in the albatross in his BBC video *Seven Worlds*. He found that if an albatross chick were to fall from its six-inch-high nest, the parent would not retrieve it. Instead, the parent would return to the nest and just sit on it; all the while the chick was cheeping pitifully, only inches below the parent. If the chick could not make its way back to the nest by itself, it would die from cold and hunger.

Clearly, "knowledge" and understanding are not required for "instinctual" behavior. The failure to emphasize this point has often left students confused about how instinctual behavior actually works.

That is not to say that birds cannot learn, they do. Learning is also basic to survival. But in the most critical of survival "instincts", the behavior is programmed into their genes, triggered by the simplest possible stimiuli.

Studying the DNA by itself tells us absolutely nothing about what the genes do. Only by comparing and contrasting the genes in one individual, with the genes in other individuals, and by observing the differences in specific traits, was it possible to learn the function of the genetic code that forms all life. Simply knowing the genetic code itself, tells us nothing.

Psychology can only learn what behavior is genetic and what behavior is learned by comparing and contrasting specific traits in each species. If we want to know what is genetic and what is learned, we must first look at the most basic *survival mechanisms* in each species. Those survival instincts most essential are (1) Survival of the individual; what food is and how to find food, and (2) Survival of the species; how to engage in sex, and what species to engage in sex with.   Low-tech observations in psychology, like low-tech observations in genetics, are absolutely basic.

2. VIOLENCE IN THE TREES

Spring. A forest glade. Leaves of tall aspens rustle in the breeze. The air is filled with miscellaneous bird calls. A hiker pauses to drink in the harmony of nature. Suddenly, a flit of red darts through the trees, a redbird in search of greener pastures. An intruder, the redbird is a stimulus for a violent act of aggression that is about to occur.

High above the head of our hiker, a second streak of red darts toward the first.

Like a scene from a World War I dogfight, the second bird zeros in on the tail of the intruder, screeching in anger, feeling out his range. Surprised, and startled, the intruder darts first left, then right. Dogged by his persistent adversary, the intruder turns and flees. The battle is over as quickly as it began. The forest assumes its illusion of peace.

In this case, the observed behavior is an act of aggression against a member of one's own species. What function does this aggression serve? Is behavior innate, instinctual, awaiting only an external cue to trigger it? Or is behavior, like knowledge, also a product of the environment?

Left: A male red rumpled swallow attacks another male swallow in his territory, much the same as male Robins and male Cardinals attack each other during the mating season. Color is the stimulus that triggers the Fight response in the Amygdala. The loser of the encounter will fly off and find another territory.

In Robins, Cardinals, and red rumpled swallows, the males have red feathers. The more colorful of the sexes is the male. The females are a dull, drab, brown, or gray color. The male will allow a female into their territory for mating, but will chase out other males. David Lack a British ornithologist found that male Robins would repeatedly attack a ball of red feathers, tearing at the inanimate object.

What is he attacking? Other males? Or the color red? Films of this attack showed savage attacks on the red dummy of his own species, only because of the red color of the dummy. Such behavior often persisted for long periods despite the bird's repeated experiences with the dummy. One hundred years ago it was not uncommon to find a news story of a woman who was attacked while coming out of the church with red feathers in her Easter bonnet.

What do you suppose would happen if we took the robin's drab mate, painted her breast red, and tossed her into the territory of her mate? He would attack her. He would drive her off. The male does not "know" a female from other birds of its species. He responds automatically, with no need for thought.

The matador uses a red cape to entice a bull to attack. However, it is not the color red that the bull is attacking. If you notice, if the matador cannot get the bull to attack, he will flick the cape up and down while the matador stands perfectly still. It is the motion of the cape that the bull is attacking.

The brain is only as complex as it needs to be to perform a function. The mechanisms governing territorial behavior in other species differ: not all attack red, not all females differ in color from their mates, and many more complex patterns of stimuli are found that trigger similar response chains.

It is not always the color red that nature uses to disperse populations. Some birds respond to songs instead of color, especially those birds that live in dense forests where you cannot always see a prospective mate or rival. Yet the nature of the responses is basically identical. Knowledge is an unnecessary complexity. No innate behavior pattern has been found that requires knowledge in the human sense of the term.

Nature's pre-programmed patterns of behavior, whether of aggression, sex, or migration are triggered by the simplest possible stimuli, they require neither thought nor understanding, and their wired-in behavior pattern is switched on inevitably like the programed instructions in a computer. There is no need for the animal to understand why it behaves as it does. Indeed, such a requirement would probably be less efficient; it is enough that the program works automatically.

> *"The Neuro-physiological organization we call instinct functions in a blindly mechanical way,*
> *especially apparent when its function goes wrong."*
> *Konrad Lorenz*

3. BIOLOGICAL PROGRAMS IN THE BRAIN

A Prewired Response

In the spring of each year, the male of a number of different species will stake out a territory, a little ecological niche in which he can mate to produce his young. If another male of the same species intrudes, he will be attacked and chased away. This territorial aggression seems to be nature's way of preventing overpopulation in any given area, by spreading out their numbers, thus ensuring that they will have sufficient food for themselves and their offspring.

The coming of spring each year resets the trigger for a chain reaction of neural responses. The male robin is primed for territorial defense and for mating. Obviously, the male must "know" enough to chase other males away from his territory and yet to admit the female. How does he "know" this?

If you observe animals from many species you will find that the most brightly colored, showiest plumage usually belongs to the male of the species. The females tend to be dull, even drab in appearance. It is the male peacock, for example, that has the showy plumage that we all associate with peafowl. Females are sparsely adorned by comparison. With the cardinal, it is the males that have bright red coloring, while females are a dull brown. If you observe the behavior of the male during spring you might see him attacking not just other males, but red scarves blowing in the wind, red feathers in ladies' new spring bonnets, and your red silk undies hanging on the clothesline.

Niko Tinbergen, awarded the Nobel Prize for his work defining what is an inborn response, found that male Stickleback fish would become excited whenever a red mail truck passed his window. He set out to find out what is happening. He made models of a stickleback fish, with a red underbelly, just like the male stickleback, and a second model without the red, just like a female stickleback.

Tinbergen found that the male stickleback in his aquarium would repeatedly attack the fake model with a red belly. Yet the stickleback model without the color red, and with the swollen belly of a female, the same male would approach with courtship rituals, trying to lead the fake female to his den.

Ounce for ounce, the chicken is among the most vicious animals on earth; second, perhaps, only to humans (human genocide, rape, and murder may involve many thousands, as in the Nazi concentration camps). Not just because of its DNA, but because of social confinement. Being kept in a cage means they cannot fly away. Both males and females in the pecking order will often peck to death a lower ranking member. That is why commercial poultry producers keep each chicken in a separate wire cage.

Cockfighting has a reputation for brutality so extreme that it has been outlawed in many states. It is made more extreme by the social conditions and training under which it occurs.

So why does this happen at all in birds? Naturalists believe in the wild it is nature's way of forcing the animals to spread out, thereby ensuring they will not exhaust the food supply in a cramped area. That means they will have more food available for their chicks.

We only see the most vicious attacks by birds when, like chickens, they are forced to live in an artificial environment, caged in a way that they cannot escape their innate aggression.

Chimpanzees and humans also fight, but not for the same reasons. See the chapter on the Social Order for details about aggression and prejudice.

The knee-jerk reaction when the doctor taps your patellar tendon with a mallet represents one of the oldest, most primitive forms of behavior. The response is prewired or preprogrammed, into your nervous system by your DNA. It is a response that does not require conscious control of your mind.

In this case, a stimulus-the pressure of the mallet that fires pressure-sensitive neurons in the patellar tendon-elicits a response, the knee jerk, which is the nervous system's automatic attempt to compensate for what it interprets as a loss of balance. This is one of the simpler of many automatic reflex responses built into the human nervous system. The visual stimuli of red and motion that elicited the aggressive response of the redbird is a similar mechanism. Although operating at a somewhat more complex level, it still is preprogramed aggressive behavior that requires no conscious control and may take precedence over conscious control.

Preprogrammed responses in lower animals may be much more complex than a simple reflex response. Wells et al. report an example of such complex behavior by an insect. In its first year of life, without ever having learned to do so, the female Sphex wasp engages in an intricate pattern of behavior at the time she gives birth.

First, she digs out a burrow for her eggs. Then she leaves the burrow and goes on a far-ranging hunt for a cricket. Finding the cricket, she stings the insect, paralyzes it, brings it back to her burrow, leaves it outside on the threshold, and goes into the burrow. When she emerges from the burrow, she drags the cricket inside with her eggs, goes outside the burrow, and seals it shut; leaving the cricket as food for her young when the eggs hatch.

Such behavior seems incredibly purposive. It is as if the wasp "knows" what she has to do to ensure the survival of her offspring. If the burrow is destroyed before she has a chance to seal it, she will immediately construct another one and repeat the entire procedure. How can such behavior be explained?

Part of the answer was provided by Jean Henri Fabre, one of the earliest of the great naturalists. You can see his influence on Watson in the following study. After the wasp brought the cricket back to her burrow, she left the cricket on the threshold and went inside. While she was inside, Fabre moved the cricket several inches away from where she had left it. When the wasp came out to get the cricket, she moved the cricket several inches back to the threshold, and again left it on the threshold and went inside. Fabre moved the cricket away from the threshold some forty times and each time the wasp would return it, never going on to the next step of dragging the cricket inside and sealing up the burrow.

The behavior of insects is not always so automatic. Some wasps will go on to the next step after a few such experiences. Nevertheless, the automatic nature of their behavior is striking. Wells et al., liken the behavior of the wasp to a series of cogwheels arranged such that each would set the next in motion but with no variation permitted in the predetermined plan. The insect, however, is much more complex than a mechanical piece. With the discovery of cybernetics and computer programs, a new explanation of its behavior is now possible.

First, the cricket-hunting behavior of the wasp may be similar to the behavior of a heat-seeking missile. The wasp probably does not seek the heat of the insect, however-more likely she seeks a specific scent, a chemical code that is characteristic of crickets.

The actual stimulus that draws the Sphex wasp is as yet undetermined, but an example of this type of behavior may be seen in the mating habits of the silk moth. During the mating season, the male moth can seek out and find a female of its species at distances of up to a mile. How?

Its sight is poor, but its sense of smell is excellent. In recent studies at the Max Planck Institute, ethologist Dietrich Schneider and his associates found that the antennae of the male silk moth have remarkably sensitive scent organs on their tips.

Chemical molecules traveling through the air trigger the insect's complex sequence of mating responses. But if his antennae are cut off, the male is unable to carry out the mating sequence. If a receptive female silk moth is placed right next to him, he ignores her. Unless the scent from her scent glands triggers the next stage in his preprogrammed mating sequence, no mating occurs.

If the scent glands of the female moth are removed and the chemicals are placed next to a normal, intact male moth, the male ignores the female and attempts to mate with the spot where the chemicals have been placed. His actions are part of a complex sequence of programmed behaviors that he cannot modify.

How does the wasp or moth "know" to go on to the next stage of behavior or to go back to a previous stage? An important clue may have been provided by Fabre's discovery that interrupting the behavior of the Sphex wasp at one point will send it back to an earlier behavior pattern.

Such behavior is remarkably similar to a computer that is caught in a feedback loop, or no LOOP. Every time the computer's program sequence comes to the IF statement, it compares two numbers to see if they match. If the numbers do not match, the computer automatically goes into the no LOOP, which returns it to a previous stage in the program's sequence for further computations. This sequence continues time after time until the computer's calculations match the preset number contained in the IF statement.

4. HYPOTHETICAL COMPUTER FLOWCHART FOR THE SPHEX WASP

A simplified computer flowchart can be designed as a model to explain the behavior of the Sphex wasp in Fabre's experiment. The· flowchart below is simplified, of course, because DO LOOPS would have to be present at each step of the program and each box shown could represent an entire subroutine in itself.

Yet such a design does provide a model for duplicating behavior patterns that may prove of value for our understanding of innate behavior. Insects may exhibit such behavior as a result of the firing or not firing of neurons in the brain in the same manner that electronic switches open and close in a computer.

NATURE'S COMPUTER SUBROUTINES

The maternal behavior of the Sphex wasp displays marked similarities to the sequential order of a computer flowchart. Next: A hypothetical computer model for a flowchart of how the Sphex wasp makes its decision to close the nest and fly off, or not.

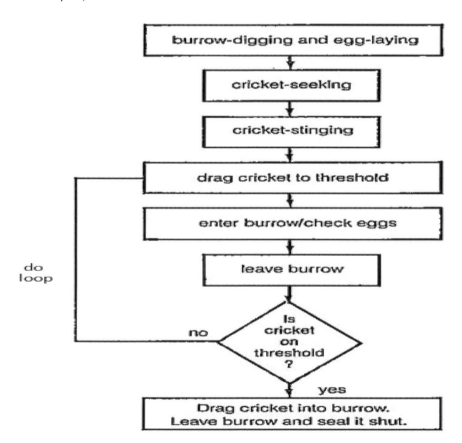

5. SURVIVAL RESPONSES:

Survival of the Newborn:
Suckling, Rooting, Crying, and Imprinting

Newborn survival reflexes are found in all mammals, and take the form of *rooting* or nipple-seeking reflexes, *suckling* reflexes, crying, and *imprinting* to the parent. For one example, if the lips and palate inside of the mouth of a newborn infant are stimulated by touch, · the reaction is an automatic sucking response. The sucking reflexes may be so powerful that if a lemon is touched to the baby's lips, the baby will automatically continue to suck, even though its facial contortions show a dislike for the bitter taste. When the infant is hungry, rooting movements of head and body orient the infant toward the nipples of the mother. If a human baby's cheek is touched on one side, it will move its head to that side.

Crying is a survival mechanism found in all mammals. Many dog and cat mothers will not retrieve a lost pup or kitten unless it cries. The human infant cries automatically when hungry or uncomfortable. The mother makes the necessary adjustments, putting the nipple in the baby's mouth, for example, and crying ceases. The end of the unpleasant wailing of the infant is a rewarding experience for the mother, and she will perform every trick she has learned until the noxious noise has ceased; not unlike the annoying buzzer that goes off in our car if the seatbelt is not connected.

One of the most important survival mechanisms is *imprinting.* Imprinting refers, in part, to the formation of the infant-mother bond. How does a newborn animal "know" its mother from any other animal in the forest? Indeed, how does it even know its own species? Would any self-respecting duck be caught dead running around with a flock of chickens?

The first thing a baby duck or baby goose usually sees after it hatches is its mother. Shortly after hatching, the infants begin following closely behind her. An Austrian ethologist named Konrad Lorenz won the Nobel prize for his work with Graylag Geese. What would happen, he wondered, if the first thing the ducklings saw was not their mother but Konrad Lorenz? The first day after the ducklings hatched, Lorenz began walking around in front of them.

Sure enough, he soon had a line of ducklings following him around the yard. After following Lorenz for several days, the ducklings had imprinted to him. What would happen when their real mother suddenly crossed their path? They would continue to follow Lorenz, and their mother would appear to them as a strange, even frightening new stimulus.

It seems to ensure that ducks will stay with ducks and chickens with chickens. When a jackdaw that had imprinted to Lorenz reached sexual maturity, like all good jackdaw males it brought a feast of worms back to its lover. The bird had difficulty getting Lorenz to accept the worms in his mouth, however, and perhaps in desperation, it tried to stuff them in his ear.

Instincts are dirt simple. They give us a chance to survive. All else is learned. Even who our mother is and what species to have sex with is learned.

6.   BLIND INSTINCT AND BEER
What do We "Know"?

Years later, Eckhard Hess and his associates conducted systematic studies of imprinting in ducks. His graduate students found that ducks would imprint to anything that moved. How about a moving beer bottle, they wondered? So, apparently after emptying some long-neck beer bottles, they tied a string around the neck, waited until the ducklings hatched, and pulled it around. The ducklings fell right in line, following the beer bottle everywhere their mother went.

It turns out that the primary stimulus for imprinting is *motion*. Furthermore, this species-specific social bond forms only during a certain critical period after birth. The tendency toward imprinting in ducks, for example,

seems greatest at about twelve to sixteen hours after hatching and if it does not occur within thirty hours from hatching, it may not take place at all.

Imprinting is not limited to birds. A sheep herder in Australia rescued an orphaned baby sheep. For weeks the baby sheep was bottle-fed and slept in the house. When the sheep got old enough, they decided to put him out to pasture, sure that he would rejoin the other sheep. But the young sheep never tried to join the other sheep. It stayed as close as possible to the house and would bleat pitifully whenever a human came out of the house. It was not a sheep in its own mind, it was attached to people.

Once imprinting occurs, it tends to be remarkably persistent.

An interesting aside from this is an example in bas relief on a stela found in one of the oldest known human civilizations at Gobekli Tepe. Gobekli has been carbon dated at 11,500 years old. Carved on a 13-foot-tall stela are three ducks, all in a row, not unlike the little goslings that followed Konrad Lorenz around.

Left: a few of twenty structures at Gobekli Tepe 11,500 years ago, some 6,000 years before Stonehenge.

Shepard has proposed that this pre-agricultural community was based on animal husbandry, dating thousands of years before farming. The twenty circular stone structures seem unlikely to have been created by hunter-gatherers, as archeologists have long assumed. Without farming, it seems unlikely that hunter-gatherers could have supported a large enough population to have built such a massive complex. *"...like a really bad episode of Naked and Afraid, the hunter-gatherers would have starved to death very quickly."* Thus, raising animals may have predated the discovery of agriculture. Next, ducks in a row carved at Gobekli Tepe.

"Tomorrow I'll teach you how to land."

Even before the work of Konrad Lorenz, our ancestors were already using cross-species imprinting to their advantage. Herdsmen, to this day, may take a puppy from its mother and place it with an ewe that has just given birth. If this is done in the first hours after birth, the new mother sheep will allow the puppy to suckle and grow up as a one of her own.

The puppy would also be double imprinted to humans. When the puppy grows up, it will have a more forceful personality than the sheep and will naturally become the leader of the pack. Sheepherders only need to train the dog to come on command, and the sheep will follow. Not only that, but the dog will now bark and chase away any other dogs or coyotes who might come looking for a meal.

Like dogs, sheep will readily imprint to any species, even our own.

Sheep raised by humans will readily attach to humans. Feral sheep, sheep reared in the wild by their mothers, would run away or avoid humans.

P. H. Gray reports a unique experiment in which he and a colleague imprinted a baby chick to a baby kitten. Both chick and kitten adapted rather well to the unusual relationship. The chick tried desperately to follow the kitten around everywhere it went. The kitten played with the chick as if it were a ball with legs, rolling it around with its paws. After about a month the kitten and chick were separated.

When the chick had grown into a large rooster, a strutting, confident cock-of-the-walk, Gray lured a stray alley cat into the same room with the rooster. Would the rooster react to the cat?

The rooster looked at the cat. The cat looked at the rooster. The rooster started for the cat, which hissed and sidestepped his advances. The rooster followed the cat under a chair, making loving noises as he approached. The cat turned and ran. The rooster, perhaps goaded by the coyness of its newfound love, took after its playing-hard-to-get friend. The rooster caught up with the cat and began to preen the cat's tail with its beak. Panic overtook the cat, and she bolted for the door with the rooster in hot pursuit.

Imprinting serves as both a survival mechanism and the basis of the social bond in herd animals such as dogs, cattle, sheep, and humans. Its function for survival is apparent. Usually, the first thing an animal experiences after birth is not a beer bottle, but its mother.

Biological imprinting to the mother ensures a degree of safety for ducklings and the young of other fowl since their mother knows when to run from danger and where to find food. Imprinting also ensures that the mating urge of the mature animal will be directed toward a member of its own species and that it will tend to flock together with its own kind for safety.

"Mother?"

Monkeys and people also develop an infant-mother bond that ensures social imprinting. The stimulus for this bond in primates is not motion, however, but contact comfort. The studies of this social bond in humans are so important to our understanding of human nature that systematic studies of this phenomenon by Harry Harlow at the University of Wisconsin.

Yet the simple nature of the stimulus that allows imprinting is so general, that virtually any similar species can imprint to another (sheep to humans, dogs to cats or humans, ducks to Lorenz, etc.). It also demonstrates that no "knowledge" or "understanding" is necessary for this behavior.

7.   SURVIVAL AND THE SOCIAL BOND

We have considered survival reflexes that occur in all mammals. Other reflexes are specific only to monkeys, apes, and humans. One is the *palmar,* or grasping, reflex. If the father extends two fingers for his newborn child to grasp, the strength of the grasping reflex in many infants is sufficient to allow it to be lifted off the bed. Fathers sometimes take advantage of this reflex to demonstrate the strength of their sons. (Muscles are not prized in daughters.) The palmer reflexes are weaker in humans than in other primates and usually disappear entirely by four to five months of age.

Complementary to the palmar reflex is the *plantar* reflex. If a pointed object is scraped along the sole of the foot from the base of the big toe diagonally to the heel, the toes will curl. In infants they curl inward. This is one of the tests neurologists use to determine if normal neural circuits are intact. Certain abnormalities of response may indicate, for example, possible damage to pyramidal nerve tracts in the brain. The reader is not advised to try this test, however, since it only seems to work for neurologists, and it would be a shame for anyone to go through life thinking that his pyramidal tracts had been damaged.

The *palmar* and *plantar* responses in humans are vestigial reflexes-remnants of reflexes that at one time were useful to humans. Infant monkeys and apes still find them indispensable. A couple of million years ago, you would have used them to cling tightly to the hair on the back of your mother as she swung through the trees. Needless to say, we do not use them much these days.

MATERNAL BEHAVIOR: Ensuring Infant Survival
SEXUAL BEHAVIOR: Ensuring Species Survival

In many mammals, such as the cat, maternal behavior may be triggered by hormonal changes within the body. These changes, in turn, act as triggers for specific stimuli. The mother cat responds to the crying or mewing of the kitten. By licking the kitten, the mother triggers nipple-seeking behavior by the kitten. If the kitten is not licked, it may not be able to find the nipple. A mother cat or dog can care for her infants, to feed, retrieve, and defend her young-even though she may never have seen an infant before. Learning seems to be important even where maternal "instincts" exist, however, the mother's ability to care for her young improves the second and third time she gives birth. Again, "learning" becomes more important at higher levels of the phylogenetic scale.

The zoologist Solly Zuckerman reports on the birth of a baby gorilla at the Berlin zoo, whose mother had been raised in captivity most of her life. Would her maternal "instincts" be sufficient to pull her and the baby through? The observers describe her reaction to the infant. What is it? She picked it up by the leg. The baby reacted with a wail. She held it away from her as if asking, "What do you do with it?" For hours, observers watched as she dragged the complaining infant around the cage. Finally, the infant was rescued and reared apart from its mother.

A similar event happened in 2019 at the Gladys Porter Zoo. A mother chimp rejected her baby. The baby was rescued and sent to a group that specializes in such events. The surrogate human mothers dressed up in "chimpanzee suits" to imprint the baby to its own species, otherwise, it would have imprinted to humans and they would not be able to put it back in the zoo with other chimpanzees.

Similar experiences have occurred in many zoos when primate mothers have been reared in captivity. Unless a primate mother has had experience in a social group, playing with other mothers' infants and watching the other mothers care for their young, she does not know how to care for her own. For this reason, most chimpanzee and gorilla infants born in captivity are taken from their mothers and reared by zoo attendants.

In the following example, a stray ginger kitten is rejected by the mother and by her other kittens. Repeated attempts to feed are met with hissing from both. This is an example not unlike human prejudice; anything that is different from the first experiences embedded in our brains is met with a "flight or fight" response. Humans react the same way. https://www.youtube.com/watch?v=1VAFyxkXNrw

On the positive side, the persistence of the ginger kitten eventually won the mother's cooperation, with a little help. https://www.youtube.com/watch?v=zMheEKbNGSU&t=61s

WHAT SPECIES TO HAVE SEX WITH, AND HOW TO ENGAGE IN SEX?

If you know anything about dogs, you know that a male dog when it reaches puberty, will attempt to mate with other than other dogs. He will even "hump" your leg. Why?

Sexual response in mammals is triggered by a variety of stimuli depending on the species. Most female mammals become sexually receptive only for relatively brief, but intensely active periods of time. Sexual behavior may occur only a few days each month or a few weeks each season. This innate control over sexual behavior is called an *estrous cycle,* a cycle of sexual periodicity. In part, it ensures that sexual activity occurs during the period of time when the female is physiologically ready for conception to occur when the egg cell is ready for the sperm.

Frequently, estrus also serves to limit sexual activity, and conception, to a specific season of the year so that weeks or months later, the offspring will be born in a climate favorable to their survival. If conception occurred in late fall and the offspring were born in the winter, when the weather was severe and food was scarce, their chance for survival would be slim. Such animals would quickly be eliminated from the breeding population. In temperate zones, spring tends to be the beginning of the mating season because it favors the later survival of the young. The mating season varies, however, depending on the particular species. In deer, for example, the gestation period is four months. Thus, the mating season begins in early fall and the fawn is dropped in spring,

When the female of any species comes into the active phase of the estrous cycle, usually called heat, she will actively and energetically seek out an available male. During the heat period, the level of general excitation is so high that if the owner of a female cat attempts to lock her indoors, she may rip a hole in a screen door with her claws to get out. If anyone doubts this, they may end up having a repair bill for their screen door. Even a very hungry cat will rarely go to such an extreme to obtain food.

Sexual behavior in the female may be triggered internally by hormones, chemical stimuli released into the bloodstream by temperature changes, day length changes, or even a biological clock-however, sexual behavior in the male is often triggered by external stimuli emitted by the female.

In many species, these stimuli are highly specific. The female dog in heat, for example, gives off a highly specific scent. Beach and Gilmore found that male dogs allowed to smell the urine of female dogs in heat reacted with marked sexual excitation. The chemical molecules of the scent, traveling freely through the air, affect the male when they fire his olfactory (smell) sensory receptors. A male dog that has scented a female in heat will pull all stops to get closer to her. If the male is kept confined and not allowed to mate, he may remain in a high state of excitement, eating little, for as long as the scent of the female reaches him.

Dogs have a highly refined sense of smell compared to humans. Many other species seem to rely even more heavily on their sense of smell. In ungulates, grass eaters such as deer, elk, and moose, the sense of smell may be intimately related to a complex ritual surrounding the mating season. Throughout the summer, these animals may travel in all-male herds with separate herds comprising the females and young. In the fall, however, the males begin the rutting season.

As any hunter knows, during the rutting season, scent glands on the legs of these male animals become so active that meat from animals in "rut" is frequently spoiled in the process of skinning. This scent seems to function to provoke rage in other males or love in females-probably both. A marked hostility develops among the males, and they begin to fight among themselves, to separate, and to establish exclusive territories from which they attack other males that happen to wander too close.

The females arrive, and their scent in turn triggers new urges in the males, something other than fighting. The female scent seems to be the ultimate "come hither stare." It drives the male to a frenzy of excitement and also ensures that he can tell a female from a male.

In a sporting goods shop, you may notice a bottle of "Buck Lure" displayed prominently on the counter. The bottle states that if the hunter faithfully dabs a little under each armpit, it will mask his atrocious human scent and bring six-point bucks running to his gun. The scent hints that it is made from the same juice that sends the bucks into action after the does-all of which should work quite well so long as you shoot him before he catches you.

This lure of smell and its effect on the male of the species has been recognized in folklore for centuries. More than a few of the perfumes marketed for the human female have hopefully contained a touch of the scent from the musk glands of exotic animals ranging from the Tibetan musk deer-the current rage-to the muskrat. A drop of each scent would be sufficient to send the male of that species into paroxysms of passion. Unfortunately, the human male has no such reflexive control over his sexual proclivities.

Sexual behavior in humans differs markedly from that in most animals lower on the phylogenetic scale and even from that of other mammals. Findings by Masters and Johnson and many others indicate that sexual behavior in humans has no significant hormonal controls. Humans are continuously sexually receptive-that is, human sexual behavior can be triggered by external, usually physical stimulation at any time, or even thoughts. The only apparent controls over human sexual behavior are social inhibitions.

Much ado is made of the human sex "drive." Folklore abounds with tales that support its power. Yet if you deprive an animal of sex, will it become or die? Countless studies indicate that no such effects occur. Depriving an animal of food eventually will produce death. Depriving an animal of sex will produce an unsatisfied animal, perhaps, but not a dead one. Sex "drive" does not necessarily increase with deprivation.

Sex in humans is an internal mechanism. It is not triggered by scent but by touch -by physically stimulating the genitals-and by the generalized excitement that accompanies the internal stimulation of thought, as in sexual fantasy.

How about sexual *behavior?* Is it innate? Is learning necessary? Or do we naturally know what the sex object should be?

Even in fairly "instinctual" animals, the stimuli that trigger sexual behavior may be grossly general. The male frog, at the beginning of the sexual season, will attempt to mate with anything that moves-from a dead leaf blown by the wind to the human hand.   Just like college freshmen.

Anthropologists Jane Goodall, Sherwood Washburn, Irven de Vore, and others have frequently observed that young male chimpanzees and baboons in the wild often engage in "sexual" mounting of other males as well as the females. These acts are now known to be only a natural form of play and social interaction that is essential for the development of normal adult sexual behavior in these primates.

Scott reared puppies in social isolation and found that, as adults, they were unable to engage in normal sexual behavior even when the female is in heat. They simply had not learned how to "behave" to complete the sex act. At the University of Wisconsin, Harry Harlow raised infant monkeys in isolation from other infant monkeys and found that as adults they, too, were woefully inept at sexual behavior. Physical contact and trial and error learning are basic. Without both, instinct has little value.

Interestingly enough, Harlow found that even rearing an infant monkey with its real mother was not sufficient social stimulation if it did not have an opportunity to interact with other monkeys its age. Of course, humans learn by reading books, word of mouth, watching movies, and by a process of fumble-and find in the back seats of cars. Animals, however, lacking these "refinements" and lacking verbal communication, must learn by trial and error. Actually, so do we.

We know now that the higher we go on the phylogenetic scale, the less the dependence on innate mechanisms and the greater the dependence on learning. In lower animals, both the behavior and the goal may be determined by innate mechanisms. However, humans are markedly dependent on learning to direct behavior and even to determine goals.

Knowledge and behavior are products of the interaction between the individual and environment, and all visual and auditory stimuli acquire meaning only through such interactions. Human knowledge does not exist · independent of these experiences, and human behavior is directed by them.

8. INNATE MECHANISMS AND LEARNED BEHAVIOR

In mammals, mechanisms are innate, but behavior is learned. The mechanism controlling hunger, for example, is innate: Deprive us of food and negative stimuli (hunger pangs) are felt. Deprive us long enough and we die. The mechanism is wired in at birth. What about behavior? Other than the suckling reflex, do we instinctively know *how* to get food? What about the food, the goal itself? Is there any innate knowledge of *what* food is?

A couple in South Africa once reared a young baboon in their home until it was nearly full grown. Baboons are rough, tough, terrestrial primates. The older they get, the rougher they become. When the animal reached adulthood, the couple decided they should take it back to its native habitat. They let it out in the wilds of Africa. For several days, they watched it.

Time passed. The baboon became hungry. More time passed. The baboon became hungrier. Eventually, it became evident that the baboon was slowly starving to death. Why? The animal was surrounded by a baboon world of plenty. Green plant shoots, tubers, and roughage of all sorts were abundant-all the makings of a gourmet dinner to any other baboon. Yet it did not eat. To this baboon, shoots, tubers, and leaves were simply not food. Food is something it got in a plastic dish twice a day. Food is table scraps, not plant roots.

The baboon got hungry but did not eat. The mechanism controlling hunger and the reduction of hunger is innate.

What reduces that hunger, the goal, is learned.

How to obtain that goal, the behavior of digging the tubers or pulling up plant shoots is learned.

Puppies will chew on anything and everything at a certain age-shoes, textbooks, table legs, even eat his own droppings. This is the way nature has programmed the puppy to learn what is edible and what is not.

Above a young Bonobo Chimpanzee watches his mother to learn about food.

Babies imitate their mother to learn how to find food, and to learn what to eat.

9. INNATE AND LEARNED BEHAVIOR
WHAT IS INNATE AND WHAT IS LEARNED?

If we want to find out what behavior is innate and what is learned, we should first look at the most important survival needs of the infant; What food is and how to find food. And what sex is and how to do sex.

	INBORN BEHAVIOR	KNOWLEDGE
1 FROGS:	Fly catching behavior	No knowledge of food.
2 PUPPIES:	Chewing behavior	No idea what food is.
3 PRIMATES:	Chewing and imitation	Not a clue.
4. HUMANS	Sucking reflex, chewing,	Not much else until imitation kicks in.

Also inborn are Taste buds (sweet tastes are generally good, bitter taste is often poison)
Stimulation (hunger pangs) = increased agitation and food seeking; eventual death if prolonged.

THE ROLE OF EXPERIENCE

The studies on vision suggested that physical maturation alone does not produce knowledge. What if the innate knowledge required priming by experience before it became available? And what forms of behavior do require learning? Does a baby walk because it *learns* to walk? Or does it simply begin walking when it is sufficiently mature physically? More important, does a baby know it can get to a wanted object by moving toward it? Is so simple a "knowledge" as this wired in at birth or does this, too, develop only through experience?

Answers to these questions are possible only through an experiment so tightly controlled that one could ensure that neither physical maturation nor experience influenced the results. Held and Hein devised a remarkably tight study of the role of experience in developing even the most basic of motor skills. In their laboratory at the Massachusetts Institute of Technology; kittens were reared in darkness since birth with their visual experiences strictly controlled. At about ten weeks of age, they were placed in a special training apparatus. A circular chamber, walls painted with vertical stripes, was their only visual stimulus-their Platonic cave.

In the center of the chamber was a sort of miniature merry-go-round, scaled down to kitten size. On one side, a kitten was strapped into a harness that allowed it to walk in a circle around the chamber and to turn left and right. The kitten could see and walk at the same time.

A second kitten was placed in a similar harness on the opposite side of the chamber, but its legs could not touch the ground. This kitten could see, but it could not walk at the same time. It was allowed to walk only in the dark. Both kittens were thus exposed to exactly the same visual stimuli, the stripes on the wall of their cave, but one kitten's leg movements were paired with visual stimuli of motion while the second kitten had no such learning experience, no opportunity to coordinate what it saw with its own body movements.

After about 30 hours of training in the chamber, the kittens were tested for visual-motor coordination. Beginning with a kitten that had received both visual and motor experience, Held moved his hand toward the kitten's eyes. The kitten blinked. Held picked up the kitten and set it down on the floor. The kitten extended its legs in anticipation of meeting the floor. Held placed it on a "visual cliff," a table-like apparatus designed to give the illusion of a visual drop-off, or "edge." The kitten avoided the drop-off. In other words, the kitten showed the adaptive behavior expected of a kitten reared under more normal circumstances.

Held repeated the experiment with a kitten that had "gone along for the ride," one that had received identical visual stimulation but without the opportunity to coordinate that experience with its own movement. He moved his hand toward its eyes. It did not blink. He picked it up and placed it on the floor. It did not extend its legs in anticipation of meeting the floor. Using a visual cliff apparatus, Held placed the kitten in a situation similar to that of the formerly blind patient looking out of a window to the ground below. As with the patient, the kitten failed to see the drop.

All kittens could walk; all kittens could see. However, the only kittens that could do both effectively were those that had received an opportunity to learn the relationship between visual stimuli and the feedback from internal stimuli from muscular movements. In the kittens deprived of that opportunity, several days of seeing and moving, moving and seeing, were required before normal visual-motor coordination developed.

The ability to see and to walk may result from innate neurological mechanisms.

But "knowing" the environment requires experience. The kittens did not know to blink their eyes or extend their legs to meet the floor unless they had previously experienced visual and muscular sensations simultaneously. Without such experience, there seemed to be no transfer of the knowledge derived from the sensation of touch to the sensation of vision. Some degree of transfer of training may have occurred, however, since the active kittens had blinked without any apparent prior experience with an object moving toward their eyes. it may be that this response was learned through their experience of stumbling around in the dark, and bumping into objects face first, combined with their experience of motion and movement in the test. The same response did not occur in the kittens deprived of the prior experience of both seeing and moving at the same time.

Body Awareness But what about the body of the organism itself? Is the animal not born with some "knowledge" or awareness of its own arms or legs-even if it does not know how to use them? Held and Bauer investigated the development of eye-hand coordination in the animal biologically closest to the human, the monkey. Although designed as a study of visual-muscular coordination, the work of Held and Bauer produced some interesting results relating to our question about an animal's knowledge of its own body.

THE VISUAL CLIFF

Gibson and Walk wanted to find out if a baby would walk off the edge of a cliff or if nature had provided an automatic control that would safeguard an infant from such a fall. They used a large sheet of clear plexiglass as a tabletop. Directly under one-half of the plexiglass, they placed a checkered tablecloth. Under the other half of the glass, but several feet below it, they placed another checkered tablecloth, creating on that side the illusion of a sudden visual drop off, a visual cliff.

They found that very young rat pups, kittens, human children, and even a newborn goat only hours old, would refuse to go onto the "deep" side. Almost every animal stayed on the side where the visual stimulus of the patterned tablecloth was closest. If Gibson and Walk used a grey tablecloth on both sides, however, the human infants showed no tendency to avoid the deep side. The experimenters concluded that there is an innate mechanism that allows "depth perception" in infants.

Another interpretation is possible, however. It is known that the eyes of very young animals focus at a very close distance, 10 inches for the human child; just about right to see its mother's face as it is nursing. It may be that the mechanism controlling the avoidance of a visual drop-off is that distance at which the baby can focus, rather than "depth." In effect, it could be that an infant will not go where its eyes cannot focus on visual support. Such an idea would suggest than no knowledge or understanding on the part of the baby is necessary. How would you test such a theory?

Imagine a small round table with a hole in the center just large enough for the head of a monkey to come through. A monkey was strapped into a seat beneath the table with only its head protruding through the top. A soft terry cloth was available so that the monkey could grasp it as a "security blanket." The animal was free to move its hands and arms, and to observe visually all of the stimuli in the laboratory, but it could not see its own body or learn to coordinate the movements of its hands with its vision.

The monkeys were reared in this condition beginning twelve hours after birth and remained there for over a month-longer than necessary for any monkey to develop visual and muscular coordination under normal conditions. They quickly learned to visually recognize the baby bottle from which they were fed. They were trained to reach for their bottle when the experimenter approached, even though they could not see their hands or the bottle under the table. Then came the day of testing. With the table removed so that the monkeys could see their hands, the baby bottle was presented. Would they reach for the bottle? Would they be able to grasp it by guiding their hands with their eyes?

When the bottle was first presented, the monkeys reached for it immediately.

But then a startling thing happened: As soon as their hands moved into view, they stopped reaching and watched their hand for minutes at a time, enraptured with the unfamiliar sight. What was it? A hairy baby bottle? A strange creature they had never met?

Eventually, after the novelty of discovering their hands abated, it was possible to observe their hand-eye coordination. Their ability to guide one hand to the bottle proved much inferior to that of normally reared monkeys of the same age. Over the next twenty days, testing continued. Not until after many trials with hand and eye could the subject monkeys achieve accuracy of reaching equal to that of normally reared ones.

After twenty sessions of visual-motor experience with one hand, the monkeys were given ten sessions of trials with the second hand, which had never been exposed to this experience. The results looked somewhat like the study of the first hand all over again. Reaching was inaccurate, and only after many trials did it become as accurate with the second hand as with the first.

10. BEYOND OUR PERCEPTION OF REALITY

An infant from our culture, reared in another culture-any culture, Russian, French, African-will grow up speaking the language of that culture. We learn our language subtly, almost as if we absorb it in growing up. We are never consciously aware of the learning process that is taking place. Once we have learned our language, and even our regional dialect, the language seems so natural, so obviously correct, that it may be difficult for us to imagine how others could speak so differently. We immediately notice even the minor differences between New England and southern accents. Once the habits are set, we may still learn another language, but it never comes to us so naturally as our original language.

Experience influences much more than our perception. Extending far beyond even language, it influences our personality, our mannerisms, our behavior, and our beliefs. In *Minor for Man,* anthropologist Clyde Kluckhohn tells of an American in China who was reared by a Chinese family after his missionary parents were killed. His physical appearance as an adult was Caucasian; he had blue eyes and light-colored hair.

Yet the Americans who met him came away with a marked feeling of his being Chinese-not simply because he spoke Chinese, but because everything about his behavior was Chinese. His mannerisms, the way he held his hands, his gestures when he spoke, the way he shuffled his feet when he walked, his deliberate movements, his gait, his deference. All were Chinese, not Caucasian. His beliefs, religion, and values were a product of his Chinese experience.

To psychologists who study learning, all human behavior and beliefs, even our very personality, are products of the same process that determine our language. From childhood on, we absorb the subtle experiences we encounter in much the same way that we perceive the language. We are never conscious of the effect of learning. We never see our experiences molding our personality. Like the process of evolution, learning operates silently, without our awareness or our cooperation. Stimuli in our environment, like words in our language, take on the meaning that experience gives them.

The study of how stimuli influence behavior is not merely a preoccupation of armchair philosophers. It is a crucial key to our understanding of human nature. How do stimuli acquire the power to control behavior? The search for the answers is one of the most important dramas in the history of psychology. And the answers are among the most important for our changing perception of human nature.

THE IDEA OF INBORN KNOWLEDGE

The one constant from all we have learned about innate mechanisms in the brain is that these mechanisms tend to be gross and general. We are not born knowing who our mother is, we do not know what species we are, we can adapt to an almost infinite variety of "mothers", we have no apparent knowledge at all of even the most basic of survival skills, it is all automatic, unthinking, programmed behavior. The studies of babies born with a cataract in only one eye showed that human babies' brains are dependent on experience before the brain itself can develop. We are, at best, a tabula rasa, a blank slate, when it comes to what John Locke and Albert Einstein called "knowledge".

Yet, this almost infinite ability to adapt has given us the ability to survive in a wide variety of situations, with only the most basic, general, in-born programs in the brain.

But there is another area of cognition that is uniquely human. The ability that most distinguishes humans from other animals is not our conscious mind, but instead is our ability to communicate knowledge by using symbols, such as words, that represent our experience. What is this unique ability that has benefited humans more than any animal; even as it has led to the vast number of superstitions, wars, and valuing entertainment more than reality?

The ability to communicate with speech propelled humans past other species. Writing and books enabled us to save trillions of bits of more data, to educate the next generation. Now, the internet and computers expand our knowledge and ability exponentially beyond what was available only a generation ago.'

Yet, each of these great abilities also became the basis of superstition, ignorance, and arrogance. Each became a source of glorifying trivia and schlock. The inability of our education system to keep ahead of the limbic system tickling of society has prevented us from benefiting fully from that great advance in knowledge.

Next, is one of the great mysteries of psychology and the brain, what is our ability to speak? How does it benefit us or prevent our ability to understand reality? What is the origin of our symbolic ability?

12 THE SYMBOL

THE UNIQUELY HUMAN ABILITY OF LANGUAGE

For many neuropsychologists, the conscious mind has long been considered one of the great mysteries of the mind. Yet, the conscious mind is not the greatest mystery of our science, instead, it is our ability to render experiences into symbols (words, gestures, sign language, etc.) to communicate.

When anthropologist Ralph Solecki began unearthing the remains of Neanderthals in the Shanidar cave in Iraq, he came upon one of the most debated issues in anthropology. It was a burial of a Neanderthal man who had suffered from severe deformity and arthritis.

What did this information mean? Why was it important? To Solecki, it meant that someone else had to catch his food for him. Someone else had to provide him with care and protection. Chimpanzees and baboons will tolerate an injured member. They will sympathize deeply with a fellow animal in pain. But they will not find food for an injured fellow; nor, with a few exceptions, will they share their own food with him. If an animal cannot keep up with the troop in its travels, he often is left behind.

Several skeletons of Neanderthals unearthed elsewhere clearly show that advanced age had left them toothless and arthritic. Yet here too they had been cared for beyond the age at which they could have been useful, productive members of the group. The finds hint at the existence of a high social order, or at least human empathy.

Solecki had unearthed nine Neanderthal skeletons, but the extraordinary nature of these people did not become evident until soil from the fourth find was sent to Paris for microscopic analysis of the soil associated with his find. A microscopic analysis of the dirt surrounding the burial of one Neanderthal was surrounded with pollen. Pollen from flowers surrounded the burial that was not found elsewhere in such abundance.

The discovery of the skull caused no immediate excitement in the anthropological world. Over a hundred and thirty such authenticated finds had already been made throughout Europe, Asia, and Africa. The Neanderthals had already acquired a well-established reputation as our predecessor on this earth.

We know much of their life. We know that they existed as a dominant species in the world from over 100,000 years ago until they seem to have evaporated mysteriously (evolved?) between 30,000 and 40,000 years ago. We know that they had a longer reign than modern humans to date, over 100,000 years. We also know that they were makers and users of tools. Their stone axes, flints, points, and knives have been found throughout the world in far greater abundance than their bones.

Neanderthals ranged farther than any other primate on this earth. Using the skins of animals, killed, gutted, and scraped clean with their tools, they endured the cold of the European winter. The remains of animal skins in Europe and Asia suggest that they made shelters from these skins, something like a tent draped over boughs of trees used as a frame. From centuries of cumulative carbon deposits found with their bones and tools, we know that they not only used fire for warmth and cooking-they apparently could make it at· will.

With so much already known about Neanderthals, the Shanidar find could only add bits and pieces to our information about the tools and techniques of our progenitors. What turned out to be significant about the Shanidar find was the piecing together of a remarkable story about the social life of this species. Placed together with bits of information from other finds, Shanidar man was to help give a new picture of the psychology of the Neanderthals. And it was to shed unexpected light on the origin of *the symbol.*

1. THE MYSTERY OF SHANIDAR MAN
The Pollen and the Symbol

The first indication that something was unique about this man came from a medical analysis of the bones. Shanidar man had suffered from a genetic defect at birth which had left bis right arm and side useless. The bones from the joints of his useful limbs indicated that he suffered from arthritis. Examination of the eye sockets suggested that he was blind in one eye. Shanidar man was not an invalid but his ability to care for himself had been severely limited. Yet he had survived his birth defect, his injury, and his arthritis for many years, only to be killed by a blow to the head that seems to have resulted from a cave-in within the cave.

What was significant was not the burial, but what was associated with the burial and the bones. The researchers hoped to find evidence of plant food common to this period. What they found instead was pollen; pollen from flowers. Clusters of pollen appeared, sometimes with parts of the flowers that supported it. In no other soil sample did pollen appear in such quantity.

Eight species of flowers were identified, ranging from the grape hyacinth to the hollyhock. Associated with the flower pollen was evidence of what must have been a pine-bough mat on which the body of the Neanderthal had been laid. Flowers growing wild on the hillsides had been collected in great number and placed on the grave.

Whatever we may have thought of the physical beauty of Neanderthals, it was evident that they were not merely walking chimpanzees who had learned to break rocks for tools. They did not fit the same mold as their older relatives, the Australopithecus of South Africa or Homo erectus of Southeast Asia. For the Neanderthals showed unmistakable signs of symbolic ability. They buried their dead, and they buried them with pomp and ceremony.

At about the same time as the Shanidar finds were coming to light, anthropologists had begun to reexamine scores of previous Neanderthal finds. Burials were not uncommon. Neanderthal skeletons had often been found lying in an unnatural position with knees drawn up to the chest and feet touching the buttocks, as if bound in this position by rawhide. It had become clear that this practice was a means of conserving burial space. By making the body as compact as possible the Neanderthals reduced the amount of digging required. For the clay earth was hard, and their wood and stone tools were inefficient.

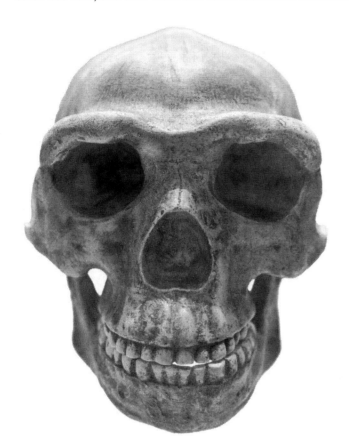

But a burial in itself tells us little, and it may have been born of necessity. For example, most animals are nomadic. Chimpanzees rarely spend more than a few nights in the same place. But if humans had taken up semipermanent residence in the caves, burials could simply have been a necessity dictated by the sense of smell.

At La Chapelle-Aux-Sainte in France, a trench grave of a Neanderthal yielded evidence of a carefully planned burial. The body was laid out with a bison leg on its chest. Flint tools and animal bones surrounded it. In a second site at La Ferrassie, France, the grave of a Neanderthal contained flint tools and bone fragments. On top of this grave had been placed a heavy stone slab. What was the purpose of including stone tools in the grave? Were they simply the possessions of the deceased? Or do they suggest a vague concept of an afterlife?

2. THE MEANING OF THE SYMBOL

Tools are practical. Their inclusion in a gravesite might simply indicate that the relatives associated them with the owner and the owner's needs. But flowers? Flowers are impractical. They take time and effort to gather. They cannot be eaten. They serve no function except one: They are a symbol. Even today we place flowers on the grave of a loved one-not for any practical purpose, but as a token, a symbol, a means of paying respect. It is significant evidence of an intellectual difference between ape and human. Furthermore, a ceremonial burial implied symbolic status-and with status, a highly developed social order. Were these Neanderthals once tribal chiefs or medicine men?

Other remarkable finds, some made many years before Shanidar man, have taken on new meaning. The now famous cult of the cave bear was practiced by early Neanderthals, and even by some present-day people such as the Ainu of Japan. The first such find was in a cave located 8,000 feet high in the Swiss Alps. Here the Neanderthals had constructed a cubical chest 3¼ feet on each side. Inside the chest were the skulls of seven cave bears facing toward the entrance. A massive slab of stone covered the chest. Deeper in the cave, six bear skulls had been placed in positions cut into the walls.

In southern France, a rectangular chest covered by a flat stone slab weighing almost a ton concealed the bones of twenty of a species of a now extinct cave bear. The bears, larger than our grizzly, had apparently been hunted by the early people as "easy" food. During the winter when the bears were in hibernation, they were very vulnerable to the weapons of early humans. The placement of the skulls suggests a ritual-perhaps intended as magic or in some way related to religious ceremonies.

We know that many tribes of American Indians had legends depicting the bear as the original man from which we all come-not an unusual idea at all considering how human the bear looks when walking on its two hind legs. The bear was worshipped, in a manner of speaking, and revered as having important powers. Did Neanderthals also attribute some symbolic power to the bear?

Anthropological data provide us with rich evidence for speculation. Did Neanderthals have a religion? Did they believe in magic and practice rituals to control the supernatural? Did they philosophize about the meaning of life? If they did, they almost certainly would have had to have language before they could develop and communicate these ideas. We can only speculate about the verbal ability of this species, but the evidence is growing that they had far greater symbolic ability than any species except today's humans.

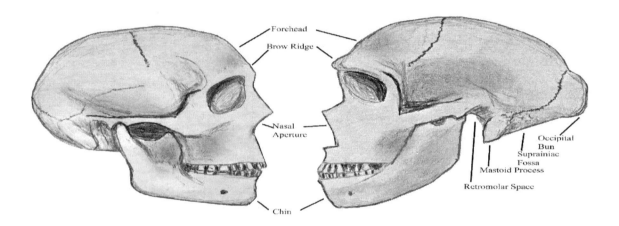

Yet, for all of their accomplishments, the Neanderthal people seem to have failed to develop pottery and basket weaving. They did not have sewing implements or the bow and arrow. Most significantly, no Neanderthal find yet uncovered has shown evidence of any lasting art form. There are no carvings in stone or paintings on cave walls. It may be that their artforms were simply too perishable to withstand time.

The earliest known art forms do not appear until Cro-Magnon man, around forty thousand years ago. And Cro-Magnon cave art is magnificent even by modem standards. Why? Was there some important evolutionary stage that the Neanderthals had not yet gone through? Or does their artwork remain to be discovered?

What is "the symbol"? The term implies first the ability to use a neutral stimulus (CS), such as a word or object (flowers), to stand for (as symbolic of) a stimulus (UCS) or concept (idea or learning set) that is not physically present. Most animals deal only with stimuli or concepts that are physically present-that they directly experience with their senses.

Only humans spontaneously use objects or words to stand for something that has been experienced but is not physically present. For example, a two-year-old human child may use a piece of wood to represent a car, plane, or boat. Children may even accompany their play with such objects with appropriate hand movements and noises. A doll may be treated as Mommy has treated the baby. It may be fed, diapered, cuddled, talked to, and punished. But the doll is not real. It is a symbol, like the piece of wood, of something the child has previously experienced.

The most dramatic discovery of archelogy is perhaps the cave paintings at Lascaux in France and elsewhere. Dating from some 30,000 years ago, these paintings showed a remarkable example of the ability to use symbolic ability to illustrate something that is not physically present.

Cro-Magnon cave art shows that symbolic ability was probably well developed by 35,000 years ago.

3. THE SYMBOL *Something That Is Not There*

However, we know that language and math are basic to the left side of the brain. Visual-motor coordination, art, and music are basic to the right side of the brain. This suggests that multiple mutations in our DNA are responsible. And that language and symbolic speech may have developed separately from visual-motor coordination. And yet, the ability to flake flint into spear points and arrowheads may have come long before the ability to speak. The unique ability to make arrowheads and art may have come first.

We have known there must be something like a Language Acquisition Device (LAS) described by Noam Chomsky since the discovery of Broca's area and Wernicke's area in the 1800s. Yet it seems to be more complex than we have expected. It is still a mystery what mutations and how many mutations may have been needed before we acquired the abilities of speech, art, and communication we now take for granted.

An ape may well know the difference between a plane, a car, and a boat when they are physically present. It may know the movements and sounds that each makes. But the ape does not use pieces of wood to represent them when it plays. It plays with objects or other animals that are physically present. Similarly, the ape may have learned the rudiments of infant care, but unless it is rewarded for doing so, it does not spontaneously make believe that a doll is a child.

To the ape, a doll is not a symbol-it is a block of wood or plastic. Both flowers and art, on the other hand, are symbolic representations of ideas or concepts. They represent ideas that no chimpanzee has yet touched with its mind. They represent the genesis of intellectual change that now begins in the mind of a two-year-old child. And that change seems to have had its origin in the mind of the Neanderthals over forty thousand years in the past.

Humans' ability to symbolize, changes the entire nature of our temporal reaction to stimuli. We can remember the past, recall the past, and, based on the past, we can anticipate the future. To other animals, only the present exists. They do not prepare for the future (unless biologically programmed to do so, such as squirrels that store nuts for the winter). They do not live with the past. They do not lay awake at night agonizing over what we should have done. An example of this came out of studies of chimpanzee behavior.

Can Chimpanzees hold a Grudge?

Anthropologist Jane Goodall studied the social behavior of chimpanzees living in the wilds of Africa. Social relations among the members of the chimpanzee troop were normally peaceful. One day, Goodall gave the group several bananas, a favorite chimpanzee delicacy. Immediately the peaceful band dissolved into a bickering, feuding group of individualists. Each wanted the bananas for itself.

The dominant male in the group managed to corner most of the bananas and even forced some of the other members to give him their bananas. Feelings ran hot and heavy. Tension was apparent. A chimp moved in to cop some of the goodies when number one was not looking. But a sustained glare from the leader was enough to force him to give back the prize. Soon the bananas were devoured. What happened then? Did ill feelings persist among the group?

Did the lower-ranking chimps harbor resentment against the higher-ranking chimps? Did anyone hold a "grudge"? No. When the existing stimulus for competition passed, so did the hostility. Unlike humans, who may carry the memory in our minds for a long time, ruminating over what we "would have, should have" done.

Similar behavior may be observed in young children, who may quarrel violently and emotionally one moment but play peacefully and cooperatively the next (or vice versa). The chimp and the child react to the stimulus as it exists for the moment. They have not yet attached symbolic meaning to the events. It is not a matter of honor. It is not a disgrace or triumph. Unless the event occurs again the next day (i.e., is physically present), they do not continue *to* react.

An adult, on the other hand, can symbolize. The events of the past may take on new meaning. The disgrace may trigger a blood feud or a smoldering resentment. We talk about it. We mull it over. We lay awake at night thinking about it. From this, future action may be planned. Revenge may be taken. The past seems to take on meaning for us because it remains in the present, encoded in our mind. Verbal tags for symbolic ideas such as disgrace or triumph can be thought over in the present. They do not simply vanish until the incident occurs again.

The "past" and the "future" do not exist in nature. Only change exists, and change is always in the present. Our human videotape equipment and our symbolic ability allow us to record the present in such a way that we can predict change. When we anticipate change, we are said to be "planning for the future." Such planning is always based on a sequence of prior experiences.

But the concept of "past" and "future" are inventions of our mind. They have proved useful only because they allow us to order and organize our experience. Adults may thus plan to take different actions in the "future" only by experiencing it, in their mind, in the present. And we experience it in the present by putting together verbal symbols (existing memory traces) that have been tagged by prior experience.

Simply put, our symbolic ability allows us to (1) *experience* mentally a stimulus or concept *in the present,* even though it is not physically present (thought); and (2) *communicate* that to others (language). Thus, the child playing with a block of wood, pretending that it is a car, is experiencing a past memory (of how a car goes) even though no such stimulus exists in the present. The child has tagged that memory trace (symbolically) to a neutral stimulus, the block of wood. A child can also emit sounds that have been tagged *to* common stimuli (noise) and associated with cars. Furthermore, children can communicate this purely mental image to others.

The symbol is perhaps still vague in our minds and somewhat difficult to grasp. So let us start with something more obvious. The most apparent and striking difference between apes and humans is that we can speak. The ability *to* communicate is an evolutionary advantage for us. How then does speech develop? And what gives us this unique ability?

> '...There's glory for you!' said Humpty Dumpty,
> 'I don't know what you mean by "glory",' Alice said.
> 'Humpty Dumpty smiled contemptuously. 'Of course, you don't—till I tell you. I meant "there's a nice knock-down argument for you!"'
> 'But "glory" doesn't mean "a nice knock-down argument", Alice objected.
> 'When I use a word,' Humpty Dumpty said in rather a scornful tone, 'it means just what I choose it to mean—neither more nor less.'
> 'The question is,' said Alice, 'whether you can make words mean different things—that's all.'
> 'The question is,' said Humpty Dumpty, 'which is to be master—that's all'

Alice in Wonderland by Louis Carroll

TEACHING ANIMALS TO SPEAK

A unique fact about teaching animals to speak is that most of the linguists who may ignore Skinner's idea of how language is learned, ended up using the same techniques identified by Skinner to teach animals to use symbols.

Still, humans have a far greater ability to learn a language without being taught, by the simple association between a word and an object, emotion, or idea.

Harlow's monkeys learned the *concept* (or learning set, schema, thought, idea, etc.) of a peanut only being under the same symbol. True, it took some 300 trials with 30 different stimuli, before they got to a 90% success rate. But that showed clearly that concepts are learned, not something that springs automatically after a certain age

Chimp Elizabeth responding to a message in symbols:

"Elizabeth give apple Amy."

"The non-talking animals are way deeper in the woods."

WORDS AS ENCODED
LEARNING SETS or CONCEPTS

In both studies, psychologists indeed seem to have taught the chimps a rudimentary grammar, not unlike that of a two-year-old human child. Even so, there is an obvious limit on what the chimps are capable of learning.

They may equal two-year-old children; but two-year-old children they remain. Their vocabulary seems to be limited to about 160 words. In contrast, M. E. Smith found the vocabulary of human children to average 118 words at 21 months and 272 words at 24 months. Two-year-old human children might do even better if they had been given the time and effort put into teaching a chimpanzee to speak.

The adult can select from an infinite variety of words, words that stand for entire concepts or learning sets composed of other concepts or learning sets. Words now become the most important stimuli in the thinking process. Formerly complex learning sets were composed of many stimuli, but by tagging them with a word, by fitting them into categories, the adult can easily manipulate these formerly complex learning sets.

This is the process we call *thinking*. Concepts or learning sets flit in and out of sequence in our thoughts as rapidly as our perception of the Necker cube can change.

The great advantage of humans is the ability to symbolize. A single word can now represent not just a specific stimulus, but a concept or series of learning sets or a perception. Complex information has been encoded and thereby simplified. A familiar but important example of the value of such encoding may be given. Suppose you had to learn all the colors of the visible spectrum of light in their proper order...

4. MNEMONIC DEVICES: Roy G. Biv

What are they? Well, there's yellow, and red, and blue, and white-no, white's not a color. Then there is green and indigo and violet. Which are the primary colors? Which colors are secondary? What is their correct order? An old mnemonic device used to aid in memory is to take the first letter of each color and arrange it into a short, more familiar word. In this case, the name Roy G. Biv, representing the three primary colors, red, green, and blue, now becomes a stimulus to elicit a variety of learning sets.

The secondary colors are represented by the lower-case letters of the name, and the spelling corresponds to the sequence of the colors in the spectrum. By learning Roy G. Biv, we can now easily call on other concepts or learning sets (our knowledge of the colors, of capital letters, and of sequence) to come up with a response on the test of Red, orange, yellow, Green, Blue, indigo and violet.

Words are a shorthand for our sensory experience. As symbols, they make learning far more rapid. And they increase the scope of our immediate experience because they are always available to represent stimuli that are not present. Thus, at exam time the student can use words to call forth a multitude of experiences that otherwise would not be available.

5. HIERARCHIES OF LEARNING SETS?
Ideas encoded in symbols

Does all verbal ability depend on *S-S* associations and learning sets? Or is there a cerebral logic, a mental ability, that exists independent of pure learning? A study of syllogisms by Wilkins provides an interesting demonstration of the importance of prior learning in working even the simplest problems of logic. Try your mental ability on the following problems:

1. All the people living on this farm are related to the Joneses; these old men live on this farm. Therefore:

    a. These old men are related to the Joneses.

    b. All the people related to the Joneses are these old men.

    c. Some people related to the Joneses are not these old men.

2. All *X's* are Y's; all Z's are *X's*.
Therefore:

    a. All Z's are Y's.

    b. All Y's are Z's.

    c. Some *Y's* are not Z' s.

3. All lysimachim is epilobium; all adenocaulon is lysimachion. Therefore:

    a. All adenocaulon is epilobium,

    b. All epilobium is adenocaulon.

    c. Some epilobium is not adenocaulon.

From the standpoint of pure logic, all the above questions should be equally easy. And the equally easy answer to each of the above is the first one. But most of us are not pure logicians. Most of us are still in the fumble-and-find stage of logic. Thus, the first question is the easiest.

Why? Because it deals with familiar learning sets. All of us have a concept for "Joneses." "Joneses" are people. More than this, it is a word used to describe a nonspecific group of people, like John Doe. We also have learning sets for "related to" and "all," and concepts of "old men" and "farm."

But in the second question, only those vaguely familiar with mathematics will know that *Xs, Ys,* and *Zs* stand for different stimuli yet can each stand for any stimuli. We can easily work this problem, however, if we substitute the familiar concept of "people" for the unfamiliar (Xs) and substitute "Joneses" for *Ys* and "old men" for *Zs.*

The last problem is the most difficult. Most of us have had some rudimentary experience with the algebraic concept of Xs and Ys, even if it often was unpleasant and forced upon us. But none of us has had experience with lysimachion or epilobium. For most, this question is incomprehensible, yet, its logic is the same as that of the other two.

These examples suggest that our thinking process depends strongly on our existing concepts or learning sets, and that our entire thought process is heavily restricted by the learning sets that we have or have not formed.

It is also apparent that we could devise a concept or learning set from many such step-by-step experiences that would enable us to work on any similar problem without prior experience. We should be able to do at least as well as Harlow's monkeys! Mathematicians who study logic have developed learning sets for these and other problems (algebra, for example). But most of us will have to muddle through unless we are required to master them.

Wilkins' syllogisms represent a hierarchy of increasingly difficult problems even though the logic of each is exactly the same.

The learning sets we use to solve the first problem will not apply to the second. However, the mathematical concepts of *X* and *Y* can be used to solve the first two easier problems. The mathematical logic represents a higher-level learning set that can be used to solve the simpler problem, even if it deals with stimuli we have never before encountered, such as adenocaulon and epilobium. Yet the understanding of a higher learning set as in algebra is not possible without repeated experience with simple, familiar situations, such as that involving the Joneses and old men, in which existing learning sets can be used.

6. USE YOUR POWERS OF INTERPRETATION

Perhaps one of the most impressive examples of an artist calling on his audience to use powers of symbolization in this way is found in the following passage from *Through the Looking Glass* by Lewis Carroll. Read it several times with feeling.

'Twas brilling, and the slithy toves

Did gyre and gimble in the wabe:

All mimsy were the borogoves

And the mome raths outgrabe.

A small child may see more "meaning" in the stanza than an adult, although the child would be hard put to explain it. For the child hangs meaning on every word through inflections in the speaker's voice, the tone of voice, the emphasis on some words, the passing over of others, the raise of an eyebrow, and the wrinkle of your nose. In this way, words become "real" to a child.

And what kind of borogoves were they? They were *mimsy* borogoves. And what happened to the mome's raths? Why, they *outgrabe-*of course!

We have been searching for a vague something-something that may be called a symbolic ability,-the factor that distinguishes humans from apes. Thus far, we have not determined its origin. We have instead found that the thread of similarity in the learning process of lower animals seems to extend even to our language.

Yet this is only part of the story. For our symbolic ability, however vague, does exist. We have touched it briefly with our minds only to have it slip elusively from our grasp. We still do not know what biological changes occurred in the transition from ape to human to make this ability possible. If we cannot catch it and hold it, why then should anyone believe such a thing exists? Could it be that humans are simply more "intelligent" than apes and that our "intelligence" gives us the ability to use language?

The most obvious difference between us and the other animals is our ability to speak. But does speech require intelligence? Parrots and Mynah birds can speak, quite distinctly, although they can understand little of grammar or word meanings. Yet a chimp cannot speak. Why? No one has even accused the parrot of having "intelligence." Compared to the chimp with its problem-solving ability, the birds are feather-brained.

Humans speak, birds speak, yet monkeys cannot. Why? The only apparent answer seems to be that humans and birds are biologically (genetically) programmed to be able to mimic and use sounds. Attempts to teach verbal speech to chimps by the Kellogg's in 1950 ended with the chimps able to say only "mama," "papa," and "cup," and the results were hardly good examples of elocution. Chimps simply seem incapable of acquiring or using speech.

7. INTELLIGENCE AND SPEECH

Is Verbal Ability Necessary for Intelligence?

Then perhaps the only difference between humans and apes is that humans have the parrot's physiological ability to speak combined with the chimp's native intelligence? We have already suggested that, as a sort of shorthand for sensory experience, speech enables people to encode and communicate ideas with a facility that itself is a major intellectual advantage over the apes. Perhaps speech itself is the only difference between ourselves and our hairy cousins. This is a logical idea-even a brilliant one. It follows superbly from a hierarchal view of the value of concepts or learning sets. But then there is Helen Keller.

At the age of eighteen months, Helen Keller was stricken by an illness that left her both blind and deaf. She had had only eighteen months in which to learn something of the world of words and sight before she was plunged into a world devoid of sound and light-a world consisting only of touch, taste, and scent.

Until the recent development of modern methods of teaching, the deaf child was at a greater disadvantage in life than even the blind. The blind could learn speech and did so well. But the deaf child could not hear speech. Because deaf children could not hear their own sounds, they could not control their own sounds. Because they could not hear words; they could not learn the meaning of words. Because they did not know that words could stand for things, they could not communicate except by gesture. Helen was not only deaf and speechless; she was also blind. Even gestures had no meaning to her. Her world was a timeless void.

When Helen was seven, Anne Sullivan became her teacher. Using the simplest of associations, Miss Sullivan (herself partly blind) would tap out the name of an object in Helen's hand and then give her the object. The first such object was a doll. Miss Sullivan tapped and presented, tapped and presented, but Helen was only able to imitate her efforts by tapping the word back, at one time tapping it onto the paws of her dog.

The breakthrough seems to have come when Anne tapped the word *water* into Helen's hand and then held her hand under a faucet. At this point, Helen seems to have "realized" that symbols (tapping) stand for objects. Once this learning set had been acquired, Helen quickly learned the symbols for thirty other objects within a matter of hours. Helen was enthusiastic about her newfound world of symbols, but learning rarely came so easily. Miss Sullivan described the process as often having been one of "merciless prodding."

Helen Keller went on to learn to write using a form of braille. Her writing was crude but grammatically correct. Although her books were not entirely of her own writing, since others aided in the translation of what she was trying to say, her ability to learn to "speak" and "hear" through touch is a remarkable achievement. What is significant about her accomplishment is that the symbols seem to be not just in speech and hearing but in touch as well. Helen's ability went far beyond the sign language of Washoe the chimp or the plastic words of Sarah.

8. BRAIN SIZE AND INTELLIGENCE

Other than speech, the most apparent physical difference between people and apes is one of sheer brain size. The average modern human brain measures 1350 cubic centimeters (cc), roughly three times the brain size of our nearest primate relatives. Chimpanzees and gorillas average only around 350 to 550 cc of brain matter.

The most convincing evidence of the importance of brain size comes from the fossil remains of our ancestors. The Australopithecus, a walking ape-man of over two million years ago, had a brain size of roughly 650cc. There is no current evidence for a primate brain size in excess of 800ccs until about one million years ago. In the next million years, Java man and Peking man upped the cranial capacity to 800 to 1000 cc and more. Two hundred thousand years ago, the Neanderthal appeared with a whopping 1500 cc brain capacity, which slightly edges our modern brain, at 1350ccs. Yet Albert Einstein had a brain size of only 1250ccs. It is not the size of the brain that creates intelligence, it is the connections that give us this powerful symbolic ability.

It is doubtful that cranial increases occurred as regularly as these examples may indicate. If recent finds in Africa are verified, it may be that a more modern form of primate existed alongside Australopithecus well over a million years ago and that a near-modern species existed during the same period as the more numerous Neanderthal types. Regardless of the specific ancestor, one thing is apparent: our brain size has increased markedly since we first appeared on earth.

The belief that brain size is related to survival is not simply a matter of fossil evidence. We know that large brains must certainly have had great survival value to the species. The human female, of all of the animals, is one of the few that experiences marked pain during childbirth. Why? In part because of her transition to upright posture, which required major engineering changes in the structure of the pelvic girdle to allow childbirth in a creature that walks on two legs instead of four. The primary factor, however, is the marked increase in the brain size of the newborn infant.

Upright posture and the large brain size of the infant complicate childbirth, making it dangerous for both the infant and the mother. A primate that had such difficulty in giving birth could only survive if the large brain size gave that species a tremendous survival advantage in some other way.

The importance of this may be seen in the so-called obstetrical dilemma. All primates except humans are born sufficiently mature physically that they can cling to their mother, suckle, and more or less make it without their mother's direct assistance. But not the human infant. The human infant is born completely helpless and dependent. The human infant is born months ahead of its time. Why? Because much of its rapid brain growth must take place outside of the mother's body. Otherwise, it could not be born at all without a cesarean section. For such a drastic change from the primate norm, brain size would have to give humans a crucial survival advantage to outweigh the tremendous difficulties that the large brain size adds to the danger of birth for both the baby and the mother.

So we know that increased brain size is associated with a survival advantage the human advantage of *symbolic ability.* But does intelligence come from brain size alone? Is this the source of our ability? We are not the only large-brained animal.

The elephant has a brain four times larger than our own three-pound mass. The brain of a whale is five times the size of our own. The dolphin has a brain slightly larger (1800 cc) and every bit as convoluted as our own.

Yet even the recent attempts to communicate with the dolphin on its own level, via sound in the water, have been no more successful than our efforts to teach chimps to use symbols.

The obstetrical problems show beyond any reasonable doubt that brain size is highly correlated with our major survival advantage-our ability to symbolize-our intelligence, if you will. Yet to know that brain size and intelligence are correlated does not prove that brain size *causes* intelligence. Indeed, it may simply be that intelligence or symbolic ability, *once it exists,* gives a selective advantage to brain size; that is, with intelligence, one must have a larger brain, greater storage capacity, to effectively use the ability to symbolize.

It is unlikely that our ability to speak is solely related to brain size. Neither is our intelligence. Neanderthals had a brain size of about 1500 ccs. Modern humans have a brain size of 1350 ccs. Einstein had a brain size of 1250 ccs.

Speech would have to have had biological programs in the brain that made possible Broca's area and Wernicke's area, but also associations between the two areas. Further, to become capable of making arrow points and art, we would have needed new biological programs in the right hemisphere, that made possible art and music. These would have required separate mutations to the biological programs in the brain.

9. THE BIOLOGICAL BASIS OF LANGUAGE

We already know from our studies of the brain, that Broca's Area allows us to process sounds into words. If this area is damaged, we can understand speech, but we cannot say words clearly.

If Wernicke's Area of the brain is damaged, we can still speak in whatever language we have learned, but we only imitate what we hear from others, something like a parrot.

Clearly, there are both biological programs in the brain that make possible pattern recognition and speech, and learned programs from our environment. Yet, what makes us better than a talking parrot, is still not entirely clear.

FOXP2: A Genetic Clue to the Origin of Language

In 2001 the discovery of the FOXP2 gene revolutionized our understanding of the origin of language. For this book it is most important to understand HOW we discovered this gene. We did not learn about it by studying the genes themselves. That road goes nowhere. Instead, we had to go back to low-tech. Scientists found a few individuals with a rare disorder that interfered with speech. By comparing their genes to the genes of those without such a disorder, it was possible to localize the specific gene that had mutated.

Further studies showed that this gene differed from the same gene found in chimpanzees. And still more studies found that this gene controlled and enhanced 61 more genes and retarded dozens more. Yet we could never have discovered the gene without going back to low-tech, much as Broca and Wernicke had done.

First, we find a difference, then we look for a cause.

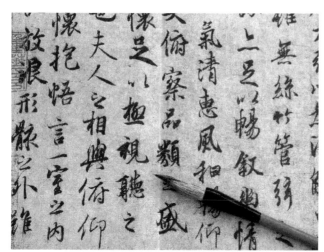

At this point, one comes away from a study of our symbolic ability feeling something like one who reached out in the middle of the night to get something off of the dresser, and suddenly touched something that should not be there. As we slide comfortably back into bed, we cannot help but believe that something else is out there, something that we have not yet seen. Something, perhaps, that we have not yet imagined.

The secret may lie in the psycholinguistic studies of Braine, or in an elaboration of the learning theory approaches of Harlow, or the cognitive research of neuropsychologists. It may lie in our genes or the neurological depths of the brain's structure. Most likely, in all of the above. At present, the ability of the brain to order and encode stimuli is one of the most important questions open to modern psychological research.

When we invented writing, that gave us the ability to transcend time. We can read the knowledge penned by Hippocrates and Herodotus and all of the failures and successes of our species. Books could educate the masses. More, we now can produce a worldwide internet that makes available a mass of information never before seen. Censorship by politicians and publishers and schools is increasingly difficult, yet it still happens.

Never in human history has there been such a thing. Nothing like it ever was. But the same methods that allow such widespread knowledge also make possible widespread lies, hatred, and misinformation. Just as words allow us to educate and communicate, those words also present us with the ability to spread misinformation, superstition, and blind belief. That is why it is so important to educate our youth to understand science, and how their mind works.

"When you put it like that, it makes complete sense."

13 MOTIVATION

beyond the puncheon floor

OLDS • MILNER • BUTLER • COWLES • ANOKHIN • ASCH • BANDURA • WALTERS

Primary Stimuli: Pleasure Centers in the Brain • Conditioned Stimuli: Learned Motives • Symbolic Stimuli: Modeling Stories

*There warn't anybody at the church, except maybe a hog or two, for there warn't any lock on the door, and hogs like a puncheon floor in the summertime because it's cool. If you notice, most folks don't go to church only when they've got to: but a hog is different. ***

Mark Twain *Huckleberry Finn*

Hogs like a puncheon floor* in the summertime because it is cool. Cool is pleasant. Pleasant is a primary reinforcer. Pleasant is a positive reinforcer. Folks avoid church or school when it is "boring.". Boring is unpleasant. Avoiding the unpleasant is reinforcing. People put up with boredom to avoid hell or social disapproval, which society has made even more unpleasant than boredom.

Seeking pleasure and avoiding pain are the most basic of animal motivations.

From Aristotle to Freud, the "pleasure principle" has been recognized as the driving force behind human motivation. Thorndike made it a basic "law" of science. Yet this principle seems to fail to explain the behavior of the monk who renounces worldly pleasure and actively seeks a life of hardship, mortifying his flesh and fasting until his skin wraps itself around his ribs and his body begins devouring its own tissue.

The principle will not explain the behavior of gamblers who consistently lose all they own, and then beg, borrow, and steal more only to race back to the gaming table. It will not explain those children in a mental institution who tear at their flesh with their fingernails so persistently that they must be kept in strait jackets. Nor will it explain the persistence of much of our normal day-to-day behavior in the face of great obstacles and little apparent reward.

Curiosity:

If you have ever tried to train a dog and have another person or dog walking nearby, you know it is almost impossible to get the dog to respond, even for food, when the overwhelming emotion of curiosity, triggered by novel stimuli, interferes with what you are trying to teach.

*Why are you reading this footnote? What is your motivation? Just because you had an "urge" to read? Was the novelty of the word puncheon enough to stimulate your curiosity? Learning the meanings of a new word may be a primary reinforcement in that it may be based on the primary reward of novel stimulation. It is also a secondary reinforcer based on a learned curiosity, Infants and animals would not pause to read this, only an organism that had learned the importance of words (or footnotes) would bother.

Thus, you may be reading this because of both primary (novel stimuli or curiosity) reinforcement and secondary or learned reinforcement. Oh yes, a puncheon floor is a split log floor.

To understand the complexities of behavior we must understand the (1) *primary stimuli* (primary reinforcers) that are the biological basis of what we seek (food, pleasure, curiosity, etc.) and what we avoid (pain, boredom, etc.); (2) *secondary* or *conditioned stimuli* (secondary reinforcers) that are positive cues (Pavlov's bell, a friendly smile, and "our" football team) or negative cues (schoolrooms, dentists' offices, and "their" football team) that have acquired their "meaning" only because of the primary stimuli they have been paired with in the past; and (3) symbolic stimuli, which affect no other animals but humans-only people respond to, or die for, causes and ideals that have no physical substance and exist only "in the mind."

The search for the origin of motivation begins in a biological laboratory with new methods of probing the brain. It then takes us to increasingly less physical realms, into the purely psychological basis of motivation. The psychological motives we share with other animals are the catalysts for the last leg of the search for the symbolic motivation that is unique to humans. Yet each stage of motivation beyond the biological depends intimately on the more basic stage that precedes it. We cannot understand the complex motives until first we understand the basic ones,

1. PRIMARY POSITIVE STIMULI:

Pleasure Centers in the Brain
Stimulation of the Brain

The surgeon made a quick incision into the scalp. Folds of skin covering the cranium were parted and held in place with stainless steel clamps. The strong membrane covering the skull was scraped away. A surgical drill whirred and a carefully preselected point on the skull was penetrated. The resulting hole was minute, only large enough to allow a tiny silver electrode to penetrate to the depths of the brain. Laboratory assistants kept constant watch on the respiration of the subject. Too much ether and the patient would die; too little and he would awaken at an acutely embarrassing moment.

The chrome-plated arm of the stereotaxic instrument was moved into position.

Precision adjustments were made on the micrometer, the alignment was checked, and more adjustments followed. The surgeon slowly lowered the exposed tip of the electrode deep into the lower midline area of the reticular system of the brain.

The surgeon missed. Instead of hitting the hypothalamus, the electrode struck a nerve tract from the rhinencephalon, or "smell-brain," area of the lower brain. This fortunate surgical accident led to the discovery of one of the most remarkable aspects of the brain's function. Deep within the brain are centers that control the primary motivation of animals and humans.

Electrode implant in the brain of a rat

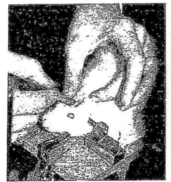

At McGill University, James Olds and Peter Milner had unknowingly probed these control mechanisms. They had blundered into a twilight zone between biology and psychology, and they uncovered the biological basis of psychological motivation.

Following the implantation, the electrode was cemented into place, and a flexible electrical wire was plugged into it. Through this wire, Olds and Milner passed a small electrical charge, approximately equal to that of a dry-cell flashlight battery. The charge was programmed to last for less than a second. When they fired an electrical impulse into the animal's brain, the animal looked up. It twitched its whiskers. It "smiled." This was hardly a spectacular beginning, but Olds and Milner found that by shooting electricity to the animal every time it leaned in one direction, it would move in that direction. If they stimulated the animal after it moved to the left, it would move to the left again.

They soon had it going from corner to corner, and running T-mazes-all for a little fire from the wire. When it reached the choice point in a T-maze, a spark would be given when it moved in the right direction. A few sparks for the proper inclination and the animal would be sucked down the runway like a moth to the flame,

What was happening? Did the animal really get a thrill from the impulse? How could they objectively measure the potency of this electrical juice? Olds and Milner hit on the idea of rigging a Skinner box in such a way that every time the animal pressed a bar it would receive a brief electrical impulse to its brain. Releasing the bar and pressing again would bring a second impulse and so on.

At first, the animal would only trip the bar by accident in the process of exploring its new cage. Such accidents normally occur at a rate of about 10 to 25 times per hour. After only a few such accidents, the animal with a rhinencephalon implant began pressing the bar at a rate of 200 times an hour, and one with a hypothalamic implant reached a rate of as much as 7,000 times per hour.

The animal would bypass food, water, and friendly animals of the opposite sex to obtain these fun shocks. Some pressed as much as 2,000 times per hour for 24 hours until they dropped from sheer exhaustion. Then they slept for a day, awoke, and after a free shock for rejuvenation, began pressing all over again. It was not uncommon to record over 55,000 responses in 48 hours.

The original study by Olds and Milner was done using rats. Since then, electrodes have been implanted in similar regions of the brains of monkeys and people. For medical purposes, dozens of humans of both sexes have had electrodes implanted in their brains. Such implants may relieve the severe depression of disturbed patients or of patients suffering incurable pain.

Dr. Robert Heath, of Tulane University, has implanted electrodes in many different regions of the human brain. Electrodes in the pleasure centers have been connected to wires leading to a battery pack on the belt. By pushing different buttons, subjects can stimulate separate areas of their own brain.

The Nucleus Accumbens is directly adjacent to the olfactory or scent part of the brain in humans and rats. In most mammals, the scent emitted by the opposite sex during estrus, the mating season, is directly associated with seeking sex.

At Tulane, Dr. Heath carried this one step further, attempting to alleviate severe depression in patients. With electrodes implanted in humans into their left anterior and right mid-septal areas, he found that humans would continually stimulate their own pleasure center. One woman described it as sexual. One man...;

> *"...stimulated himself to a point that, both behaviorally and introspectively, he was experiencing an almost overwhelming euphoria and elation and had to be disconnected, despite his vigorous protests."*

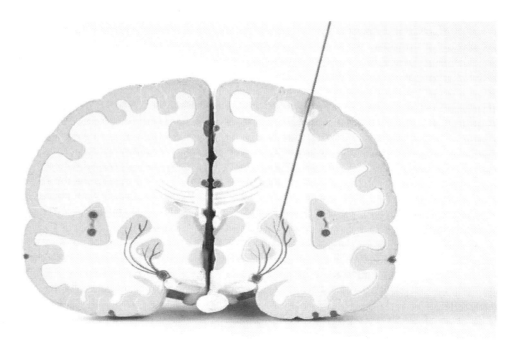

Above is a schematic of an electrode being implanted in the human brain.

Human subjects have an advantage over rats in that they can report their subjective impressions of what this stimulation feels like. What do they report? Depending upon the area stimulated, the sensations may be described as warm, pleasant, or sexual. Feelings range from mildly relaxing to that of a sexual orgasm.

Such implants have had significant clinical value. They have proven successful in reducing the unending pain experienced by terminal cancer patients without the side effects of drugs, and in eliminating the danger of severe psychomotor seizures in some epileptics who do not respond to drugs.

2. Natural Positive Stimuli

Novel stimulation is one of the more powerful primary reinforcers. Consider the excitement of the dog going for a walk or-a child getting ready for a vacation.

Like Pavlov's bell associated with food, merely the jingle of a dog's chain, something associated with getting to go for a walk, can send a dog into dramatic excitement. The dog may excitedly wag his/her tail, leap toward the chain, eagerly let the leash be attached, and bolt toward the door in anticipation of getting to go for a walk. The novel stimuli of the walk are the only excitement needed to trigger this massive response of excitement. Even in movies and books, the novelty of the plot or the unexpected turn of events is one of the most effective attention-getting stimuli for humans.

3. THE PIT: sensory Deprivation

Brain stimulation is by no means the only form of pleasure. Moderate levels of novel stimulation are also pleasurable. Robert Butler, at the Walter Reed Army Hospital, caged monkeys in isolation booths with no sight of the outside world. The monkeys were allowed to get a brief 10-second glimpse of another monkey, an electric train, or even just the inside of the laboratory, if they were willing to work for it. And they were. They spent over 40 percent of their time in an hour peeking out at these stimuli. Time after time, they worked diligently at a task or learned new tasks with their only reward being a bit of sensory stimulation," temporary relief from boredom, like that afforded the academically sated student checking out passersby through a window. Or, us watching sports, movies, TV, Politics, etc. to relieve our boredom.

Pleasure, hunger, thirst, and an exciting level of stimulation are all primary "drives," preprogrammed into our nervous system by our genes. Sex, food, water, and sensation are primary "natural" rewards; they are innately reinforcing and require no experience.

We learn how to seek food to satisfy the primary motive of hunger. We learn to seek novel sensations for the excitement they bring, and we invent elaborate fantasies to escape our mundane reality. When our genitals are stimulated, we learn to seek the source of stimulation, and the study of an animal's stimulation of the pleasure centers of the brain is, by analogy, the classic story of the adolescent's discovery of masturbation and sexuality.

We seek pleasant sensations. The stimuli that produce these pleasant sensations are already determined by our biology. But pleasure-seeking is only one basis of our biological motivational system. We also seek to avoid the unpleasant.

Psychology departments often have a variety of equipment to test human responses. In one department's basement laboratory, sophisticated studies are conducted into the physiological, perceptual, and learning processes of humans and animals. In the laboratory are Skinner boxes controlled by minicomputers to automatically program the sights, sounds, and reward schedules of the animals, stereotaxic instruments to implant electrodes, jars of pickled brains for dissection, and even a laser.

Of all the attractions on the guided tour, none has proven as interesting as The Pit. Coming off the elevator into the basement, the tour group heads straight down a gray alley runway and zigs right at the first choice point. Past the doors of the physiological laboratories; past the rat breeding colonies, past the one-way mirror rooms, and past the locked room to which no one has a key, we come to the second choice point in the underground maze.

Unlocking the first door, we enter into a waiting room strewn with electronic equipment, tape recorders, a laser, and sundry magic boxes. Two more doors, set back-to-back, separate this room from The Pit-a nontechnical term for an anechoic chamber, a sound-deadened room.

Entering The Pit, one is met by row after row of jagged foam baffles.

When the doors are closed and the light is turned off, the room is as pitch black as Carlsbad Caverns during an energy crisis. In The Pit, however, there is no rock wall to echo our sounds, for the air vibrations are effectively absorbed by the foam baffles. It would seem like the perfect place to study or contemplate the meaning of life. No distractions, no noise, only silence. It is so quiet that if you listen, you can hear the vibrations of the filament in the light bulb as the electrons are thrown off.

Elaborate studies have been conducted to determine the effects of sensory deprivation. In one such study, Bexton, Heron, and Scott paid college students $20 a day to remain in a similar isolation chamber. That was way back when the minimum salary was only $1.00 an hour. Today, the minimum wage is $15.00 an hour. Inflation in action. The students were asked to lie on a bed in a partially sound-deadened room. Translucent goggles were placed over their eyes to minimize pattern vision. Gloves on their hands and padding on the arms minimized tactile sensations. Time out was given for meals, of course. How long do you think you could stand this degree of sensory deprivation? A week? Two weeks? The price of peace turned out to be more than most could bear.

Before the end of the first day, the students became restless, irritable, and eager to end the experiment. Many had already begun hallucinating. Only a few stubbornly held out for two to three days.

During the experiment, Bexton, Heron, and Scott tested the attention span of the students by exposing them to such spellbinders as an old stock market report and a lecture for children about the evils of alcohol; stimuli hardly likely to enrapture a college audience. In their sensory-deprived state, however, the students found such trivia the nectar of life and later reported having eagerly awaited each testing session.

No subjective report of the reactions of others can be as lucid as one written by those who have entered The Pit. In a separate study, Heron, Coone, and Scott followed up on the reports of their students by experiencing the same sensory-deprived conditions. Sleep made the conditions tolerable, but one could not sleep forever.

Being awake proved to be intolerable. By the end of the first day, the researchers reported hallucinations. At first, rows of dots and geometric patterns danced before their eyes. Later, people, scenery, and bizarre mosaics moved across their visual field. The hallucinations swerved, separated, danced from side to side, and sucked in and out like a visual whirlpool of illusion. They reported their eyes were tired from trying to focus on the hallucinations. Were these hallucinations the brain's attempt to self-stimulate, much as dreams in sleep provide self-stimulation?

Different subjects react in different ways to sensory deprivation. Perception of time and space are frequently distorted. Yet there are no reports of anyone having lost contact with reality during the relatively brief study periods. The hallucinations seem to be the mind's attempt to self-stimulate. One is tempted to draw a parallel between deprivation-induced hallucinations and the natural state of dreaming during sleep. Sleep is also a relatively low level of sensory stimulation. In both conditions, the mind seems to creatively "free associate" to produce an unreal fantasy world that goes beyond any physical basis in reality.

Subjects unanimously report that sensory deprivation is unpleasant and that almost any stimulation may be reinforcing. Such extremes of sensory deprivation are rarely found under normal conditions. At a normal level of stimulation, we find old stock market reports and moral lectures on alcohol boring. When forced to endure this level of sensory deprivation, we may daydream rather than hallucinate, but very low levels of stimulation are innately unpleasant and we avoid them if possible. Escaping from the unpleasant is a primary reward.

4. CENTERS OF FEAR AND RAGE

Just as there are centers of the brain for pleasure, hunger, and thirst, there are also centers for fear, pain, and discomfort. Even before Olds and Milner's famous discovery, Swiss psychologist W. R. Hess had probed the brain and found centers of rage and fear in the hypothalamus that can be triggered electrically. The effect of electrically stimulating these areas is exactly the opposite of stimulating the pleasure centers. The animal will frantically work to escape or avoid such stimulation, even though no physical damage results from the electrical impulses.

In one classic study, a mouse was presented to a cat after an electrode had been implanted in the cat's "fear" center. The cat's first reaction to the mouse was to approach, sniff, and start to play roughly with the mouse. When the cat approached the mouse, an electrical stimulus was delivered to the fear center. The cat jerked back in surprise, keeping its eye on the diabolical mouse. Then the mouse, apparently terrified by its own uncertain future, suddenly began running frantically around the cage. When the mouse accidentally ran in the direction of the cat, the cat panicked. The cat raced to one corner. The mouse made a suspicious move in the cat's direction and the cat bolted for another corner.

To the observer, films of this encounter make it appear as if the cat was running scared; running from the mouse. And it was. So long as the electrical current was applied, the cat reacted with fear. Usually, stimulation of such centers will elicit a feeling of discomfort, fear, or pain, without reference to a source. Yet the mouse was the stimulus present when the fear occurred. It was the stimulus the cat was attending to. The cat apparently associated this stimulus with the fear it experienced and actively fought to avoid the mouse for as long as the electrical stimulation lasted.

Of all primary negative stimuli, pain is the most obvious in its effects. Pain is an extreme level of physical discomfort, usually the body's signal that tissue destruction is taking place. The evolutionary advantage of this biological fact is evident. Yet most of our behavior is motivated by more subtle feelings of discomfort; a cramp in the muscle from sitting too long in one posture, a tight feeling in the gut from eating too much, the tension of a full bladder, the early pangs of hunger, the restlessness of boredom. Long before these subtle stimuli become painful, we act to do something about them. We often react even before we become conscious of their pressure, their power to motivate.

5. PRIMARY NEGATIVE STIMULI

Pain seems to be at the opposite end of a scale of stimulation from that of sensory deprivation. Pain seems to involve intense levels of stimulation. The higher the level of stimulation, the greater the number of pain-sensitive neurons that are triggered and the greater the discomfort or pain. A hard slap fires more neurons than a light slap. Between the extremes of too little and too much stimulation, however, many paradoxical effects need to be explained.

The level of stimulation seems to be partly associated with the emotional reaction we have. Modest levels of stimulation result in curiosity. We seek stimulation for enjoyment. Moderate levels of stimulation result in caution, as in having to give a speech in a classroom full of strangers. High levels of stimulation result in fear. Phobias may result.

Very high levels of stimulation result in triggering aggression, as in the Fight or Flight response. A cornered animal will be afraid, but fight more ferociously.

6. PARADOXICAL EFFECTS

Robert Butler and others have found that novel stimulation is a positive stimulus that animals will actively work to obtain. But many studies have found that novel stimuli also can be frightening to animals. Rats, cats, monkeys, and people often react with fear to any sudden change in stimulation. Young children left alone in a strange house may be panic-stricken by the novelty, yet would be quite comfortable alone in their own home.

The reaction of pleasure or fear seems to be a matter of degree. The greater the intensity of novel stimulation, the greater the difference in the reaction. Very high levels of stimulation may be avoided. We do not like intense stimuli that we cannot control. If we feel that we have sufficient control over the situation, however, we may actively seek high levels of stimulation, as do daredevils such as Evel Knievel.

There is a limit to how much human behavior we can explain as either seeking pleasure or avoiding pain. Most day-to-day human behavior does not bring us biological satisfaction. Yet our behavior may persist even where there is no primary reinforcement. Most human behavior is based on conditioned stimuli. Instead of reacting only to biological pleasure or biological pain, we react to conditioned pleasure and conditioned pain.

7. WHAT IS *A* REINFORCER?

When Is a Stimulus Reinforcing?
A stimulus is considered a reinforcer if an animal is motivated to go out of its way to obtain that stimulus. This is often criticized as a circular definition, but the conditioned emotional responses connected to any stimulus, as in Picasso's paintings or Scarlett Johansson's "snot", show just how powerful any stimulus can be, when associated with fame. It is not just food, as behaviorists used in laboratory studies, that motivates behavior.

Primary reinforcer Stimuli that naturally (biologically) increase pleasure or reduce pain. (e.g., food, sex, novelty, and escaping from boredom, pain, or anxiety) are stimuli we will go out of our way to obtain.

Conditioned reinforcers Any stimulus that has been paired with a primary reinforcer may become a conditioned, or secondary, reinforcer (e.g., Pavlov's bell, paper money; gold, noise in vacuum cleaners, or political rallies) even though the conditioned reinforcer has no actual value.

Symbolic reinforcers   Any stimulus (including a thought or idea) that is paired with a conditioned reinforcer (Which could also *be* a thought of an idea) may become a symbolic reinforcer (e.g., national flags, religious symbols, thoughts of our own success, the imagined effect that our behavior has on the minds of others).

Some primary grade schools may use a gold star for a reward for a child's correct behavior and a black mark, for their naughty behavior. A student of mine told of how she was implementing the same method with her own daughter. One day her daughter did something naughty, and she told her daughter she was going to have to give her a black mark. The "black mark" is only a symbol of something negative.

The child; "No, don't give me a black mark!"

Parent: "Would you rather have a spanking or would you rather have a black mark?"

The child, crying, "I'd rather have a spanking!"

It is not clear just how much experience the child had ever had with spankings, but it does show just how this method may work better than I would have expected.

Even in the Boy Scouts, they give out merit badges for accomplishments, and they may wear these merit badges on their uniform as a symbol of having achieved some degree of proficiency. Often the young will work hard to achieve these merit badges, even though there are no primary positive stimuli associated with them.

At a higher level, in the military, soldiers often receive good conduct ribbons, sharpshooter badges, and campaign ribbons, worth virtually nothing themselves, but as symbols of their achievement. At a still higher level, they may receive medals for being wounded (purple heart), and courage under fire (silver star, bronze star, Congressional Medal of Honor, etc.). In the Navy they have "hash marks" on the sleeve of their uniform indicating years of service.

Most of these have no inherent value by themselves, they are a symbol that has been associated with the emotion we call pride. Even just a word of appreciation is often powerfully stimulus to motivate our behavior.

8. HOW ARE SYMBOLIC STIMULI OR REINFORCERS LEARNED?

Direct learning-using words. For example, if an animal were conditioned to fear bugs, the animal would fear only the stimulus of a bug; but humans would fear both the bug and the *thought* of the bug (symbolic stimulus) crawling on their skin'. Avoiding such thoughts is reinforcing. Now if you were told in.so many words (Symbolic stimuli) · that there are bugs in the food that you just ate, you would avoid eating more: of that food and possibly even vomit what you had just eaten. Avoiding such food reduces your anxiety. *Avoiding* such stimuli is therefore, reinforcing.

Indirect learning-using modeling stories (containing symbolic/stimuli) For example if a society wants its children to avoid bugs (or drugs, sex, communism, _witches 'bad thoughts," the devil, or the deep blue sea) then the society will tell its children modeling ~' · stories, containing symbolic stimuli or examples of reinforcers, that of someone Who got involved with bugs (or whatever) and ended up suffering a "fate worse than death" (or something similar).

If the society wants its children to be brave (or obedient, thrifty, law-abiding; and courteous}, the modeling stories will tell of someone who triumphed on the battlefield and received the admiration of all for his courage.

Thinking such thoughts (daydreaming), or trying to achieve such a triumph (imitation) is reinforcing: Seeing such a success is reinforcing. Symbolic stimuli are effective quite independent of any reality.

9. POSITIVE SECONDARY REINFORCEMENT

When Pavlov's bell was paired with food, the bell came to control the behavior of the dog. The bell became a secondary, conditioned stimulus. The bell could now be used in place of the food to control the dog's behavior. Russian psychologist Peter Anokhin described an example of the power of such stimulus control. He trained a dog to find food behind a partition on either the left or right side of the room. If the food was behind the left partition, a bell would be sounded on the left side and vice versa. The dog quickly learned to go to the side where the bell sounded and avoid the unrewarding side.

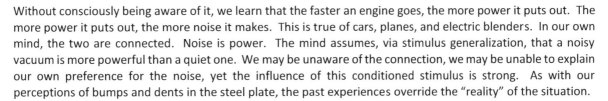

After training, the psychologist sounded the bell on the right side and the dog went behind the right partition and began eating. While the dog was eating, the bell was sounded behind the unrewarded left partition. The dog immediately stopped eating and ran over to the left partition. The conditioned stimulus had acquired such control over the behavior of the dog that at least for a time or two, the dog gave up a 'bird in the hand" without even a hope of finding "two in the bush."

Most of us assume that there must be at least a promise that "the grass is greener...," but the dog had never received a greater reward on one side than the other. The dog should have "known" better. The power of the conditioned stimulus overcame the satisfaction of a sure thing.

Our mind is as effectively controlled by such conditioned stimuli as was Anokhin's dog. For example, some time back, a company test-marketed a "noiseless" vacuum cleaner. The noiseless wonder worked as well as the noisy model and had the advantage of doing its work quietly. Placed side by side with the standard model, it did an equally good job but housewives would not buy it. They preferred the noise! Why? Noise is a conditioned stimulus signifying power.

Without consciously being aware of it, we learn that the faster an engine goes, the more power it puts out. The more power it puts out, the more noise it makes. This is true of cars, planes, and electric blenders. In our own mind, the two are connected. Noise is power. The mind assumes, via stimulus generalization, that a noisy vacuum is more powerful than a quiet one. We may be unaware of the connection, we may be unable to explain our own preference for the noise, yet the influence of this conditioned stimulus is strong. As with our perceptions of bumps and dents in the steel plate, the past experiences override the "reality" of the situation.

When a teenage boy gets his first car, he may find that it has a smooth quiet engine. Often the first change he makes will be to punch holes in the muffler to give it that deep-throated "varoom" sound. Noise is power. On a less superficial level, the same conditioned stimulus is used in political campaigns. Hitler perfected the technique. In massive political rallies at Nuremberg, tens of thousands of brown-shirted men would cheer his presence and chant their approval in unison, "Zeig Heil. Zeig Heil. Zeig Heil." Even in our own political process, we use noise in the form of sustained applause, brass bands, and cheering. In this case, noise is approval.

Any stimulus paired with a primary stimulus may take on the power of the primary stimulus. Such conditioning is most effective when we are not consciously aware of it. However, it would be a mistake to assume that behavior based on such conditioned stimuli is "irrational." The fact is that most of our behavior is based on such conditioned stimuli. We call such behavior "rational" if it brings us a "real" primary reward, and "irrational" if it can be shown that there is no "real" primary reward.

Yet the mind makes no practical distinction between rational and irrational responses. Both are conditioned. The only reason for emphasizing the "irrational" stimuli, such as noise, is to make it clear to the reader that a great amount of our behavior is controlled by conditioned stimuli. People often attribute such motivation to conscious "wants," "needs," or "drives." We are only beginning to understand the origin of these "wants," "needs," and "drives."

A classic study of conditioned reinforcers was done by John Cowles. Cowles trained a chimpanzee to put a poker chip into a slot machine and pull a lever. The machine would then drop a dried grape into a food cup at the bottom of the vending machine. Cowles next trained the chimp to work at a task, discriminating between small and large objects. If it picked the correct size, it was rewarded by being given a poker chip. After each testing session, the chimp was allowed to exchange the chips for a grape. Chimps learn to value poker chips (secondary reinforcers) the way humans value money.

The chip (CS) had been paired with a grape (USC). The chip now became a conditioned reinforcer. It had acquired value. And now the chimp worked hard to obtain the chips. Groups of chimps trained on such a schedule quickly learn to hoard chips and steal chips from other chimps. Humans, being more intelligent than the chimpanzee, have devised more diverse means of working to obtain "poker chips" and, in the process, more ingenious methods of stealing them.

In the book *Alas Babylon,* novelist Pat Frank writes a shattering story of an American town in the days following a nuclear holocaust. In the first few hours after the bombs rain on the major cities, the roads become clogged with motorists driving as far and as fast as they can from the major cities. Merchants in the smaller towns began to make tremendous profits on items in short supply. Food and gasoline prices skyrocket. Gasoline is cheap at $50 a gallon, sugar at $20 a sack. But gradually, like a cloud of doom, the merchants begin to become aware that, without a stable government, the money they have made is no longer of any value. When the vending machine breaks down, the poker chips lose their value.

People will go to great lengths to obtain their conditioned reinforcers. Anyone who has watched the TV giveaway show "Let's Make A Deal" has seen hundreds of people dressed up like the Great Chicken, Superman, a frog, a fairy, a donkey, and so on. They hop up and down, croak, shriek, and otherwise make a spectacle of themselves merely for the outside hope that, out of the hundreds in the audience, they might be chosen for a chance to choose door number one, door number two, or door number three. They might win thousands of dollars or only a stuffed muskrat, but the thoughts of winning (CS) is in itself sufficient to motivate their behavior.

In our schools, teachers may give out gold stars for being good. At a higher level, Sports jackets, Prom Queen, Valedictorian, and more are symbols of achievement.

In the Boy Scouts, Merit badges are given for achievement. They can be worn on their uniform.

In the Army, Merit badges are given for marksmanship, campaigns, combat. At a higher level, one can be awarded a Purple Heart for wounds, a bronze, silver, or gold medal for heroism, even a Congressional medal of honor. And a Presidential medal can be awarded as well.

While we may "swell with pride" at our merit badges, they have no actual value in real life other than that they have been associated with something our society has labeled "good".

10. NEGATIVE REINFORCEMENT

Negative "drives" may also be conditioned. Neal Miller trained a rat to run from a white compartment into a black compartment by shocking the rat when it was on the white side. Very quickly the rat learned to avoid the white side (negative CS) and to stay on the black side (positive CS). Then Miller put a partition between the two sides. A door in the partition could be opened by turning a wheel. Miller placed the rat in the white compartment. The rat, its path to freedom blocked, had to learn to turn the wheel to escape the white room into the black room. Its speed of escape increased from trial to trial.

Without any further shocks, Miller then changed the conditions so that his rats could only escape by pressing a bar. Soon wheel turning no longer worked. The rats' wheel-turning activity became extinct. Quickly they learned to press the bar to escape from the white room. Again, no further shocks had been given, yet they pressed the bar with increasing speed over the next ten trials. The rats were not learning to escape the shock, for no shocks were given. They were learning to escape the conditioned stimulus of the white room.

Two facts are important in the Miller study. First, the study differs from that of Watson's conditioned fear study with little Albert because the rats were learning to work a completely new task in order to escape. The rats had acquired more than a conditioned fear, they had acquired a conditioned "drive"; a "motive" to work. Second, they did not work to escape the primary stimulus of shock, but to escape the secondary conditioned stimulus of the white compartment (CS). Fear of the compartment was a conditioned "drive."

People rarely have to work to escape shock, but we work to escape many such "white rooms." At an early age, we condition our children with warnings about "what will people think!" Our anxiety over what people think of us leads us to learn ego-defensive mechanisms that reduce this anxiety. We may learn to brag, or to rationalize our behavior, or place the blame for our inadequacy on someone else. We may even learn to repress our thoughts and avoid anxiety by not thinking certain thoughts.

11. SCHOOL
AS A SOURCE OF
LEARNING GOOD MANNERS

Schools are useful in teaching good manners and consideration of the feelings of others.

SCHOOL AS A SOURCE OF FEAR AND LOATHING

School itself is a source of learned conformity. From the fear of rejection to the pleasure of attention, schools provide a dramatic example of how humans are subject to the same positive and negative emotions.

**"My day at school? Oh, the usual.
Bullying and cliques."**

More indirect evidence of the power of such emotions may be seen in the play of young children. Imagine the feelings of a young boy who wants *to* be accepted by an older group of children. He may "play the fool" hoping to be accepted. He may tag along behind the older boys, trying to join in their play. After repeated rebuffs, there is finally a hint of acceptance:

"Okay, okay," the other boys say, "we'll let you play with us, but you gotta play our way; you gotta play hide and seek, and you're it." The boy is elated! He has to be "it,", but he doesn't mind. He would do this and much more for the feeling of elation that comes with social acceptance. So, he covers his eyes and counts to one hundred by twos. Then he looks, he hunts, he calls, and with a sinking feeling in his gut he realizes-no one is there. Society conditions us to want to be accepted and *to* fear rejection.

The fear of going against the group often begins in school. Even if bullying never happens to us, we see it happen to others. We know what may happen to us if we are different.

12. THE SOLOMON ASCH STUDY OF CONFORMITY

Anxiety over what people will think dictates a remarkable amount of human motivation. Often, the effect is devastating. More direct evidence of the power of this conditioned drive is found in a classic study by Solomon Asch. Seven college students were asked to help in a study involving human judgment of the length of lines. A single line, drawn on a large poster, was presented to the group of students.

They were asked to state out loud, and one at a time, which of the three lines on another poster was the same length as the first line. The judgments were all quite easy-so easy, that a separate study had found an error rate of only I percent. However, unknown to one of the seven students, six of the students had been told in advance to unanimously give an incorrect answer on every judgment following the first two. Would their judgment pressure the other student to conform?

Asch found that social pressure has a profound impact on what we say we see. When the lines are presented, the first student calls out his answer: "line two." The second student calls: "line two"; the third student; "line two."

The uninformed student who has been chosen as the subject of this investigation suddenly startles. He looks again at the lines. He looks at the other students. He looks back at the lines. Clearly, line one is the correct answer. Then the fourth student calls: "line two." It is now the turn of the "outsider" to answer. No one looks at him. No one says anything to him. Will he conform? Will he call it as the others say, "line two"? Or will he call it as he sees it and say, "line one"? He squints, he squirms, but with less than a second's hesitation he calls out, "line two."

Sixty-seven percent of all students placed under such indirect pressure will conform to the consensus of the group on one or more trials. Only thirty-three percent will resist the pressure to conform. Without such pressure, there is a total error rate of only 1 percent. With the pressure, the error rate jumps to 36.8 percent of all calls. Of course, once a student has read about such studies in his psychology book, he will have been counter-conditioned to "watch out for sneaky psychology experiments!"

Still, others may have been conditioned to "never follow the group, -do your own thing." And in such cases, it has been found that some students-just to prove their independence, -will take a negative approach, going against the group even when the group may be correct. Both conditioning patterns would cause fewer students conforming in this type of study. However, without such counterconditioning, the results are remarkably predictable.

Nowhere is this more obvious than in our politics where the great majority of some politicians go along with the ideas of their constituents, even when they know what they are doing violates their most basic oath of office.

What is disturbing about the Asch experiment is that such results occur even though the experiment involved: (1) a simple objective judgment of (2) measurable differences in lengths of lines, (3) without any direct pressure from other students, (4) whom the subject did not know and probably would never have seen again.

Can you imagine the effect of such pressure when it involves: (1) a complex, controversial subject Such as politics, religion, abortion, pornography, gun control, or free speech, that (2) cannot be easily and objectively measured as can lengths of lines, when (3) there *is* direct verbal pressure, complete with temper and emotion directed against the nonconformer by (4) other people that the non-conformer must live with, in society and even depend on for their livelihood?

"I will of course yield to whomever agrees with me."

The courage of a Socrates, a Galileo, or a Darwin comes all too rarely to a world in which many of us not only will not speak out against the group, or the sacred cows of the group but may refuse even to think; that is, repress such thoughts ourselves. Yet even these three men had others who believed as they did to help counter the weight of the criticism they had to bear.

On a more mundane level, the effectiveness of such pressure is greatest when the nonconformist believes that the group is at least partly right. To be most effective, the group must appeal to a principle more noble than one's self. Nowhere is this technique applied with greater effectiveness than the yearly United Fund Drive. Once each year the employees of many large firms receive a card with their paycheck that tells them none too subtly what "fair share" of their paycheck they should contribute to charity.

In many, if not most, companies these cards are collected from each individual by "the boss" along with the contributions. Much fanfare and tambourine rattling accompanies such drives. In almost every company a count is kept of those contributing to the fund, sometimes by name and sometimes by a conspicuous display of a "percent contributing" poster. Departments within the company are encouraged to compete with each other to make the 100 percent quota.

 "Bosses" do not like to see their department come in low on the rating scale. More than once, supervisors of large groups have ended up by making contributions from their own pocket for those who failed to contribute. Their departments must be 100 percent. And more than once a supervisor has been quietly mad at the nonconformers for "making" the supervisor pay "their" share.

"My last comment 'appeared' to be inviting feedback.
Do not be fooled."

What is true in childhood and adulthood certainly holds true in adolescence.

During the 1950s, teenage males played a game known as "chicken." One boy would take his hotrod to the end of the block. A second boy would take his car to the opposite end. At a signal, they would gun their engines and race madly toward each other in the same lane. The boy who was first to swerve his car off the road was "chicken." The behavior of the "winners" was motivated by the positive social reinforcement of other boys who thought him brave and skillful. But some boys rarely patted him on the back for every such "victory," so much of the reinforcement took place symbolically, in the imagination of the winner.

But what of the loser? What reinforcement motivates the continued efforts of boys who try time and again only to lose? In many such cases, the only reward they receive by playing "chicken" is to avoid the social stigma of being thought a bad sport or the anxiety of believing that others will think they are not game. By going along with the gang, one's anxiety over being disliked is reduced.

The boy who pats himself on the back for playing "chicken," or who worries about what others will think of him, is engaging in a behavior that is uniquely human and derives from our symbolic ability. Other animals do not self-reinforce. Other animals do not think about how their mates view them.

Symbolic stimuli can control human behavior even though they have never before been paired with a primary stimulus and can never bring us any primary reward. We have seen this again and again in Kamikaze pilots, suicide bombers, and even our own politics.

When children perform some act and say, in effect, "Look at me, look at me!" they are seeking the conditioned stimulus of social approval. The social approval itself may not benefit the child, but it has been paired with primary stimuli such as contact comfort, food, positive physical stimulation, and anxiety reduction.

We are conditioned to believe that people who are liked by others are good people. We strive to be liked by others. In part, this striving produces primary stimuli. That is, the others reinforce us by giving us better jobs, which ensure food and physical comfort, or they blow in our ear, which gives us pleasurable primary sensations.

We seek social approval because it can bring us primary reinforcers. Yet we are capable of responding to symbolic meaning as well. We may react to a symbol as if it were more important than a primary stimulus even though it can never bring us any primary reinforcement. One of the best examples of such a purely symbolic stimulus is provided by the philosopher-mathematician Bertrand Russell in his Nobel Prize acceptance speech:

> *"Vanity is a motive of immense potency. Anyone who has much to do with children knows how they are constantly performing some act and saying, "Look at me." "Look at me" is one of the fundamental desires of the human heart. It can take innumerable forms, from buffoonery to the pursuit of posthumous fame. There was a Renaissance Italian princeling who was asked by the priest on his deathbed if he had anything to repent of. 'Yes,' he said, 'there is one thing. On one occasion I had a visit from the Emperor and the Pope simultaneously. I took them to the top of my tower to see the view, and I neglected the opportunity to throw them both down, which would have given me immortal fame.' History does not relate whether the priest gave him absolution."*

If the prince had achieved "immortal fame," what would he have gained? He could not physically benefit from the fame. He would receive no primary reinforcement for it during his life and certainly none after his death. The only benefit he could have received is the psychological one, in the present, while he was still alive. The symbolic stimulus, the idea of immortal fame, is self-conditioned. It has never been paired with primary stimuli. Rather, its power derives from pairing with other conditioned stimuli-stimuli signifying admiration, the posthumous fame of other people in history, the glory of those who have lived before us reflected in our books and our myths.

A symbol, like a conditioned stimulus, is a powerful control over behavior by itself. To many people, the American flag is such an important symbol that they may encourage the jailing of someone who wears it as a shirt, even though this harms no one. The sign of the cross is widely believed to have supernatural power in itself and in many cultures, it is worn to ward off evil, disease, demons, and of course, Count Dracula.

"Our" football team may be so symbolic of our self that it becomes a part of us. We revel in its glory when it wins and feel downcast when it loses, though in no way can we be physically affected by its fortunes. In a more grandiose vein, we also pay homage to our own country and we privately cheer when we win a contest with another country (the space race, Olympic games). Yet, as with our football team, we feel glory only because of the side our conditioned stimuli are paired with, not because our country is better than another; though we may readily convince ourselves that this is true.

Our schools dramatically encourage the idea of "our" football team against "their" football team using emotionally charged cheerleading, weekly "pep" rallies for "our" team, and encouraging spirit in "our" school against "their" school, even in school "pride".

The unspoken idea is that "we" are better than "you".

This emotional devotion to "our" side shows up again in our politics and our religions, with groups and even nations instilling pride in their flag, their national anthem, and their religion. All of which is accompanied by dramatical emotional outpourings.

The same is true of all of our symbolic conditioning whether Democrat or Republican, Catholic or Protestant, American or Russian. Indeed, in the war between Catholics and Protestants in Northern Ireland in the 1960s, the importance of these symbolic stimuli is all too apparent. The Catholics blame the Protestants for the war; the Protestants blame the Catholics. Yet, as with "our" football team, the group one rallies behind depends on which group the positive conditioned stimuli have been paired with. The significant others in our lives are paired with the symbols representing "our" team.

When a deadly epidemic hit the world, people divided up into two sides; the pro-vaccine and the anti-vaccine groups. Despite the evidence from over 70 years that vaccines were the single most important product of medical science. The one thing that has most increased our life-span is not end of life care, but vaccines against the diseases that killed so many of our young. Evidence meant nothing when up against emotions.

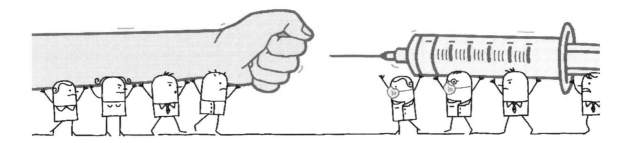

Even when former President Trump, at one of his own rallies in September 2021, suggested that his people should get the vaccine, he was greeted with a chorus of "boos" from his crowd. People expressed pride in their refusal to get the vaccine, they saw it as standing up for their "rights", even as over 800,000 Americans had already died from the disease, often spread by the unvaccinated.

Crowds of people throughout the world gathered to protest the Covid-19 mask or vaccine requirement. In America, school boards who were considering requiring the vaccine for school children were greeted with anger and threats, even though their children had been required to take other vaccines for over 70 years, before they could go to school. The police had to provide protection from the angry people.

People were more outraged over their "rights" than over the rights of others who might sicken and die from infection the protesters could spread. All of this protest over their "rights" had been triggered by a handful of politicians and press, few of whom ever commented on the over one million Americans' who died from Covid, many of whom might have been saved by masks or vaccines. They only focused on their "rights".

13. SYMBOLS AS EMOTIONAL RALLYING CRIES

The Nazis had the swastika; every country has a Flag. Every country rewards its soldiers, athletes, even boy scouts with medals that are paired with honor. The medals may do nothing for the individual, yet they may be a greater source of "pride" than anything else in his life. Every football team has a symbolic name (Detroit *Lions,* L.A. *Rams,* Denver *Broncos,* Dallas *Cowboys)* that serves as a rallying point, that focuses our attention and emotion onto a single stimulus. Religious institutions have their Cross, Star of David, image of Buddha, sign of Confucius, or Tower of Islam.

These symbols are powerful emotional rallying points for each group. And each group consciously strives to indoctrinate its members with a "team spirit" in football, "patriotism" in one's country, or the "spirit of God" in one's religion. If the pairing of the symbol or idea with the appropriate conditioned stimuli is successful, the members will fight harder for "their" school team, die more bravely for "their" country, or believe more devoutly in "their" religion.

In Vietnam in the 1960s, a number of Buddhist monks doused themselves with gasoline, assumed the lotus position, and set themselves on fire to protest a real or imagined political grievance. As with the Italian princeling, they received no positive reinforcement, except the imagined effect in their mind.

Young Buddhist monk stoically keeps cross legged posture as flames engulf him in a ritual suicide to protest policies of the Ngo Dinh Diem government in Viet Nam in 1963. gained no primary reinforcement for this act. The reinforcement existed only in the mind of the individual. No animal on earth except humans is capable of such self-reinforcement. While other animals will respond only to physical stimuli that are present (food or a bell paired with food), humans can condition themselves and their children to react to stimuli that do not exist outside of their own minds. Only people fear the dark, the bogeyman, witches, demons, ghosts, and "what other people will think." Only human beings die for, or kill for, country, religion, beliefs, "truths," or causes. All these stimuli exist as symbolic ideas within the human mind.

Our ability to imagine things that never were has allowed us to rise above other animals and to experience intellectual stimulation not available to other animals. At the same time, however, this ability has proven to be the source of a truly remarkable propensity for self-delusion. We prefer to emphasize the importance of our symbolic ability by pointing out our creative ability and our imagination. However, a count of the relative number of human acts in each category shows that as much or more human behavior will fall under the rubric of self-delusion than in the category of creative contributions. The ease with which we ignore this fact seems to have consistently prevented us from doing anything to change it. Such symbolic stimuli often become the sacred cows of culture that no one dares to question.

14.EXTINCTION OF STIMULI THAT EXIST ONLY IN THE MIND

One reason symbolic stimuli do not lose their "power" as easily as Pavlov's bell may be that they are strongly controlled by a complex series of conditioned stimuli. However, a second reason may be more important. Simply put, you cannot easily extinguish a behavior based on a stimulus that does not exist. If the animal is not able to discover that the stimulus does not exist, new learning cannot occur. In little Albert's conditioned fear of the white rat, time alone would not reduce his fear. Only by repeatedly exposing Albert to the white rat without following it with the frightening noise, could his fear be extinguished. If he could run away every time he saw the rat, new learning could not occur.

So long as we can avoid bugs, snakes, or triskiadektas, we will not lose our fear of them. Fears of werewolves, Dracula, ghosts, demons, and devils cannot be easily extinguished precisely because they do not exist outside of the mind. Since they do not exist, we cannot confront them in situations in which new learning could occur. We cannot meet "friendly" ghosts, demons, werewolves, or devils as we might meet a "friendly" white rat. Of course, it is sometimes possible to desensitize such fears if enough "significant others" in a society assure the person such stimuli do not really exist.

15.OBSERVATIONAL LEARNING: Modeling Stories

Symbolic stimuli are consistently reinforced by being paired with other conditioned fears. Actual primary stimuli, such as "things that go bump in the night," are often paired with the symbolic idea of ghosts. If we sleep in a strange house alone, myriad natural sounds become arousing if not frightening stimuli. We may fear that the sounds are made by ghosts, and months after we leave the house we may tell others of our personal experience with ghosts, which may reinforce the fear of the listener. Fictional movies that hint they are based on fact are powerful symbolic conditioners of such fears.

Following *"The Exorcist,"* for example, many psychiatrists reported a marked increase in the number of patients who believed they were possessed by demons.

Much the same is true of positive symbolic stimuli. The behavior of the kamikaze pilot never was challenged during his lifetime. Why? (1) The belief that his sacrifice would ensure him a place by the emperor in the afterlife could never be proved wrong. It was a one-trial learning experience. (2) during his lifetime, this symbolic belief received repeated confirmation from his peers, who congratulated him on his courage and clearly respected him for his noble intentions, even though they may not have envied his choice of death.

A male undergraduate was the subject. A young female was the experimenter. *Modeling Behavior* The male was told that he would be shown a series of 13 slides of people that were being considered for advertising campaigns. Some of the slides showed people in everyday poses, looking something like Whistler's Mother. Other slides showed pictures of naked males and females that bore scant resemblance to Whistler's Mother. In the background of each picture were a number of unrelated objects.

The undergraduate was told that he could operate a switch that would change the slides and that he could leave them on as long as he wished. The experimenter then placed a helmet over the subject's head which contained a recording camera that was specially designed to keep track of the subject's eye movements. This made it possible to determine exactly which part of the picture the subject observed and how long he spent looking at each part (Walters, Bowen, and Parke).

Sixty undergraduate males were tested on the same apparatus. What do you suppose they spent the most time looking at Whistler's Mother or naked people? And in the slides with naked people, what do you suppose they looked at the most, the nude males and females or the background? Wrong! The group was split. Roughly half of the 60 males spent more time looking at the bodies than the background, in contrast to the other half who spent comparatively more time looking at the background than at the sexually-oriented pictures.

Why? Were the two groups of males from different cultures? No. Was one group from the divinity school and the other from the psychology department? No. The males were selected at random. The only difference was in the models they had been exposed to just before the study.

All the young men had been shown an example of the type of recording that the eye-marker camera makes. A film was shown in which a dot of light, indicating the eye movements of a subject, wandered across one of the slides. For half of the males, the example showed the dot of light spending more time wandering over a naked figure than the background. The other half saw the dot of light wandering mostly over the background with relatively fewer glances at the naked figures.

When shown the 13 slides the males then had an opportunity to exercise "free will." They were not told to follow the model, yet they did. Further, the modeling effect worked only on the slides with sexual content; they did not follow the model on the neutral slides. Why? When we are in a situation that we have never before experienced and we feel anxious, we will tend to follow the lead of someone who seems to know what to do (a model). Modeling reduces our anxiety and our uncertainty.

Modeling behavior is conditioned from an early age. We learn that we must behave differently at school than at home and differently at church than at school. At the home of our friends, we learn that they follow varying rules in their daily behavior-eating, sleeping, doing chores, and the like. We learn to look for these cues without waiting for the other person to tell us how to behave.

We seek to avoid disapproval and seek approval when we "perform" for our in-laws, our boss, our "significant others." We watch others to learn how to hold our fork at the banquet; to learn what opinion we should or should not express; to learn how to obtain the primary and secondary stimuli we want. Modeling is a timesaver. If we can learn from others, then we do not have to go through the trial-and-error process of learning.

Children quickly master the cues signifying reinforcement. These cues are essential to modeling; they also are quite arbitrary. Children who grow to maturity in the rough backstreets of the Bowery are exposed to markedly different models than if they grew up as children of a well-to-do merchant or a rich philanthropist. Children of poverty may see their fellow schoolmates laugh and joke about cutting school: "What do I care about school, man. That won't put money in your pocket." They may see their friends congratulate others when they get away with stealing hubcaps or breaking street lights. "Hey man, look at the cool set of caps Harry popped right under the nose of the cop down the block." Because they see this behavior being rewarded and admired by their peers, they, too, may seek the rewards.

So, they pop hubcaps and imagine to themselves what "the guys" will think if they see what we "got away with," or they may break out street lights-all with no hope of a primary reinforcer. They do it only for the imagined effect that this will have on the mind of others. The imagined admiration of "the guys" is a symbolic reward sufficient to overcome the threat of primary punishment if caught.

In their concern about the effects of modeling, parents often go to great lengths to "set a good example." Over the centuries, parents have invented myths and modeling stories in the hope that they can motivate their children: (I) Behave, or the bogeyman will get you; (2) don't tell tales-remember what happened to the little boy who cried wolf; (3) honesty and hard work pay off, as in Horatio Alger stories of the poor boy who, through honesty, hard work, and self-sacrifice, received success and glory in the end.

Whenever his boss praised him, he broke into the biggest smile.

As the child becomes an adult, the threats and rewards change, but the themes remain the same: (1) Behave, or God will get you for it (Sodom and Gomorrah myths); (2) don't tell tales, or the law will get you for it (Watergate sagas); (3) If you work hard and sacrifice for the good of the company, you too, can have a key to the executive washroom (the "Organization Man" syndrome).

We model our behavior after others when we see that their behavior is admired.

Some admire war heroes for their bravery or patriotism. Still others admire the medical profession for their self-sacrifice for humanity. Honesty and forthrightness may be held as symbols of the highest esteem. By imitating the behavior of the models, children or adults may increase the chance that others will see them as similar to the model. Cues paired with the model become secondary reinforcers. The child strives to reproduce the cues. Thus, the child comes to identify with the model, and the model becomes a part of the child.

In summary, all human motivation appears to have its origin in the most basic of biological processes. All creatures are biologically programmed to seek pleasure and avoid pain. On a higher level, we seek stimuli that have been associated with pleasure, and we avoid those that have been associated with pain. These are the conditioned stimuli studied by Pavlov and Thorndike. But of all the animals only humans respond to stimuli that have never been paired with a biological stimulus. Only humans respond to stimuli that do not exist in nature, and only humans seem to be capable of self-reinforcing.

Symbolic stimuli acquire their power to motivate because they have been associated with other conditioned stimuli. Motivation thus involves a complex chain of associations between

(1) biological stimuli, positive and negative areas of the brain

(2) conditioned stimuli, what is associated with something positive or negative, and

(3) symbolic stimuli. Each higher order of conditioned stimuli acquires its power to reinforce behavior only because it has been associated with more basic stimuli.

Our culture has a tremendous number of rewards to motivate shoppers to spend more. We value some rewards more than others. Generally, a CASH or DISCOUNT PRICE is more likely to grab our limited attention and motivate our behavior than something as vague as REDEEMABLE POINTS.

Our military awards achievement ribbons and medals for bravery. The Boy Scouts award MERIT BADGES, and rank, not unlike the military. Bonuses may be given for years of service, even in universities, to encourage professors to stay.

This is only part of the picture of motivation. We now know something of the origin of the many reinforcing stimuli in our world. Next comes the question of control. How does the environment program behavior? Why is it that people behave so differently even when they have identical conditioned reinforcers? Why are some of us doggedly persistent at a task when others give up readily? Why is there a marked difference in the same person's motivation at different tasks?

14 PROGRAMING BEHAVIOR

SKINNER, FERSTER, FINDLY, BRADY, VEGAS, TLALOC, APPLE SUICIDES,

SWEATSHOP LABOR, SUPERSTITION

Skinner: Man and Myth •, Monkey on a Chain • Successive Approximations • Chaining • Humanity in a Cage •
Sweat Shops • Gambling • Persistence in the Face of Adversity • Society

Belief, belief. You've got to augment my belief in life or people mightily or cross it uglily. I'm awfully sure of this tonight.

Robert Frost In a note to B. F. Skinner *Selected Letters of Robert Frost*

Most of us find it remarkable that an electrode implanted in the pleasure centers of an animal's brain has such powerful control over behavior that the animal will slap a lever thousands of times an hour without stopping, literally until complete exhaustion. But this is not so remarkable. C. B. Ferster and B. F. Skinner have been able to obtain the same behavior without wires, without electrodes, with virtually no reinforcement.

With pigeons used as subjects, response rates as high as 12,000 per hour have been obtained on less food than it took to survive. They had to be fed separately to continue the experiment. Similar behavior may be produced in rats, monkeys, and people (as in sweatshop labor).

A scandal resulted for Apple computers over sweatshop workers in China in the Foxconn factory where the iPhone is produced. They were on a schedule of piece-work pay similar to what the pigeons were being given, where they were not paid enough to survive. They were treated so badly, not even allowed to go for breaks without docking their already poor pay, that girls from the company were going up to the top floor and committing suicide by jumping off.

The Apple suicides made front page headlines only briefly here. Apple was not happy.

Left; when humans are put in the same position of being unable to escape the conditions at Foxconn, some went to the top of the building and jumped off to commit suicide.

To prevent the girls from committing suicide, the company, Foxconn, in China put up nets all around their building to catch the girls if they tried to kill themselves. Hard to believe they thought that was the solution.

Above: Relatives of some of the girls at Foxconn who committed suicide protest in front of the nets, above their heads, that Foxconn put up to prevent the girls from dying by catching them when they jumped.

See the Apple suicides:

https://www.theguardian.com/technology/2017/jun/18/foxconn-life-death-forbidden-city-longhua-suicide-apple-iphone-brian-merchant-one-device-extract

Or Google, *Images* for the *Apple Suicide nets*.

HOW THE ENVIRONMENT CONTROLS OUR BEHAVIOR

More important than this, Skinner had uncovered a sequential orderliness in nature that underlies much of human and animal behavior. Skinner and his associates have discovered how such behavior is subtly and effectively programmed by our environment.

With an understanding of how the environment controls behavior came the realization that we can exercise the same control over behavior. Based on this knowledge, B. F. Skinner has called for the development of a technology of behavior that would allow us to order intelligently the controls in our environment.

Partly because of his role in the discovery of the schedules of reinforcement and partly because of his voluminous writings on the study and control of behavior, Skinner has become one of the most discussed psychologists in history.

Although most textbooks cover Reinforcement theory as a theory of leaning, it was never a theory of learning it is a theory of motivation; what motivates us to persist at a task? Skinner himself only called it a theory of behavior, not a theory of learning.

In a poll conducted at Southern Methodist University in the 1970's, today's ranking psychologists were asked to rate their own colleagues: Who are the greatest minds in the history of psychology? Of the ten names that received the highest acclaim, the only living psychologist was B. F. Skinner. A Johns Hopkins University poll of psychology faculties and graduate students reportedly found B. F. Skinner the scientist most respected by his fellows. Few have received such historical recognition in their lifetime.

Today, forty years later, Skinner is still regarded by many as a major *influential psychologist.*

https://www.verywellmind.com/most-influential-psychologists-2795264

Skinner's fame and his contribution are two different things. Even in psychology, what he is most known for are his Schedules of Reinforcement, that is, his research, which we will cover here.

Yet it was Skinner's book, *Science and Human Behavior*, that impressively showed how it was possible to make a science of psychology, simply by *observing behavior.*

Even today, we know very little about how the brain itself produces behavior. We cannot trace its wires and its connections. Our famed fMRIs and PET scans show only a grossly general picture of what is happening in what area of the brain. But psychology has learned a great deal about how the environment affects behavior, just by studying the relationship between stimuli and responses. Skinner added "sequence" and "timing" to the picture.

Day of the Zombie Performance Reviews

Skinner used food to motivate pigeons to perform. Businesses, from fast food to universities, use Performance Reviews, usually yearly, to motivate people. Unlike pigeon food, Performance Reviews cost little.

HIGH-TECH RELIES ON LOW-TECH.

Skinner's success has the makings of a legend in an era when legends are considered fantasy. His followers often revere him with a muted, detached hero worship at a time when hero worship is regarded as naive. Many see his work as having mightily augmented our belief in ourselves by showing us a method of understanding the "laws" of behavior and a means of controlling our destiny. But, his detractors have damned him for his portrait of humanity that crosses "uglily" with our belief in our freedom and dignity. No psychologist since Freud has been the target of more intense criticism. No scientist since Darwin has been less understood by the public.

Among the public, those who have heard of Skinner know him best for his books: *Walden Two,* a novel about a utopian community based on scientific principles; and *Beyond Freedom and Dignity,* a controversial criticism of our culture's sacred cow of "free will." Both books generated a fury of debate that catapulted Skinner into the public arena.

"Catchy motivational poster."

"Despite all my rage, I am still just a rat in a cage." Smashing Pumpkins

Contrary to what many think, Skinner did not advocate more control, he wanted more positive reinforcement instead of the threat we now use to motivate behavior.

Yet these books represent Skinner's philosophy, not his science. In science, no one achieves lasting recognition simply by being controversial. Recognition by one's fellow scientists is given only to those who have produced pure research, usually uncontroversial, and often dull, research that sheds light on the laws of nature that govern behavior. Let us take a look at the reasons for Skinner's recognition by his peers.

In the mid-1800s, Gregor Mendel unveiled his discoveries of the underlying order in successive generations of smooth and wrinkled peas. No one noticed. After all, who cares about the sex life of smooth and wrinkled peas? Why did Mendel waste his time on such seemingly trivial studies? Why not study people rather than peas?

Human genetics is relevant to most of us, the genetics of smooth and wrinkled peas is not. Yet if Mendel had begun with so complex an organism as the human being, it is unlikely that he would have discovered the underlying order in genetics. In the complex organism, many complicated interrelationships hide the simple effect of genetics and mask the underlying order of nature in an infinite number of different combinations.

Before we can successfully study human nature, we must understand the simpler, more basic elements of nature. From the simple beginning of Mendel's discoveries, it has been possible for others to discover the underlying order in increasingly more complex organisms. While others have tried to begin with the most complex organism and work backward to more basic processes, Skinner, like Pavlov and Thorndike before him, realized the importance of beginning with the simple. The pigeon and the albino rat have since become the traditional laboratory subjects, second only to the ubiquitous college freshman.

More than a simple subject is needed. A simple measure of the results is basic. Gregor Mendel measured smooth and wrinkled peas. From this measure, he uncovered an underlying order that would not have been apparent without systematic observation. Empedocles measured air bubbles. Pavlov measured saliva. Thorndike measured the number of trials and errors of animals in a puzzle box. Skinner measured responses.

Skinner devised a measure of the actual behavior of the animal. As the animal pressed a lever, or pecked a disk, a recording apparatus automatically counted the responses. The animal's response would also drop a food pellet into a cup. This behavior was found to vary predictably, based on how Skinner programmed the schedule of food pellets (reinforcement for behavior). This apparatus is now famous in the literature as the Skinner Box. See this example on YouTube.

https://www.youtube.com/watch?v=X-lgMnvPDQ0

Now Skinner had an ingeniously simple means of studying an isolated act of behavior. The great number of different responses may mask the underlying order of complex behavior. By separating one schedule of reinforcement from those complex interactions, Skinner was able to focus on the hidden controls of behavior

https://www.youtube.com/watch?v=ne6o-uPJarA

The Skinner box provided a measure of the effect of control on behavior. The problem now became one of varying the controls and observing the effect. One of the first controls to be varied was the partial reinforcement effect. Partial reinforcement is more effective in sustaining behavior than consistent reinforcement.

1. **PARTIAL REINFORCEMENT EFFECT**:

Try, Try Again

A rat is placed in a Skinner box. Sniffing and shuffling its way around the cage, the rat explores its new environment. By accident, the rat puts its paw on a lever projecting from the wall. Click . . . cashonk, thud . . . . a food pellet drops into the tray next to the lever. The rat eats the food and again sniffs its way around the box. A second time it stands on the lever, click . . . cashonk, thud, and it eats again. Before long the rat stops exploring and fixes attention upon the lever. A rapid series of clicks ... cashonks, and thuds follow. Each is punctuated by a brief period of silence as the rat consumes the food pellet. Every time the rat presses the lever it receives a reinforcement *R*. A series of reinforced responses *(RRRR)* is called a continuous reinforcement schedule *(CRF)*.

Imagine what would happen if the machine went out of order. Imagine that pressing the lever was only occasionally followed by *R*. Now, the rat might have to press for several nonreinforced trials NNN before it got an *R* trial. Surely learning would be less efficient on such a schedule. And this is exactly what happens. More trials are required to learn on a partial *R* schedule than on a continuous *R* schedule. But after even a brief period of training, say only a series of *NRNR-* (50 percent partial reinforcement schedule)-what would happen if the food were turned off altogether? How long will the rat persist at its lever pressing?

Remarkably, the rat that receives only one reinforcement for every four responses *NNNR* (25 percent partial) will continue to respond, without reinforcement, more persistently than one on a 50 percent partial reinforcement schedule,-that is, receiving an *R* every other trial *(NRNR)*. And both groups will continue to respond much longer into the extinction period, when no food is given, than a continuously rewarded group *(RRRR)*. So, we are left with an interesting paradox. The more inconsistent the reward, the less effective the learning. However, once the organism has learned an appropriate response, the more inconsistent the reward, the more persistent the behavior.

Most of our experience is on just such a partial reinforcement schedule.

The evolutionary advantage of such increasing persistence is apparent. When primitive people went out to hunt, sometimes their efforts paid off *(R)* and, most of the time they did not *(N)*. During some years, the game was plentiful; during others, however, long periods of famine passed in which game was scarce, and the frequent *N* trials were felt as pain in the gut. If the hunters were to survive, nature had to program it to persist in the face of great discouragement. The inconsistency of the reinforcement in training pays off during long periods of failure.

2. OPERANT CONDITIONING AND EXTINCTION

Operant or instrumental, conditioning is the type of learning studied by Thorndike and Skinner, Operant conditioning is different from the classical conditioning studied by Pavlov, at least in their sequence.

In Pavlov's Classical Conditioning the environment is operating on the individual. Like Steven Spielberg in the movie JAWS playing that deep bass just before someone gets eaten by a shark.

In Thorndike and Skinner's Operant Conditioning, the individual is operating on the environment. By Trial-and-Error learning, the individual learns what works and what does not work. It is the action of the individual that determines the outcome.

The animal must first make a *response,* before learning (conditioning) occurs. If the response is followed by a reinforcer, the response will tend to be repeated. Operant · conditioning also requires that the animal operate on its environment, while classical conditioning may occur without any participation by the animal. Both forms of conditioning are involved In most learning experiences, however.

Extinction of a response: If reinforcement no longer follows a response, the response begins to weaken; that is, it will go into extinction. Suppose that a rat has learned that every time it presses a bar in a Skinner box, food will be delivered into a food cup. We now prevent food from being delivered, and, after more attempts, eventually the rat will stop pressing the bar. Pressing is only wasted energy when.no reinforcement follows.

Skinner states that we can tell if a stimulus is a reinforcer by removing the stimulus and observing the. behavior of the animal, If the behavior goes into extinction, the stimulus was maintaining the behavior of the animal.

As an example, in the 1970's a college fad called "streaking" started across the nation. A college student would take off all of his clothes and streak naked across the campus, to be picked up by an accomplice on the other side of campus, if the other student showed up; often they did not. Why would anyone take off all his (or her?) No, you never saw women taking off their clothes, only men. Unless the women got paid well.

What could reinforce such behavior? What do you think would happen if there was no one at all on the campus?

Suppose that we removed all the students, fraternity members, friends---everyone except the streaker. Would the streaker still streak? Or would the streaker only perform for the imagined effect of this behavior on the minds of others? Or to impress their fraternity brothers?

"For another buck I'll distract the pigeons while you run."

3. *RESISTANCE TO EXTINCTION:*

If behavior is no longer followed by reinforcement the behavior will be likely to continue much longer in an animal that has received only occasional or partial reinforcement in the past, than it will in the animal that has received continuous reward.

"Behavior is shaped and maintained by its consequences."
B. F. Skinner

4. SHAPING BEHAVIOR

Shaping of behavior is continually used in our school system. We do not start by teaching quadratic equations. We must first start by teaching the 1, 2, and 3s. Then we teach addition. Next, we teach subtraction. Then division. Then multiplication. Eventually, we will have shaped the mind of a child to the point where geometry and algebra can finally be taught.

In physical therapy and speech therapy we do not begin by expecting the individual to complete the full task. We start with baby steps and gradually work up to what we want to accomplish.

Skinner's use of shaping animal behavior is quite similar. If you have ever seen an Organ Grinder's monkey, you have seen the end product of shaping, where the monkey holds a little tin cup and goes from one person to the next begging for dimes. You have not seen the beginning of the method.

To produce such behavior the owner began by rewarding the monkey consistently simply for holding the cup *(RRRR).* Then he gradually increased the amount of time the monkey must hold the cup before it was rewarded with a peanut *(R).* The increase in time represents increased *N* lengths.

The reinforcement schedule *-RRRRNRNNRNNNN-* finality reached the point that the monkey was no longer rewarded at all for holding the cup. Now it was rewarded only for presenting the cup to a donor *(RRRR).* Then the reward was given only after presentation to several *donors-RRRRNRNNNRNNNNNR-until* the reward was only rarely given.

  As a result, the animal would work for long periods of time without stopping, for peanuts. Skinner has found that animals trained on similar variable reinforcement schedules will work continually, even though they cannot earn enough food this way to sustain life, and had to be fed separately to continue the experiment.

To see an exceptional example of how one young woman used shaping to train rats to do tricks see:

https://www.youtube.com/watch?v=7g2rxtWu_FM&t=71s

https://www.youtube.com/watch?v=0jo_EG7XqZQ

Or search on youtube.com for "rat tricks".

Humans, like dogs on David Letterman's "Stupid Pet Tricks", will "act like an idiot" for nothing more than a chance to win on a reality TV show. Whether it is for a chance to win a prize, or a date on *The Batchelor*, or to be on *The Real Housewives of ....*" We do bizarre things for little or no primary profit. Often, we just want validation or our "*15 minutes of fame.*"

5. FIXED RATIO SCHEDULE:
Pay For Play-The Sweat Shop

On a fixed ratio schedule, we only get paid for how much work we do. There was a minor scandal some years ago when a rap singer was selling his P-Diddy t-shirt for $15 and it came out that these t-shirts were being manufactured in Honduras by 14-year-old girls who were being paid .15 cents for every t-shirt they produced. Even working ten hours a day, six days a week, they could not make enough money to survive.

Despite its disrepute with the labor unions, the fixed-ratio schedule is frequently used in nonunion jobs. Humans on a fixed-ration schedule of pay, getting paid for how many apples they pick, or how many products they produce, can never get ahead. They may make just enough to pay their rent but never enough to escape the "rat race".

Today, we think that that kind of treatment is horrific. Yet, in America, until the labor union movement began in the 1920's, American workers were also paid in piece work wages. The wealthy businesses could pay workers whatever they wanted. And, guess what, they did not want to pay them much, they wanted to keep all the profit for themselves. It took decades, and more than a few lives lost, to change the American situation. Does anyone really want to go back to the "good old days"?

How much work would an animal put out for an occasional reward? If it gets an *R* every third response *(FR 3)*, this is easy. But would it continue to respond if we gradually increase to 100 *(FR 100)* the number of unrewarded responses it must make? In part, the answer depends on the ache in one's gut at feeding time. A chimpanzee may be worked up to dependably pull a lever 5,000 times for a grape. Yet, it may refuse to pull a lever 5,500 times for a grape. Enough is enough.

Findley and Brady wanted to find out if applying a conditioned stimulus (noise or light) in place of the grape could increase the chimp's motivation. They paired light (a CS Like the Bell in Bell-Meat) with food early in training. Pull lever-light-food, pull lever-light-food, etc. On a rewarded trial, every time the chimp pulled the lever, the light would come on and food would follow. When the chimp pulled the lever on unrewarded *(N)* trials, no light came on and no food followed.

When the chimp would press 4,000 times for a grape *(FR 4,000)*, they then stopped giving food after every 4,000 responses and instead presented only the light. What was the result?

The chimps would work to obtain the light every 4,000 responses and kept on working even though they got nothing but the light every 4,000 responses. They did not get the grapes until after 120;000 responses. A handful of grapes after each 120,000 responses was enough to sustain a reliable *FR-120,000* schedule.

High fixed-ratio schedules produce a post-reinforcement pause after each rewarded response. The animal puts out hundreds of responses, gets a reward, and then takes a coffee break before it begins responding again. Its behavior is not unlike that of the employee who, after the vacation, just cannot seem to get going again on Monday morning.

This post-reinforcement pause produces a characteristic break in a cumulative response curve that makes it easy to distinguish this schedule from others. The cumulative response curve shows the total number of responses the animal has made at any point in training. The steep slope of the response line indicates a high rate of responding in a very short period of time.

After a number of responses pass without reward, an animal trained on a fixed ratio schedule will begin to respond increasingly more rapidly than before, as if it fears losing the golden goose.

6. VARIABLE RATIO SCHEDULES:
Las Vegas-a Skinner Box for Humans

On a variable-ratio *VR* schedule," one never knows how many responses must be made before his behavior will be rewarded. It may be that we have one successful response right after another, only to find that we might not be paid off again for several hundred responses. Ferster and Skinner worked a pigeon up to a VR-110 schedule in which the reinforcement varied, but averaged once every 110 trials.

One reinforcement might come after a previous reinforcement, the next reinforcement might not come until 57 or 128 or even 500 responses. On average, however, the reinforcement came after 110 responses, hence a *VR* 110. The pigeon never knew when its response would be paid off. Pigeons have pecked a disc at a rate of 12,000 times per hour, or between three and four pecks per second, for this random reinforcement.

Identical schedules of reinforcement govern all forms of gambling. The poker player never knows which hand will pay off. The crapshooter never knows if the throw of dice will win or lose the pot. Sometimes they have a "run of good luck" with two or more wins in a row. Sometimes they have a "losing streak" with a great many *N* trials. Most often, the payoff is somewhere between the two extremes. Such a schedule can produce very persistent behavior in the face of losses.

Skinner's Pigeons at Las Vegas

Poker games have been known to last well into the morning with each player believing the next hand could be the big win. Such behavior may not go into extinction until the players have lost more money than they ever intended to lose. After someone has lost heavily, he may increase the intensity of his gambling. The gambler may get a loan on his car or house because he has now lost so much that he "must win it back." Pigeons on variable schedules may peck intensely for days even though the amount of food they get is not sufficient to sustain life. People too, can be programmed to respond long after having passed the point of diminishing returns.

Because of the powerful effect of variable-ratio schedules, gambling has been made illegal in most states, that is until politicians discovered they could promise voters a tax break by having a State Lottery. Many parents have even attempted to counter condition their children in advance of the temptation by warning them to watch out for the "evils" of gambling. Response rates on variable-ratio schedules are high, although not as high as on fixed-ratio schedules.

Unlike the fixed-ratio schedule, which always pays off, the variable-ratio schedule pays off so unpredictably that tremendous rates of responding may be maintained over a long period of time, even when the payoff does not occur at all. Pigeons must be slowly worked up to such a schedule by gradually increasing the number of nonreinforced trials. People, being more intelligent than the pigeon, can be started with virtually no training.

Las Vegas is one enormous Skinner box for people--the ultimate human experimental psychology laboratory. The author was in Las Vegas some years ago (doing research, of course) and was struck by the sight of row after row of slot machines lined up back-to-back, with row after row of laboratory animals eagerly feeding the slot machines, pulling the lever, and watching the wheels spin.

From the nickel slots, where the payoff rate was very high, one might be seduced into working one's way up to the increasingly big money; the $0.25, $0.50, $1.00 slots, and from there to the gaming tables where the house wins big. As the amount of money goes up, the odds of winning go down. The nickel slots have mostly disappeared, as a quarter is only worth a nickel today (inflation).

Pay your money, pull the lever, and the little wheels spin and spin. Whirr... click, click, click... an orange, an orange, oops, a plum. Close. You almost got it that time. The little wheels on the machine tell you that you are getting warmer. Although every company sets its own rates, the average casino slot will let you win back three out of every four dollars you insert. Perhaps surprisingly, that allows most people to come away "feeling like winners".

Much of the reinforcement of the first few pulls is in the novelty of the spinning wheels. As the first wheel whirrs to a stop, there is a brief pause before the second stops, and a whirr until the third. The pause allows a buildup of suspense not unlike that which maintains a high rate of reading through a good suspense novel.

7. CONDITIONED STIMULI:

Flashing Lights And Sirens Are The Key

Next to every few pairs of slot machines is a flashing light. Some casinos have red lights like those on police squad cars. Some have a siren that goes off every time a player wins a mini jackpot. The flashing lights and bells act as powerful conditioned stimuli because they are paired with the payoffs, much like the light paired with food by Findley and Brady.

Yet the greatest effect of the conditioned stimuli is not on the winner, but on those who are playing nearby. The stimuli let everyone else know that someone is making money. The effect is pronounced.

It provides moral support for the other players and potential players. Their enthusiasm increases, and their response rate picks up. Again, the proof is in the performance: Casinos that use these conditioned stimuli rake in substantially larger profits than before they began using them.

The casinos make so much money from the gambling profits that everything else can be offered at seductive rates. One of the famous Vegas casinos has a special twenty-nine cent breakfast. The breakfast, like the casino's $1.00 Vodka Collins and inexpensive but top-flight entertainment, is excellent. At that casino, one day there was an elderly couple who looked as if they were on their first fling since retirement. The wife had several dollars' worth of quarters and was tenderly feeding a one-armed bandit.

She seemed determined to have her try at instant wealth. Her husband, evidently more skeptical than she, stood behind her muttering obscenities under his breath. The crowd that morning was sparse after the heavy bettors had retired. Yet in the fifteen minutes it takes to eat breakfast, four payoff alarms and flashing lights went off at scattered points throughout the casino. As the crowd got heavier, more people began to play the machines and the alarms began going off with increasing frequency, up to several times a minute.

Most of the payoffs are teasers, or handfuls, rather than jackpots. One of these mini jackpots was hit by the woman in our story. Sirens wailed, lights Hashed, players whooped and shrieked. Ten minutes later, the woman had a sackful of quarters and was energetically feeding another slot machine. Next to her stood her husband, just as enthusiastically feeding a second machine. One cannot help but think that with just a little more programing, they would be up to 12,000 pecks per hour,

Variable-ratio schedules are common in our social life. We go to parties that are sometimes fun (R) and sometimes boring (N). Our social interaction with others sometimes pays off with a stimulating conversation (R) and sometimes with little more than numbing repetition (N). Our performance on the job is sometimes noticed favorably by the boss (R) and often ignored (NNN). But the variability of R adds a spice to life. No matter how many N trials we must face, we will persist in expectation of another R tomorrow.

Such variable schedules prevent satiation of the organism too early in its history of responding-that is, a full pigeon does not respond as dependably as a hungry one. However, the availability of alternative dispensers of reinforcement may prevent the development of highly persistent responding during long periods of extinction-that is, if one pellet dispenser in a social environment fails to deliver, we can always turn to another one.

A variable-ratio schedule may yield persistent responding at very high rates, as indicated by the smooth, steep slope of the response line. The responding may be so dependable that the post reinforcement pause of the fixed ratio schedule does not develop. In extinction, the response rates may be even more persistent than in any other schedule.

8. FIXED INTERVAL SCHEDULE: The Student's Dilemma,

In strictly technical terms, getting a reinforcement becomes a discriminative stimulus that indicates that another reward is *not* forthcoming if the animal presses soon after. In a similar fashion, employees may learn that when the boss is not looking, they may safely engage in more reinforcing activities, such as grooming or gossip, without missing out on their paycheck.

So, after each feeding, the animal no longer presses. Instead, it licks its paws and fur if it is a rat, preens its tail feathers if it is a bird, or puts on makeup or reads a novel if human. The time between rewards is now taken up with something "more rewarding" than wasting energy on bar pressing.

Ferster and Skinner report that a pigeon responded over 40,000 times in an 18-hour period on an *FI* 2-min schedule. After 500 reinforcements, the response rate began to slow down, but the pigeon still kept going. Although response rates are consistent during reinforcement, the rate of responding falls off rapidly when reinforcement stops.

Does the schedule produce similar behavior in people? Imagine the following situation. Early in the semester, the professor assigned the students the first few chapters in the textbook. Bob eagerly devoured the required reading within the first week of class. Then the next few chapters were assigned and these, too, he absorbed, although it took a little longer to get around to reading them. But after the first scheduled exam, the semester began to drag on and when the next assignment came, he glanced through the chapters and then put them off to go bowling.

9. SOCIAL EXPERIENCES AS
REINFORCED (R) OR NOT (N)

Even in dating and marriage, a statement by our date early in the relationship may leave us wondering. If we have had many experiences with this person, the statement may be of no consequence. But the same statement by a stranger might leave us cold and wondering if the stranger isn't just a little peculiar. Similarly, a long period of silence in conversation is not viewed with discomfort between friends, but may be so embarrassing between two new acquaintances that one or both may feel an acute discomfort. In fact, they may be so embarrassed that they feel a need to talk about anything at all.

It has been said that marriage is the strongest test of friendship. This may be illustrated by comparing the resistance to extinction (separation) of married couples who had known each other for a long time before marriage to that of couples who marry after only a brief, whirlwind courtship. Generally, the longer the courtship, the more persistent the marriage.

One major reason for this seems to be that in longer courtships, the series of happy times *(Rs)* and conflict *(Ns)* is in better balance than in short courtships where couples tend to know each other only through a series of purely positive encounters, both partners putting their 'best foot forward."

Short courtship RRRNRRNR
Long Courtship RRRNRNNRRNNRR RRRNR
Marriage RRNNRRNNN NNRRNNR
The result should be predictable. Marriage is more like an extinction period NNNN than it is like the acquisition period of courtship. Now that the couple is married, they no longer put out quite as much effort as before. The husband lets the wife open her own doors, and rarely flatters or brings gifts. The wife rarely gives her husband the undivided, eye batting, smiling attention she gave to him when he was a suitor.

Even more to the point, now they see each other every day, morning and night, in sickness and in hair curlers, in unshaven stubble and cold cream, whereas during courtship, they had at least some time to prepare before meeting. Further, the time between meetings may have reduced the probability of conflict: The less you see of each other, the less the opportunity for conflict. Now, the number of conflicts increases. The delay and frustration become frequent.

To the couple with the short courtship, total togetherness in marriage may be all too sudden. Financial and other worries and irritating personal habits overwhelm the inadequate preparation of courtship. The marriage may begin to go into extinction.

We can speculate about how useful this knowledge of human nature might be. Could we intentionally program tolerance between individuals in the same way that such tolerance is accidentally programmed by capricious experiences? Could such tolerance programming in children be of value in reducing the frustrations of interpersonal interaction? Could we develop children with such persistence in the face of adversity that they could endure in the face of great discouragement?

Skinner was not as interested in speculating about the application of such schedules as he was in scientifically exploring how the specific schedules affect behavior. In *Schedules of Reinforcement,* Ferster and Skinner explore two basic variations of control. First, one can control the *ratio* of responses to reinforcements-that is, how many responses are made. Or one could control the interval of rewards, or how much time may pass before responding brings a reward.

10. VARIABLE INTERVAL SCHEDULES:

Fishermen, Dating, and the Rain God Tlaloc.

A Variable Interval Schedule is like a fisherman waiting for a fish to bite. He never knows how long he must wait before his behavior is reinforced. Even though this requires little actual work, it can sustain behavior for many hours, even days.

TLALOC Aztec Rain God

When the Aztecs prayed to Tlaloc the rain god to bless their crops with rain, they never knew how long they would have to wait before Tlaloc decided to perform. They might have to sacrifice more and more to appease the god before he would grant fertility to their crops and themselves. Tlaloc was fickle. After a number of responses pass without reward, an animal trained on a fixed ratio schedule will respond increasingly more rapidly than before. When our sacrifices to TLALOC fail to bring us rain, we may fear we have not sacrificed enough. So, we may sacrifice even more in hope of getting TLALOC to give us rain.

If you are waiting for a phone call from your boyfriend, you may not know how long you have to wait before he might call. If the male has been a strong reinforcer for her interest, she may wait long hours for a call. If not, she may have her roommate tell him that she is out. If the interval between her calls or dates is short, she is said to be popular, but she cannot usually increase her popularity be reverting to a male variable-ratio schedule and asking out the boys. Some say that is changing.

The "etiquette" of our culture requires that the reinforcers emitted by girls be more subtle than those of the boys. Subtle reinforcers would consist of emitting smiles, eye batting, and exclamations of "My, aren't you strong! Handsome! Helpful!" This form of variable-ratio programming is like "flirting."

The rate of responding may be lower on *VI* schedules than on other schedules, as indicated by the gradual slope of the response line. The persistence of responding across long periods of time, however, is very great. In extinction, the rate of responding is also low, but we may return to the fishing hole time and again before we give up entirely.

11. DIFFERENTIAL RATES OF RESPONDING DRH

If you differentially reinforce only increasingly faster rates of responding, it is possible to develop incredibly high rates of responding. Skinner reports that by requiring increasingly high response rates before giving out reinforcement, a pigeon can be made to respond as rapidly as ten to fifteen times per second.

Similar *DRH* schedules (differential rate high) can be found in most forms of athletic competition. In amateur sports, we have classes of competition that represent increasing levels of speed and ability, From the Little League to the Olympic Games, we reward athletes for increasingly more able performance. In the professional ranks, from the rookie ballplayer to the old pro with years of experience, value and pay are determined by speed of reaction in the game. How fast can they run? How quickly can they move around the court or skate down the ice?

At some stages, we measure the high rates of one athlete against those of others. An athlete may measure his personal high rate against his own previous top performance, but all strive to attain increasingly higher rates. If the required *DRH* cannot be attained, athletic behaviors may become extinct-that is, the athlete may go into a business that is based on a different schedule of reinforcement.

Other permutations operate as well. Most human behavior is a complex combination of these simple schedules. Car salespeople may be paid a commission on each car they sell (fixed ratio), yet they may also get a base salary every two weeks (fixed interval) to protect them against extinction during the off season for sales. In addition, they never know how long they must wait (variable interval) before a customer will come by or how many customers they must perform for (variable ratio) before their responding will pay off.

Such complex schedules tend *to* be the rule rather than the exception. Even if we work on a fixed-interval pay scale in a factory, other schedules influence our performance. We work harder when the boss is watching (fixed ratio), but we never know for sure when the boss may drop by (variable interval). We may like our job because of the variable ratio of social reinforcement we enjoy from our fellow employees. Or, as in police or emergency service, we may like it for the occasional exhilaration and excitement of the novel emergencies that occur, unpredictably, on a variable interval schedule.

Salesmen, real estate agents, and others who work on a fixed percent or commission rate may be paid only if they make a sale. The more sales, the greater the pay. If no sales are made, no pay is given. But even commission work is not a pure fixed-ratio schedule. The salespeople never know how many customers they must perform for before one will buy. Such a schedule does not work a person as hard as a pure fixed-ratio schedule does, because there is a limit to the amount of physical work that can produce results.

One of the criticisms of Skinner's work was that he talked about controlling people like we do rats. Actually, we are all controlled, even by the ideas others embed in our mind. Much of this control is in plain sight, yet we are so used to it we never notice. Skinner was talking about making control more positive, not about having more controls.

12. A TECHNOLOGY OF BEHAVIOR
Permutations of Schedules: But... But ...

In *Walden Two* and *Beyond Freedom and Dignity,* Skinner calls for improved methods of controlling behavior. He notes we all control others; if we speed, we get a ticket, if we don't work, we get fired, if our friend is mad at us, they may stop speaking to us.

Skinner's call for more effective controls has resulted in some of the most vituperative criticism yet leveled against a scientist. Much of this criticism, however, is a gut-level reaction against control. No one likes *to* be controlled. Few of us would vote for controls that would take away our freedoms. But this reaction ignores the issue. We already use control on a massive scale.

We punish our children for "bad" behavior, and we often do it capriciously and without understanding the long-term consequences. We pass laws requiring compulsory attendance at school. We control the behavior of students with our schedules of testing and grades. We control the behavior of each other with our dispensing of social reinforcers, often at a petty and irrational level.

Control already exists. And in many cases, it is far from subtle, although we are so used to control that we barely notice it exists. Parents may control children by the obvious technique of spanking or withholding privileges. Or we may punish one another by the "silent treatment", the sulking of the "wounded ego" or the outrage of moral indignation. "How could you?" But are we really aware of the effect of such punishment?

Suppose that a six-year-old is told not to play with a ball inside the house. Yet while the parents are away, the child disobeys the order and ends up breaking a window. When the parents come home the deed is discovered. "Did you play with the ball after I told you not to?" A parent scolds.

What does the child say? Does the child admit that he/she did? And if so, what happens". Do the parents punish the child now? To the parents, they are punishing the child for disobeying. Yet the child may not see things that way, they may see that they are being punished for telling the truth.

Punishing someone for telling the truth may seem irrational. Yet it happens often. And it is hardly limited to the discipline of a child. Suppose that a politician takes a position on something we feel strongly about? Do we punish them by voting for someone else? And what if someone else is just lying to get your vote?

Skinner was not suggesting more control, he was suggesting that we apply scientific principles to our existing controls—that we improve our technology of conditioning so that we may eliminate the problems that result from the capricious and irrational controls we now use. In theory, such improved control, and our awareness of the consequences of that control, could improve child-rearing, business-labor relations, and even interpersonal relations.

"Who's just happy to be employed?!"

ORIGIN OF THE INDIVIDUAL
THE PSYCHOLOGY OF PERSONALITY
AND CHILD PSYCHOLOGY

Why do people behave irrationally? Are there "unconscious" processes within us that determine our behavior? And what about our "self," the part of us that is conscious and aware? How does our self-concept come into being?

From the experimental studies of psychology, we move into an area that involves more observation than experimentation. It is also a somewhat more speculative area but one that is often more directly applicable to our everyday experiences.

Our use of ego-defense mechanisms, for example, has been widely studied by Freudian, behavioral, and humanistic psychologists. Chapter 16 deals with the origin of our self, which many psychologists consider crucial to our understanding of human behavior.

Why are children fearless or aggressive, shy or passive? What is there in the genes of a child or in the early formative experiences of a child that could produce a genius? What is the source of our individual differences?

Our discussions of child psychology begin with the important questions of the nature of the biological and social influences that determine the temperament of the individual.

Chapter 18 addresses the question of how two children growing up in the "same" environment can develop markedly different beliefs, goals, and aspirations. Finally comes adolescence and the problems associated with sexual adjustment. In no other subject is the effect of social conditioning as apparent as in the once-taboo area of sexual behavior.

Chapter 16 • Probing the Unconscious: ego-defense mechanisms

Chapter 17 • Personality and Temperament:

the biological and social basis of individuality

Chapter 18 • The Environment of the Child: as the twig is bent

Chapter 19 * Love, Sex, and Society

16 PROBING THE UNCONSCIOUS

Unconscious Processes • Ego Defenses • Repression • Denial of Reality • Displacement • Projection • Reaction Formation • Rationalization • Emotional Insulation • Confession and Atonement • Internalization

I'm sure I have a noble mind, with honesty and tact
And no one's more surprised than I, To see the way I act
Rebecca McCann
Complete Cheerful Cherub

It may long be debated in scientific circles whether we are capable of the average person's concept of "free will." But one thing seems certain: So long as we are unaware of how our motives are conditioned by our society, so long as we are unaware of how our behavior is controlled by others in our environment, so long as we are unaware of the distortion of reality that is a product of our own mind, we can never be "free", we can never exercise intelligent control over our own behavior.

Only with an awareness of the effect of these controls, only with an awareness of our own marked propensity for self-delusion, can we hope to free ourselves from an existence dominated by our learned responses and seek to selectively control our own destiny.

Throughout our history, we have been inclined to invent myths, more to glorify our accomplishments than to acknowledge our failures, more to magnify our rationality than to study our irrationality, and to emphasize our virtue over our vanity. We tell our children stories about how hard work always brings success, of the importance of rational thought, of how virtue always triumphs and the good guys win in the end.

Yet, failure, irrationality, and the bad guys winning occur far more frequently in our history than accomplishment, rationality, and virtue. At the turn of the century, the Viennese physician Sigmund Freud became one of the first to attempt a serious study of the dark, irrational side of our nature. By concentrating on our mistakes, our vanity, our irrationality, Freud began to uncover what he called the "unconscious" nature of our mind. Freud discovered that we are largely unaware of why we behave as we do, and that there are processes that occur within our minds that selectively distort reality.

Freud's concepts are not always accepted by psychology today. But of all of Freud's ideas, the ones that have stood the test of time are his ideas of Ego Defense Mechanisms. Behaviorists John Dollard and Neal Miller reinterpreted his defense mechanisms in terms of learning theory. Humanist psychologists Carl Rogers and Abe Maslow used the Ego Defense mechanisms as a step we must go through on our way to Self-Actualization in Maslow's Hierarchy of Needs.

EGO DEFENSE MECHANISMS

1. DENIAL OF REALITY

Avoiding the unpleasant may temporarily reduce our feelings of anxiety

Anna Freud, Freud's daughter and also a psychoanalyst, wrote the book on defense mechanisms. She noted the tendency in our culture to avoid or deny the unpleasant in what we tell our children.

There is a "Peanuts" cartoon by Charles Schultz in which Linus explains to Charlie Brown his personal philosophy for coping with overwhelming problems. Linus says, in effect, that he has found that no problem is so big or so complex that one can't run away from it.

Denial of reality involves "running away" from something on a cerebral level, or distorting something to make it seem more pleasant than it is. This process is similar to repression in many respects. For example, the thought that our own death is inevitable must surely occupy everyone's mind at one time or another. Yet to really consider the uncertainties of life is a frightening thing. Most of us accept uncertainties and inevitability on a cold, intellectual level, but few of us really seem capable of conceiving of a world going on without us. Death is still a traumatic question. And when om· children ask their innocent questions after the death of a pet or grandparent, we often grab at straws for our answers. We may tell them that the departed has "gone to sleep" or has gone away for a long time to some vague place.

The origin of our tendency to deny reality is aptly described by Anna Freud:

> It is a curious thing that adults are so ready to make use of this very mechanism in their intercourse with children. Much of the pleasure which they give to children is derived from this kind of denial of reality. It is quite a common thing to tell even a small child "what a big boy" he is and to declare, contrary to obvious facts, that he is as strong "as Father," as clever "as Mother," as brave "as a soldier" or as "tough" as his "big brother." It is more natural that, when people want to comfort a child, they resort to these reversals of the real facts. The grown-ups assure him, when he has hurt himself, that he is "better now" or that some food which he loathes "isn't a bit nasty" or, when he is distressed because someone has gone away, we tell him that he or she will be "back soon. "

Anna Freud's comments bring back to the author vivid childhood memories of shots of penicillin, tetanus vaccine, polio vaccine, and whatever else happened to be available. The nurses must have had a "Nurse's Manual of Standard Usages," because many of them would jab needles into arms as if they were jabbing practice grapefruits and follow up the shot with, "There now, that didn't hurt, did it?" Has anyone ever been convinced? Nonetheless, children never contradict the adult's statement. They accept this discrepancy between verbal reality (words) and physical reality (pain) without even thinking to question it.

It is easy to find similar examples on a cultural level of our culture's acceptance of verbal statements that conflict grossly with physical reality; of how we can have verbal ideals of justice and equality for all, yet fight for almost 200 years to prevent minority groups from being educated with our children; of how we can express the verbal ideals of "love thine enemy" and "Do unto others ." yet fail to accord common decency to those who are strangers, or who are not of our faith or politics or opinion.

Denial of reality may prevent us from seeing the unpleasant in those we love.

Parents of teenagers are fond of quoting the old adage "Love is blind" when their children become strongly attracted to someone whose faults are "obvious" to the parents yet so blithely ignored by a son or daughter. The same parents, on the other hand, are often blind to the faults of their own flesh: They may ignore behavior in their own child that they would find outrageous in someone else's child.

The situations we have discussed involve only a mild amount of anxiety. What about the person in a situation where his or her life were about to end and nothing could be done about it? Just such a situation developed during the riot at New York's Attica prison in 1971. Prisoners overcame the guards, took their guns, and liberated a large percentage of the inmates. Other guards sealed off the prison from the outside. Using the captured guards as hostages, the prisoners forced a standoff. Tense hours passed as the prisoners, their rioting uncontrolled, tore through the prison, ripping apart furniture, burning mattresses, and terrorizing the captured guards.

Hours passed into days as the prison administration threatened to storm the prison and the prisoners threatened to kill the guards; demands were made on both sides, compromise failed, hot words were exchanged. Finally, a decision came from the governor to storm the prison. In the moments that followed, ten guards and twenty-nine prisoners were killed. It was later determined that the guards had died from a fusillade of bullets fired by their fellow guards and state troopers trying to rescue them.

One of the surviving guards later described for the news media his experiences as a captive. For days, he recalled, the inmates had threatened him with knives and heaped abuse on him. Some of the more hardened prisoners described to him in vivid detail how he would die if the police attacked. Bound and helpless, he could only accept their abuse. What did he feel as the minutes ticked by? Was he frightened? Remarkably, the guard described not fear, but resignation. He said that throughout his ordeal it seemed as if he were sitting back and observing, in a detached fashion, a situation unfolding on television, A feeling of unreality that this really isn't happening, -is a common reaction to a frightening situation when an individual is unable to change the situation.

Psychologists who examined the concentration camp prisoners of Hitler's Germany after World War II found that prisoner after prisoner described the experience in much the same terms. Uprooted from their homes without warning, herded into crowded cattle cars, the prisoners were shipped to concentration camps in massive numbers.

Paul Chodoff describes the reaction of one of his patients who survived the ordeal: Feelings of disbelief at what was happening to them were common. At the camps they were stripped naked, deloused, their bodies shaved of hair, and finally crowded into barracks to await the daily decisions on who would be the next to die. The elderly and ill were the first to meet the gas chambers.

> *It appears that the most important defenses among concentration camp inmates were denial and isolation of affect. As might be expected in the case of this probably most ubiquitous of all defenses there was widespread employment of denial as manifested by my patient who would not see the corpses she was stepping over, and by the poignant picture of her fellow inmates who refused to believe that the smoke arising from the crematorium chimneys came from the burning corpses of their mothers.*

> *Isolation of affect, which could be so extreme as to involve a kind of emotional anesthesia, seemed to have functioned particularly to protect the ego against the dangers associated with the feelings of hostility toward an external object which treats the self as if it were an inordinate object and not a person. My patient who says, "It didn't bother me. I had no feelings whatsoever," when being shaved while naked in front of SS troops, was certainly isolating her affect from her cognition.*

Thus, there seem to be two aspects of denial of reality: (1) conflicting learned behavior patterns, as when we learn to believe in a concept of brotherly love, yet practice patterns of behavior that are just the opposite, without ever thinking to question the discrepancy between the two reactions; and (2) emotional insulation, as when our experiences are terrifying, but because we cannot do anything to escape the situation, we repress the anxiety-producing stimuli. This amounts *to* fatalistic resignation, but in such cases, the reaction of denial may be very adaptive for the individual.

2. DISPLACEMENT

Involves a shift of emotion from an unacceptable object to a more acceptable object. The most frequently used example involves a man who is berated by his boss for something that happened at work. The man cannot talk back to his boss without risking being fired. So he bottles up his resentment, he swallows his pride, and he keeps his hostility inside, until, until he can find someone who cannot fight back on whom to displace his hostility. When he gets home, he may yell at his wife over a trivial incident. His wife can't fire him or beat him up, so his aggression is "safely" displaced. The wife, so the story goes, then displaces her hostility onto the children, who kick the dog, who chases the cat, who claws the rat, who eats the cockroach.

Two of the nation's leading primatologists, Sherwood Washburn and Irven DeVore, recently took their cameras to Africa to capture the obscure mating habits of the Chacma baboon. In their movie *Baboon* Behavior, they filmed a convincing demonstration of how basic the mechanism of displacement is, even to our primate relatives. To test the hierarchy of dominance within the troop, they tossed tidbits of food to the baboons.

The most dominant males grabbed the treats for themselves and chased off the lower ranking males. One of the less dominant males made repeated attempts to grab some of the tidbits for himself. Two of the dominant males ganged up on him and chased him ignominiously from the field. Frustrated and full of rage, the defeated baboon could not attack the source of his frustration without getting severely mauled. Nearby, a small female baboon was quietly munching leaves and paying no particular attention to the fracas. Without warning the disgruntled male baboon attacked her. She ducked, dodged left, right, raced across the field, and scampered up a tree, all the while without the slightest hint as to what had brought this wrath down on her.

The learning concepts of discrimination and stimulus generalization play a role in determining the object on which the aggression is displaced. The male baboon did not displace his aggression onto a tree or rock, he displaced it onto another baboon. The smaller female baboon was the most acceptable substitute, she couldn't fight back, a discriminative cue. And she was an object most similar, stimulus generalization, to the source of the original frustration.

Our democracy began as an attempt to go past the "might makes right" of human history and give everyone an equal chance at life.

Do humans really engage in this type of behavior? How often have you seen someone skin his or her shins on some inanimate object and then curse or kick that object? Why do we blame the object rather than ourselves? How many parents have tripped over a child's toy and then displaced their rage onto the toy or even the child? Would we react the same way in our boss' house if we tripped on his child's toy? Or would we suppress our rage and seek to excuse this mishap as "my fault" or "kids will be kids"?

Counterconditioning may change our reaction. If we are counter conditioned with the idea that kicking an object we have tripped over is "silly" or "immature," then we may avoid this behavior-at least when anyone is watching. Motivation is also a factor. We may inhibit our aggression easily so long as the levels of frustration are low and readily dealt with, yet we may "let it all hang out" after a prolonged period of such frustration.

Not everyone learns to displace his aggression to the same object. One man may displace his frustration onto his wife, if she has served as an accepting stimulus in the past. In contrast, another man may have learned that if he takes it out on his wife, she may give him more hell in return than he bargained for. Still a third man may have found his wife to have been a source of comfort and understanding in the past, confiding his troubles *to* her rather than being aggressive. For some parents, the children may become the object of displacement for their frustration. And when children get older, they may use the parents as objects of their hostility when they are hurt or frustrated by their peer group.

As with all ego-defense mechanisms, sometimes we are unaware of why we snap at the innocent comments of others when we are frustrated. Other times we may realize what we are doing, yet react reflexively with an uncontrolled burst of temper. And sometimes we are fully aware of what we are doing, yet continue to do so anyway.

Displacement of positive emotions may also occur. A lover who is frustrated by being dropped in an intense love affair may react by marrying "the first thing that came along." This love affair on the "rebound" may have been "set up" by the emotional frustration of the first rejection. It is difficult to avoid drawing an analogy between this reaction and a well-known phenomenon in laboratory animals. A hungry rat may be trained to run down an alley runway to food at the end of the runway. After many trials, it settles on a given speed of running, which can be measured with photoelectric relays placed along the runway.

But what happens if we suddenly remove the food the rat has been getting? We now have a hungry rat that no longer gets the food it has come to expect. If this frustration continues over a number of trials, like a frustrated lover with continued frustrations in love, the rat would eventually give up and the response would reach extinction. On the first trial after the rat's discovery that the food is gone, however, an interesting thing happens: It runs even faster to the empty food box, as though its frustration had temporarily spurred it to greater effort.

Sometimes frustrated goals are channeled into more socially acceptable goals.

The natural sexual curiosity of teenagers may be frustrated by social attitudes or by their own lack of experience. Teenagers might fear expressing such curiosity openly so they may sublimate their curiosity by taking up painting, sculpturing, or photography, where nudity is considered an acceptable art form. What originally began as a sublimation of their sexual curiosity may turn their energy into a creative and satisfying hobby or even a profession. Of course, not all school teachers, artists, or photographers began this way, but it may well be more common than they might admit.

3. PROJECTION: He Did It, It's His Fault, He Did It …

"There's not enough blame to go around … there's only enough for you."

At a very early age we learn that if our unacceptable behavior is at least partly the fault of someone else, then we are not as much to blame. If we are not so much to blame, then our anxiety over our unacceptable behavior is lessened. Parents will punish a child more severely if the child's destructive behavior is aggressive or intentional than if the same results were to occur through an unavoidable accident. Thus, it is hardly surprising that two boys interrupted in the midst of a knockdown, drag-out fight will protest:

"He started it!"

Projection serves to reduce our own anxiety by (1) attributing socially unacceptable motives to others that are actually our own; and (2) shifting the blame for our own mistakes and shortcomings to others. We learn to relieve our own anxiety or guilt by projecting the cause of that anxiety on another person. We can always find a "reason" for disliking another person: "He deserves it!" -that is, "He started it!"

We see this repeatedly in our politics, where one political party accuses the other party of doing exactly the same things that they are doing; as in accusing one party of stealing the election when that is what your own party is trying to do.

Of course, it is sometimes true that an incident *is* entirely the fault of one person: A bully may pick on a boy and start a fight. This fact itself provides good rationale for a belief that we are always right and others are wrong. But the history of conflict, whether a trivial domestic argument or an international conflagration, clearly shows that projection is the rule, whether it is warranted or not.

If we feel anxiety over our own poor performance, there is often a reflexive tendency to project the guilt to others. In effect, "I'm good; it's her fault that I look bad." We reduce our anxiety by blaming others for our own mistakes-the underlying, unstated feeling being: "Hit is her fault, I can't be held to blame."

Sometimes we reduce our anxiety over our own feelings of inferiority by actively looking for anything at all to criticize in the behavior or ideas of others. We may find faults in others that we easily ignore in ourselves. To admit one's own shortcomings is to face an anxiety-producing stimulus; such an admission drops us a notch, in our own estimation, on our internalized social yardstick. So we may avoid thinking of the mistake or shortcoming as our own fault, and project the blame to another.

We may also avoid the anxiety over our own shortcomings by projecting shortcomings to others. A young woman who feels insecure about her attractiveness to men might intentionally damage the reputation of another young woman by saying, "Of course she has a lot of dates; I wonder what she does to get them?" The unstated implication being: "She is popular because she is doing something I certainly wouldn't do. But if I did, I would be popular too."

By cutting down the other girl, she avoids the feelings of anxiety over her own status, and probably even allows herself some feeling of superiority. We may thus seek to reduce our own feelings of inferiority by making the accomplishments of others look less honorable.

Projecting unacceptable motives to others may reduce our own anxiety over the feeling that we are to blame for our failures.

4. RATIONALIZATION: Always a "Good" Reason

In the Hollywood movie *John Wick,* John Wick kills 36 men to get to kill the man who killed his puppy. Why? Because they "KILLED HIS PUPPY!" At least he had a "good" reason. What is remarkable is how few people who watch this movie even consider that this is not a good reason, it is a rationalization; Hollywood has been able to get away with this kind of rationalization for generations.

Rationalization involves thinking up logical, socially acceptable reasons for our behavior or beliefs. When we are unable or unwilling to see the underlying reason for something that has happened, we may invent a reason that sounds more logical, more noble, or more rational than the actual reason.

If someone questions the motive for our behavior or beliefs, "Why did you do...?" or, "Why do you believe ..." and we are unable to consciously explain, we may react guiltily by saying, "Why? Why just *because,* that's why!" Such a reaction suggests the "unconscious" nature of our motives. We may not know "why."

But rationalization is even more subtle. Instead of emitting a vacuous "because ...," we instead insert a reason that sounds so rational that we are firmly convinced it is the "true" reason. Precisely because our rationalization sounds so much more convincing than "just because," we may be unable to see our actual motives.

How many parents have been uptight, angry, or "on edge" and then reacted to some minor transgression of their children by punishing them? How many then rationalize their overreaction by saying, "They have to learn to behave," or "I did it for their own good," rather than admitting that the punishment amounted to a displacement of parental anger?

When hurt by a criticism from someone we respect, we may "punish" our critic with the "silent treatment" or by saying something to hurt his or her feelings. We may then rationalize our behavior by thinking, in effect, "He deserved it." Are we likely to admit, even to ourselves, that the only reason we "punished" the person was that we reacted to our own hurt by lashing out to hurt the other person in return? When our motives are socially unacceptable, we often cannot admit them even to ourselves.

Rationalization may also be a means of reducing the impact of our failure. Over two thousand years ago, a Greek storyteller named Aesop wrote an allegory that has proven to be one of the more memorable of what we now call Aesop's fables. In the story, a fox spies some luscious grapes hanging from a vine. Time and time again he leaps, trying to grab the grapes, but time and again he fails. Finally, the fox gives up. Walking away from the prize, he muses to himself, in effect, "Oh, they were probably sour anyway!" This common ego-defense mechanism is called "sour-grapes" rationalization.

Imagine two people in competition for the same thing-for example, a promotion. Only one of the two competitors will succeed in obtaining the desired goal. What about the one who fails-who loses out? That person may well be expected to feel some degree of ego deflation. To be turned down is a slur on one's personal ability.

It is as if "the boss" were saying that only one of the contenders measures up. The person who was not promoted may ease his or her feelings of anxiety by rationalizing that the promotion really is not worth the extra worries and responsibility, or even that it may be better not to have gotten the promotion.

Another excuse may be that the boss is simply unable to recognize superior abilities, instead promoting someone without them. If these rationalizations are not sufficient, an individual may resort to the ultimate in "sour grapes": the suggestion that the other person did not win the promotion in an honorable fashion but obtained it by buttering up the boss, greasing the skids with fine words, or accumulating some imagined wealth of brownie points.

All these forms of "sour grapes" are common. With very little effort we should be able to recognize in ourselves just such rationalizations over our own failures. Of course, sometimes people *are* promoted for the wrong reasons, passing up persons of greater ability. That it does happen gives us a "justification" for feeling that our rationalization is correct.

One does not have to be a personnel director, however, to notice that in most cases, if any two people are in competition for the same goal, the one who fails to obtain it, regardless of which of the two fails, will tend to find a justification for the failure that will reduce his or her feelings of inadequacy. A smart personnel director may go out of the way to provide both with a softening rationale for the choice even before the choice is made and thus may prevent or reduce bitter feelings within the company.

Many of us have been conditioned since early youth not to use the "sour grapes" reaction. And if we feel uncomfortable when searching for excuses, we may *suppress* any tendency to use this mechanism. If we have never learned to use this anxiety reducer, we may not even relate it to our behavior. But those who feel they never use the "sour grapes" mechanism can usually be caught using the "sweet lemon" rationalization. For an example, imagine that someone is thinking about buying a new car. Suppose that he is relatively poor.

Suppose that he has some difficulty making ends meet on his present salary. If he decides that he cannot afford the payments, he may rationalize that the "old klunker" really gets him where he wants to go and that by keeping it in good repair, he can easily save money he would otherwise blow on the fast depreciation of a new car. He really has a "sweet lemon."

On the other hand, what would he think if he went ahead and bought the new car in spite of his financial worries? Would he not then think, "Well, if I had kept the 'old klunker' I would be out so many repair bills that I had just as well be making monthly payments. And a new car is less likely to break down when I need it most." So the heavy monthly payments become a "sweet lemon" because they give him a "dependable car" and "no repair bills."

In each case, we rationalize our choice by saying, in effect, "It's all for the better anyway," Since we now believe we have done the "right thing," we no longer worry over our choice.

Never underestimate the power of a "sweet lemon." For hundreds of years, our philosophies have been dominated by this logic. We can endure any hardship so long as we can believe "it will all turn out for the best in the end." We can suffer any misfortune if we believe that "every cloud has a silver lining." And centuries of oppression have been easier to bear when we believe that "God has willed it," the implication being that God will eventually reward us for our submission or suffering, and that all our distress has a purpose.

The "sour grapes" rationalization can be seen in our reaction to the simplest forms of failure. If a baseball player, golfer, tennis pro, etc., swings at an easy shot and misses, he may suddenly stop and intently examine his instrument, as if expecting to find it hinged in the middle. Or, he may glare at a "too bright" sun that spoiled his aim, brush the hair out of his face, grimace at the wind, and rub his eyes as if to say, "If it hadn't been for the ... sun, hair, wind, that speck of dust, etc., I would have made that shot."

We learn at an early age that there are reasons (extenuating circumstances) that sometimes account for our failures. Having a reason reduces our anxiety over our personal inadequacy. A few of these reasons may be valid. So, we may generalize from a few situations to a great many situations.

The origin of the "sweet lemon" rationalization may be more closely related to what B. F. Skinner calls "superstitious reinforcement." From past experience, we learn that when we feel very depressed or worried, something good often may follow this period of trauma. By the laws of chance this occurs with some frequency. (There is roughly a 50 /50 chance that something good will follow something bad.) It is only a short step from this to the learning set of: "Everything turns out for the best," which we may then generalize to a great many other situations.

Making up a rational excuse and also projecting the blame protects our ego from feelings of failure.

5. REACTION FORMATION I Love You, I Hate You

When we react with an emotion that is the opposite of what we "really feel," we are engaging in a paradoxical behavioral reaction called a *reaction formation.* A young man or woman may be strongly attracted to someone of the opposite sex, but past experiences with subtle cues in similar situations may have led him/her to fear rejection. If the fear of rejection is strong, they may act in a haughty and disinterested manner when out on a date. In this case her action, contrary to what they really feel, is a way of saying, "You probably won't like me anyway; well, just see if I care!"

We saw this come from the world of politics in the election of 2020. Those who most tried to steal the election for Donald Trump were the ones most vocal in accusing the other side of "stealing the election".

A well-known line from Shakespeare is, "Methinks the lady doth protest too much." A reaction formation may often be recognized by the extreme form of protest it takes.

Examples of conscious reaction formation are more apparent than examples on an unconscious level. Psychologists who have tested males and females for pain threshold tolerance have long known that males do not report that increasing levels of shock intensity are "painful" until the level of shock goes far beyond the level that females report as "painful." Why? Are males biologically more resistant to pain than females? Not necessarily. It is not uncommon to see a male flinch at a high shock level and then report through gritted teeth, "No, that's not painful at all."

This effect is increased markedly if the male is being shocked by an attractive female experimenter of about the same age. In our culture, males are conditioned from an early age to believe that "boys don't cry; that's sissy stuff." And when we feel that others would think less of us (anxiety-producing thought) then we may reduce that anxiety by going to the opposite extreme,

Sometimes fears of homosexuality tend to be ingrained in us by our culture. In a recent news program, a camera news team was covering a gay liberation parade as it marched flamboyantly down the major streets of a large California city. After filming the parade, the news crew began sampling the reactions of the pedestrians on the sidewalk who had paused to look at the parade. Almost everyone had a comment to make; some good, some bad. Finally, the cameras were turned on one startled construction worker who had paused to watch. "Huh!" he exclaimed, throwing his hand up in front of his face, "I'm just a spectator, I'm just a spectator!" And he hurriedly melted back into the crowd.

We often tell others something that is just the opposite of what we really feel: "Oh, darling, I just love your dress (that I can't afford), hairdo (that looks better than mine), facelift (that makes you look younger than me), new baby (that looks just like my husband), etc. Well, I'm glad to hear about your raise (that I didn't get), promotion (that I wasn't considered for), new book (that I could have written better), etc." Sometimes we may bask in a feeling of personal glory over our self-sacrificing altruism: "Well, I just couldn't hurt his feelings by telling him what I really thought." Of course, it is often very good diplomacy to avoid telling others what we "really think." But are we doing so in deference to the feelings of others?

Or are we doing so to avoid making an enemy, being disliked, or being thought insensitive or jealous?

Modesty is often a reaction formation. If someone flatters our ego and tells us how attractive we are, we may bask in the praise. Yet we often react by insisting that we really aren't "that" attractive, or competent, or intelligent. We condition our children to avoid bragging and showing off. So, if one feels guilt at being told he is better than average, he may overreact in the opposite direction, even to the extent of pointing out some of his own minor Haws. Unconsciously, he may be saying, "I'm not only good looking (or intelligent or competent), I'm also modest about it."

6. EMOTIONAL INSULATION: I Expected as Much ...

At an early age we learn that our highest aspirations are not always realized. We learn that if we expect too much we may be severely disappointed. To avoid the anxiety of disappointment we learn to "insulate" ourselves from possible hurt. A student who takes an exam and is really unsure of how he did may react by saying "Oh, man I really blew it!"

When he gets the exam back, he may find that he really did "blow it." If so, the hurt is not as great as if he had not been prepared for it. More likely, he will find that he did better on the exam than the worst he had feared. The relationship of this mechanism to the "elation-depression effect" discussed in the chapter on Learning is apparent.

By expecting to do worse than we really expect to do, we can insulate ourselves against the possibility that, as sometimes happens, our "worst possible" expectancy may come true. It is interesting to find that the better students, those who often worry the most about grades, seem to make use of this mechanism more often than other students. Much of the time, the worst we fear is not as bad as the actual outcome.

7. CONFESSION AND ATONEMENT: I Did It, I'm Sorry ... Have Some Candy...

Confession is the opposite of the mechanism of projection. Confessing one's guilt, instead of blaming it on someone else, can reduce anxiety. It might seem inconsistent to expect confession of guilt to reduce anxiety, but this is often the case. If we are conditioned to believe that blaming something on someone else is "cowardly" and "despicable" (negative conditioning) and that "owning up" and admitting one's faults or guilt is the "only honorable way" (positive conditioning), then we may seek to confess rather than hide our faults. In our culture, we actively seek to inculcate just such reactions in our children.

If little Jimmy pulls sister Suzie's hair, then mother may punish little Jimmy. As often as not, the "punishment" consists of making Jimmy apologize to his sister. Jimmy may well feel embarrassed at the indignity of asking forgiveness, but mother stands over him and "psychologically' twists his arm until he does. After his confession of guilt, mother may give him an assurance of forgiveness, or at least stop twisting his arm. The act of apologizing relieves his anxiety and thus may become a means of escaping guilt in other situations.

Religions frequently use the confessional and penance as a means of atoning for one's guilt. Freely confessing one's shortcomings, with the accompanying assurance of forgiveness, relieves one of anxiety. In fact, Freud himself made use of a similar mechanism as the basis for the techniques of psychoanalysis. Freud encouraged his patients to "free associate" and talk about anything that came to mind. Eventually, the patients would hit on the underlying "cause" of the anxiety.

Simply talking about the anxiety producing worries seemed to give his patients relief. This "talking cure," as one of Freud's patients called it, came to be the primary technique of psychoanalysis. More recently, behavioral psychologists have used this with a somewhat different twist. By talking about our worries, by getting them out in the open, stimulus desensitization or counterconditioning can occur. These fears, once faced, can then be counter conditioned.

As the child grows up in a society or family, the child internalizes (takes on) the values of the group. In taking on these values he learns to avoid behavior that would result in punishment and to emit behavior that would result in approval. The child may even take on aspects of the parents' personalities. Sometimes this internalization may serve to reduce anxiety. For example, a daughter who intensely dislikes the quick temper of her father may display this disliked quality in her own personality. It may be that the father represented a frightening figure to the daughter during her childhood. To reduce anxiety, such children may become like the father, as if to say: "If I am like you, then you cannot dislike me." Or, put another way, "If I am like you, then you will like me."

8. INTERNALIZATION: If I Am Like You, You Must Like Me.

In more extreme circumstances, anxiety about acceptance may lead one to adopt attitudes and behavior that we otherwise would not adopt. Studies of people caught up in lynch mobs provide an example. What we saw in the behavior of the attack on Congress on January 6, is another. One such subject described his feelings after the incident. As he walked down the street, he was suddenly caught up in a group of people who were screaming that the election was stolen. He knew nothing of the incident or the people involved, but as the temper of the crowd became increasingly hostile, he found himself yelling out the same slogans as the crowd.

In part, he was caught up in the emotion of the moment, but he may also began to fear that if the crowd thought he was not in sympathy with their cause, they might turn their wrath on him. Although he would probably not have been harmed by staying silent, he nonetheless internalized the motives and emotions of the crowd to avoid any feeling of anxiety. The feeling that "If I am like them, they will not dislike me" seems to be a major element in mob psychology.

Perhaps the most common form of internalization, and certainly the most frightening, is its use as a technique in ideological or religious conversion. This technique of conversion was widely practiced during the cultural revolution in Red China in the early 1970s. Thousands of people were accused of being reactionaries or of being anti-Mao. In the months that followed, such people were first terrorized by the rampaging Red Guard; students deeply ingrained in Maoist thought, who subjected them to great indignities. In the inquisition that followed, the accused were forced to sign confessions admitting the error of their ways. Finally, they were given an opportunity to recant and denounce their anti-Maoist feeling and accept the "true" Maoist doctrine. Even without the ritual confession and psychological abuse, most of them did so willingly, even eagerly. The dissidents not only came to sing the praise of Chairman Mao, they seemed to come to believe it.

People have often internalized the values and emotions of a lynch mob, even though they knew nothing about the crime of the accused.

9. INTERNALIZING RELIGIOUS AND POLITICAL VALUES

People may internalize the values and beliefs of another in an attempt to reduce their own anxiety. This technique has been used throughout history by politicians and preachers to convert people to their beliefs. The technique involves several steps. The first of these is to implant a feeling of fear in the mind of the individual. Try to imagine the effect of the following sermon from the Puritan preacher Jonathan Edwards on the minds of children and adults in a more superstitious era of our culture:

> *The God that holds you over the pit of hell, much as one holds a spider or some loathsome insect over the fire, abhors you, and is dreadfully provoked; His wrath towards you burns like fire; He looks upon you as worthy of nothing else, but to be cast into the fire ....*

> *If we knew that there was one person, and but one, in the whole congregation, that was to be the subject of this misery, what an awful thing it would be to think of! If we knew who it was, what an awful sight would it be to see such a person. How much all the rest of the congregation might lift up a lamentable and bitter cry over him! But alas! instead of one, how many is it likely will remember this discourse in hell! And it would be a wonder, if some that are now present should not be in hell in a very short time, before this year is out.*

> Jonathan Edwards, *Sinners in the Hands of an Angry God,* 1809

After the fear of their future has been implanted in the minds of the children, the remaining steps were relatively simple. They would be told that they could avoid this horrible fate if only they believe in A, B; and C, or behave in manner X, Y, and Z. More often than not, such tactics have been effective in producing conversions, especially when such conditioning begins in childhood.

But it is not necessary to begin with the mind of a child to produce such an effect. Politics is rich with examples.

Adolph Hitler effectively used such tactics. By portraying all people who were Jewish or communist as horrible criminals, Hitler painted a terrifying picture to the German people of what would happen to law, order, and decency if something were not done to correct the problem.

As Chancellor of Germany, Hitler did not officially take on absolute power until February 28, 1933. On February 27, the Reichstag (the German Parliament) was burned to the ground by arson. The next day Hitler's propaganda machine blamed the act on the communists and played it up as a senseless act of destruction.

Hitler claimed that he must have absolute power to deal with this threat to law and order and immediately called a meeting of the members of the German Parliament, and with the cheering and approval of its members, Hitler was voted absolute power to deal with this menace to society.

Today, some historians believe that Hitler ordered the burning of the Reichstag to give him an excuse to take total power. Regardless of the origin of the fire, the fear in the minds of the German people had been planted. To reduce this fear, they readily gave away what little freedom they still had in order to reduce their fear of the communists.

It may seem that such confession and conversion is merely a verbal tribute to the new order. But this is not always the case. An occasional Galileo may publicly recant in the face of this torture while privately continuing to rebel, but often the conversion is complete and unquestioning.

The effectiveness of the conversion depends in part on the nature and extent of one's childhood experiences. Whether in Nazi Germany, Maoist China, or in our own country, the psychodynamics of the conversion are remarkably similar: If the stress is sufficient, the mind will take the route of greatest anxiety reduction.

Similar techniques are practiced by police departments throughout the country.

A suspect who has been caught will be psychologically conditioned by one officer who, with great disgust and feeling, tells the subject how horrible was the crime and how great should be the punishment for it. He implies that so much damning evidence is available that the suspect's own mother would convict him. Such inter-rogation may continue for hours. Then a second officer comes in and tells the suspect that all he need do is to confess his sins, sign here, and he will be spared the ordeal of a courtroom trial.

A person who has killed someone by accident or after provocation, for example, may be so frightened that he or she will agree to confess to murder in spite of the extenuating circumstances. A prosecutor may even promise total immunity to the subject if he will testify against others who may or may not have been involved in the crime.

As both the Supreme Court and the American Civil Liberties Union are aware, such techniques are so effective that many innocent people have been led to confess without the use of a single rubber hose. Others, hoping to be pardoned, may testify eagerly and with great moral indignation about the behavior of their co-conspirators, real or imagined, who had formerly been their closest friends.

Such techniques, common among police departments, were responsible in part for the famous Miranda decision by the Supreme Court in which the court ruled that anyone arrested for a crime must be read his rights and allowed to have a lawyer present during questioning. One need only read through the court records of charges of witchcraft and heresy that were common up through the seventeenth century to gain m1 appreciation for the effectiveness of such interrogation techniques. Tens of thousands of innocent victims were convicted of witchcraft by such techniques and many came to believe that, "If everyone says I am a witch, then I must be a witch."

10. MULTIPLE DEFENSE REACTIONS:

Lots of Good Reasons ...

To summarize the use of the ego-defense mechanisms, take as an example the emotion of hate. In our culture, we strongly censure the open expression of hostility. In fact, there are a great number of religious and secular prohibitions against hostility. For example:

1."Do unto others   "
2."Love thine enemy   "
3."Turn the other cheek...   "
4."Love thy neighbor .... "

If we violate a taboo that we accept as true, then we may feel guilt for doing so. But at the same time, we have a number of religious and secular ideas that encourage hostility:

1."Eye for an eye, a tooth for a tooth .... "
2."Vengeance is mine .... "
3."Those who believeth not are condemned already."
4."Stand up for your 'rights,' fight for what you believe in."

It seems inevitable that some conflict between our opposing sets of emotional beliefs will result. We hate, but we feel guilty about hating. Anxiety results, and the anxiety must be reduced. To reduce our guilt, we use an ego-defense mechanism:

"It threw him off when I turned the other cheek.
So then I hit him."

Repression "I have no feelings about X at all." Here, we repress our true feelings and perhaps even deny that we hate X. If we repress our emotional bias, we cannot feel guilt.

Reaction Formation "I love the guy." Here, we insist that not only do we not hate X, we really think well of him. Have you ever heard anyone say something to the effect: "I really like the guy, it's his... personality I can't stand." If we feel guilty about saying something bad about someone, we may feel a need to preface our dislike by saying something nice about him or her. It is as if we were saying: "See, I'm not prejudiced, I can see both sides of the coin."

Projection "I don't hate X; other people do." Gossip is a common means of cutting someone else down without appearing to have any hostile intent oneself. In gossiping, one can pretend that the hostility comes from someone else: "You'll never believe what Harry told me about X." Gossip is often used as a means of reducing one's own feeling of inferiority as if we were saying: "See how inadequate X is. Because X is so inadequate, I am better by comparison."

Rationalization "X deserves to be hated." If we think about all the bad things we notice about X, then we can rationalize our dislike of X. We dislike X because X is bad (i.e., X deserves to be hated). It may be that X hurt our feelings or insulted our secondary reinforcers, but to us X is bad. We tend to ignore the fact that we do not apply the same strict standards of judgment to those we like as we do to those we dislike.

The ego-defense mechanisms are not necessarily as clear cut as the classifications might suggest; there is considerable overlapping among them. Repression and denial are both forms of avoidance conditioning; projection and rationalization both involve learned methods of reducing anxiety and stimulus generalization to similar situations; and reaction formation, atonement, and internalization may all involve a conditioned abhorrence of one behavior that leads to an exaggerated reaction to the opposite extreme. All the mechanisms involve learned methods of reducing anxiety.

Our ego-defense mechanisms seem to lose some of their effectiveness when we become aware that we are using them to reduce anxiety. Because of counterconditioning, we may feel we are being dishonest with ourselves by using them. Without an awareness of these mechanisms, however, how can we hope to mature beyond a childhood world dominated by fears and wishful thinking? Recognizing our use of such irrational mechanisms is essential. If we are unaware of why we behave as we do, we cannot change for the better.

EGO-DEFENSE

Unconscious In its simplest definition, *unconscious* refers to the fact that we are often unaware (unconscious) of why we behave as we do. Some psychologists would extend this definition to include actual thought processes that occur in our "unconscious mind." However; the existence of an *independent* unconscious mind is largely speculation.

An *ego-defense mechanism* is any method by which the "mind" protects itself from anxiety; in effect, it defends the self-concept from feelings of failure, guilt or other anxiety producing thoughts. Such mechanisms are considered unconscious in the sense that we tend to be unaware of why we behave as We do. Freud considered many of these mechanisms Jo be natural, even innate. Dollard and Miller consider the mechanisms to be largely learned means of avoiding anxiety.

Repression Unpleasant or unflattering facts may be forgotten or ignored. If we do not think about them, we avoid anxiety over them.

Denial of Reality When reality. is too unpleasant, we tend to distort it by telling ourselves or our children that the unpleasant is really not that bad, In extreme cases. concentration camp inmates felt resigned to their fate and often felt as if their situation -were "not real, more like a dream."

Projection - To remove our own feelings of failure or guilt, we may project the blame to someone else, sometimes even: to an inanimate object.

Displacement If we cannot release our emotion. onto the source of our emotion, we may react by displacing, or redirecting, the emotion onto someone or-something that is more' acceptable without realizing that we are doing it ("You jilted me, but I don't care, I found someone I like even better").

Reaction Formation We are using a. reaction formation when we pretend to feel something that is just the opposite of what we actually feel. (Thought- "These people may not like me if they knew how I really felt, so I will think more like they think I should think.")

Emotional insulation. When we· fear being disappointed; we may reduce the anxiety by reducing our expectations. ("Well, r expected to lose anyway/')

Confession Feelings of guilt may be reduced by confessing our guilt if we believe that all will be forgiven. ("I did it. I'm sorry. Do you hate me?")

Identification Feeling that we are one with a very important person (ex. parent, God, nation, or a friend) makes us feel more secure. We come .to perceive ourselves as a part of that person or thing.

Internalization. · We may take on the same values or behavior as someone powerful or admired. By uncritically accepting their values as our own we *may* feel that they will like us more.

Rationalization By using a logical. Sounding reason, we can Justify our behavior; ("Whatever I have done is all right because of reasons X, Y, 'and Z.")

11 THE CONCEPT OF UNCONSCIOUS PROCESSES

It is sometimes disturbing to read descriptions of Freud's ideas in the popular press. Freud is known for what he said that was sensational and shocking, not for what he did that was important. Freud's concepts of Oedipal complexes, penis envy, psychosexual stages of development, and, of course, the id, ego, and superego seem to dominate our memory of him. Yet many of these concepts never achieved scientific respectability, for science, like nature, takes a severe toll of its philosophical creations. When future historians evaluate the contributions of Freud, it seems probable that his most significant contribution will be his insight into the "unconscious" nature of human behavior-specifically, his concept of our *ego-defense mechanisms.*

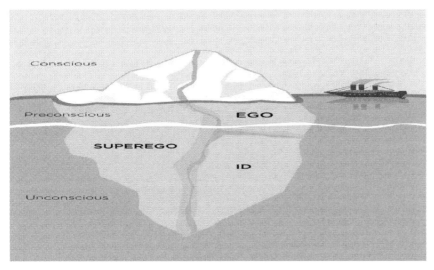

Freud obtained many of his insights into the unconscious nature of the mind from observing the paradoxical behavior of people under hypnosis and patients suffering from hysteric paralysis. From his studies of hypnosis with the French physicians Charcot, Liebault, and Bernheim, Freud came to believe that much of human behavior we consider conscious was actually determined by prior experiences of which we are unaware. A person under hypnosis may be told that a half hour after he awakens, he will go over to the coat rack, take off an umbrella, and open the umbrella, and that he will not remember having been told to do this. When he is brought out of the trance, he will carry out these instructions to the letter, yet he will not be able to explain why he did so. Freud notes (vol. IV, 23);

> *A person is put into a hypnotic state and is subsequently aroused. While he was in the hypnotic state, under the influence of the physician, he was ordered to execute a certain action at a certain fixed moment after*

his awakening, say half an hour later. He awakes, and seems fully conscious and in his ordinary condition; he has no recollection of his hypnotic state, and yet at the pre-arranged moment there rushes into his mind the impulse to do such and such a thing, and he does it consciously, though not knowing why. It seems impossible to give any other description of the phenomenon than to say that the order had been present in the mind of the person in a condition of latency, or had been present unconsciously, until the given moment came, and then had become conscious. But not the whole of it emerged into consciousness: only the conception of the act to be executed. All of the other ideas associated with this conception-the order, the influence of the physician, the recollection of the hypnotic state-remained unconscious even then.

The impact of these observations on Freud's thinking was marked. To Freud it was apparent that our behavior could be controlled by a process of which we are totally unaware. Years later, he wrote in his autobiography (1938, 28): " *...I received the profoundest impression of the possibility that there could be powerful mental processes which nevertheless remained hidden from the consciousness of men,"*

Freud gathered additional evidence of unconscious processes from his studies of *parapraxes,* the so-called "Freudian" slips of the tongue. If you were out on a date and called your new girlfriend by another girl's name, to Freud, the other girl's name would have been evidence that, for all his well-meant sincerity, the boy was probably thinking of someone else while he was talking to his date. Most of us are guilty of such slips of the tongue, often with embarrassing consequences. Psychologists today may be more likely to attribute this to stimulus generalization from a similar situation, rather than to an ongoing unconscious thought process. But Freud felt that such slips were significant evidence of our lack of awareness of our unconscious processes. Freud's ideas are well illustrated by a comment from his own experience that somehow sounds all too familiar (Freud, 1938, 86):

One evening, wishing to excuse myself for not having called for my wife at the theater, I said: "I was at the theater at ten minutes after ten." I was corrected: "You meant to say before ten o'clock." Naturally, I wanted to say before ten. After ten would certainly be no excuse. I had been told that the theater program read, "Finished before ten o'clock." When I arrived at the theater, I found the foyer dark and the-theater empty. Evidently, the performance was over earlier and my wife did not wait for me. When I looked at the clock, it still wanted five minutes to ten. I determined to make my case more favorable at home, and say that it was ten minutes to ten. Unfortunately, the speech-blunder spoiled the intent and laid bare my dishonesty, in which I acknowledged more than there really was to confess.

12. DEFINING THE UNCONSCIOUS

Freud's studies led him to infer that there are unconscious processes that determine our behavior. Freud's concept of an "unconscious" sometimes took on an almost mystical quality of an inner man or id, ego, and superego within the individual. However, evidence for any ongoing unconscious process is lacking. Psychologists today are more likely to simply note that much of our behavior is "unconscious," in the sense that we are unaware of why we behave as we do. However, the "unconscious" processes inferred by Freud may be as legitimate a construct as the "conscious" processes most people cite in explaining our behavior. In a remarkably perceptive analysis of "conscious" and "unconscious" behavior, Freud wrote (1949, vol. IV, 102):

By the medium of consciousness each one of us becomes aware only of his own states of mind; that another man possesses consciousness is a conclusion drawn by analogy from the utterances and actions we perceive him to make, and it is drawn in order that this behavior of his may become intelligible to us. (It would probably be psychologically more correct to put it thus: that without any special reflection we impute to everyone else our own constitution and therefore also our consciousness, and that this identification is a necessary condition of understanding in us.) This conclusion-or identification-was formerly extended by the ego to other human beings, to animals, plants, inanimate matter and to the world at large, and proved useful as long as the correspondence with the individual ego was overwhelmingly great; but it became more untrustworthy in proportion as the gulf between the ego and non-ego widened. Today, our judgment is already in doubt on the question of consciousness in animals; we refuse to admit it in plants, and we relegate to mysticism the assumption of its existence in inanimate matter. But even where the original tendency to identification has withstood criticism-that is, when the non-ego is our fellow-man-the assumption of a consciousness in him rests upon an inference and cannot share the direct certainty we have of our own consciousness.

"Sometimes a cigar is just a cigar" Freud

Freud recognized that his concept of "unconscious" processes was founded on the same type of inferences as our belief in "conscious" processes. Our concept of behavior as "consciously" directed is no more or less valid than the inferences that led to Freud's postulation of "unconsciously" directed behavior. Freud also recognized, however, that our past beliefs that animals, plants, and objects have consciousness like our own are no longer considered valid. Many psychologists, led by B. F. Skinner of Harvard and Donald O. Hebb at McGill University in Canada, have noted that human consciousness is itself nothing more than an inference from our observation of our own conditioned responses and the interaction of nerve cells in the brain. Indeed, the general trend of physics, medicine, and psychology has been to disassociate themselves increasingly from concepts based on inferences rather than hard data.

At the time Freud made his inferences, few supporting data were available. As the years have passed, however, more sophisticated observations and experimental designs have been applied to Freud's ideas. Many changes in our knowledge of behavior have made it necessary to drop out some of Freud's ideas and to add many new ones.

Sigmund Freud planted the seeds of an idea about the unconscious mechanisms of the mind. It would be unfair to give Freud sole credit, however, for his daughter Anna did as much to popularize the concepts as her more famous father. Anna Freud's publication of *The Ego and the Mechanisms of Defense* in 1946 was a significant, though often ignored, milestone. The seeds planted by the Freuds reached fruition as viable scientific constructs in the 1950 publication of *Personality and Psychotherapy* by Yale psychologists Dollard and Miller. Dollard and Miller put Freud's ideas to the test, reinterpreting Freud's ideas in terms of modern learning concepts. They and many others deserve credit for developing the concept of the ego-defense mechanism.

Because science must change with new knowledge, our concept of ego-defense mechanisms as summarized here has changed greatly since Freud first wrote of these mechanisms. In fact, current views in some cases bear only a slight resemblance to the original writings of Freud. The basic functions of the mechanisms remain the same, however:

(1) to reduce anxiety by removing unpleasant or ego-devaluing thoughts (negative conditioning or reinforcement); and

(2) to substitute more acceptable or pleasant thoughts in their place (positive conditioning or reinforcement). In addition, these mechanisms are said to operate "unconsciously" in the sense that we are often unaware that we are using them.

Imagine the behavior of a small boy who feels insecure in a social confrontation with another boy. The anxiety may trigger a defensive reaction. And the boy may brag, "I can lick you!" or his bravado may be less direct, "My dad can lick your dad." Bragging about one's physical strength may act as something of an anxiety reducer, and so long as the boy's bluff is not called, his primitive ego defense is successful and he may even feel a sense of superiority.

As the child grows older, however, definite changes occur in ego-defensive reactions. A ten-year-old child may have learned that bragging is not socially acceptable: braggarts are not liked. If so, the older child may gain satisfaction indirectly, by bragging about a perceived superiority of father, mother, home, or possessions. If the child's father, home, or possessions are 'better" than those of other children, the child becomes "better" than the others. If the child identifies with his father, father's successes become the child's. Time may have changed the wording, but some years ago it was not uncommon to hear a boy saying something like, "My dad won the Purple Heart in World War II, fighting the Germans at Fort Lauderdale." In effect, "I bet you can't top that."

But then comes college. College students are bright; college students are sophisticated; college students are worldly. If a college student wants to brag about his physical prowess, he can't be obvious. Subtlety is the key. In the midst of a conversation with his dorm-mates about the relative merits of the philosophies of Kant and Sartre, he suddenly pauses, slaps his forehead and exclaims, "Oh gosh, I forgot to stop by the cleaners to pick up my black Karate belt!"

Subtlety is the key. The ego-defense mechanisms are rarely so obvious as the examples of masculine braggadocio would imply. To Freud, the mechanisms are so subtle that even the person using them is unaware of it. In fact, today it might be useful to recognize three levels of awareness in our use of these mechanisms: (1) unconscious use, when we are unaware that we have acted defensively, or bragged, or repressed an idea; (2) reflexive use, when we may be aware that we are acting defensively, but the habit is so strong from past usage we cannot consciously overcome the reflexive tendency to blurt out something defensive or ego enhancing; and, (3) intentional distortion, when we deliberately are defensive or distort reality with the intention of creating a certain reaction in the mind of the hearer. Although ego-defensive reactions may be similar at all levels of awareness, Freud usually spoke of ego-defense mechanisms only in the first sense- of their occurrence without our conscious awareness.

Ego-defense mechanisms can be understood only when one can see them operating in oneself. We can easily see such defensive reactions in the behavior of others, but unless we can also recognize them in our own behavior, we cannot fully understand how we use these mechanisms.

Individuals react differently when they are made aware of their defensive reactions. Some adopt the "medical students' syndrome," identifying with every mechanism of which they are aware-to the extent that they develop an "empathic illness" or fear that everything they do is defensive, unconscious, or "wrong." Others are unable to see in themselves the defenses they readily see in others. Neither extreme is desirable, but the more common of the two seems to be the inability to see in ourselves the defenses we readily see in others. In Freud's words (1949, vol. IV, 102):

"...experience shows that we understand very well how to interpret in others (i.e., how to fit into their mental context) those same acts which we refuse to acknowledge as mentally conditioned in ourselves. Some special hindrance evidently deflects our investigations from ourselves and interferes with our obtaining true knowledge of ourselves. "

Neither of these extreme reactions is desirable. But the more common of the two seems to be the inability to see in ourselves the defenses we readily see in others. The "special hinderance" preventing this is the ego defense mechanism of repression.

13. REPRESSION

When thoughts become too uncomfortable, they must be censored from the mind. ff they are not censored; anxiety or discomfort may result. ff the mind successfully censors the anxiety-producing thoughts, they are said to be repressed, and are not available to conscious recall.

Repression can be a valuable ego-defense mechanism. If a loved one dies, we may feel a tremendous sense of loss and anxiety. Yet we cannot live our lives with so intense a level of anxiety. Gradually, our unpleasant memories of the death are repressed. Memory of the departed person fades, and normalcy returns to our life. The basic axiom seems to be that we tend to forget (avoid recalling) stimuli that are unpleasant (negative). As Freud notes (1938, 96):

> *The uniform result of the entire series of observations I can formulate as follows: The forgetting in all cases is proved to be founded on a motive of displeasure.*

Although Freud believed we repress traumatic experiences, today, more psychologists are concerned with the fact that we seem to be unable to suppress traumatic experiences. Post Traumatic Stress Disorder, experienced by soldiers of victims of abuse, seem unable to let go of their negative experiences. It is unclear if repression of traumatic experiences is common.

Repression can be a valuable psychological means of reducing anxiety. Unfortunately, however, the mind does not discriminate between harmful anxiety and anxiety-producing stimuli that can lead to important knowledge. The mind may repress anything that is unpleasant. Freud noted that Charles Darwin had formulated a "golden rule" of science based on his realization that we tend to fail to recall anything disagreeable. Darwin states in his autobiography (1898, 71):

> *I had, during many years, followed a golden rule, namely, that whenever a published fact, a new observation or thought, came across me which was opposed to my general results, to make a memorandum of it without fail and at once; for I had found by experience, that such facts and thoughts were far more apt to escape from my memory than favorable ones.*

We tend to recall and enhance facts that we consider to be flattering to ourself, our personal adequacy. This effect does not seem to be innate; it depends on whether we have been conditioned to believe that something is damning or enhancing. The Rosenzweig effect is seen only if we are conditioned to believe that the puzzles represent a true measure of our I.Q., and if we have already been conditioned to perceive I.Q. as an important secondary reinforcer. Once this conditioning has occurred, the tendency to avoid the unpleasant takes over.

An example of repression is provided by Sigmund Freud in a story from his own experience. Freud has been accused of many things but never modesty. When Freud gained what he believed were important insights into sexuality, he withstood great criticism and deserved the praise for great courage. He considered his insights into human sexuality to be among the most important in his life. Therefore, it must have been with great pain and courage that he wrote the following (1938, 101):

In the summer of 1901, I once remarked to a friend with whom I was then actively engaged in exchanging ideas on scientific questions: "These neurotic problems can be solved only if we take the position of absolutely accepting an original bisexuality in every individual." To which he replied: "I told you that two and a half years ago, while we were taking an evening walk in Br---. At that time, you wouldn't listen to it."

It is truly painful to be thus requested to renounce one's originality. I could neither recall such a conversation nor my friend's revelation. One of us must be mistaken; and according to the principle of the question cui prodest? I must be the one. Indeed, in the course of the following weeks, everything came back to me just as my friend had recalled it. I myself remembered that at that time I gave the answer: "I have not yet got so far, and I do not care to discuss it." But since this incident, I have grown more tolerant when I miss any mention of my name in medical literature in connection with ideas for which I deserve credit.

Freud may have been overly self-critical. It is quite possible that the "forgetting" was an actual lapse of memory rather than self-deception. But Freud believed that the frequency of such occurrences is greater than "forgetting" alone would explain.

Freud's story is an example of the fact that selective distortion may also occur because sometimes we remember only what it pleases us to remember. For example, if students are asked to write down their test grades at the end of the semester without a chance to look at their tests again, they tend to recall slightly different grades than they actually received. Their grades appear consistently better in memory than they appear on the official grade sheets. Students who make a 78 may remember it as an 80, an 81 is remembered as an 86, an 86 is remembered as "a high B" or a "low A," and grades of D and F are frequently forgotten entirely- "gosh, I didn't think I did *that* bad!" Students then go back through the collection of old exams only to discover that the gradebook is usually right.

Although students frequently remember their grades accurately, they rarely under-estimate.

And teachers seem to remember their own lectures as more exciting and inspiring than their students do.

Perhaps the most effective description of how repression operates was provided by John Dollard and Neal Miller. In *Personality and Psychotherapy,* they note a familiar example of suppression (a sort of conscious repression) in which people who are engaged in conversation may drift into talking about death, disease, gall bladder trouble, or some such topic. Someone suddenly says "How did we ever get on this awful subject? Let's talk about something else!" And the conversation is then consciously directed onto some other topic. Here, we have intentionally *suppressed* an unpleasant stimulus.

Anxiety reduction thus can occur in much the same way as it does when little Albert runs away from the white rat. The unpleasant stimulus can be a thought as easily as it can be specific words in a conversation or a white rat. Any cues leading to unpleasant thoughts can produce anticipatory anxiety. These thoughts would then be avoided. When we avoid even thinking such thoughts, we are said to have repressed them. Here, we have "unconsciously" *repressed* an unpleasant stimulus.

For a simpler example, just as *talk* of excrement, sex, or death may be *suppressed* at the dinner table so that eventually we automatically avoid such conversations at dinner, the unpleasant *thoughts* may be *suppressed* until avoiding them becomes automatic. A thought that is automatically avoided is said to be *repressed.*

17 PERSONALITY AND TEMPERAMENT

The Biological And Social Basis Of Individuality

SCHEINFELD • HALL • SPELT • THOMPSON • BENEDICT • MEAD • MONEY

Genetics and Individual Differences • The Law of Chance • Biological Differences in Temperament • Early Experience and Temperament • Culture and Personality • Sex Role Development

"Never forget that each of you is a distinctly unique individual.   Just like everybody else."

Margaret Mead

Not in innocence and not by design is the child conceived. In a single ejaculation, more than 200 million sperm cells are propelled into a long, dark, and uncertain journey, the cells are driven in every direction by blind, unconscious force. In a matter of hours, thousands of them will have made their way to the fallopian tubes. Millions of others will have dropped out of the race or will be lost in a capricious fold of skin.   For the survivors, this is the last leg of a marathon race in which only one of the hundreds of millions of entrants may win. Only one will contribute its unique genetic material to the formation of an individual.

If two parents were to live forever, what is the chance that some of their children would be identical? Each male sperm cell or female egg cell contains exactly half of the genetic material, 23 chromosomes, that is combined at conception to produce the individual. Yet each such cell is as unique as an individual fingerprint. Each chromosome may contain from 20,000 to 40,000 or more gene locations that determine specific physical traits. The biologist Amram Scheinfeld determined that in any spoonful of sperm cells there could be 8,388,608 distinctly different individual combinations! The number of different combinations of the two sets of 23 chromosomes each is almost as Infinite as the stars in the sky.

All these possible variations result from the combinations of the unique genetic contribution of the male's own parents. They are, of course, distinctly different from those of any other male. Although the female supplies only one or a few eggs per month, on average, the same uniqueness applies to each individual egg. Scheinfeld has calculated that the chance of the recombination of the same male and female chromosomes would be less than once in 64 trillion times.

In simpler language, no matter how prolific two parents might have been, it is probable that every one of their own children would have been unique. Except for identical (same egg) twins, all would have had brothers and sisters that were in some ways uniquely different from each other. They would have differed in the shape of the nose, chin, or head, the color of hair or eyes, their height, weight, and bodily proportions, and perhaps, their temperament.

1. WE START OUT AS A BUNDLE OF EMOTIONS.

AS WE GO THROUGH LIFE THOSE EMOTIONS ARE CHANNELED INTO SPECIFIC RESPONSES

To see a remarkable example of the range of responses of a baby, go to this YouTube video of a mother whose baby is constantly changing from shock to pleasure in seconds, as the mother changes her behavior.

https://www.youtube.com/watch?v=HX8mIHeuaf0

This baby goes from fear of novelty, of the mother blowing her nose, to hysterical giggling when it recognizes its mother.

The following baby cries when his mother sings a sad song. It shows clearly, just how little it takes to trigger an emotional reaction in another person.

https://www.youtube.com/watch?v=vOYwagmZ4yw

As we go through life those emotions are channeled one way or another by the experiences we have. How much of our personality is a result of the biology of those emotions and how much is due to experiences?

The study of personality is a study of individual differences. Each of us is an individual because each varies somewhat from every other person. These variations are not just physical variations of height, weight, and shape, they are also variations in temper. Some of us are either slow or quick to anger, some are shy or fearful, while others readily go "where angels fear ..." some are adept at physical sports while others are quick of mind. Yet if these variations are so random, so unpredictable, so capricious, how is it possible to study them?

The answer is that even capricious disorder conforms to a certain order-in this case, the law of chance, the probability curve. All genetic traits may vary. But the variation is distributed in much the same manner as the roll of dice. We cannot predict the outcome of a single shot in the dark that leads to conception. We cannot predict the unborn child's height, weight, or I.Q. Yet for great numbers of such rolls of the dice, we can predict the end result with admirable accuracy.

Everyone who has seen the rows of newborn infants at a hospital has noted the individual differences they display-not only physical differences, but differences in temperament as well. Some cry readily while others sleep, oblivious to any holocaust that might occur around them.

While one baby responds with giggling and cooing to the sound of the mother's voice, others may react with a cool detachment to the same stimulus by their mother, while still others display the same intense wide-eyed interest in everything that trips their auditory sensors. The temperament or responsiveness that is basic to personality is beginning to gel. But what is the origin of the differences in emotional reactions?

Are these differences a product of caprice from the gene pool? Or are they an end product of how the different mothers treat their children from the very first? The nature-nurture controversy is revisited. Now the questions change. What is the evidence that temperament is inherited?

2. BREED DIFFERENCES SHOW DISTINCT TEMPERAMENT TYPES

The most convincing observation of innate, biological differences in emotion comes from observing breed differences in dogs. Across the centuries, in the process of breeding for individual differences in physical characteristics, we have also bred, intentionally or accidentally, marked differences in temperament.

The Chihuahua is a feisty, emotional little terror that barks ferociously at any and every newcomer and runs and hides behind its master at any move a stranger makes in its direction.   The Cocker Spaniel is a calm, even-tempered family dog whose reaction to strangers is not so extreme. The German Shepherd, a one-man or one-family dog, is fiercely loyal and will defend its home and family from strangers. In contrast, the well-known hound dog" is so affable and outgoing that it easily makes friends with all comers, including unwanted late-night intruders.

Above: The end result of only a few hundred years of humans selectively breeding for individual differences in dogs has produced over 189 AKC registered breeds of dogs, out of only six original breeds. Darwin realized that nature had been doing for hundreds of millions of years, what humans have been doing for a few hundred years.

Human personalities seem to be mirrored in the breeds of dogs. The Chihuahua is a model of the nervous, excitable person who snaps at others or reacts with suspicion to their attempts at friendship. The calm, easygoing, imperturbable family man could be symbolized by the spaniel. The ambitious, aggressive yet fiercely loyal businessman bespeaks the worldly-wise behavior of the reserved shepherd. While the gregarious, outgoing "extrovert," who could sell refrigerators to Eskimos, or be taken advantage of by everyone, is the soul of the hound. With only a little imagination, each of these classifications could be expanded into many types and subtypes.

But are choleric chihuahuas and phlegmatic hounds really inborn personality types? And if they are, do they apply to people?

C. S. Hall reasoned that if emotional reactivity is influenced by heredity, it should be possible to breed for increasingly more "fearful" or less "fearful" animals in the same way that we breed for physical traits. If we want only shepherds with black and tan coats, we allow only black and tans to mate. Shepherds with tinges of white, gray, or red are excluded from breeding; hence, we have artificial selection.

Eventually, we can breed a group of dogs with only black or only tan coats by selectively breeding dogs with such genes. So, we should be able to select the most fearful animals out of a litter and allow only these to mate. Then take the most fearful pups from their offspring and allow only these to mate, and so on. If fearful temperament is genetically based, we should end up with animals that produce offspring that are nearly always fearful or emotionally reactive.

But how do you tell if an animal is more or less fearful? Subjective judgments have proven too unreliable. Before Hall could begin his study, he needed an objective measure of emotionality, measures that would be free from the bias of his own judgment. He decided on the "open-field" test. Hall used rats as subjects. The animal would be placed in an unfamiliar room full of novel stimuli.

The natural reaction of animals in such a new environment is to freeze or cry, perhaps urinate or defecate (autonomic nervous system reactions to fear), and slowly, ever so slowly, begin to explore. Such reactions are characteristic of all animals in strange situations from rats to human children.

Some animals lose their fear of strangeness quite readily. Animals classified as fearless or nonreactive began to explore quickly, rarely defecated, and crisscrossed every square inch of the room in their exploration. In contrast, fearful or reactive animals froze, took a long time before beginning to explore, frequently defecated at novel changes in noise or lighting, and kept to the corners of the room, rarely exploring the many areas of the room.

By measuring the (1) amount of time before the animal began to explore, (2) frequency of defecation, and (3) amount of area explored (how many grids the animal crossed), one could obtain a good measure of emotionality.

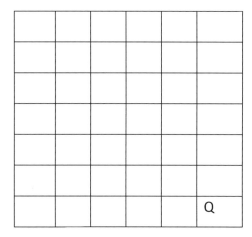

Hall proceeded to mate two types of rats from the same breed of rats. He carefully measured the frequency of defecation and the time that elapsed before a hungry animal would relax enough to begin to eat in an unfamiliar room. He then took the most fearful rats and bred them with other fearful rats. Next, he bred the least fearful with other least fearful rats. Within seven generations he had bred two strains of rats that could be identified as fearful and non-fearful. Fearful strains were approximately three times as fearful as non-fearful strains on Hall's measures.

Of course, one should be careful of the value judgment we place on such emotions. It might seem better to be fearless than to be fearful, but fearless rats in the real world would quickly be eaten by fearless cats. Fear does have value because it produces caution.

Hall's pioneering studies were later expanded by P. L. Broadhurst who carefully controlled for environmental influences. Two separate personality types had been bred; they seem to have reached their maximum differences after about seven generations. Further breeding did not noticeably affect their differences.

Soon, other investigators began to find genetic links to aggressive traits (Guhl, Langerspertz). The role of genetic differences in human temperament was still unclear but none could deny that individual differences in temperament were linked to the genetic throw of dice.

3. PERSONALITY AND TEMPERAMENT FROM THE ENVIRONMENT

The success of breeding studies should have been enough to put the nurture sympathizers on the defensive. But environmental psychologists had not been napping. Psychologist David Spelt had already begun to investigate the role of conditioning in the prenatal environment. He found that the unborn fetus in a human mother would react with jerking, twitching, and ail increased heart rate when a loud unpleasant noise (UCS) was sounded near the mother's stomach.

Spelt then took a neutral CS, a vibrator that did not disturb the fetus, and paired it with the noise; vibrator-noise, vibrator-noise, etc. in the classical CS-UCS conditioning sequence. After 15 to 20 such pairings, the fetus would jerk and twitch measurably to only the touch of the vibrator on the mother's stomach. The unborn human child of about seven months was capable of learning from the environment. The question now became, what might he learn?

The first breakthrough for the environmentalist camp came from a carefully controlled study by W. R. Thompson at Wesleyan University. Thompson subjected virgin female rats to a fear-producing shuttle box problem. For one group of females, a buzzer (CS) sounded, and a few seconds later an electric shock was delivered to the grid floor they were standing on.

The buzzer came to elicit a fear response. By running into the next compartment, the rats could escape the shock, A second group of females, the control· or baseline group, received the same treatment except that the buzzer never signaled shock. Instead, the buzzer was sounded purely at random so that it could never come to elicit fear. Both groups received the same number of shocks, but only one group came to fear the buzzer.

After this conditioning, Thompson discreetly ensured that each of the females would become pregnant. After pregnancy began, each female was put in the shuttle box. The buzzer was sounded. But the escape to the other side was prevented. The door had been sealed shut.

Yet no shock followed the buzzer for any of the rats. This was to ensure that only the fear of the buzzer would affect the emotionality of the mothers. Thompson repeated this procedure three times each day. Would the heightened fear in the pregnant mothers affect the temperament of their unborn offspring?

When the rat pups reached thirty days of age, testing began. One by one, the rat pups were given the open field test. Measures were taken of the distance the animals moved in, exploring the new environment. As the data came in, it was apparent that the rat pups of the frightened mothers covered only about two-thirds as much ground as the rat pups born to normal mothers.

In fact, the rat pups of frightened mothers took an average of 15 minutes before they would leave their home cage to enter the outside world. That contrasts with only 5.2 minutes for rat pups born to mothers who were not frightened. Furthermore, the effect seems to have persisted late into adulthood. As adults of 130 to 140 days old, the rats born to fearful moms took 4.8 minutes before leaving their cage compared to 2.1 minutes for the controls.

Here was clear-cut evidence that environment influences temperament. The results were as impressive as anything produced by the genetic studies. However, this fear does dissipate with experience.

4. MATERNAL EMOTIONS

We know that the differences between the two groups of rats were produced by the differences in the environment of their mothers. The electric shock, the buzzer, the mother's fear, and what might have happened during her lifetime-none of these factors could have influenced the genes of the unborn rats. We also know that the feat in the rat pups was not produced by either the shock or the buzzer. First, the rat mothers were never shocked after they became pregnant; and second, the buzzer did not affect the emotionality of offspring born to rat mothers that had not first been conditioned to fear the buzzer.

Evidence of both genetic and environmental influence on temperament is significant. Yet both the genetic studies and the environmental studies are extreme examples. It may be unlikely that the biological differences in temperament between individual people are as great as the temperamental differences between breeds of dogs or rats, simply because we have not bred people for specific traits. Indeed, the biological similarities between humans might strongly outweigh the differences. The studies tell us that heredity can influence temperament, but they do not tell us how much heredity influences temperament.

The studies of differences in the prenatal environment also present problems, it seems that fear in a pregnant mother may also produce stress in the fetus that may make the unborn child more fearful. But how fearful would a human mother have to be before this influenced her unborn child? It is unlikely that only a few frightening experiences during pregnancy could have much effect. Unless it were prolonged, the anxiety of the mother would probably not affect the fetus. But how prolonged? Would it likely only the children of mothers who were suffering from chronic anxiety? Or would it also affect the fetus if the mother were only shy?

Again, the evidence of the effect of the environment on temperament is important, but it does not make clear how its influence may change under changing conditions. We must know the circumstances under which it influences temperament and the degree of its influence. At present our knowledge is limited. To learn more about the effects of the environment on temperament we must study the effect of specific experiences on animals that are more like humans in their temperament.

5. AGGRESSIVE OR PEACEFUL PERSONALITIES
RESULTS FROM EARLY EXPERIENCE

Suppose we were to take closely bred puppies from the same genetic mold, the same litter, and subject each one to a slightly different environment. Suppose that one pup was frightened by strangers, kids throwing rocks, etc., another had only positive petting experiences with people, a third was roughhoused with (not enough to be scared, just enough to be stimulated), puppies lough to rough house, and a fourth was teased. What you might well find is that from the same litter one dog would grow up timid and fearful, the second would grow up comparatively happy and playful; the third would love to roughhouse, even when too big to handle, and the fourth would have an exaggeratedly hostile reaction to strangers.

The effect of experience on temperament can be dramatic. The army and police have succeeded in conditioning dogs to become so fearless that they will attack a group of men armed with guns or knives with no thought of their own safety and no regard for the consequences. Sentry dogs and police dogs are fearless because they are conditioned to be fearless. Their training begins at about one year of age, just after they get over the "puppiness" in their behavior.

They are first habituated to one man, the man who will be their master throughout the training. When attack training begins, a second person will play the role of the aggressor. Dressed in a bite-proof suit, the aggressor will tease the dog, first by flailing at the dog in a feigned attack and then by quickly retreating and allowing the dog to chase after him.

This S-R series of attack-retreat, attack-retreat interaction has two purposes.

The dog is first aroused by being teased in the attack phase. If the dog were teased or attacked with too much gusto it could, however, become frightened and end up as an animal who cowed in the face of the aggressor. But a good trainer never lets this happen. The trainer knows that the dog must never be beaten. In fact, the dog must consistently and repeatedly win. Each time the feigned attack by the aggressor ends with the aggressor fleeing in mock terror and being subdued by the dog. More than any other factor it is this sense of successful aggressive encounters that gives the dog the courage to tackle anyone at any time.

Later in training, the dog learns this same behavior under a wide variety of conditions. It is positioned downwind of a hidden aggressor so that the scent may become an anticipatory stimulus for what happens next, the aggressor's jumping out in front of the dog in mock attack and then fleeing. In this way, the dog quickly learns to be on guard for the scent of any hidden enemy such as a burglar hiding in a building or a sniper hiding under a grass hut in a Vietnamese village. With a little more training, the dog easily learns to distinguish the scent of a Vietnamese from that of an American or the scent of a male from a female. It could then be conditioned to attack one but not the other.

How did this dog come by his aggressive personality?

Such training takes advantage of the tendency that all predatory animals have to attack anything that runs away from them. The initial conditioning seems to involve associating the aggressor, with the teasing followed immediately by his running away, which elicits an innate aggressive response.

Equally as important, the dog's attack behavior is reinforced because it wins every encounter. If the dog were teased or abused until it was frightened, rather than just angered, or if it lost more encounters than it won, it would have been conditioned to have a fearful and timid "personality."

Human children may be affected by a similar experience. The child who is allowed to win, to tackle jobs that allow success, will develop self-confidence. The child who is browbeaten by parents and peers, who rarely succeeds in jobs or social encounters, may become fearful of trying. Not just aggression, but an attitude of success or failure can be conditioned by the child's early experiences.

Yet we cannot assume that constant winning is a key to success. In the real world, failure is far more common than success. Being able to tolerate failure, to make it through failure, is also important in our lives.

6. TRAINING CAN MAKE A DOG INTO A SEEING EYE DOG WITH A CALM PERSONALITY

The police dog is only one example. If you wanted to train the same breed of dog to be a seeing-eye dog, you would want quite a different temperament. Such training would require them to get used to children and cats from a very early age, to ensure that they would not be aggressive toward them or distracted from helping their owner.

Much of the behavior of animals that are considered natural may depend upon the early experience of the animal. Cats and dogs are often considered "natural" enemies. Yet if you raise a kitten and puppy together, they will be tolerant and even playful when they are together.

The author once had a Persian kitten that was reared with a Cocker Spaniel puppy. Predictably, they grew up to be playmates. The cat lived to a ripe old age of 16 years and in the process outlived three new dogs. But she made friends only with the spaniel. When a new dog was brought home, she reacted with hostility. She refused to befriend him, and when the innocent puppy tried to sniff at her, she raked him across the nose with her claws. From that time on, the puppy treated all cats as if they were lions, even though he came to outweigh them by a good 60 pounds.

Note that this only works when the animals are raised together from a very early age. It would be a serious mistake to leave an infant with an older dog, even if that dog is friendly most of the time.

The cat never made friends with another dog; perhaps they looked so different from the spaniel that she did not even recognize them as similar. When another puppy showed up, the cat's reaction to this new stimulus was intense. It was as if letting this strange animal live in the house was a violation of our contract between cat and human. For days, she refused to eat. She ran away from home and seemed to return only after hunger became overpowering. Finally, her hunger strike subsided and she came to tolerate the strange intruder, but she never became his friend.

7. EARLY EXPERIENCE PROFOUNDLY AFFECTS PERSONALITY

Mouse with a cat friend. Aggression and affection are personality traits powerfully influenced by our early experiences.

Perhaps the outstanding research on the effects of early social experience began in the 1920s. Zin Kuo reared young kittens with rat pups. Normally, an adult cat will kill and eat a rat. But when these kittens grew up, they not only did not kill other rats, but they actually were friendly with them. The former enemies now played together. Kuo also found that if he shaved the hair off of a rat then all social amenities vanished. Hairless rats were not in the memory banks of the cats. The cats killed and ate the naked rats.

Perhaps this reaction is not too different from that of the cat who refused to make friends with a puppy that did not resemble the spaniel she had come to know. More than this, Kuo found a remarkable degree of imitation in the killing behavior of the kittens. If kittens were raised by mother cats that, for whatever reason, killed but did not eat a rat, these kittens would also learn to kill but would usually not eat their prey.

If people were asked to observe adult cats from each of these different backgrounds, what conclusions do you think would be reached? If One cat kills and eats a rat, would the cat have an average cat personality? A second cat sees a rat and plays with it as if it were another kitten. Is this an overly friendly cat? Or A third cat kills the rat but does not eat it. Is this a sadistic cat that kills for pleasure? Is it perhaps, an incompetent cat?

A psychologist, observing the same behavior without knowing its origin, might begin to analyze it into personality types or traits. A biologist, seeing the same patterns of behavior, might suspect that inborn genetic differences in the cats' wiring diagrams have led to differences in how they adapt to their environment. Only by carefully controlling all conditions from the beginning is it possible to separate one "cause" from another.

The effect of experience on the temperament of animals is apparent. It is more difficult to determine the effect of experience on human temperament. One way is to observe the differences in temperament between different human cultures.

Biologically, there is little difference between Germans, French, Italians, Americans, or any other groups of people. Anthropologists such as Ruth Benedict have studied different American Indian tribes. Others, such as Margaret Mead have studied neighboring tribes in New Guinea. In such cases, the neighboring groups of natives are very close biologically. Any differences between tribes of American Indians or tribes of New Guinea natives must be due to the experiences of the child growing up in the culture, and not a result of biological differences.

8. THE FIRE IN YOUR BELLY:

Conditioned Enthusiasm: Our Goals in Life

Author and Supreme Court Justice Oliver Wendel Holmes said success in life depends upon the *"fire you have in your belly"*. The following example from Shepard tells of a psychologist who describes how such subtle conditioning may have a powerful effect on our future preferences.

> *All of my life I have had a thing for thunderstorms. Some people are terrified of them, but for as long as I can remember I have found them exciting and exhilarating. I could sit on the porch for hours listening to the rumble of thunder in the distance, breathing in the rain freshened air, and watching the lightning dance across the sky making living silhouettes out of the fast-moving storm clouds. I can remember having been surprised to find that not everyone shared my fascination with thunderstorms; it seemed so natural, but it was not until late in life that I learned the origin of my interest.*
>
> *My mother was herself frightened of storms. But when she became a mother, she decided that her son would not grow up with the same fear.*
>
> *So, when I was very young, every time a storm was brewing in the distance, she would take me out on the back porch and introduce me to the thing that frightened her as if it were the most fascinating discovery that we had made:*
>
> *Mom: (with feeling) Ooh! Listen to the thunder in the distance! Me: (with empathy) Yeah! Thunder!*
>
> *Mom: Mmmm! Smell the air! ·*
>
> *Me: Yeah! Air!*
>
> *Mom: Look! Look at the pretty lightning! Me: (with gusto) Go, lightning, go!*
>
> *Actually, I remember absolutely nothing of the event. If my mother had not told me about these little sessions years later, I would have no idea why I have such a feeling of exhilaration associated with thunderstorms. Yet to this day, thunderstorms give me a vague but heady sense of power. "*

Since that was written, the former First Lady, Betty Ford, wrote in her memoirs of an almost identical incident happening to her. Her mother was also afraid of thunderstorms, and she wanted to be sure her daughter did not grow up the same. So, she used her positive emotions to condition her daughter to love thunderstorms. To this day, Betty Ford says, she gets a feeling of exhilaration around a thunderstorm.

Unfortunately, society does not place a premium on having an interest in thunderstorms. But if the same type of conditioning were applied, by parents or peers, to develop an interest in books. "Ooh! Look at the pretty pictures!" or "The secrets of the ages are to be found in books!"), would the child not come out with an attitude toward reading and study that would make that child different from the ones who received no such conditioning?

Would it have an effect such as that described by John Paul Sartre who said of his grandfather's words about him becoming a great writer; *"it flowed into my bones. It directed my life."*

And would this show up in the child's study habits, grades, and interests in school? What if the same type of conditioning were applied by parents or peers to an interest in hotrods, chess, members of the opposite sex, their religion, their politics, their values, attitudes, and opinions? So, we do praise certain behavior and shame other behavior. We direct the course of our children's lives, often without any awareness of what shapes their future.

Such subtle conditioning seems to play a crucial role in molding the child's interests, for better or worse. For the most part, this conditioning is unplanned and often unintended. It may depend on nothing more than a series of capricious experiences with parents or in the peer group of a child during a critical period of life. But the direction the child's interests take may be determined by experience, and the question now becomes, "What different experiences are children likely to face?"

9. INFLUENCES ON TEMPERAMENT

What contributes most to our individuality-our heredity or our environment? At present, such a question cannot be meaningfully answered. Both heredity and environment make major contributions. However, one general difference can be noted. Heredity makes its major contribution to our general temperamental or activity level. Environment determines our specific likes and dislikes, and our reactions to specific environmental situations.

How does heredity affect temperament? At birth, genetic differences are already present in certain traits that we sometimes call activity, fearfulness, aggressiveness, and probably many others that have not yet been identified. One example of hereditary influences on temperament can be seen in temperamental differences. of breeds of dogs. Yet, humans have never been bred for differences as dogs have.

How does the environment affect temperament? Anthropologists have found that neighboring tribes of genetically identical individuals may have markedly different temperaments, with members of both sexes displaying predominately "feminine" behavior in one tribe and even a complete reversal of "expected" sex roles in a neighboring tribe. Some psychologists have found that rearing rat pups with a fearful mother will make the rat pups more fearful and just the opposite with rearing the pups with a non-fearful mother. Other studies indicate that early conditioning experiences may even determine the sex role preference of a child.

What happens when heredity and environment interact? Suppose that a quiet, passive baby was born to parents who were expecting an active, enthusiastic baby. Suppose that the parents' efforts to interact with the baby were not greeted with giggles and· coos the way that the parents had been led to expect from watching their neighbor's happy baby. In such a case, some parents might curb their interaction with their baby; leaving it with less interaction, which could add to the baby's own tendency to not be active.

In contrast, if an active baby were born to parents who were so busy, with so many problems, that they wanted to be bothered as little as possible by the infant, a different interaction might occur. The active baby might be ignored by the parents or even punished for its curiosity: "That child just will not learn to stay out of things!" In some parents, the frequent crying of an active child might go unheeded or even be punished. In contrast, an active baby born to parents who do well with such babies, or a passive baby born to parents who do well with a passive child, might have an entirely different interaction with its environment

We know so little about the interactions of a baby and its mother that it is difficult to say with certainty how the interaction between the two may influence temperament in an individual, we only know that it may.

"Emphasize our unique differences, pass it down."

18 AS THE TWIG
IS BENT.
THE ENVIRONMENT OF THE CHILD
WATSON • TOMAN • HILTON • SCHACTER • WEBER

Social Influences on the Child • Birth Order. Sibling Interaction.

Sex and Age Interaction • Socioeconomic Environment

Give me a dozen healthy infants, well formed, and my own specified world to bring them up in and I'll guarantee to take any one at random and train him to become any type of specialist I might select-doctor, lawyer, artist, merchant-chief and, yes, even beggarman and thief, regardless of his talents, penchants, tendencies, abilities, vocations, and race of his ancestors... I am going beyond my data and I know it, but others have been going far beyond their data with considerably less data.

John B. Watson, *Behaviorism*

In the 1930s, John B. Watson's statement strongly summarized the rapidly growing realization of the importance of a child's environment. To Watson, we are what we are conditioned to be. If we change the environment, we change the child. It was a difficult pill to swallow for a generation that still believed that people were "born" doctors, "born" geniuses, or "born" to be poor or criminal. "Blood will tell.' was a dominant theme among the populace. Today, the same idea has gained ascendence again. Today, we hear "it's all in the DNA", as if we had all the evidence already.

When Watson said that even race did not matter, America was far more racist than it is today, yet Watson was at least a hundred years ahead of his time. He deserves more credit than his critics in understanding the importance of the environment.

We know that one race is not that biologically different from another. Scientists have begun to look for the answer to the difference in "personality" and behavior in the differences in the child-rearing practices and cultures of the groups. The end of racial myths has not solved the question of what "makes" a doctor, lawyer, merchant-chief, or even a beggarman and thief. But here, too, we have increasingly come to look to the environment of the child rather than the bloodline.

1. FAMILY INTERACTIONS

In a family of many, a boy named Albert became enthralled with the idea of knowledge. He wanted to understand the secrets of nature, and his interest in mathematics led him to become a famous scientist. His brother Frank, who had no such ambitions, was satisfied to settle down and rear a family. His life satisfaction came from his family, not from his work. A third brother, Charles, became disenchanted with life at an early age, rejected the system, and spent much of his life wandering from one job to another without lasting satisfaction. Why?

All came from the same house. All had the same education, religion, and middle-class values. All had the same environment. Or did they? One of the great problems of psychology has been the fact that people from apparently identical environments may turn out so differently. Part of the answer to this mystery is that the mystery is an illusion. No two children are ever exposed to the same experiences, not even members of the same family. Each child develops a different social fingerprint.

Sociology and psychology merge in their interest in their study of different environments and the individual. The areas of greatest interest have been (1) *birth order,* or whether you are first born, middle born, or youngest in the family; (2) *family interaction,* which includes family size, sibling rivalry, and parental child-rearing patterns; and (3) *socioeconomic status,* the upper, middle, and lower economic strata of society.

Each of these areas interacts in a complex and still uncertain way to produce marked differences in the children they touch. The following pages contain many generalizations. There are no certainties in our knowledge of how these different experiences affect the child. But the generalizations have been found to contain important kernels of truth.

2. BIRTH ORDER

In 1874, Sir Francis Galton published a study of *English Men of Science. G*alton reported that significantly more of the British men of science were either only sons or firstborn sons. Since then, studies of *Who's Who in* America and numerous similar sources have also been found to contain a preponderance of firstborns (Altus, 1967). *Newsweek* reported in 1969 that twenty-one of the first twenty-three astronauts to travel in space were either only children or firstborn children. The ratio of firstborn to later born is rarely anything like the extreme of the astronaut sample, but the findings suggest that somehow firstborn children differ importantly from those born later in a family.

Firstborns also differ from later born in emotional behavior. Not only do they tend to be more successful, but they also tend to be somewhat more anxious and dependent than younger siblings (Schachter).

Do parents react to firstborn in a way that is different from later-born? In one study, Hilton had three groups of four-year-old children work on a series of puzzles. The groups consisted of (1) only children (2) firstborn with a young sibling, and (3) later born. Hilton found that firstborn and only children were significantly more likely to run to their mother for help between tests even though told not to leave their seats. Firstborns also tended to seek the reassurance or approval of others more often than later-born children. Again, the question is why?

We know enough about genetics to rule out heredity as a cause of birth-order differences. No two children can indeed have exactly the same genetic combination, but the genetic throw of dice is determined by the same law of chance in both first- and later born. Differences in intelligence and temperament must therefore be a result of differences in environment. We do not know what produces these effects. Humans cannot easily be studied in a laboratory, but we can study the obvious environmental differences that first- and later-born children will encounter. Eventually, we may discover more of the cause of the differences in success and temperament.

3. THE FIRST: The New Toy Effect

It walks, it talks, it wets its pants... there is a certain thrill, a new toy effect that comes with having your first child that may be quite different with later children. Imagine the difference in how we react to the person who is first at anything. Were there many Americans who did not notice the first manned landing on the moon? Can you remember how you felt? How about the second landing? Important perhaps, but not quite the same feeling. And the third, fourth, fifth, and sixth lunar landings?

How about the parent's reaction to the first child? The enthusiasm of the new parents is unbounded. The infant's first smile, first goo goo, first word, all are greeted with the glory we gave to the first man landing on the moon. When the child takes its first wobbly steps, often with dad holding both hands, the child's success is met with exclamations of "Hey, come look, come look, baby's walking! Ooh, that's a girl, come to daddy." Daddy laughs, giggles, and coos. Baby responds in turn. But what happens when number two begins to take the first steps? "Say, have you noticed the baby is walking already?" And by the time number three begins toddling across the kitchen landscape, the parental response is, "Hey, get that kid outa the garbage can!"

The oldest child is the first to walk, to talk, to run around the block, to go to the dentist; the first to drive a car, ·date, get a job, go to college, get married, etc. All the child's successes may be magnified in importance in the eyes of the parents.

But all is not sweetness and light. All of the firstborn's failures to live up to parental expectations may also be magnified. Parents pay close attention to the faults of the firstborn. They worry over minor details. They often are overly concerned about making sure that the firstborn is properly disciplined, and this overconcern may lead to particularly strict rules that later-born children may not have to put up with.

4. THE PROVING GROUND

The firstborn provides the training ground for the parents in their early attempts at parenthood. Firstborns are also the objects of intense parental anxieties. At the first bad case of colic, the child may be rushed to the doctor, while the later-born child is more likely to simply be burped. During the first bout with measles, the mother spends long hours brewing chicken soup for the child, and hovering over the bed of her firstborn as if to ward off the angel of death. Later born may end up being fed by an older sister or brother.

The firstborn is the testing ground for parental theories of childrearing; the trail breakers for all who come after. Parents may exhaust their pet child-rearing theories on this child, and may well excuse later born from such experimentation. Discipline will vary from one child to the next.

Then comes the time of the firstborn's first date. Dad's rules for the firstborn *Privilege and* daughter tend to be the strictest of all. Mom and Dad spend many restless hours waiting for her to return from the clutches of a sinister-looking seventeen-year-old boy. All older boys seem to look a little sinister.

But things come easier for those who follow. If the firstborn daughter had to wait until age 16 to date, the second daughter may be allowed to date at 15 or even 14. Mom and Dad are beginning to relax. If the number one son got to use Dad's car at 17, number two may get it at 16, and with more free time and gas.

Mom and Dad are becoming a soft touch. In fact, by the time Mom and Dad become grandparents they may well find it difficult to deny anything to their grandchildren. Mom and Dad are becoming pushovers.

Responsibilities may be pushed on to the number one child. This child is not only the first to have certain privileges, but the first to have to take out the garbage, get a paper route, and babysit with (ugh) a kid brother. Parents may expect the first child to act more mature at any age than number two will be expected to act at the same age. To the parents, delegating jobs and responsibilities to the number one child is viewed as a way of training the child to become an adult. Later, after some children have left home, the youngest child may get much the opposite treatment. If this child is viewed as their last child, the parents may attempt to prolong childhood and be more lenient in their child's training. After all, with a few successes to their credit, they can afford to relax.

5. THE RIVALRY: Mom Always Liked You Best

Jealousy is a prime mover in the world. It has been recognized as a force in the control of behavior since the earliest times. Cain was the firstborn son of Adam and Eve in the biblical story of creation. He grew up to be a farmer. Cain's brother Abel, the second born, became a herdsman. Both took the fruit of their labor as an offering to God. God looked with favor on Abel's sacrifice of the young of his flock. But God ignored the fruit of the ground offered by Cain. "And Cain was very wroth, and his countenance fell" (Genesis 4:5). The result is well known to every Sunday school child. Cain rose up in anger against his brother Abel, and slew him.

Such stories occur repeatedly in our biblical history. Joseph (Genesis 37), the youngest child of Jacob, was favored by his father over all the older brothers. Jacob clearly showed his favoritism by giving Joseph a gift of a coat of many colors. Joseph himself seems to have been a little struck by his own importance, and he tells his already envious brothers of a dream in which he and his brothers were binding sheaves of grain in the field when his sheaf arose and stood upright, while the sheaves of his older brothers bowed down to it. The result? His brothers hustled him out of the way at the first opportunity and sold him into slavery.

The rivalry between sisters is also of historical interest. Leah· and Rachel, the two wives of Jacob, were sisters (Genesis 30) who competed to see which one could give Jacob the most sons. When Rachel found herself unable to bare children, she gave Jacob her handmaid Bilhah to bear children in her place. When Leah eventually found that she too, could no longer bare children, she gave Jacob her handmaid Zilpah to continue bearing him children in her name. Today, of course, our culture is unlikely to encourage this type of competition between sisters. But competition over more common values and goals may be expected.

6. AGE AND SEX: Older versus Younger, Male versus Female

Walter Toman has suggested that perhaps one's brothers and sisters are more important molding forces in their own world of little people than even the parents.

Toman believes that how we relate to other people is strongly influenced by our early experiences with brothers and sisters. The only child may be prominent in the literature about famous people, but the lack of siblings may prevent him or her from learning how to deal with others-knowledge that is fire-formed in the combat of sibling rivalry and nurtured by the close interpersonal contact and daily give and take of companionship. The ability to develop social relations is formed by interaction with peers, not with parents.

Walter Toman noted a considerable number of permutation effects related to age and sex. Being an only child or a child among many is only one possible permutation. One could be the:

1. older brother of brother(s)
2. younger brother of brother(s)
3. older sister of sister(s)
4. younger sister of sister(s)
5. oldest brother of sister(s)
6. youngest brother of sister(s)
7. oldest sister of brother(s)
8. youngest sister of brother(s)

The effects of each situation are not certain. Toman provides some impressive speculation about the differences in personality that they may produce. Let us consider simply the differences in experiences that children might face in each situation without speculating as to how those differences might affect their personalities.

The above permutations affect the experiences of each child in a different manner. It is not easily predictable. The boy who is an older brother in a family of brothers will meet different experiences than the youngest brother in a family of brothers. The oldest state of competition as brother and sister vies for the attention and affection of the parents. They then tend to compete for the tidbits of reinforcement (who gets the toys or new clothes, or the praise) doled out by the parents.

The oldest sister of brothers also has an excellent training ground for her later role in life as a wife and mother. She has an opportunity to learn much about handling males, and she often becomes a confidante of her younger brothers, who tend to tell her their problems rather than turn to their parents. In contrast, the younger sister of older brothers will also learn how to handle herself with males, but her age may make her lower on the sibling-dominance hierarchy. Unlike the older sister of brothers, she may learn a role relationship with males that is closer to the male-female role expectation of our culture. Males outside the family may more easily relate to her as a companion than as a confidante. Her older brothers will tend to be very protective of their kid sister when she begins to date, though their protectiveness may not extend to other people's kid sisters.

We have few studies that can clearly show how these differences in the birth order, age, and sex of siblings interact to form the child's personality. Pure studies of complex interactions are difficult to perform. It is fun to speculate how these experiences may shape the child, but we cannot be certain. What *is* important is an awareness of the interaction of a very large number of influences, only one of which is parental behavior, on the development of the child.

Equally important is the realization that no two children can ever have exactly the same history of experience any more than they can have the same fingerprints or genetic makeup. Such is the stuff of which the individual is formed.

Class, status, and power are never equally distributed in any society. Socialistic countries may attempt to distribute these qualities evenly among their people, yet there are always those among the equals who are "more equal" than others. Children born to families of wealth and status are exposed to quite different environments than those of the working class. Children of white-collar workers have different home environments than children of blue-collar workers. All differ from the experience of those on the welfare rolls.

The eminent sociologist Max Weber exerted a strong influence on the thinking of modern social psychologists. Weber keyed social inequality to the differences in the distribution of class, status, and power. The most important determinants of these are the wealth and occupational status of the parents. Simply put, the inequality is that some people have them and some people do not. How do these differences affect the experiences of the child?

It is hardly an accident that a vast majority of the great men in history have come from the upper and upper-middle socioeconomic classes. Copernicus and Darwin, in science, Voltaire and Bertrand Russell in philosophy, and many others were either independently wealthy or were supported by wealthy relatives. Although a Freud or Einstein might arise from the middle class, they might have a harder time making it to success, the majority of famous people in the past, Washington, Jefferson, Adams, and more came from the wealthy class of landowners and aristocrats. Benjamin Franklin and Abe Lincoln were "poor boys who made good," but these much-touted symbols of success were less common in our past than our cultural myths would admit. In fact, Franklin and Lincoln both came from middle-class families, not from the poor.

Even today, when we are less tied to our family's money, the vast majority of PhDs came from families who were rich enough, at least, to afford to support them through the arduous task of eight or more years of college; not something all of us can afford.

To qualify as being in the upper socio-economic group, one must be wealthy enough that one can enjoy all of the comforts of modern life without their children having to work to support themselves. Rich children have access to the best universities and, in theory, the best teachers, and the best recommendations.

Yet despite the apparent value of going to an ivy league or well-respected university, studies suggest that, even though they have a better chance of getting a high-paying job, their contribution to science and literature is no greater than that of those going to a state university.

7. CULTURE: Personality on a Grand Scale

There are dramatic differences in temperament between cultures. A study of cultural differences is, therefore, a study of personality on a grand scale.

What do we find if we look at cultural differences in temperament? From the beginning, anthropologists have found drastic differences in temperament between cultures. In *Patterns of Culture,* Ruth Benedict provides an extensive evaluation of the personality differences of several major tribes. The differences in temperament are marked.

Benedict reports that the Zuni Indians of the American Southwest are relatively calm and even-tempered. For example, while adultery by a woman in a neighboring tribe may result in her being beaten or even having her nose cut off, among the Zuni, her behavior causes no great stir, and she may leave her husband at will. Zuni women are also-moderate in their reactions to an adulterous husband. In one case, Benedict writes (107-108):

> ... *The season before one of Dr. Bunzel's visits in Zuni, one of the young husbands of the household in which she lived had been carrying on an extramarital affair that became bruited about all over the pueblo. The family ignored the matter completely. At last the white trader, a guardian of morals, expostulated with the wife. The trader set forth with great earnestness the need of making a show of authority and putting an end to her husband's outrageous character. So, his wife said, "I didn't wash his clothes. Then he knew that I knew that everybody knew, and he stopped going with that girl." It was effective, but not a word was passed. There were no outbursts, no recriminations, not even an open recognition of the crisis.*

In contrast, the Dobuan society studied by Benedict valued aggression and hostility. Benedict notes (pp. 168-169):

> *The Dobuan, therefore, is dour, prudish, and passionate, consumed with jealousy and suspicion and resentment. Every moment of prosperity he conceives himself to have wrung from a malicious world by a conflict in which he has worsted his opponent. The good man is the one who has many such conflicts to his credit, as anyone can see from the fact that he has survived with a measure of prosperity. It is taken for granted that he has thieved, killed children and his close associates by sorcery, cheated whenever he dared. As we have seen, theft and adultery are the object of the valued charms of the valued men of the community.*

One of Ruth Benedict's students was Margaret Mead.. In *Sex and Temperament in Three Primitive Societies,* Mead challenged even the belief that the temperamental differences between males and females are inborn. Mead studied the Arapesh culture in which males and females both develop traits that are considered feminine in western culture. The males often performed the same jobs as the females, including child care. Neither sex was expected to be aggressive, and the ideal was one of cooperation and nonaggressive behavior.

In a second tribe, the Mundugumor, both males and females were physically and sexually aggressive. Tenderness was looked upon as of no value. Both sexes were ruthless in pursuing their goals. In yet another tribe, the Tchambuli, the women took on the role of being dominant in sexual and business matters. The males tended to be vain about their looks, emotionally dependent, and passive, and they stayed at home to gossip and care for the children while their wives went to work in the fields.

For another example of a female run society, this one in China, see *The Land Where Women Rule* :Here, women do all the work, just the opposite of America in the 1950s, where women stayed home and raised children.

https://www.youtube.com/watch?v=t_l9D7tEixc

Can temperament be controlled by the expectations of the culture? History seems to bear out the conclusions of Benedict that it can. For example, at one time the most feared nation of warriors in Europe were the Swiss pikemen. They were the most capable and fearless warriors in the mercenary armies of Italy and France until the advent of guns ended the advantage of their weapons. Today, Switzerland is a symbol of neutrality and peace.

Can temperament be conditioned in males and females by the expectations of culture? Mead's findings seem supported by recent work by Money, Hampson, and Hampson at Johns Hopkins University, who studied the sexual behavior and temperament of nearly one hundred children born as hermaphrodites, with the sexual apparatus of both males and females. The researchers found that twenty-three of their patients had actually been reared in a sexual role that was opposite of what their biological sex type would indicate, and all but one continued in the sex role in which they had been reared.

The pink and blue blanket syndrome that greets the newborn infant in our culture influences much more than the female and male preference for color; it influences their behavior, their sex desires, and their temperament. But how can our culture have such a pronounced effect on our likes and dislikes? How does culture mold the individual to prefer one pattern of behavior over another or one temperament over another?

We reward males for "masculine" traits such as bravery, encourage them to play rough-and-tumble games, and shame them as "sissies" when they cry or play with "female" toys. At the same time, females are encouraged to take an interest in "Little Suzie Homemaker" toys, discouraged or shamed for playing rough-and-tumble or dirty games, and allowed to cry. Our culture encourages such differences from the very moment that we select the pink or blue blanket for the infant's bed.

THE PEER GROUP CAN DRAMATICALLY INFLUENCE THE BEST INTENTIONS OF PARENTS

"Thank you for everything, Dad, the lessons, the lectures,
it's all been good, but now I must bid you adieu,
for I am like the wind, and Rusty here is like the coolest guy around."

19 LOVE, SEX, *AND* SOCIETY

Social Norms, Sexual Behavior, And Interpersonal Attraction

MOWRER • KINSEY • MASTERS AND JOHNSON • SORENSEN • ARONSON Changing Sexual Behavior • The Sex Researchers • The Origin of Sexual Preference • Marriage and Love • Theories of Interpersonal Attraction

> *Laws are coldly reasoned out and established upon what the lawmakers believe to be a basis of right. But customs are not. Customs are not enacted, they grow gradually up, imperceptibly and unconsciously, like an oak from its seed. In the fullness of their strength, they can stand up straight in front of a world of argument and reasoning, and yield not an inch. We do not know how or when it became custom for women to wear long hair, we only know that in this country it is custom, and that settles it. Maybe it is right, maybe it is wrong-that has nothing to do with the matter; customs do not concern themselves with right or wrong or reason. But they have to be obeyed; one may reason all around them until he is tired, but he must not transgress them, it is sternly forbidden. Women may shave their heads elsewhere, but here they must refrain or take the uncomfortable consequences. Laws are sand, customs are rock. Laws can be evaded and punishment escaped, but an openly transgressed custom brings sure punishment. The penalty may be unfair, unrighteous, illogical, and a cruelty; no matter, it will be inflicted, just the same .... Custom is custom; it is built of brass, boiler iron, granite; facts, reasonings, arguments have no more effect upon it than the idle winds have upon Gibraltar.*

> Samuel L. Clemens,
> *Letters from the Earth*

Standards of sexual behavior have changed drastically throughout the years. But few people seem to be aware of just how drastic the changes have been. In a study of changing patterns of childrearing, Martha Wolfenstein discusses a 1914 publication *Infant Care,* put out by the U.S. Government's Children's Bureau, which purports to tell parents how to deal with the early sexual behavior of the infant:

> *. . . The infant appeared to be endowed with strong and dangerous impulses. These were notably autoerotic, masturbatory, and thumb-sucking. The child is described as "rebelling fiercely" if these impulses are interfered with. The impulses "easily grow beyond control" and are harmful in the extreme: "children are sometimes wrecked for life." The baby may achieve the dangerous pleasures to which his nature disposes him by his own movements or may be seduced into them by being given pacifiers to suck or having his genitals stroked by the nurse. The mother must be ceaselessly vigilant; she must wage a relentless battle against the child's sinful nature. She is told that masturbation "must be eradicated . . . treatment consists in mechanical restraints." The child should have his feet tied to opposite sides of the crib so that he cannot rub his thighs together; his nightgown sleeves should be pinned to the bed so that he cannot touch himself." Similarly for thumb-sucking, "the sleeve may be pinned or sewed down over the fingers of the offending hand for several days and nights," or a patent cuff may be used which holds the elbow stiff.*

It may be difficult today to believe that such advice was taken seriously. Yet our Puritan ancestors were quite serious about it. In 1900, one of the outstanding news stories of the day dealt with two women who were arrested on the beach for wearing bathing suits that showed their naked ankles. In great grandmother's day, "all decent women" were covered from the tip of their toes to the collar around their neck, whether in swimming or in public. Sex was simply not discussed in polite society, and as late as 1934 Massachusetts had a law that prohibited doctors from giving birth control information to patients who wished to know.

In the 1960s sex education began to creep into the American classrooms, albeit in a Mickey Mouse form. Resistance to such education frequently was violent. Those who opposed it argued that sex education should be given in the home and the church. But is it? As early as 1959 Bandura and Walters, in a study of adolescents, found that few children learned their sex information from either parents or church. Most of them picked it up from older children, backroom gossip, or reading books (Fig. 19-1). This seems to contrast sharply with how children in most societies learn about sex.

In *Patterns of Sexual Behavior,* C. S. Ford and Frank Beach reviewed a mountain of data on sexual behavior among primitive tribes. They found that primitive societies often allow their children free sex play and participation in discussions of sexual behavior. In fact, such children have opportunities to observe adult sexual behavior: very little can be hidden in an igloo or grass hut. There is no evidence that the sexual adjustment of the children is harmed by this exposure.

How much of our culture's sexual morality is the result of custom? How much is universally practiced? To answer these questions, we must examine sexual behavior in other cultures and in our own culture at earlier periods of our history.

Many of the world's cultures allow some form of premarital sexual behavior. Some cultures even allow extramarital sexual behavior. Cultural attitudes toward sexual behavior are so diverse that anthropologists have been unable to find a single universal sexual taboo except, perhaps, the incest taboo. All cultures appear to have some regulations prohibiting sexual behavior between members of an immediate family: father-daughter, mother-son, and brother-sister.

Even incest is not the universal taboo it might seem, however. Among the ancient Egyptians, the Incas, the royalty of Hawaii, and many other great civilizations, brother-sister marriages were a common means of keeping royal lineage strictly pure. Furthermore, such themes recur frequently in both literature and religion. In literature, Oedipus fulfilled a prophecy by killing his father and marrying his mother. The story of Oedipus was made infamous by Sigmund

HISTORICAL CHANGES IN SEXUAL TABOOS:

Freud in his concept of the Oedipus complex: that every child develops a sexual attachment to the parent of the opposite sex. Freud's view of the sexuality of the child shocked Victorian society.

Few psychologists today consider the Oedipus complex as having major importance, but Freud was not just fantasizing. Such stories of incest are common even to great religions, including those of our own culture and from our own sacred past. One of the more famous is the Egyptian legend of Isis and Osiris, from about 1500 B.c. As the legend goes, the good King Osiris was killed by his brother Set. His sister Isis came upon his body by the banks of the Nile and began weeping over it. As she embraced her brother's body Osiris suddenly came to life long enough to impregnate her, whereupon he promptly died again. Isis gave birth to Osiris' son and later reared him secretly in the Nile Delta. The son later became the lord of the upper world.

In the biblical story of Sodom and Gomorrah, God destroys the two cities with fire and brimstone but he saves the life of Lot, his wife, and two daughters, telling them to flee the city. On leaving the city they are told not to look back, but Lot's wife look behind her and is turned into a pillar of salt. The Sunday School version ends at this point, but the biblical version does not. Lot is left with a problem. He has only two daughters. He has no sons to carry on his name. Lot's daughters conspire to find a solution. They proceed to get their father drunk and one at a time they rape him. Both become pregnant, and both bear male children. Their children go on to found two of the major tribes of Israel-the Moabites and the Ammonites. The story ends at that point without censure or recrimination (Genesis 19:26-38).

Later in biblical times, incest became punishable by death, but in the earlier part of our history, it seems to have evoked remarkably little wrath. The question of incest has always been a problem for Western religions that interpret the Bible literally, because the story of creation is itself an incest story, In the beginning, God created Adam and Eve. Adam and Eve had sons, Cain and Abel, and presumably daughters. There was no one else around at the time, so with whom did the sons of Adam mate to propagate the species?

Our concept of what is "normal" in sex and marriage has also changed markedly.

Some consider King Henry VIII a lecher for having had six wives. But King Henry practiced serial monogamy-he had one wife at a time. In our religious history, this has rarely been the case. Abraham had many sons by his mistresses (Genesis 25:6). Jacob had two wives, both sisters, who competed with each other to give him the most children. As we have seen, both loaned Jacob their handmaids so that he could have more children (Genesis 30:1-30). The biblical book

I Kings begins with a story of how King David, who was getting old and impotent, was unable to have sex with his wives. As a cure, his servants brought him a young virgin. The cure was ineffectual. But the ultimate in Old Testament lovers was King Solomon, who, they say, had some seven hundred wives and three hundred concubines (I Kings 11:3).

Long before the time of Christ, the Middle East came under the rule of the Roman Empire. In Rome, polygamy was forbidden, although concubines were still allowed. Over three hundred years after the death of Christ, Christianity was made the official state religion of Rome. Roman laws remained predominant, however, and polygamy did not return, although for hundreds of years even the popes had mistresses. A thousand years passed before celibacy became a virtue.

With the coming of the Victorian era and the Puritan lifestyle, sexual attitudes became rigid and restricted. The influence of this Puritan attitude toward sex is so pervasive that it persists to this day. Biblical stories, for example, still are judiciously censored or even altered to fit the prevailing moral climate. They have been washed clean of all references to sex that might hint at any type of behavior not in keeping with the prevailing moral code. Yet every generation continues to teach its children that whatever moral values are currently fashionable are somehow the will of God.

THE SEX RESEARCHERS

The public silence regarding sexual behavior has been imposing. So much so that for centuries little has been known of human sexual behavior. Early sex researchers met with great resistance. One of the first was 0. H. Mowrer, a graduate student at the University of Missouri. The story *is* told in detail by Erwin Espar.

Hoping to graduate with honors, Mowrer devised an original survey of sexual behavior for a course in marriage and family living taught by a popular teacher H. 0, Degraff. The project was approved by Max Meyer, an outstanding psychologist in his own right, who went out of his way to loan Mowrer university envelopes to help in his collection of data. But local citizens and the news media began to hear rumors of strange goings-on at the University of Missouri. Rumors led to such a furor that the college board met to discuss disciplinary action. The result was that both Max Meyer and H. 0. Degraff were fired for their role in allowing Mowrer's survey. Meyer was later reinstated, but Degraff was unable to find another teaching position. Mowrer himself escaped relatively unscathed. Since he was only a student at the time, he was not held responsible.

Mowrer's sex survey was quite mild compared to what would be instituted twenty years later by Alfred Kinsey, but during the 1920s, its questions dealing with premarital sex were considered shocking. Mowrer went on to become one of the biggest names in psychology, writing books on learning theory, social psychology, psychiatry, religion, and many other areas. But in all that Mowrer wrote, he never wrote another article on sex.

The first breakthrough in sex research came with the studies of Dr. Alfred Kinsey and his associates in their studies of the sexual behavior in the human male and female. Kinsey was a well-known research biologist before he entered the field of sex research. His own reputation, plus the fact that his books were published by one of the outstanding medical textbook publishing companies, lent respectability to Kinsey's report, even in the face of tremendous adverse criticism.

Over thirty years, Kinsey and his associates conducted interviews with more than 18,000 people. Fewer than ten of them refused to continue the interview once they started (Pomeroy, 1963). Although Kinsey's subjects were not drawn from a random sample of the population, Kinsey did manage to get entire groups of P.T.A. members and church groups to participate in this study. Overall, it was a massive undertaking. Kinsey and his coworkers have sometimes been accused of bias in their sampling, yet most subsequent studies have shown Kinsey's results to have been conservative rather than liberal. Regardless, Kinsey shocked the nation.

Kinsey found that 83 percent of the males and 50 percent of the females interviewed reported having engaged in premarital intercourse. In addition, extramarital sexual relations were reported by 50 percent of the males and 27 percent of the females. The occasional use of masturbation was reported by 92 percent of the males and 62 percent of the females. Homosexual experiences to the point of orgasm were reported by 37 percent of the males, with 18 percent of the males displaying as much homosexual as heterosexual behavior, but only 4 percent of the males being exclusively homosexual. Less than 10 percent of the females had had homosexual experiences to the point of orgasm. Equally as important, a great many so-called "deviant" sexual behaviors were found to be "normal" in the Kinsey group.

Studies since Kinsey indicate that his results were probably not exaggerated.

Vance Packard surveyed 2,200 unmarried juniors· and seniors in colleges and universities throughout America. He found that 57 percent of the 21-year-old males and 43 percent of the 21-year-old females reported having engaged in premarital sexual intercourse. Kinsey earlier had reported 51 percent and 27 percent for males and females, respectively, in the same age group of unmarried college students. In 1972, a sex survey reported in the *British Medical Journal* found that of 1,500 freshmen girls at the University of Aberdeen, over 45 percent had engaged in premarital sexual behavior. Furthermore, nearly 40 percent of the coeds who reported engaging regularly in sexual relations noted that they did not use any contraceptive devices. Many of them were afraid to go to a doctor for such information. Others were afraid that the use of contraceptives would suggest to their partners that the coeds had "planned" to have sex.

Adolescence is a mixed picture of tolerance and ignorance, pleasure, and fear. Such research is of great value in evaluating the type of sex information needed by teenagers, and in determining how to help them with the problems they will encounter.

SEXUAL CONDITIONING Pavlov and Sex

There is a wide variety of sexual responses given to seemingly inappropriate objects. Some males are sexually aroused by the sight or feel of the panties or other clothing of the opposite sex (a fetish). Still, others may be aroused by the sight or thought of members of their own sex (homosexuality). Comparatively little is known of the origin of the first sexual awakening in the adolescent. Less still is known about how one develops a sexual attachment to clothing, members of one's own sex, or even members of the opposite sex.

A partial answer to the question of how sexual preference may be established was found by Rachman, who attempted to reproduce the origin of a fetish-a sexual attraction to a nonsexual object. Rachman's subjects were male volunteers whose normal sexual preferences had already been established. Sexual arousal was measured by a mercury-activating rubber tube that could be fitted around the subject's penis. The apparatus was vaguely similar to the device doctors place around a patient's arm to measure blood pressure. When sexual arousal occurred, the penis became enlarged and erect, and the response registered on the mercury recorder.

Each subject was then seated in front of a viewing screen. Rachman flashed on the screen a picture (CS) of some neutral object, in this case, a picture of black knee-length boots. The subjects gave no response to this picture. After fifteen seconds, this CS would be followed by the UCS, which was one of six slides of an attractive nude woman. The slide of the nude woman normally produced a sexual response by itself.

After thirty to sixty-five pairings of the picture of the boots (CS) with pictures of nude women (UCSs), the picture of the boots could now be shown alone and the subject would experience sexual arousal, even though this slide was no longer followed by the slides of the nude women. Furthermore, this sexual response generalized-that is, pictures of other boots would produce a similar response.

To be sure, this sexual response to boots probably was short-lived (went into extinction) outside of the testing situation. It is unlikely that any long-term sexual response of this type would be as pronounced as in a true fetish, or in a homosexual or heterosexual attachment. But suppose that the same conditioning occurred during a very sensitive critical period of puberty. Would conditioning then have a more profound effect on sexual preference than in Rachman's subjects, whose sexual preferences had already been established?

There are no available studies on the origin of sexual preference in puberty. However, the evidence of the first experiences with fetishes among those who have fetishes, and of homosexual seduction and heterosexual seduction all suggest that the effects of such conditioning during puberty may be far more profound than if the same conditioning occurs later. Thus, a child who experiences his or her first sexual awakening or orgasm while being spanked, which is not as uncommon as it sounds, might later experience a strong desire to be punished as a part of lovemaking.

But this may be only a part of the origin of sexual preferences. Sexual fantasies, when associated with sexual arousal, may also play a part in directing the sexual interest of the child. Even the aura of mystery surrounding the clothed body seems to be important in stimulating sexual curiosity about members of the opposite sex. This is especially true when, as in males, there is a strong peer group interest in such censored knowledge. Future studies in psychology will have to examine all these aspects of beginning sexuality in detail before the questions can be answered with certainty.

MARRIAGE AND LOVE

Other sex "problems" also appear to be at least partly a creation of society. In ancient Greece, homosexuality was both common and accepted. In modern America, homosexuality was branded as a crime until very recently. It: was not until 1974 that the American Psychological Association removed homosexuality from the list of psychological disorders. One's sexual orientation is, to a very large extent, determined by one's early sexual experiences, both in fantasy and reality.

One explanation of how homosexuality develops is that in adolescence a child may "imprint" to the same sex partner as readily as to a partner of the opposite sex, just as Konrad Lorenz's ducklings "imprinted" to Lorenz rather than their real mother. But unless there are additional psychological maladjustment most psychologists would not place homosexuality in the category of being a mental problem. Of course, the fact that society reacts quite negatively to homosexuals makes 'it likely that the homosexual will have additional problems."

Among the sexual problems most easily dealt with by psychologists are those concerning personal sexual adjustment. Individuals who are unable to perform sexually with a partner, even though they may be able to achieve orgasm by masturbation, have responded quite well to psychological treatment. So long as the individual is willing to participate in therapy, and hopefully the individual's partner as well, therapy has proved quite successful in most cases.

Throughout most of our history, young people have rarely had to worry about seeking a marriage partner. Traditionally, marriages occurred shortly after puberty. The Romans and Hebrews permitted marriage at the age of twelve for girls and a year or two older for boys. Most marriages were arranged by the parents of the young people involved. The rule of the day in early America was first and foremost to get married. You could fall in love *afte1·* marriage, not before. Romeo and Juliet notwithstanding, marriage was considered the province of parents, not poets.

SOCIAL AND ABNORMAL PSYCHOLOGY

Some of the most important issues raised in modem social psychology concern the origin of human aggression, wars, and social order (including questions of individual freedom and social control).

Chapter 20 Explores the nature of Prejudice and War. From WWII to the experimental evidence of prejudice. It continues with the social order of nonhuman animals and the implications of new field studies of primate social behavior that show how chimpanzees of Jane Goodall went to war. It covers Obedience studies, Social Pressure, and the Stanford Prison Experiment.

Chapter 21 takes up the question of what cements the social bonds between an individual and the nation, between two people, and between a mother and infant. Do such social bonds have anything in common? Such questions are the province of the social psychologists who study the origin of social interaction, prejudice, and the attachment of a child to its mother.

In Chapter 22, the emphasis is on the origin and treatment of common psychological problems such as depression and anxiety. The humanistic approach of Carl Rogers and Abraham Maslow and the existential approach of Victor Frankl and Rollo May provide important insights from their clinical observations. In addition, the studies provide important experimental evidence of the origin of these problems.

Chapter 23 examines the dramatic emotions and feelings of those who have been diagnosed as mentally disturbed. Their thoughts and behavior provide important clues *to* our understanding of the social and emotional origins of their problems. This section ends with an examination of antisocial behavior and the personal and cultural origins of drug-related problems in our culture.

Chapter 20 • THE SOCIAL ORDER: Social Order In Animals And Humans
Chapter 21 • THE SOCIAL BOND: Tribes, Nations, and The Infant-Mother Bond
Chapter 22 • PSYCHOLOGICAL PROBLEMS OF THE INDIVIDUAL: Origin And Treatment
Chapter 23 • PSYCHOSIS AND SOCIETY Social Norms And Abnormal Psychology

20 THE SOCIAL ORDER
FROM CONFLICT TO WAR

Hitler * Theories of Prejudice * The Robber's Cave Exp. * The Dominance Hierarchy * Prejudice * Conformity *
Aggression * Public Opinion * The Chimpanzee Wars * Stanford Prison Exp. * Politics

"An intimate coupling of nationalism and a sense of social justice must be implanted in the young heart. Then a people of citizens will someday arise, bound to one another and forged together by a common love and a common pride, unshakable and invincible forever.

Care must be taken not to under estimate the force of an idea. I should like to remind those who become fainthearted... of a time whose heroism represented the most overpowering proof of the force of idealistic motives. For what made men die then was not concern for their daily bread, but love of their country, faith in its greatness, a general feeling for the honor of the nation...

...I believe I am acting in accordance with the will of the Almighty Creator... I believe I am fighting for the work of the Lord."

Adolph Hitler
Mein Kampf

The greatest atrocities ever committed have not been committed in the name of evil. Virtually without exception, they have been committed in the name of doing good.

The thousands of years that we tortured our grandmothers into confessing they were witches, and burned them alive at the stake, was all done in the name of saving the little children, and the frightened adults, from evil. It was done by people who believed they were doing good. They saw themselves as "heroes"; as did most of their society.

You cannot get people to destroy others in the name of evil. They will not do it. But they are eager and enthusiastic for a chance to be a hero; to destroy those who have been labeled "evil."

The attack on the Twin Towers in America in 2001 was done in the name of God, against Americans they believed were infidels.

The hundreds of years we slaughtered the Native Americans and relegated the survivors to concentration camps (reservations), in the deserts and badlands, was all done in the name of saving our good Christian settlers from the "heathen savages".

Over 14 million soldiers died in WWII. Over 50 million more civilians died of starvation and disease and bombs from that war. Everything Hitler did was done in the name of Patriotism and Country; saving Germany from those they had labeled the enemies of Germany. Constantly, they were warned that they were surrounded by enemies. The people themselves demanded that action be taken.

The violent purges of hundreds of thousands by Stalin in the Soviet Union, were done in the name of destroying the "Enemies of the People". Now, the same phrase has been repeated by politicians in our own country to attack the press they do not like.

The attack on America's Congress on January 6 was done in the name of saving our country from those who would "steal" the election, despite all evidence to the contrary. Some 57 court cases had been thrown out or canceled due to no evidence. The reason for hatred had simply been invented.

The argument that the human mind is at the mercy of irrational, aggressive impulses is not without merit. In every country, in every generation, the call to aggression and the appeal to prejudice has seemed to overpower even the most basic survival need. At the beginning of each war-the American Civil War, the Spanish American War, the First Great War to *End All Wars WWI*, and even the Vietnam War, tens of thousands of men have assembled in taverns, meeting halls, and town squares to cheer the declaration that their government has decided to have every fourth one of them killed.

The carnage is not exaggerated. In the American Civil War, out of approximately 2.4 million men at arms, some 618,000 died, a ratio of more than one of every four (Williams, et al.,). In World War II, casualties were even higher. In Russia, an estimated thirty million men, women, and children died, and many more died from starvation and disease, not just from bullets and bombs.

Six million Jews were put to death. Over three million German soldiers and about twice as many German civilians died. Not counting civilian casualties, an estimated 14,000,000 men at arms met their death. Of this total, 322,000 were Americans (Williams, et al.).

The number of Americans killed in World War II often surprises Americans who have been led to believe by Hollywood that Americans won the war single-handed, with other nations making only minor efforts. Citizens of Russia, France, England, and many other countries would be surprised to hear the American version.

What is it that makes it so easy to hate or attack those who believe or behave differently? This was the question that fueled American social psychology in the decades following WWII. What causes prejudice?

1. HOW HITLER GAINED CONTROL OF GERMANY

Words Used To Inspire Conquest And Hate

We know something about the stimuli that produce aggression in animals and people. You can make a dog angry by teasing it. By a series of attack and retreat actions, the aggressor who trains police guard dogs will first threaten the dog and then coax it into attack by a swift retreat. As soon as the dog in turn threatens the trainer, it is made to feel that it can now emerge victorious by its attack.

Politicians have used similar techniques to tease the populace into an aggressive fury. In playing on the deepest fears of the masses-their fears of crime, of anarchy, of witches, of drug addicts, and even fear of immigrants, - politicians have presented a threat and followed it up with the promise that society will emerge victorious if only they vote for that politician.

Any situation always looks clearest when viewed with the benefit of hindsight, usually decades or even centuries later. But the question remains: Could we have predicted Hitler's rise to power? Could we have predicted the American era of McCarthyism? Could we have predicted Watergate? Could all these situations have been avoided if the public had been educated in a different way?

Again, we must begin with the simple and work up to the more complex. In retrospect, it is perhaps not difficult to see how the fiery rhetoric of an Adolph Hitler could capture the minds and imaginations of the German people by playing on their fears on the one hand and on their deep patriotism on the other.

But here, as in other areas of human psychology, more basic underlying processes may well be masked by the complexity of the problem. What would the social order be like without the rhetoric of politicians? Without appeals to conditioned emotional responses? To find out, we must look first at social orders in animals that do not have the elaborate rules of ritual and rhetoric found in human societies.

CBS newsman William Shirer was assigned to Germany before, during part of, and after WWII. He summarized a remarkable chronicle of how Hitler rose to the position of a beloved dictator who started a war that took the lives of tens of millions of people. His three-inch-thick book, **Rise and Fall of the Third Reich,** is a classic of information.

Among the techniques used by Hitler that led to his success:

• **Torchlight parades of thousands** of his devoted followers to impress the masses with his strength, dutifully recorded by the press.

• **A technique scholars called "the Big Lie".** If you tell a big lie, and you tell it often enough, people will come to believe that lie.

• **A constant barrage of criticism** against the democratic government, the Weimar Republic, blaming others for losing the last war, blaming the republic for creating the great depression and labeling others as traitors, for ignoring the greatness of Germany.

• **The "Bully Boys", Hitler's Brown Shirts,** attacked and beat critics, broke up rallies by other parties, and created a fear to criticize the Nazis by their constant verbal attacks.

• **Glorification of "heroes"** When a young Nazi, Horst Wessel, was killed in a clash with communists, Hitler made him into a national hero. Even a song was devoted to his supposed heroism; the Horst Wessel Song. The music was played as the Nazis enthusiastically marched off to war.

- **Patriotism was an issue in almost every speech.** Hitler constantly rallied the German people with statements about how they did not lose WWI, but were betrayed by some of their leaders who stabbed them in the back. Restoring the glory of Germany was a major theme throughout his oratory.

There were at least five major events that led to what happened in Germany:

1. **FEAR AND HATE**: Hitler played up the fear of anarchy. Tens of different political parties, especially the communists, were repeatedly portrayed as a threat to Germany. He would excite the crowds with tales of communists, but also Jews and labor union leaders and socialists taking over their country, and then enrage them with anger over what was supposedly happening; not unlike the way guard dogs are trained; they were teased to anger them, then unleashed against their perceived enemies

2. **CHANCE:** Even though Hitler came in second in the election to the WWI war hero, von Hindenburg, his NAZI party had the most members in the German parliament. He had enough control to force Hindenburg to name him as Chancellor, second only to President Hindenburg. Shortly after, Hindenburg died, the NAZI party voted to give Hitler both the title of Chancellor and President of Germany.

3. **THE REICHSTAG FIRE**: The moment he seized all power came after the infamous Reichstag Fire, when the German parliament burned to the ground. Scholars believe the NAZIs themselves set the fire. Immediately, the NAZIs blamed the communists. The members of the Reichstag were called into an emergency meeting the next day and voted to give the government supreme power to deal with the threat. Thousands were arrested in the next days, although there was never evidence as to their guilt.

4. **CRYSTAL NIGHT**: Night of The Broken Glass--a young Jewish man who was studying in Paris, learned that his parents had been arrested and sent to a concentration camp. He took a gun and killed the German ambassador to France. Hitler played this up as evidence that the Jews were a threat to Germans. His Brown Shirts used this as an excuse to arrest Jewish individuals and break the windows in Jewish shops across Germany (which led to the term Crystal Night).

5. **PLANTING STORIES IN THE PRESS**, using a ruse to justify attaching other countries. Hitler's propaganda ministry spread lies about Germans living in the Sudetenland, in Czechoslovakia, were being beaten by the Czechs. Some might have been real, those things happen. But it was hyped in the press by Hitler and Goebel to channel the minds of the German people.

   An identical ruse was used by Putin as a false flag to excuse their already planned invasion by saying the Ukrainian forces had attacked their Russian supporters in the Donbas, and were engaged in "genocide"

   And yes, in America, Donald Trump falsely claimed the election had been stolen to justify an attempt to whip a crowd into storming the capital and prevent the certification of the actual votes. 140 police officers were injured, one died and four committed suicide. And then, many supporters in Congress claimed the attack was just like a group of "tourists".

6. **STORIES AND THREAT;** Stories of atrocities against them. Hitler's driver later described how they had been sitting around joking about how their fellow Germans were supposedly badly treated by the Czechs; *"A poor 70-year-old German woman, her wooden leg on fire, swimming across the river to escape the Czechs."*

   When Hitler was ready to attack Poland, they staged a fake attack, supposedly by Polish troops, on a German radio station. They left behind, not only dead Germans, but the bodies of dead Polish soldiers they had killed to make people think that Polish troops had attacked them. This is known now as a "false flag operation".

7. **EMOTION** Adolph Hitler was adored by large numbers of Germans. How could a dictator who caused so much human suffering have had such control over the minds of people? The answer, in part, is that

Hitler knew how to tell the German people what they wanted to hear. He inspired them to feats of aggression by the use of heroic modeling stories of patriotism;

8. **PROJECTING THE BLAME:** By accusing others, democrats and communists, of attempting to overthrow their government, they blamed others of doing the same thing they were trying to do.

... Our educational system lacked the art of picking a few names out of the historical development of our people and making them the common property of the whole . . . thus tying. a uniform, uniting bond around the entire nation. They did not understand how to make the really significant men of our people appear as outstanding heroes in the eyes of the present. to concentrate the general attention upon them and thus create a unified mood. They were not able to raise what was glorious for the nation above the level of objective presentation, and fire the national pride by such gleaming examples .... Adolph Hitler *Mein Kamp*

One of the most significant descriptions of what ultimately led to the success of the Nazis is described by a protestant clergyman, Martin Niemoller, who served time in a concentration camp himself:

"In Germany, the Nazis first came for the Communists. I did not speak up because I was not a Communist. Then they came for the Jews, and I did not speak up because I was not a Jew. Then they came for the trade unionists, and I didn't speak up because I was not a trade unionist. Then they came for the Catholics, and because I was a Protestant, I did not speak up. Then they came for ME... by that time there was no one left to speak up for anyone."

Anyone who was different, anyone who criticized or failed to support their cause was labeled unpatriotic. Anyone who opposed them was labeled a criminal. Even their own members who did not fall in line with the party were taken out. Our educational system has failed to teach the reality of what happened in Germany, their only explanation is to label Hitler a madman. Now, we see similar behavior in our own country, yet few have any understanding of how this can happen.

Democratic societies have tried to change the nature of society by making it more equal, yet in human history, this has been far more rare than we might suppose.

2. THE ORIGIN OF PREJUDICE

Social psychology in America had as a major goal; to explain how the atrocities in Nazi Germany in WWII could possibly have happened. How could the good people of Germany have so readily worked in the concentration camps, sending people to the gas ovens on weekdays, played with their kids on Saturday, gone to church on Sunday, and back to the gas ovens on Monday? They did not do so because they were forced, they often did so with the enthusiasm of someone who wants to be a hero, to do so for patriotism; for God and Country.

Gordon Allport published a study of adult prejudice that has since become the outstanding text on the subject of beliefs, values, attitudes, and opinions. In *The Nature of Prejudice,* Allport penned an exhaustive but remarkably readable classic in the field of human psychology. This book, along with his Psychology of Rumor, was to make Gordon Allport one of the most respected psychologists in history.

Prejudice means to prejudge. Based on our past experience, we all generalize to new people and new situations. In effect, we prejudge both people and events even before we have had experience with them. We may prejudge them to be good or we may prejudge them to be bad. In its normal usage today, prejudice also includes discrimination. When we discriminate, we behave differently toward one person than we do toward another. If we make a prejudgment that some people or things are bad, we may treat them in an unfair way.

Allport has conducted exhaustive studies in which he evaluated the following major theories of prejudice: (I) conflict, (2) personality type, (3) displacement of aggression, or scapegoating, and (4) learning.

Conflict has often been a historical source of hatred. If two people compete for the same thing, one will emerge as the victor. When the issues are important to the individual, the losers are rarely known for their sportsmanship. The conflict may be for jobs. In a normal job market, such competition may be fierce enough, but in a depression, the effects of being passed over are likely to be even greater. Applied to race relations, the theory would be that we not only fight fiercely for our own jobs, but we fight for those with whom we identify. If a member of our race is competing for a job with a member of another race, there is often a strong tendency to pick those of our in-group over the others.

Our in-group may not be based simply on race; religion or politics or sports, or any of many other affiliations may cause us to root for an individual whose views are most in accord with our own and discriminate against someone whose views are different. Rather than engage in a personal competition with another individual, we tend to identify with an in-group and to support all its members against members of another group with which we identify less.

Competition may occur over more things than jobs. Competition may be over the "hearts and minds of men." Such competition has produced some of the greatest and most violent wars of history. The religious wars of the Middle Ages, the ideological differences between fascism, communism, and democracy, and even opinions as to the books that should be used in our schools produce issues of conflict. None involves a physical prize to be fought over, but each has proven an even more powerful symbolic prize. The fact that history has little good to say about such conflicts centuries later has never dampened the ardor with which each generation has fought for its in-group.

PSYCHOLOGY AND "MIND CONTROL"

Public opinion has a subtle effect on all of us. We learn that others will think less of us if we behave in thus and such a manner. We learn that cries of outrage come from our peers if we violate the rules of the game. We may find it difficult to escape from such conditioning. Worse still, we may find that we are no longer conforming to others, we are conforming to the dictates of our own minds, dictates that are the product of social conditioning. The subtle effects of social learning may, in fact, prove to be more effective controls over the mind than either the threat of physical punishment or the harangue of public opinion.

If we choose to do something of our own free will, without physical coercion and without the pressure of public opinion, then our decision must surely be "free"? Never in history has this question been asked by so many; increasingly it is becoming the question of the twenty-first century. In some cases, it is asked because people fear the effects of advertising, or television violence, or other forms of propaganda on their own decisions. In some cases, the question reflects a fear that psychologists may use their newfound knowledge of the mind to control the minds of the masses. In fact, the fear of control by psychologists is overrated.

No psychologist has yet discovered a technique for mind control that has not long been used by church, state, and parents to produce "desired" behavior in others. At any rate, if one were going to use such knowledge to control the minds of others, one would not go about telling them how it is done. *Learning how it is done, makes it increasingly less likely to be an effective control.* The question of mind control is new-not because mind control itself is new, but because we are only now realizing the extent to which such control exists.

If you learn how mind control has been used in the past, it makes you somewhat less likely that you will fall for it when others use it.

Consider how societies have used fear to control the behavior of others, from children to adults:

- If you don't behave the boogeyman will get you!

- If you don't do as I say the Chupacabra will drag you off!
- Santa will only leave you a lump of coal if you are naughty.

    Santa *"knows if you are sleeping, he knows if you are awake, he knows if you've been bad or good..."* Santa is the FBI of misbehaving children.

- Believe what I tell you, or God will send you to burn in the eternal fires of Hell.
- If you aren't a loyal supporter, your political party will publicly shame you.

Mind control is everywhere.

In a sense, a book on psychology is a book on mind control; not a book on how to control minds, but a book that explains the controls that have been observed and recorded by psychologists and historians.

Out of such knowledge an entirely new concept of freedom is beginning to emerge. It may no longer be enough to be free from an arbitrary use of power and from the arbitrary opinions of others. Can we be free if we are unaware of the controls that our early conditioning and experiences that others have embedded in our own mind?

Children learn to fear more than bugs. They are, in fact, taught at a very early age, consciously and unconsciously, to avoid certain types of people, people whose political, religious, or other behavior may be different from their own. You see the sad result of this in today's politics of hate.

They are conditioned to love, fear, and hate. By the time they are adults, there is scarcely any area of their behavior that is not affected by the early social control.

3. THEORIES OF PREJUDICE

1. AUTHORITARIAN PERSONALITY TYPES:

One of the very first theories of where prejudice originates is the idea that, unlike the rest of us, some people are just naturally prone to becoming authoritarian. They defer to authority and expect that others will defer to their authority. Many hundreds of studies were cranked out by psychologists. As we will see, prejudice and cruelty are too common to be explained by just a "Type" theory. Yet, to this day, it is all too common to see, for example, school shooters labeled as "mentally ill" or even evil, with no consideration for other factors.

2. LEARNING THEORY: Prejudice As Learned

We learn negative emotions and rational reasons for judging others from our peers and society.
There is a classic example of this; a picture of the Grand Dragon of the Ku Klux Klan at a cross burning, standing alongside his son. The man is dressed in a white sheet with a white pillow case over his head. Two eye holes are cut out of the pillowcase. Next to the man is his son, roughly ten years old, wearing a white sheet, with a white pillowcase over his head.

Anyone who has seen this can see that this child is growing up in an environment where he is learning prejudice. He is surrounded by neighbors and friends who share the same hatred of others who are different. He hears the same reasons, that others are controlling the country, that others are taking our jobs, going to replace us, part of a secret cabal of evil that runs the country.

3. CONFLICT THEORY: Competition over jobs, etc.

This is the theory that, because people may have to compete with other groups over jobs, they will develop prejudice against others. We saw this in Texas and elsewhere following the Vietnam war. Vietnamese who immigrated to America often took up fishing as their only source of income. Fishermen who were already fishing here would trash the nets of the Vietnamese and sabotage their boats.

4. GENERALIZED PREJUDICE:

Psychologist Gordon Allport wrote the book on prejudice, called *THE NATURE OF PREJUDICE*. In it, he describes a remarkable experiment on prejudice. Is conflict always necessary to produce prejudice? Must we have had a bad experience with a member of another group before we will display prejudice to a member of another group?

In a study with college students by E. Earl Hartley, he provides an answer. Hartley designed a questionnaire to provide data on the extent to which students liked or disliked various ethnic groups. The students were asked whether they would like or dislike someone of a given race to be admitted to our country, live next door, work together on a job, etc. Questions were asked about members of thirty-two nations and races, including French, English, Jews, Italians, Indians, Armenians, Daniereans, and Wallonians. The questionnaire barely stopped short of asking, "Would you like your sister to marry one?"

The findings indicate that those who tended to be prejudiced against familiar ethnic groups, tended to be prejudiced against all ethnic groups, including the Daniereans, and Wallonians.

Who are Daniereans, and Wallonians?

There are no such people. He made them up.

How can you be prejudiced against people who do not even exist? You cannot have had any bad experiences with such people, because they do not exist. You cannot even have heard anything bad about these people, because they do not even exist.

Gordon Allport suggests that this reaction represents a *generalized* attitude of prejudice. That is; since we are the best, anyone who is not "we", must not be as good as we are.

Our attitude may result, not from conflict, but from a culturally inculcated feeling of pride for one's own country, combined with an almost inevitable feeling that since we are the best, other groups must be inferior to us.

5. IN GROUP VS. OUT GROUP CONFLICT

Us Guys against Them Guys

There is a remarkable example of how prejudice can be created just by separating people into two different groups. This is based on earlier studies by Tajfe and Billig, In a similar deceptively simple experiment, subjects were given the task of judging how many dots were in a series of slides they were shown. There were so many dots and the slides were presented so fast, that no one could count them, they could only guess.

They wrote their guess down on a piece of paper. The experimenters then collected their responses, took them into another room, and threw the responses into a waste basket. The psychologists had no interest at all in what their responses were.

Next, they went back into the room, and, purely at random, they told the subjects that "you, you, you, and you" were over estimators. And that the others remaining were under estimators. It was in no way true, the psychologists were only interested in what would happen next, just because the subjects were divided into two groups.

Then they separated the two groups, gave them each a series of puzzles, and at the end, they asked them to rate their group, and then to rate the other group. Each group rated their own group as "above average". But each group rated the other group as only "average."

Students sometimes say, that this is not prejudice. Yet this is the very essence of prejudice: the belief that our group is better than their group.

If a member of one group were later to have a job opening, and they had a choice of who to give that job to, what would they choose? They are likely to give that job to the people in the group they consider "above average" and not the "other" group.

What would happen if we took a group of human children and turned them loose on an island on their own, much as Carpenter did with the rhesus monkeys on Santiago Island? Suppose, too, that we artificially divided the children into two separate groups. Would they stake out a territory and defend it against each other? Or would they come together and meet and talk amiably simply as humans and not as groups? And what would happen within the groups? Would they establish a dominance hierarchy? Or would democracy reign supreme?

Unfortunately, it is not possible to develop a pure study of this type with human children. Any children used would have to be old enough to volunteer for such a project, and by that time, they would have had some influence from their culture. Already they would have experienced the ideals of a democracy, the structure of a school system, the social order of a gym class, and the ties of friendship.

Such a study would not tell us what human nature is "naturally" like, but it would tell us much of what children in our culture are like. Just such a study has been done by Muzafer Sherif, O. J. Harvey, B. Jack White, William R. Hood, and Caroline W. Sherif of the University of Oklahoma in what has become a classic study in intergroup conflict.

4. THE ROBBER'S CAVE EXPERIMENT

A Study in Group Conflict

What would happen if we took a group of human children and turned them loose on an island on their own much as Carpenter did with the rhesus monkeys on Santiago Island? Suppose, too, that we artificially divided the children into two separate groups. Would they stake out a territory and defend it against each other? Or would they come together and meet and talk amiably simply as humans and not groups? And what would happen within the groups? Would they establish a dominance hierarchy? Or would democracy reign supreme?

Unfortunately, it is not possible to develop a pure study of this type with human children. Any children used would have to be old enough to volunteer for such a project, and by that time, they would have had some influence from their culture. Already they would have experienced the ideals of a democracy, the structure of a school system, the social order of a gym class, and the ties of friendship. Such a study would not tell us what human nature is "naturally" like, but it would tell us much of what children in our culture are like. Just such a study has, in fact, been done by Muzafer Sherif, O. J. Harvey, B. Jack White, William R. Hood, and Caroline W. Sherif of the University of Oklahoma in what has become a classic study in intergroup conflict.

The setting is an isolated 200-acre tract in the Sans Bois Mountains of southeastern Oklahoma. Robber's Cave is a densely wooded area with a small cave rumored by the local inhabitants to have been the hideout for famous old-time train robbers Sam Bass and Jessie James.

Now a Boy Scout camp, the Robber's Cave area had bunkhouses and a mess hall, and several swimming spots made by damming up a natural creek. It was an ideal setting for a study in the prepubescent social order.

The experimenters carefully selected 22 fifth-grade boys averaging eleven years of age. All were selected to be as nearly alike as possible. They came from the same racial, religious, socioeconomic, and educational backgrounds. All were well adjusted in school and at home and all had similar I.Q.s.

Similar backgrounds were important in evaluating the studies of differences between groups. If any differences developed between groups, they would not be the result of racial, religious, or national differences between the boys. None of the boys knew each other at the beginning of the experiment. This was important, too, because the experimenters wanted to observe the structure of the group as it was forming.

The boys were assigned at random to two separate groups. Each group had its own bunkhouse at some distance from the other. At the beginning of the experiment, neither group knew of the existence of the other group. The experimenters now sat back to observe and record some of the spontaneous activity of the newly forming groups.

Group Norms Begin to Form

Beginning early in the first week, group norms began to appear. In one of the groups, later named the Rattlers, one of the boys injured his foot, but showed no sign of crying or undue concern over the injury. When the injury was discovered by other members of the troop, they expressed admiration over the boy's toughness, and soon a norm began that members of their group were tough and not crybabies. Injured members later continued the norm by refusing to cry or complain even in the most trying circumstances. Along with this norm of being tough, the group widely adopted and approved the practice of cursing. In contrast, the second group did not adopt the norm of toughness but instead adopted a norm that cursing was taboo. This norm was reinforced within the second group, even in the face of being cursed out by the other group.

Group Identity is Established
The Status Hierarchy
Territorial Behavior

By the end of the first week, both groups had adopted names as separate forms of identity. From the Australian aborigine to the American high school student, it seems to be a common practice to associate one's own group with a particular animal, which then becomes the totem or symbol around which the group rallies. One group spontaneously named themselves the Rattlers. The second group, on discovering that another group was also in the area, asked the staff members if the other group had a name. The staff replied that they did not know, whereupon the second group decided to name themselves, quickly coming up with the name, Eagles.

Early in the first week, cliques began to develop within the groups. Two or more of the higher-ranking boys tended to side with each other while a number of others developed friendship preferences. A status hierarchy had begun. The hierarchy was evident in the way the members of the group reacted to different boys under similar conditions. When lower-ranking members complained about the rules of the game or the proposed activities they were largely ignored by the other members of the group. Yet higher ranking members who complained about similar problems were usually always listened to, even though they may have been unable to get their own way in the group.

The status hierarchy within each group was already tacitly recognized by the group members themselves, although they might not have been able to verbalize what it was. The status hierarchy had its effect, and as early as the second day, expectations were evident. The Eagles had constructed a rope bridge across a stream. The first boy to attempt to walk the bridge was one of the leaders. He made about 15 feet before falling in. Other high-ranking members followed but none did better.

Finally, a lower-ranking member tried. A member of the group commented, "He won't make it very far." But to everyone's amazement, the lower-ranking member crossed the bridge. The group's reaction seemed more surprised that a low-ranking member had succeeded than that the bridge itself had been crossed.

"Looks like this beach has already been claimed."

By the end of the week, the Rattlers had adopted certain areas as their own. The group had "their" swimming hole, "their" hideouts, and even "their" flag, which consisted of a T-shirt on which they had drawn the design of a rattlesnake.

At one point, three of the lower ranking members of the group returned to one of their hideouts to find trash around "their" cave. They were outraged that others had been in "their" cave.

Although the psychologists say the trash had been left by other members of their own group, the three members expressed resentment over the feeling that "outsiders" had been in their territory. Later, the Rattlers wandered close enough to the territory of the Eagles to hear them playing on the baseball diamond.

The reaction was immediate. Some members of the group threatened to "run them off." Others proposed that they "challenge" them. The next day when the Rattlers played on the diamond themselves, the Rattlers noticed changes that they had made to improve the baseball field and some of them declared, "Now this is our diamond."

Social control within the group appeared almost spontaneously. One of the Social controls is seen in how one of the boys in the Eagles had been overbearing and antagonistic in his comments toward the other Eagle boys. Later he overheard the other boys talking about him and cutting him down for his behavior. Thereafter, he went out of his way to be agreeable to the boys and to win their favor.

Not all the social control exerted was so subtle. Two of the boys became homesick and eventually were allowed to go home. Their constant desire to go home had dropped the status of one of them from a previous high. After the two had both gone, the remaining boys made repeated derogatory remarks about those who "chicken out." Another boy commented that "Things are going to be better around here now." While still a third, who himself had also talked about going home earlier, volunteered the statement that, "No one else in this camp will do the same."

The derogatory comments about the two departed members seemed to have served effectively as a modeling story within the group: Now, other boys who had been homesick ended their talk of going home. Peer group pressure inaction.

GROUP NORMS DEVELOP

After the first week, the group norms had become sufficiently well established that the differences between the two groups were marked. At times the staff had to check on various minor squabbles among the Rattlers because the norm of "toughness" was so firmly established that few of the members complained of their injuries. The only member of the group who did cry was ignored by the other members of the group.

In contrast, the Eagles had not adopted this norm. Even the leader of the group commonly cried over injuries. The Eagles had, however, adopted a· norm that prevented complaining. Members of the Eagles who were homesick were ridiculed, two of them for as long as three days. Furthermore, the Eagles adopted the practice of swimming in the nude, something that was not taken up by the Rattlers.

The members of both groups came from similar backgrounds. Despite their similarities, differences began to develop almost immediately. What would happen in the long run? Would two completely separate cultures emerge from these two groups? As adults; left to grow up on their own in the wilderness, would we end up with two tribes living nearby with their own separate customs, their own separate rules, and their own identities?

Does this spontaneous development of social norms account for the differences between entire nations? Are the national stereotypes of German "efficiency," "industrious" Japanese, French "lovers of wine, women, and song," and the "easygoing" Italians all products of equally spontaneous adoptions of norms that have come to be accepted within their groups? Perhaps it is a little much to generalize from two handfuls of boys to the entire world population, but the suggestion is strong.

By the eighth day, the interaction between the two groups began for the first time. The Eagles, on learning that a second group was at camp, issued a challenge to the Rattlers to a game of baseball. The challenge was carried by one of the staff members and eagerly accepted by the Rattlers. Each group arrived with its own flag, When the two groups came together for the very first time, they immediately began to hurl a few insults, even though they had not yet had any bad experiences with each other

The staff arranged a tournament between the two groups. For days, Rattlers and Eagles would compete with each other in baseball, tug-of-war, and a variety of activities to determine which of the two teams would win the prizes. The prizes consisted of much admired four-bladed pocketknives, one for each member of the winning team. The stakes were perhaps not as high as those fought for by nations, but to these boys, the prizes might as well have been the crown jewels.

SUPERSTITIOUS REACTIONS TO LOSING

Before the meeting of the two groups, there had been some discussion among the Eagles about "good sportsmanship," but when the first meeting took place all bets were off.

The member of the Eagles who had displayed the greatest amount of verbal goodwill before the game ended up doing the most catcalling and razzing. It was as if stating the intention of good sportsmanship made it all the easier to be derogatory to the other group. Even before the game got underway, name-calling by one side was countered with claims of, "We can do better than you,' by the other.

"You're not Eagles, you're pigeons," cried a Rattler.

When the smoke had cleared, the Rattlers had won the game. They were exuberant. The Eagles were downcast.

For the second part of the tournament, a tug-of-war was planned. Again, the Eagles lost. The Rattlers felt good enough about winning to cheer the Eagles, noting that "That shows that we are good sports." But they also razzed the dejected Eagles unmercifully.

At the end of this game, the Rattlers left the field. One of the Eagles noticed that the Rattlers' flag had been left behind. The Eagles ran to the flag, tore it down, found some matches, and set it on fire.

AN EAGLE BANNER
SUPERSTITIOUS REACTIONS TO WINNING

The Eagles unexpectedly won the next two games. One member of the Eagles attributed it to their prayers. Another decided that the Rattlers had lost because of all the cursing they did. Still, a third Eagle decided the Rattlers cursed so much that the Eagles should not even talk to them anymore.

Group Solidarity Against a Threat

The Rattlers now decided that it was their turn to strike. Late at night, the Rattlers snuck over to the cabin of the Eagles. Banging and yelling, the intruders turned over beds, ripped mosquito netting, and yelled challenges at the Eagles. The Eagles were too stunned to retaliate immediately. The Rattlers, fleeing home, told each other exaggerated stories of their bravery, and talked of the booty; comic books, and blue jeans-they had pilfered from the Eagles. It seemed as if only a lack of time and a Hollywood sound stage prevented these escapades from being turned into stories of the glories of the Great Wars.

The next day, the Eagles retaliated. While the Rattlers were eating lunch, the Eagles stormed the Rattlers' cabin, turning over their beds and scattering their possessions to the wind. When the Rattlers returned to see the holocaust, the cursing began. "Communists," yelled two of the Rattlers, referring to the Eagles, and all agreed that the Eagles were the lowest.

For days, the raids continued back and forth. The situation had all the makings of a new version of the Hatfields and McCoys. It was a feud that might well be passed on from generation to generation had it been allowed to continue. Each group thought the other to be the very devil. But what did the groups think of themselves? Sherif et al. noted.

> The Eagles bragged to each other they were "good sports" who did their best and who prayed and didn't curse. Later, they refrained from bragging in the presence of the out-group since this was agreed to bring bad luck. The Rattlers were constantly telling each other, and all within hearing distance, that they were brave, winners, not quitters, tough, and (naturally) good sports.

After the contests and raids, stories were told over and over of the accomplishments of this person and that person, blisters acquired in a tug-of-war were compared both in winning and losing groups, and these tales of individual feats grew with each telling.

Having an enemy seemed to increase group solidarity. When confronted by the out-group, even the lowest ranking group members displayed an increased sense of belonging to "their group." Indeed, the lowest ranking members of the group were frequently the most vociferous in their condemnation of the other group.

Could it be that having an out-group to hate increases the pride and the prejudice of all the members of the group? Certainly, each team glowed and reveled in unanimous victory when they won over their opponents. Backslapping, bragging, and even occasional condescending bits of goodwill toward the losing team were common bedfellows of victory.

In losing, the picture was sometimes different. Occasionally there were recriminations directed toward members of the in-group. But often the loss was glossed over by rationalizing the loss as due to 'bigger guys" on the other team, the Rattlers going so far in one case as to rationalize that they lost the game because their bats were heavier than the bats of the Eagles.

Members of one team frequently accused members of the other team of cheating or bad sportsmanship, even when staff members present knew that such charges were without foundation; much like the claims that the election of 2021 was "stolen" in America. With or without foundation, the charges were readily believed by the accuser and members of his group.

AN OUTSIDE THREAT LEADS TO INSIDE SOLIDARITY.

Increased solidarity within an in-group is often observed in times of conflict with an out-group. Hitler took advantage of this common reaction by filling the German people's press with stories of the threat to Germany, usually an imaginary threat, that was posed by the neighbors that he wished to attack. Austria, Czechoslovakia, Poland, Russia, and France all became victims of a similar degree of xenophobia.

Within the country that feels threatened, a feeling of solidarity also exists. Sociologists have long noted that during times of war even the suicide rates go down. Having an out-group to hate seems to give a sense of urgency and purpose to even the more menial preparations for confrontation.

So, what produces conflict? In a group of children already touched by years of our culture, two things seem to be involved. First, merely separating individuals into two distinct groups seems almost sufficient. Shirts and skins or Eagles and Rattlers, the acquisition of an identity seems to occur rapidly, and the identity takes the form of two learning sets of "us-guys" and "them-guys."

Beyond this miniature culture, the world at large already has many such divisions. We identify ourselves by nations, by religions, by beliefs, and by ideology. By politics. By Red vs. Blue. Further, nature has already provided a unique classification of shirts and skins by the subtleties of skin coloring and minor differences in features that lead to racial distinctions,

Our young grow up in a world of good-guy and bad-guy stereotypes. Cowboys and Indians, cops and robbers, narcs and pushers, etc., divide the world into convenient categories in which individuals can feel solidarity with their own in-group while at the same time hating the guys in the other group.

The list of shirts and skins relationships sanctioned by society goes on endlessly: the witches and witch hunters, the slaves and masters, the communists and patriots, and the nonbelievers and believers. In the absence of officially approved sanctions for hatred, we seem to invent our own; -not just the apparent differences of whites and people of color, but also the artificially created differences of labor and management, students and teachers, democrats and republicans, and other designations for those who are with us and those who are against us.

We do not hate all of these to the same degree. The greater the degree of fear that our culture or subculture associates with the out-group, the greater the degree of hatred that seems to be felt toward them.

Here, competition becomes a factor. We compete with "them guys" to end our fear that the other guys will get what we want. When such competition exists within a society, the goods end up being distributed according to the existing status hierarchy of that culture.

The competition between groups often does not have any such Rules of Hoyle to go by. Between nations, races, or religions, the strongest has traditionally played the tune to which the weaker must dance. When the nations are more evenly matched, the outcome may be a series of Hatfield and McCoy-type reprisals, with neither side fully gaining the upper hand. The goal for which the battle is waged seems remarkably unimportant. Whether engaged in a life-or-death struggle, a battle for human souls, or the victory in a game of baseball, the emotions that play on the minds of the participants are remarkably similar.

It is as if we "love to hate" our enemies. Unfortunate as it may be, the hatred of an out-group is often the basis for a powerful form of social bond. The fear we feel when facing an enemy seems somewhat reduced when we face it with someone else who shares our fear and hate. It matters little what the enemy may be or who is in the right. What matters is that we felt a common bond with those who agree with our hatred.

Common goals, like common hatreds, produce a feeling of comradeship within a group. If we have struggled long and hard for a common goal, we share a social bond with those who have shared our struggle. Sherif, and his associates at the University of Oklahoma investigated whether such a formula could eliminate hostility between the warring Rattlers and Eagles.

They had already determined the amount of conflict between the groups could not be reduced through increased interaction of the two groups in noncompetitive situations. Quite the opposite occurred: The more times the groups met, even where competition was not allowed, the greater the hostility between them.

Now the researchers tried a new ploy. They arranged a series of problems that neither group could solve by itself: Cooperation between the groups would be essential to solve the task. The simplest cooperative task required that all the boys from both groups pool a certain amount of money to enable them to view a movie that both groups wanted to see.

More complex tasks required that all the boys fan out to see whether they could find a leak in the camp's waterlines that had cut off the water supply to the camp. Still, another task required that twenty of the boys pull together on ropes to start the engine of a truck that had supposedly become stalled.

After a half dozen such cooperative ventures, group identities began to break down. Catcalling gave way to talking and joking between members of the two groups, and by the end of the cooperative sessions, group identities had disappeared sufficiently that none of the original hostility was apparent.

The effectiveness of such cooperation for a common goal is unquestioned. In the world at large, however, it is difficult to imagine anything that could bring all the nations together for a common cause except, perhaps, an invasion of flying saucers.

But what happens to adults? Is the behavior of an adult automatically more rational than that of the children studied by Sherif and associates? Unfortunately, the reverse is often true. We know from centuries of experience that instead of becoming more rational, adults often exhibit behavior that is increasingly violent and less amenable to change.

5. THE MILGRAM OBEDIENCE STUDY

How Far Would You Go?

Although not designed as a study of prejudice, one study suggests that a willingness to hurt others, as in Hitler's treatment of Jews, is not limited to any simple personality type. Stanley Milgram, at Yale University, wanted to determine the extent to which subjects would continue to obey an authority figure, even when that authority figure told them to do something that could cause physical harm to another person.

The question in the back of his mind came from the atrocities committed by otherwise normal German citizens, who were issued uniforms and put in charge of concentration camps in Hitler's Germany. Were some people more likely than others to obey authority figures when asked to harm someone else?

The experiment began with subjects who answered an ad asking for people to participate in a study that purported to be investigating the effects of punishment on learning. One subject was strapped in a chair, wired with electrodes, and asked to correctly memorize a wordlist. Another subject tested the first and administered punishment for any mistakes. The punishment consisted of an electric shock.

The subject being "tested" never actually received any shocks. He was, in fact, an experimenter's helper, who had been instructed to make mistakes at various points throughout the learning process. The real subject was the one who was doing the testing-and the shocking.

The person who was to administer the test and the shocks was shown a machine in which electric shocks beginning at 15 volts could be increased all the way up to 450 volts. Each increase was approximately 15 volts. The shock board was clearly labeled from "mild" at 15 volts up to "*danger severe*" at 450 volts. Every time the fellow in the chair made a mistake, the real subject was instructed to raise the intensity of the shock another 15 volts.

The person giving the shock never knew that the shock victim was not actually being shocked. The "shocked" victim had been trained to react appropriately every time the subject administered the punishment. At 75 volts he would grunt in reaction to the apparent shock; at 100 volts he complained about the shock; at 150 volts he demanded his release; at 285 volts he screamed, then fell silent.

The question was who would go how far in administering what was apparently a very harmful degree of punishment to the victim. Would any subjects go all the way? Or would all of them stop the experiment as soon as the fellow receiving the shocks began to complain that they were painful? After all, none of the subjects knew that the person being shocked was anything other than a person like themselves. As it turned out, of the 40 original subjects, 62 percent of them went all the way up to 450 volts!

Why? Unlike the soldiers in charge of the concentration camps in Germany, none of these subjects' jobs or lives depended on obeying the voice of authority. The subjects went on with the shocking simply because they were told to do so.

Do only men behave with such disregard for their fellow humans? In a remarkable experiment by Phillip Zimbardo of Stanford, he had girls in a similar situation, shocking a fellow student for mistakes they made. Again, the student being shocked was never really shocked and was acting as if she was when a light went on.

Zimbardo found that girls would rarely shock a fellow student when they were sitting right across from them. Yet in a bizarre twist, Zimbardo repeated the same experiment with one change. Now the student doing the supposed shocking was allowed to wear a pillowslip over their face so that the student pretending to be shocked would not know who they were.

When the girls who were shocking the other "student" for making mistakes could be anonymous, all vestiges of civility vanished. The girls would now shock the bejebees out of her fellow "student".

Think of gossiping behind someone's back, saying things you would never say to their face. We see this in using mean tweets to trash another. Being anonymous makes it easier to hurt others because you do not have to face them..

Think of how readily political followers or soldiers can harm another when they feel their actions are anonymous, when no one else will know. We see this in the behavior of those who attacked the capital on Jan. 6, feeling they were anonymous as part of a mob. Often, they were surprised when they were held relponsible.

What was surprising about the Milgram result is not that there were some authoritarian personality types who would readily obey the command to harm others, but that so many people would go so far, so often.

Such results indicate clearly that we need not postulate any specific authoritarian type to explain such behavior: The behavior is a phenomenon that is readily elicited in the great majority of people.

What would you have done if you had been at My Lai in South Vietnam and had been told to take no prisoners? What would you do if you were a narcotics agent and were told that Mr. X had been repeatedly reported to the Heroin Hot Line as a suspect, and that "we want to fix the pusher"?

What would you do if you were told by someone in our government to do something illegal for the "cause"? Would most people be likely to use their sense of decency and fair play? Or would they obey the voice of authority that told them to leave no survivors, fix the pusher, or hurt their political enemies? Whatever one may think of the ethics that Milgram used in conducting such a study, it is clear that his results sent a chill of fear up the spines of all who read them.

How much of human prejudice can we account for by the theory of personality type? Prejudice is not limited to a few people of a given personality type. All people display prejudice of some type or another, and a disconcertingly large number of people will quite readily discriminate against others when they think they can get away with it. A personality-type theory is useful, but most psychologists consider the authoritarian personality only one of many factors that would explain the nature of prejudice.

6. THE GOMBE CHIMPANZEE WARS
The Outcome of Our Biology?

Perhaps the most important, and the most censored, of the discoveries of Jane Goodall was her description of the war between two groups of neighboring chimpanzees. This account was so disturbing that it was censored by the media in favor of the far more tame idea that chimpanzees could make and use tools. Many refused to believe that the kindly-looking chimpanzees could behave with the cruel intent of destroying their fellow species, just as humans have done in thousands of years of war.

Many doubted her description of the chimpanzee wars, to this day it is absent from our media; yet every study since has confirmed her early reports.

Two groups of chimpanzees, the Kahama in the South, the Kasakela in the North, shared close territories. Over years, after a new Kasakela leader took over, the Kasakela males would isolate and kill the Kahama males in the South, one by one. Even the Kahama male, who had been most friendly to the killer tribe, was "mercilessly" killed.

That left only one young male, and eventually, he too was murdered. The males from the North took over the females, and the Southern territory, killing some of the females and beating others. It seems a microcosm of human history, too often reflected in the atrocities of Nazi Germany, Kosovo, Myanmar, and now Putin's atrocities in Ukraine.

It is too strikingly familiar to the many more incidences of genocide in the world, to this day, by humans: It is even similar to the lessor conflict between red and blue politics in America. No quarter is given, no agreement is possible.

Consider the behavior of the four police officers as one of them kneeled on George Floyd's neck for over nine minutes as he cried "mother" and begged for his life as he struggled to breathe. All four officers lied about what happened in their reports, to cover up their behavior. Had it not been for the video recordings of many bystanders, we would never have known what really happened. This is a striking comparison of our similarity to the apes, and how cruel we can be.

We can learn better. At least, that is the theory that democracy, justice, and psychology are based on. But we cannot learn better as long as we censor the truth from our children. Our schools have failed to teach what is important to know at every level.

Even though only three of the "guards" behaved with cruelty toward their fellow students, not one of the other "guards" spoke out, and not one tried to stop it. We see this echoed in the police, who stood by and watched as their fellow officers beat and killed a civilian.

Unfortunately, the censorship of Goodall's most important work by the media, and its absence from our educational system, detract from our understanding of what we are seeing all around us. Goodall says she experienced "horrific nightmares" from this in the years to come. Many refused to believe Goodall's account of the murderous behavior in chimpanzees, just as many refused to believe that police officers could behave with such callous disregard for others and their oath of office. Or that politicians could value getting re-elected more than truth.

Since then, other scientists have confirmed what Goodall honestly showed. That is science at its best, in the ability to confirm or deny such evidence based on new studies, including observational studies, that *replicate the evidence*. See *The Gombe Chimpanzee War 1974-1978* at

https://www.youtube.com/watch?v=fxWY7rosS-0

7. THE MYTHS OF CULTURE

Each country has its own mythology about war. In Russia, children are taught that Russia won WWII alone while the Allies bided their time, hoping that Germany and Russia would destroy each other. Russians believe that the Allies invaded France only when it became apparent that Germany was beaten. German children, in contrast, may read books by Paul Carell hinting in colorful language that German soldiers could have won the war *"If only..."*

Every country that participated has its own stories of martial bravery, and its citizens seem to believe that their nation did the most.

In the agony and ecstasy of World War I, the troops marched to Europe to the tune of "When Johnny Comes Marching Home." Implicit in the parade atmosphere that saw the doughboys off to war was the promise of the "... hurrah, hurrah" of glory that would greet them on their return.

But the trench warfare that greeted them in Flanders Field was unlike the glory they may have imagined. Time after time the Ailed troops leaped from their trenches and charged the German lines. Time after time the German machine guns decimated the ranks of the Allies. Between the Allied charges, the German soldiers were ordered to charge, and the machine guns of the Allies would end the German hopes of triumph. This stalemate continued unabated month after month.

The Viennese physician Sigmund Freud found it difficult to explain the carnage of World War I-so difficult that he found it necessary to suggest the existence of *Thanatos,* an aggressive instinct, a "death wish," a drive to self-destruction. Thanatos was presumably the opposite of Eros, the drive to procreate.

To Freud, such an instinct seemed the only possible explanation of how humans, like the lemmings, could regularly march in unison to their deaths. Lemmings march to the high cliffs of Dover and dive off into the ocean. This is also a myth. During mating season, many thousands of them crowd together at Dover and elsewhere. It is the crowd of Lemming bodies that pushes some of their own off of the edge. They do not intentionally commit suicide.

One century and several wars later, Freud's conclusion that humans are innately aggressive is echoed in the writings of the ethologist Konrad Lorenz, who views our aggressive folly as programmed into our genes. Along the same lines, the author Robert Ardrey writes convincingly of modern human's descent from a line of killer apes who scavenged their way across the Pleistocene plains of Central Africa over a million years ago. In *African Genesis*, Ardrey proposes that our single greatest drive is that of the "territorial imperative," the drive to stake out a territory of our own, to acquire possessions, and to defend what is ours from all comers.

Yet for each proponent of the view that human nature is innately aggressive, there seems to be another who will say it isn't so. The French philosopher Jean Jacques Rousseau argued vehemently that we are born good but are corrupted by society. Rousseau originated the concept of man as the "noble savage" corrupted by society

Even when 'public opinion does not conspire to harass or publicly censure the individual, its effects may be telling. We saw in the study by Solomon Asch, how the opinion of others could produce marked changes in the verbal reports of an individual. Two-thirds of the subjects who disagreed with the group opinion nevertheless acquiesced purely because of what they imagined the others would think of them if they did not conform. The subjects who refused to conform were not argued with, ignored, or rejected, but even without this rough treatment, the pressure was strong.

John Stuart Mill, in his essay *On Liberty,* was among the first to argue for more than freedom from the threat of physical or economic sanctions against the individual. Mill argued that no one's opinion, no matter how absurd it may seem, should be subjected to censure by the majority. To Mill, to censure someone else's opinion is to assume one's own infallibility. Mill argued that each person should have the right to express even the most outrageous opinions and beliefs without fear of public censorship. He thought this to be true, not because of any inherent value in the opinion of the individual, but precisely because all opinions are fallible and hence no opinion, not even that of the majority, should prevail. In Mill's words:

> *Unfortunately for the good sense of mankind, the fact of their fallibility is far from carrying the weight in their practical judgment, which is always allowed to in theory; for while everyone well knows himself to be fallible, few think it necessary to take any precautions against their own fallibility, or admit the supposition that any opinion, of which they feel very certain, may be one of the examples of the error to which they acknowledge themselves to be liable. Absolute princes, or others who are accustomed to unlimited deference, usually feel this complete confidence in their own opinions on nearly all subjects.*

> *People more happily situated, who sometimes hear their opinions disputed, and are not wholly unused to be set right when they are wrong, place the same unbounded reliance only on such of their opinions as are shared by all who surround them, or to whom they habitually defer: For in proportion to a man's want of confidence in his own solitary judgment, does he usually repose, with implicit trust, on the infallibility of "the world" in general. And of the world, to each individual, means the part of it with which he comes in-contact; his party, his sect, his church, his class of society: The man may be called, by comparison, almost liberal and large minded to whom it means anything so comprehensive as his own country or his own age. Nor is his faith in this collective authority at all shaken be his being aware that other ages, countries, sects,*

churches, classes, and parties have thought, and even now think, the exact reverse. He devolves upon his own world the responsibility of being in the right against dissentient worlds of other peoples; And it never troubles him that mere accident has decided which of these numerous worlds is the object of his reliance, and that the same causes which make him a Churchman in London, would have made him a Buddhist or a Confucian in Peking. Yet it is as evident in itself, as any amount of argument can make it, that ages are no more infallible than individuals; every age having held many opinions which subsequent ages have deemed not only false but absurd; and it is as certain that many opinions now general, will be rejected by future ages, as it is that many, once general, are rejected by the present. life. Within all species, the more aggressive members of the group are the ones who have access to the food. The more aggressive members are also the ones most likely to reproduce. In the wilds of nature, these are survival advantages. Our modem world of technology has changed all this: In a push-button world, the least aggressive can often succeed as well as the most aggressive.

The traditionally subservient world of women has always been based on their lack of physical strength and on the fact that they bear and rear the young of the species. In the twentieth century, however, these factors are no longer handicaps. And in a world where knowledge is more important than strength, the importance that nature has placed on aggression now threatens our existence with the attention-getting specter of a nuclear holocaust.

8. THE STANFORD PRISON EXPERIMENT

A classic study of the abuse of power was done in the early 1970s by Phillip Zimbardo and his associates at Stanford University. Zimbardo paid college students to participate in a two-week study of the effects of a prison environment.

Eighteen students were selected from a number of applicants based on their personality test scores. They were selected to be representative of normal, well-adjusted students. The students were then divided at random into two groups of nine "guards" and nine "prisoners." The prison was constructed in the basement of Stanford's psychology department.

The "prisoners" were arrested, fingerprinted, and booked according to the standard criminal procedure at the local police department and then moved to the Stanford "prison." They received no special instructions. The "guards," working three at a time, were instructed to 'keep order" in their prison. The first day passed uneventfully. Both groups were feeling somewhat silly in their new roles and still uncertain about how to behave. The "guards" were feeling out their power by having the "prisoners" repeatedly "sound off" their prison numbers, army style.

On the second day, the unexpected happened. The "prisoners" rebelled against the authority exercised by the guards. As a group, they refused to cooperate. Jeering and cursing, they taunted the "guards." They stuffed mattresses and beds against the doors of the cells to keep the "guards" out. For a while, the rebellion seemed to be a success, but finally, the guards decided to assert their authority.

They called in the off-duty "guards." After a bull session on how to deal with the situation, they took action. Using a CO_2 fire extinguisher as a weapon, the "guards", decided, on their own, to shoot a chilling blast of CO_2 over the "prisoners" in each cell. The "guards" forced their way into each cell, stripped the "prisoners" naked, and began to enforce discipline in their own way.

As punishment, the "guards" made the "prisoners" do pushups, and clean out toilet bowls with their hands, and Zimbardo notes, singled out certain "prisoners" as "troublemakers" deserving of special punishment. The "prisoners" who were least involved in the rebellion were given especially good treatment in a privilege cell. Later, the "guards" devised a way to psychologically break the will of the "prisoners." They took the prisoners who had led the rebellion, removed them from their cells, arid suddenly began giving them special treatment. The effect was that the other "prisoners" thought they had been "sold out," that their fellow prisoners had become lackeys for the "guards." The solidarity of the "prisoners" had been destroyed in only hours.

Interestingly, the psychological technique used by the "guards" to break the solidarity of the "prisoners" is similar to those used by the North Korean Communists as part of their 'brainwashing" program during the Korean War. Zimbardo notes, this technique is used in American prisons today. Real guards may use such methods to prevent prisoners from developing group solidarity.

The greatest fear of the average prisoner is that other prisoners might consider him or her a "stool pigeon" and decide to execute the prisoner. The threat appears to be effective.

What does it mean? Remember, these were college students-presumably well-educated and presumably average. When they later saw the films and heard the tapes of their behavior, many of the "guards" expressed shock at what they had become.

But here they knew that the "prisoners" were only students. What happens in "real life" where real prison guards or real policemen are told to "keep order"? What happens in mental institutions where the major concern of the poorly paid attendants is not the well-being of the patients but to "keep order?" What happens in Washington when the President of the United States tells his staff to "cover up" a crime as we now know President Nixon did? Will these "real-life" people behave more honorably than the college students in Zimbardo's study? Will they understand their own motives any better than the students?

Some have criticized Zimbardo's study as artificial and not representative of what we would do in a similar situation. But we have to note that the entire of human history, from Hitler to Putin's invasion of Ukraine, from the death of Floyd, and hundreds of others, at the hands of the police to the harsh behavior of American soldiers at Abu Grebe prison in Iraq, we see much worse in the "real" world.

If anything, Zimbardo's study was mild.

9. DEMOCRACY AS AN EFFORT TO GO BEYOND THE DICTATES OF OUR BIOLOGY

Who shall make the laws? Is the power to be invested in the people themselves?

If the rule of the majority is absolute, then what is to prevent a majority from passing laws or in other ways banning minority groups or individuals whom they view as irreligious, immoral, or simply inferior? What is to prevent a majority rule from becoming merely a "dictatorship of public opinion"? In the great democracy of Athens, Socrates was put to death by just such a majority vote. The philosopher John Stuart Mill penned a poignant commentary on such a tyranny of the majority in his famous essay, *On Liberty*

Like other tyrannies, the tyranny of the majority was at first, and is still vulgarly, held in dread, chiefly as operating through the acts of the public authorities. But reflecting persons perceive that when society is itself a tyrant-society collectively, over the separate individuals who compose it-its means of tyrannizing are not restricted to the acts which it may do by the hands of its political functionaries. Society can and does execute its own mandates: And if it issues wrong mandates instead of right, or any mandates at all in things with which it ought not to meddle, it practices a social tyranny more formidable than many kinds of political pressure, since, though not usually upheld by such extreme penalties it leaves fewer means of escape, penetrating much more deeply into the details of life, and enslaving the soul itself. Protection, therefore, against the tyranny of the magistrate is not enough: There needs protection also against the tyranny of the prevailing opinion and feeling; against the tendency of society to impose, by other means than civil penalties, its own ideas and practices as rules of conduct on those who dissent from them: To fetter the development, and, if possible, prevent the formation, of any individuality not in harmony with its ways, and compel all characters to fashion themselves upon the model of its own

One group's concept of freedom has often ignored the freedom of others.

It was a remarkable thing for the framers of the Constitution to admit that the people of the United States could not be trusted with absolute power any more than a king. The realization of this led to the inclusion in the Constitution of a Bill of Rights, which guaranteed freedom of speech, religion, freedom from police persecution, and many other freedoms. It was hoped that the Bill of Rights would prevent the people and their representatives from taking these freedoms away from dissident individuals or minority groups. The civil rights of the individual have not been as absolute as we have believed. But the idea that there were inalienable rights of the individual had been planted.

In the wake of Watergate, story after story has come to light of illegal and semi-illegal activities conducted against American citizens by government agencies. Psychological issues have been involved in such behavior. For example, what would happen if you were a member of a government agency and had the power to use against those whose political or ideological views you feared? What would be the psychological effect of having such power? Would the average person be tempted to use this power?

What does it mean? Remember, these were college students-presumably well-educated and presumably average. When they later saw the films and heard the tapes of their behavior, many of the "guards" expressed shock at what they had become.

But here they knew that the "prisoners" were only students. What happens in "real life" where real prison guards or real policemen are told to "keep order"? What happens in mental institutions where the major concern of the poorly paid attendants is not the well-being of the patients but to "keep order?" What happens in Washington when the President of the United States tells his staff to "cover up" a crime as we now know President Nixon did? Will these "real life" people behave more honorably than the college students in Zimbardo's study? Will they understand their own motives any better than the students?

Even when public opinion does not conspire to harass or publicly censure the individual, its effects may be telling. The study of obedience by Milgram showed how the opinion of others could produce marked changes in the verbal reports of an individual. Two-thirds of the subjects who disagreed with the group opinion nevertheless acquiesced purely because of what they imagined the others would think of them if they did not conform. The subjects who refused to conform were not argued with, ignored, or rejected, but even without this rough treatment the pressure was strong.

John Stuart Mill, in his essay *On Liberty,* was among the first to argue for more than freedom from the threat of physical or economic sanctions against the individual. Mill argued that no one's opinion, no matter how absurd it may seem, should be subjected to censure by the majority. To Mill, to censure someone else's opinion is to assume one's own infallibility. Mill argued that each person should have the right to express even the most outrageous opinions and beliefs without fear of public censorship. He thought this to be true, not because of any inherent value in the opinion of the individual, but precisely because all opinions are fallible and hence no opinion, not even that of the majority, should prevail. In Mill's words:

Unfortunately for the good sense of mankind, the fact of their fallibility is far from carrying the weight in their practical judgment, which is always allowed to in theory; for while everyone well knows himself to be fallible, few think it necessary to take any precautions against their own fallibility, or admit the supposition that any opinion, of which they feel very certain, may be one of the examples of the error to which they acknowledge themselves to be liable.

Absolute princes, or others who are accustomed to unlimited deference, usually feel this complete confidence in their own opinions on nearly all subjects, People more happily situated, who sometimes hear their opinions disputed, and are not wholly unused to be set right when they are wrong, place the same unbounded reliance only on such of their opinions as are shared by all who surround them, or to whom they habitually defer: For in proportion to a man's want of confidence in his own solitary judgment, does he usually repose, with implicit trust, on the infallibility of "the world" in general. And of the world, to each individual, means the part of it with which he comes in- contact; his party, his sect, his church, his class of society: The man may be called, by comparison, almost liberal and large minded to whom it means anything so comprehensive as his own country or his own age. Nor is his faith in this collective authority at all shaken be his being aware that other ages, countries, sects, churches, classes, and parties have thought, and even now think, the exact reverse, He devolves upon his own world the responsibility of being in the right against dissentient worlds of other peoples; And it never troubles him that mere accident has decided which of these numerous worlds is the object of his reliance, and that the same causes which make him a Churchman in London, would have made him a Buddhist or a Confucian in Peking. Yet it is as evident in itself, as any amount of argument can make it, that ages are no more infallible than individuals; every age having held many opinions which subsequent ages have deemed not only false but absurd; and it is as certain that many opinions now general, will be rejected by future ages, as it is that many, once general, are rejected by the present.

10. LEARNING: The Sociocultural Environment

The social order is something a child learns in the process of growing up. A sociologist once described a moment in her life in which she became acutely aware of the social order. At a very young age, she began to set the table all by herself for the first time. She jubilantly went from one place to the next, setting out a plate without seeing who the plate was for. Finally, she got to one extra plate and she set it on the table, announcing that this plate was for "Sunny," the family's black maid. All of a sudden, the room got quiet. Her father said, "Sunny doesn't eat with us." The maid, who was present in the room at the time, cheerfully overlooked the whole incident, but a deep People and problems often affect us differently when we meet them face to face than when we only hear about them.

A lifelong impression was left on the girl that she had embarrassed everyone present. Sunny ate in the kitchen. Subtle as the incident was, it was an acute moment of embarrassment that she recalled for decades after it happened.

For better or worse, it is from such instance that children learn the relationship between themselves and the other people in their society. They learn that each is different. And they learn that each is different in ways other than simply physical appearance.

The structure of society often has even more obvious differences. In almost every American city, there are separate areas where different racial and ethnic groups live. Social groups are divided by custom and tradition into ghettos of "shirts" and "skins" and many things in between. Children hear their parents talk about "that" kind of people or people who live in "that" kind of area. The nuances are subtle but effective.

Perhaps even more remarkable than the obvious physical stratification of Western society is the degree of segregation that formally existed in the child's primary source of information about the outside world, the mass media.

Who were the first black actors to make it big in the media? Not just with a role, but with an actual hero image? In the movies, it was Sidney Poitier; in television, it was Bill Cosby of the I Spy series. These two were in the vanguard of innumerable black heroes. Until Poitier and Cosby, however, nearly 200 years had passed in America in which no black child had a hero to identify with. The seriousness of the problem was demonstrated by a psychological study in the 1950s:

When black children were given a preference in playing with black dolls or white dolls, they usually picked the white ones.

Equally as important as the structure of society are the attitudes the children learn toward other groups. Can the association of a group with a good word or a bad word cause that group to take on the same good or bad connotation as the word?

R. Rosenthal, a professor at Harvard University, provides a remarkable answer. Rosenthal distributed some rats among a group of students. He explained to the students that some of them would get a "maze-bright" rat that had been bred for generations, specifically for its ability to learn. Other students would be given a "maze-dull" rat that had been bred for generations to produce a strain that was resistant to learning.

After randomly assigning the rats, Rosenthal sat back to observe the progress of the students. At the end of a series of tests, sure enough, the "maze-bright" rats did markedly better than the "maze-dull" rats. The results came out exactly as expected-except that there had been no difference at all between the two groups of rats at the beginning. The only difference was that some students had been told that their rat was "maze-bright," while others had been told that their rat was "maze-dull."

Then why did the two groups of rats perform so differently if there was no difference in their genetic backgrounds? The difference seemed to lie in the way the students treated their rats. Those who had been given "maze-bright" rats picked them up tenderly, stroked them repeatedly, whispered sweet nothings in their ears, and treated them like the choicest product of evolution. In contrast, those given the "maze-dull" rats seemed considerably less enthused with their subjects, whose ignorance had apparently already been proven.

The keepers of the "maze-dull" rats played with them less, picked them up roughly, and sometimes slammed cage doors on their tails, frightening the rats. In short, there was a considerable difference in the learning environment of the "maze-dull" rats compared to that of the "maze-bright," rats which were treated like kings.

The principle is far-reaching. We react much differently to those we perceive as intelligent than to those we perceive as dull. First impressions, sometimes based on hearsay and sometimes based on inadequate information, carry a tremendous amount of weight. Comments we have heard from others about people we have never met may well prejudice our behavior toward them even more than the objective evidence. We like those we are told are likable. We also dislike those whose names have been associated with something undesirable.

Harold Kelly, of the University of California, Los Angeles, provides an example of how pervasive such a simple association can be. A guest lecturer was invited to talk to a group of students. Before the talk, Kelly handed out a biographical sketch about the speaker's background, his interests, and something of his personality. All the students received exactly the same description of the lecturer, with one important difference. At random, half of the students received a description that included a comment to the effect that the lecturer is a "rather warm person," while the other half received a description noting that the man is a "rather cold person."

At the end of the lecture, Kelly asked the students to fill out a set of rating scales about the lecturer. Students who had received the biographical sketch with the "rather warm" comment rated the lecturer as significantly more sociable, popular, good-natured, humorous, and even humane than did the students who received the "rather cold" insertion.

But the proof was in their behavior. Of the students who received the "rather warm" insertion, 56 percent of them interacted with the lecturer by asking him questions or talking with him after class. In contrast, only 32 percent of those who had been given the "rather cold" description did so.

Statements about religion, politics, sex, war, drugs, and so on that are implanted early in childhood later arise to color our liking or disliking of people, even before we meet them. And our liking or disliking of them may determine whether we are likely to offer them a job, treat them with equal justice, or even provide them with a civil greeting. More than this, such preconceived descriptions, attached to a wide variety of religious, political, or social ideas, bias us for or against ideas even before we have a chance to consider them on their merits. If fears are strong, if the early conditioning has been effective, it may prove impossible for us to change our mind even in the face of objective evidence to the contrary.

The effect of such conditioning may be "guilt by association." The words that are associated with an individual tend to "rub off" on him regardless of his merit. Gordon Allport (1954, p. 256) describes an example of such stimulus generalization from our own era of McCarthyism.

> Thus, the striking feature of red scapegoating is its grease spot effect. Almost anyone who is disliked or is suspected of holding any contrary values of almost any subject can be, and is, called a Communist-especially those who advocate liberal, pro-labor, tolerant, or even analytical views of Communism and its policies. College professors are suspect because whenever emotion is in control, anti-intellectualism prevails.

During the witch-hunting of the fifteenth century, Pope Innocent VIII saw fit to denounce liberals and rationalists who "with most unblushing effrontery" contended that witchcraft is not a real thing. Anyone who called for a critical and differentiated appraisal of Communism and of Communist phobia in the middle of the twentieth century similarly laid himself open to abuse from high sources (Senate committees, Senate legislatures, boards of college regents).

The McCarthy senate hearings in 1950 destroyed the reputations and careers of many innocent people who were blacklisted as communists or communist sympathizers.

11. CONFLICTING BELIEFS: COGNITIVE DISSONANCE

We have seen what happens when different groups of people come into conflict over an issue. But what happens when the conflict exists between two ideas within the same individual?

Some years ago, a prophet of a small religious sect received a revelation that, on December 21, their world would be destroyed by a great disaster. According to the prophet, the members of this sect would be saved at the last moment because of their belief in the forces from another world. Anguished, but hopeful of a new life, some of the members of the sect quit their jobs, others spent their savings, and all waited for the end to come. On the night of the great event, the faithful gathered with the· prophet to await the inevitable.

What would happen if, when the day came, the world went on as usual? Leon Festinger, Henry Riecken, and Stanley Schachter wanted to find out. After discretely questioning the members of the sect, the psychologists sat back to observe the reaction of the faithful to the coming of the end. Doomsday came and went. Nothing happened.

Now the believers experienced the unpleasant state known as cognitive dissonance. They had two dissonant cognitions, two conflicting beliefs:

First, they believed that their faith in the prophet was correct and that they were not fools for believing.

Second, they saw that doomsday did not produce the disaster they expected.
Clearly, both cognitions could not be correct.

Festinger and his associates found that the change in the followers' belief could be predicted by knowing their degree of commitment to the belief. Those who had believed in the prophecy, but had not quit their jobs or awaited the end with the group, decided that the prophecy was probably wrong. Those with the greatest commitment came to an entirely different conclusion: Not only were they correct all along-quite the contrary, but the prophet also declared, it was their vigilance and faith that had saved the day! Secure in the belief that they had triumphed, these members felt, not downcast or foolish, but exuberant.

The experimenters concluded that when experiencing the unpleasant state of cognitive dissonance, if we cannot change our thoughts or behavior, as in the case of those who had already gone to await doomsday, then we will invent an excuse that will justify our behavior to ourselves or to others.

Perhaps the most convincing-and the most frightening-evidence of cognitive dissonance comes from studies of what is sometimes called the "innocent victim" effect. Berscheid, Boyd, and Waister conducted a study in which college student volunteers were required to administer electric shocks to other students.

After completing this unpleasant task, each was asked to rate their "victim" as to how nice a person they believed him or her to be. Under normal circumstances, most college students will give a stranger they have just met the benefit of the doubt, usually rating him as better than average. After having shocked the innocent stranger, however, their reactions change. *They now rate the person they have hurt less favorably than they would a stranger they have not hurt.*

How can people come to dislike someone they have hurt? One possible explanation comes from the cognitive dissonance interpretation of similar studies by Lerner and Simmons: The students who administer the shocks seem to have two dissonant cognitions. First, the students believe themselves to be fine, honest people who would not intentionally hurt anyone who did not deserve to be hurt. Second, they have just hurt someone who did not deserve to be hurt.

Their thinking could now take two possible directions. They could believe that they are not as fine and honest as they thought, and were capable of hurting someone who did not deserve to be hurt. Or they could reason that the person they have just hurt was not so fine and honest, and perhaps deserved to be hurt. The result suggests that, rather than change their perception of themselves as fine and honest, the students came to believe that their victims must have deserved to be hurt.

Interestingly, Berscheid and her associates could find no such dislike of the victim in a control group where the students believed that the person they were shocking would later have a chance to shock them back. Here, it appears that the students felt, "Well, I know I am a fine fellow, and I am going to get shocked just like this other fellow, therefore, we must both be fine fellows." Of course, such thoughts do not have to occur to the individual on a conscious level. Everyone automatically assumes that they are good and that they would not hurt anyone without cause. Given this basic belief, the opinion may follow automatically.

The reaction of the first group of subjects seems remarkably common. Guards in the prison camps in Nazi Germany aided in inflicting suffering and death on over ten million innocent victims. Yet how do you suppose the guards viewed themselves? Do you think they considered themselves to be evil and cruel? Or do you think they considered the victims as evil people who deserved their fate? Before he committed suicide, Adolph Hitler wrote a last testament in which he declared that all he had tried to do was to make the world a better place to live by getting rid of the "undesirable" people in the gas ovens at the concentration camps.

12. THE "JUST WORLD" HYPOTHESIS

Criminals often justify their actions against an innocent victim by saying that the person was so rich they "deserved" to be robbed or beaten. Public officials. who inflict severe penalties on prostitutes or drug users, who hurt no one but themselves, must come to believe that such people are so despicable that they deserve anything that society does to them, a view often supported by the media. If we believe the World to be a "Just World" then we may often have to change our opinion of the injustices that we see to make the injustice conform to our own view of the world.

In *The Social Animal*, Eliot Aronson notes that we may justify the behavior of conflicting Ideas with others in a manner very similar to the way we justify our own beliefs and actions. During a student protest movement at. Kent State University in the late 1960s, the National Guard was called out to keep order. Students were intimidating the Guard by throwing rocks. The Guard retaliated. They fired into the students, killing a number of them. As it turned out, several students who were merely walking at a distance from the scene were shot to death.

Aronson notes that in the days that followed, those who were sympathetic to the Guard came to believe unpleasant rumors that were circulating about some of the victims: for example, that two of the dead girls were pregnant and their families now were spared anguish and shame, and that bodies of the dead students were filthy, lice-ridden, and infected with syphilis.

None of the rumors was true, but believing them helped many people to rationalize that the victims had deserved their fate. Belief in such rumors as a means of rationalization represents an extreme example, yet similar rationalizations, on a milder level, are used at some time by everyone.

"In my opinion, the flimsy construction of their homes indicates the pigs desire to be eaten."

Cognitive dissonance may be viewed as a form of approach-avoidance conflict on a cognitive, decision-making level. The principle is still the same. We tend to choose (approach) the belief (or rationalization) that pleasures most or hurts least. We avoid the belief that is the most unpleasant.

Although the conflict is described as "cognitive," the term may be somewhat misleading, for conscious thought is not necessary. We do not normally think to ourselves, "I am basically a good person who would not intentionally harm someone who did not deserve it." Although we do not consciously think about it, the unstated belief may guide Our perception of reality.

13. THE USE OF POWER

Every year in America an average of 50 police officers are killed in the line of duty; the average has ranged from 27 to 72. https://www.nature.com/articles/d41586-019-02601-9 Every time a law enforcement officer is killed, his associates in similar agencies join in a caravan through town in tribute to the fallen officer. The news media covers the tribute.

But hardly any attention is given to the fact that over 1,100 civilians are killed by the police every year on the average; based on the FBI's own statistics. 450 of those are shot, the rest die in police custody. Even this number is not complete because there is no requirement that police agencies have to report every death through police shootings and in police custody. https://www.nature.com/articles/d41586-019-02601-9 The article in *Nature* believes the actual number is over 3,000. All but a few, are ignored by the media. Unless there is video evidence of misconduct, even the statistics are ignored. There is rarely a tribute, just an automatic assumption that they must have deserved it.

"We don't believe your story.
A wolf would never attack a sheep."

14. ANARCHY AND EDEN:

THE DOMINANCE HIERARCHY AND THE IN-GROUP

What might society be like without the corrupting effects of culture and the social inhibitions of society, without the politicians and preachers? For the answer, psychologists turn to the societies of animals, animals that have no culture.

Throughout the animal kingdom, aggression tends to be ordered into two primitive structures. Aggression among the members of a group is ordered into a *dominance hierarchy.* Aggression between social groups tends to lead to the division of physical space into *territorial* enclaves of in-groups, or "us guys," and out-groups, or "them guys."

THE PRIMATE SOCIAL ORDER

Robert Yerkes of Yale University is among the most outstanding historical figures in the study of primate social behavior. Yerkes describes dominance among chimpanzees as follows:

The dominance drive as expressed in the endeavor to gain superior social status is little in evidence during the first months of life, becomes common during childhood, and is a conspicuous and highly important chimpanzee characteristic during adolescence and maturity, As soon as two unacquainted individuals who are well grown are brought together they proceed to settle their social status by looking one another over appraisingly, by trial of physical prowess and courage, or by a combination of the two.

...A serious chimpanzee fight for supremacy is likely to be fast and furious. The animals are likely to rush at one another, and with teeth, arms, hands, and feet inflict all the punishment of which they are capable.

...My experience in this whole matter may be summarized thus:

Whether they be primarily physical or mental, contests for social supremacy may be brief and decisive or long continued and indeterminate. It is more likely the former when there is great disparity of traits between individuals; the latter if they are evenly matched. In some pairs which I have known the struggle for social status is perennial, and each time individuals meet after a period of separation the question of priority has to be settled anew. Needless to say, under these circumstances' life is neither readily predictable nor continuously peaceable. At times it seems as if the presence of the urge to gain and hold superior social status creates perpetual unrest in a group of chimpanzees.

When dominance becomes firmly established one can place a banana between two chimpanzees without fear of initiating a battle: Rather than fight over the banana, the subordinate animal will simply sit where it is and allow the dominant animal to take its time about going over to pick up the banana. Once status has been established, the subordinate animal will no longer challenge the dominant one. Yet when two chimps meet for the first time, there is always a certain testing out, a sizing up, complete with threats and counterthreats, until one either decides that the other is obviously superior or until a test of strength determines the winner.

Are young human children different from chimpanzees? Or is our apparent reserve, the relative lack of combat, a product of socially conditioned norms? Samuel Clemens, whose pseudonym Mark Twain earned him a reputation as one of history's most astute judges of human nature, tells a story drawn from life by Mark Twain in his classic *Tom Sawyer*:

"Well why don't you do it then? What do you keep saying you will for?
Why don't you do it? It's because you're afraid."
"I ain't afraid."
"You are."
"I ain't."
"You are."
Another pause, and more eyeing and sidling around each other. Presently they were shoulder to shoulder. Tom said:
"Get away from here!"
"Go away yourself!"
"Won't."
"I won't either."

So they stood, each with a foot placed at an angle as a brace, and both shoving with might and main, and glowering at each other with hate. But neither could get an advantage. After struggling till both were hot and flushed, each relaxed his strain with watchful caution, and Tom said:

"You're a coward and a pup. I'll tell my big brother on you, and he can thrash you with his little finger, and I'll make him do it, too."

"What do I care for your big brother? I've got a brother that's bigger than he is-and what's more, he can throw him over that fence, too." (Both brothers were imaginary.)

"That's a lie."

"Your saying so don't make it so."

Tom drew a line in the dust with his big toe and said:

"I dare you to step over that and I'll lick you till you can't stand up."

Anybody that'll take a dare will steal sheep." The new boy stepped over promptly, and said:

"Now you said you'd do it, now let's see you do it."

"Don't you crowd me now: you better look out."

"Well, you said you'd do it-why don't you do it?"

"By jingo! For two cents I will do it."

The new boy took two broad coppers out of his pocket and held them out with derision. Tom struck them to the ground. In an instant both boys were rolling and tumbling in the dirt, gripped together like cats; and for the space of a minute they tugged and tore at each other's hair and clothes, punched each other's noses, and covered themselves with dust and glory. Presently the confusion took form and through the fog of battle Tom appeared, seated astride the new boy, and pounding him with his fists.

"Holler 'nuff!" -said he.

The boy only struggled to free himself. He was crying- mainly from rage.

"Holler 'nuff!" -and the pounding went on.

At last the stranger got out a smothered "Nuff" and Tom let him up and said:

"Now that'll learn you. Better look out who you're fooling with next time."

The new boy went off brushing the dust from his clothes, sobbing, snuffling, and occasionally looking back and shaking his head and threatening what he would do to Tom the "next time he caught him out." To which Tom responded with jeers, and started off in high feather, and as soon as his back was turned the new boy snatched up a stone, threw it and hit him between the shoulders and then turned tail and ran like an antelope.

"The more I learn about people, the more I like my dog."
Mark Twain

One of the most dangerously vicious circles menacing the continued existence of all mankind arises through that grim striving for the highest possible position within the ranked order, in other words, the reckless pursuit of power which combines with an insatiable greed of neurotic proportions that the results of acquired power confer."

Nobel Laureate Konrad Lorenz

Much like politics.

Yet, we do have some ability to learn better, *if we learn better*. The censorship of reality in our schools, at every level, makes it difficult to learn.

To paraphrase George Santayana, Historian and philosopher;
Those who are ignorant of the past, are doomed to repeat it.

CHAPTER 21
THE SOCIAL BOND

The Infant-Mother Bond, Social Learning, Therapist Monkeys, Any Two Groups,

"Here they come! Here they come!" Gun locks clicked. Across the smoke-infested fields came a brown swarm of running men who were giving shrill yells. They came on, stooping and swinging their rifles at all angles. A flag, tilted forward, sped near the front.

As he caught sight of them the youth was momentarily startled by a thought that perhaps his gun was not loaded. He stood trying to rally his faltering intellect so that he might recollect the moment when he had loaded, but he could not.

The man at the youth's elbow was mumbling as if to himself:

"Oh, we're in for it now! Oh, we're in for it now!"

The captain of the company had been pacing excitedly to and fro in the rear. He coaxed in schoolmistress fashion, as to a congregation of boys with primers. His talk was an endless repetition. "Reserve your fire boys-don't shoot till I tell you-save your fire-wait till they get close up -don't be damned fools-"

Perspiration streamed down the youth's face, which was soiled like that of a weeping urchin ....

He suddenly lost concern for himself, and forgot to look at a menacing fate. He became not a man but a member. He felt that something of which he was a part-a regiment, an army, a cause, or a country-was in a crisis. He was welded into a common personality which was dominated by a single desire. For some moments he could not flee, no more than a little finger can commit a revolution from a hand.

If he had thought the regiment was about to be annihilated, perhaps he could have amputated himself from it. But its noise gave him assurance. The regiment was like a firework that, once ignited, proceeds superior to circumstances until its blazing vitality fades. It wheezed and banged with a mighty power. He pictured the ground before it as strewn with the discomfited.

There was a consciousness always of the presence of his comrades about him. He felt the subtle battle brotherhood more potent even than the cause for which they were fighting. It was a mysterious fraternity born of the smoke and danger of death.

Stephen Crane The Red Badge of Courage

That *"subtle battle brotherhood... born of the smoke and danger of death"* is a powerful description of the attachment formed between humans. We see it in war, in politics, in our school pep rallies for "our" team. Where does this social bond come from? How does it affect our lives?

The emotions of war described by Stephan Crane create fear. Fear creates that subtle battle brotherhood. Fear is also the basis that establishes the bond between infants and their mother. From Harlow's study of motherless monkeys, to a child lost in a supermarket when his mother goes around the corner, fear makes a social bond.

THE INFANT-MOTHER BOND
The Linus Blanket

We have seen the effect of conflict between groups and within an individual, but what about the social bond with people?

In the primate laboratory at the University of Wisconsin, a long-term study has been under way to determine the origin and effect of early social bonds. The research has been conducted over four decades by Harry Harlow and his wife Margaret Harlow and later by Stephen Soumi. It is impossible to use human children to investigate the effect of early social bonds, so the Harlow's adopted a relative of ours whose psychological development is now known to be remarkably similar in many respects to our own. For their study they picked the rhesus monkey. Many psychologists today consider the Harlow's findings to be among the most significant and far-reaching in the field of child psychology.

Isolated from its mother soon after birth, a baby rhesus monkey lay in a bare wire cage clutching a soft cheesecloth pad. By isolating infant monkeys from their mothers, Harlow had hoped to rear a colony of disease-free monkeys. What they discovered instead was a psychological need as important as any biological need for food or air. So long as the monkey could hold to its pad, its behavior was alert and wide-eyed, like a human infant taking in all the happenings of its world. But when the pad was removed for cleaning, its behavior changed drastically.

From out of nowhere, a human hand came into its cage and picked up the monkey's cheesecloth pad. Screeching in dismay, the infant monkey vainly struggled to grasp and hold the pad, its fingers clinging to the pad as desperately as a mountain climber who has lost his footing on a ledge. Forcibly separated from its pad, the infant monkey was a picture of terror and depression- huddling against the floor of the cage, clutching itself, and whimpering plaintively.

https://www.youtube.com/watch?v=_s1YdEZkHIo

For as long as the infant monkey was without its pad, it was anxious and fearful. Only when the pad was returned did the monkey at last find comfort and security. If the pad had been permanently removed, the infant would have become listless and apathetic and might have reacted to people or other monkeys only as fear stimuli. Over a prolonged period of time, the infant monkey might have wasted away and even died.

Quite similar reactions are found in human infants deprived of their parents.

Infants orphaned under the age of two years are particularly susceptible. At the turn of the century in America, the institutionalized orphan child was far more likely to die than to live. Improved nutrition and better maternal care in modem institutions have markedly reduced the death rate among orphans, but as late as 1945, Rene Spitz reported that the emotional development of institutionalized infants was often severely impaired. Some children withdrew, showed signs of depression, and became more susceptible to disease. In such institutions, it was not uncommon for a single worker to be responsible for thirty or more infants. Under such conditions, the infants could hardly receive the amount of maternal care that they would normally get.

Harlow set out to systematically investigate the relationship between the infant and its mother. They began by rearing infant monkeys under specially designed conditions: (1) social isolation, in which infants were reared alone in a bare wire cage with no social contact; (2) nursing wire mothers, in which the infants were reared in social isolation but were able to cling to a substitute mother constructed of wire that provided them with milk; and (3) contact com¬f01t, in which a similar substitute mother constructed of wire had a piece of terrycloth towel wrapped around it to provide the infant with contact comfort.

https://www.youtube.com/watch?v=hsA5Sec6dAI

The results were pronounced. Infants reared with no contact comfort were psychologically devastated. They clasped their heads in their hands and sat and rocked convulsively back and forth. Other times, they sat and stared fixedly into space. A few of the monkeys developed compulsive habits of picking or chewing at their skin until it bled. Anything new terrified the infants, and a few bit themselves when approached by a human. Their behavior appeared grossly pathological. Harlow had not expected this aberration. They had reared fifty-six animals in this condition, and when the monkeys became adults, some five to eight years later, their behavior was still abnormal. The monkeys were distinctly different from any normally reared animal.

1. Contact Comfort:
A Fear Reducer

The most important discovery by Harlow is not often noted in textbooks. It is not that the baby seeks contact comfort, but that the baby's fear of novelty, fear itself, is dramatically reduced just by contact comfort with a terrycloth mother. You can see this most important part in the following film, about halfway through.

https://www.youtube.com/watch?v=OrNBEhzjg8I

When the baby monkey is taken away from its terrycloth mother and placed in a "fear stimulus" room, it is terrified. It huddles in a corner, clutches itself, rubs itself, but is too frightened to explore.

But as soon as Harlow puts the terrycloth mother in the room, its behavior changes dramatically. It runs to its terrycloth mother. It rubs up and down against her (for contact comfort). Then, it begins to explore. It picks up a piece of paper, the paper scares the monkey, he touches base with his mother quickly, but then goes back to exploring.

STIMULUS	RESPONSE
Novel stimuli------------------------------	Arousal--Fear
Contact Comfort--------------------------	Fear Reduction

This is an important survival mechanism. In the wild, if there was a leopard nearby, members of the troop would let out a whoop. This would scare the monkey baby, it would run to its mother, grab hold of her fur, and the mother could except to the trees. The mother cannot hold the baby and escape, the baby must cling tightly to her as she escapes.

The fear of new or novel stimuli ensures that the baby will stay close to the mother and not wander off.

Effect of Total Social Isolation

And what of the monkeys reared with a nursing wire mother? Breast feeding is considered by some psychologists to be the basis of the infant-mother bond, but nourishment did not help. They were as psychologically devastated as the first group of monkeys. Furthermore, they showed no interest in the wire mother. Even though all the monkeys were able to see and hear other monkeys of their kind in cages, this visual and auditory experience seemed of little value.

Harlow found that monkeys without a cloth pad to cling to were terrified. They huddled in the corner clutching themselves for comfort.

Monkeys reared without contact comfort were severely disturbed. One was biting himself in defensive aggression brought on by a fear reaction to the approach of the photographer.

Sexual behavior was also markedly aberrant. On reaching sexual maturity, the monkeys were placed together for prolonged periods of time, sometimes as long as seven years, but they were unsuccessful at mating. The problem was not for want of trying. Zoologists often note that animals in zoos often do not mate. Without early experience with their peers, they may fail to learn the social skills needed.

They made repeated but clumsy attempts at intercourse, but posturing was inadequate both by males and females. Monkeys normally learn sexual behavior by a process of fumble and find that begins early in childhood. These monkeys seem to have failed partly because they were fearful and to a large extent because they simply had not learned how to engage in sexual behavior. The flesh was willing, but the mind was weak.

Harlow tried group psychotherapy. A group of nineteen males and females, which had been isolated as infants, were used to stock the monkey island at the local zoo in Madison, Wisconsin. These monkeys had never before played with other monkeys. How would they react? At first, they fought frequently. A dominance hierarchy 'developed and fighting was reduced. Although some friendship pairs were formed, their social and sexual behavior was primitive.

At this point, Harlow decided to introduce the number one breeding male from their normal breeding colony. Could the Don Juan from the breeding colony succeed where the more inept males had failed? With a dogged persistence, the big male set about approaching the females. Time after time he tried again, time after time he was greeted with the utmost indifference. Sex was impossible without a willing and knowledgeable partner.

In a later study, Harlow finally succeeded in impregnating some of the isolated females, but after giving birth, the mothers exhibited grossly inadequate maternal behavior. They had no knowledge of how to care for the infants. Furthermore, they actually seemed to fear the infants. When the infants attempted to make contact, the mothers pushed them away, sometimes even biting an infant or stepping on its head. Despite persistent attempts by their infants to make contact, the mothers continually refused the infants' attention. They did not even "know" what their own infant was.

The monkeys reared on the terrycloth substitute mother presented a different picture. Totally devoted to the cloth mother, they clung to her sixteen to eighteen hours per day. The cloth-covered piece of wire had become their mother, and if their real mother was suddenly presented, they reacted to her with fear. If enogh time had passed, nothing could change their attachment to the cloth mother.

What would happen if a mature infant monkey, raised on a cloth mother, were to be removed from its cloth mother and kept in isolation for two years? Would it still show the same attachment to its cloth mother? The answer is a resounding yes. After a separation of two years and longer, these monkeys ran to their cloth mother and grasped her tightly to them at the first opportunity.

For as long as these monkeys had their terrycloth mother with them, they displayed none of the abnormal behavior of the isolated monkeys. But the importance of the cloth mother is not evident in the laboratory. Its importance is best seen in the open field test developed by Robert Zimmerman (Harlow and Zimmerman, at the University of Wisconsin). The open field test involves placing the monkey in an unfamiliar room that is full of a number of new, and hence, frightening objects.

If a cloth-reared monkey is placed alone in such a room, it is immediately fear-stricken. The monkey shrieks and clutches itself with its hands, moves cautiously around the room, and finally stops, huddling by itself on the floor This is normal behavior for a very young monkey or a very young human child who is suddenly removed from a familiar environment and thrown into a new world without Mother.

Alone in the room, the infant monkey is too frightened to explore its new surroundings. When the terrycloth mother is placed in the room with it, however, the infant monkey's behavior changes dramatically. Instantly, it rushes to the mother, grasps her firmly, and rubs its body against hers. After a few moments, the infant monkey begins to relax. It begins to look in the direction of the formerly frightening objects in the room. It may even put its thumb in its mouth as it clings to the mother with one hand.

Within a minute or so, the infant monkey may leave the mother and go out to explore the new objects. Picking up one of the objects, the infant may play with it briefly. Suddenly something frightens the monkey, and it races back to its terrycloth mother. It touches her as if to assure itself that she is still there, and then goes back out to explore. The presence of the mother gave the infant the security it takes to explore.

When taken away from their cloth mother and exposed to this "open field" test, the monkeys huddled in fear without their mother.

Monkeys reared with contact comfort were secure and happy as long as they could run to their cloth mother when frightened, then they go back to play with the objects. For as long as its "mother" is there, the monkey will play with the objects freely and with no concern whatsoever.

The contact comfort of the terrycloth mother reduces the infant monkey's fear. Without the contact comfort the infant is terrified, but with the contact comfort, it is brave and assured and will even threaten moving objects that would otherwise terrify it. Remarkably, so long as the monkey knows that the terrycloth mother is there, it has comparatively little need of her. The monkey will explore without fear for hours only occasionally touching base with its "mother." The monkey's need for security is somewhat like our need for air: We never notice our need for it until someone cuts off our supply.

What about the isolates? After six months of isolation, could they now develop a love for a terrycloth mother? Harlow found such infants would come to associate with the terrycloth mother. But problems remained, even after a prolonged association with a terrycloth mother. These monkeys could never feel secure, even in the presence of the cloth mother. In the open field tests, they ignored her and lay huddled by themselves on the floor.

Given the opportunity to run away from a frightening mechanical toy, or to run to a cloth mother for comfort, the isolates always ran away from the fearful toy. In contrast, the monkeys reared with cloth mothers invariably ran to the cloth mother, even if the cloth mother was closer to the fear stimulus. From these studies, Harlow concluded that there is a critical period in the life of an infant monkey during which the social bond with the mother normally forms, usually within the first three months of life.

Strikingly similar behavior is observed in human infants under the same conditions. In human infants, the critical period appears to be within three months to one year of age. By about six to nine months of age, human infants begin to develop a fear of novelty. This fear is evident in their crying when approached by strangers or in their fear of being alone away from their mother.

Before six months of age, infants are not especially particular about being handled by strangers. They can often sit or lie by themselves in their crib for hours. If they cry, they cry because they are uncomfortable. But by six months of age, they begin to cry for another reason: They begin to cry because they are alone and they want mom to entertain them.

Even at six months of age, human infants are still sometimes uncertain as to who their mother is. if a working mother leaves her six-month-old infant at the babysitter's home, the infant may cry when the mother goes away. But if the babysitter happens to take enough time to play with the infant during the day, a strange thing happens. The infant has now become "imprinted" to the babysitter and may well cry when Mama comes in the afternoon to take the infant home. Such a reaction appears to be quite normal.

"I think we bonded a little."

There is no evidence that it is harmful to the infant to have multiple moms, at least so long as the infant gets enough cuddling and attention. Having multiple moms might even be beneficial. Although the evidence is unclear, it may be that multiple mothering, as in the Israeli kibbutz, might be beneficial in that it tends to reduce stranger anxiety at an earlier age and perhaps even makes the infant more secure in social situations.

2. HUMAN BABIES: SOCIAL BONDS

By eight to twelve months of age, human infants have firmly "imprinted" to their mother. If their mother has been an adequate source of contact comfort, they will seek her out any time they are anxious or fearful. Even children who seem to delight more in playing with Daddy than with Mother will often end up running to Mom when they are hurt rather than to Daddy.

A normal dependence relationship will continue for a great many years.

As with the infant monkeys, the Mother reduces fear in many strange situations. A child is normally quite fearless at the grocery store-so long as Mother is there. But if that child should suddenly wander down an aisle while Mother is busy shopping and look up to discover that Mother is not there, frantic efforts to find her, often coupled with crying, are frequent manifestations of the strength of the infant-mother bond.

The implications of Harlow's studies for human child-rearing practices are great. It means nothing to the human child if the Mother loves him from a distance. No matter how intense her love may be, the child does not understand it. The child understands only contact comfort and the fear reduction that contact comfort brings. Except for adequate nutrition, there is no single act of parenthood that is more necessary for a child than the fulfillment of the need for security. Freedom from fears and anxieties should be as much the birthright of a child as is food and shelter.

Hugging a teddy bear gives a child a sense of security.

When does a child stop needing contact comfort? The first year of life is undoubtedly critical for the child to learn to relate to other humans, but the need for contact comfort continues long after this. Some children have outgrown the need for contact comfort by the time they are of school age, most appear to seek contact comfort in times of stress well into adolescence. Even though children may outgrow their need for contact comfort, there is no indication that we ever outgrow a need for security and a feeling of belonging.

Cloth mothers provide the infant with a feeling of security, but security is not enough. When the monkeys reared with cloth mothers reached sexual maturity, they were unable to mate. Their social behavior was primitive, and their sexual behavior was inept. They had not learned to interact with other monkeys. They did not seem to know what the other monkey was. It was just a novel fear stimulus.

Harlow then tried a variety of infant-rearing techniques: (1) with the real mother but without peer group contact, (2) with a cloth mother but with peer group contact, and (3) without a mother but with peer group contact. On reaching sexual maturity, the monkeys were tested for their social Interaction.

Remarkably, the infant monkeys were reared with their real mother but without any other social contact were inept at social and sexual behavior. In contrast, monkeys reared with a cloth mother and peer group contact, as well as monkeys reared with nothing but peer group contact, were quite capable of sexual and social behavior. Their performance was much the same as that of normal monkeys. The infant monkeys that had been reared without a mother but with peer group contact, held on to each other for their contact comfort. As they matured, the social, play, and sexual behavior developed more or less spontaneously.

The together-together experiment of Harlow demonstrated that infant monkeys reared with each other to cling to grew up better adjusted socially than monkeys reared with their real mothers but without peer group contact.

3.MONKEY PSYCHOTHERAPISTS

For normal psychological development, peer group play (with close physical contact and comfort) appears to be essential. In infant monkeys, it may be even more important than the infant-mother bond. Without such experience, an infant monkey, reared with its real mother or with a cloth mother, does not react to another monkey as a social object. In fact, it reacts to the new monkey as a fear stimulus.

One might expect that the intellectual ability of the social isolates would be impaired, but this does not seem to be the case. Harlow found little evidence of intellectual impairment in isolated monkeys they studied. The monkeys can work complex tasks with the same proficiency as normally reared monkeys or monkeys in the wild.

Later studies by Harlow in conjunction with Stephen Suomi of the University of Wisconsin, indicate that the emotional plight of the isolated monkeys is not hopeless. Monkeys that had been reared in social isolation for as long as six months were markedly emotionally disturbed. However, it proved possible to partly reverse the emotional disturbance through the use of "therapist" monkeys to help bring the isolates out of their depression.

The "therapist" monkeys were chosen from normal animals three to four months of age. Their age and size were such that they would be no threat to the isolated monkey. They were still at an age where they desired to cling to another monkey. At first, the isolated monkeys were afraid of the smaller monkey. But the new monkey was persistent in wanting to cling to the isolated monkey. In a matter of weeks, the isolated monkeys were clinging to the smaller therapists in return, and active play between the two soon began. Following six months of such therapy, the experimenters considered the isolated monkeys to have recovered from their early trauma.

4. CHILD ABUSE AND THE AFTERMATH

What happens to infants who are punished by their mothers? In a unique series of experiments, the Har lows subjected the infant monkeys to a harsh and rejecting mother. After the infants had become attached to a terrycloth mother, Harlow introduced a new source of fear. This time the fear came not from the environment, but from the mother herself. Now, when the infant monkey ran to its mother seeking protection, it was hit by a sharp blast of compressed air. The compressed air could not physically harm the infant monkey but was intensely frightening to it. Did the monkeys change their mind about their love for the mother? Quite the contrary. When hit repeatedly by the blasts of compressed air, they did not shy away from the mother but clung more tightly to her. It was as though the compressed air increased the monkeys' dependency on their mother. When the monkeys were frightened by the air blast, they reacted the only way they knew how: Clinging to their mother had always reduced their fear in the past, so now they clung even more tightly.

Dogs demonstrate the same need for contact comfort as infant monkeys and humans. In a study cited by Scott, A. E. Fisher, at Pennsylvania State University, found that punishing dogs for approaching their master or their mother resulted in greater dependency, not less.

In one study puppies were subjected to painful stimuli every time they approached their mother. As a control, other puppies received no such harsh treatment on their approach to their mother. The result of this conditioning is disturbing. Rather than dislike the punishing mother, the puppies became more attached to her. When they grew up, their period of dependence on their mother lasted significantly longer than for dogs who were not punished for approach responses.

Instead of becoming independent and leaving their mother at an early age, they become more dependent on her. As with Harlow's infant monkeys, they appear to have done the only thing they knew how to do to reduce their fear: They intensified their ·approach reaction to their mother. More remarkably, the effect of such early conditioning may last long beyond the infantile period.

This finding may account for the fact, often observed by social workers, that the "battered child" who has suffered from consistent parental abuse may still very much want to return to its parents. Exaggerated dependency of this type is not uncommon in such children. This fact could account for a great deal of seemingly "masochistic" behavior, perhaps even in adults.

Harlow refers to the relationship between the infant and its mother as one of "love." They have chosen not to speculate about the role of fear in forming this bond. But it may be suggested that fear is one of the more important elements in producing the social bond. In infancy, fear seems to intensify the "love" or (dependency on) the mother. The more frightened the infant is, the greater and more persistent the attachment.

5. FEAR, LOVE, AND DEPENDENCY:

Is Fear Reduction Love?

The Battered Child versus the Secure Child

Some people believe that giving a child too much love and comfort will spoil the child or make the child too dependent on the mother. Just the opposite appears to be true: The infant that receives comfort and freedom from fear is going to become independent earlier, and need less attention from Mom than the child who is left alone with its fears. The child who is frequently punished or frightened by its parents, on the other hand, would be expected to become the most dependent on them.

One of the most important contributions of the Harlow studies may not be on the nature of love as much as on the effects of fear and our understanding of them. Harlow has painted a clear picture of the things that infants and children fear and what is necessary to bring them security and healthy psychological development.

Fear of the Unfamiliar makes a child stay close to its mother for safety. We do not need contact comfort all of our lives. As children get older, their unknown fears may be reduced by the stimuli that have been associated with contact comfort.

If an infant monkey is placed in a room full of novel stimuli, it is utterly fear-struck and too inhibited to explore. If its terrycloth mother is placed in the same room, the infant monkey's behavior changes drastically: It runs to her, rubs up against her, and in a matter of minutes begins to explore the room fearlessly.

What would happen if a monkey accustomed to a terrycloth mother were prevented from touching her? What would happen if it could only see her? Harry Harlow put a clear plexiglass shield over the terrycloth mother and observed the reaction of the infant. Coming into the room full of unknown stimuli, the infant monkey's first reaction was to attempt to make contact with its terrycloth mother. Unable to physically contact the mother, would it get any security from the sight of her?

The answer appears to be yes. Such infants were not as bold as those who could make contact with the mother, but they were far less fearful than if they had not had the visual stimulus-the sight of the mother to comfort them. It may be that the association of the familiar visual stimulus of the mother with the fear reduction that normally accompanies contact was enough to give the visual stimulus itself some fear-reducing properties.

A familiar environment also seems to serve as a source of comfort. Human children are frightened when they are first taken away from home to go to school. The unfamiliar environment may be terrifying. But if some of the same stimuli, the strangers and the unfamiliar children, were introduced to the child in his own home the child might be quite unafraid.

As the child grows older, the fear of novelty becomes less important. Learned fears began to take precedence. Fears of the unknown, fears of the dark, to fears of the bogeyman, of witches, of dirty old men, of people who have the "wrong" politics or the "wrong" religion, of the "bad guys."

These fears may be reduced by getting home before dark to a familiar environment, being on guard against witches, avoiding old men, or staying with our own familiar religion, politics, or whatever makes up our familiar belief in what is "good." Some fears, of course, are fully justified, but in childhood, they are more often than not, merely fears of the unknown quantities that we have picked up from the subtle conditioning, the "watch outs" that are a part of our subculture.

By adolescence, a new round of fears is ready to overtake the child. Children are beginning to learn that they are judged by other people, and they are beginning to judge themselves as they imagine others will judge them. If we lived alone on a desert island, our failures would have no meaning to us. But our failures take on new meaning in a world where other people judge us by looks, talent, popularity, and many other changing standards.

Now, what we fear most is personal inadequacy. It is a feeling that we rarely put into words and probably rarely even think about in concrete terms. We worry about how people react to us. We fear not being loved, not being "in" with the group, not being competent at our work or in other activities, being disliked by the boss, not being religious enough, being oversexed or undersexed, the outcome of the rating-dating games, and our current status in the gossip among the students or coworkers.

Not everyone experiences the same fears, nor does everyone worry to the same degree. But everyone worries. The thought that brings a chill of terror to one person's mind may be shrugged off by another. But all have their own personal fears and their own ways of dealing with them.

Fears may change with time. Things that filled us with a chill of terror in the past may seem of little consequence today. Think back to what bothered you the most five years ago. Think back to a time when you were "in trouble." Do the things that bothered you then seem nearly as bad today? How about last year? What was it that gave you the greatest degree of discomfort or anxiety? Does it bother you as much today?

More often than not the things that bother us become less intense as the years pass. Perhaps it is the greatest hope for the future that no matter how bad things may seem at the present, all things must pass. The worries that seem so potent today may seem trivial and unimportant some years hence.

Fears of Personal Inadequacy seem to result when we compare ourselves to others, often to those more successful around us. This comparison begins at home and in the public school system. How do we rate on a scale of 1 to 10? Who gets picked first or last in choosing up sides in the gym? Are you number one in the gym or only a wanna-be? How do we score in the school systems ranking of A to F? all of these are artificial comparisons. They have little meaning in the world outside of school. Yet they may cause us feelings of inadequacy.

6. CONFLICT IN SOCIETY

In the microcosm of the adolescent gym class, coaches have devised an ingenious method of studying the primitive art of war-making. It has taken psychologists a long time to improve on their techniques. In gym class, a ritual "choosing up sides" is followed by an equally stylized division of the two sides into two separate camps. To tell who is the enemy, boys of one group remove their T-shirts to become the "skins," who pit themselves against their newfound rivals, the "shirts." The two newly formed nations then work their pubescent energy into a sweat over the possession of a synthetic rubber ball, all the while wondering aloud how the girls' teams tell each other apart.

The controlled conflict of sports seems a muted version of the centuries-old conflicts between tribes, races, and nations. Hemmed in by rules, padded for safety, and carefully watched over by the whistle-blowing gods of war, the revelry of violence is carefully restrained. Civilization tempers its trophy of victory with the Rules of Hoyle. Order prevails. Yet even among high school teams, there is often fierce competition between rival schools. What would social order be like without the rulebook?

7. TERRITORIAL CONQUEST

Many species of animals will stake out a territory, an area of land, and defend this area from any other animals of the same species that approach within this territory. The male chaffinch, a familiar bird with an orange-brown breast, will stake out a nesting site, perhaps using visual cues such as a fence line or trees, and will attack any other bird with an orange-brown breast that comes within a given distance of his nesting site. Since male chaffinches have orange-brown breasts and females do not, this selective factor is an obvious evolutionary advantage in that it limits population density during the breeding season. Perhaps more importantly, only the males who have a territory will mate, and since maintaining a territory requires a healthy and fit animal, nature has a way of ensuring that only the fittest will mate and produce offspring.

The aggressive behavior that leads to "territorial" defense in the chaffinch is triggered by a very specific cue and can be considered an innate reaction. But some of the forms of behavior in higher animals are not so easily explained. C. R. Carpenter, a zoologist, captured some 350 rhesus monkeys in India and transported them to Santiago Island, a 36-acre dot off the coast of Puerto Rico.

Initially, social disruption was intense. Mothers abandoned their young, and fights were frequent. But within a year the rhesus monkeys had trooped across the island, dividing themselves into groups and the land into territories. Each group tended to stay within its own area. The areas were poorly defined but quite observable.

If one troop of monkeys wandered away from its home base and encountered another troop far afield, verbal battles would erupt. As the troops came nearer, tension became apparent within each of the two groups. The animals looked anxiously and nervously toward the strangers. Occasional verbal threats and gestures erupted from the dominant males in each group. Sometimes entire troops had screaming matches with each other. The troop that was farthest from its home base usually was the first to withdraw.

The second troop sometimes followed for a way, continuing its verbal threats. Not all primates display such territorial behavior. Some species of baboons, chimpanzees, and gorillas are considerably less possessive about land, yet the fact that it is common among primates, and the rule among most mammals, poses an interesting problem. We know what triggers territorial behavior in the· case of the chaffinch. Yet no specific stimulus has ever been found that will trigger aggression among primates. Territorial behavior in birds and territorial behavior in primates appear to be quite different phenomena.

Groups of primates appear to intentionally stake out territories of their own that they defend from others of their own species. But do they? Or is it a figment of the imagination of the observer? E. Mayr, while working at Harvard University, suggested that there is nothing at all intentional in the territorial behavior of primates. Given two basic concepts of (1) **philopatry,** an attachment to a familiar area not unlike a child's attachment to a blanket or a surrogate mother or a dog's attachment to its own familiar backyard, and (2) **xenophobia,** a mutual fear of strangers, it is possible to account for the observed territorial behavior of primates without, in any way, having to assume that they possess a "territorial instinct."

A dog becomes attached to its own backyard. So long as the dog remains within the safe confines of its fenced-in area, it may snarl and growl with great fury at the approach of postmen and garbagemen. Remove that fence and the dog's manner may be markedly changed. Now it may approach the strangers with a wagging tail and head somewhat lowered. The human child, too, may be frightened and insecure when removed from familiar home surroundings to a strange place. It may be only natural to prefer a familiar area over an unfamiliar area, especially if there is hostile resistance from others in a new area. The xenophobic fear of strangers would then reinforce the tendency to stay in a familiar area.

Is xenophobia sufficient to produce such a marked hostility between two groups of the same species? This reaction to strangers is no exaggeration. Irven De Vore and Sarel Eimerl, note an observation made by S. L. Washburn at the Berkeley Primate Laboratory when he introduced a small female macaque into a cage containing an established group of macaque monkeys. The reaction was violent: *"The other Macaques, normally quite placid, responded with the utmost vehemence. They shook the netting, they threatened furiously, they screamed."* The small female could be of no possible threat to the members of the troop, She was cowering in the arms of the anthropologist. Yet she was met with marked hostility. Such reactions might well account for the supposed territorial defense observed in primates in the wild.

Why would primates hate or fear a member of their own species that had never before harmed them and could not harm them? How deep are the roots of such prejudice? The question is made even more complex by Carpenter's observation that the monkeys that generate a white heat toward strange members of their own species may live in peace with a separate group of monkeys of a different species only a few yards away. Such observations have been repeatedly confirmed. Why then such a specific hatred?

Thomas Struhsaker has suggested that hostility between groups results from conflict. Two groups of the same species may compete over the same sleeping spaces or the same food sources. In the process of competing, hostility develops between the groups just as it does between individuals. This observation is partly confirmed by the fact that some troops of monkeys seem to develop a dominance hierarchy in which troop A will be dominant over troop B, which will be dominant over troop C and so on.

Perhaps the best-known theoretical view of territorial behavior has been given by C. R. Carpenter, who attempted to explain its occurrence in primates.

> *The process of territoriality may be explained by a hypothetical example with a more familiar animal: The white rat. If a group of white rats were thoroughly conditioned to a complex labyrinthian maze by various kinds of incentive, allowed to live in the maze for a long period of time and then given the opportunity to range into mazes occupied by other groups, what would happen? The chances are that the strange situation and animals would be avoided, especially if competition with the other animals occurred and the rats would tend to remain in familiar territory with their localized food supply, water, nests, etc.*

Carpenter's hypothesis may explain a significant portion of territorial behavior, but the conflict hypothesis does not adequately explain why conflict occurs between troops of the same species but not between troops of different species. Carpenter notes that howler monkeys may feed peacefully in the same trees with capuchin monkeys, and macaques with langurs. Even where the two species eat the same foodstuffs, no conflict may occur. In contrast, conflict may occur between groups of rhesus monkeys-even when they have more than sufficient foods provided by nature or by the caretakers on Santiago Island. Conflict between groups may well be important in maintaining territorial behavior, but apparently, there is more to it than this.

An alternative theory may be suggested. Hostility between groups may result from hostility within groups. Stimulus generalization may then occur. One generalizes experiences with the members of one's own group to stimuli presented by members of the other group. Within a troop of macaques, each individual has engaged in combat or exchanged threats with other macaques. But each macaque has not exchanged threats with langurs or capuchin monkeys. The macaque growing up within its troop learns to expect to have a certain relationship with another macaque; it does not learn to have a certain relationship with capuchin monkeys or langurs.

If the macaque is now presented with an unfamiliar macaque monkey from a neighboring tribe, stimulus generalization would occur, as well as a fear of the "novel" monkey from another troop. The macaque "knows" he has been threatened with conflict by other members of its troop but does not know these strangers and so expects to have conflict with them. From the macaque's past experience within the troop, the stranger is perceived as a potential threat. Hostility results.

If this theory is true, then one might expect that the greater the degree of conflict within a given troop, the greater would be the tendency to display territorial behavior. A troop of monkeys in which the competition was hot and heavy might be expected to be markedly hostile toward an unfamiliar troop that it encountered. In contrast, a troop similar to that observed by Rowell, in which conflict was minimal, would exhibit a less hostile reaction to a strange troop of monkeys.

One thing seems apparent: We cannot explain hostility between troops of monkeys in the same way that we can explain hostility between nations. Monkey leaders cannot excite members of their troop by telling them of atrocities allegedly committed by the other side. They cannot appeal to patriotism, pride, and honor. Whatever causes the hostility between the troops seems to be more basic, deriving from the fact that the two troops are simply two separate troops. They are both different. They are "shirts" and "skins." Once they have become two distinct groups, other natural forces seem to produce territorial behavior.

The social bonds that are the strongest, are those formed in emotion: From a child's fear of novel stimuli, to the adult's fear and anger against those who have a new opinion (as in Galileo and Darwin), a different religion, another political belief, or even of Daniereans, and Wallonians, who do not even exist. The ease with which we hate without reason and reject others, makes for a sad comment on our culture. Our educational system has failed to teach us reasons to be tolerant of others.

22 PSYCHOLOGICAL PROBLEMS OF LIFE

Origin And Treatment

LINCOLN * OPRAH * SHAKESPEARE * FREUD • SPITZ • MASSERMAN • BANDURA • ROGERS • SKINNER *
MASLOW • FRANKL• MAY• LIDDEL • PREVENTIVE PSYCHOLOGY

Psychoanalytic, •Behavioral • Humanistic Psychology: Self-Theory, Hierarchy of Needs • Existential
Psychology: Existential Crisis, Search for Meaning • Behavioral and Cognitive Behavioral, Experimental
Neuroses,

It is important to understand that everyone goes through problems in life. From Abraham Lincoln to Oprah
Winfrey, from the most famous to the least known of us, life is hard. If we ignore the problems of life, then
when they happen to you, it may seem as if you are alone, that no one else has ever felt that bad, that no one
else would understand. You are not alone.

Abraham Lincoln is remembered as perhaps the greatest American president. Yet what is left out of our history
books are the frequent episodes of anxiety and depression that he endured for most of his life.

Even as a young man Lincoln had periods of depression
not uncommon to youth. So much so that his friend was
afraid he might commit suicide. Joshua Shenk wrote of
this in his book. *"Lincoln's Melancholia"*. One of his two
suicidal periods came about as a result of lost love as a
young man.

An even more telling event occurred when Lincoln went through what might be called a midlife crisis when he was a lawyer in his forties. Then he compared himself to a man who was perhaps the most successful politicians of his time, Stephen Douglas, a man of universal fame.

Lincoln wrote that, compared to Douglas, *"My life is a failure. A flat failure"*

1. COMPARING OURSELVES TO OTHERS

That Road Goes Nowhere

Comparing our own success to that of others is a mistake we often make in life. We never know that so many others have been through this. Even successful athletes and scholars often end up comparing themselves to those who are the most successful in their field, to their own detriment.

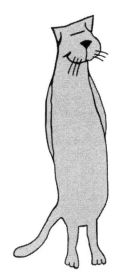

Happiness is found when you stop comparing yourself to dogs

Sometimes such comparison is useful. Yet too often, it can be detrimental to our well-being. Much of our society creates such comparisons; Facebook, glamor magazines, bullying, rejection, and name-calling, all contribute to the value judgments that others use against us, or we use against ourselves.

School itself forces this on students; who gets picked first or last in choosing sides in gym, who is the class princess, the best liked, the homecoming queen, the head cheerleader a majorette. Even in class, we grade others on a system of A to F. Who gets to be class Valedictorian, who gets a scintilla of recognition?

Songwriter, singer, and author, Rick Springfield wrote in his autobiography, *Late, Late at Night* about how he attempted suicide at the age of seventeen. After another argument with his mother about not wanting to go to school, he went into the garage and tried to hang himself. Fortunately, the rope unwound and he fell to the ground. He said he felt relief.

Why would he want to kill himself? He says nothing about being bullied, although males are often ashamed to tell anyone if they are, but he says he *"felt like a failure in the only life arena I knew (school)"*. All too many young people feel like failures in school. The only criteria that they judge themselves on, or are judged by others, is socializing or sports. If you are not good at either, you may feel like a failure. If you do not know anyone else has been there and gone on to succeed, you may feel alone and without hope.

Unfortunately, our school system leads us to think in terms of how we compare to others. Not just in grades, how you score from A to F, but in gym, how good you are at athletics, who gets picked first, or last, in "choosing up sides" in gym, who is the prettiest, who has the most "likes" on Facebook, how many "followers do we have, etc., ETC...

Even during his greatest success in life, as he became President of the United States, just days before the Civil War began, he would go on to have severe periods of doubt. He was seen prowling the halls of the White House at night, his head down, saying in effect, *"I must have relief from this anxiety or it will kill me."*

Most of Lincoln's depression is censored from our history books. But it has the meat of understanding that should be taught to all. Making it through life is full of problems. There will always be problems. Understanding this makes it somewhat less likely that we will feel, if we are alone, that no one else would understand.

Yet our school system is often the source of the elation-depression effect of life. We are forced to compare ourselves with others; in athletics, in grades, in social success (whether we have a date for the weekend), and in many other, often superficial, criteria. Those criteria become embedded in our minds. They become part of the mirror by which we judge ourselves.

Oprah Winfrey is one of the most successful, and certainly the richest women on earth. In an interview with Piers Morgan, she opened up about the three most traumatic events in her life; one of which left her feeling suicidal.

Her first trauma, not unlike Lincoln's, occurred from lost love. She described the feelings of being put down. Today, looking back on it, she holds no animosity and no longer feels bad about it. Looking back from great success, it is easier to remember the bad times that we thought would never end.

The second trauma was when she was betrayed by a friend who sold a story about her to a scandal sheet. She was so crushed and probably worried her career would end, that she took herself to bed. Now, looking back on it, it seems much less of a trauma.

The third and most traumatic, the one that led her to think of suicide, occurred when she was young. She spoke of being sexually molested at the ages of 9, 10, 11, 12, 13, and pregnant at 14.

When she was sent away to live with her father in another town, her father did not know of her pregnancy and set the rules down hard. He told her that he would rather see his daughter floating down the Cumberland River (dead) than to bring disgrace to this family by having a child out of wedlock. She thought; "I will just have to kill myself".

This was in an era of American history where society and parents felt they had to use fear, shame, and guilt over sex, as a form of birth control. It led to an enormous degree of pain and suffering among many. Whatever "rational" reason society may have had for this, it quickly lost any rational feeling, and left only anger and emotion in society, and shame and guilt among so many young women.

The judgmental attitudes of our peers, of Hollywood, of our society, all come to be a part of the negative self-judgment, embedded in our minds by others throughout our lives. Yet, when problems arise, we tend to blame the individual, and sometimes even label them as "mentally ill". Yet most of this shame and guilt are a product of society itself and what it chooses to label with emotions.

Our censorship of reality by our public schools has failed our young. Even today, stories such as the above are censored from their education.

Life has been made harder to deal with by such censorship. Oprah's openness about her own life problems may do more good than psychotherapy by desensitizing young people from feeling their life is doomed to shame and failure. Life is hard. All of us go through problems in life. Even the most wealthy and famous of people all go through problems in life. The psychological effects of those problems is often "normal", it is not a "mental illness"; it is the brain reacting to whatever creates anxiety and depression.

When we have a history of repeated anxiety-producing experiences, or depression-producing experiences, this sets up a pattern of expectation. The brain begins to anticipate that we will have more such experiences. This can get to a point where we cannot easily escape the emotions that we anticipate will follow new experiences. When this is embedded in our mind, we may need professional help to go beyond our expectations; to counter condition or desensitize us, or to find new goals in life that will give our life meaning.

2. ANXIETY AND DEPRESSION

" The human race is a race of cowards, and I am not only marching in that parade,

but carrying a banner."

Mark Twain

Most such fears are as arbitrary and unnecessary as our culture's common fear of bugs or our former fear of witches. But this fact does not make the fear any less real to those who experience it. Fears of external stimuli may be easily dealt with: If we fear bugs, we call an exterminator. However, if we fear an internal stimulus; a feeling of-personal inadequacy, or failure, or feelings of guilt; we call a psychologist. We may be able to avoid, escape or exterminate an external fear, but an internal fear, a feeling of shame or guilt, cannot be escaped.

Cures for such conditioned reactions vary. Desensitization is perhaps the most common. The rape victim must be desensitized to the fear of the incident; to the feeling of guilt by association. Unless she feels she is still accepted by all, that this silent, undiscussed horror is not a stigma against her, the anxiety and consequently the depression cannot be reduced.

Similar techniques are often effective in cases of feelings of failure. A person who is depressed as a result of feelings of failure may be greatly relieved to discover a simple fact of life that virtually every great individual in science, business, politics, preaching, or music has suffered many series of failures and events of personal tragedy. The realization that one is not alone in one's misery, that failure is a common occurrence, can often aid greatly in eliminating that feeling of isolation, that feeling that one is the only individual in the world who has experienced the terrible feelings of isolation and failure.

HISTORICAL FEELINGS OF ANXIETY AND DEPRESSION

At the height of his success, after publishing his classic "*War and Peace*", Leo Tolstoy, approaching the age of 50, suddenly suffered a loss of hope; a feeling that life has no meaning; what psychologists might call an existential crisis. He describes this depression in his book, *My Confession*.

My life had come to a sudden stop. I was able to breathe, to eat, to drink, to sleep. I could not, indeed, help doing so; but there was no real life in me. I had not a single wish to strive for the fulfillment of what I could feel to be reasonable. If I wished for anything, I knew beforehand that, were I to satisfy the wish, nothing would come of it, I should still be dissatisfied. Had a fairy appeared and offered me all I desired; I should not have known what to say. If I seemed to have, at a given moment of excitement, not a wish, but a mood resulting from the tendencies of former wishes, at a common moment I knew that it was a delusion, that I really wished for nothing. I could not even wish to know the truth, because I guessed what the truth was.

The truth lay in this, that life had no meaning for me. Every day of life, every step in it, brought me nearer the edge of a precipice, whence I saw clearly the final ruin before me. To stop, to go back, were alike impossible; nor could I shut my eyes so as not to see the suffering that alone awaited me, the death of all in me, even to annihilation. Thus I, a healthy and happy man, was brought to feel that I could live no longer, that an irresistible force was dragging me down to the grave. I do not mean that I had an intention of committing suicide. The force that drew me away from life was stronger, fuller, and concerned with far wider consequences than any mere wish; it was a force like that of my previous attachment to life, only in a contrary direction. The idea of suicide came as naturally to me as formerly that of bettering my life. It had so much attraction for me that I was compelled to practice a species of self-deception, in order to avoid carrying it out too hastily. I was unwilling to act hastily, only because I had determined first to clear away the confusion of my thoughts, and, that once done, I could always kill myself. I was happy, yet I hid away a cord, to avoid being tempted to hang myself by it to one of the pegs between the cupboards of my study, where I undressed alone every evening, and to cease carrying a gun because it offered too easy a way of getting rid of life. I knew not what I wanted; I was afraid of life; I shrank from it, and yet there was something I hoped for from it.

Leo Tolstoy *My Confession*

At the height of his literary career the author of W*ar and Peace,* Leo Tolstoy, began to suffer a series of depressive attacks that lasted for a period of over five years. Why? Tolstoy describes himself as having a good and loving wife, fine children, and a well-to-do estate. He is in excellent health, he is at the peak of his fame, and he describes his mind as neither deranged nor weakened.

Yet Tolstoy was experiencing feelings of listlessness, hopelessness, and despair that characterize the acute depressive reaction. Such reactions may vary greatly in the degree of depression that the individual feels, but they are not at all uncommon. In fact, some psychologists have considered depressive reactions so common that they have taken to referring to it as the "common cold" of psychology.

3. HISTORIC FEELINGS OF GUILT, IMPOTENCE, AND DISPAIR

Feelings of impotence and an inability to change the mistakes we have made are common psychological worries. The problem is well stated in *The Rubaiyat* by the twelfth-century poet Omar Khayyam:

The moving finger writes; and, having writ,

Moves on, nor all your piety nor wit

Shall lure it back to cancel half a line,

Nor all your tears wash out a word of it.

And neath that inverted bowl we call the sky;

Whereunder, crawling coop'd we live and die,

Lift not your hands to it for help;

for it as impotently moves as you and I.

Yesterday this Day's Madness did prepare;

To-morrow's silence, triumph, or despair:

Drink! for you know not whence you came, nor why:

Drink! for you know not why you go, nor where.

4. ANXIETY AND THE CAUSES OF DEPRESSION

Underlying most cases of depression seem to be two basic phenomena: The first is an emotional reaction that can best be described as prolonged anxiety or resignation, and the second is the effect of prior experiences or conditioning.

Anaclitic Depression Anaclitic depression refers to a depression born of dependence. For example, infants that are separated from their mothers may undergo extreme anxiety. Puppies will whimper, monkeys will shriek and whine, and the human child will cry out loud. In nature, this function is highly adaptive. The cries of the infant are nature's insurance that the mother will attend to its needs. The fear experienced by the infant when left without its mother ensures that it will stay close to its mother in the wild and instantly run to her in times of danger. The combination of fear and contact comfort helps cement the bond between the infant and its mother.

But what happens if the dependency needs of the infant are not met? In the human child, between the ages of six months and one year, these needs become acute. R. A. Spitz notes that an infant separated from its mother will go into a state of what he refers to as anaclitic depression. Left without its mother, the baby may weep and cry violently. Attempts by others to console the baby may be unsuccessful. The baby may cry itself to sleep. This behavior lasts, Spitz notes, for about three to four weeks. But at this point, things begin to change. If the mother has not returned, the infant will gradually go into a state of severe depression. To quote Spitz's description of its behavior:

The child lies quietly on its stomach, does not even look up if the observer enters the room, does not play with any toy, does not even grasp for it. It is passive and dejected, has eating difficulties, sleep disturbances, loses weight, and becomes more susceptive to colds and eczema.

In an attempt to prevent this reaction, Spitz provided a substitute mother for each child that he found separated from its real mother. Of one hundred and twenty-three cases in which this was attempted, the substitution of a mother was successful in all but forty-five cases. Six months to one year of age seemed to be the most critical period. Beyond one year of age, similar reactions occurred, but separation for as long as three months appeared to be reversible if the infant were given a mother.

Anaclitic depression is not limited to infants. We come to depend on those around us, even though we may not be aware of it while it is happening. We experience a marked sense of loss and depression at the loss of a loved one.

On a different level, a similar reaction may occur at the breakup of a high school romance or in the depression following a lonely divorce. The feeling of loneliness of a jilted lover may be an even more intense state of depression. The anxiety of losing someone on whom one depends may be increased by the feeling that perhaps one's own inadequacies caused the lover to leave for someone else. Even the parting of long-time friends may be accompanied by a marked feeling of loss and sadness.

Some forms of depression seem to be related to the early conditioning of the *Conditioned Guilt* child. If a child is conditioned to fear white rats or any other external stimulus, this fear is referred to as a *phobia*. But if the same degree of fear is attached not to an external stimulus but to an internal one- to the individuals themselves- the reaction may be one of guilt. Children who are conditioned to believe that lustful thoughts are "evil," and that anyone who experiences such thoughts is sinful, may inevitably come to experience some such thoughts of their own.

As a result of their behavior or their thoughts, they may then commit acts that they have come to believe are terrible. Now they must carry the fear of having committed such acts with them. They cannot run away from their fear as Little Albert could run away from the white rat. No matter how hard they try, the fear is now attached to them. The fear is no longer a product of an external source that can be escaped; it is an inescapable fact of their being. The shame, the guilt, the feelings of unworthiness and inadequacy that can result from this type of experience may lead to feelings of depression and worthlessness.

Society often conspires to intensify and even encourage such feelings. The case of rape is a notable point. The victim of rape often experiences intense feelings of depression and anxiety. The victim may feel personally guilt-ridden and experience feelings of worthlessness. Why? Not merely because of the act of rape itself.

Decades of social conditioning in which girls are warned about that "fate worse than death" and are conditioned to believe that "no right-thinking boy would want a girl who was not chaste" have produced an intensified and exaggerated fear of such events. Now, after the fact, through no fault of her own the victim must carry with her an inescapable fact of life and an almost inevitable feeling of anxiety and depression produced by decades of conditioned emotional reactions.

Traumatic events are not necessary to produce this feeling, however. Children are often conditioned to feel that unless they are a success socially, athletically, in marriage, or in business, there must be something wrong with them personally. You see some of this in the successful performer Rick Springfield, who described the feelings that led to his suicide attempt as a teen as *" feeling like a failure in the only life arena I knew."* School. A major failure in any such area may lead to a feeling of personal inadequacy that closely resembles feelings of guilt. The anxiety resulting from a repeated series of failures may produce a degree of fear and insecurity rivaling that of an infant deprived of its mother.

5. ELATION-DEPRESSION EFFECTS

Depression may also be an effect of differences in the magnitude of reward. In the process of growing up, all of us develop at least a vague image of what life will be like when we finally finish our education, get a job, and marry. But what happens if this image we have developed turns out to bear little similarity to the end result?

What happens if one's job is not rewarding or stimulating? What happens if one's marriage is unsatisfactory? If there is a substantial discrepancy between the ideal one has come to expect and the reality of one's life, anxiety and depression may result. Day after day, the individual receives few if any reinforcements and those that are received occasionally are inadequate compared to what he or she has come to expect or believes others to be getting. Unhappiness sets in. If this situation continues for a prolonged period of time, feelings of dejection and depression may follow.

If we have unrealistic expectations of life, that alone may create a feeling of depression.

The individual may have some choices for changing the source of depression. With or without professional help it may be possible to reevaluate one's job or one's course in life; either to attain more satisfaction or to convince oneself that it is a successful achievement. It may be possible to reevaluate one's marriage to find ways of reviving the sources of reinforcement. Unfortunately, other people in the environment often do not cooperate or, even if they are aware of the problem, they may be unable to provide help.

Yet it may not always be possible to "count your blessings" as a way out of a depression. Such cliches are of very little value when you are caught in a situation that makes you feel tied to, or dependent on, your job or marriage. In the end, it may sometimes be necessary to drastically change the situation by changing the job or even the marriage partner. Such changes, however, may be insufficient to resolve the basic difficulty, and therapy may be necessary to help the individuals change their goals and direct their interests into areas that may provide appropriate reinforcement.

Clinical psychologists, such as Carl Rogers, often trace anxiety and depression to a discrepancy between the individual's *self-ideal,* which is what individuals believe they should be and how they should behave, and the individual's *self-image,* which is how individuals see themselves as being. From the demands and appraisals of parents and peers, children construct an ideal self. This ideal self is their perception of what they should be like if they are to be respected and liked by others.

From the same series of demands and appraisals, children also develop an image of what they are actually like as individuals, whether they are treated with respect or indifference, whether they are regarded as a success or failure, and an infinite variety of other views of their social, sexual, and personal abilities. If children fail to live up to the goals for success that they have internalized, they may make a self-judgment of their own ability. Their self-esteem may fall, and with it their desire to achieve and their will to continue.

6. SELF-CONCEPT AND PSYCHOLOGICAL PROBLEMS

Carl Rogers, one of the outstanding clinical psychologists in America, evaluated the problems of many everyday people who came to him looking for help with their problems of living. Rogers found that the clients who had problems often had a great discrepancy between their self-ideal and how they saw themselves. People who had fewer problems had a smaller discrepancy between their self-ideal and how they perceived themselves.

From his observations, Carl Rogers developed a technique of working with his clients to improve their self-image. He found that his clients would often benefit if they were bathed in an atmosphere of what Rogers called "unconditional positive regard." Acting as a sounding board, Rogers reflected the feelings of his clients back to them, giving the clients a feeling that the therapist understood them and did not judge them. He also provided the clients with a starting point in self-understanding that would allow them to work their own way out of their problems.

To Carl Rogers, the most important factor in determining human behavior is the individual's own unique perception of reality. Each of us exists in a world of experience that may differ from that of others. Each reacts, not to "reality," but to his or her own subjective perception of reality.

Rogers believes if allowed to do so, we will seek our own paths of personal psychological growth and strive to exercise our greatest human potential. Such a view of human nature goes beyond anything discussed. It implies that we are capable of "free will," of making decisions on our own by a process of rational thought.

As in Rogers' client-centered therapy and Maslow's self-actualization (a cognitive approach). This is a *self-concept* approach that:

1. Rogers noted that many problems result due to a discrepancy between their "ideal self" and how they have come to see themselves (their self-concept).

2. Emphasizes Unconditional Positive Regard: all of us grow up in a world of conditional positive regard; our parents like us if we are obedient, our friends like us if we are positive toward them, etc. To change to a more positive self-concept, Rogers talks about bathing the individual in an atmosphere of "unconditional positive regard". That does not mean agreeing with everything they do or say, it means treating them as worthy of positive regard no matter what. Rogers emphasizes self-acceptance and realistic self-praise.

3. Emphasizes helping the client on the road toward actualization of their greatest potential for growth to a higher level of self-acceptance and self-actualization.

Humanistic Psychology A number of influential psychologists such as Kurt Lewin, Gordon Allport, Abraham Maslow, and Carl Rogers have advocated just such a broad view of the intellectual capabilities of human nature. Even though we are often the product of conditioned behavior and irrational patterns of thought, we can go beyond our conditioning, beyond our irrationality, to achieve a far higher level of development. Maslow has referred to this higher development as *self-actualization*. Such concepts are part of an area of psychology that is referred to as *humanistic* psychology.

7. A HUMANISTIC COMMENT ON THE CAUSE AND CURE OF PSYCHOLOGICAL PROBLEMS

Let people realize clearly that every time they threaten someone or humiliate or hurt unnecessarily or dominate or reject another human being, they become forces for the creation of psychopathology, even if these be small forces. Let them recognize that every man who is kind; helpful, decent, psychologically democratic, affectionate, and warm, is a psychotherapeutic force even though a small one.

Abraham Maslow *Motivation and Personality*

The most basic needs of the human being are those of self-preservation. We *Self-Preservation* must first meet the biological needs of food, water, shelter, and comfort. In a primitive society, where one must cope daily with the problem of filling his stomach, there is little time for philosophical speculation on the nature of humanity or the universe. Someone who is hungry cannot even worry about what others think of him or her (self-enhancement).

#Maslow's hierarchy of needs

#self-actualization

#B-cognition

#D-cognition

#humanistic psychology

One example of the humanistic approach to psychology is provided by Maslow in what he refers to as a hierarchy of needs. To simplify Maslow's hierarchy of needs, in line with the concepts of both Maslow and Rogers, the striving of the human being can be seen as a series of striving~ for basic needs. Maslow has included in his hierarchy a number of basic needs, which can be grouped into perhaps three basic categories: (1) self-preservation, (2) self enhancement, and (3) self-actualization.

What happens to humans when the need for self-preservation is not met? In extreme conditions, people may be deprived of food for long periods of time. In such circumstances, however, some of the most basic aspects of civilized behavior may break down. In the early history of the westward movement, there is a famous story of the Donner party en route to California, Along the way, they became marooned in a snowstorm as they attempted to cross the high Sierra. For weeks the party was unable to find food.

As time passed, the members of the party began to die one by one. When the survivors were finally rescued, they told a chilling story of having survived by eating the bodies of those who had died. Social inhibitions that would be considered inviolable under normal conditions broke down rapidly under conditions in which people were deprived of their most basic biological needs.

More recent cases can be cited. The most recent one involved an athletic team whose plane crashed in the Andes and who survived for over a month by eating the dead. Even the most primitive of human cultures are rarely subjected to such extremes, however. Except for the backwaters of the world, the needs of most of us for food and shelter are adequately met. When our need for self-preservation is satisfied, we can go on to the next stage *Self-Enhancement* of development, the stage of self-enhancement. According to Maslow's concept, self-enhancement in the individual involves a development of competence, along with feelings of being loved, feelings of belonging, and a feeling of self-esteem and self-worth.

The failure to feel competent or loved or worthy may result in resort to ego defense mechanisms as a means of covering feelings of insecurity. Or it may involve doing things that we believe will make us more attractive or better liked by others. Simple examples may be the use of cosmetics or clothes to enhance our attractiveness, or the use of whatever resources we have to better our position in life, our power, our prestige, our reputation, or the size of our home.

But according to Maslow, if we are still trying to enhance our attractiveness and our prestige, we have not reached the stage at which we are at our best. Only after we have satisfied our basic needs for feeling secure, for self-esteem and self-worth, can we go on to the next stage.

Maslow's theory could be applied to nations as well as to individuals. Although humans have been on this earth for hundreds of thousands of years, it has only been within the past ten to twenty thousand years that we have begun to develop cities, agriculture, and a complex economic structure. Not until the development of agriculture were we able to progress much beyond the state of the hunting and gathering tribes. With the development of farming techniques, we came to rely on grain, a stable food supply that could be stored as surplus throughout the winter. As the techniques of farming progressed, the surplus increased. Agriculture allowed-in fact forced-people to settle in permanent communities. More than this, it allowed them a surplus of food so that they no longer had to seek their sustenance each day.

Maslow's Hierarchy of Needs

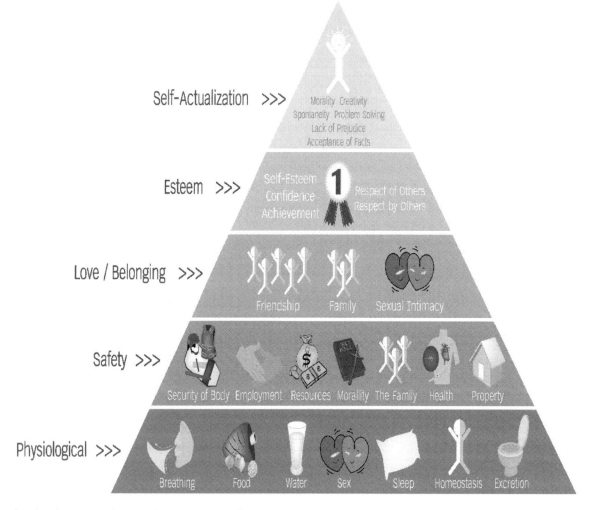

The development of a complex social order followed rapidly. It was no longer necessary for all members of the community to seek their own food. Instead, some now could devote their time to art, astronomy, the priesthood, and war. Such was the beginning of an aristocracy, a specialized group of soldiers, an organized religion, and the rudiments of science. Not until the surplus of grain had assured people freedom from the need for worry about hunger could communities go to the next step of self-enhancement, of supporting the specialists who have molded civilization. For example, a nation might achieve self-enhancement by increasing its army and conquering neighboring peoples to increase its feeling of security.

Most human needs for self-preservation and self-enhancement would be agreed on by all psychologists. But at this point, Abraham Maslow, Carl Rogers, Gordon Allport, and others within the humanistic psychology movement propose that humans are more than the end product of their biology and the environmental forces that act on them. To many psychologists, the picture of humans as being mere pawns in their social environment is inadequate. They point out that we are capable of going far beyond nature. We are capable of building things that never were, of changing even the most basic structure of social order, of improving ourselves by our own efforts. Thus, just as we have changed nature through our conscious efforts, we can also change ourselves through our conscious efforts.

Self-Actualization To Maslow, the stage of self-actualization represents the ultimate in one's psychological strivings. With our basic needs for self-preservation and self-enhancement satisfied, we can now go on to actualize our greatest potential. Maslow has completed biographical studies of a great many individuals whom he considers to be in the stage of self-actualization.

These are the people that he believes to be the most psychologically healthy individuals. Albert Einstein, Albert Schweitzer, Eleanor Roosevelt, Abraham Lincoln, and a number of individuals who had never achieved such degrees of fame are some of the people who Maslow believes successfully satisfied their more basic needs and went on to what he calls *meta needs* where they sought truth, beauty, justice, and the higher values and goals of humanity.

Not all psychologists would be willing to admit that we can accurately distinguish between the so-called self-actualizing individuals and just any ordinary individuals. Yet there is a feeling in a great many psychologists that there is, in fact, a stage of psychological development in which the individual is capable of going beyond his more basic strivings and developing a conscious, reasoned striving toward such values.

To Maslow, only a small percentage of individuals ever reach a high level of self-actualization. Most of us :6nd that self-enhancement is still a consuming need. The difference between these stages of development resembles the difference between a Supreme Court Justice and a minor county official who is elected by the public. Sitting at the post for life, the Supreme Court Justice is assured of both salary and prestige. Having reached an age at which he can feel personally secure, the Justice does not find it necessary to seek the symbols that would lead to self-esteem.

Because his position is secure, he does not find it necessary to seek the goodwill of the powerful. In contrast, lower-ranking elected officials must test the wind of their constituents and bend in the direction that will assure reelection. Being young, they may have strong emotional causes that they feel are more important than general principles. In short, they are more likely to be the pawn of the powerbrokers, their constituents, and even their own emotional reactions.

8. THE EXISTENTIAL CRISIS

Philosophy majors, who may now be thoroughly confused, should note that existential psychology is somewhat closer to humanism in *philosophy* than it is to humanistic psychology. Psychologists have given these terms their own definitions.

Perhaps the ultimate fears are the sources of existential anxiety. These are the worries about self-identity, about where we are headed and what our future may be, and about the meaning of life itself. Such fears may be precipitated by a sudden crisis: the loss of a job, the death of a loved one, a sudden realization that one's philosophy of life is irrevocably in error. In the existential crisis, the individual may be caught up in a confusing and frantic search for meaning and purpose in life. We long for something or someone to give us a purpose in life: a cause, a love, a sense of belonging.

Such fears are common, the evidence indicates that the majority of people do experience some of these fears in varying degrees. To be effective, psychologists must somehow find answers to the causes and cures of such human problems-the problems of the individual.

Existential psychology is a branch of modern psychology that concerns itself with the human need for meaning in life. As in existential philosophy, existential psychologists believe that the only meaning and purpose in life is that which people themselves give to it. They see humanity as alone, unable to depend on God or science to provide life with the meaning and purpose that earlier generations felt from their faith in God or science. Consequently, the individual must strive to give life meaning and purpose." This off-beat but very important branch of psychology is championed by two well-known figures in the field of psychoanalysis and psychology, Victor Frankl and Rollo May.

The existential crisis is perhaps not easily seen by college students who are just on the brink of the rest of their lives. Yet the existential crisis is not uncommon at any age. It is perhaps most familiar to the average person as the "Paul Bryant syndrome" of the old television show *Run [or Your Life.* Paul Bryant, a well-to-do lawyer, was suddenly told by his doctor that he has only a short time to live. Feeling that he had not yet tasted life, Bryant left his law practice and set out to find what life is all about, all the while quoting the great philosophers of the past who had similarly engaged in a search for the meaning and purpose of life.

AN EXISTENTIAL CRISIS

A profound expression of the feelings of an existential crisis is found in the following quote from Shakespeare:

To-morrow, and to-morrow, and to-morrow,
Creeps in this petty pace from day *to* day
To the last syllable of recorded time:
And all our yesterdays have lighted fools
The way to dusty death.
Out, out, brief candle!
Life's but a walking shadow,
a poor player
That struts and frets his hour upon the stage,
And then is heard no more; it is a tale
Told by an idiot, full of sound and fury,
Signifying nothing. –
Macbeth Act V, Scene V

William Shakespeare.

Two of the major existential psychologists have suffered a similar crisis in their lives. Viktor Frankl was imprisoned in the Nazi concentration camps during World War II. Here, prisoners who had been uprooted from their homes and separated from their families faced the problem of sheer survival day after day. Each day they awoke not knowing whether they would be among those who would die or whether they would survive to work for another day. God did not help, science did not help, politics, philosophy, and religion were of little value.

Under such circumstances, all sense of purpose in life, all sense of meaning in life seemed to evaporate. None could have known what the outcome of the war would be or even if they would survive the night. But many did survive. Frankl himself was able to survive, in part by the purpose provided by his belief that when it was all over, he could write of his experiences from the standpoint of a psychoanalyst who had seen human suffering at perhaps its most extreme. This feeling helped give Frankl a sense of meaning, a goal for life.

Rollo May faced a similar crisis. May contracted tuberculosis and was confined to the hospital for a long period of time. During his hospitalization, May began to question the meaning and purpose of his life. It was then that he picked up a book by Jean-Paul Sartre, the French existential philosopher, and began to identify with the feelings that Sartre expressed of one alone caught up by an uncaring universe with no one to depend on. From his experiences and his readings, May began to formulate a belief that one of the major problems an individual must face in life is a confrontation with the questions of a meaning and purpose to his or her life.

Both humanist and existential psychologists have painted a graphic picture of the individual in the twentieth century in search of answers to the philosophical questions Who am I? Where am I going? Why? It speaks to the questions of self-identity, hope for a future, and purpose in life.

But these questions are not asked only by those who have faced some sort of personal tragedy. They are the same questions asked by Leo Tolstoy in his autobiography and by Ernest Hemingway in his novels and his life.

They may be seen in the strivings of Marilyn Monroe, Janis Joplin, and countless well-known celebrities. The same feelings are expressed in the writings and thoughts of Leo Tolstoy and Abraham Lincoln, whose outstanding contributions have tended to mask their unhappy marriages and their feelings of self-dissatisfaction. Many famous people, often at the height of their careers, have felt the existential confrontation with the questions of the purpose and meaning of it all. Many have been unable to find the answers.

The psychologist who must deal with such existential crises may concentrate on helping the individual to find goals to strive for in life. These goals vary with each individual. No two people will necessarily be able to find meaning with the same goals. But having a goal, a view of something better to achieve tomorrow, is crucial to the problem of daily living. It would be a very bleak psychological future if we felt that each day we lived would be exactly the same as the one before, with no hope for improvement, no hope for novelty, merely a continuous unending series of routine and ritual. Goals provide a spice for life. But each person must find his own.

9. PSYCHOANALYTIC THEORY

Of all the approaches to psychological problems, the first and oldest are the psychoanalytic theories that had their origin in the observations of Sigmund Freud. It is difficult to present an accurate summary of Freud's theory in a textbook. Few psychologists have written as much literature as Freud, and his theory has evolved and changed over a period of seventy years.

Most textbooks supply a modernized version of Freud and ignore entirely the overwhelming emphasis that he placed on sexual energy as the prime driving force in human behavior. This book is no exception. In many ways, such an updated version of Freud is easier to relate to than the original, but at the same time it loses some of the flavor of the authentic Freud. Readers must keep this in mind if they are exposed to a quite different-sounding Freud in later courses.

Id   Freud believed that the human mind is shaped by three general forces: the *id, ego,* and *superego.* The newborn child is represented by Freud as being only a bundle of instincts composed of energy and needs- the id. The id is primarily seen as the sexual and aggressive energy that provides the drive and desires of the infant.

The energy operates on a principle of immediate gratification-the pleasure principle. When hungry, the infant screams for satisfaction; when angry or frustrated, it lashes out in undirected rage. The principal motive of the infant is to satisfy its instinctual urges. The id instincts have no conscious awareness of their existence or of the outside world. The instincts have no interest in anything except to take what gives pleasure and to respond with rage to what gives pain.

Ego   The id must have a conscious link with the outside world if it is to be successful in gratifying its needs. The ego provides such a link. The ego provides direction that allows the energy to be channeled toward the appropriate external objects. In contrast to the id, the ego is based on the *reality principle*. Thus, reality may require that the child wait, or delay his gratification, until the appropriate object is available. The child must learn how and when it can release pleasurable energy or direct aggressive energy.

The id may be conceptualized as a source of instinctual energy forces striving for expression. Freud believed that when humans became civilized animals, the automatic *Superego* release of sexual and aggressive impulses presented a problem. If we were to live together in relative peace, we had to inhibit our sexual and aggressive reactions. This was done by means of the superego.

The superego represents the child's internalization of all of the taboos and prohibitions-the "Thou shalt nots"- that parents and society impose on the individual to restrict his impulses for immediate pleasure or rage. Some people refer to the superego as a conscience, a sort of watchdog that prevents us from acting out our impulses.

The ego evolves as a reality-oriented control to channel the id energy into acceptable outlets. It mediates between the id and superego.

The superego evolves as a control over the expression of socially unacceptable drives of sexual and aggressive behavior that arise in the id. Freud believed that when conflict occurs between the id and superego, the ego would protect itself by using the ego-defense mechanisms of repression, and displacement. etc.

The Superego creates some problems of its own. Freud believed that the sexual and aggressive energy could now be bottled up within the mind. Under the prohibitions of the superego, the energy of the id, which Freud considered to be not unlike hydraulic pressure, creates a state of tension or anxiety. The pressure must be vented. If is not, the energy may be converted into a physical illness, as in hysteric paralysis or blindness (see conversion hysteria, Chap. 23). Repression of the tension-producing thoughts may only temporarily reduce the anxiety.

Freud believed that in our dreams, this energy sometimes seeped through the censorship of the superego. The energy then takes a very different form, as symbols of sex and aggression. If you burn a piece of wood, the energy of the fire changes the chemicals within the wood into a greatly altered, even unrecognizable, form of carbon, ash, and vapor. Freud believed that sexual energy and aggressive energy similarly is transformed into symbols within the dream whose meaning can then be interpreted by the psychoanalyst. Freud's theory of the meaning of dreams has never been proven scientifically, but it excited a tremendous amount of interest.

One of Freud's major contributions to the problem of anxiety was his development of the process of *psychoanalysis*. Freud's partner in medicine in 1895 was a physician, Joseph Breuer. Breuer had a patient, the famous "Anna O." in the literature, who was suffering from hysteria. As she talked to Breuer about her problems, she noted that simply talking them out relieved her anxiety. She came to call this *"the talking cure."*

Freud was quick to recognize the importance of this 'talking cure". Freud tried allowing his patients to "free associate" -that is, to say whatever came into their mind. He believed that by free-associating the patients would reveal the underlying cause of their problem. Then, in the process of talking out their problem, the underlying tension or energy could be released. To Freud, the "talking cure" was a catharsis, a means of purging the mind of anxiety. Today, both free association and catharsis are basic to the process of psychoanalysis.

Not all feelings of depression and anxiety result from discrepancies between one's self-ideal and self-concept, as some humanists propose, or from one's confrontation with an existential crisis as the existentialists suggest, or from inner conflict between the id, ego, and superego, as psychoanalysts believe. Many, perhaps most, of the average person's fears and moments of depression result from conditioned emotional reactions we face in the daily conflicts with family or peer groups, or at work. Such conflicts occur when we must interact with others in situations that make us feel anxious and uptight.

"Like many of you, I've had difficulty adjusting to life in the modern forest."

10. THERAPY

PSYCHOLOGICAL PROBLEMS OF THE INDIVIDUAL

When patterns of negative experience become predominate, we may need professional help to overcome those problems.

Studies by Liddell have found that animals exposed to levels of anxiety, as in anticipating a shock, will develop patterns of anxiety similar to those of people. One might argue that the studies of Liddell seem too artificial to apply to people. Most of us do not worry about getting hit with a blast of air when we start to eat our morning cornflakes. Yet the anxiety produced by an air blast or an electric shock is identical to that produced by having to face an unpleasant boss with an inadequate or uncompleted work report or having to face the demands and nagging of a spouse. Our worries about our self-ideal, our imagined judgment by the minds of others, even our anticipatory anxiety about "Who am I?", "Where am I going?", and "Why?" are a product of similar conditioned anxieties.

The anxieties of the employee are the same basic anxieties, even though produced by different experiences. But people are not caged like animals and subjected to such conditions, are they? Cannot they escape? Cannot they exercise free will and break through such conditions? Perhaps. But the human being is as time-bound by society as Liddell's sheep are bound by a restraint harness. The restraints are not physical, but psychological. If your job is the source of our anxiety, we cannot stop work. We must always go back to the same position on Monday.

If social interaction is the source of our anxiety, we cannot avoid people without becoming a hermit. And if the source of the anxiety exists purely in one's own mind, it may be impossible to escape from it even temporarily. Physicians may send patients suffering from "nervous breakdowns" to the country for a "rest cure," but such a cure may only be temporarily effective. We must eventually return to the job, the family, the people, or problems that are the source of the anxiety.

Treatment may be effective only when it is possible to successfully remove the source of the anxiety. It is not enough to treat disturbed children-their parents and schools must be involved.

Children who are afraid of other children will not be helped by therapy unless they can go back into a world where others react to them positively, without criticism or condemnation.

People who feel inadequate or insecure on the job cannot do an effective job if they must worry about the reaction of their boss or fellow employees. Treatment of such problems thus requires more than simply a psychologist. It would be most effective if it were accompanied by a restructuring, or at least a reeducation, of the entire society to make society less aversive-less anxiety-producing.

ANTICIPATORY ANXIETY

How many times do we worry about the outcome of a test grade, an encounter with the boss or a fellow employee, or the outcome of a personal argument, only to feel relief that the worry is over-even if the outcome is, in fact, the worst that we had imagined? Young lovers may be worried about losing their love, but once the certainty of loss is apparent, they can perhaps rationalize that it is all for the best and go on to something else. People who worry about losing their jobs may spend more time suffering the agony of uncertainty than they would if they actually lost the job. One of the greatest problems of anxiety thus is that of anticipatory anxiety.

FIVE APPROACHES TO THERAPY

11. BEHAVIORAL PSYCHOLOGY
APPLIED PSYCHOLOGY Therapy

Beyond any doubt Mary Cover Jones classic use of Pavlovian conditioning was perhaps the first dramatic success in applying the principles Pavlov discovered to a human problem.

She took a child named Peter (little Peter) who was already terrified of dogs, a not uncommon childhood fear—dogs bark, dogs are big, etc. Peter's fear had already generalized to all furry animals. Starting with a furry rabbit, at a distance, she waited until Peter looked up and saw the rabbit, then stuck a spoon with ice cream onto his lips, then took the rabbit away.

This is **counter conditioning**; the pleasure of the ice cream was used to counter the fear of furry animals.

Then, she **gradually** moved the rabbit closer each time (**gradual desensitization**) and each time Albert saw the rabbit—a spoonful of ice cream was touched to his mouth.

After several short sessions over a week, Peter was able to pet the formerly frightening stimulus. His fear had been *counter conditioned* by a process of gradual desensitization. Associating the positive emotion of ice cream countered the negative emotion of fear.

TECHNIQUES OF BEHAVIORAL PSYCHOLOGY
1. Functional Analysis of Behavior

In a Functional Analysis of Behavior, a psychologist would attempt to find the specific elements of a behavior. One psychologist was concerned that his daughter had developed a fear of the dark. That is actually a common fear in children, but it is not natural. So, he looked at what was happening at night. He would go into his daughter's bedroom, read her a bedtime story, kiss her good night, and then, turn out the light.

So, turning out the light (the dark) was *associated* with her security leaving and the end of a fun time.

To solve the problem, he simply reversed the *sequence* of events. Now, he would turn out the light (the dark) as soon as he went into her room, read her a bedtime story, kiss her good night, and leave. The dark was now associated with something positive and fun times. It ended her fear of the dark.

Of course, we do not always know why a child is afraid of the dark; it may be because he watched a scary movie, or his older brother told him that Freddy Kruger was hiding under the bed and would grab him at night. But the technique he used would be useful, even if one did not know the "cause" of the problem.

2. Anticipatory behavior

Our brain comes to anticipate anxiety or depression from a series of negative experiences. If the brain has come to expect that something bad will likely result (from social interaction or life) then this emotion may dominate their thoughts.

To counter this, a technique similar to that of Albert Bandura, showing them examples of others who have been through similar experiences and gone on to succeed (such as the above examples of Lincoln, Springfield, Oprah, and so many others) can be used to counter the anxiety or depression.

3. Approach-Avoidance

If we have unrealistic expectations of life, love, success, and we get hit with something unexpectedly negative (such as divorce, a miscarriage, PTSD by exposure to blood and death in war) this can contribute to depression. Beautiful, successful, model and actress Brooke Shields, in her book *Down Came the Rain*, tells of repeated feelings of depression over being unable to have a baby. She said, "Why am I being punished?"

Then she gets pregnant and feels great. But that ends in a miscarriage and more feelings of guilt. That shows some feeling of guilt you often see in women who have had a miscarriage. Yet it is not their fault. About 20% of pregnancies result in a miscarriage, even when you have done everything right. If we taught girls in school this simple fact, it might prevent much of the guilt that so many feel, as if it is their fault. But this is part of reality that is censored from our children.

When she finally does have a baby, she then goes into a post-partum depression, unable to carry on. If we have unrealistic expectations of having a baby being all giggles, coos, and happy times, then when we are hit with the reality of a baby, feeding, burping, and wiping, this can be more depressing than people realize.

Simple education might have prevented much of the problems. But the censorship in our schools is so great that few are ever exposed to reality.

4. Behavior Modification:

Behavior-modification approach As in Mary Cover Jones or Joseph Wolpe's desensitization or Skinner's use of reinforcement to shape behavior (a conditioning approach). Counterconditioning and desensitization and reinforcement of appropriate behavior are three basic principles. Conditioning and reinforcement techniques are used for removal of phobias through counterconditioning, and use of reinforcement to establish desired behaviors.

O. H. Mowrer was one of the first to use Classical Pavlovian Conditioning to apply to changing a problem.

The problem: enuresis What do you do if you *are* a young person, and you still wet the bed? This is a very real question for young people who have a problem known as *enuresis*. Their body control systems have no difficulty in holding their urine during the day, but the systems fail at night while the subject's sleep.

The therapy: conditioning O. H. Mowrer was one of the first to apply the new knowledge of conditioning to human problems-specifically, enuresis. The subjects Were young people, many of whom had been taken to several specialists without success. The problem was how to condition the subjects to wake up *before* they wet the bed, To do this, Mowrer devised an ingenious apparatus, a urine-sensing, buzzer-blanket, which is laced with wires. The subject sleeps on the blanket, and when it becomes wet with urine, an electrical contact is created between the wires.

A small electric charge then sets off an alarm clock. The alarm (UCS) elicits an innate *response-arousal* (UCR)-arid the child wakes up. The stimulus *wet* occurs just before the alarm sounds and therefore, is paired with the *alarm* (UCS). The CS *wet* will now come to elicit *arousal* (CR), which formerly had been elicited only by the *alarm* alone. Of course, many other stimuli, as in dreams, may *have* occurred just before the *alarm,* but the only stimulus that is experienced every time the *alarm* is triggered is the stimulus *wet,* which becomes the CS.

The result: What have we got? So far, we have a child who now wakes up *every* time urination occurs-not much of an improvement. More is involved, however. Other stimuli occur just before the stimulus *wet.* Specifically, the body experienced the stimulus *bladder tension,* which is paired with the *wet* on every trial. Since *wet* (CS_1) now elicits *arousal* by itself, any stimulus paired with it will come to be a CS (CS_2). After a number of pairings, the CS_2 of bladder tension will come to elicit *arousal* and the child will wake up before, rather than after, the accident occurs.

Mowrer's technique proved to be remarkably successful. After conditioning was complete, the electric, urine-sensing, buzzer-blanket could be thrown away, the "bond" of *bladder tension-arousal* now being maintained by the reinforcement of bladder release.

No conscious understanding of the process is necessary. Indeed, most of us go to the bathroom without being aware of the internal sensory stimuli. If asked how we knew we had to go, we might reply, "Oh, I just had the urge." Yet our behavior is triggered by the internal stimulus of bladder tension whether or not we are conscious of it.

		TIME...	
Trial		*Learned*	*Innate*
1.	BLADDER TENSION	WET------	ALARM - AROUSAL
2.	BLADDER TENSION	WET------ *arousal*	- ALARM - AROUSAL
3.	BLADDER TENSION	Wet - Arousal	- ALARM - AROUSAL
4.	BLADDER -TENSION	Arousal -	ALARM - AROUSAL
5.	BLADDER TENSION	AROUSAL	

5.*Change the environment, and you change the behavior.*

One of the most successful forms of behavior modification, from the works of Skinner and others, involves changing the environment to reward positive behavior and ignore negative behavior.

These techniques have been used in everything from group therapy to token economies to change behavior.

12. BANDURA'S BRIDGE BETWEEN BEHAVIORAL AND COGNITIVE BEHAVIORAL PSYCHOLOGY

One of the most important and least known of all therapies is a bridge between behavioral and cognitive behavioral psychology by one of the all-time greats in psychology, Albert Bandura. Bandura took 44 children who were already terrified of dogs, and, instead of using individual therapy, he showed them a series of four short videos of a boy playing with a cocker spaniel. The boy was feeding, walking, and interacting with the dog.

After only four short videos, over four days, of a boy playing happily with a dog, it was possible to get these boys, individually, to pet the dog, much as Mary Cover Jones had done, only using modeling films, a cognitive form of *gradual desensitization* and *counter conditioning* (the happy boy and dog countering the fear of the dog).

This was a remarkable study that suggested that visual examples could be used to change our emotions, and even used with large numbers of individuals at the same time. Unfortunately, its value has been largely ignored and is missing from our education of clinical practice. This is a technique that could be used in our schools, not for fear of dogs, but to protect children from the effects of bullying and peer group pressure.

13. COGNITIVE BEHAVIORAL APPROACH:

Aaron Beck was a pioneer in the development of cognitive behavioral therapy. Basic to his approach is the belief that psychological problems result from distorted and counterproductive thinking. "Thinking" is the Cognitive in Cognitive Behavior Therapy (CBT).

CBT works with clients to **identify their irrational thought patterns**, evaluate and work through their dysfunctional patterns of thought. Among many things this involves;

Repetitive thought patterns; we may stay up at night worrying over what others think of us, or mulling over and over what we should have done differently, or blaming ourself for things we did, or should have done.

However common the above patterns of thinking are, they are self-defeating, irrational, and useless. By forcing the client to think about how unnecessary and invalid those thoughts are, it may allow the client to replace their negative thought patterns with more realistic ideas.

Overthinking and Catastrophizing; We tend to overthink simple issues. We may believe that others dislike us, when they are only preoccupied with their own problems and ignore us. We may tend to "catastrophize" simple problems of living as if they were major problems, when most of them may go away on their own.

"Let's put that nasty word 'plummet' out of our minds."

Sometimes CBT involves visualizing yourself in an anxiety producing situation and how you could behave differently. This can be useful to help the individual think about alternative ways of responding to difficult situations.

"Visualize yourself not falling off the wall."

Problems such as depression and ulcers are common in our culture. Millions of us endure these products of anxiety with little apparent interruption of our lives and with no display of abnormal behavior. Many of the most successful and admired people in the world are coping daily with these types of stress.

But there is another area of psychology, poorly defined, in which the problems are beyond the individual's ability to cope. When the problems begin to disrupt the life of the individual or the lives of those around him, the problems may cease being those of the individual and become problems of society. Such problems may involve psychosis or antisocial behavior-the subjects of our next chapter.

14. EXISTENTIAL APPROACH

As in the work of May and Frankl (also a cognitive approach). This is a *goal-oriented* approach that places an emphasis on individuals having to give life meaning by their own choices, to encourage individuals to set their own goals in life.

"I woke up one day and said to myself, 'Why do I keep chasing the bone?'."

This is the existential crisis of Shakespeare's soliloquy challenging the meaning of life; "*Life is a tale...full of sound and fury, signifying nothing*"

The point of existential therapy is to find goals that give your life meaning. The previously discussed trauma of Victor Frankl and others suggest that this is not a unique problem in life. For young people it may be a feeing of being left out of the few things their peers value, sports and socializing, and giving them hope that they can succeed in other areas. For adults, it may be having to go beyond the feeling that their work has no purpose, or the empty nest syndrome. Goals give purpose. Purpose gives hope.

15. PREVENTIVE PSYCHOLOGY

One Of the least supported ideas in psychology is that of preventing psychological problems before they begin. Actually, almost all psychologists agree with the idea of preventive psychology, but there is surprisingly little support for the idea.

Both the World Health Organization (WHO), and the American Psychological Association have produced massive tomes on the idea of preventing psychological problems but the main emphasis in both groups is to (1) identify problems early (by going into schools to find problem) and (2) Get them help. Help consists of providing psychotherapy and psychiatric medication to assist the individuals through the problem. That would certainly provide for plenty of jobs for psychologists and psychiatrists.

The difficulties with these proposals is that there is no money for such a grand project and no will to actually implement it. It is unlikely that parents would be thrilled with the idea that their child might be screened for "mental illness" and there is serious concern that children would be "labeled" with a tag of "mental illness"; even if we invented a tamer term for their problem. We have enough problems with name calling and bullying that lead to school shootings and suicide among students that we already have.

Alternatives to the problems of cost and labeling have been covered in *Forces of Life*, by Shepard, such as educating all students to understand the problems of living, much as the earlier discussion of the depression of Abe Lincoln, Rick Springfield, Mark Twain, Oprah Winfrey and many more. Simply educating students to understand that they are not alone in feeling anxiety and depression, that these are universal problems, helps free them from the fear that there is something wrong with them. Letting them know that others have been through the same feelings, suffered and survived, and go on to succeed in life, is a powerful medicine of hope.

Educating students to understand how peer group pressure and concepts such as a "scale of 1-10) create problems because we often compare ourselves to others, to our own detriment. Or we assume that the concepts of beauty and success presented to us by the schools and our peers (as in the chapter on Perception and Beauty (chapter 9) are relative to the culture we grow up in.

16. ECLECTIC PSYCHOLOGY

Most psychotherapists do not limit themselves to one school of therapy or another. Most are Eclectic. This approach simply involves the use of any form of treatment that seems to work best for a given client. Most therapists do not feel it is necessary to use only one technique but will instead accept whatever seems to work best from any of the other approaches.

But there is another area of psychology, poorly defined, in which the problems are beyond the individual's ability to cope. When the problems begin to disrupt the life of the individual or the lives of those around him, the problems may cease being those of the individual and become problems of society. Such problems may involve psychosis, severe personality disorder, or antisocial behavior; -the subjects of our next chapter.

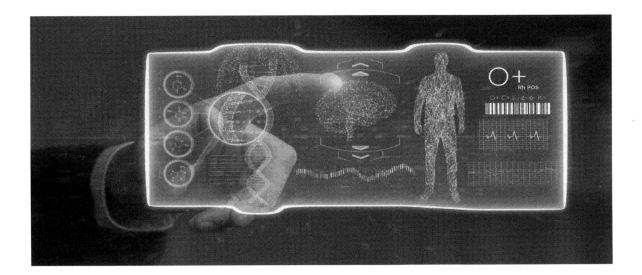

23 PSYCHOSIS AND SOCIETY

Psychoses: Schizophrenia (Paranoia, Catatonia, Disorganized); Manic-Depressive Reactions; Autism; Problems in Diagnosis • Neuroses: Obsessions, Compulsions, Conversion hysteria, Antisocial Behavior: Crime and Delinquency, Drugs and Society

We call each other crazy and are all in the same boat together... We cannot cope with life as we find it, nor can we escape it or adjust ourselves to it. So, we are given the power to create some sort of world we can deal with. The worlds created are as varied as there are minds to create them. Each one is strictly private and cannot be shared by another. It is much more real than reality. For nothing that happens to a sane mortal in the common-place world of ordinary living, can approach the startling intensity of things going on in delusion. There is a sharpness-a shrillness-a piercing intensity which thrusts itself through the consciousness and is so much more convincing than the blunt edge of reason, that even if the two are conflicting there is no choice between them. Reason is beaten, dismissed and defeated at the very outset; it cannot contend with the saber edge of delusion.

I can understand now how the girl felt who was locked in the side-room, alone with her madness; in such despair that she tried vainly to rip her skull apart. In three days, she had torn every strand of hair out by the roots, handful by handful. This left her head as bald as her palm; and still she tore at it in the starkest madness imaginable.

At least I have learned this: nothing is as terrible when it is actually happening to us as when we are dreading, fearing and anticipating it. It is the fear we build in our minds which gives a thing the power to cause us greater pain.

Lara Jefferson
These Are My Sisters

Lara Jefferson recovered from her fears. The notes from her long period of mental illness produced a remarkable document of the delusions, anxieties, and fearful anticipation of unknown horrors that can only be described by someone who is acutely aware of his or her own terror. No psychiatrist, no armchair theorist, has ever produced a more compelling record of the thoughts and emotions of such problems than those who have been there.

This chapter deals with psychological problems of the individual-but they are also social problems of the culture. These problems may be divided into three broad categories: (1) *psychosis,* a severe psychological disorder characterized by anxiety and often delusional thinking that prevents the individual from functioning normally in society; (2) *psychological problems,* a less severe problem that produces psychological distress in the individual but does not prevent adequate social or economic adjustment; and (3) *antisocial* behavior such as crime, delinquency, and drug use, which may involve no psychological distress by the individual, yet may be a problem for the society as a whole.

Are these really social problems? They are not as obvious as the often-discussed problems of war, Inflation, recession, and pollution. Yet the magnitude of these psychological problems is astounding when put into perspective. According to government and health officials there are approximately a quarter million Americans hospitalized for psychosis each year, while an additional three million have been diagnosed as psychotic.

There are approximately twenty-four thousand known suicides each year in the United States. Many authorities believe the actual number is probably double this, but many cases are disguised as an "accidental overdose of drugs" or as automobile accidents with no apparent cause. In addition, almost two hundred thousand people attempt suicide each year.

Approximately nine million Americans are alcoholics. Nineteen million have been treated for severe depression or anxiety. Twenty million more are believed to suffer from some form of neurosis. Federal Bureau of Investigation statistics indicate that nearly two million juveniles are arrested each year, and as recently as 1974 there were over 430,000 arrests in one year for simple possession of marijuana. Clearly, the social consequences of psychological problems are enormous.

At one time it was believed that people could be divided into categories of normal and abnormal. It was thought that these two conditions were as distinct as the conditions of sickness or health, of being pregnant or not pregnant. Psychological adjustment is now known to be a matter of degree: It is not an either/ or condition. One is not either sane or insane. In fact, the symptoms of psychosis also appear in normal individuals. The question is to what degree. does it interfere with their life or of others' lives?

Furthermore, an individual may be very disturbed at one time in his life, but be normal at all other times. Perhaps the only viable definition of psychosis is that individuals in this category may be unable to help themselves. They may not be able to hold a job or interact with others successfully. They may be placed in an institution or helped by family and friends for their own protection. Two major categories of such problems are *schizophrenia* and Bi-Polar.

1. SCHIZOPHRENIA

We have studied schizophrenia for over 100 years, since it was described by Emil Kaplan in the late 1800s. Today, we see at least a partial genetic cause, yet we still do not know why, even with genetically identical twins, if one has schizophrenia, the odd that their genetically identical twin will have schizophrenia is only about 40%. Despite evidence of a genetic cause, we still have only an incomplete understanding of it.

In fact, much like an "upper respiratory infection" in medicine (which could be one of a hundred varieties of the cold, the flu, pneumonia, allergies, Hantavirus, Anthrax, etc.) the symptoms of schizophrenia are common to many other disorders. We have Schizo-affective disorder, which is a mood disorder, but not schizophrenia, and Schizoid personality disorder, which is not schizophrenia, and Paranoid personality type. Even bi-polar and anti-social personality types have some symptoms that are similar. All of these and more have similar symptoms, but are not schizophrenia.

There is some doubt among many psychologists that all of the things we call schizophrenia are actually the same thing, or have different origins. The most basic symptoms of schizophrenia are (1) Disorganized thinking and (2) Delusions or hallucinations, usually auditory hallucinations such as hearing voices and (3) flattened emotions. Today, we have medications to help control those symptoms. The following is an early account of such a case, by the individual himself:

> *Only a short time before I was confined to my bed I began to hear voices, at first only close to my ear, afterwards in my head, or as if one was whispering in my ear, or in various parts of the room. These voices I obeyed or endeavoured to obey, and believed almost implicitly, especially after my mind was entirely deranged; I understood them to be the words of the Lord or of his Spirits. Afterwards, when I was very faint and ill, I saw visions of various kinds, the countenances of my friends and relations now white, now red as in flames, venerable countenances with flowing locks and silvery beards-the hand and arm of death stretched over me, and processions, beautifully delineated, like those of the ancient pagans.*

> *Those voices commanded me to do, and made me believe a number of false and terrible things. I threw myself out of bed-I tried to twist my neck, -I struggled with my keepers. When I came to Dr. Fox's I threw myself over a stile, absolutely head over heels, wrestled with the keepers to get a violent fall, asked them to strangle me, endeavoured to suffocate myself on my pillow, etc. threw myself flat on my face down steep slopes. and upon the gravel walk, called after people as my mother, brothers, and sisters, and cried out a number of sentences, usually in verse, as I heard them prompted to me-in short for a whole year I scarcely uttered a syllable, or did a single act but from inspiration; though I now know that scarcely one of the things I said, or one of the things I did was I intended to perform.*

> *. . . I suspect that many of the delusions which I laboured under, and which other insane persons labour under, consist in their mistaking a figurative or a poetic form of speech for a literal one; and this observation may be of importance to those who attend to their cure,*

> *... For this, again, is one species of lunacy, to mistake a spirit of humour enjoining an act which is an evident absurdity, for a spirit of sincerity, or, as the French say, to take it "au pied de la lettre"; as if a father were to say to his child in fun, "Now run into the puddle,"-or, "Now put your fingers into the fire," -or, "Now put yourself into a passion," meaning the very contrary, and the child were to take his words as if meant in earnest. So, I was ordered to throw myself head over heels over stiles-to throw myself · to the right, and left, or flat on the face on the floor or upon gravel walks; these forms of thought may have been meant as absurdities, for me to do the very contrary; they may also, however, have a spiritual meaning, comprised in these words-recollect yourself-remember where you are, what you are about, what you want to do, and act accordingly.*

John Perceval, Esq.

A Narrative of the Treatment Experienced by a Gentleman, During a State of Mental Derangement, 1840

John Perceval, the son of a British Prime Minister, is describing symptoms that psychologists have labeled schizophrenic. What are the voices he hears? They seem to be only the thoughts within his own mind. Or, they may be the brain triggering the thoughts in a way that is more than simple thoughts. The nature of this disorder is such that these thoughts take on a type of superstitious power-a power not unlike that which compels normal people of some cultures such as in Haiti to believe that the voices they hear in their dreams or in their self-induced trances are actually the voices of spirits. If they believe that the words in a voodoo chant have the power to control their bodies, then they will act accordingly.

How can delusion have such power over the mind of an individual? In *Hamlet,* Shakespeare has one of his characters say "... *for then is nothing either good or bad but thinking makes it so."* In the human mind, with apologies to Shakespeare, nothing is either true or false, but thinking makes it so. If the individual believes that something is true, he or she will act accordingly.

For hundreds and hundreds of years, we have believed and taught our children that spirits or demons can possess the human body. If you read through the literature of medical journals of an earlier era, you will find case after case of people that believed that they were possessed by demons. Such cases have become more rare in the past hundred years.

Today, the demons have been replaced by radio waves and electric wires: people are likely to believe that such control emanates from electric wires embedded in their brain, or by radio waves emitted by some external power, or even by people from another planet. The implication is very important: the beliefs that we learn in our culture determine the nature of the symptoms we develop. The symptoms themselves can be learned.

Thus, two important aspects of schizophrenia are the effect of belief on behavior and the learning of symptoms. But neither of these alone suggests the third and perhaps most important element-the fear, anxiety, and sensitivity of the patient.

Perceval puts it very well:

> *The lunatic doctors appear to think that patients do not feel their position: Now, I know that many lunatics are extremely sensible to ridicule; this sensitiveness is, indeed, one of the phenomena of an unsound mind; and I know that lunatics are very much pained and embarrassed by exposure under their misfortune, and I suspect that this is common to all. But they are not able to bear up against the feeling, and therefore fly for relief to boisterousness and impudent boldness, or sink from it into an apathy and passiveness, which is supposed to betray absence of feeling, when it really betrays incapability to meet such feeling. I have noticed in another volume my having been, during the progress of my recovery at Dr. Fox's, completely thrown off my balance by the fear of meeting strangers; but it was not until I reflected, that I knew the cause of my own silly conduct.*

Schizophrenia is characterized by withdrawal from people and reality into the individual's own world of thought. It may be accompanied by hallucinations or distortions in logic and reasoning. Emotional responses are often inappropriate. News of misfortune may be greeted with giggling and laughing, or the individual may turn off to life entirely and respond to everything in much the same way, speaking in a dull monotone voice. The symptoms may vary greatly from one individual to the next. Some of the most common symptoms of schizophrenia are: (1) *catatonia*, (2) *paranoia*, (3) disorganized, and (4) *simple reactions*.

Catatonia People who are catatonic may sit or stand for hours in one posture, never moving, never speaking, and rarely reacting to anything going on around them. If the doctor were to raise the arm of a catatonic patient, the patient might hold the arm suspended in the air or remain for long periods of time in whatever posture the doctor arranged. This plasticity of behavior is perhaps one of the more remarkable characteristics of catatonia. Patients will hold even very uncomfortable postures for far longer periods of time than the average person could ever endure. Immobility is not the only characteristic of catatonia. The patient may go through periods of rage or manic behavior and in some cases may be destructive, although usually not toward other people.

The unresponsiveness of the catatonic should not be taken at face value. In one case, a psychologist came onto a ward where a new catatonic patient had just been admitted. As he went into the office to sign in, he noticed the patient looking at him out of the comer of his eye. As the psychologist entered the office, he left the bottom half of a split door slightly ajar. Suddenly the patient leaped from his seat, ran over toward the psychologist, stopped at the door, and gently closed it. The patient immediately returned to his seat and continued with his immobile posture. Such an intense, compulsive need for order is common in catatonic schizophrenia.

When such patients have been returned to normal, they can often describe in vivid detail everything they observed during the period when they appeared to be unresponsive to their environment. In one case, an individual described his feelings as a fear that moving would disturb some universal harmony or bring about some calamity as a result of his behavior. It is as if a catastrophe might happen if they moved.

Paranoia

The person with paranoid experiences may have strong feelings that other people are against him or her. Why? What do we do to those who are different? We ostracize them. We make fun of them, we treat them like dirt.

It should not be too much of a surprise that they become paranoid. Even average people may feel that others are talking about them behind their back. It is a feeling learned from the sad experiences with reality in our culture. The symptoms may be a product of our society, not of the individual.

In some cases, the individuals may believe that they are being controlled by forces from another world or by wires embedded in their brain; perhaps an impression coming from stories of psychologists implanting wires in the brains of rats to study their emotions.

More coherent individuals may believe that other people around them are plotting against them and trying to do them harm. The latter feeling is not uncommon among normal people, however. The expression that "our ears are burning" has long signified that feeling that someone is talking about us behind our back. It may be a feeling that the boss does not appreciate us or that other people we know make fun of us when we are not around.

We know from past experience that such things do happen. Criticizing people behind their backs is a national pastime. Because we know that unkind remarks are not uncommon-perhaps because we too may make them-we may assume that such gossip is happening even when we have no evidence for that assumption. In paranoia, the individual attributes critical thoughts to others, and may even attribute acts and behavior to them that are physically impossible.

As with a detective who slowly builds a damning case on the basis of circumstantial evidence alone, accumulated circumstantial evidence becomes overwhelmingly in paranoia.

*Disorganized Schizo*phrenic reactions involve a distortion of emotional affect and may be accompanied by infantile behavior. Nervous giggling, for example, may intrude on conversations at inappropriate times. Disorganized schizophrenia may have delusions and hallucinations of a disorganized type. They may believe that they are dead, or that something has happened to various parts of their body. They may stop caring for themselves, even to the point of soiling themselves, and may have to be cared for by others.

Simple reactions: Undifferentiated: One example of this came as a surprise one day as I was sitting in my office. A young woman suddenly came into my office, sat down, and started talking. I had no idea who she was or what she came for. As she started talking, she sounded perfectly rational until she came to the end of her first sentence. She never came to the end of her sentence, she continued talking, often switching from one subject to another, making little sense. This is more characteristic of the simple type of *disorganized thinking* often associated with schizophrenia. This is often a good candidate for psychoactive medication.

The individual suffering from simple schizophrenia may not experience delusions or marked behavioral abnormalities. Rather, the person's behavior is characterized by apathy and withdrawal. His or her thinking may not be bizarre so much as it is limited and inadequate. Such individuals may make a marginal adjustment to life, and many of them may drift through life as tramps or hobos, sometimes as prostitutes, or as members of a "hippie" culture.

Heredity In the 1950s, researchers found that if an individual who developed symptoms of schizophrenia happened to have a genetically identical twin brother or sister, the likelihood that the twin would develop the same symptoms was high. Research in the 1960s and 1970s failed to show such high results. In an extensive European study in 1966, E. Kringlen found 45 percent rates for identical twins and 15 percent for nonidentical pairs. Psychiatrist E. Fuller Torey found in a study of identical twins, if one twin had schizophrenia, then there was a 50% chance the other identical twin would have schizophrenia. Others have found 60%.

Furthermore, Donald Hebb has noted that similar figures can be found for the development of tuberculosis, which is emphatically *not* a genetic disorder: among identical twins (87 percent) and among nonidentical twin brothers and sisters (26 percent). One possible explanation may be that identical twins spend more time together than fraternal twins, hence, exposed to the same environment, and stress.

Hereditary studies of schizophrenia are inconclusive. However, many psychologists believe that some people may be genetically predisposed to be sensitive to stress or to other factors that may cause schizophrenia. For example, lung cancer is not caused by genetics, yet of any hundred people who smoke packs of cigarettes each day, some will develop lung cancer quickly and some will not. Irritation of the lungs such as that caused by cigarette smoke, an environmental factor, is believed to cause lung cancer, but some people may be genetically more sensitive to this factor than others. The same type ·of genetic factor might predispose one person to develop schizophrenia under environmental conditions where another would not.

Biochemical factors For decades, scientists have been examining schizophrenic patients to attempt to find a biochemical difference between schizophrenics and "normals." A major breakthrough seemed about to occur when a physician announced that a chemical stimulant, the drug caffeine, was found to be present in the urine of schizophrenic patients in five to twenty times the amount that it is in the urine of "normal" individuals.

Do high concentrations of stimulants cause schizophrenia? Hopes were quickly demolished when it was discovered that just the opposite was true; schizophrenia causes caffeine. That is, the patients who were placed on psychiatric wards had so little to do during the day that they sat around drinking abnormally large amounts of coffee and cokes, which contain caffeine, that was naturally released into their urine.

In over fifty years of research such disappointment has been the rule rather than the exception. Yet almost every year, at least one newspaper article is likely to appear that suggests that a biochemical cause of mental disorder has been found. LSD, stimulants, and vitamins have at one time or another been suggested as a cause of mental disorder. At present, no such statement can be made. Eventually, biochemical factors may be found to be important in the problems of mental disorder, but many years of research must follow before a firm statement could be made. Furthermore, if a chemical is found that is present only in schizophrenics, the next question would have to be, "What causes the chemical to be present?"

Social theories emphasize the role of the family or faulty interpersonal relations in the development of mental disorders. The patients themselves often cite problems in interpersonal relationships as a cause of their difficulty. Studies of the families of schizophrenic patients have sometimes found parents who are too restrictive, while other studies find parents who are too permissive. Studies have found some parents to be aloof while others are overly protective. But did the parent's attitude toward the child cause the mental problem? Or did the fact of the child's mental problem cause the parents to react differently to the child than they otherwise would have? As with the biological theories, it is difficult to separate cause from effect.

Such studies can be of value only if they can follow the development of both normal and disturbed children from before the child develops the symptoms and through the time the mental problems arise. Such studies are easier to do with other animals than with human children, Harlow, Masserman, Liddell, and others suggest that bizarre behavior, including self-destructive behavior, stereotyped movements, and generalized fear of the environment, can be produced by the environment of the animal.

Studies of the environment of humans who are schizophrenic do not show the marked degree of social isolation that was imposed on Harlow's monkeys. Also, not all children who are exposed to stressful or fearful environments develop severe psychological problems. These facts present some problems for an environmental approach, it may be that the most important factor in Harlow's studies was not the isolation of the animals per se but the fear that the monkeys experienced when they were isolated. If true, the social isolation would not be necessary to produce such a reaction. At present, not enough evidence has been collected to prove that fearful experiences are a "cause" of schizophrenia. But, judging from the patients' own comments on the fears that they feel, such fear must play a crucial role.

Other researchers suggest that the bizarre behavior of schizophrenia is learned by the patient through environmental conditioning. Self-destructive children are often found to tear at their skin or bang their heads on the floor because parents or other people in the environment will take notice and will sympathize with them. Some studies have shown, ironically, that such behavior can be eliminated by ignoring the destructive behavior and rewarding the child with attention for more productive behavior. It may be possible to generalize from such findings to other cases, but, at present, no one has demonstrated that such an explanation can apply to all forms of bizarre behavior.

It may be that both biological and psychological factors combine to produce schizophrenia, but we do not yet have a means of separating heredity and environment that would allow us to determine the contribution of each separately.

We have been discussing psychological problems that relate to severe psychological disorders. Another important area of psychological problems relates to severe feelings of anxiety of the individual. Such personal problems are sometimes called *neuroses.* A neurosis may be characterized by feelings of anxiety, obsessional thoughts, compulsive acts, or physical complaints with no apparent cause.

2. AUTISM SPECTRUM DISORDER

Infantile autism represents a form of mental disorder that produces a striking effect on a child. Behavior of the child may be normal during the first year or so. Beginning by the age of two, the disorder may be characterized by a withdrawal of the infant from social contact. Living in its own inner world, the child fails to develop normal social or intellectual ability.

Autism has four main characteristics. The first is withdrawal from social interaction. The child may react to people with fear, or may treat them merely as objects or obstacles to be avoided in the environment, or simply as food-dispensing machines, much as one might regard a coke machine. The withdrawal is so extreme that the child may fail even to make eye contact, glancing at a person as we might glance at a table in the room.

Second, speech development is halted. The child may be incapable of speech if severe autism develops by the age of two. In less severe cases, the child may speak only in a dull, drawn-out monotone with an almost mechanical quality. This monotone is similar to that found in some cases of schizophrenia and is somewhat reminiscent of a case of severe stage fright in a normal child.

Third, self-stimulatory behavior is common. Such children may rock back and forth repeatedly, or rapidly fan their hands in front of them over and over again. This behavior is also found in otherwise normal children who are blind or deaf-children who have been deprived of normal sensory input. In the autistic child, such behavior becomes more common and extreme.

Finally, self-destructive behavior is sometimes found as well. This may include face slapping, biting of the child's own hand or arm, and in some cases the repeated banging of his head against a floor or wall. Such behavior may sometimes result from being placed in a fear-producing situation, or it may be a means of getting attention and comfort from a parent or attendant.

The following case study is from the records of an autistic child studied by the author. The child's parents had maintained extensive records, including pictures and films, of his development up to the time of his first admission as a patient. The entire history of this subject, from his educated and concerned parents, to the age of the onset and symptoms of the disorder, are remarkably similar to other early onset cases of autism.

Jimmie's parents report that his birth was at term and was normal except for some apparent difficulty in breathing. Reportedly he was administered oxygen for 30 minutes after birth. From this time on, however, his development appeared normal. He has always been a handsome and well-formed child. Jimmie reportedly progressed at a faster than normal rate of development and his parents seem to have believed that he was precocious, learning to stand and walk before the average child his age was expected to do so. By one and one-half years of age he was speaking six to eight words and had learned to hum tunes. He reportedly could work a new thirty-piece jigsaw puzzle in five minutes.

By two years of age things reportedly began to change dramatically.

Whether or not it occurred as suddenly as the parent's recall, is difficult to determine. Parents may miss such unusual behavior until it becomes extreme. But by two, Jimmie had stopped speaking even the few words he had earlier known. He became hyperactive. He displayed jealous fits over his younger brother. He would bite himself on the hand when stressed and sit rocking by himself for hours. His parents took him to specialist after specialist, looking for an answer to his problems. Two diagnosed him as emotionally disturbed. One EEG report indicated brain damage; a second did not. Depressant drugs had no effect on his hyperactivity. Amphetamines reportedly had a temporarily beneficial effect.

Ten years passed with the specialists unable to help. Today, Jimmie still displays the characteristic symptoms of autism. The back of his head has been worn bald as a result of his habit of self-stimulating by lying on his back and rolling his head from side to side, over and over. There is a large callus on the thumb-joint area of his right hand where he has repeatedly bitten himself. He bites himself and screams in response to any new or stressful situation, as when we drove him to the medical center for an EEG.

There is no evidence that he uses this self-destructive behavior as an attention getting device at present. He displays no aversion to physical contact or petting by the head nurse, but he seems to form no lasting social attachment even after over a year of repeated attempts by the nurse. But if anyone were to hold out the promise of candy to him, he would do anything to obtain it. He responds to candy the way most children respond to attention and affection.

Jimmie's parents have repeatedly said that they believe that he understands far more than he lets on. They feel that he is just being negative much of the time. In fact, he would occasionally display behavior that suggested that he might have some hidden ability, as when he would "decide" to obey a command even after repeatedly having refused to pay attention, or when he would work a jigsaw puzzle faster than most adults. These not uncommon traits in autistic children brings up the question of whether he may actually understand what is asked of him but is prevented from acting by his disorder, as is sometimes true of catatonic schizophrenics. How much of an inner world of thought might lie beneath his behavior?

To test his ability required his undivided attention, something he rarely gave to people. Bribery was necessary. Gumdrops proved to be an attention getter that was far beyond anything else used to attempt to gain his attention. To see if he really knew what people were saying I began by getting him to hand me an object, a pencil, book, or glass. He caught on quickly, learning that a gumdrop awaited when he handed me the object. But when he was asked for a specific object by name he failed. In spite of the fact that he clearly wanted to do anything for the reward, when asked for a book he ended up by handing me anything and everything until he finally got it right. After extensive testing his ability to understand words turned out to be at the level of an eighteen-month-old child.

TESTING ON AN IQ TEST

Then came testing for his puzzle-fitting ability. Interestingly enough, he did surprisingly well on the puzzles on the WAIS adult I.Q. test but failed miserably at the puzzles on the WISC test for children. This seeming paradox is a key to his level of ability, however. Some of the adult puzzles can be worked by anyone who can fit together the pieces. The children's puzzles, in contrast, can only be worked if the subject recognized that they are a picture of an object, a car or animal, etc.

His puzzle-working ability turned out to be only one of putting together the pieces that fit. He has little or no understanding of the pictures in a puzzle. When we reached a point where the puzzles became too difficult to work, he immediately lost interest and turned away in frustration.

Not all autistic children show the same lack of verbal ability as Jimmie. Some can show remarkable progress in training. All can benefit to some extent from techniques of behavior modification. It is even possible, though it is not well demonstrated, that if such children are discovered early enough, before the age of two perhaps, that a diet of love and affection can prevent or reverse some of the more serious emotional symptoms of the disorder, such as self-destructive behavior and the underlying emotional disturbance.

What causes such a severe emotional and intellectual problem? There is no general agreement among psychologists as to its source. Some psychologists have noted the similarity between the autistic behavior (rocking, self-biting, fearfulness) found in Harlow's monkeys that were deprived of contact comfort. Yet the studies of the home life of such children do not show such extreme neglect. It may be, however, that it is not the lack of contact comfort or maternal care that causes these symptoms. Anything that produces prolonged fear or anxiety may have the same effect. This could be a problem with the biology of his brain where contact comfort fails to reduce fear as it normally would.

Yet more is involved than this. Harlow and Suomi found that infant monkeys who were totally isolated and emotionally devastated were, nonetheless, as able· to learn to work the same complex tasks to obtain food as normal monkeys could. The isolated monkeys displayed no loss of intellectual ability as a result of their deprivation. The clear majority of autistic children do display marked impairment of their verbal abilities.

Medical evidence of brain damage, as might result from Jimmie's failure to breathe normally at birth, is found in many such cases. An equally large number display no evidence of brain damage, but our neurological methods for detecting brain damage are crude, and only gross damage can be detected by most tests. Furthermore, a small but significant number of cases suggest a genetic defect as indicated by a recurring syndrome involving an abnormal head and jaw shape including spaced front teeth, and a buck-toothed appearance.

All of this may mean that there are multiple causes involved in this disorder.

In other forms of Autism Spectrum Disorder, you do not find the lack of intellectual ability you may find in early onset autism. In some cases, formerly known as Asperger's Syndrome, you may find good intellectual development, but a failure of the individual to be able to seek or understand interpersonal relationships. One possible example of this is that of Sheldon from the TV series *The Big Bang Theory*. The actor who plays Sheldon does a credible job of illustrating some of the characteristics, including a failure to understand sarcasm, a lack of social skills, and an almost compulsive interest in one subject to the exclusion of social interests. In most cases, anxiety is not uncommon.

At present, psychologists do not agree on any specific cause of autism, but few areas of emotional disturbance have attracted as much study and interest. The wealth of data coming out of behavior modification and clinical studies may eventually produce a more satisfying answer.

Problems in Diagnosis It is often said by clinical psychologists that when they finally leave the classroom and begin practicing with actual patients, they spend the first several months unsuccessfully trying to fit the patients into the textbook descriptions of the disorders. It is rare that any case ends up being as cut and dried as the textbook description makes it seem.

3. Bi-Polar Disorder

Besides the schizophrenic pattern of psychosis, there is a category first identified by the physician Emil Kraepelin *in* 1899, which he called the *manic-depressive psychosis, now called the Bi-Polar disorder.* Patients may be predominately manic for long periods of time. In this condition, they may display excessive elation, irritability, extreme talkativeness, flights of fantasy, and, sometimes, delusions of grandeur (manic phase) or guilt (depressive phase) not unlike that found *in* paranoia.

They may have unlimited enthusiasm and energy and involve themselves in all manner of things. At the same time, they are easily distracted and have a great deal of difficulty following through on one train of thought. They may suddenly switch to a depressive reaction and may display a profound sense of sadness, avoiding people and sometimes going into a stooped position as if the weight of the world were on their shoulders. The patients may suffer strong feelings of guilt. They may believe that they have committed unpardonable sins.

Hallucinations occur in extreme cases. An individual may believe that he has spoken to God or the devil. In the manic phase, he may 'hear voices" saying he has been chosen for a glorious purpose, while in the depressive phase, the "voices" may accuse him of crimes or misbehavior. Manic-depressive reactions are more likely to be characterized by extreme mood swings, often very sudden, between feelings of extreme elation and talkativeness to moods of great depression and silence. The following case study is of a manic-depressive patient examined by the author. This patient refuses to walk, an unusual reaction in such cases, and has to be moved about in a wheelchair.

James is fifty years old. He looks like a distinguished businessman with handsome facial and physical features. Muscle tone in his legs appears good, judging from his frequent leg movements while in the wheelchair. However, he refuses to walk. James displays marked mood swings similar to those found in manic-depressive reactions. His behavior may be described as usually manic, but he is not physically active during these periods. Instead, he sits in his wheelchair and, using gestures and phrases full of profanity, he free-associates about God, sex, and his past. Following is a typical exchange:

Examiner "Why do you not try to walk?"

James "God doesn't give me the right." *or* at another time: "I am not able to walk, because I'm crippled; I would fall."

During his frequent periods of free-association, James came up with numerous spontaneous comments such as: "You can't depend on Jesus Christ, because God is older than he." And, "The doctors gave me some little black poison pills."

In a display of adolescent braggadocio, he told the examiner which nurses were "good in bed" and why. This was accompanied with frequent exclamations of "I know! *I* know!" P.S. He did not know. Perhaps of interest he seemed to have picked up aspects of his personality from his family and his brothers.

Some days following testing, the examiner had an opportunity to meet some of James' relatives. According to his mother, he had "seizures" up to the age of two years when he "stopped" and did not have any more until the age of fourteen. When asked to describe one of the later seizures, it was clear that she was describing a manic episode rather than a seizure. Another relative stated that one could be talking to James and he would suddenly get a look on his face "like he was mad." He would then start fighting and cursing and throwing things.

When first brought in to see his relatives, James was sullen and withdrawn. He refused to speak out loud for over one hour. Toward the end of the hour, he began to speak in a hoarse whisper. A male relative suddenly remembered that James used to frequent a place called the "Pub" and spent many hours talking to the bargirls there. At the mention of "Pub," James began smiling and saying in a loud voice "*I* know! *I* know!" He then became quite talkative and apparently continued this way for some time, for he was still sitting, smiling, and talking happily to himself several hours after his relatives had left. The latter behavior is characteristic of James' manic-depressive reaction.

His mother reports that the doctor they consulted when he began having his "seizures" told them that what James needed was to get married. So, by hook or crook, James was married to "a very pretty little thing." The marriage lasted approximately one year, during which he apparently became quite depressed and "neglected his wife," who then seems to have packed her bags and left. James speaks often of her leaving, but rarely of her as a person. He frequently stated, "But I don't hold it against her, I love everybody," as though he were obeying a commandment of God,

According to his relatives, James was once cheated out of a small inheritance by a relative. This relative apparently took James home for a stay and convinced him to sign away his interest in the inheritance. Whatever the truth may be, James speaks *with* unmistakable dislike whenever this relative's name is mentioned.

Some of James' comments are paranoid in nature. However, the overall picture of his problem is more closely associated with manic-depressive behavior. Paranoid-like ideation is common in many forms of psychosis. However, James' comments lack the well-organized, coherent structure of the delusions of the "true" paranoid. There is nothing in the content of his statements that would imply that he believes he is being persecuted. The statements were made while he was smiling, even laughing, and there is no evidence of a fear reaction.

Some statements were spontaneous and some were in response to questions. Most, however, involved a marked degree of irrelevant free-association. James' emotional reactions, while only grossly appropriate, were not flat as is often found in schizophrenia. While in the "manic" phase, he is not aggressive, but could be described as happily "possessed." He greatly enjoys talking about God, sex, and his hometown. His manic state is accompanied by numerous gestures; pointing up when he speaks of God, and various appropriate gestures when he speaks of sex. During a depressive phase, he may not speak at all or may speak in a barely audible whisper.

DIAGNOSES ARE OFTEN DIFFICULT WHEN SYMPTOMS OVERLAP

The difficulty of making a diagnosis, as well as the difficulty of seeing into a patient's mind, is apparent in the following example of Clifford Beers (1908), a Yale University graduate who developed a serious psychological disorder that resulted in his being institutionalized. Beers recovered and had sufficient insight into his condition to write the following critical account of his two years of delusion. The story picks up at the point where Beers has just written a letter to his brother asking him to come for a visit, and to bring the letter as a "passport" to identify himself:

The thought that I might soon get in touch with my old world did not excite me. I had not much faith anyway that I was to re-establish former relations with it, and what little faith I had was all but destroyed on the morning of August 30th, 1902, when a short message, written on a slip of paper, reached me by the hand of an attendant. It informed me that my conservator would call that afternoon. I thought it a lie, I felt that any brother of mine would have taken the pains to send a letter in reply to the first I had written him in over two years. The thought that there had not been time for him to do so and that this message must have arrived by telephone did not then occur to me. What I believed was that my own letter had been confiscated. I asked one of the doctors to swear on his honor that it really was my own brother who was coming to see me, This he did. But abnormal suspicion robbed all men in my sight of whatever honor they may have had, and I was not fully reassured. In the afternoon, as usual, the patients were taken out of doors, I among them. I wandered about the lawn and cast frequent and expectant glances toward the gate, through which I believed my anticipated visitor would soon pass. In less than an hour he appeared. I first caught sight of him about three hundred feet away, and impelled more by curiosity than hope, I advanced to meet him. "I wonder what the lie will be this time," was the gist of my thoughts.

The person approaching me was indeed the counterpart of my brother as I remembered him. Yet he was no more my brother than he had been at any time during the preceding two years. He was still a detective. Such he was when I shook his hand. As soon as that ceremony was over, he drew forth a leather pocketbook. I instantly recognized it as one I myself had carried for several years prior to the time I was taken ill in 1900. It was from this that he took my recent letter.

"Here's my passport," he said.

"It's a good thing you brought it," I replied, as I glanced at it and again shook his hand-this time the hand of my own brother.

"Don't you want to read it?" he asked, "There is no need of that. I am convinced,"

After my long journey of exploration in the jungle of a tangled imagination, a journey which finally ended in my finding the person for whom I had long searched, my behavior differed very little from that of a great explorer who, full of doubt after a long and perilous trip through real jungles, found the man he sought and, grasping his hand, greeted him with the simple and historic words, "Dr. Livingstone, I presume?" The very instant I caught sight of my letter in the hands of my brother, all was changed. The thousands of false impressions recorded during the seven hundred and ninety-eight days of my depression seemed at once to correct themselves, Untruth became Truth, A large part of what was once my old world was again mine. To me, at least, my mind seemed to have found itself, for the gigantic web of false beliefs in which it had been all but hopelessly enmeshed I now immediately recognized as a snare of delusions.

That the Gordian knot of mental torture should be cut and swept away by the mere glance of a willing eye is like a miracle. Not a few patients, however, suffering from certain forms of mental disorder, regain a high degree of insight into their mental condition in what might be termed a flash of divine enlightenment.

Though insight regained seemingly in an instant is a most encouraging symptom, power to reason normally on all subjects cannot, of course, be so promptly recovered. My new power to reason correctly on some subjects simply marked the transition from depression, one phase of my disorder, to elation, another phase of it. Medically speaking, I was as mentally disordered as before-yet I was happy

. . . Yet had I failed to convince myself on August 30th, when my brother came to see me, that he was no spy, I am almost sure that I should have compassed my own destruction within the following ten days; for the next month, I believed, was the fatal one of opening courts. You will recall that it was death by drowning that impended. I liken my salvation itself to a prolonged process of drowning. Thousands of minutes of the seven hundred and ninety-eight days-and there were over one million of them, during which I had been borne down by intolerably burdensome delusions -were, I imagine, much like the last minutes of consciousness experienced by persons who drown. Many who have narrowly escaped that fate can testify to the vividness with which good and bad impressions of their entire life rush through their confused minds, and hold them in a grip of terror until a kind unconsciousness envelops them. Such had been many of my moments. But the only unconsciousness which had deadened my sensibilities during these two despondent years was that of sleep itself. Though I slept fairly well most of the time, mine was seldom a dreamless sleep. Many of my dreams were, if anything, harder to bear than my delusions of the day, for what little reason I had was absolutely suspended in sleep. Almost every night my brain was at battledore and shuttlecock with weird thoughts. And if not all my dreams were terrifying, this fact seemed to be only because a perverted and perverse Reason, in order that its possessor might not lose the capacity for suffering, knew how to keep Hope alive with visions which supplied the contrast necessary for keen appreciation.

No man can be born again, but I believe I came as near it as ever a man did. To leave behind what was in reality a hell, and immediately have this good green earth revealed in more glory than most men ever see it, was one of the compensating privileges which make me fell that my suffering was worthwhile.

I have already described the peculiar sensation which assailed me when, in June, 1900, I lost my reason. At that time my brain felt as though pricked by a million needles at white heat. On this August 30th, 1902, shortly after largely regaining my reason, I had another most distinct sensation in the brain. It started under my brow and gradually spread until the entire surface was affected. The throes of a dying Reason had been torture. The sensations felt as my dead Reason was reborn were delightful. It seemed as though the refreshing breath of some kind Goddess of Wisdom were being gently blown against the surface of my brain. It was a sensation not unlike that produced by a menthol pencil rubbed ever so gently over a fevered brow. So delicate, so crisp and exhilarating was it that words fail me in my attempt to describe it. Few, if any, experiences can be more delightful. If the exaltation produced by some drugs is anything like it, I can easily understand how and why certain pernicious habits enslave those who contract them. For me, however, this experience was liberation, not enslavement.

Clifford Beers *A Mind That Found Itself*

This account by Beers has elements of several symptoms already discussed. There is a paranoid mistrust of everyone around him. He believes the doctor has lied to him, that his letter was confiscated. The thought process here is a characteristic type of delusional thinking found in schizophrenia. Beers believes his brother is actually a spy in disguise until the sight of his own letter (" passport") suddenly produces a marked change in this delusion. The suddenness of this change from depression and suspicion to one of elation and mania is characteristic of the sudden mood swings of a manic-depressive reaction. And finally, until the meeting with his brother he had remained mute for two years. He had refused

to speak to anyone because of his belief that everyone was lying to him and conspiring against him. This silence is most commonly found in catatonic schizophrenia.

What kind of diagnosis can be given in this case? None really. The diagnosis is unimportant. What is important is recognizing the way in which Beers' beliefs influenced his behavior. Thinking that he was unable to believe in anyone, he reacted with suspicion and hostility and silence. Such a sudden recovery of reason as Beers describes is rare. However, sometimes a new way of looking at things, an environment with less anxiety, or a change of one's view of the future may produce a sudden change in one's view of reality.

Approximately 80 percent of all the individuals admitted to mental hospitals are released within one year. Many of them recover spontaneously without help. Nonetheless, a small percentage must spend their entire lives as wards of the state. Contrary to the image portrayed by certain movies and television shows, individuals suffering from a psychosis are more dangerous to themselves than to others. Some are categorized as "criminally insane," but they are not representative of the average person who suffers from mental disturbance. Most mentally disturbed individuals are, in fact, quite harmless.

In the field of psychology today there is no general agreement as to the cause of psychotic behavior. Two factors do appear to be common to most forms of psychosis, however. First, the symptoms appear to be determined by the past experiences of the Individual. The symptoms represent a greatly intensified form of thoughts or behavior that are probably found in most of us. Secondly, the *anxiety*, which may result from guilt feelings, feelings of personal inadequacy, or simply a fear of others, appears to be so intense that the patient is unable to deal with it in a normal way. The result is a breakdown of the individual's ability to relate to reality and to conduct himself in a way that would allow him to function in society.

Schizophrenia is characterized by strong feelings of anxiety, disorganized thinking, and sometimes by bizarre behavior and hallucinations. The cause(s) of these symptoms is still being debated. The most productive theories of schizophrenia are the *biological* and *social, psychological* theories.

4. PERSONALITY DISORDERS

OBSESSIVE *COMPULSIVE DISORDER (OCD)*

One disturbance is the *obsessive-compulsive reaction.* An *obsession* is the thought one cannot get out of one's mind, a tune one hums over and over. Hitler, for one example, developed an obsessive hatred of the Jews. People may also have thoughts of sex or aggression that they cannot get out of their minds. Such thoughts may continue over and over, even though they produce great anxiety and unpleasantness.

A *compulsion.* is an obsession with repeating a certain behavior. This reaction may appear in compulsive acts such as repeated handwashing or behavior such as apologizing or confessing when one has nothing to apologize or confess for. Each major publicized murder case, such as the Boston Strangler or the skid row slasher, produces a great many individuals who feel a compulsion to confess to a crime, perhaps to be absolved of guilt for some imaginary crime they have committed.

On a lesser scale, individuals may confess or feel guilt over comparatively minor and even imaginary misdeeds. At the opposite extreme, compulsive reactions may induce people to go out of their way to prove they are right about an issue, continually insisting that others recognize their viewpoint. Obsessive-compulsive reactions may appear in normal people as a matter of course, though they may have little effect on their lives. That song or tune that we cannot get out of our mind is perhaps not disturbing, but it is a minor version of what the obsessive-compulsive reaction is,

The childhood game of avoiding stepping on cracks in the sidewalk may be a mild compulsion. In the days of Tom Sawyer, boys would frequently take a stick and run it along a picket fence, hitting each picket with a stick. If they missed a picket they would sometimes stop and go back to it. Picket fences are rare in today's society, but you can occasionally find the same behavior in schools where students may go by the lockers, touching each locker and, on missing one, going back to it before continuing. Such behavior only becomes an *obsessive-compulsive* symptom, however, if it gets to the point where it interferes with the individual's ordinary daily activity or if it becomes a problem.

Hysteric reactions may be a very debilitating form of neurosis. When Sigmund Freud began his studies of the mind with Joseph Breuer, the type of patient they encountered most often was suffering with what Freud came to call *conversion hysteria.* The hysteric may suddenly be struck blind or deaf, or become paralyzed in a leg or arm. In many cases, the limbs may become numb enough that a prick with a pin evokes no reaction.

Yet all this, the sensory defects, the paralysis, and the numbness, occur with no physical problem whatever. The French neurologist Jean Charcot found that he could reproduce symptoms of hysteria, including the numbness to pain, in patients under hypnosis. But Charcot failed to recognize this as a psychological problem. He believed that such people were suffering from a "weak" or degenerated brain. It remained for Sigmund Freud to recognize that the symptoms of hysteria were psychological in nature, a product of the mind of the individual.

Conversion hysteria was a fairly common phenomenon up through the early 1900s, but since the time of Freud it has declined markedly in frequency. If you want to find cases of conversion hysteria today it is necessary to go to the backwoods of Appalachia or to the less educated areas of the country.

One thing that appears to have contributed to the decrease in hysterical symptoms is the increasing sophistication of the average citizen. Most people are aware today that one cannot simply be "struck blind" or "struck deaf" for no reason. There must be some physical cause for illness. In an era when we believed that such things could happen, perhaps as punishment by God, they occurred more frequently. Among people who do not believe in such things, however, these symptoms do not occur.

People who are hysteric tend to be highly suggestible. Their personalities may be outgoing and friendly, even seductive, but they find it difficult to cultivate deep emotional relations with others. They tend to become extremely enthusiastic and elated over even minor issues. At the same time, they appear to feel a great deal of inadequacy and guilt. It may be that there has been no decrease in the number of people who are hysteric since the time of Freud but only that the symptoms have changed.

Freud and Breuer managed to bring patients out of their paralysis or sensory defect, first by hypnotizing them and telling them they would no longer experience this problem, and later by allowing them to talk their problems out in therapy. Faith-healers have experienced some success in alleviating these symptoms in their followers by using faith as a similar form of the power of suggestion.

Faith-healing, like hypnosis, has its limitations. Psychological cures only work for psychological causes. A number of years ago, a nurse at a state institution told the author of a difficult problem that she had encountered. She was in charge of a dorm of patients, many of whom were children suffering from cerebral palsy, a physical condition that left them unable to coordinate muscle movements, and sometimes unable to speak because they could not control the muscles of their tongue. These children had been watching a television show the night before and, on the show, they had seen a faith-healer who had used the "power of the Lord" to help members of his audience who were paralyzed.

After laying his hands on them and going through a series of rituals, the crippled suddenly began to walk. The children had seen it happen themselves, on television, and now they wanted to be cured. They wanted her to write a letter to the faith-healer asking him to come to the hospital to cure them.

This was perhaps the most difficult problem that could be imagined. What do you tell the children? Would the faith-healer even pay any attention to the letter? If he came, could he help? And what would he tell them if he were unsuccessful? Would he tell them that they did not have enough faith?

Unfortunately, we know the answers to these questions. It was a very difficult thing for the nurse to explain to the children that, as with other television shows, you simply cannot believe all that you see. All the children received for the letter the nurse wrote to the faith healer, was a series of replies asking for money.

NARCISSISTIC PERSONALITY DISORDER

NARCISSISTIC PERSONALITY DISORDER

CAUSES

Environment

Genetics

Neurobiology

PREVENTION

Child Therapy

Family Therapy

Attend Parenting Classes

NARCISSISTIC PERSONALITY DISORDER SYMPTOMS

Expectations of Superior Treatment from Other People

Fixation on Fantasies of Power, Success, Attractiveness

Self-perception of Being Unique, Superior

Need for Continual Admiration from Others

Sense of Entitlement to Special Treatment and to Obedience from Others

Exploitation of Others to Achieve Personal Gain

Unwillingness to Empathize with the Feelings, Wishes, and Needs of Other People

Intense Envy of Others, and the Belief that Others are Equally Envious of Them

Constantly Demeans, Bullies and Belittles Others

5. ANTISOCIAL BEHAVIOR:
Crime and Delinquency

In America today, there are approximately twenty million young people between the ages of fifteen and nineteen. According to statistics from the Federal Bureau of Investigation (FBI), just under two million young people in this age group are arrested each year.

Judges are sometimes criticized for turning loose criminals immediately after they are caught. Yet our prisons are crowded to overflowing. The judges have little choice. The numbers arrested each year are staggering. According to FBI statistics, in 1974, there were 445,600 arrests. Ninety-three percent of these arrests were for simple possession, not sale *(U.S. News and World Report,* Dec. 2, 1974).

Even today, with many states making marijuana legal, the statistics have not changed much. 663,000 were arrested in 2018, although the arrests have started going down recently.

https://www.pewresearch.org/fact-tank/2020/01/22/four-in-ten-u-s-drug-arrests-in-2018-were-for-marijuana-offenses-mostly-possession.

Police agency claims that the police primarily use drug laws to go after "pushers", are not substantiated by the evidence. Officers are often eager to make an arrest, to get another notch on their sleeve; it aids them in getting a raise, or in getting a promotion. If you have ever seen a single car stopped with half a dozen police cars around it, often from different agencies, you may have witnessed a feeding frenzy of officers eager to get their name on an arrest, for their own benefit.

Newspaper accounts of the rising crime rate have terrified many Americans. Politicians have used this fear to claim they would put more people in jail, build more jails, since the 1970s.

No one has any simple solution to the problem. However, a few facts can be pointed out. One of the great problems with the judicial system has been that of repeat offenders. Unfortunately, it is not true that once a person has served time, he is free to make a fresh start. Someone with a felony conviction on his record can never be a teacher or a lawyer, even a member of the plumbers' union. Is it surprising that as many as 75 percent of former convicts return to a life of crime within five years?

Another problem in the judicial system is the distinction between so-called "victim" and "victimless" crimes. Victim crimes involve an antisocial act against another person, such as murder, rape, and robbery. The victimless crimes are those against one's self, such as suicide and drug use. For offenses in the first category, few people would deny that imprisonment is often necessary to protect society. The second category is not so easily dismissed. Does society have the right to forcibly confine someone for something he does to himself? In our society, the answer has been yes.

Drugs such as heroin have been banned from the market, and anyone possessing even a small quantity of this substance may be subject to a severe prison sentence. Few doctors would disagree that heroin is an extremely dangerous drug. The dangers come from three major sources: (1) the danger of a fatal overdose due to the ease with which an excessive amount of the drug may be injected; (2) diseases, such as hepatitis, which tend to be transmitted easily by needles that have not been thoroughly sterilized, and (3) a rapidly acquired physical and psychological dependence on the drug, which may develop into a lifelong addiction.

The body builds a tolerance to heroin with continued usage. Because the body adapts to it, increasingly greater amounts of the drug are required to produce the desired psychological effect. If an individual has been taking daily injections for as long as three weeks, the body will also develop a physical dependence on the drug. Tolerance to the drug, which results from the body's attempt to maintain an internal balance, brings about a new balance within the body. If the drug is now suddenly withdrawn, the body must rapidly adjust to this change. The result is what is known as "withdrawal symptoms." Withdrawal symptoms may include abdominal cramps, diarrhea, and muscle spasms lasting for one to two weeks.

Dr. David Ausubel notes that the withdrawal symptoms bear little resemblance to the exaggerated version seen in movies and on television. Ausubel describes the symptoms as being about the same as a case of the flu. Ausubel notes that physical dependence on the drug cannot account for the *psychological* dependence that occurs. Long after addicts have undergone the treatment they **still** return to the drug. Some studies found as many as 90 percent of former addicts followed over a five-year period have done so. This suggests a degree of psychological dependence quite independent of the physical effects.

Distinguish between:
1. Physical Dependence
2. Psychological Dependence

Ausubel also notes that addiction is not an "all or none" state of being but varies greatly from one individual to the next. The survey showing a 90 percent return to the use of drugs by former addicts was done on a group of down-and-out, impoverished addicts. Studies of professional individuals who have become addicted shows strikingly different results. Among professional groups, the highest incidence of drug addiction occurs among physicians, who have ready access to the drugs. Yet Thorwald Brown indicates a cure rate of 92 percent among addicted doctors in California. Brown also cites an 8 percent suicide rate for the same group.

Researchers tend to agree that major reasons for the psychological dependence on drugs such as heroin seem to be a combination of a euphoric effect and the fact that drugs, like alcohol, are effective reducers of anxiety and tension.

Perhaps the biggest complaint against such drugs is the problem associated with crime and the addict's need to obtain money to support the habit. Profits from heroin sales in the United States are estimated by Leech and Jordan to reach seven hundred million dollars a year. But does it have to be so? Leech and Jordan report that Great Britain has been experimenting with the legalization of drugs on a limited basis for dispensation to addict through their physicians.

In Great Britain, it is not necessary for an addict *to* steal *to* support his habit. The British experiment has not reduced the problem of addiction; many people prefer *to* obtain their drugs from the underground rather than openly. However, it has reduced black market control of drugs and with it, the need for the addict to commit crimes to support his habit. The famous $100-a-day drug habit results only because the drug must be obtained illegally. The actual cost of manufacturing these amounts of drugs is only a few dollars at most. If we are really interested in helping solve the problem of crime and drugs it may be necessary to explore new approaches, perhaps those similar to Great Britain, to find a solution. America's thirteen-year experiment with the prohibition of alcohol in the 1920s and 1930s served only *to* produce organized crime; it did not reduce crime. The classic solution of building more jails has clearly not worked.

Few scientists have questioned the harmfulness of heroin, but marijuana is a different problem. In the 1930s, the United States government sponsored a campaign against marijuana. Posters were published warning people to beware because a cigarette may be handed *to* them "by the friendly stranger.

"Opium was legal in the United States until the Harrison Act of 1914. In fact, opium was widely and freely sold *over* the counter and advertised as virtually a cure-all for any problem (which it was not). The Sears catalog of 1902 lists among its "miracle" drugs one that was designed to cure the craving for opium (which it did not). Morphine and heroin are derived from opium and are basically identical to opium In their effects.

Posters were widely distributed in the 1930's warning children of the supposed dangers of marijuana.: "It contains the killer drug 'marijuana's-a powerful narcotic in which lurks Murder! Insanity! Death!" (Grinspoon, 1969). In Texas, possession of a single marijuana cigarette was sufficient to send a person to jail for life until the laws were finally amended in 1973, In fact, a number of persons were sentenced to life for just such a minor charge.

Not until the late 1960s did the government seriously begin to investigate whether marijuana was harmful. President Eisenhower appointed a commission consisting of some of the most respectable men in the country to investigate and report on marijuana and drug abuse.

After a thorough study of the situation the commission reported its findings, including the recommendation that all criminal penalties for possession of marijuana be abolished. (Presidential Commission Report on Marijuana and Drug Abuse, 1970, U.S. Government). Furthermore, the National Commission on the Causes and Prevention of Violence, chaired by Dr. Milton Eisenhower, the brother of former President Eisenhower, reported finding no reliable scientific evidence of harmful effects of marijuana nor any evidence that marijuana is the stepping stone to hard narcotics.

As soon as the reports on marijuana became public, they were condemned by law enforcement officials, judges, and even the President of the United States, who proceeded to reject the findings. Several years and over a million arrests later, a few studies did find evidence that marijuana may be harmful. A report released by the Department of Health, Education, and Welfare notes that smoking marijuana may reduce the level of male sex hormones and possibly interfere with other biological functions. These reports did not show evidence of marijuana actually being harmful. The fact that male sex hormone levels may be reduced under some circumstances tells us nothing about how harmful smoking marijuana may be. Perhaps the question we should be asking at this point is not simply is marijuana harmful, but how harmful and harmful in comparison to what?

Is marijuana as dangerous as alcohol? According to government statistics, over half of the 24,000 traffic fatalities each year result from drivers who have been drinking. This would seem to represent a clear and present danger. Yet no one goes to jail for possessing alcohol. Studies indicate that marijuana does reduce one's concentration in driving, but not as much as alcohol. No one has suggested that marijuana is responsible for anything like the death rate attributed to alcohol or cigarettes.

Uniform Crime reports from the Federal Bureau of Investigation show that 445,600 arrests were made in 1974. This is up 6 per cent from the 1973 figure of 420,700. The 1974 figure represented 69 percent of all drug arrests. By 2020, despite some states making it legal, there were some 663,000 arrests for marijuana.

By 2010, out of 8.2 million reported marijuana arrests between 2001 and 2010, 88% were for simple possession. https://www.aclu.org/gallery/marijuana-arrests-numbers

Despite the current trend toward legalization of marijuana, both the number of arrests and the-percentage figure were all-time records, marking the continuation of a steady climb from 1965, when 18,815 arrests for marijuana represented 40.8 per cent of drug arrests. Widely accepted estimates indicate that about 93 per cent of marijuana arrests are tor private possession arid use. This was not an offense warranting arrest in some states last year and since has been reduced to the status of a non-criminal "violation" in five others. '

All of this does not mean that marijuana is harmless. Smoking marijuana, like smoking cigarettes, may cause cancer and possibly even have unforeseen consequences. Yet we have known for fifty years that cigarettes kill over 250,000 Americans a year, yet, we do not arrest people for smoking cigarettes.

The major danger of smoking marijuana may be the fact that prolonged exposure to a prison cell is known to be damaging to one's psychological well-being. To quote Dr. Thomas Bryant, President of the Drug Abuse Council (*U.S. News and World Report,* Dec. 1974, p. 80): "Even if marijuana were shown to be as dangerous as alcohol or tobacco, giving a criminal record to the user only exacerbates the potential harm to society and to the values you and I hold."

We have been mass-producing hardened criminals out of petty ones. We have stigmatized hundreds of thousands of people as drug users and given them criminal records-records that impede if not block progress toward positions of responsibility in our society and indirectly may divert many persons to a life of crime.

Our society is only beginning to weigh the benefits of our laws against their consequences. Marijuana is perhaps the only drug whose harmfulness is still in doubt. We know beyond any doubt that cigarettes and alcohol kill far more Americans each year than even the 80,000 deaths attributed to oxycodone.

How much evidence would you consider necessary before you would ban such a product from the public? How much evidence should be necessary before people are put in jail for using the drug? How long a jail sentence should a pusher receive for selling diet soda to minors.

No, the questions are not absurd: For decades the same questions have been asked, and answered, by authorities on a variety of drugs,' most notably marijuana. The evidence of harmful effects from marijuana has been based on the same type of evidence as the ban on saccharin. The news media and the government have been quick to point out that marijuana has been found harmful in some studies, but both have been negligent in informing the public about precisely how such evidence was obtained.

There is a double danger in this negligence. Not only is there the problem of the harm that the resulting laws have done to other people, but there is the danger of "crying wolf ". College students, who have long been aware of the government's tendency to exaggerate, may not believe when warned about real dangers.

The problems of the individual are a creation of the interaction between the mind of the individual and the social environment in which we must live-a world of anxiety, beliefs, and social norms. Psychologists have not proposed any simple solutions to these problems. The first step we must take before we solve the problems is to understand those problems. And this we are only beginning to do.

Is there a future in prophylactic psychology? Considering how much more successful medicine has been in *preventing* diseases (plague, smallpox, malaria) than it has in treating the problems after they arise, this is an area too long neglected by psychology.

6. On the Forces That Shape Human Behavior

Applying Known Principles; it is perhaps astonishing that so much of psychology's literature has been devoted to treating problems and so little to preventing them. This may be the single most ignored area of psychology, and perhaps the most promising.

The first step toward preventing psychological problems is to understand the workings of the mind. If we are ignorant of our use of ego defense mechanisms, our tendency to engage in witch-hunts, our superstitions, our human fears, and our conditioned social beliefs, then we are at the mercy of our environment.

PSYCHOLOGICAL AND SOCIAL PROGRESS

Human technology has made tremendous advances in the centuries between the witch-hunts of the past and the psychological traumas of today's world. Yet for all of the advances in technology, we have made little progress in teaching our children to understand their own mind. Progress in social change has not kept pace with progress in computer technology.

Psychologists should perhaps be excused for believing that the future of humanity lies, not in the mysteries of outer space, but in an understanding of the human mind. Yet this is not merely a preoccupation with our own subject matter. Throughout human history, no single fact has been more evident than that we have been a captive of the inventions of our own mind. Unaware of the forces that shape our thoughts, we have been blown about by social and environmental forces like a leaf in the wind. The endless wars, prejudice, and witch hunts may seem different, yet they are often a failure of our educational system.

We are only beginning to become aware of the forces that shape our minds. As we gain new knowledge of why we behave as we do, it should become possible for us to understand and to improve our educational system and our society.

"We're not hibernating this year.
Too much cultural change to keep up with."

EPILOGUE

TOWARD A
UNIFIED FIELD THEORY

Sometimes psychologists have made a name for themselves by criticizing another point of view and establishing their own as superior (brain, behavioral, developmental, cognitive, perceptual, neuropsychology, etc., etc.). Yet all have found some important pieces. What we need is to put the best pieces together.

- The brain itself is biologically programmed by our DNA to process learning by simple associations, generalization, and emotions, that are processed into concepts or learning sets. That includes *patterns and sequences* of visual and auditory data.

- There are unique biological programs in the brain for speech, and much more. However, John Locke's idea of a tabula rasa or "blank slate" referred only to knowledge amd understanding, no one ever denied the biological processes, such as Broca's area and Wernicke's area, or other brain mechanisms.

- And yet the evidence shows that, when it comes to knowledge and understanding, the mind begins as very much a tabula rasa, a blank slate, requiring stimulus impression from experience to even begin to develop the brain itself (as demonstrated by the recent studies of single cataracts in babies and Blakemore and Cooper's study of how vertical and horizontal lines cannot be perceived without experience, as well as the origin of illusions, trapezoidal, etc.).

- Experience structures the brain so effectively that we are unable to easily adapt to completely different realities. Experience creates a "reality" in the brain from which we interpret all experiences, as shown by visual illusions and by how we respond to words, p. 213, etc. The brain's experiences form a "reality" is the basis of our value judgments of everything we experience. We see this in our reactions to politics, religion, interpersonal relations, and nearly every experience we have.

- PERMUTATIONS: The many permutation effects, from the Primacy effect, generalization, emotions, approach-avoidance, and an infinite number of others, shows that there are many permutations to learning. Human behaviors in all areas is so varied that, as an analogy, they are not unlike the way the way simply changing the frequency of electromagnetic radiation can produce everything from radio and radar to visible colors, to infrared and ultraviolet radiation. Or how changing the atomic structure can change the very nature of matter.

- Yet psychology has gone more toward a philosophy of differing opinions, instead of a unity of purpose. Psychology cannot be a science if we are just a gaggle of conflicting ideas. We are something more; a Unified Field.

The most basic sensory impressions can combine with the S-S associations to become sensory perceptions. The basic perceptions can combine to become concepts (or learning sets, or schema, or cognitive maps, or reason, or ideas, or thoughts, etc.)

S-S associations can combine with trial-and-error learning to become ideas or concepts or perceptions, as Harlow demonstrated.

WHAT LEARNING THEORY CONTRIBUTES

- **PSYCHOLOGY CAN CONTROL OUR BIOLOGY:** Pavlov's simple association between a Stimulus and a Response (S-R psychology), began an understanding of the link between biology and psychology. The beginning of the S-R and S-S paradigm gave psychology a foundation with biology and reality it had never had before. It clearly showed how even our brain's powerful Flight or Fight response could be "rewired" to produce saliva and even pleasure.

- **EMOTIONS:** Watson's realization that Pavlov's paradigm would also apply to emotion, the most powerful motivation of our species, should have opened the floodgates to our understanding of, not just Little Albert's emotional reaction to furry animals, but to everything from some 700 phobias and 450 paraphilias, to our political and religious opinions. But it did not. Instead, the implications of the study are censored in our textbooks to this day. Censored, perhaps, because we do not want to think of our political and religious beliefs being controlled by the emotions others embed in our brains.

- **PARADIGM:** The S-R or S-S paradigms provide the most powerful paradigm for understanding how the brain is programmed by the environment. It is, at least potentially, *a paradigm that, like mathematics, applies to an almost infinite number of stimuli, being associated with an emotion* that determines our beliefs, what we seek, what we will die for, and even the value of big lips or tiny feet or large breasts, to produce a sexual response (re. Rachmann's experiment or Vonnegut's example).

- **THOUGHTS:** It applies to the very thoughts in our brain (as in S-S associations). Neal Miller's study of anxiety responses, measured by a "lie detector" or GSR, dramatically showed how even our thoughts fall under the S-S paradigm.

WHAT LEARNING THEORY CANNOT EXPLAIN

Critics of the S-R, and S-S approach have pointed out problems that cannot be explained by this simple approach.

- Consider a "flashbulb" memory. Almost everyone can remember where they were the first time they heard of the Kennedy assassination or the attack on the Twin Towers on September 11. I can not only remember the event; I vividly remember the road I was on when I first heard of these events on my car radio and exactly where I was when I saw it on television later. It is not just a stimulus-response memory it is like a general impression of everything going on at the time. An image is implanted in my brain. It is like Darwin saying, "*...I remember the very spot in the road whilst traveling in my carriage...*" when he had his great insight. What kind of memory is a flashbulb memory? Is Sensory Impression the most basic form of learning?

- Studies show that we do better on exams if we take the exam in the *same* room we study in instead of a different room. Why?

- Edward Tolman noted we learn by what he called "Cognitive Maps" and "Latent" learning. How?

- We can condition an adult to fear a word in a laboratory, by giving a mild electric shock associated with that word, yet he will not fear that word outside of the laboratory. Why?

- You cannot teach an adult to fear a furry animal as easily as you can a child. Why?

- Perceptual psychology offers a bridge between behavioral and cognitive psychology, along with Harlow's study of "learning sets".

COGNITIVE PSYCHOLOGY

Cognitive Psychologists often see themselves as having replaced Behavioral Psychology, yet it is more accurate to say that they added an important new dimension to psychology. Cognitive psychology could never explain what Behavioral Psychology could explain, and Behavioral Psychology could not explain what Cognitive Psychology demonstrated.

Perhaps more likely, both saw a portion of how the mind works, but not the whole picture.

- COGNITION: Wolfgang Kohler's extensive study of "insight" in chimpanzees was a major step toward recognizing that something was going on at a higher level inside the brain, although trial an error learning was clearly a part of the puzzle.

- SELECTIVE ATTENTION, demonstrated by Donald Broadbent having students wear headphones, playing different stories into each ear, were told to pay attention to only one story. When asked questions about what was happening in both ears, they were able to effectively answer those questions that were about the story only happening in the ear they were attending to.

- COGNITIVE MAPS Tolman's studies of latent learning and "cognitive maps" strongly suggested that we learn far more than just a simple stimulus-response association. This presaged the realization that we may learn all sensory input, not just an S-R relationship. Estes Stimulus Sampling theory, suggested that S-R learning may develop out of overall sensory impressions.

- DEVELOPMENTAL: Piaget's experiments with human children provided a rich source of understanding of how children understand reality differently than adults; from their own experiences, and how this understanding changes throughout life.

- MEMORY: Studies of memory and the fallibility of memory by Elizabeth Loftus and others have found our memory is vague and easily re-written. Eyewitness testimony, often considered the best evidence, is a serious problem that has led to the jailing of innocent people. The number one cause of innocent people being convicted of crimes they did not commit, is eyewitness testimony

.https://www.oxfordbibliographies.com/view/document/obo-9780199828340/obo-9780199828340-0026.xml

- COGITO, ERGO, COGITO, COGITO Studies demonstrated that our cognitive thoughts are dependent on the ideas embedded in our brains first (the Primacy Effect) and the failure of our brain to be able to connect two simple ideas we have already learned. Thoughts seem to actually be learned *perceptions* that flit in and out like looking at the top or bottom of a Necker cube.

The major contributions of cognitive psychology are important, but not paradigm-changing. They add to the paradigm.

WHATCOGNITIVE PSYCHOLOGY CANNOT DO

The failure of cognitive psychology to provide a bridge between simple learning, such as conditioned emotions, trial and error, learning sets and their own area of cognitive processes, left their theories without a hard science support.

• Piaget's concepts of Schema, Accommodation, and Assimilation are subject to the problem of the Nominal Fallacy: the belief that, by having named something, we have somehow explained it.

• Harlow's study of "learning sets" provided a hard evidence ground for going from simple association to cognitive psychology, but has been largely ignored by cognitive psychologists.

• More important, they have not considered the most recent discoveries of cataract studies in babies that show the brain itself is profoundly molded by experience. Without visual experience, the brain itself will never develop the ability to see. Experience itself changes the biology of the brain and our perceptions.

• Cognitive psychology sometimes gives students the mistaken idea that there are magical-mystical processes working in the mind. Yet these processes are subject to the same error noted by Lorenz in his comment on instincts: *The Neuro-physiological organization we call instinct functions in a blindly mechanical way, especially apparent when its function goes wrong.*

• The excitement of working with children, instead of rats and pigeons, has led many psychologists to accept the idea that this is more important, which helped extend cognitive psychology to a point where many think what they do is more important than anything else in psychology.

COGNITIVE NEUROSCIENCE
OR NEUROPSYCHOLOGY

The relatively new area of Neuropsychology has provided us with the shock and awe of beautiful multicolored pictures (artificially colored) to show the inner firing of groups of nerve cells. The use of fMRI and PET scans provide a dramatic view of the interaction of parts of the brain we could never otherwise have known. It is now being used to map the human brain.

• These studies have shown, for one example, that nerve tracts are going from the temporal cortex and Wernicke's area, to the Motor cortex and Broca's area. These areas "light up" (the neurons absorb more oxygen or use more energy) when we engage in speaking.

• Cognitive Neuroscience is being used to map the brain.

• Professor Nancy Kanwisher of MIT has a remarkable series of lectures describing how this has been used to tease out how we know there are many specialized areas of the brain that respond to faces, language, and music. These are a series well worth watching if you are fascinated with the function of the brain itself. Not since the initial discoveries of Broca and Wernicke have we had such a complete view of how the brain works. Professor Kanwisher has used her own brain to demonstrate how the brain functions.

• https://www.youtube.com/watch?v=5Yj3nGv0kn8

• https://www.youtube.com/watch?v=ZueXhzQS1k4

• One perhaps surprising discovery at MIT is the relationship between language and thought. Her associate, Rebecca Saxe, found that there are specific parts of the brain that "light up" when we *think about what other people are thinking about us*.

https://www.youtube.com/watch?v=1AiB6kmnxeM

Or search youtube.com for "Special Parts of the Human Brain".

WHAT NEUROPSYCHOLOGY CANNOT TELL US

No matter how complete our map of the human brain becomes, it will never tell us about the origin of our knowledge, beliefs, or emotions. It cannot explain the behavior of a Kamikaze pilot or a suicide bomber, it cannot tell us why we speak English or Swahili, or where our prejudices or interests come from.

• Cognitive neuropsychology has taken over what is researched in the major institutions of this country. If you look at the areas of psychology at MIT, Stanford, and others, there is virtually no psychologist who has any interest other than cognitive neuropsychology.

• This narrow focus on the brain could set psychology back a quarter of a century by ignoring the vast importance of simple learning and the role of experience in even the most basic programming of the brain, as in the studies that showed the brain itself cannot develop the ability to see (cataract studies in babies a PBS video and Blakemore and Cooper's study of vertical and horizontal line perception). Even more, the studies of the most basic perception of reality in trapezoidal illusions and in our perception of beauty.

• Neuropsychology gives us no insight into personality differences, what makes for genius, and why we love or hate or feel the emotions of shame or guilt.

• Only the low-tech methods of basic psychology, sociology, and cultural anthropology can provide us with an understanding of the uniquely human thoughts that control our mind.

• Even if we know everything possible about the functioning of the neurons in our brain, about every part of the brain and how they interconnect, it will tell us nothing about basic human behavior. In every final analysis, we have to go on to the simple associations that are encoded in our minds by experience.

COMPUTER SCIENCE AND ITS CONTRIBUTION

Although the brain is not like a hardwired computer, it shares remarkable similarities to a computer.

• SWITCHING: The Neurons that power the brain work in a simple ON or OFF function, much like a computer, with the addition of graded potentials and excitatory plus inhibitory neurotransmitters.

• DECISION MAKING: Perhaps the most dramatic similarity is how both computers and the brain make decisions. Computers use an IF-THEN decision diamond or DO LOOP to make a decision. In a flowchart, in the Decision Diamond, the computer compares two numbers or patterns (IF X = Y, THEN go on to the next step. IF X does not equal Y, THEN go back to a previous step in the program.)

• CONTRAST and COMPARISON: In a similar way, the human mind compares and contrasts two variables. This allows the brain to make a "choice" whether the two variables (or stimulus patterns) are similar or not. This is evident in Approach-Avoidance conflict or seeing a solution to a problem, or the Necker cube perception.

• PREPROGRAMMED PROCESSING: Like a computer, the brain is biologically structured to process information. Just as a computer must have DOS or a Disk Operating System loaded into itself before new programs or information can be fed into it, so does the human mind. Experience creates the models from which we understand reality.

DESPITE THE SIMILAR FUNCTIONS
OF THE COMPUTER AND THE BRAIN,
THERE ARE ALSO DRAMATIC DIFFERENCES.

• EMOTION: This is the primary force that controls human motivation. There is no comparable method in the computer. Curiosity, Pleasure, Fear, Anger, and all of the various combinations of these that produce excitement, shame, guilt, etc. are a unique product of the brain and experience.

• Although it is possible to simulate emotion on a computer, this tells us absolutely nothing about the programs and emotions that life and society feed into the human mind.

• Only the low-tech methods of learning in *psychology, sociology and cultural anthropology* can tell us how the brain uses emotion and comparison to make the brain into a useful, programmed mind.

• Psychology (Learning) picks up, where biology leaves off. Sociology and Cultural Anthropology come in to provide the next step of information.

• The mind itself is structured by its experiences in a way that is quite unlike a computer. The information and perception provide the raw material on which our mind depends. The structure of the brain itself (as in our unique perceptions), determines what the brain is capable of "seeing" or experiencing.

In effect: We need all of these areas, from History to Psychology to Culture, in a Unified Field Theory, to be able to understand the human mind and to be able to alter such forces for our benefit.

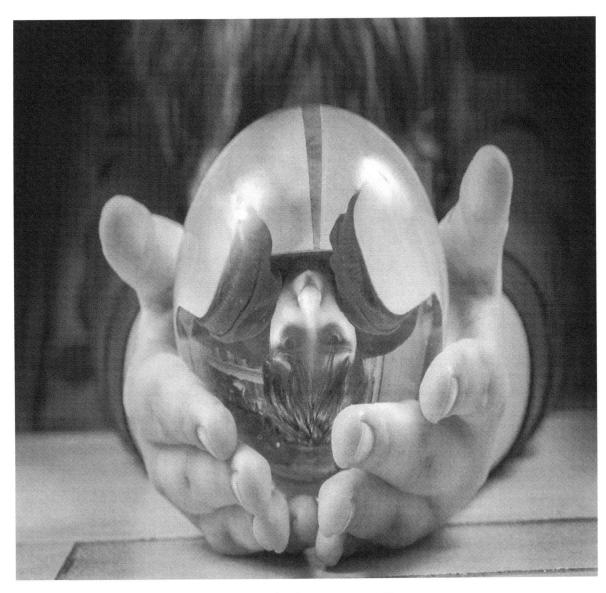

Our perception becomes our reality.

ACKNOWLEDGMENTS

Cover background by askandrew
Photos licensed from shutterstock
Photos licensed from depositphoto
Or from YAYimages
Illustrations from depositphoto
Additional photos and illustrations as indicated
References are given throughout the book and attributed to the
original source.
Cartoons by Andrewgenn unless noted
Youtube videos as noted
Apologies if anyone has been missed.

Prologue
Bear cartoons by Andrewgenn
All the cool stuff is in the deep woods from YAYimages

Stress about the test by Andrewgenn

Burning of "witches" from Shutterstock
Salem witch trials from Shutterstock
Militants celebrate by zabelin
Qanon by zimmytws
Dragon by Denismile
Blind men and elephant by leremy
Full page part opening to brain by paulistano

End of chapter hand holding brain by Sergey Nivens
Erase the frontal lobe by Andreus
Group examining brain on screen by DragosCondreaW

Frog cartoons by Julos

Man surrounded by sharks tintin75
Hypnosis dream images by agsandrew
Washington by Ruain Lytvyn
DNA and Computer by Andreus
Sensation
Eyes by Srecko80
Line and motion by Dragovich

PAVLOV marusyachaika
Pavlov's tank maxtor7777
Picasso art works by Mayaartworks
Starving Artist Cartoon andrewgenn
Never Heard of Picasso andrewgenn
Eye against computer background by Sergeynivins
Picasso style example pepeemilio2
Artist's hunger for recognition   andrewgenn
Hake fish fotoall
Cow in India mzuuzu
Hypnosis opening BrianAJackson
Sleeping child by sSplajn
Cartoons by andrew

Ape and you thought I was dumb by andrewpotyseiv
Apes begging for food by Gudkovandrey

Upside down lens by sirer61
Illusion lines Furian
Illusion Multiple Boxes Necker Cube Alisher
Line and Motion circle SvetlanaParsh
Spinning circles by anutuno
Necker cube by panimoni
Zulu Hut Round Dendenal
Dr. viewing EEG yacobchuk1
Necker Cube Variation Iconscout
EEG Record dusan964
EEG WIRE EXAMPLES tumponkrit
EEG WAVE LENGTH Polina_po
Cataract surgery Bork
Focus illusion 4eyed by Alexanderpokusay
Upside down woman Nikiteev
Invisible square by Youri Valensko

Tattooed Couple AllaSerebrina
Lesbian Cows Haylight
Mursi woman with lip plate LuisaPuccini
Chinese women with tiny feet by ChinaImages
Mursi tribe, Woman with Liip Plate miroslav_1
Mursi woman with child by itpow
2 Mursi women with lip plates   luisapuccini
Child in Thailand with Neck Rings agiampiccolo
Woman in Thailand with Neck Rings agiampiccolo
Woman and child with neckrings agiampiccolo
Girl with piercings sucher

Theater Masks top of chapter   Morphart
Robert Boyle georgios
Vouban Georgios
heel boot bersenvstudio
Jaws shark by Andreus

Cognition
Part opening for cognition by Matt_photography
Chinese symbols by melanjurga
Ape head left OlgaTropinina
Sultan sulks head in hand onot
Sultan last bdnz

Sultan chimp thumbs up Cundrawan703
Rat Maze edesignua
Broadbents study with headphones by Stokkette
Developmental children lemony
2-7 yr girl developmental Victoria Novak
Happy 12-year-old OlgaTropinina
Computer programmer in moment of frustration by
AndrewLozovoi
Bad karma Memory by Andrewgenn
The Perceiver by davisales
Developmental stages to 12 mo by lipmic

Lorenz Goslings following Mother rhamm
Lorenz duck Victoria_Novak
Kittywaiet on a nest frankff
Frogs Morphart
Puppy chewing toy eriklam
Baboon baby imitates mother WittkePhotos
Harlow rhesus adult andrevoleynik
Rhesus mom with baby Ukususha
Frightened chimp harlow turaevgeniy
Social Smile Baby sborisovHigh
Baby eating shoe by Couperfield

The symbol
Primitive man Lurii
Cave painting by bereta
Cave painting by rdinar
Cave man with torch by ddsign stock
Neanderthal skull by Creative marc
The non-talking animals are deeper by Andrewgenn

Masks in series by rolffimages
Astonished baby by alekseyth
Cute babies by Gekaskr
Series of babies by rawpixel
Cute rat Hall Temperament Pakhnyushchyy
Cute puppies temperament Miraswonderland
Cute rat front temperament 2 Pakhnyushchyy
George Washington Pony Tail   DepositNovic
Thomas Jefferson Pony Tail   lenschanger
Color chimp baby on board watman
Police dog trainingby SergeyTikomarov
Young seeing eye dog girls zoeytoja
Seeing Eye Dog Training Belish
Cat and Mouse Friend bloodua
Dog and Cat Friend pyotr021
Dog and cat by websubstance
Kitten on bulldog willeecole
Child with teddy bear by EdZbarzhyvedski
Male Awareness Weekend   andrewgenn

Principles of behavior
Women working at Foxconn by ChinaImages
Relatives of suicide at Foxcomm by ChinaImages
Cartoon on Zombie performance review by YAYimages
Sign on slots Re2deer
Bullying at school by Andrewgenn

XY Genetics chapter opening perig76
Egg cell surrounded by sperm   phonlamai
Stork bringing Baby Dazdraperma
China Golden Lotus foot ChinaImages
Chinese Golden Lotus Shoe oqba
Very last chimp hurrumpp DenisPotysiev
Chapter 20 social

Cartoon this beach is already claimed by Andrewgenn
Cartoon yield to whoever agrees with me by Andrewgenn
Killer ape illustration by Denis Potysiev
Photo angry ape by jonnysek
3little pigs by Andrewgenn
No wolf would eat a sheep by Andrewgenn
Chapter 22
Cartoon I think we bonded by Andregenn
Crying eye by lightsourse
Kitten hanging from rope by natulrich
Happiness is when you stop comparing yourself with dogs by Andrewgenn
That nasty word plummet cartoon YAYimages
Iceberg metaphor by crystaleyemedia
Freud by Georgios
Freud with cigar by fogbird
Visualize yourself not falling off a wall Andrewgenn
Existential crisis Shakespeare by Ricku
Upside down image by sirer61

BIBLIOGRAPHY

Attenborough, David 2019, *Seven Worlds,* BBC documentary.

Ader, R., and Conklin, P. M. 1963. Handling of pregnant rats: Effects on emotionality of their offspring. *Science* 142:411-12.

Adorno, T. W., Brunswik, E. F., Levinson, D. J., and Sanford, R. N. 1950. *The authoritarian personality: Studies in prejudice* N. Y: Harper & Row.

Allport, G. W. 1954. *The nature of prejudice.* Boston: Beacon Press.

Allport, G. W., and Pettigrew, T. F. 1957. Cultural influence on the perception of movement: The trapezoidal illusion among Zulus. *Journal of Abnormal and Social Psychology* 55:104-13.

Allport, G. W., and Postman, L. 1947. *The psychology of rumor.* New York: Holt.

Altus, W. D. 1967. Birth order and its sequelae. *International Journal of Psychiatry* 3:23-32.

Anokhin, P. K. 1971. Three giants of Soviet psychology: Conversations and sketches by Michael and Sheka Cole. *Psychology Today* 4, 10:43.

Aronson, E. 1972. *The social animal.* San Francisco: **W. H.** Freeman.

Asch, S. E. 1956. Studies in independence and conformity: A minority of one against a unanimous majority. *Psychological Monographs* 9:70.

Ausubel, D. 1958. *Drug addiction.* New York: Random House.

Azrin, N. H., Hutchinson, R.R., and Hake, D. F. 1967. Attack, avoidance, and escape reactions to aversive shock. *Journal of Experimental Analysis of Behavior* 10:131-48.

Bandura, A. 1969. *Principles of behavior modification.* New York: Holt, Rinehart, & Winston.

Bandura, A., Ross, D., and Ross, S. A. 1963. Imitation of film-mediated aggressive models. *Journal of Abnormal and Social Psychology* 66:3-11.

Bandura, A., and Walters, R. H. 1959. *Adolescent aggression.* New York: Ronald Press.

Beach, F. A. 1941. Female mating behavior shown by male rats after administration of testosterone propionate. *Endocrinology* 29:409-12.

Beach, F. A. 1942. Analysis of factors involved in the arousal, maintenance, and manifestation of sexual excitement in male animals. *Psychosomatic Medicine* 4: 173-98.

Beach, F. A. 1955. The descent of instinct. *Psychological Review* 62:401-10.

Beach, F. A. 1968. Coital behavior in dogs: Effects of early isolation on mating · in males. *Behavior* 30:218-38.

Beach, F. A., and Gilmore, R. W. 1949. Responses of male dogs to urine from females in heat. *Journal of Mammalogy* 30:391-92.

Beers, C. 1934. *A mind that found itself* New York: Longmans Green.

Belmont, L., and Marolla, F. A. 1973. Birth order,family size, and intelligence. *Science* 182:1096- 1101. Benedict, R. 1934. *Patterns of culture.* Boston: Houghton-Mifflin.

Bernstein, I. 1969. Lecture on primate behavior. Arlington, Texas.

Berquist, E. H. 1972. Role of the hypothalamus in motivation: An examination of Valenstein's reexamination. *Psychological Review* 79 (6):542-46.

Berscheid, E., Boyd, D., and Walster, E. 1968. Retaliation as a means of restoring equity. *Journal of Personality and Social Psychology* 10:4.

Birch, H. G. 1945. The relation of previous experience to insightful problem-solving. *Journal of Comparative Psychology* 38:367-96.

Bishop, M. P., Elder, S. T., and Heath, R. G. 1963. Intercranial self-stimulation in man. *Science* 140: 394-96.

Boring, E. G. 1950. *A history of experimental psychology.* New York: Appleton-Century-Crofts.

Boring, E. G., and Lindzey, G. 1967. *A history of psychology in autobiography,* vol. V. New York: Appleton-Century-Crofts.

Brace, C. L. 1968. Ridiculed, rejected, but still our ancestor, Neanderthal. *Natural History* 77:38-45.

Braine, M. D.S. 1963a. The ontogeny of English phrase structure: The first phase. *Language* 39:1-13.

Braine, M. D. S. 1963b. On learning the grammatical order of words. *Psychological Review* 70:323-48.

Breland, H. M. 1973. Reply to Schooler's article on birth order. *Psychological Bulletin* 80, 3:210-12.

Broadhurst, P. L. 1960. Experiments in psychogenetics. In *Experiments in personality,* vol. 1, ed. H. J. Eysenck. London: Routledge and Kegan

Broca, P. 1878. Anatomie, compares des circonvolutions cerebrales. Le grand lobe limbique et la scissure limbique dans la se des mammifere, *Review of Anthropology* 1:385-498.

Brown, R., and Bellugi, U. 1964. Three processes in the child's acquisition of syntax. Hasoard *Educational Review* 34: 133-51.

Brown, T. T. 1961. *The enigma of drug addiction.* Springfield, Ill.. Charles C. Thomas.

Bruner, J. S. 1962. The conditions of creativity. In *Contemporary approaches to creative thinking,* eds. Gruber, Terell, and Wertheimer. New York: Atherton.

Bruner, J. S., and Kenney, H. J. 1966. On multiple ordering. In *Studies in cognitive growth,* eds. Bruner, Olver, and Greenfield. New York: Wiley & Sons.

Buckhout, R. 1974. Eyewitness testimony. *Scientific American* 231, 6:23-32.

Butler, R. A. 1953. Discrimination learning in rhesus monkeys to visual exploration motivation. *Journal of Comparative and Physiological Psychology* 46: 95-98.

Butler, R. A. 1954. Incentive conditions which influence visual exploration. *Journal of Experimental Psychology* 48: 19-23.

Carel, P. 1965. *Hitler moves east, 1941-1943,* trans. E. Osers. Boston: Little, Brown.

Carpenter, C. R. 1964. *Naturalistic behavior of nonhuman primates.* University Park: Pennsylvania State Univ. Press.

Carpenter, C. R. 1965. The howlers of Barro Colorado Island. In *Primate behavior: Field studies of monkeys and apes,* ed. I. DeVore. New York: Holt, Rinehart, & Winston.

Carrel, A. 1939. *Man the unknown.* New York: Harper Brothers.

Carroll, L. 1946a. *Through the looking glass and what Alice found there.* New York: Random House.

Carroll, L. 1946b. *Alice's adventures in wonderland.* New York: Random House.

Chodoff, P. 1970. The German concentration camp as psychological stress. *Archives of General Psychiatry* 22, 1:78-87.

Chomsky, N. 1965. *Aspects of the theory of syntax.* Cambridge: **MIT** Press.

Chomsky, N. 1967. The formal nature of language. In *Biological foundations of language,* ed. Lennenberg. New York: Wiley & Sons.

Chomsky, N. 1968. *Language and mind.* New York: Harcourt Brace Jovanovich.

Clemens, S. L. 1923. *The adventures of Huckleberry Finn.* New York: Harper Brothers.

Clemens, S. L. 1958. *The adventures of Tom Sawyer.* New York: Dodd.

Clemens, S. L. 1962. *Letters from the earth,* New York: Harper & Row.

Collias, N. E. 1944. Aggressive behavior among vertebrate animals. *Physiological Zoology* 17:83-123

Collias, N. E. 1951. Problems and principles of animal sociology. In *Comparative psychology,* ed. C. P. Stone, pp. 388-422. Englewood Cliffs, N. J.: PrenticeHall.

Cooley, C. H. 1909. *Social organization.* New York: Scribner.

Cooley, C. H. 1927. *Life and the student: Roadside notes on human nature, society, and letters.* New York: Knopf.

Cooley, C. H. 1964. *Human nature and the social order.* New York: Schocken Books.

Coopersmith, S. 1968. Studies in self-esteem. *Scientific American* 218, 17:96-100.

Cowles, J. T.1937. Food-tokens as incentives for learning in chimpanzees. *Comparative Psychology Monograph* 14:5.

Crane, S. 1964. *The red badge of courage.* New York: Bantam Books.

Crespi, L. P. 1942. Quantitative variation of incentive and performance in the white rat. *American Journal of Psychology* 55:467-517.

Cushing, H. W. 1936. *From a surgeon's journal.* Boston: Little, Brown.

Darwin, C. 1859. *On the 01'igin of species by means of natural selection.* London: J. Murray.

Darwin, C. 1887. *The autobiography of Charles Da1Win.* London: Collins.

Darwin, C. 1909. *Voyage of the Beagle.* New York: Collier & Son.

Davis, K. 1947. Final note on a case of extreme isolation. *American Journal of Sociology* 52:432-37.

Descartes, R. 1961. *Meditations on the first philosophy,* trans. L. 0. Lafleur. New York: Liberal Arts Press.

DeVore, I., and Eimerl, S. 1965. *The primates.* New York: Time, Inc.

DeVore, I., and Hall, R. L. 1965. Baboon social behavior. In *Primate behavior,* ed. I. DeVore, pp. 53-110. New York: Holt, Rinehart, & Winston.

Dollard, J., Doob, L., Mlller, N. E., Mowrer, 0. H., and Sears, R.R. 1939. *Frustration and aggression.* New Haven: Yale Univ. Press.

Dollard, J., and Miller, N. E. 1950. *Personality and psychotherapy: An analysis in terms of learning, thinking, and culture.* New York: McGraw-Hill.

Doty, R. W., and Giurgea, C. 1961. Conditioned reflexes established by coupling electrical excitations of two cortical areas. In *Brain mechanisms and learning,* eds. Fessard, Gerand, Konarski, and Delafresnaye, pp. 133-52. Springfield, ill.: Charles C. Thomas.

Durant, W., and Durant, A. 1961. *The story of civilization: The age of reason begins.* New York: Simon & Schuster.

Eccles, J. C. 1953. *The neurophysiological basis of mind.* London: Oxford Univ. Press.

Eccles, J. C. 1957. *The physiology of nerve cells.* Baltimore: Johns Hopkins Univ. Press.

Eccles, J. C. 1973. *The understanding of the brain.* New York: McGraw-Hill.

Edwards, J. 1809. *Sinners in the hands of an angry God. The works of President Edwards in eight volumes,* vol. 7. Worcester, Mass: Isaiah Thomas.

Engel, B. T. 1972. Operant conditioning of cardiac function: A status report. *Psychophysiology* 9: 161-77, 207.

Espar, E. A. 1967. Max Meyer in America. *Journal of the History of the Behavioral Sciences* 3, 2: 107-31.

Ferrier, D. 1886. *The functions of the brain.* London: Smith, Elder.

Ferster, C. S., and Skinner, B. F. 1957. *Schedules of reinforcement.* New York: Appleton-Century-Crofts.

Festinger, L. 1957. *A theory of cognitive dissonance.* Stanford: Stanford Univ. ·Press.

Festinger, L., Riecken, H. W., and Schacter, S. 1956. *When prophecy fails.* New York: Harper & Row.

Findley, J. D., and Brady, J. U. 1965. Facilitation of large ratio performances by use of conditioned reinforcement. *Journal of Experimental Analysis of Behavior* 8:125-29.

Flynn, J. P. 1967. The neural basis of aggression in cats. In *Neurophysiology and emotion,* ed. D. C. Glass, pp. 40-60. New York: The Rockefeller Univ. Press.

Ford, C. S., and Beach, F. A. 1951. *Patterns of sexual behavior.* New York: Harper & Row.

Frank, P. 1959. *Alas, Babylon.* New York: Bantam Books.

Frankl, V. E. 1963. *Man's search for meaning,* trans. Ilse Lusch. Boston: Beacon Press.

Franklin, B. 1950. *The autobiography of Benjamin Franklifl and selections from his other writings.* New York: Modem Library.

Franzblau, A. N. 1958. *A primer of statistics for non-statisticians.* New York: Harcourt, Brace.

Freud, A. 1946. *The ego and the mechanisms of defense.* New York: International Universities Press.

Freud, S. 1920. *A general introduction to psychoanalysis.* London: Bonji and Liveright, Inc.

Freud, S. 1935. *Autobiography.* New York: Norton. Freud, S. 1938. *The basic writings of Sigmund Freud.* The Modern Library. New York: Random House.

Freud, S. 1949. *Collected papers,* vol. IV. London: Hogarth. (Also published by Basic Books, N.Y., 1959)

Gallistel, C.R. 1964. Electrical self-stimulation and its theoretical implications. *Psychological Bulletin* 61:23-34.

Gallup, Gordon C. 1971. It's done with mirrors chimps and self-concept. *Psychology Today* 4, 10:58.

Calton, F. 1869. *Hereditary genius: An inquiry into its laws and consequences.* London: MacMillan Gardner, R. A., and Bardner, B. T. 1967. Teaching sign language to a chimpanzee. *Science* 165:664- 72.

Gazzaniga, M. S. 1967. The split brain in man. *Scientific American* 217:24-29.

Gazzaniga, M. S. 1970. *The bisected brain.* New York: Appleton-Century-Crofts.

Gazzaniga, M. S., and Sperry, R. W, 1967. Language after section of the cerebral commissures. *Brain* 90:131-48.

Gebhard, P.H., Gagnon, J. H., Pomeroy, W. B., and Christenson, C. U. 1965. *Sex offenders: An analysis of types.* New York: Harper & Row.

Gibbon, E. 1896. *The history of the decline and fall of the Roman empire.* London: Methuen & Co.

Gibson, E. J., and Walk, R. D.1960. The "visual cliff." *Scientific American* 202:67 - 71.

Goodall, J. 1965. Chimpanzees at the Gombe Stream Reserve. In *Primate behavior,* ed. I. DeVore, pp. 423- 73. New York: Holt, Rinehart, & Winston.

Goodall, J. 1971. *In the shadow of man.* Boston: Houghton-Mifflin.

Gray, P. H. 1966. *The comparative analysis of behavior.* Dubuque, Iowa: Brown.

Gregory, R. L. 1966. *Eye and brain: The psychology of seeing.* New York: McGraw-Hill.

Gregory, R. L., and Wallace, J. G. 1963. *Recovery f1'0m early blindness: A case study.* Experimental Psychology Society Monograph

Grinspoon, L. 1969. Marijuana. *Scientific American* 221:6.

Grossman, S. P. 1975. Role of the hypothalamus in the regulation of food and water intake. *Psychological · Review* 82, 3:200-24.

Guhl, A. M. 1961. The development of social organization in the domestic fowl. *Animal Behavior* 6:92-99.

Guthrie, E., and Horton, G. 1946. *Cats in a puzzle box.* New York: Holt, Rinehart, and Winston.

Hall, C. S. 1941. Temperament: A survey of animal studies. *Psychological Bulletin* 38:909-43.

Hall, C. S.1951. The genetics of behavior. In *Handbook of Experimental Psychology,* ed. S. S. Stevens. New York: Wiley & Sons.

Haney, C., Banks, C., and Zimbardo, P. 1973. Interpersonal dynamics in a simulated prison. *International Journal of Crime and Penology* 38:909-43.

Hansen, C. 1969. *Witchcraft at Salem.* New York: Braziller.

Harlow, H. F. 1949. The formation of learning sets. *Psychological Review* 56:51-65.

Harlow, H. F. 1958. The nature of love. *American Psychologist* 13:673-85.

Harlow, H. F. 1962. The heterosexual affectional system in monkeys. *American Psychologist* 17:1-9.

Harlow, H.F., and Harlow, M. K. 1949. Learning to think. *Scientific American* 181:36-39.

Harlow, H.F., and Harlow, M. K. 1962. Social deprivation in monkeys. *Scientific American* 207:137-46.

Harlow, H. F., and Harlow, M. K. 1966. Learning to love. *American Scientist* 54:244- 72.

Harlow, H. F., and Suomi, S. J. 1971. From thought to therapy: Lessons from a primate laboratory. *American Scientist* 59:538-49.

Harlow, H.F., and Zimmerman, R.R. 1959. Affectional responses in the infant monkey. *Science* Aug. 21, 1959:421-31.

Harlow, J. M. 1868. Recovery from the passage of an iron bar through the head. *Publications of the Massachusetts Medical Society* 2:327.

Hartley, E. E. 1946. *Problems in prejudice.* New York: Kings Crown Press.

Haskins, F. H. 1908. *Adolphe Quetelet as statistician.* New York: Columbia University.

Heath, R. G. 1963. Electrical self-stimulation of the brain in man. *American Journal of Psychiatry* 120, 6:571-77.

Hebb, D. 0. 1949. *The organization of behavior.* New York: Wiley & Sons.

Heidbreder, E. 1933. *Seven psychologies.* New York: Century.

Held, R., and Bauer, J. A., Jr. 1967. Visually guided reaching in infant monkeys after restricted rearing. *Science* 155:718-20.

Held, R., and Hein, A. 1963. Movement-produced stimulation in the development of visually guided behavior. *Journal of Comparative and Physiological Psychology* 56:872- 76.

Herodotus. 1956. *The history of Herodotus,* trans. G. Rawlinson. New York: Tudor.

Heron, W., Coone, B. K., and Scott, T. H. 1956. Visual disturbances after prolonged perceptual isolation. *Canadian Journal of Psychology* 10:13-18.

Heussenstaemm, F K. 1971. Bumper stickers and the cops. *Transaction* Feb.

Hess, E. H. 1959. Imprinting: An effect of early experience. *Science* 130:133-41.

Hess, W. R. 1954. *Diencephalon: Autonomic and extrapyramidal functions.* New York: Grune & Stratton.

Hess, W. R. 1957. *The functional organization of the diencephalon.* New York: Grune & Stratton.

Hill, N. 1966. *Think and grow rich.* New York: Hawthorn.

Hilton, I. 1967. Differences in the behavior of mother toward first- and later-born children. *Journal of Personality and Social Psychology* 7:282-90.

Hippocrates. 1952. On the sacred disease. In *The great books of the western world,* vol. 10, ed. R. M. Hutchins. Chicago: Encyclopedia Britannica.

Hitler, A. 1943. *Mein kampf.* Eng. ed. Boston: Houghton-Mifflin. (First edition, 1924.)

Hooten, E. 1937. *Up from the ape.* New York: Macmillan.

Houdini, H. 1920. *Miracle mongers and their methods: A complete expose of the modus operandi of fire eaters, heat resisters, poison eaters, venomous reptile defilers, sword swallowers, human ostriches, strong men, etc.* New York: E. P. Dutton.

Houdini, H. 1924. *Houdini exposes the tricks used by the Boston medium "Margery" to win the $2500 prize offered by The Scientific American. Also, a complete exposure of Argamasilla, the famous Spaniard who baffled noted scientists of Europe and America with his claim to X-ray vision.* New York: Adams Press.

Hovland, C. I. 1937. The generalization of conditioned responses: The sensory generalization of conditioned responses with varying frequencies of tone. *Journal of General Psychology* 17:125-48.

Hubel, D. H., and Wiesel, T. N. 1965. Receptive fields and functional architecture in two non-striate visual areas (18 and 19) of the cat. *Journal of Neurophysiology* 28:229-89.

Hudgins, C. V. 1933. Conditioning and the voluntary control of the pupillary light reflex. *Journal of General Psychology* 8:3-51.

Inhelder, B., and Piaget, J. 1958. *The growth of logical thinking from childhood through adolescence.* New York: Basic Books.

Inhelder, B., and Piaget, J. 1959. *The early growth of logic in the child.* New York: Harper & Row.

Iverson, G. R., Longcor, W. H., Mosteller, F., Gilbert, J. P., and Youtz, C. 1971. Bias and runs in dice throwing and recording: A few million throws. *Psychometrica* 36: 1-17.

James, W. 1892. *Psychology: The briefer course.* New York: Henry Holt & Co. (Later edition, Harper Torchbooks, Harper & Row, 1961.)

Jefferson, L. 1948. *These are my sisters.* Tulsa, Oklahoma: Vickers Publishing Co.

Jones, M. C. 1924. The elimination of children's fear. *Journal of Experimental Psychology* 1:328-90.

Kahl, J. A. 1953. Educational and occupational aspirations of "common man" boys. *Harvard Educational Review.* 23: 188-201.

Katz, D. 1953. *Animals and Men,* trans. H. Steinberg and A. Summerfield. London: Penguin.

Kellogg, W. N., and Kellogg, L. A. 1933. *The ape and the child.* New York: McGraw-Hill.

Kelly, H. H. 1950. the warm-cold variable in the first impression of persons. *Journal of Personality* 18: 431-39.

Kendler, H. H., and Kendler, T. S. 1962. Vertical and horizontal processes in problem solving. *Psychological Review,* 69:1-16.

Kendler, T. S., and Kendler, H. H. 1962. Inferential behavior in children as a function of age and subgoal constancy. *Journal of Experimental Psychology* 64:460-66.

Kinsey, A. C., Pomeroy, W. B., and Martin, C. E. 1948. *Sexual behavior in the human male.* Philadelphia: W. B. Saunders.

Kinsey, A. C., Pomeroy, W. B,, Martin, C. E., and Gebhard, P. H. 1953. *Sexual behavior in the human female.* Philadelphia: W. B. Saunders.

Klukhohn, C. 1949. *Mirror for man: The relation of anthropology to modern life.* New York: Whittlesey House.

Kohler, W. 1925. *The mentality of apes.* New York: Harcourt, Brace.

Kringlen, E. 1966. Schizophrenia in twins: An epidemiological study. *Psychiatry* 29, 2:172-84.

Kuo, A. Y. 1930. Genesis of cat's response to rats. *Journal of Comparative Psychology* 2:1.

Lack, D. L. 1933. *The life of the robin.* London: H.F. and G. Whitherby.

Langerspertz, K. 1961. Genetic and social causes of aggressive behavior in mice. *Scandinavian Journal of Psychology* 2:167-73.

Leech, K., and Jordan, B.1970. *Drugs for young people: Their use and misuse.* Oxford: Pergamon Press.

Lerner, M. J., and Simmons, C. H. 1966. Observers' reactions to the "innocent victim": Compassion or rejection? *Journal of Personality and Social Psychology* 4:2.

Levine, S., and Mullins, R., Jr. 1964. Estrogen administered neonatally affects adult sexual behavior in males and females. *Science* 14:185-87.

Levine, J., and Murphy, G. 1943. The learning and forgetting of controversial material. *Journal of Abnormal and Social Psychology* 38:507-17.

Liddell, H. S. 1954. Conditioning and emotions. *Scientific American* Jan.

Lindberg, D., and Seigfried, R. 1972. Students leaning toward the occult. United Press International, Nov. 12.

Locke, J. 1924. *Essay concerning human understanding.* Oxford: Clarendon Press.

Lorenz, K. 1952. *King Solomon's ring.* London:

Lorenz, K. 1966. *On aggression.* New York: Harcourt, Brace, & World.

Lorenz, K. 1970- 71. *Studies in animal and human behavior,* vol. 18. Cambridge: Harvard Univ. Press.

Luria, A. R. 1966. *Human brain and psychological processes,* trans. Basil Haigh. New York: Harper & Row.

Luria, A. R. 1973. *The working brain: An introduction to neuropsychology,* trans. Basil Haigh. London: Allen Lane.

MacDonnell, M. F., and Flynn, J.P. 1966. Control of sensory fields by stimulation of the hypothalamus. *Science* 152:1406-8.

Magoun, H. W. 1958. *The waking brain.* Springfield, ID.: Charles C. Thomas.

Maier, N. R. F. 1945. Reasoning in humans: The mechanisms of equivalent stimuli and of reasoning. *Journal of Experimental Psychology* 35:349-60.

Malmo, R. 1966. Psychological aspects of frontal gyrectomy and frontal lobotomy in mental patients. In *The frontal lobes,* Association for Research in Nervous and Mental Disease. Hafner Publishing Co.

Malinowsky, B. 1954. *Magic, science, and mligion.* New York: Doubleday.

Maslow, A.H. 1954. *Motivation and personality.* New York: Harper & Row.

Maslow, A. H. 1963. Self-actualizing people. In *The world of psychology,* vol. 2, ed. G. B. Levitas. New York: Braziller.

Masserman, J. H. 1950. Experimental neurosis. *Scientific American* Mar.

Masters, W. H., and Johnson, V. E. 1960. *Human sexual response.* Boston: Little, Brown.

May, R. 1953. *Man's search for himself.* New York: Norton.

May, R. 1961. *Existential psychology.* New York: Random House.

Mayr, E. 1963. *Animal species and evolution.* Cambridge: Harvard Univ. Press.

McDougall, W. 1908. *An introduction to social psychology,* 16th ed. London: Methuen.

Mead, G. H. 1934. *Mind, self, and society.* Chicago: Univ. of Chicago Press.

Mead, M. 1935. *Sex and temperament in three primitive societies.* New York: William Morrow.

Milgram, S. 1963. Behavioral study of obedience. *Journal of Abnormal and Social Psychology* 67:371-78.

Milgram, S. 1968. Some conditions of obedience and disobedience to authority. *International Journal of Psychiatry* 6:259- 76.

Mill, J. S. 1865. *On liberty.* London: Longmans, Green, &Co.

Miller, G. A., Galenter, E., and Pribram, K. H. 1960. *Plans and structure of the brain.* New York: Holt, Rinehart & Winston.

Miller, N. E. 1941. The frustration-aggression hypothesis. *Psychological Review* 48:337-42.

Miller, N. E. 1948. Studies of fear as an acquirable drive: Fear as motivation and fear reduction as reinforcement in the learning of new responses. *Journal of Experimental Psychology* 38:89-101.

Miller, N. E. 1951. Learnable drives and rewards. In *Handbook of experimental psychology,* ed. S. S. Stevens. New York: Wiley & Sons.

Miller, N. E. 1969. Learning of visceral and glandular responses. *Science* 163:434-45.

Miller, N. E., and Banuazizi, A. 1968. Instrumental learning by curarized rats of a specific visceral response, intestinal or cardiac. *Journal of Comparative and Phy8iological P8ychology* 65: 1- 7.

Miller, N. E., and DiCara, L. 1967. Instrumental learning of heart rate changes in curarized rats:
Shaping and specificity to discriminative stimulus. *Journal of Comparative and Physiological Psychology* 63:13-19.

Miller, N. E., and Dworkin, B. R. 1973. Visceral learning: Recent difficulties with curarized rats and significant programs for human research. In *Contemporary trends in* cardiovascular *psychophysiology,* ed. P. Obrist et al. New York: Aldine-Atherton,

Milner, G., and Penfield, W.1955. The effect of hippocampal lesions on recent memory. *Transactions of the American Neurological Association,* 42-48.

Mind of Man, Film: NET Audio-Visual Center, Office for Academic Affairs, Indiana University, Bloomington, Indiana, 47401.

Money, J. 1961. Hermaphroditism. In *The encyclopedia of sexual behavior,* ed. A. Ellis. New York: Hawthorne Books.

Money, J., Hampson, J. G., and Hampson, J. L. 1956. Sexual incongruities and psychopathology: The evidence of human hermaphroditism. *Bulletin of the Johns Hopkins Hospital* 98, I:43-57.

Monier-Williams. 1891. *Brahminism and Hinduism,* p. 318. London: MacMillan.

Monkeys, apes, and man. 1971. National Geographic Television Special.

Morgan, C. I. 1894. *An introduction to comparative psychology.* London: Scott.

Moruzzi, G., and Magoun, H. W. 1958. Brainstem reticular formation and actuation of the EEG. *Electroencephalography and Clinical Neurophysiology,* 1:455-73.

Mowrer, 0. H. 1938. Enuresis: A method for its study and treatment. *American Journal of Orthopsychiatry* 8:436-59.

Mowrer, 0. H. 1939. A stimulus-response analysis of anxiety and its role as a reinforcing agent. *Psychological Review* 46:553-65.

Mowrer, 0. H. 1960a. *Learning theory and behavior.* New York: Wiley & Sons.

Mowrer, 0. H.1960b. *Learning theory and the symbolic processes.* New York: Wiley & Sons.

Mowrer, 0. H., and Mowrer, W. M. 1965. Enuresis an etiological and therapeutic study. *Journal of Pediatrics* 67:436-59.

Neisser, U. 1967. *Cognitive Psychology.* New York: Appleton-Century-Crofts.

Newell, A., and Simon, H. A. 1972. *Human problem solving.* Englewood Cliffs, N.J.: Prentice-Hall.

Newton, G., and Levine, S. 1968. *Early experience and behavior: the psychobiology of development.* Springfield, Ill.; Charles C. Thomas.

Niemoller, M. 1968. Speech cited in *Choose life,* ed. B. Mandelbaum. New York: Random House.

Oesterreich, T. K. 1930. *Possession, demoniacal and other: Among primitive* races *in antiquity, the Middle Ages, and modern times.* New York: Richard R. Smith.

Olds, J. 1958. Self-stimulation of the brain. *Science* 127:315-23.

Olds, J., and Olds, M. 1965. Drives, rewards, and the brain. In *New Directions in psychology,* ed. T. M. Newcomb. New York: Holt, Rinehart, & Winston.

Packard, V. 1968. *The sexual wilderness.* New York: McKay.

Pascal, B. 1958. Pensees, New York: E. P. Dutton. Pavlov, I. P. 1927. *Conditioned reflexes: An investigation of the physiological activity of the cerebral* cortex, trans. G. Anrep. London: Oxford Univ. Press.

Pavlov, I. P. 1928. *Lectures on conditioned reflexes,* trans. H. Grant. New York: International Publishers.

Penfield, W. 1959. The interpretive cortex. *Science* 129: 1719-25.

Pen6eld, W., and Jasper, **H.** 1954. *Epilepsy and the functional anatomy of the human brain.* Boston: Little, Brown.

Penfield, W., and Roberts, L; 1959. *Speech and brain mechanisms.* Princeton, **N.J.:** Princeton Univ. Press.

Perceval, J. Esq. 1840 *A narrative of the treatment of a gentleman during a state of mental derangement.* London: Effingham Wilson. (Later edition, 1961, ed. G. Bateson. Stanford: Stanford Univ. Press.)

Piaget, J. 1930. *The child's conception of physical causality.* New York: Harcourt, Brace.

Piaget, J. 1948. *The moral judgment of the child.* Glencoe, Ill.: The Free Press.

Piaget, J. 1951. *The child's conception of the world,* New York: Humanities Press.

Piaget, J. 1954. *The construction of reality in the child,* trans. M. Cook. New York: Basic Books.

Plato. 1928. *The works of Plato,* ed. I. Edman. (Jowett trans.) New York: Modern Library.

Pomeroy, W. B.1963. Human sexual behavior. In *Taboo topics,* ed. N. L. Forberow. New York: Atherton.

Powley, T. 1977. The ventromedial hypothalamic. syndrome, satiety, and a cephalic phase hypothesis. *Psychological Review* 54, 1:89-126.

Premack, A. J., and Premack, 0. 1972. Teaching language to an ape. *Scientific American* Nov.

Pribram, K. 1971. *Languages of the brain.* Englewood Cliffs, N.J.: Prentice-Hall.

Pruetz, Jill D., and Paco Bertolani. "Savanna Chimpanzees, Pan Troglodytes Verus, Hunt with Tools." Current Biology, vol. 17, no. 5, 2007, pp. 412–417., doi:10.1016/j.cub.2006.12.042.

Rachman, S. 1966. Sexual Fetishism: An experimental analogue. *Psychological Record* 16:293-96.

Reeves, A., and Plum, F. 1969. Hyperphagia, rage, and dementia accompanying a ventromedial hypothalamic neoplasm. *Archives of Neurology* 52:68-73.

Reynolds, V., and Reynolds, F. 1965. Chimpanzees of the Budongo forest. In *Primate* behavior, ed. I. DeVore, pp. 425-73. New York: Holt, Rinehart, & Winston.

Rogers, C. R. 1951. Client-centered *therapy: Its current practice, implications, and theory.* Boston: Houghton-Mifflin.

Rogers, C. R. 1961. *On becoming a person.* Boston: Houghton-Mifflin.

Rosenthal, R. 1966. *Expe1'imenter effects in behavioral* research. New York: Appleton-Century-Crofts.

Rosenzweig, S. 1943. An experimental study of "repression" with special reference to need-perceptive and ego-defensive reactions to frustrations. *Journal of Experimental Psychology* 32:64- 7 4.

Roth, M. 1957. Interaction' of genetic and environmental factors in the causation of schizophrenia. In *Schizophrenia: Somatic aspects,* ed. D. Richter. New York: Macmillan.

Rowell, T. E. 1967. A quantitative comparison of the behavior of a wild and a caged baboon group. *Animal Behavior* 15, 4:499-509.

Russell, B. 1950. Nobel Prize acceptance speech. Stockholm.

Sackett, G. P. 1965. Effects of rearing conditions upon the behavior of rhesus monkeys. *Child Development* 36:855-68.

Sartre, J. P. 1964. *The words,* trans. B. Frecthman. New York: Braziller.

Schachter, S. 1959. *The psychology of affiliation* : Stanford Univ. Press.

Schachter, S. 1963. Birth order, eminence, and higher education. American *SociologicalReview28:757* ~68.

Scheinfeld, A. 1965. *Your heredity and environment.* Philadelphia: J. P. Lippincott.

Schjelderup-Ebbe, T. 1935. Social behavior of birds. In *Handbook of social psychology,* ed. Carl Murchinson, pp. 947-72. Worcester, Mass.: Clark Univ. Press.

Schlipp, P. A. 1970. *Alben Einstein-philosopher-scientist.* Library of Living Philosophers. La Salle, Ill.: Open Court Publishing Co.

Schmeidler, G. R., and McConnell, R. A.1958. *ESP and personality patterns.* New Haven: Yale Univ. Press.

Schneider, D. 1974. The sex-attractant receptor of moths. *Scientific Ame1'ican* 231, 1:28-36.

Schooler, C. 1972. Birth order effects: Not here, not now! *Psychological Bulletin* 78:161-75.

Scott, J.P. 1958. Critical periods in the development of social behavior in puppies. *Psychosomatic Medicine* 20:42-54.

Scott, J.P. 1962. Critical periods in behavioral development. *Science* 138:949-58.

Scott, J.P. 1963. The process of primary socialization in canine and human infants. *Monogram of Social Research in Child Development* 28, 1:1-47.

Shepard, D.L. 1977 PSYCHOGY: The Science of Human Behavior, Science Research Associates (SRA) IBM's college publishing division, Palo Alto CA.

Shepard, D.L. 2020 *Forces of Life: Success and Failure--preventing psychological problems and inspiring success.* SLG

Shepard, D.L. 2021 *MIND Psychology; the Untold Story of how Your Mind Works...* Amazon

Shepard, D.L., *The New PSYCHOLOGY A Unified Field of Brain, Mind, Behavior, Perception, Culture, and Life...*

Shepard, D.L. Psychology and *The Origin of* Civilization Imprinting and Animal Husbandry at Gobekli Tepe SLG Amazon

Sherif, M., Harvey, 0. J., White, B. J., Hood, W. R., and Sherif, C. W. 1961. *Intergroup conflict and cooperation: The Robbers Cave Experiment.* Norman, Okla.: Univ. of Oklahoma Press.

Skinner, B. F. 1948. *Walden two.* New York: ⁰ Macmillan.

Skinner, B. F. 1951. How to teach animals. *Scientific American* 185, 6:26-

Skinner, B. F. 1953. *Science and human behavior.* New York: Macmillan.

Skinner, B. F. 1957. *Cumulative record.* New York Appleton-Century-Crofts.

Skinner, B. F. 1961. *Verbal behavior.* New York: Appleton-Century-Crofts.

Skinner, B. F. 1971. *Beyond Freedom,_and dignity.* New York: Knopf.

Skinner, B. F. 1976. *Particulars of my life.* New York: Knopf.

Smith, M. E. 1926. An investigation of the development of the sentence and the extent of vocabulary in young children. *Univ. Iowa Studies of Child Welfare*, 3, 5 ..

Solecki, R. 1971. *Shanidar, The First Flower People.* New York: Knopf.

Solomon, R. L., Kamin, L. S., and Wynne, L. C. 1953. Traumatic avoidance learning: The outcomes of several extinction procedures with dogs. *Journal of Abnormal and Social Psychology* 48:291-302.

Solomon, R. L., and Wynne, L. C. 1953, Traumatic avoidance learning acquisition in normal dogs. *Psychology Monog1'aphs* 67, 4:354.

Sorensen, Robert. 1972. *Adolescent sexuality in contemporary America.* New York: World Publishing.

Spelt, D. K. 1948. The conditioning of the human fetus in utero. *Journal of Experimental Psychology* 38:338-46.

Sperry, R. W. 1964. The great cerebral commissure. *Scientific American* 210:42-52.

Sperry, R. W. 1966. Brain bisection and mechanisms of consciousness. In *Brain and conscious experience,* ed. J. C. Eccles. New York: Springer-Verlag, Sperry, R. W. 1968. Hemisphere deconnection and unity in conscious awareness. *American Psychologist* 23:723-33.

Spitz, R. A. 1945a. Anaclitic depression. In *The psychoanalytic study of the child,* ed. 0. Fenichel et al., vol. 2, pp. 313-42. New York: International Universities Press.

Spitz, R. A. 1945b. Hospitalism. In *The psychoanalytic study of the child,* ed. by 0. Fenichel et al., vol. 1, pp. 54-74. New York: International Universities Press.

Statts, A. W. 1968. *Learning, language, and cognition.* New York: Holt, Rinehart & Winston.

Stewart, J., and Palfaik, T.1967. Castration, androgens, and dominance status in the rat. *Psychosomic Science* 7, 1:1-2.

Storie, L. J., and Church, J. 1968. *Childhood and adolescence,* 2d ed. New York: Random House.

Stratton, G. M. 1897. Vision without inversion of the retinal image. *Psychological Review* 4:341-60.

Struhsaker, T. T. 1967. Social structure among vervet monkeys. *Behavior* 29: 110-21.

Suomi, S. J., and Harlow, H. F. 1972. Social rehabilitation of isolate reared monkeys. *Developmental Psychology* 6:487-96.

Szasz, T. S. 1961. *The myth of mental illness.* New York: Harper & Row.

Teitelbaum, P. 1961. Disturbances in feeding and drinking behavior after hypothalamic lesions. In *Nebraska symposium on motivation,* ed. M. R. Jones. Lincoln, Neb.: Univ. of Nebraska Press.

Teitelbaum, P., and Epstein, A. N. 1952. Random and food directed activity in hyperphagic and normal rats. *Journal of Comparative and Physiological Psychology* 50:486-90.

Teitelbaum, P., and Epstein, A. N. 1962. The lateral hypothalamic syndrome: Recovery of feeding and drinking after lateral hypothalamic lesions. *Psychological Review* 69:74-90.

Terman, L. M. 1925-59, *Genetic studies of genius: Mental and physical traits of gifted children,* vols. 4 and 5. Stanford: Stanford Univ. Press.

Theios, J. 1962. The partial reinforcement effect sustained through blocks of continuous reinforcement. *Journal of Experimental Psychology* 64:1-6.

Thiel, R. 1957. *And there was light.* New York: Knopf. Thompson, W. R.1957. Influence of prenatal maternal anxiety on emotionality in young rats. *Science* 125:698-99.

Thorndike, E. L. 1911. *Animal intelligence.* New York: Macmillan.

Thorndike, E. L. 1931. *Human learning.* New York: The Century Co.

Tinklepaugh, .0. L. 1928. An experimental study of representative factors in monkeys. *Journal of Comparative and Physiological Psychology* 8:197-.

Toland, J. 1966. *The last 100 days.* New York: Random House.

Tolstoi, L. 1887, *My confession.* New York: Crowell. Toman, W. 1969. *Family constellation: Its effects on personality and social behavior,* 2d ed. New York: Springer.

Twitmyer, E. B. 1905. Knee-jerks without stimulation of the patellar tendon. *Journal of Philosophy, Psychology and Scientific Methods* 2:63.

U.S. Government. 1969. *Crimes of violence: A staff report submitted to the National Commission on the Causes and Prevention of Violence,* vol. 12, pp. 670-77. U.S. GPO.

U.S. Government. 1970a. *Marijuana: A signal of misunderstanding.* First Report of the National Commission on Marijuana and Drug Abuse. U.S. U.S. Government. 1970b. *The 1'eportof the Commission on Obscenity and Pornography,* vol. 1, Y3 Ob 7, 1/970. U.S. GPO.

Valenstein, E. S., Cox, V. C., and Kakolewski, J. W. 1970. Hypothalamic motivational systems: Fixed or plastic neural circuits? *Science* 163:1084.

Von Senden, M. 1960. *Space and sight: The perception of space and shape in the congenitally blind beforeand after operation,* trans. P. Heath. Glencoe, Ill.: The Free Press.

Wald, G. 1950. Eye and camera. *Scientific American* 182:32-41.

Wald, G. 1964. The receptors of human color vision. *Science* 145: 1007-17.

Walters, R.H., Bowen, N. V., and Parke, R. D. 1964. Influence of looking behavior of a social model on subsequent looking behavior of observers of the model. *Perceptual and Motor Skills* 18:469-83.

Warner, L. 1955. What the younger psychologists think about ESP. *Journal of Parapsychology* 19: 228-35.

Warner, L. 1957. The study of social stratification. In *Review of sociology: Analysis of a decade,* ed. J. Gittler, pp. 221-58. New York: Wiley & Sons.

Washburn, S. L. 1960. Tools and human evolution. *Scientific American* 3:3.

Washburn, S. L., and De Vore, I. 1962. Social behavior of baboons and early man. In *Social life of early man,* ed. S. L. Washburn, pp. 91-105. New York:

Wason, P. C., and Johnson-Laird, P. N. 1972. *Psychology of reasoning.* Cambridge: Harvard Univ. Press.

Wason, P. C., and Shapiro, D. 1971. Natural and contrived experience in a reasoning problem. *Quarterly Journal of Experimental Psychology* 73:63- 71.

Watson, J.B. 1925. *Behaviorism.* New York: Norton.

Watson, J.B., and Rayner, R. 1920. Conditioned emotional reactions. *Journal of Experimental Psychology* 3:1-14.

Watson, J. D. 1968. *The double helix.* New York: Atheneum.

Watson, R. I. 1968. *The great psychologists.* Philadelphia: J. P. Lippincott.

Weber, M. 1948. *The theory of social and economic organization,* trans. A. N. Henderson and Talcott Parsons. Glencoe, ID.: The Free Press.

Weber, M. 1958. *The Protestant ethic and the spirit of capitalism,* trans. Talcott Parsons. New York: Scribners.

Weiner, N. 1948. *Cybernetics.* Cambridge: MIT Press. Weiner, N. 1963. Nerve, brain, and memory models. *Symposium on cybernetics of the nervous system,* ed. N. WeinerandJ. P. Schade. New York: Elsevier.

Wells, H. G., Huxley, J. S., and Wells, G. P.1934. *The science of life.* Garden City, N.Y.: The Literary Guild, Country Life Press.

Wendt, H. 1963. *In search of Adam.* Chicago: Collier Books.

Werblin, F. S. 1973. The control of sensitivity in the retina. *Scientific American* 228, 1:70-9.

Whitehead, A. N. 1926. *Science and the modern world.* New York: MacMillan.

Wilkins, M. C. 1928. The effect of changed material on ability to do formal syllogistic reasoning. *Archives of Psychology,* 102.

Williams, T. H., Current, R. N., and Freidel, F. 1969. *A History of the United States to 1865.* New York: Knopf.

Williams, T. H., Current, R. N., and Freidel, F. 1969. *A History of the United States since 1865.* New York: Knopf.

Wolfenstein, M. 1951. The emergence of fun morality. *Journal of Social Issues* 7: 15-25.

Wolfenstein, M. 1953. Trends in infant care. *American Journal of Orthopsychiatry* 23:120-30.

Wolpe, J. 1969. *The practice of behavior therapy.* New York: Pergamon Press.

W oodburne, L. S. 1967. *The neural basis of behavior.* Columbus, Ohio: Charles E. Merrill.

Yerkes, R. M. 1929. *The great apes.* New Haven: Yale Univ. Press.

Yerkes, R. M. 1943. *Chimpanzees: A laboratory colony.* New Haven: Yale Univ. Press.

Zajonic, R. B., and Marcus, G. B. 1975. Birth order and intellectual development. *Psychological Review* 82, 1:74-88.

Zeaman, D. 1949. Response latency as a function of the amount of reinforcement. *Journal of Experimental Psychology* 39:446-82.

Zeigarnic, B. 1927. Uber das Behalten von erledigten und unerledigten Handlungen. *Psychol. Forsch.* 9: 1-85. Trans. W. D. Ellis in *A source book of gestalt psychology.* Boston: Routledge.

Zimbardo, P. G. 1972. Pathology of imprisonment, *Society* 9, 6:4-8.

Zuckerman, S. 1932. *The social life of monkeys and apes.* New York: Harcourt, Brace